FINANCIAL MANAGEMENT

HARCOURT BRACE COLLEGE OUTLINE SERIES

FINANCIAL MANAGEMENT

H. Kent Baker

Department of Finance
The American University

Harcourt Brace College Publishers
Fort Worth   Philadelphia   San Diego
New York   Orlando   Austin   San Antonio
Toronto   Montreal   London   Sydney   Tokyo

Printed in the United States of America

LIBRARY OF CONGRESS CATALOGING IN PUBLICATION DATA

Baker, Kent.
    Financial management.

    (Harcourt Brace Jovanovich college outline series)
    (Books for professionals)
    Includes index.
    1. Corporations—Finance—Management. I. Title. II. Series.
III. Series: Books for professionals.
HG4026.B234 1987   658.1′5   86-7625
ISBN 0-15-601645-1

First edition

9 0 1 2 3 4 5 145 9 8 7 6

PREFACE

Financial management is vitally important to the success of any business firm. Thus, everyone contemplating a career in business should be familiar with the subject. The purpose of this book is to provide an introduction to financial management in the clear, concise, and practical format of an outline. The unifying concept of the book is that financial managers make decisions in order to achieve the firm's primary goal of maximizing shareholder wealth. Each of these decisions involves a set of risk-return tradeoffs. The book focuses on what business firms, especially corporations, should do to achieve their financial goals rather than merely describing what firms actually do in practice. Special attention is given to examining the concepts and analytical techniques that are used in financial decision making.

The book has five parts. Part 1 (Chapters 1 through 5) presents the *foundations of financial management,* which include the finance function, the operating environment of financial management, and key concepts such as time value of money, risk and return, and valuation that are used throughout the outline. Part 2 (Chapters 6 through 8) covers key concepts and tools of *financial analysis and planning.* Part 3 (Chapters 9 through 13), called *utilization of funds,* examines the management of current assets or working capital management and fixed assets. Part 4 (Chapters 14 through 16) concentrates on *cost of capital, capital structure, and dividend policy.* Finally, Part 5 (Chapters 17 through 20) concerns the *acquisition of funds* and describes the process by which firms raise money and manage liabilities and equity. Because the book is an introduction to financial management, it does not focus on special topics such as international finance, mergers and acquisitions, and business failure.

The outline is comprehensive enough to be used independently, but you will find that many of its features make it an ideal supplement to college courses and textbooks on financial management. One of these features is a *Textbook Correlation Table* that begins on the inside of the front cover. The table shows how the topics covered in this outline correspond by topic to the pages of several leading textbooks on financial management used at major colleges and universities. If the sequence in this outline differs from your textbook, you can easily find the corresponding topic by consulting the table.

Another feature is the sample *examinations* included with this outline. The three examinations are designed not only to measure your retention of information, but also to test your ability to apply the concepts and tools you have acquired. Each sample examination includes different types of questions that you are likely to encounter on a typical college exam including true-false, multiple choice, fill in the blank, and problems. Other features include the outline format itself, numerous examples in every chapter, and a glossary of key terms provided at the back of the book.

There are several other features at the end of each chapter that are specifically designed to supplement your textbook and course work in financial management.

RAISE YOUR GRADES This feature consists of a checkmarked list of open-ended, thought-provoking questions to help you assimilate the material you have just studied. By inviting you to compare concepts, interpret ideas, and examine the whys and wherefores of chapter material, these questions help you to prepare for class discussions, quizzes, and tests.

SUMMARY This feature consists of a brief restatement of the main ideas in each chapter, including definition of key terms. Because it is presented in the efficient form of a numbered list, you can use it to refresh your memory quickly before an exam.

RAPID REVIEW Like the summary, this feature is designed to provide you with a quick review of the principles presented in the body of each chapter. Consisting of true-false and multiple choice questions, it allows you to test your retention and reinforce your learning at the same time. Should you have trouble answering any of these questions, you can locate and review the relevant sections provided.

SOLVED PROBLEMS Each chapter of this outline concludes with a set of problems and their step-by-step solutions. Undoubtedly the most valuable feature of the outline, these problems allow you to apply your knowledge of financial management to the solution of both numerical and essay questions. Along with three examinations, they also give you ample exposure to the kinds of questions that you are likely to encounter on a typical college exam. To make the most of these problems, try writing your own solutions first. Then compare your answers to the detailed solutions provided in the book.

CONTENTS

THE FINANCE FUNCTION

1-1. Nature of Financial Management

Financial management, also called *managerial finance*, *corporate finance*, and *business finance*, is a decision-making process concerned with planning, acquiring, and utilizing funds in a way that achieves the firm's desired goals. This process involves evaluating assets, liabilities, and equity and making decisions based on that evaluation. Financial management is part of a larger discipline called **finance** which is a body of facts, principles, and theories relating to raising and using money by individuals, businesses, and governments. The individual charged with financial management is called the **financial manager**. This book concerns financial management of profit-oriented business organizations, especially the corporate form of business, however, many of the tools and concepts discussed are applicable to individuals and to governments.

There are three functions in the financial management process: financial analysis and planning, acquisition of funds, and utilization of funds.

A. *Financial analysis and planning* **involves examining the firm's financial position and determining the actions needed to achieve its goals.**

Financial analysis and planning are a prerequisite for making sound financial decisions. This broad function includes monitoring and modifying the firm's current actions to ensure that its goals are met. Financial managers use numerous techniques to perform financial analysis and planning. These techniques are presented throughout this text.

B. *Acquisition of funds* **involves determining the firm's best financing mix.**

The financing function is concerned with managing the firm's financial structure which consists of liabilities and owners' equity. The term **funds** in financial management refers to the financial capital a firm needs in order to operate. Funds are provided by a firm's creditors and owners in the form of short-term funds (less than one year) and long-term funds (one year or more). These funds may be obtained externally, by borrowing from financial institutions or by issuing securities, or internally, by having profits reinvested in the firm. Because all funds are not equally desirable, the financial manager must determine the most appropriate mix of short-term and long-term financing at a given point in time. This requires analyzing the available alternatives, their costs, and their implications.

C. *Utilization of funds* concerns determining where to invest funds.

The investing function deals with managing the firm's assets. Because the firm has numerous alternative uses of funds, the financial manager strives to allocate funds wisely within the firm. This task requires determining both the mix and type of assets to hold. The asset mix refers to the number of dollars invested in current and fixed assets. Within these two asset categories, the financial manager must determine which specific assets to hold, such as plant and equipment.

1-2. Evolution of Financial Management

Financial management has changed dramatically over time. Until 1900, finance was considered a part of applied economics. For the next thirty years, financial management centered on obtaining funds primarily to finance the wave of mergers and consolidations. During the 1930s and 1940s, finance focused on legal matters associated with bankruptcy and on planning for survival and recovery. By the end of the 1950s, finance expanded to include using funds or asset management. The character of finance also shifted from a descriptive framework to an analytical framework emphasizing financial theory and decision making. Since then finance has focused on the policies and decisions that affect the value of the firm and placed increased emphasis on quantitative methods and computer technology to assist in financial decision making.

1-3. Goals of the Firm

Firms have numerous goals, but not every goal can be attained without causing conflict in reaching other goals. Conflicts often arise because of the different goals of the firm's many constituents, who include stockholders, managers, employees, labor unions, customers, creditors, and suppliers. There are those who claim that the firm's goal is to maximize sales or market share; others believe the role of business is to provide quality products and service; still others feel that the firm has a responsibility for the welfare of society at large; and there are some who believe that business should be run in the interests of its owners. The financial manager must have some goal or objective to guide decisions involving the management of the firm's assets, liabilities, and equity. Hence, priorities must be set to resolve conflicting goals.

A. **The primary goal of the firm is to maximize the wealth of its existing stockholders.**

The overriding premise of financial management is that the firm should be managed to enhance stockholder well-being. Stockholder wealth depends on both the dividends paid and the market price of the common stock. Wealth is maximized by providing the stockholder with the largest attainable combination of dividends per share and stock price appreciation. Because stock prices already reflect both current and expected future dividend payments, maximizing stockholder wealth really means maximizing the market price of the stock. This is not a perfect measure of shareholder wealth, but it is the best available measure.

B. **Shareholder wealth maximization only serves as the operational guide for financial decision making.**

Financial decisions should be made to benefit the firm's owners or holders of common stock. For several reasons, however, financial managers are constrained in achieving this goal.

1. The financial manager operates within an environment that restricts financial decision making. These constraints include numerous laws and regulations involving taxes, selling securities, and public disclosure of information. Some social

objectives such as pollution control, safe working conditions, fair hiring practices, and antitrust actions are formal legal obligations and serve as constraints under which firms operate. Thus, the "rules of the game" become constraints, and firms should strive to maximize stock prices subject to these constraints.

2. The financial manager can only partially influence the firm's stock price. Financial decisions affect stock prices but maximizing stock price is not totally within the firm's control. The market price of a firm's stock represents the total judgment of all market participants about such factors as:

- the firm's ability to earn profits over time
- the timing, distribution, and riskiness of the firm's earnings stream
- the manner of financing the firm
- the firm's dividend policy
- the quality aspects of the firm, including management, diversification, and potential growth

Market perceptions actually determine stock prices.

C. Economic theory assumes that profit maximization is the goal of the firm.

Profit maximization is not the same as shareholder wealth maximization. **Profit maximization** is the goal of increasing the firm's total profits as much as possible in the shortest time period. Although the goal of profits maximization has the advantage of providing a clear link between financial decisions and profits, maximizing total corporate profits may not automatically maximize stockholder wealth. Thus, shareholder wealth maximization is considered a more appropriate corporate goal.

Profit maximization does not provide an ideal basis for financial decision making for several reasons.

1. *Emphasizes profits.* Profit maximization focuses on total profits rather than earnings per share or stock price. **Earnings per share** (EPS) are the earnings available to common stockholders divided by the number of shares of outstanding common stock. A firm with higher total profits may actually have lower earnings per share and stock prices than a similar firm. The owner's wealth in a firm is better reflected by its earnings per share or stock price and not its profits. However, maximizing earnings per share will not always maximize stockholder welfare because it does not consider risk or the timing and distribution of returns.

EXAMPLE 1-1: Three years ago Don Myers bought 100 shares each of Abell Company and Bartell Company for $20 per share. Both firms are in the same line of business. Abell Company has spent considerable money during the past few years to develop innovative products and to automate and expand its production facilities. These developments are expected to improve the firm's competitive position and to increase future profits. Abell had $100,000 in profits during the past year and 40,000 shares of outstanding common stock. Over the same time period, Bartell Company has invested little money in product development and production capacity. However, during the past year Bartell earned $150,000 on 75,000 shares outstanding. Neither company pays cash dividends but reinvests all profits. The stock of Abell Company is currently selling for $30 per share while Bartell's stock is selling for $20 per share.

The difference in stock prices between the two companies can be explained as follows. Abell Company has lower profits but higher earnings per share and stock price than Bartell Company. Abell's lower profits may be attributed to the higher expenses incurred to improve its competitive position. However, the market perceives that the Abell Company is in a better position than Bartell Company to compete and to generate increased profits in the future. The wealth position of Don Myers is greater in Abell Company than Bartell Company despite Bartell's larger profits.

	Abell Company	Bartell Company
Profits or net income......................................	$100,000	$150,000
Number of shares outstanding	40,000	75,000
Earnings per share (EPS)	$ 2.50	$ 2.00
Stock price...	$ 30.00	$ 20.00

2. *Ignores the distribution of returns.* Profit maximization fails to consider how the firm's returns are distributed or the preferences of stockholders in receiving returns. Stockholders may prefer one form of return over another. Some stockholders may prefer dividends to future price appreciation because they need current income. Profit maximization also does not consider the potential impact of dividends on stock prices.

EXAMPLE 1-2: Dynamic Technologies is a rapidly growing company that requires large amounts of capital. The firm's stockholders are wealthy individuals in high income tax brackets. The stockholders probably have little need for current income from dividends because they are wealthy. Thus, they may prefer that the firm reinvest all or most of its earnings to boost future profits and stock prices.

3. *Lacks a time dimension.* Unlike maximization of shareholder wealth, profit maximization has no explicit way of comparing long-term versus short-term profits or considering the timing of returns. Profits earned today are treated in the same manner as profits earned in the future. Profit maximization ignores the *time value of money* in which a dollar received today is worth more than a dollar received tomorrow. Profit maximization is also oriented toward the short term. A firm may take actions, such as failing to replace obsolete equipment, that increase profits in the short term but reduce the firm's performance and hurt the shareholders' wealth position in the long term. Time value of money is discussed in Chapter 3.

EXAMPLE 1-3: Lamone Pharmaceuticals wants to choose between two projects. Both projects cost the same, are equally risky, and are expected to increase the firm's earnings per share as shown below.

Additions to Firm's EPS	Year	Project A	Project B
	1	$2.00	$0.50
	2	0	0.50
	3	0	0.60
	4	0	0.60
	Total	$2.00	$2.20

Project B is preferred under profit maximization because it provides a $2.20 increase in EPS versus $2.00 for Project A. Profit maximization ignores the fact that Project A provides its returns sooner than Project B. Project A could be worth more than Project B by the end of four years if the earnings generated by Project A could be reinvested to earn even higher profits.

4. *Ignores risk.* Profit maximization assumes that risk or uncertainty is of no concern to stockholders. Financial decisions involve a **risk-return tradeoff**, which means that in exchange for taking greater risk, the firm expects a higher return. **Risk** is the probability that the actual return will differ from the expected return. Profit maximization does not consider risk, but shareholder wealth maximization does. The concept of risk is discussed in Chapter 4.

EXAMPLE 1-4: Haslem Corporation must choose between two projects. Both projects cost the same. Project C is certain to add $1.00 per year for the next four years to Haslem's earnings per share. Project D is expected to add $1.25 per year for the next four years, but this investment is very risky. That is, Haslem is not certain that the annual increase in earnings per share will be $1.25.

On the basis of profit maximization, Project D is more attractive because it adds more to the firm's total profits than Project C. Yet, profit maximization ignores the risk associated with this project's expected returns. Project C could be more attractive due to its lower risk.

Year	Project C	Project D
1	$1.00	$1.25
2	1.00	1.25
3	1.00	1.25
4	1.00	1.25
Total	$4.00	$5.00

1-4. The Role of the Financial Manager

In striving to maximize shareholder wealth, the financial manager makes decisions involving planning, acquiring, and utilizing funds which involve a set of risk-return tradeoffs. These financial decisions affect the market value of the firm's stock which leads to wealth maximization. In the short run, many factors affect the market price of a firm's shares which are beyond management's control. Some of the changes in market price do not reflect a fundamental change in the value of the firm. In the long run, increased prices of the firm's stock reflect an increase in the value of the firm. Hence, financial decision making should take a longer-term perspective. Figure 1-1 shows the financial manager's role in achieving the primary goal of the firm.

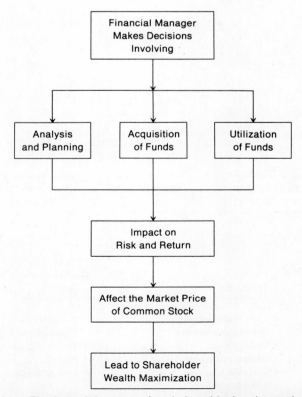

Figure 1-1   The financial manager's role in achieving the goal of the firm.

A. The financial manager interacts with other functional managers to achieve the firm's goals.

Finance is one of the major functional areas of a business. For example, the functional areas of business operations for a typical manufacturing firm are manufacturing, marketing, and finance. Manufacturing deals with the design and production of a product. Marketing involves the selling, promotion, and distribution of a product. Manufacturing and marketing are critical for the survival of a firm because these areas determine what will be produced and how these products will be sold. However, these other functional areas could not operate without funds. Since finance is concerned with all of the monetary aspects of a business, the financial manager must interact with other managers to ascertain the goals that must be met, and when and how to meet them. Thus, finance is an integral part of total management and cuts across functional boundaries.

B. The finance function is performed by a separate department within larger business firms and usually by the accounting department within smaller firms.

Financial managers rely heavily upon other managers, such as accountants and economists, to provide information for decision making. As shown in Figure 1-2, in a large organization the chief financial manager, typically called the vice-president of finance, reports directly to the president and has authority over the treasurer and controller.

1. The *treasurer* is responsible for handling *external* financial matters, such as cash and credit management, raising funds, capital budgeting, and financial analysis and planning. The treasurer needs input from manufacturing and marketing to carry out these activities.
2. The *controller* is responsible for *internal* matters, such as accounting, budgeting, taxes, payroll, and data processing.

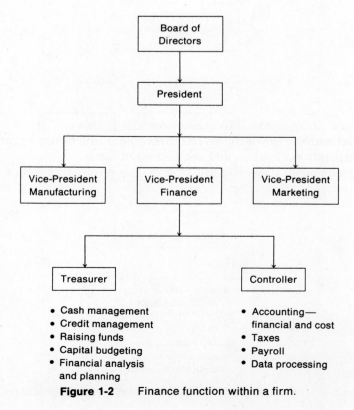

Figure 1-2 Finance function within a firm.

C. A difference may exist between financial theory and practice.

Financial theory presumes that stockholder well-being *should be* the major goal of the firm. As an agent of the firm's stockholders, the financial manager should strive to maximize shareholder wealth. In practice, the interests of owners and managers may not always be the same. Although small businesses are usually managed by their owners, most large corporations are characterized by a separation of ownership and control. That is, most owners do not directly run the firm but select managers to operate the firm for them. Conflicts between managers and shareholders may arise because managers place their own interests ahead of those of the shareholders. Managers may seek to maximize their own welfare by granting themselves large salaries and other benefits. Or management may seek short-term results and profits rather than take a long-term perspective because their bonuses are tied to short-term performance. Such actions may be harmful to stockholders. Several mechanisms are available that protect the shareholders' position. For example, stock options plans that make managers part owners may help align the interests of management and shareholders. The possibility of replacing managers through shareholder action and outside takeover of the company may also serve as a deterrent for mismanagement.

RAISE YOUR GRADES

Can you explain ...?

☑ the meaning of financial management
☑ the three functions of the financial management process
☑ how financial management has changed over time
☑ the primary goal of the firm
☑ the limitations of profit maximization as a goal
☑ the place of finance in the business firm
☑ the different responsibilities of the treasurer and the controller

SUMMARY

1. Financial management is a decision-making process concerned with planning, acquiring, and utilizing funds to achieve desired goals.
2. The financial management process has three major functions: financial analysis and planning, utilization of funds, and acquisition of funds.
3. Financial management has evolved from a descriptive framework focusing on the financing function to a broader analytical framework encompassing the planning and investing functions.
4. The primary goal of the firm is to maximize the wealth of its stockholders. Shareholder wealth maximization is achieved in a public corporation by maximizing the market price of the firm's stock.
5. A limitation of stockholder wealth maximization is that a firm can only partially influence its stock price.
6. Profit maximization is a less appropriate firm goal than shareholder wealth maximization. Unlike wealth maximization, profit maximization focuses on profits rather than earnings per share, fails to consider the distribution of returns, lacks a time dimension, and ignores risk.
7. Financial decisions involve a risk-return tradeoff in which higher expected returns are accompanied by higher risks. The financial manager determines the appropriate risk-return tradeoff in order to maximize the value of the firm's stock.

8. The financial manager interacts with other functional areas such as manufacturing and marketing to achieve desired goals.

9. The organization of the finance function depends largely on the size of the firm. Larger firms have a separate finance department whereas smaller firms typically combine the finance and accounting areas.

10. The financial manager reports directly to the president and has authority over the treasurer and controller. The treasurer is responsible for most of the firm's general financial activities whereas the controller's functions center on accounting and taxes.

11. Conflicts may arise between managers and shareholders because of the separation of ownership and control. These differences may be reduced by several factors, such as stock option plans that make managers part owners or the possibility of replacing managers.

RAPID REVIEW

True or False?

1. Financial management is the study of financial decision making related to the efficient use of financial capital to achieve desired goals. [Section 1-1]

2. The financial manager plays a major role in the firm's financial and investing decisions. [Section 1-1B-C]

3. Financial management has remained largely unchanged over the past 30 years. [Section 1-2]

4. The primary goal of the firm is to maximize the wealth of its shareholders. [Section 1-3A]

5. The maximization of shareholder wealth is measured by the market price of the firm's stock. [Section 1-3A]

6. The financial manager has full control over its firm's stock price. [Section 1-3B]

7. Profit maximization is the same as shareholder wealth maximization. [Section 1-3C]

8. Profit maximization aims at maximizing earnings per share. [Section 1-3C]

9. Profit maximization emphasizes the preferences of stockholders in determining how profits are distributed. [Section 1-3C]

10. A problem associated with profit maximization is that it ignores the timing of returns. [Section 1-3C]

11. The goal of shareholder wealth maximization ignores risk. [Section 1-3C]

12. The risk-return tradeoff suggests that as the risk of a course of action increases, its expected return should also increase. [Section 1-3C]

13. The financial manager's chief responsibility is to the owners of the firm. [Section 1-4]

14. Financial management is an independent business function that requires little interaction with other functional areas. [Section 1-4A]

15. The treasurer is primarily responsible for a firm's accounting and tax activities. [Section 1-4B]

Multiple Choice

16. Financial management during this century has:

   (a) changed little
   (b) changed dramatically
   (c) changed from an analytical to a descriptive framework
   (d) None of the above

   [Section 1-2]

17. Which of the following are functions of the financial management process?

    (*a*) Financial analysis and planning
    (*b*) Utilization of funds
    (*c*) Acquisition of funds
    (*d*) All of the above

[Section 1-1]

18. Which phrase best describes the goal of the firm?

    (*a*) Profit maximization
    (*b*) Risk minimization
    (*c*) Maximization of earnings per share
    (*d*) Shareholder wealth maximization

[Section 1-3A]

19. A limitation of shareholder wealth maximization as the goal of the firm is:

    (*a*) lacks a time dimension
    (*b*) not totally within a firm's control
    (*c*) ignores risk
    (*d*) None of the above

[Section 1-3B]

20. Which activity is typically *not* performed by the controller?

    (*a*) Accounting
    (*b*) Taxes
    (*c*) Capital budgeting
    (*d*) Data processing

[Section 1-4B]

Answers

True and False				*Multiple Choice*
1. True	6. False	11. False		16. b
2. True	7. False	12. True		17. d
3. False	8. False	13. True		18. d
4. True	9. False	14. False		19. b
5. True	10. True	15. False		20. c

SOLVED PROBLEMS

PROBLEM 1-1: What is the difference between *finance* and *financing*?

Answer: Finance is a body of facts, principles, and theories relating to raising and using money by individuals, businesses, and governments. Financing is one of the functions of financial management that involves raising funds.   **[Sections 1-1]**

PROBLEM 1-2: What are the three primary functions of financial management?

Answer: The three key functions are financial analysis and planning, utilization of funds, and acquisition of funds. These functions are performed in order to achieve the firm's goals, especially maximization of stockholder wealth.   **[Section 1-1A-C]**

PROBLEM 1-3: How has financial management changed over the past several decades.

Answer: The emphasis in financial management has changed from a descriptive frame-work to an analytical framework. Greater attention is now placed on financial theory and decision making. Quantitative methods and computers have become increasingly important in financial management. The role of the financial manager has become considerably broader to include all aspects of managing and controlling the firm's financial operations. **[Section 1-2]**

PROBLEM 1-4: What is the primary goal of the firm? How can achievement of this goal be measured?

Answer: The primary goal of the firm is to maximize the wealth of its stockholders. This goal is achieved by maximizing the value of the owners' interests in the firm. Stock-holders receive returns from dividends and stock price appreciation. The market price of a share of stock reflects the perceived value of both current and expected future dividends. Hence, stockholder wealth is measured by the market price of the firm's common stock. **[Section 1-3A]**

PROBLEM 1-5: What factors influence the market price of a firm's common stock?

Answer: A firm's common stock price is influenced by many factors over which the financial manager has only partial control. Factors influencing stock price include: the timing, distribution, and riskiness of the firm's earnings; its investment, financing, and dividend policies; qualitative factors including the quality of management; and general economic conditions. **[Section 1-3B]**

PROBLEM 1-6: Does the goal of maximization of the value of the owners' interest in the company ignore social considerations?

Answer: No. Social considerations are not ignored but they are constrained by the goal of shareholder wealth maximization. Shareholders are primarily interested in maximizing the monetary returns from their ownership interest. Investors may avoid companies that incur unnecessary social costs because this reduces their returns. Firms do exercise social responsibility, but many of the actions taken to benefit the social welfare are mandated by law. **[Section 1-3B]**

PROBLEM 1-7: What are the limitations of profit maximization as the goal of financial management?

Answer: Profit maximization suffers from several limitations which make it inappropriate as the major corporate goal. First, profit maximization focuses on total profits rather than earnings per share. Stockholders are more concerned with earnings per share than profits because earnings per share better represents their wealth. Second, profit maximization fails to consider the distribution of returns. Third, profit maximization lacks a time dimension because it fails to reflect differences in the timing of returns. Finally, profit maximization ignores the amount of risk taken to increase profits. Stockholder wealth maximization does not suffer from any of these limitations. **[Section 1-3C]**

PROBLEM 1-8: What does the risk-return tradeoff mean?

Answer: The risk-return tradeoff means that higher returns are expected for taking greater risks. Risk is the probability or likelihood that the actual return will differ from the expected return. Investors are not indifferent between the firm's time-adjusted profit and risk. They may drive down the firm's stock price if management's decisions are not to their liking. Thus, risk-return tradeoffs taken by management affect the market price of common stock. **[Section 1-3C]**

PROBLEM 1-9: What is the importance of the finance function in a business firm?

Answer: Finance is one of the major functional areas of a business. Finance deals with all the monetary aspects of the firm. Money is important throughout the firm. Thus, the finance function is integral to the overall operation of the firm. **[Section 1-4A]**

PROBLEM 1-10: Which type of firm is more likely to be a shareholder wealth maximizer—one in which the owners are managers or one in which there is separation of ownership and management?

Answer: The premise of financial theory is that firms should operate for the well-being of their owners. Although there is considerable debate on the issue, firms are more likely to operate for the benefit of their owners if the goals and interests of the owners and managers are similar. In large corporations, there is greater separation of ownership and control than in smaller business organizations. **[Section 1-4C]**

2 BUSINESS ORGANIZATION AND TAXES

THIS CHAPTER IS ABOUT

☑ **Forms of Business Organization**
☑ **Taxes**

Financial decision making does not exist in a vacuum. Business firms operate in a complex environment of legal, political, economic, and financial forces that affect decision making. The financial manager's goal of maximizing shareholder wealth is influenced and constrained by the environment in which the firm operates. Two of the most important factors making up the firm's operating environment are its legal form of business organization and taxes.

2-1. Forms of Business Organization

The form of business organization affects the firm's ability to obtain financing. It also affects both the personal and tax liability of its owners. The three primary forms of business organization are the sole proprietorship, the partnership, and the corporation. This book focuses on corporations, but most of the general financial principles developed in this book are also applicable to other forms of business organization.

A. A *sole proprietorship* is a business owned by one person.

One individual is solely responsible for all aspects of the business. This individual owns all the firm's assets and is responsible for all its liabilities. Sole proprietorships are generally small businesses and are common in wholesale, retail, and service industries. More businesses are sole proprietorships than any other form of business organization.

1. Advantages of a sole proprietorship are:

   - *Ease of entry and exit.* A sole proprietorship requires no formal charter and is inexpensive to form and dissolve.
   - *Full ownership and control.* The owner has full control, reaps all profits, and bears all losses.
   - *Tax savings.* The entire income generated by the proprietorship passes directly to the owner. This may result in a tax advantage if the owner's tax rate is less than the tax rate for a corporation.
   - *Few government regulations.* A sole proprietorship has the greatest freedom from government regulation of any form of business organization.

2. Disadvantages of a sole proprietorship are:

   - *Unlimited liability.* The owner is personally responsible for any and all business debts. Thus, the owner's personal assets can be claimed if the firm defaults on its obligations.

- *Limitations in raising capital.* Fund-raising ability is limited by the small size of most sole proprietorships.
- *Lack of continuity.* A proprietorship ceases to exist when the owner dies.

B. A *partnership* is a legal arrangement in which there are two or more owners.

Partnerships may operate under varying degrees of formality. For example, a formal partnership may be established using a written contract known as the *partnership agreement.* Partnerships are most common in professions such as accounting, law, consulting, and medicine.

1. Partnerships may be either general or limited.

   - A *general partnership* is one in which each partner has unlimited liability for the debts incurred by the business. General partners usually manage the firm and may enter into contractual obligations on the firm's behalf. Profits and asset ownership may be divided in any way agreed upon by the partners.
   - A *limited partnership* is one containing one or more general partners and one or more limited partners. The personal liability of the general partner for the firm's debts is unlimited but the personal liability of limited partners is limited to their investment. Limited partners cannot be active in management.

2. Advantages of a partnership are:

   - *Ease of formation.* Forming a partnership may require relatively little effort and low start-up costs.
   - *Additional sources of capital.* A partnership has the financial resources of several individuals.
   - *Management base.* A partnership typically has a broader management base than a sole proprietorship.
   - *Tax implications.* As in a sole proprietorship, the income passes directly to the owners and is normally taxed as direct income of the partners, whether or not it is actually distributed to them. The tax impact can be less than that of a corporation, depending on the tax position of the owners.

3. Disadvantages of a partnership are:

   - *Unlimited liability.* General partners have unlimited personal liability for the debts and litigations of the business.
   - *Lack of continuity.* A partnership may dissolve upon the withdrawal or death of a general partner, depending on the provisions of the partnership.
   - *Difficulty of transferring ownership.* It is difficult for a partner to liquidate or transfer ownership.
   - *Limitations in raising capital.* A partnership may have problems raising large amounts of capital because many sources of funds are available only to corporations.

C. A *corporation* is a separate legal entity created by the state.

This legal entity may own assets, borrow money, and engage in other business activities without directly involving its owners. In most large corporations, owners, who are also called shareholders or stockholders, do not directly run the firm. Instead they select managers to run the firm for them. The firm's managers are considered agents of the corporation and are authorized to act in the corporation's behalf. Thus, a corporation is a distinct and separate entity from its owners. Most middle- and large-size businesses are corporations. The corporation is the dominant form of business organization in the United States in terms of asset size and sales volume.

1. A corporation is incorporated in a particular state which is not necessarily the one in which it is located. The corporate founders file with the appropriate state officials

articles of incorporation, which provide information about the proposed business. If approved, the state issues a **charter** which establishes the corporation as a legal entity. The corporate **bylaws**, which are rules that govern the internal management of the company, are established by the board of directors and approved by the stockholders. A corporation is subject to the laws of both the state in which it is incorporated and the state in which it is located.

2. Advantages of a corporation are:

   - *Limited liability.* Stockholders are liable only to the extent of their investment in the corporation. Thus, stockholders can only lose what they have invested in the firm's shares, not any other personal assets.
   - *Unlimited life.* Corporations continue to exist after the death of owners.
   - *Transferability of ownership.* Shareholders can easily sell their ownership interest in most corporations by selling their stock.
   - *Ability to raise capital.* Corporations can raise capital through the sale of debt securities, such as bonds, to investors who are lending money to the corporation, and equity securities such as common stock to investors who are the owners.

3. Disadvantages of a corporation include:

   - *Time and cost of formation.* Registration of public companies with the Securities and Exchange Commission (SEC) may be time-consuming and costly.
   - *Regulation.* Corporations are regulated by numerous state and federal government agencies, and public corporations must comply with securities law.
   - *Taxes.* Corporations are the only type of business organization wherein earnings are subject to double taxation at the federal level. A corporation is taxed on its income as it is earned. Part of the corporate income which remains after taxes may be paid as cash dividends to shareholders. For individual shareholders, these dividends are included in their personal income, and, as such, are taxed a second time if they exceed the dollar amount allowed by the Internal Revenue Service as a dividend exemption. For corporations who own stock in other corporations, a portion of the cash dividends received may also be taxed.

2-2. Taxes

The financial manager must have an understanding of tax matters because almost every financial decision has some tax implications. This task is difficult because tax rules are complex and change frequently. There are many different types of taxes and tax rules vary depending on the form of organization. For example, the owners of sole proprietorships and partnerships are taxed on their total personal income less a variety of exemptions, deductions, and exclusions. Both personal and corporate income taxes are progressive up to a specific level (that is, the tax rate increases in graduated steps as taxable income rises), but the Tax Reform Act of 1986 institutes a flat tax at certain levels.

The following discussion is limited to corporate federal income taxes and oversimplifies some aspects of the tax laws. Personal income tax regulations differ significantly from corporate income tax regulations in many ways. The tax regulations discussed are based on the Tax Reform Act of 1986. (For a more detailed discussion of current tax regulations, see either *Federal Tax Course* published by Harcourt Brace Jovanovich, Publishers, or West's *Federal Taxation*, both published annually.)

A. *Ordinary taxable income* for a corporation is equal to ordinary gross income minus deductible expenses.

The Tax Reform Act of 1986 sets the top corporate tax rate at 34 percent, effective for taxable years beginning on or after July 1, 1987. Figure 2-1 shows that there are three corporate federal income tax brackets. In the case of a corporation that has taxable income in excess of $100,000 for any taxable year, the amount of the tax is increased by 5 percent on such excess or $11,750, whichever is less. The effect of the surtax is to tax

Taxable Income	Marginal Tax Rate
$50,000 or less	15%
Over $50,000 but not over $75,000	25
Over $75,000*	24

* For a corporation with taxable income in excess of $100,000 for any taxable year, the amount of the tax is increased by (1) 5 percent of such excess, or (2) $11,750, whichever is less. A flat tax of 34 percent begins at $335,000 in taxable income.

FIGURE 2-1   Corporate federal income tax rates.

every extra dollar of taxable income in the $100,000 to $335,000 range at a 39 percent rate. Thus, a corporation with taxable income of more than $335,000 will pay, in effect, a flat tax rate of 34 percent on all taxable income. Positive taxable income is multiplied by the tax rate to obtain income taxes due. (Corporations may also be subject to an alternate minimum tax (AMT), which is treated in taxation textbooks.)

The **effective tax rate**, also called the *average tax rate*, is the percentage of total taxable income paid in taxes. The effective tax rate is calculated by dividing the tax liability by total taxable income. The **marginal tax rate** is the tax rate on the next dollar of taxable income. The effective and marginal income tax rates become the same for taxable income of $335,000 or more. In making financial decisions, the marginal tax rate is used because the firm is concerned with the tax impact of the additional income or deductions resulting from the decision.

1. *Ordinary gross income* includes sales revenue and other income. For example, *interest income* received by a corporation is taxed as ordinary income at regular corporate tax rates. *Dividend income* received by a corporation is subject to a tax break. A corporation may exclude 80 percent of the dividends received from another corporation from its taxable income. The remaining 20 percent of the dividends received is taxed as ordinary income. Thus, the maximum effective tax rate becomes 6.8 percent (20 percent [amount of dividend income subject to tax] × 34 percent [maximum rate]). The dividend exclusion eliminates most of the double taxation of dividends at the corporate level.

2. Deductible expenses are either cash or noncash expenses incurred in generating income.

   • **Cash deductible expenses** are expenses that are deducted from the firm's operating income for tax purposes and which involve an actual outlay of cash. These expenses include cost of goods sold; selling, general and administrative expenses; and lease and interest payments. *Interest paid* is deducted from ordinary income to obtain taxable income but *dividends paid* are not tax deductible. Thus, interest is paid with before-tax dollars, while dividends are paid with after-tax dollars. In this way, the tax system favors debt financing over equity financing.

   • **Noncash deductible expenses** are expenses that are deducted from the firm's operating income for tax purposes but which do not involve an actual outlay of cash. Depreciation, amortization, and depletion allowances are examples of such noncash charges. Depreciation expenses are the most common noncash deductible expense.

EXAMPLE 2-1: Alpha Corporation, a calendar year taxpayer, has taxable income of $90,000 for 1988.

(*a*) Using the tax rates in Figure 2-1, Alpha's income tax liability is $18,850.

$$\text{Income tax liability} = (0.15)(\$50,000) + (0.25)(\$25,000) + (0.34)(\$15,000)$$

$$= \$7,500 + \$6,250 + \$5,100 = \$18,850$$

(*b*) Alpha Corporation's effective tax rate is:

$$\text{Effective tax rate} = \frac{\$18,850}{\$90,000}$$

$$= 0.2094 \text{ or } 20.94 \text{ percent}$$

Its marginal tax rate is 34 percent.

EXAMPLE 2-2: Beta Corporation's ordinary taxable income for 1988 is $400,000. It also has $10,000 in dividend income.

(*a*) Using the information in Figure 2-1, Beta's income tax liability is $136,000.

$$\text{Income tax liability} = (0.34)(\$400,000) = \$136,000$$

Because Beta's taxable income is greater than $335,000, a flat tax of 34 percent applies.

(*b*) The effective tax rate paid by Beta Corporation is:

$$\text{Effective tax rate} = \frac{\$136,000}{\$400,000}$$

$$= 0.3400 \text{ or } 34.00 \text{ percent}$$

The marginal tax rate is also 34 percent.

(*c*) Beta Corporation would have to pay taxes on 20 percent of the dividends received, or $2,000 (0.20 × $10,000). At a marginal tax rate of 34 percent, Beta Corporation would pay $680 (0.34 × $2,000) in taxes on these dividends.

B. *Depreciation* is a systematic allocation of the cost of an asset over time.

The tax laws permit a firm to write off the costs of a depreciable asset over a period of years to better match costs and revenues in each accounting period. Depreciation is a tax-deductible expense but it is not necessarily related to either the economic life or the market value of the asset. For example, a building may depreciate for accounting and tax purposes while its market value actually appreciates.

The Economic Recovery Tax Act (ERTA) of 1981 completely overhauled the depreciation rules and created the **Accelerated Cost Recovery System (ACRS)**, which is mandatory for tax reporting only after December 31, 1980. This law substitutes the term *cost recovery* for the more familiar term *depreciation*. The Tax Reform Act of 1986 modified the structure of ACRS by adding more classes, reclassifying certain assets, and reducing the early write-off of most real estate. In computing the cost recovery under ACRS, firms ignore the asset's salvage value and expected useful life.

The Tax Reform Act of 1986 increases the expense option to $10,000 for property placed in service after December 31, 1986. That is, a firm may expense up to $10,000 in business property rather than use ACRS. There is, however, a dollar-for-dollar reduction for amounts invested in business property in excess of $200,000 during the year.

1. The ACRS establishes recovery periods for various classes of property. A **recovery period** is the length of time over which the cost of an asset is recovered. Under the new ACRS rules, each type of property is classified into eight classes. The 3-year, 5-year, 7-year, and 10-year classes use 200 percent declining balance (DB) with a switchover to straight-line. The 15-year and 20-year classes use 150 percent DB with a switchover to straight-line. The switchover occurs at the point which maximizes deductions. Residential rental real estate is in a 27.5-year class using straight-line. Nonresidential real estate is in a 31.5-year class using straight-line. The new ACRS method is used for tax purposes and applies to assets placed in service after December 31, 1986.

2. The annual depreciation amount depends on the asset's depreciation rate and depreciable basis. Equation 2-1 is used to calculate the annual depreciation amount.

$$\frac{\text{Annual}}{\text{depreciation amount}} = \text{Depreciation rate} \times \text{Depreciable basis} \qquad \textbf{(2-1)}$$

- The **depreciation rate** is usually the annual percentage rate at which an asset is depreciated or cost recovered. This rate is determined by the cost recovery class of the asset and the appropriate year in that recovery period.
- The **depreciable basis** is the original cost of an asset plus costs related to an asset's purchase, such as transportation, insurance during shipping, and installation.

3. Business personal property may be depreciated under the accelerated (ACRS) method or straight-line method. The accelerated method provides for more rapid write-off than the straight-line method. The total amounts of depreciation taken under the accelerated and straight-line methods are the same. However, the more rapid depreciation taken under the accelerated method results in a higher present value of the tax savings, due to the time value of money. (The concept of time value of money is discussed in Chapter 3.) That is, the firm realizes the tax savings earlier rather than later during the recovery period. Both residential rental property and nonresidential real property must be depreciated using the straight-line method. The Tax Reform Act of 1986 does not specify the depreciation percentages and the taxable year of switchover to the straight-line method but merely indicates the two depreciation methods. Figure 2-2 presents the *unofficial* depreciation percentages for the accelerated depreciation. (A separate recovery schedule is used for real estate, but it is not shown.)

Recovery Year	ACRS Class					
	3-Year	5-Year	7-Year	10-Year	15-Year	20-Year
1	.3300	.2000	.1428	.1000	.0500	.0375
2	.4500	.3200	.2449	.1800	.0950	.0723
3	.1500	.1920	.1749	.1440	.0855	.0668
4	.0700	.1152*	.1249	.1152	.0769	.0628
5		.1152	.0893*	.0922	.0693	.0572
6		.0576	.0893	.0739	.0623	.0538
7			.0893	.0655*	.0590*	.0489
8			.0446	.0655	.0590	.0446*
9				.0655	.0590	.0446
10				.0655	.0590	.0446
11				.0329	.0590	.0446
13					.0590	.0446
14					.0590	.0446
15					.0590	.0446
16					.0300	.0446
17						.0446
18						.0446
19						.0446
20						.0446
21						.0250
Total	1.0000	1.0000	1.0000	1.0000	1.0000	1.0000

* Assumes switchover to straight-line method over remaining useful life.

FIGURE 2-2 Unofficial depreciation percentages for personal property placed in service after December 31, 1986, assuming the half-year convention applies.

4. Property other than real estate is generally depreciated using a half-year convention in the first and last tax year. The **half-year convention** treats the property

as placed in service or as disposed of in the middle of service. For example, the statute assumes that the recovery period for 5-year property begins in the middle of the year in which an asset is placed in service, and that it ends five years later. The effect of this rule is that taxpayers must wait an extra year to recover the cost of depreciable assets. Thus, the actual write-off periods are increased by one year to 4, 6, 8, 11, 16, and 21 years. (The Tax Reform Act of 1986 allows for modifying the half-year convention rule, depending on the pattern of property acquisitions during the year.)

EXAMPLE 2-3: Perry Corporation buys and places into service $100,000 of light trucks that qualify as 5-year property under the ACRS rules.

(*a*) The depreciable basis is $100,000.
(*b*) The annual depreciation amount is determined by substituting the depreciable basis of $100,000 and the ACRS recovery rates for 5-year property shown in Figure 2-2 in Equation 2-1.

Recovery Year	Depreciation Rate (1)	Depreciable Basis (2)	Depreciation Amount [(1) × (2)]
1	.2000	$100,000	$ 20,000
2	.3200	100,000	32,000
3	.1920	100,000	19,200
4	.1152	100,000	11,520
5	.1152	100,000	11,520
6	.0576	100,000	5,760
Total			$100,000

C. An *operating loss*, for tax purposes, is the excess of deductible expenses over ordinary gross income.

A firm with negative taxable income has a loss for the year and pays no income taxes. A net operating loss of a corporation may be carried back three years and forward fifteen years to offset taxable income for those years. Losses that are carried back are deducted first from the earliest year and then brought forward on a year-by-year basis until either the loss is offset or the allowable time period is exhausted. A corporation may forgo the carryback option and elect, instead, to carry forward the loss. This choice would be preferred by taxpayers whose marginal tax rate is expected to be higher in the future than it was during the past three years.

1. A **loss carryback** is a loss applied against the taxable income of a previous year so as to produce a refund to the firm of taxes previously paid.
2. A **loss carryforward** is a loss applied against a subsequent year's taxable income.

EXAMPLE 2-4: Sampson Plastics, Inc. had a $300,000 operating loss in 1987. The firm's taxable income and taxes paid from 1984 through 1988 are shown below.

	1984	1985	1986	1987	1988
Taxable income	$125,000	$100,000	$50,000	−$300,000	$150,000**
Tax payments	37,250*	25,750*	8,250*	0	41,750**

* *Based on tax rates in effect prior to the Tax Reform Act of 1986.*
** *Before operating loss carryforward.*

If the firm elects to use the carryback provision, Sampson Plastics would file an amended tax return for 1984 through 1986. The operating loss experienced in 1987 would be carried back and used to offset a total of $275,000 ($125,000 + $100,000 + $50,000) in taxable income for the preceding three years. The firm would receive a tax refund of $71,250 ($37,250 + $25,750 + $8,250) for the full amount of taxes paid. The remaining $25,000 in operating losses would be carried forward as a tax deduction. It would reduce Sampson Plastics' 1988 tax liability by $9,750 (0.39 × $25,000). (Note: The 5 percent additional tax means a 39 percent marginal tax rate for every dollar of taxable income from $100,000 to $335,000.)

D. The sale of corporate assets may have several tax consequences.

The Tax Reform Act of 1986 does not change the character of a corporate taxpayer's gains which remain either capital or ordinary. Section 1231 (plant and equipment) is also left intact by the Tax Reform Act of 1986, even though there is no long-term capital gain deduction or a difference between ordinary and capital gain tax rates after 1987. Thus, the Tax Reform Act of 1986 eliminates the preferential alternative tax rate for net capital gains of corporations. The tax consequences of corporate asset sales depend on whether the asset sold is an ordinary asset, plant and equipment, or a capital asset.

1. Ordinary assets are inventory, stock in trade, or other property sold to customers in the ordinary course of business. Ordinary assets also include notes and accounts receivable resulting from the sale of such assets. Income from the sale of ordinary assets is ordinary income taxable at the corporation's regular tax rates. Losses from such sales are deducted in full from ordinary income.

2. Plant and equipment owned for more than six months get special tax treatment under Section 1231 of the Internal Revenue Code. Each year, gains from sales of such assets are offset against losses. If the result is a net Section 1231 loss, it is fully deductible from the corporation's ordinary income. If the result is a net Section 1231 gain, it is treated as a long-term capital gain unless the corporation has deducted Section 1231 losses during the past five years. If losses have been deducted in those years, the gain is treated as ordinary income to the extent of the losses deducted.

EXAMPLE 2-5: In 1988 Bulmash Corporation has two sales of Section 1231 assets: the first producing a gain of $2,000, and the second producing a loss of $5,000. For tax purposes, the gain of $2,000 and the loss of $5,000 are offset, resulting in a net Section 1231 loss of $3,000, which is fully deductible from ordinary income.

EXAMPLE 2-6: If, in Example 2-5, the gain had been $5,000 and the loss $2,000, the gain of $5,000 and the loss of $2,000 would result in a net Section 1231 gain of $3,000, which is treated as a long-term capital gain. However, the Tax Reform Act of 1986 provides no preferential treatment for long-term capital gains, which are taxed at ordinary rates.

EXAMPLE 2-7: If, in Example 2-6, Bulmash Corporation had deducted $1,700 of Section 1231 losses during the period 1983–1987, the $3,000 gain would be treated as follows: $1,700 is ordinary income and $1,300 is long-term capital gain.

3. Capital gains and losses result from the sale of capital assets. After eliminating inventory, receivables, and plant and equipment, very few corporate assets are classified as capital assets. A **capital asset** is an asset that is not bought or sold in the ordinary course of business. In practice, they are usually limited to purchased goodwill and investments in real estate or securities not used for normal business operations. Other intangible assets, such as copyrights, patents, and capitalized research and development expenses, get special tax treatment. Capital gains and losses are either long-term or short-term. *Long-term gains* and *losses* result from sales of capital assets held for more than six months, and *short-term gains* and *losses* result from sales of capital assets held for six months or less. Short-term gains and losses are first netted, as are long-term gains and losses. If the result is a net short-term loss and a net long-term gain, or vice-versa, these are further netted. The

results of this netting process can be as follows:

- A *net short-* and/or *long-term capital loss* cannot offset ordinary income, but is carried back as a short-term loss and is offset against short- and long-term capital gains incurred in the past three years, which are applied to the earliest year in point of time. If any loss remains, it is carried forward for a period of five years from the year of the loss and is offset against capital gains.
- All net short- and/or long-term capital gains are subject to regular corporate income tax rates.

Figure 2-3 summarizes the capital gain and loss treatment of corporations for taxable years beginning after December 31, 1986.

Item	Corporate Tax Treatment
1. Short-term capital gain	Taxed at ordinary rates
2. Long-term capital gain	Taxed at ordinary rates
3. Short-term capital loss	No deduction against ordinary income
4. Long-term capital loss	No deduction against ordinary income
5. Capital loss carryback	3 years; treated as short-term
6. Capital loss carryforward	5 years; treated as short-term

FIGURE 2-3   Summary of capital gain and loss treatment of corporations for taxable years beginning after December 31, 1986.

EXAMPLE 2-8: Davidson Company had $50,000 of ordinary taxable income and $30,000 in net long-term capital gains for 1988. The firm had no tax loss carryforwards. Both the $50,000 in ordinary taxable income and the $30,000 in net long-term capital gains are taxed at the ordinary rates shown in Figure 2-1. Thus, for 1988 Davidson Company would pay $15,450 in taxes, as shown below.

$$\text{Income tax liability} = (0.15)(\$50,000) + (0.25)(\$25,000) + (0.34)(\$5,000)$$

$$= \$7,500 + \$6,250 + \$1,700 = \$15,450$$

E. All of the gain resulting from disposition of the corporate plant and equipment is treated as ordinary taxable income.

Recapture of depreciation results when a corporation sells depreciable property for more than its *adjusted basis*, which is the property's purchase price plus capital additions less its accumulated depreciation.

1. *Business personal property.* Gain from disposition of business personal property, such as machinery, equipment, and furniture, is treated as ordinary income to the extent of *all* depreciation (or ACRS) previous deducted, regardless of whether an accelerated method or an alternative straight-line method is used. Any excess of gain over the amount of depreciation recaptured as ordinary income is a Section 1231 gain and is treated as discussed above. Thus, total gain from the sale of plant and equipment may be split into two parts: recaptured depreciation, which is taxed as ordinary income, and a Section 1231 gain, which is treated like a long-term capital gain and is also taxed at ordinary rates. The reason for making the distinction in the gain is that a net long-term capital gain must be netted against a net short-term loss, whereas recaptured depreciation is simply treated as ordinary income.

EXAMPLE 2-9: Davidson Company purchased a 5-year recovery class asset in 1988 for $50,000, and sold it two years later for $75,000. During ownership, a total of $26,000 accelerated ACRS was deducted. The adjusted basis of the asset is $24,000 ($50,000 − $26,000) and the total gain is $49,000 ($75,000 − $26,000). Of the total gain, $24,000 is recaptured as ordinary income (the amount of ACRS deducted), and the remaining $25,000 is Section 1231 gain, which is treated as long-term capital gain and taxed at the regular corporate rates.

  2. *Real estate.* Under the Tax Reform Act of 1986, only the straight-line method is allowed on residential and nonresidential real estate. There is no recapture of such depreciation deductions claimed for property placed in service after December 31, 1986.

RAISE YOUR GRADES

Can you explain...?

☑ the three primary forms of business organization
☑ the advantages and disadvantages of each form of business organization
☑ the difference between the liability of a general partner and a limited partner
☑ how a corporation is created
☑ why a corporation is called a legal entity
☑ double taxation of corporate income
☑ the difference between the tax treatment of corporate earnings and those of a sole proprietorship or partnership
☑ how ordinary income, dividend income, and capital gains are taxed in a corporation
☑ the tax implications of interest expense compared to dividend payments
☑ the difference between the effective tax rate and the marginal tax rate
☑ why depreciation is a noncash expense
☑ how to determine the annual depreciation of an asset under the Accelerated Cost Recovery System (ACRS)
☑ the difference between an ordinary asset and a capital asset
☑ how an operating loss and a capital loss are treated for tax purposes
☑ how a gain and loss on Section 1231 assets are treated for tax purposes

SUMMARY

1. The three primary forms of business organization are the sole proprietorship, the partnership, and the corporation.
2. A sole proprietorship is owned by one individual, whereas a partnership is owned by two or more people.
3. A corporation is a separate legal entity created by the state.
4. There are more businesses organized as sole proprietorships than any other form of business organization, but corporations dominate in terms of dollar volume of business activity.
5. Corporations, which require registration with the Securities and Exchange Commission, are usually more costly to form than sole proprietorships and partnerships.
6. Advantages of corporations include limited liability, unlimited life, transferability of ownership, ability to raise capital, and managerial flexibility.

7. Income from sole proprietorships and partnerships is treated entirely as the personal income of the owner(s).

8. Corporate income is taxed first at the corporate level and then the distributed portion is taxed again as the owners' personal income. Thus, owners are subject to double taxation on income distributed as cash dividends.

9. All forms of business organization are subject to a progressive tax rate until a specific level of taxable income is reached.

10. The Tax Reform Act of 1986 sets the top corporate tax rate at 34 percent.

11. The effective tax rate is the percentage of taxable income paid in taxes.

12. The marginal tax rate is the tax rate on the next dollar of taxable income. The marginal tax rate is generally used in financial decision making.

13. Interest payments are treated as tax-deductible expenses, but cash dividends paid are not. Thus, interest expenses receive favorable tax treatment relative to dividend expenses.

14. A corporation may exclude from its taxable income 80 percent of the dividends received from another corporation.

15. Cost recovery (depreciation) is a tax-deductible expense allowed to firms for certain types of business assets. The Accelerated Cost Recovery System (ACRS) determines the depreciation rate, based on the recovery period assigned to certain types of property.

16. A business incurring a net operating loss may carry the loss back three years and/or forward fifteen as a deduction against taxable income.

17. The sale of a corporate asset has different tax consequences, depending on whether the asset sold is an ordinary asset, plant and equipment, or a capital asset.

18. Long-term gains and losses result from the sale of capital assets held for more than six months; short-term gains and losses result from the sale of capital assets held for six months or less. Capital losses may be carried back three years and carried forward five years.

19. The sale of corporate plant and equipment for a gain may result in the recapture of depreciation, which is treated as ordinary taxable income. Any excess of gain over the amount recaptured as ordinary income is Section 1231 gain, which is treated as a long-term capital gain.

RAPID REVIEW

True or False

1. Sole proprietorships are the most common form of business organization. [Section 2-1A]

2. A sole proprietor has limited personal liability for any business debts. [Section 2-1A]

3. Both general and limited partners may actively manage a partnership. [Section 2-1B]

4. A partnership must be established by filing a partnership agreement. [Section 2-1B]

5. A corporation is a distinct and separate legal entity from its owners. [Section 2-1C]

6. Corporations are the dominant form of business organization in terms of size and sales. [Section 2-1C]

7. The corporate charter is issued by the federal government. [Section 2-1C]

8. Stockholders are liable only to the extent of their investment in the corporation. [Section 2-1C]

9. Double taxation is associated with the distribution of corporate earnings to a firm's owners. [Section 2-1C]

10. Partnership income is normally taxed as direct income of the partners, whether or not it is actually distributed to them. [Section 2-2]

11. According to the Tax Reform Act of 1986, the highest marginal federal tax rate on ordinary corporate taxable income is 34 percent. [Section 2-2A]

12. Dividends received by one corporation from another are taxed at a 20 percent marginal tax rate. [Section 2-2A]

13. Both interest and dividend payments are tax deductible expenses from a corporation's ordinary gross income. [Section 2-2A]

14. Depreciation is a noncash tax-deductible expense. [Section 2-2A]

15. The Accelerated Cost Recovery System refers to the increase of the corporate tax rate in graduated steps as taxable income rises. [Section 2-2B]

16. The Tax Reform Act of 1986 eliminates the use of the straight-line method of depreciation. [Section 2-2B]

17. An operating loss is the excess of tax-deductible expenses over capital gains. [Section 2-2C]

18. A long-term capital gain or loss occurs from the sale of a capital asset held for more than six months. [Section 2-2D]

19. For tax purposes, a capital asset is an asset that is not bought or sold in the ordinary course of business. [Section 2-2D]

20. A recapture of depreciation resulting from the sale of a capital asset is taxed as ordinary income. [Section 2-2E]

Multiple Choice

21. All of the following are advantages of a sole proprietorship *except*

   (*a*) ease of entry
   (*b*) limited liability
   (*c*) direct control over the business
   (*d*) few government regulations

   [Section 2-1A]

22. Upon the death of the sole proprietor, the firm technically

   (*a*) ceases to exist
   (*b*) continues as usual
   (*c*) operates under the jurisdiction of the court
   (*d*) none of the above

   [Section 2-1A]

23. Which types of owners have unlimited liability in a business?

   (*a*) Sole proprietors
   (*b*) General partners
   (*c*) Corporate shareholders
   (*d*) Both a and b

   [Section 2-1A through 2-1C]

24. Which form of business organization generally has the greatest ability to raise capital?

   (*a*) Sole proprietorship
   (*b*) General partnership
   (*c*) Limited partnership
   (*d*) Corporation

   [Section 2-1C]

25. Which of the following statements is *true* under the Accelerated Cost Recovery System (ACRS)?

   (*a*) Salvage value is subtracted from the cost of the asset in calculating the depreciable basis.

(b) Cost recovery is based on the expected useful life of the asset.
(c) Neither a or b
(d) Both a and b

[Section 2-2B]

26. An operating loss may be carried back three years and carried forward

(a) 3 years
(b) 5 years
(c) 10 years
(d) 15 years

[Section 2-2C]

27. Long-term gains and losses result from sales of capital assets held for more than

(a) 3 months
(b) 6 months
(c) 1 year
(d) 2 years

[Section 2-2D]

28. A net capital loss is

(a) deducted from ordinary income for tax purposes
(b) used only to offset capital gains
(c) carried back three years and carried forward five years
(d) Both b and c

[Section 2-2D]

29. Which of the following statements is *true* about capital gains?

(a) Capital gains receive preferential tax treatment.
(b) Capital gains are taxed at ordinary corporate income tax rates.
(c) Capital gains result from the sale of ordinary assets.
(d) None of the above

[Section 2-2D]

30. Recaptured depreciation is taxed as

(a) a short-term capital gain
(b) a long-term capital gain
(c) ordinary income
(d) None of the above

[Section 2-2E]

Answers

True or False

1. True	11. True	
2. False	12. False	
3. False	13. False	
4. False	14. True	
5. True	15. False	
6. True	16. False	
7. False	17. False	
8. True	18. True	
9. True	19. True	
10. True	20. True	

Multiple Choice

21. b	
22. a	
23. d	
24. d	
25. c	
26. d	
27. b	
28. d	
29. b	
30. c	

SOLVED PROBLEMS

PROBLEM 2-1: A corporation has taxable income of $75,000.

(*a*) What is the firm's federal income tax liability?
(*b*) What is the firm's effective tax rate?

Answer:

(*a*) Using the tax rates in Figure 2-1, the firm's income tax liability is $13,750.

$$\text{Income tax liability} = (0.15)(\$50,000) + (0.25)(\$25,000)$$
$$= \$7,500 + \$6,250 = \$13,750$$

(*b*) The effective tax rate is:

$$\text{Effective tax rate} = \frac{\$13,750}{\$75,000} = 0.1833 \text{ or } 18.33 \text{ percent}$$

[Section 2-2A]

PROBLEM 2-2: Textilease Corporation had $500,000 in taxable income in 1988.

(*a*) What is the firm's tax bill?
(*b*) What is the effective and marginal tax rates?

Answer:

(*a*) Texilease Corporation's tax bill is:

$$\text{Income tax liability} = (0.34)(\$500,000) = \$170,000$$

(*b*) Both the effective and marginal tax rates are 34 percent.   **[Section 2-2A]**

PROBLEM 2-3: Brigham Enterprises, Inc. received $20,000 in dividends from stock owned in Campsey Construction Company. If Brigham Enterprises is in the 34 percent marginal tax bracket, what is its income tax liability for the dividends?

Answer: Brigham Enterprises, Inc. owes taxes on $4,000 (0.20 × $20,000) of the dividends received. With a 34 percent tax rate, the firm's tax liability is $1,360 (0.34 × $4,000).

[Section 2-2A]

PROBLEM 2-4: Mountain Gift Company earned $800,000 before interest and taxes during 1989. During that year the firm paid $100,000 in interest and $75,000 in cash dividends. How much in federal income taxes did the firm pay?

Answer: Interest payments are a tax-deductible expense, whereas cash dividends are paid after taxes. The corporation's taxable income was $700,000 ($800,000 − $100,000) and its income tax liability was $238,000 [(0.34)($700,000)].   **[Section 2-2A]**

PROBLEM 2-5: In 1988, Stempler Towel Company had net sales of $200,000 with cost of goods sold of $100,000, depreciation of $25,000, and other operating expenses of $30,000. The firm also received $10,000 in dividend income, and paid $20,000 in interest and $5,000 in cash dividends. What is the firm's taxable income and its tax liability?

Answer: As shown on page 26, Stempler Towel Company has $27,000 in taxable income and paid $4,050 (0.15 × $27,000) in federal income taxes.

Stempler Towel Company
Income Statement
For the Period Ending December 31, 1989

Sales	$200,000
Taxable dividends	
(0.20 × $10,000)	2,000
Gross income	$202,000
Operating expenses:	
Cost of goods sold	100,000
Depreciation expense	25,000
Other operating expenses	30,000
Earnings before interest and taxes	$ 47,000
Interest expense	20,000
Earnings before taxes	$ 27,000
Taxes (15%)	4,050
Net income	$ 22,950

[Section 2-2A]

PROBLEM 2-6: Barton Products purchased several light trucks for a total cost of $40,000. These trucks are classified as 5-year property under the Accelerated Cost Recovery System (ACRS). What is the annual cost recovery amount using ACRS?

Answer: Substituting the ACRS recovery rates for 5-year property shown in Figure 2-2 in Equation 2-1, the annual cost recovery is as follows:

Recovery Year	Depreciation Rate (1)	Depreciable Basis (2)	Depreciation Amount [(1) × (2)]
1	.2000	$40,000	$ 8,000
2	.3200	40,000	12,800
3	.1920	40,000	7,680
4	.1152	40,000	4,608
5	.1152	40,000	4,608
6	.0576	40,000	2,304
Total			$40,000

[Section 2-2B]

PROBLEM 2-7: Carrington Corporation started business in 1987 and experienced a $40,000 operating loss. In 1988, the corporation has $60,000 in taxable income before adjusting for its previous operating loss. What is Carrington Corporation's income tax liability in 1988?

Answer: The operating loss incurred in 1987 is carried forward and applied against the taxable income. Thus, the corporation would pay taxes on $20,000 ($60,000 − $40,000). Its federal income tax liability is $3,000 (0.15 × $20,000). **[Sections 2-2A & C]**

PROBLEM 2-8: Norris Corporation sold three Section 1231 assets during 1988, each of which had been held for over six months. The first two sales produced gains of $10,000 and $8,000, respectively, while the third sale resulted in a loss of $14,000. The firm had not deducted Section 1231 losses during the prior five years. The firm's ordinary taxable income before any gains and losses is $60,000. How much, if anything, would Norris Corporation pay in taxes on the sale of Section 1231 assets?

Answer: Norris Corporation has a net Section 1231 gain of $4,000 ($10,000 + $8,000 − $14,000), which would be treated as a long-term capital gain. With taxable income of

$60,000, the firm has a marginal tax rate of 25 percent. Since a long-term capital gain is taxed at ordinary rates, the firm would pay $1,000 (0.25 × $4,000) in taxes on the sale of Section 1231 assets.

PROBLEM 2-9: If, in Problem 2-8, Norris Corporation had a net Section 1231 loss of $5,000 in 1988, how much tax would the firm pay?

Answer: A net Section 1231 loss of $5,000 is fully deductible from ordinary income. The corporation's taxable income would be $55,000 ($60,000 − $5,000). Its income tax liability is $8,750.

$$\text{Income tax liability} = (0.15)(\$50,000) + (0.25)(\$5,000)$$
$$= \$7,500 + \$1,250 = \$8,750$$

PROBLEM 2-10: Colby Corporation sells, for a gain of $10,000, some securities that it has held as an investment for four months. The corporation's marginal tax rate is 34 percent. The firm has $2,000 in short-term losses but no long-term capital gains or losses. How would Colby Corporation treat these sales for tax purposes?

Answer: Colby Corporation realized a short-term capital gain on the sale of the securities because they were held for fewer than six months. The short-term capital gains and loss are netted to produce a net short-term capital gain of $8,000 ($10,000 − $2,000), which is taxed at ordinary rates. Colby Corporation would pay $2,720 (0.34 × $8,000) in taxes on the short-term capital gain. **[Section 2-2D]**

PROBLEM 2-11: Powers Corporation experienced the following capital gains and losses for the year:

Short-term capital gain	$25,000
Short-term capital loss	10,000
Long-term capital gain	20,000
Long-term capital loss	50,000

How would these capital gains and losses be treated for tax purposes?

Answer: Short-term capital gains and losses are netted to produce a net short-term capital gain of $15,000 ($25,000 − $10,000). Likewise, long-term capital gains and losses are netted to produce a net long-term capital loss of $30,000 ($20,000 − $50,000). The net short-term gain and the net long-term loss are netted to produce a net long-term capital loss of $15,000 ($15,000 − $30,000). Capital losses can be used only as an offset against capital gains. Corporations may carry back net capital losses to three preceding years, applying them first to the earliest year in point of time. Carryforwards are allowed for a period of five years from the year of the loss. When carried back or forward, a long-term capital loss becomes a short-term capital loss. **[Section 2-2D]**

PROBLEM 2-12: In 1987 Morris, Inc. bought $100,000 in equipment that was classified as ACRS 7-year property. The firm has already deducted $56,260 in accelerated depreciation. The firm's marginal tax rate is 34 percent. If the firm sells the asset for $60,000, what is the firm's tax obligation as a result of the sale?

Answer: The entire $16,260 gain is considered recaptured depreciation and is taxed as ordinary income.

$$\text{Adjusted basis} = \$100,000 - \$56,260 = \$43,740$$
$$\text{Total gain} = \$60,000 - \$43,740 = \$16,260$$
$$\text{Income tax liability} = 0.34 \times \$16,260 = \$5,528.40$$

[Section 2-2E]

PROBLEM 2-13: Morris, Inc. purchased another machine in 1987 for $60,000 and sold it two years later for $80,000. The machine is classified as 7-year property. The firm has already deducted a total of $23,262 in accelerated ACRS. What is the tax obligation of Morris, Inc. for the sale?

Answer: Morris, Inc. would realize a total gain of $43,262, which is divided into $23,262 ($60,000 − $36,738) as recaptured depreciation and $20,000 as a Section 1231 gain. Assuming the firm has no capital losses, the total gain would be taxed at the firm's marginal tax rate.

$$\text{Adjusted basis} = \$60,000 - \$23,262 = \$36,738$$
$$\text{Total gain} = \$80,000 - \$36,738 = \$43,262$$

$$\text{Income tax liability} = 0.34 \times \$43,262 = \$14,709.08$$

[Section 2-2E]

3 THE TIME VALUE OF MONEY

THIS CHAPTER IS ABOUT

- ☑ **Meaning of Time Value of Money**
- ☑ **Future Value**
- ☑ **Future Value of a Stream of Payments**
- ☑ **Present Value**
- ☑ **Present Value of a Stream of Payments**
- ☑ **Perpetuities**
- ☑ **Growth Rates**
- ☑ **Sinking Fund**
- ☑ **Loan Amortization**

3-1. Meaning of Time Value of Money

You may have heard the expression, "A bird in the hand is worth two in the bush." In a way, this refers to the *time value* of birds; that is, it is better to have a single bird in hand now than the possibility of catching two birds in the future.

Money also has a time value. *Time value of money* means that a dollar today is worth more than a dollar tomorrow. Ask yourself, "Would I prefer getting $1,000 today, or $1,000 one year from now?" If you answered $1,000 today, then you realize that money has a time value. By having $1,000 today, you could do something with the money today, such as spend, save, or invest it.

Time value of money involves two major concepts: *future value* and *present value*.

3-2. Future Value

The first key concept about the time value of money is **future value**. Future value, sometimes called *compound value*, is the amount to which a present amount of money or a series of payments will grow over time when compounded at a given interest rate.

A. Future value involves three factors.

1. **Principal** is the amount of money borrowed or invested today.
2. **Interest** is the amount paid for (in the case of borrowed money) or earned by (in the case of invested money) the use of money. The percentage of the principal that is paid or earned in interest is called the **interest rate**.
3. **Time period** is the length of time or number of periods during which interest is paid or earned.

EXAMPLE 3-1: Suppose a firm deposits $1,000 in a bank at 10 percent interest a year. One year later the $1,000 will have grown to $1,100: $1,000 is principal and $100 is interest. The amount of interest is determined by multiplying the interest rate of 10 percent (0.10 in decimal notation) by the principal of $1,000 (0.10 × $1,000 = $100). Thus, the value of a dollar today can increase in the future because of the interest. This is illustrated below and in Figure 3-1.

Principal (beginning balance)	$1,000.00
Interest for year 1 at 10 percent (0.10 × $1,000 = $100.00)	100.00
Future value at the end of year 1	$1,100.00

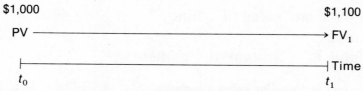

FIGURE 3-1 Future value of $1,000 invested at 10 percent for one year.

EXAMPLE 3-2: Now suppose that the firm leaves its $1,000 on deposit for two years in a bank paying 10 percent annual interest. At the end of the first year, the initial deposit becomes $1,100, as shown in Example 3-1. During the second year, the firm will earn 10 percent on this $1,100, or an additional $110 in interest. The firm is earning interest on the changing balance. Hence, at the end of the second year, the firm will have $1,210 in its account as shown below and in Figure 3-2.

Balance at the beginning of year 2	$1,100.00
Interest for year 2 at 10 percent (0.10 × $1,100 = $110.00)	110.00
Future value at the end of year 2	$1,210.00

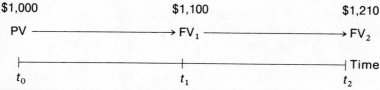

FIGURE 3-2 Future value of a $1,000 invested at 10 percent compound interest for two years.

B. Interest may be simple or compound.

Essentially, there are two types of interest. **Simple interest** is the interest paid or earned on the initial principal only. **Compound interest** is the interest paid on both the principal and the amount of interest accumulated in prior periods. The process of determining future value when compound interest is applied is called **compounding**. Using compound interest usually results in a greater future value than using simple interest.

EXAMPLE 3-3: Suppose that the financial manager has the choice of leaving $1,000 with a bank paying 10 percent simple interest or 10 percent compound interest for five years. With simple interest the financial manager earns 10 percent interest each year on the principal of $1,000 for a total of $500 (0.10 × $1,000 × 5). With compound interest the amount of interest earned increases each year because the beginning amount upon which the interest is calculated increases each year. Compound interest totals $610.51 after five years. The $110.51 difference in interest favors compound interest. The calculation of simple and compound <u>interest</u> is shown below:

Year	Beginning Amount (1)	Simple Interest [0.10 × (1)] (2)	Ending Amount [(1) + (2)] (3)	Beginning Amount (4)	Compound Interest [0.10 × (4)] (5)	Ending Amount [(4) + (5)] (6)
1	$1,000.00	$100.00	$1,100.00	$1,000.00	$100.00	$1,100.00
2	1,000.00	100.00	1,200.00	1,100.00	110.00	1,210.00
3	1,000.00	100.00	1,300.00	1,210.00	121.00	1,331.00
4	1,000.00	100.00	1,400.00	1,331.00	133.10	1,464.10
5	1,000.00	100.00	1,500.00	1,464.10	146.41	1,610.51
Total interest		$500.00			$610.51	

C. Future value can be found by using a formula.

The general formula for calculating future value is shown in Equation 3-1. In this formula, future value (FV_n) is equal to the initial principal amount, PV, compounded at the interest rate i for n periods.

FUTURE VALUE ANNUAL COMPOUNDING

$$FV_n = PV(1 + i)^n \qquad (3\text{-}1)$$

EXAMPLE 3-4: Using Equation 3-1, the future values of $1,000 compounded at a 10 percent annual interest rate at the end of one year, two years, and five years are computed as follows.

Substituting PV = $1,000 and $i = 0.10$ for different values of n in Equation 3-1 produces the following results:

Year	Calculation	Future Value
1	$FV_1 = (\$1,000)(1 + 0.10)^1 =$	$1,100.00
2	$FV_2 = (\$1,000)(1 + 0.10)^{2*}$	
	$= (\$1,000)(1.21) =$	1,210.00
5	$FV_5 = (\$1,000)(1 + 0.10)^{5**}$	
	$= (\$1,000)(1.61051) =$	1,610.51

* $(1.10)^2 = (1.1)(1.1) = 1.21$
** $(1.10)^5 = (1.1)(1.1)(1.1)(1.1)(1.1) = 1.61051$

These results are identical to those shown in Examples 3-1, 3-2, and 3-3.

D. Future value can be found by using a table.

Instead of computing the value of the term $(1 + i)^n$ by using Equation 3-1, you can use a table to find this value. The value is called the **future value interest factor** or $FVIF_{i,n}$ and may be viewed as the result of investing or lending $1 at interest rate i for n time periods. The values of the FVIFs for different interest rates and time periods are shown in Appendix A. Three things should be noted about Appendix A:

1. The FVIFs are greater than 1.0, except for time period 0.
2. The FVIFs increase as the interest rate for a given period increases.
3. The FVIFs increase as the time period associated with each interest rate increases.

Equation 3-1 can be rewritten as Equation 3-2:

FUTURE VALUE USING A TABLE

$$FV_n = PV(FVIF_{i,n}) \qquad (3\text{-}2)$$

EXAMPLE 3-5: Using Equation 3-2 and Appendix A, the future value of $1,000 compounded for five years at a 10 percent interest rate is computed as follows.

First, you need to find the value in Appendix A that corresponds to the intersection of a 10 percent interest rate with compounding for five years, that is, $FVIF_{0.10,5}$. This value is 1.611 and represents the calculation $(1.10)^5$. Now, substitute 1.611 in Equation 3-2 to find the future value.

$$FV_5 = (\$1,000)(1.611) = \$1,611.00$$

It is important to note that $1,611.00 is slightly different from the $1,610.51 computed in Examples 3-3 and 3-4 for the same problem. This is because the values in Appendix A are rounded to three decimal places, which may understate or overstate the true value.

EXAMPLE 3-6: Using Appendix A, how long would it take to double money at a 10 percent interest rate?

The first step would be to search the 10 percent column in Appendix A to locate the future value interest factor that is closest to 2.0. The closest number is 1.949. Hence, money doubles in slightly over seven years when compounded at 10 percent annually.

E. Compounding can be more frequent than once a year.

Compounding that occurs more than once a year is called **intraperiod compounding**. The calendar period over which compounding occurs is called the **compounding period**. For example, compounding may occur annually, semiannually, quarterly, or monthly. When using intraperiod compounding, the future value formula shown in Equation 3-1 must be modified to reflect the number of times per year compounding occurs, denoted by m. This change is presented in Equation 3-3.

FUTURE VALUE WITH INTRAPERIOD COMPOUNDING
$$FV_n = PV\left[1 + \frac{i}{m}\right]^{mn} \qquad \text{(3-3)}$$

EXAMPLE 3-7: Instead of placing $1,000 in the First National Bank that pays 10 percent interest annually, the financial manager decides to put the money in the Second National Bank that pays 10 percent interest compounded semiannually. Between the two banks, there would be a difference in the future value of your investment after one year.

The future value of the deposit at each bank is shown below:

First National Bank Annual Compounding	Second National Bank Semiannual Compounding
$FV_1 = (\$1,000)(1 + 0.10)^1$	$FV_1 = (\$1,000)\left(1 + \dfrac{0.10}{2}\right)^{(2)(1)}$
$\quad = (\$1,000)(1.10)$	$\quad = (\$1,000)(1.1025)$
$\quad = \$1,100.00$	$\quad = \$1,102.50$

Now subtract $1,100 from $1,102.50 to find the difference in future values of $2.50. Thus, more interest is earned with semiannual compounding than with annual compounding.

F. The more frequently interest is compounded, the greater the future value.

Increasing the frequency of the compounding period makes the future value grow more rapidly because more interest is earned on the changing balance. Figure 3-3 shows the results of different compounding periods on an initial investment of $1,000 for one year.

G. Interest rates may be either nominal or effective.

The **nominal interest rate** is simply the stated rate, such as 10 percent. The **effective interest rate**, also called the *annual percentage rate* or *APR*, is the true interest rate and may differ from the nominal rate depending on the frequency of compounding.

Equation 3-4 is used to find the effective interest rate. In this equation, i is the nominal rate and m is the number of compounding periods per year.

EFFECTIVE INTEREST RATE
$$\text{APR} = \left[1 + \frac{i}{m}\right]^m - 1 \qquad \text{(3-4)}$$

EXAMPLE 3-8: A firm deposits money in a bank that pays a 10 percent nominal interest rate and compounds interest semiannually.

Substituting $i = 0.10$ and $m = 2$ values in Equation 3-4 results in an APR of 10.25 percent. This result is also shown in Figure 3-3.

$$\text{APR} = \left[1 + \frac{0.10}{2}\right]^2 - 1$$
$$= (1.05)^2 - 1$$
$$= 1.1025 - 1$$
$$= 0.1025 \text{ or } 10.25 \text{ percent}$$

Initial Investment	Compounding Period	Future Value	Effective Annual Interest Rate
$1,000	Annually	$1,100.00	10.00%
1,000	Semiannually	1,102.50	10.25
1,000	Quarterly	1,103.81	10.38
1,000	Monthly	1,104.71	10.47
1,000	Daily	1,105.16	10.52

Figure 3-3   Comparison of results of different compounding periods for $1,000 invested at a 10 percent interest rate for one year.

3-3. Future Value of a Stream of Payments

The concept of future value can be extended beyond compounding a single payment to compounding a series, or *stream*, of payments.

A. Future value determination may involve a stream of unequal payments.

Calculating the future value of an unequal stream of payments involves finding the future value of each payment at a specified future date and then summing these future values. The calculation is shown in Equation 3-5 and illustrated in Figure 3-4.

FUTURE VALUE OF AN UNEQUAL STREAM OF PAYMENTS
$$\text{FV}_n = \sum_{t=0}^{n} P_t(1 + i)^{n-t} \qquad \text{(3-5)}$$

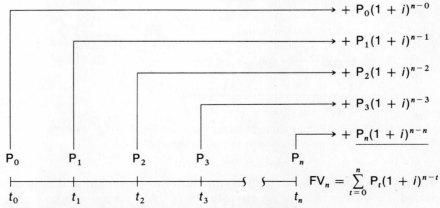

Figure 3-4   Future value of an unequal series of payments.

The sigma (Σ) notation is a mathematical symbol for summing a series of values. In Equation 3-5, the future value for a time period (FV_n) is found by adding up each payment (P_t) adjusted for the number of periods in which interest is earned. The exponent ($n - t$) indicates the number of periods in which interest is earned.

EXAMPLE 3-9: A firm plans to deposit $2,000 today and $1,500 one year from now at Liberty Bank. No future deposits or withdrawals are made and the bank pays 10 percent interest compounded annually. Using Equation 3-5 and Appendix A, the future value of the account at the end of four years is computed to be $4,924.50.

$$FV_4 = (\$2,000)(1.10)^4 + (\$1,500)(1.10)^3$$
$$= (\$2,000)(1.464) + (\$1,500)(1.331)$$
$$= \$2,928.00 + \$1,996.50 = \$4,924.50$$

B. Future value determination may involve a stream of equal payments.

A stream of equal payments made at regular time intervals is an **annuity**, sometimes called a *fixed annuity*. There are two types of fixed annuities.

1. An **ordinary annuity** is one in which the payments or receipts occur at the *end* of each period. This type of annuity is also called a regular, or *deferred*, annuity. The *future value of an ordinary annuity* ($FVOA_n$) is shown by Equation 3-6. The term A is the amount of the fixed annuity payment and $FVIFA_{i,n}$ is the *future value interest factor of an annuity* for interest rate, i, and time period, n. Appendix B shows the FVIFAs for various values of i and n.

FUTURE VALUE OF
AN ORDINARY ANNUITY $$FVOA_n = A(FVIFA_{i,n})$$ (3-6)
USING A TABLE

EXAMPLE 3-10: A firm deposits $1,000 at the end of each of three consecutive years in a bank account paying 10 percent interest compounded annually. The value of the account at the end of the third year is computed by first substituting $A = \$1,000$, $i = 0.10$, and $n = 3$ in Equation 3-6. After $FVIFA_{0.10,3}$ is located in Appendix B, the equation can be solved. The FVIFA of 3.310 is the value in Appendix B where the 10 percent interest rate and three-year time period intersect. The results are shown in Figure 3-5.

$$FVOA_3 = (\$1,000)(FVIFA_{0.10,3})$$
$$= (\$1,000)(3.310) = \$3,310$$

Compounded two years → $1,210

Compounded one year → $1,100

No compounding → $1,000

$1,000 $1,000 $1,000 $3,310 = FVOA_3

Time

t_0 t_1 t_2 t_3

FIGURE 3-5   Future value of an ordinary annuity ($FVOA_n$) for three years with 10 percent annual compounding.

2. An **annuity due** is one in which payments or receipts occur at the *beginning* of each period. The *future value of an annuity due* ($FVAD_n$) is found by using Equation 3-7.

FUTURE VALUE OF		
AN ANNUITY DUE	$FVAD_n = A(FVIFA_{i,n})(1 + i)$	**(3-7)**
USING A TABLE		

This equation is identical to Equation 3-6 except that in Equation 3-7 each payment is compounded for one extra year. The reason for this additional compounding is that figures in Appendix B are based on the assumption that payments are made at the end of the year, but an annuity due requires payments to be made at the beginning of the year.

EXAMPLE 3-11: Instead of depositing $1,000 at the end of each year for three consecutive years, as done in Example 3-10, the firm makes deposits at the beginning of each year. Interest is compounded annually at 10 percent. How much will you have in your account after three years?

Substitute A = $1,000, $i = 0.10$, and $n = 3$ in Equation 3-7, locate $FVIFA_{0.10,3}$ in Appendix B, and solve the equation. The results are shown in Figure 3-6.

$$FVAD_3 = (\$1,000)(3.310)(1.10)$$
$$= (\$1,000)(3.641) = \$3,641$$

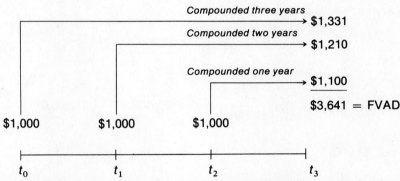

FIGURE 3-6 Future value of an annuity due ($FVAD_n$) for three years with 10 percent annual compounding.

The future value for the annuity due ($3,641 in this example) is greater than that for the ordinary annuity ($3,310 in Example 3-10) because each deposit is made one year earlier and consequently earns interest one year longer.

3-4. Present Value

The second key concept regarding the time value of money is **present value**. Present value is the current value of a future amount of money, or series of payments, evaluated at an appropriate discount rate. A **discount rate**, sometimes called the *required rate of return*, is the rate of interest that is used to find present values. The process of determining the present value of a future amount is called **discounting**.

A. Discounting is the reverse of compounding.

Future value determination compounds money forward in time to determine its worth in the future. Present value determination discounts money that will be received in the future back in time to see what it is worth in the present. This relationship is shown in Figure 3-7 on the following page. You can find present value by rewriting the future value formula (Equation 3-1) to solve for PV. You will recall that the future value formula is $FV_n = PV(1 + i)^n$. To find present value, divide both sides of the equation by $(1 + i)^n$, which yields the present value formula.

Future Value (Compounding)

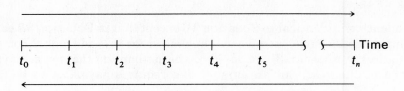

FIGURE 3-7   Comparison of future value to present value.

PRESENT VALUE $PV = \dfrac{FV_n}{(1 + i)^n}$ or $FV_n\left[\dfrac{1}{(1 + i)^n}\right]$ (3-8)

PV, FV, i, and n are defined as before.

EXAMPLE 3-12: Suppose that a firm expects to receive $1,100 one year from now. What is the present value of this amount if the discount rate is 10 percent?

Substitute $i = 0.10$ and $n = 1$ in Equation 3-8. $FV_1 = \$1,100$. Now solve the equation. The results are shown in Figure 3-8.

$$PV = \frac{\$1,100}{(1.10)^1} = \$1,000.00$$

or

$$PV = (\$1,100)\left[\frac{1}{(1.10)^1}\right] = (\$1,100)(0.9091) = \$1,000.01$$

FIGURE 3-8   Present value of $1,100 received at the end of one year discounted at 10 percent.

As shown in Example 3-1, compounding $1,000 at a 10 percent interest rate for one year provides a future value of $1,100. This example shows that discounting $1,100 at 10 percent yields a present value of $1,000. The $0.01 difference is caused by rounding the term in brackets.

B. Present value can be found by using a table.

Instead of computing the term in brackets in Equation 3-8 for various values of i and n, Appendix C, which incorporates these calculations, can be used. Each value in Appendix C is called a **present value interest factor** for discount rate i and time period n, or $PVIF_{i,n}$.

Three things should be noted about Appendix C:

1. The PVIFs are less than 1.0 except for time period 0.
2. The PVIFs decrease as the interest rate for a given period increases.
3. The PVIFs decrease as the time period associated with each interest rate increases.

Use Equation 3-9 to find present values using a table.

PRESENT VALUE
USING A TABLE $PV = FV_n(PVIF_{i,n})$ (3-9)

EXAMPLE 3-13: A firm expects to receive $1,000 five years from now and wants to know what this money is worth today. The value today of $1,000 to be received five years from now discounted at 10 percent is calculated as follows:

Substitute $i = 0.10$ and $n = 5$ in Equation 3-9. $PV_5 = \$1,000$. Locate $PVIF_{0.10,5}$ in Appendix C, and solve the equation.

$$PV = (\$1,000)(0.621) = \$621$$

3-5. Present Value of a Stream of Payments

Like future value, present value can also be applied to a stream of payments or receipts rather than to a single amount.

A. Present value determination may involve a stream of unequal payments.

To find the present value of an unequal, or mixed, stream of payments, simply calculate the present value of each future amount separately and then add these present values together. This procedure is identical to the one described by Equations 3-8 and 3-9 except that the individual present values are summed. Although either Equation 3-8 or 3-9 may be rewritten to represent a stream of payments, we will use Equation 3-9 because it is easier to apply.

PRESENT VALUE OF AN UNEQUAL STREAM OF PAYMENTS
$$PV = \sum_{t=1}^{n} P_t(PVIF_{i,t}) \tag{3-10}$$

EXAMPLE 3-14: Miller Company expects to receive payments of $1,000, $1,500, and $2,000 at the end of one, two, and three years, respectively. The present value of this stream of payments discounted at 10 percent is computed as follows.

Substitute $i = 0.10$ and $t = 1, 2,$ and 3 in Equation 3-10. Locate each value of PVIF in Appendix C, and solve the equation.

$$PV = (\$1,000)(0.909) + (\$1,500)(0.826) + (\$2,000)(0.751)$$
$$= \$909 + \$1,239 + \$1,502 = \$3,650$$

B. Present value determination may involve an equal stream of payments.

The present value of an equal stream of payments, PV_n, is found by using Equation 3-11. In this equation, the annuity payment, A, is multiplied by the term in brackets, which is the sum of the individual present value interest factors.

PRESENT VALUE OF AN ORDINARY ANNUITY
$$PVOA_n = A\left[\sum_{t=1}^{n} \frac{1}{(1 + i)^t}\right] \tag{3-11}$$

A table can also be used to solve for PV_n. To do this, rewrite Equation 3-11 by replacing the term in brackets with a calculated value called the **present value interest factor of an annuity**, $PVIFA_{i,n}$. The rewritten version is shown in Equation 3-12. Appendix D presents these values for various discount rates and time periods. In this table note that the $PVIFA_{i,n}$ is always smaller than the number of periods of the annuity, n.

PRESENT VALUE OF AN ORDINARY ANNUITY USING A TABLE
$$PVOA_n = A(PVIFA_{i,n}) \tag{3-12}$$

EXAMPLE 3-15: A company expects to receive $1,000 at year's end for the next three years. The present value of this annuity discounted at 10 percent is computed as follows.

Substitute $i = 0.10$, $n = 3$, and $A = \$1,000$ in Equation 3-12. Locate $PVIFA_{0.10,3}$ in Appendix D, and solve the equation. The result is shown in Figure 3-9 on the following page. The $1 difference between the answer in Figure 3-9 and the one below is due to rounding.

$$PVOA_3 = (\$1,000)(PVIFA_{0.10,3}) = (\$1,000)(2.487) = \$2,487$$

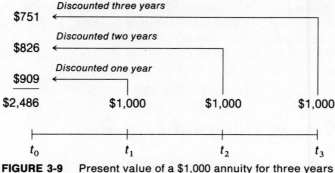

FIGURE 3-9 Present value of a $1,000 annuity for three years with a 10 percent discount rate.

3-6. Perpetuities

The time value of money concept has many applications besides finding the future or present value of a single amount or of a stream of payments or receipts. One application is determining the present value of a perpetuity. A **perpetuity** is an annuity with an infinite life; that is, the payments continue indefinitely. The present value of a perpetuity is found by using Equation 3-13.

PRESENT VALUE OF A PERPETUITY

$$\text{PV of a perpetuity} = \frac{\text{Annuity}}{\text{Discount rate}} = \frac{A}{i} \qquad (3\text{-}13)$$

EXAMPLE 3-16: Jackson Fashions wants to deposit an amount of money in a bank account that will allow it to withdraw $1,000 indefinitely at the end of each year without reducing the amount of the initial deposit. If a bank guarantees to pay the firm 10 percent interest on its deposit, the amount of money the firm has to deposit is computed as follows:
   Substitute A = $1,000 and i = 0.10 in Equation 3-13 and solve.

$$\text{PV of a perpetuity} = \frac{\$1,000}{0.10} = \$10,000$$

3-7. Growth Rates

Another application of the time value of money concept is calculating the compound annual growth or interest rate, i, of a stream of payments or receipts. Equation 3-14 shows how to compute this rate when the growth rate is constant. In this equation, n represents the number of compounding periods during which the growth takes place.

COMPOUND ANNUAL GROWTH RATE

$$\text{FVIF}_{i,n} = \frac{\text{Ending amount}}{\text{Beginning amount}} = \frac{FV_n}{PV} \qquad (3\text{-}14)$$

Dividing the ending amount by the beginning amount gives the $\text{FVIF}_{i,n}$. Appendix A is used to locate the growth rate, i, corresponding to the $\text{FVIF}_{i,n}$.

EXAMPLE 3-17: Track Lighting Company has steadily increased its dividends per share from $1.00 in 1985 to $1.36 in 1989. The annual compound growth rate of these dividend payments over the four years is computed as follows.
   Using Equation 3-14, divide the ending amount, $1.36, by the beginning amount, $1.00, which gives a $\text{FVIF}_{i,4}$-1.36. Now locate 1.36 in the 4 period row in Appendix A. Notice that 1.36 is in the 8 percent column when n equals four years; thus, the annual compound growth rate of the dividend payments is 8 percent.

3-8. Sinking Fund

Another application of the time value of money concept is determining the annuity amount that must be deposited each year to produce a certain lump sum in the future, an arrangement usually called a **sinking fund**. For example, a sinking fund may involve a required annual payment designed to provide funds for the retirement of a bond. To find the amount of the sinking fund payment, rewrite Equation 3-6 and solve for the annuity payment, A, as shown in Equation 3-15.

SINKING FUND
$$A = \frac{FVOA_n}{FVIFA_{i,n}}$$
(3-15)

EXAMPLE 3-18: Adam Smith wants to have $50,000 available in five years to start his own business. If he makes five equal payments into an account paying 10 percent interest annually, the amount he must deposit at the end of each year to achieve his objective is computed as follows. (Recall that an annuity with payments at the end of the year is an ordinary annuity.)

The value of $FVOA_{0.10,5}$ = $50,000 is given. Using Appendix B you will find that $FVIFA_{0.10,5}$ = 6.105. Substitute these values into Equation 3-15 and solve.

$$A = \frac{\$50,000}{6.105} = \$8,190.01$$

3-9. Loan Amortization

An *amortized loan* involves a series of equal installments over the life of a loan, each of which includes both interest and the repayment of principal. Mortgage loans, automobile loans, and many business loans are amortized or liquidated on this type of installment basis. To determine the amount of the periodic payment, rewrite Equation 3-12 and solve for the annuity payment, A, as shown in Equation 3-16.

LOAN AMORTIZATION PAYMENT
$$A = \frac{PVOA}{PVIFA_{i,n}}$$
(3-16)

EXAMPLE 3-19: A partnership borrows $10,000 from a bank for five years at an interest rate of 10 percent. If the partnership repays the loan including interest in five equal, year-end installments, the amount of each payment is computed as follows:

Substitute $PVOA_5$ = $10,000 and $PVIFA_{0.10,5}$ = 3.791 (Appendix D) in Equation 3-16 and solve.

$$A = \frac{\$10,000}{3.791} = \$2,637.83$$

Each of these $2,637.83 payments includes interest and partial repayment of principal.

RAISE YOUR GRADES

Can you explain . . . ?

☑ why money has a time value
☑ the meaning of the terms principal, interest, and time period
☑ the relationship between future value and present value
☑ how compounding differs from discounting
☑ the difference between simple interest and compound interest

☑ the effect of more frequent compounding on future value
☑ the difference between nominal and effective interest rates
☑ the difference between an ordinary annuity and an annuity due
☑ how to use the future value and present value tables
☑ how to use the annuity tables
☑ the difference between an annuity and a perpetuity
☑ how to determine a growth rate
☑ how to determine the amount of a sinking fund payment

SUMMARY

1. Money has a time value because a dollar received today is worth more than the same dollar received in the future.
2. Time value of money involves two major concepts: future value and present value.
3. Future value is the amount to which a present amount of money or a series of payments will grow over time when compounded at a given interest rate.
4. Present value is the current value of a future amount of money or a series of payments evaluated at an appropriate discount rate.
5. Compound interest is interest paid on both principal and accumulated interest and results in a greater future value than does simple interest.
6. More frequent compounding results in greater future value.
7. The nominal interest rate is the stated rate, while the effective interest rate is the true rate and will differ from the nominal rate if there is compounding.
8. An annuity is a stream of equal payments made at regular time intervals.
9. A perpetuity is an annuity with an infinite life.
10. An ordinary annuity involves payments at the end of each period, whereas an annuity due has its payments at the beginning of each period.
11. Discounting is the reverse of compounding. With discounting, values decrease whereas with compounding, values increase.
12. A sinking fund involves a required periodic payment designed to produce a certain amount of money in the future.
13. An amortized loan is one requiring a series of equal installments over the life of the loan, each of which includes interest and repayment of principal.

RAPID REVIEW

True or False?
1. The time value of money means that money received today is worth the same as money received in the future. [Section 3-1]
2. Computing the future value of an amount of money for any specified time period requires knowledge of the amount of principal and the interest rate. [Section 3-2A]
3. The process of determining future value when compound interest is applied is called compounding. [Section 3-2B]
4. Using simple interest generally gives the same future value as using compound interest. [Section 3-2B]
5. Future value interest factors are usually less than 1.0. [Section 3-2D]
6. The more frequently interest is compounded, the greater the future value. [Section 3-2F]

7. The terms *effective interest rate* and *annual percentage rate* mean the same thing. [Section 3-2G]

8. A characteristic of an annuity is that an equal sum of money is deposited or withdrawn each period. [Section 3-3B]

9. An ordinary annuity is one in which the payments or receipts occur at the beginning of each period. [Section 3-3B]

10. The future value of a $1,000 three-year ordinary annuity is smaller than the future value of a $1,000 three-year annuity due, assuming the same interest rate. [Section 3-3B]

11. The process of determining the present value of a future amount is called discounting. [Section 3-4A]

12. The present value interest factor is equal to 1.0 divided by the future value interest factor. [Section 3-4A]

13. Present value interest factors (PVIFs) are usually less than 1.0. [Section 3-4B]

14. A perpetuity is an annuity in which payments continue indefinitely. [Section 3-6]

15. An amortized loan involves a series of annuity payments which contain the repayment of principal only. [Section 3-9]

Multiple Choice

16. The formula for compound value is:

    (a) $FV_n = PV(1 + i)$
    (b) $FV_n = PV/(1 + i)$
    (c) $FV_n = PV(1 + i)^n$
    (d) $FV_n = (1 + i)/PV$

    [Section 3-2B]

17. What is the future value of $1,000 compounded annually at 8 percent for five years?

    (a) $1,080
    (b) $1,400
    (c) $1,469
    (d) $1,800

    [Sections 3-2C and 3-2S]

18. Approximately how long does it take money to double at an 8 percent interest rate?

    (a) 4 years
    (b) 7 years
    (c) 9 years
    (d) 11 years

    [Section 3-2E]

19. If a bank pays a 12 percent nominal interest rate, what is the effective interest rate assuming quarterly compounding?

    (a) 12.0 percent
    (b) 12.3 percent
    (c) 12.6 percent
    (d) 13.0 percent

    [Section 3-2G]

20. At the end of ten years, how much is $1,000 deposited yearly in an ordinary annuity paying 11 percent interest worth?

    (a) $11,000
    (b) $13,856

(c) $15,927
(d) $16,722

[Section 3-3B]

21. What is the present value of $1,000 to be received in eight years discounted at 9 percent?

(a) $500
(b) $502
(c) $550
(d) $607

[Section 3-4B]

22. What is the present value of a ten-year $1,000 ordinary annuity discounted at 6 percent?

(a) $4,886
(b) $6,145
(c) $7,360
(d) $10,000

[Section 3-5B]

23. If $1,000 invested for eight years is worth $1,594 at the end of the eighth year, what is the annual compound growth rate for this investment?

(a) 6 percent
(b) 7 percent
(c) 8 percent
(d) 10 percent

[Section 3-7]

24. Parents want to save $100,000 for their child's college education. They plan to make fifteen equal year-end payments and expect to earn an 8 percent annual interest rate. How much will they have to invest annually to accumulate the $100,000?

(a) $2,542
(b) $3,683
(c) $6,139
(d) $7,285

[Section 3-8]

25. If you borrowed $120,000 to buy a house and financed it at 10 percent annual interest for thirty years, what is your annual mortgage payment assuming that you make equal year-end payments?

(a) $4,000
(b) $6,527
(c) $8,336
(d) $12,729

[Section 3-9]

Answers

True or False			*Multiple Choice*	
1. False	6. True	11. True	16. c	21. b
2. True	7. True	12. True	17. c	22. c
3. True	8. True	13. True	18. c	23. a
4. False	9. False	14. True	19. c	24. b
5. False	10. True	15. False	20. d	25. d

SOLVED PROBLEMS

PROBLEM 3-1: At the end of five years, how much will an initial deposit of $500 be worth at the following annual interest rates?

(a) 6 percent
(b) 10 percent
(c) 15 percent

Answer: This problem involves the future value of a single amount. Substitute the appropriate future value interest factors ($FVIF_{i,n}$) in Appendix A in Equation 3-2 and then solve as shown below.

(a) $FV_5 = (\$500)(FVIF_{0.06,5}) = (\$500)(1.338) = \$669.00$
(b) $FV_5 = (\$500)(FVIF_{0.10,5}) = (\$500)(1.611) = \$805.50$
(c) $FV_5 = (\$500)(FVIF_{0.15,5}) = (\$500)(2.011) = \$1,005.50$ **[Section 3-2D]**

PROBLEM 3-2: You are offered an investment opportunity that is supposed to double your money in four years. For this to be true, what must the compound annual rate of return be on this investment?

Answer: This is a future value, or compounding, problem. Use Appendix A to find the rate that is closest to an FVIF of 2.0 for four years. The closest FVIF for this time period is 2.005, which represents a 19 percent compound annual return. **[Section 3-2D]**

PROBLEM 3-3: Two different banks offer the following rates for similar savings plans: Bank A pays 9 percent interest compounded annually; Bank B pays 8 percent interest compounded quarterly. Which plan would earn more for your investment if you intended to deposit $5,000 for six years?

Answers: This problem involves intraperiod compounding. Use Equation 3-3 and Appendix A.

$$\text{Bank A:} \quad FV_6 = (\$5,000)(1 + 0.09)^6 = (\$5,000)(1.677)$$
$$= \$8,385$$

$$\text{Bank B:} \quad FV_6 = (\$5,000)(1 + 0.08/4)^{(4)(6)} = (\$5,000)(1.02)^{24}$$
$$= (\$5,000)(1.608) = \$8,040$$

Bank A's plan would result in a higher future value by $345 ($8,385 versus $8,040). **[Section 3-2E]**

PROBLEM 3-4: Find the annual percentage rate (APR) for 12 percent compounded

(a) semiannually
(b) quarterly
(c) monthly

Answer: This problem involves finding the effective interest rate using Equation 3-4.

(a) $APR = (1 + 0.12/2)^2 - 1 = (1.06)^2 - 1$
$= 1.124 - 1 = 0.124$ or 12.4 percent
(b) $APR = (1 + 0.12/4)^4 - 1 = (1.03)^4 - 1$
$= 1.126 - 1 = 0.126$ or 12.6 percent
(c) $APR = (1 + 0.12/12)^{12} - 1 = (1.01)^{12} - 1$
$= 1.127 - 1 = 0.127$ or 12.7 percent **[Section 3-2G]**

PROBLEM 3-5: You plan to invest $2,000 a year in an Individual Retirement Account (IRA) for the next 20 years. You would like to know the effect of investing this money at the beginning of each year rather than waiting until the end of each year. Calculate the difference in the future value of your IRA at the end of 20 years as an ordinary annuity versus an annuity due, assuming a 10 percent interest rate.

Answer: To find the future value of an ordinary annuity, use Equation 3-6 and Appendix B:

$$FVOA_{20} = (\$2,000)(FVIFA_{0.10,20}) = (\$2,000)(57.275)$$
$$= \$114,550$$

To find the future value of an annuity due, use Equation 3-7 and Appendix B:

$$FVAD_{20} = (\$2,000)(FVIFA_{0.10,20})(1 + 0.10)$$
$$= (\$2,000)(57.275)(1.10) = \$126,005$$

The annuity due is worth $11,455 more ($126,005 versus $114,550) because the payments are made at the beginning of the period and earn interest one year longer than they do in the ordinary annuity.   **[Section 3-3B]**

PROBLEM 3-6: Find the present value of $5,000 to be received in four years discounted at the following rates:

(*a*) 5 percent
(*b*) 10 percent
(*c*) 15 percent

Answer: For this present value problem, use Equation 3-9 and Appendix C:

(*a*) $PV = (\$5,000)(PVIF_{0.05,4}) = (\$5,000)(0.823) = \$4,115$
(*b*) $PV = (\$5,000)(PVIF_{0.10,4}) = (\$5,000)(0.683) = \$3,415$
(*c*) $PV = (\$5,000)(PVIF_{0.15,4}) = (\$5,000)(0.572) = \$2,860$ **[Section 3-4B]**

PROBLEM 3-7: Jacoby Manufacturing Company is considering an investment in a new machine costing $25,000. The machine is expected to provide the following returns over the next five years: year 1 = $5,000, year 2 = $6,000, year 3 = $7,500, year 4 = $7,500, and year 5 = $9,500. These returns are assumed to be received at the end of each year. If the firm requires a 20 percent return on its investment, should it purchase the machine?

Answer: This problem involves finding the present value of a stream of unequal payments by using Equation 3-10 and Appendix C.

$$PV_1 = (\$5,000)(PVIF_{0.20,1}) = (\$5,000)(0.833) = \$\ 4,165.00$$
$$PV_2 = (\$6,000)(PVIF_{0.20,2}) = (\$6,000)(0.694) = \$\ 4,164.00$$
$$PV_3 = (\$7,500)(PVIF_{0.20,3}) = (\$7,500)(0.579) = \$\ 4,342.50$$
$$PV_4 = (\$7,500)(PVIF_{0.20,4}) = (\$7,500)(0.482) = \$\ 3,615.00$$
$$PV_5 = (\$9,500)(PVIF_{0.20,5}) = (\$9,500)(0.402) = \underline{\$\ 3,819.00}$$

Total present value $20,105.50

Jacoby Manufacturing should not purchase the machine because the present value of the returns is less than the cost of the machine by $4,894.50 ($20,105.50 − $25,000). Thus, the machine does not meet Jacoby's investment return criterion of 20 percent.

                                                                           [Section 3-5A]

PROBLEM 3-8: You have won a sweepstakes and are offered the option of receiving either $50,000 today or $12,500 at the end of each of the next five years. Ignoring taxes and assuming a discount rate of 12 percent which option would you prefer.

Answer: Use Equation 3-12 and Appendix D to find the present value of a $12,500 annuity for five years discounted at 12 percent, and compare this to $50,000.

$$PVOA_5 = (\$12,500)(PVIFA_{0.12,5}) = (\$12,500)(3.605) = \$45,062.50$$

You would prefer to receive the $50,000 today because the present value of the stream of payments is worth only $45,062.50. **[Section 3-5B]**

PROBLEM 3-9: Your bank offers to lend you $20,000 to be repaid in six equal year-end installments of $5,142.71. What interest rate is the bank charging you on this loan?

Answer: Rewrite Equation 3-12 and use Appendix D to solve for the interest rate. Recall that Equation 3-12 is $PVOA_n = A(PVIFA_{i,n})$. Dividing both sides of the equation by A gives a new equation: $PVIFA_{i,n} = PVOA_n/A$. Now, solve the new equation as follows:

$$PVIFA_{i,6} = \$20,000/\$5,142.71 = 3.889$$

Look up the PVIFA of 3.889 for six years in Appendix D, and the result is an interest rate of 14 percent. **[Section 3-5B]**

PROBLEM 3-10: What is the present value of a stream of payments of $500 per year forever, assuming interest rates of

(*a*) 5 percent
(*b*) 10 percent

Answer: To solve this perpetuity problem, use Equation 3-13:

(*a*) PV of a perpetuity = $500/0.05 = $10,000
(*b*) PV of a perpetuity = $500/0.10 = $ 5,000 **[Section 3-6]**

PROBLEM 3-11: You are considering the purchase of a bond for $1,000 that will not pay any interest during its ten-year life but will be worth $2,839 when it matures. If you buy this bond and hold it until maturity, what rate of return will you earn?

Answer: This growth rate problem can be solved by using Equation 3-14 and Appendix A. The ending amount of $2,839 is divided by the beginning amount of $1,000 to produce a FVIF for ten years.

$$FVIF_{i,10} = \$2,839/\$1,000 = 2.839 \qquad \textbf{[Section 3-7]}$$

Look up the value of *i* for an FVIF of 2.839 in Appendix A for ten years and the result is an annual compound growth rate of 11 percent.

PROBLEM 3-12: Eagles, Inc. wants to retire a $30,000,000 bond issue in five years. It plans to make five equal year-end payments to an account that pays 9 percent interest starting with the first installment, beginning one year from today. How large is each installment?

Answer: To solve this sinking fund problem, use Equation 3-15 and Appendix B:

$$A = FVOA_5/FVIFA_{0.09,5} = \$30,000,000/5.985 = \$5,012,531.33$$
[Section 3-8]

PROBLEM 3-13: Dixie Corporation obtains a $25,000 loan that carries a 13 percent interest rate. If the firm repays the loan in three equal year-end installments, how large is each installment?

Answer: To solve this loan amortization problem, use Equation 3-16 and Appendix D:

$$A = PVOA_3/PVIFA_{0.13,3} = \$25,000/2.361 = \$10,588.73 \qquad \textbf{[Section 3-9]}$$

RISK AND RETURN

In Chapter 1 the primary goal of the firm, and therefore of its financial manager, is stated to be shareholder wealth maximization. The financial manager's task is to make financial decisions that maximize the price of the firm's common stock, given legal and other constraints. Each of these financial decisions has certain risk-return characteristics that affect stock price. This chapter explores the meaning of risk and return and how they can be measured.

4-1. Basic Risk and Return Concepts

A. *Risk* is the variability of an asset's future returns.

Risk is present whenever future outcomes are not completely certain or predictable. From an investor's viewpoint, the uncertainty of, or variability in, an asset's future return creates risk. Thus, if an asset's actual return could differ from its expected return, the investment involves risk. The greater the variability, the greater the risk. Although the actual return may vary both above and below the expected return, risk is typically considered to be the probability of loss or of getting less than expected.

B. *Probability* is the percentage chance that an event will occur.

Probabilities range between 0 to 1.0.

1. A probability of 1.0 is the same as a probability of 100 percent and indicates an event is certain to occur.
2. A probability of 0 or 0 percent indicates an event is certain *not* to occur.
3. A probability between 0 and 1.0 or 100 percent indicates the likelihood of an event's occurrence. For example, a weather report that predicts a 60 percent chance of rain means that the event has a 0.6 probability or 60 percent chance of occurring.
4. The sum of the probabilities of all possible outcomes of any given set of circumstances is equal to 1.0 or 100 percent.

C. A *probability distribution* is a list of all possible outcomes and the probability associated with each.

1. A probability distribution may be objective or subjective. In reality, probability distributions often combine both objective and subjective probabilities.

- An *objective* probability distribution is generally based on past outcomes of similar events.
- A *subjective* probability distribution is based on opinions or "educated guesses" about the likelihood that an event will have a particular future outcome.

2. A probability distribution may be discrete or continuous.

- A *discrete* probability distribution is an arrangement of the probabilities associated with the values of a variable that can assume a limited or finite number of values (outcomes). Figure 4-1 shows bar charts, or discrete probability distributions, for Project A and Project B based on data in Example 4-1.

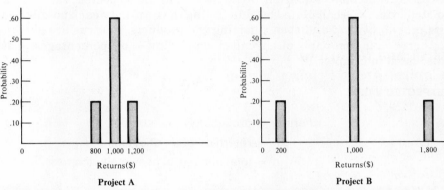

Project A   **Project B**

FIGURE 4-1   Discrete probability distributions for Project A and Project B

- A *continuous* probability distribution is an arrangement of probabilities associated with the values of a variable that can assume an infinite number of possible values (outcomes). Figure 4-2 shows continuous probability distributions for Project X and Project Y.

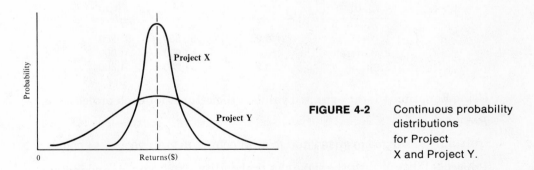

FIGURE 4-2   Continuous probability distributions for Project X and Project Y.

The flatter or less peaked the probability distribution of expected future returns, the higher the risk of the project. The **range** of a probability distribution is the difference between the highest and lowest possible outcome. A flat probability distribution has a wider range than a peaked distribution.

Figure 4-1 shows that Project B has a flatter probability distribution of cash flows and therefore a wider range than Project A. Thus, Project B is riskier than Project A.

D. Riskiness increases with time.

The accuracy of forecasted returns generally decreases as the length of the project being forecast increases. This increases the variability of an asset's returns and therefore risk.

4-2. Risk and Return of a Single Asset

In making investment decisions, two values are computed using a probability distribution of an asset's returns: the asset's expected return (value) and its risk. Common risk measures include the standard deviation and coefficient of variation.

A. *Expected value* or *expected rate of return, $\bar{r}$,* **is the weighted average of all possible returns from an investment, with the weights being the probability of each return.**

In a more general sense, expected value is a type of average or *mean* of the outcomes of a probability distribution. Thus, expected value can be used as a measure of an expected outcome. Equation 4-1 shows that the expected value of a probability distribution, $\bar{r}$, is calculated by multiplying the return for each possible outcome, r_i, by its probability, p_i, and then summing the products. Returns are generally stated in either dollar amounts, often called **cash flows**, or percentages. Cash flows are discussed in Chapter 12.

EXPECTED VALUE
$$\bar{r} = \sum_{i=1}^{n} p_i r_i \qquad \text{(4-1)}$$

where p_i = probability of outcome, *i*

r_i = return or value of outcome, *i*

n = total number of possible outcomes

EXAMPLE 4-1: Seldin Company plans to invest in one of two projects, each requiring the same initial investment. Estimates of next year's dollar returns (cash flows) on these investments depend on the *state of the economy*. The firm estimates these returns based on a weak, moderate, and strong economy and attaches probabilities to each state of economy.

State of the Economy (i)	Probability (p_i)	Returns Project A (r_i)	Returns Project B (r_i)
1 Weak	0.2	$ 800	$ 200
2 Moderate	0.6	1,000	1,000
3 Strong	0.2	1,200	1,800

Using Equation 4-1, the expected value of the returns for each project is shown below:

Project A

$$\bar{r}_A = (0.2)(\$800) + (0.6)(\$1,000) + (0.2)(\$1,200) = \$1,000$$

Project B

$$\bar{r}_B = (0.2)(\$200) + (0.6)(\$1,000) + (0.2)(\$1,800) = \$1,000$$

Generally, the higher the expected return, the more attractive the investment. Ignoring risk, the projects are equally attractive because they have the same investment and expected value. However, one problem with the expected value is that it does not indicate the variability of outcomes.

B. *Standard deviation, σ,* **is a statistical measure of the variability of a probability distribution around its expected value.**

The standard deviation can be used as a measure of the amount of absolute risk associated with an outcome. *Absolute risk* does not consider the relationship of the variability of outcomes to its expected value. Standard deviation also measures the tightness of a probability distribution. A tight probability distribution is one in which the set of possible returns is close to the expected value of the returns. If a probability distribution is tight, then the range or difference between the highest and lowest value in the distribution will be relatively small. Thus, the smaller the standard deviation, the tighter the probability distribution, the smaller the range of returns, and the lower the risk.

Standard deviation is an appropriate risk measure of the variability if the probability distribution is reasonably symmetrical. A **symmetrical distribution** is one in which each half of the distribution is a mirror image of the other half. A **skewed distribution** is a distribution which is not symmetric. When comparing different investments using the standard deviation, the size of the initial investments and the expected value of their probability distributions should also be equal in order to making meaningful risk comparisons. Unless these conditions are met, use of the standard deviation may be misleading. As shown in Equation 4-3, the standard deviation is calculated as follows:

1. Compute the expected value, $\bar{r}$.
2. Subtract the expected value from each possible return to obtain the deviations, $(r_i - \bar{r})$.
3. Square each deviation, $(r_i - \bar{r})^2$.
4. Multiply each squared deviation by its probability of occurrence, $p_i(r_i - \bar{r})^2$, and then sum. The result is called the **variance**, σ^2, which is the standard deviation squared.

VARIANCE
$$\sigma^2 = \sum_{i=1}^{n} p_i(r_i - \bar{r})^2 \qquad \text{(4-2)}$$

5. Take the square root of the variance to get the standard deviation.

STANDARD DEVIATION
$$\sigma = \sqrt{\sum_{i=1}^{n} p_i(r_i - \bar{r})^2} \qquad \text{(4-3)}$$

EXAMPLE 4-2: Using data given in Example 4-1 and Equation 4-3, the standard deviations for Project A and Project B are computed as follows:

Project A

$$\sigma_A = \sqrt{(0.2)(\$800 - \$1,000)^2 + (0.6)(\$1,000 - \$1,000)^2 + (0.2)(\$1,200 - \$1,000)^2}$$
$$= \sqrt{(0.2)(-\$200)^2 + (0.6)(\$0)^2 + (0.2)(\$200)^2}$$
$$= \sqrt{16,000} = \$126.49$$

Project B

$$\sigma_B = \sqrt{(0.2)(\$200 - \$1,000)^2 + (0.6)(\$1,000 - \$1,000)^2 + (0.2)(\$1,800 - \$1,000)^2}$$
$$= \sqrt{(0.2)(-\$800)^2 + (0.6)(\$0)^2 + (0.2)(\$800)^2}$$
$$= \sqrt{256,000} = \$505.96$$

EXAMPLE 4-3: The standard deviations of Projects A and B can be compared directly because their probability distributions are symmetrical and their initial investments and expected values are equal. Project B has a larger standard deviation than Project A by approximately \$380, and is therefore riskier. Figure 4-1, page 47, confirms this finding because Project B's probability distribution is flatter and hence reflects greater risk than Project A's peaked distribution.

EXAMPLE 4-4: The expected returns and standard deviations of Project C and Project D are given below. The probability distribution of each project is symmetrical.

	Project C	Project D
Expected Value	$10,000	$100,000
Standard Deviation	5,000	5,000

Although both projects have the same standard deviation, they are not equally risky. In fact, Project C is riskier than Project D. In this case, using the standard deviation to compare project riskiness is misleading because their expected returns differ. A relative measure called the coefficient of variation, rather than an absolute measure, is needed to compare project riskiness in this example.

C. *Coefficient of variation, cv,* **is defined mathematically as the ratio of the standard deviation to the expected value.**

The coefficient of variation is a relative measure of risk that shows the amount of risk per unit of return. It is an appropriate risk measure for comparing projects in which the expected values differ and for which, therefore, using the standard deviation would be misleading. The higher the coefficient of variation, the greater the relative risk. Equation 4-4 is the formula for the coefficient of variation.

COEFFICIENT OF VARIATION $$cv = \frac{\sigma}{\bar{r}}$$ **(4-4)**

EXAMPLE 4-5: Using data in Examples 4-1 and 4-2 and Equation 4-4, the coefficients of variation for the projects are:

Project A	Project B
$cv_A = \dfrac{\$126}{\$1,000} = 0.13$	$cv_B = \dfrac{\$506}{\$1,000} = 0.51$

Project A's coefficient of variation indicates that there is $0.13 risk per dollar of expected return whereas Project B has $0.51 risk per dollar of expected return. Thus, Project B is riskier than Project A. The same ranking of riskiness occurred in Example 4-3 using the standard deviations.

EXAMPLE 4-6: Using data in Example 4-4 and Equation 4-4, the coefficients of variation for Project C and Project D are:

Project C	Project D
$cv_C = \dfrac{\$5,000}{\$10,000} = 0.50$	$cv_D = \dfrac{\$5,000}{\$100,000} = 0.05$

Project C is riskier because it has a higher coefficient of variation than Project D.

D. A *standard normal distribution* **is the distribution of a normal random variable with an expected value (arithmetic mean) of zero and standard deviation equal to one.**

The normal distribution or **normal curve** is a bell-shaped distribution, such as the distributions of Project X and Project Y in Figure 4-2, that is dependent upon the mean and the standard deviation of the population under investigation. Since the normal distribution is a continuous rather than a discrete distribution, it is not possible to speak of the probability of a point but only of the probability of falling within some specified range of values. Thus, the area under the curve between any two points must then also depend upon the values of the mean and standard deviation. However, it is possible to standardize any normal distribution so that it has a mean of zero and a standard deviation of one, using the transformation in Equation 4-5.

NUMBER OF STANDARD DEVIATIONS $$z = \frac{r_i - \bar{r}}{\sigma}$$ **(4-5)**

Equation 4-5 is used to compute the number of standard deviations, z, that a particular outcome, r_i, is from its mean, $\bar{r}$. In a standard normal distribution, about 68 percent of the outcomes lie within ± 1 standard deviation of the mean, about 95 percent of the outcomes lie within ± 2 standard deviations, and over 99 percent within ± 3 standard deviations. Figure 4-3 illustrates these characteristics of a standard normal distribution. Once the number of standard deviations is calculated, Appendix E gives the probability or area under the standard normal distribution corresponding to $\Pr(Z < z)$ for values of z from 0.0 to 3.0. Although Appendix E contains only positive z values, it also applies for negative z values because the standard normal distribution is symmetrical about its mean.

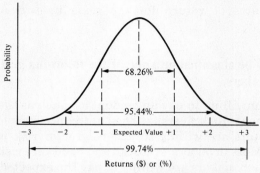

FIGURE 4-3   Normal probability distribution curve

EXAMPLE 4-7: As calculated in Examples 4-1 and 4-2, Project B has an expected return of $1,000 and a standard deviation of about $506. Given a normal distribution with $\bar{r} = \$1,000$ and $\beta_B = \$506$, find the value of z_1 and z_2 such that $\Pr(\$400 < X < \$1,400) = \Pr(z_1 < Z < z_2)$. Solving this problem involves three steps. First, Equation 4-5 is used to compute the z values for $400 and $1,400.

$$\text{If cash flow} = \$400, \text{ then } z_1 = \frac{\$400 - \$1,000}{\$506} = -1.19$$

$$\text{If cash flow} = \$1,400, \text{ then } z_2 = \frac{\$1,400 - \$1,000}{\$506} = 0.79$$

Therefore, $\Pr(\$400 < X < \$1,400) = \Pr(-1.19 < Z < 0.79)$. The $\Pr(-1.19 < Z < 0.79)$ is given by the area of the shaded region in Figure 4-4. Next, Appendix E is used to find the probabilities associated with each z value. $\Pr(-1.19 < Z < 0)$ is obtained by going down the z column to 1.1 and across the row to 0.09 to find 0.3830. Similarly, $\Pr(0 < Z < 0.79)$ is 0.2852. Finally, the combined probabilities indicate that there is about a 67 percent chance $(0.3830 + 0.2852 = 0.6682$ or 66.82 percent) that Project B's actual cash flow will fall between $400 and $1,400.

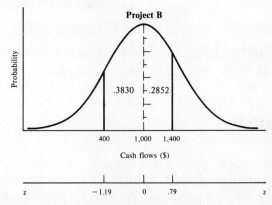

FIGURE 4-4

Probability of obtaining cash flows between $400 and $1,400 for Project B in Example 4-7

EXAMPLE 4-8: Continuing from Example 4-7, what is the range of values within which the actual expected value will fall approximately 68 percent of the time?

A 68 percent probability represents 1 standard deviation above and below the expected value. Thus, there is a 68 percent probability that the actual expected value will be between $1,000 \pm $506 or between $494 and $1,506.

4-3. Risk Preferences

A. Decision makers have different views about risk and return.

Decision makers want to be compensated for the risk associated with an investment. The greater the risk, the more the demanded return. The actual amount of compensation demanded, which is called the **required rate of return**, is influenced by the individual decision maker's attitudes toward risk. Thus, decision makers have different required rates of return for the same investment because their risk preferences differ.

B. Decision makers may be classified into one of the following groups: risk averters, risk neutral, or risk takers.

1. *Risk averters* are unwilling to pay an amount as much as the expected value of an uncertain investment. Risk aversion does not imply complete avoidance of risk. Risk-averse investors are willing to accept greater risk provided the return is sufficiently high. Most investors in stocks and bonds are risk averse.
2. *Risk-neutral* decision makers are willing to pay the expected value.
3. *Risk takers* are willing to pay more than the expected value.

EXAMPLE 4-9: Data from Examples 4-1, 4-2, and 4-5 are summarized below:

State of the Economy (i)	Probability (p_i)	Returns Project A (r_i)	Returns Project B (r_i)
1 Weak	0.2	$ 800	$ 200
2 Moderate	0.6	1,000	1,000
3 Strong	0.2	1,200	1,800
Expected Value ($\bar{r}$)		1,000	1,000
Standard Deviation (σ)		126	506
Coefficient of Variation (cv)		0.13	0.51

A risk averter would select Project A because it involves the same expected return as Project B but has less risk. A risk-neutral investor would be indifferent between the two investments. A risk taker would prefer Project B. Although the expected value of each project is equal, Project B has a greater potential return and more risk. That is, with a strong economy the maximum return for Project B is $1,800 compared with only $1,200 for Project A.

The risk-averse investor would be unwilling to pay Project B's expected value of $1,000. A risk-neutral investor would be willing to pay exactly $1,000, and a risk taker would be willing to pay more than the expected value.

4-4. Risk and Return of a Portfolio

Until this point, risk-return analysis has focused on a single asset. Firms rarely hold a single asset but rather a **portfolio** or collection of two or more assets or securities. *Portfolio theory* involves the selection of efficient portfolios. An *efficient portfolio* provides the highest return for a given level of risk or the least risk for a given level of return. Portfolio theory originated in the context of financial assets such as common stocks, but the general concepts apply to physical assets such as the capital budgeting projects discussed in Chapter 13.

A. The *expected portfolio return,* $\bar{r}_p$, **is the weighted average of the expected returns from the individual assets in the portfolio.**

Equation 4-6 is the formula for the expected portfolio return.

EXPECTED PORTFOLIO RETURN $$\bar{r}_p = \sum_{i=1}^{n} w_i \bar{r}_i \qquad \text{(4-6)}$$

where $\quad w_i$ = proportion of portfolio invested in asset, i

$\bar{r}_i$ = expected return of asset, i

n = number of assets in the portfolio

EXAMPLE 4-10: Kokus Properties is evaluating two opportunities, each having the same initial investment. The project's risk and return characteristics are shown below.

	Project E	Project F
Expected return ($\bar{r}_j$)...	0.10	0.20
Standard deviation (σ_i)......................................	0.08	0.08
Proportion invested in each project (w_i).....................	0.50	0.50

Using Equation 4-6, the expected return of a portfolio combining Project E and Project F is:

$$\bar{r}_p = (0.5)(0.10) + (0.5)(0.20) = 0.15 \text{ or } 15 \text{ percent}$$

B. *Portfolio risk,* σ_p, **is the variability of returns of the portfolio as a whole.**

The riskiness of a portfolio may be less than the riskiness of any individual assets contained in the portfolio because of diversification. **Diversification** is investing in more than one type of asset in order to reduce risk. Diversification could also be several different assets of the same type, but this would be less effective. The concept of diversification follows the old dictum, "Don't put all your eggs in one basket."

1. Diversification reduces risk by combining assets, such as securities, with different risk-return characteristics. This favorable interaction among assets is known as the **portfolio effect**. The amount of risk reduction achieved through diversification depends on the correlation of the individual assets' returns with one another. The **correlation coefficient**, ρ or rho, is a relative statistical measure of correlation in the degree and direction of change between two variables. It ranges from $+1.0$ to -1.0.

   • If $\rho = +1.0$, the two variables move in the same direction exactly to the same degree and are *perfectly positively correlated.*
   • If $\rho = -1.0$, the two variables move in opposite directions to exactly the same degree and are *perfectly negatively correlated.*
   • If $\rho = 0$, the two variables are uncorrelated or independent of each other.

2. Risk reduction is achieved through diversification whenever the returns of the assets combined in a portfolio are not perfectly positively correlated. In other words, greater benefits are achieved with less positive or more negative correlation among asset returns.

C. **Portfolio risk is measured by the portfolio standard deviation.**

Unlike the expected portfolio return, the **portfolio standard deviation** is only the weighted average of the standard deviations from the individual assets when the two assets' returns are perfectly positively correlated. Otherwise, the portfolio standard deviation is a function of the risk of the individual assets, their weights in the portfolio, and the correlations among the individual assets' returns. Equation 4-7 solves for the standard deviation of portfolio returns for a two-asset portfolio.

PORTFOLIO STANDARD DEVIATION FOR TWO ASSETS

$$\sigma_p = \sqrt{w_1^2\sigma_1^2 + w_2^2\sigma_2^2 + 2w_iw_2\rho_{1,2}\sigma_1\sigma_2} \qquad \text{(4-7)}$$

where

w_1 = proportion invested in asset 1

w_2 = proportion invested in asset 2

σ_1 = standard deviation of asset 1

σ_2 = standard deviation of asset 2

$\rho_{1,2}$ = correlation coefficient between asset 1 and asset 2

EXAMPLE 4-11: Based on the data in Example 4-10 and using Equation 4-7, the portfolio standard deviations are:

For $\rho_{1,2} = +1.0$

$$\sigma_p = \sqrt{(0.5)^2(0.08)^2 + (0.5)^2(0.08)^2 + (2)(0.5)(0.5)(1.0)(0.08)(0.08)}$$
$$= \sqrt{0.0016 + 0.0016 + 0.0032} = \sqrt{0.0064} = 0.08$$

Risk is not reduced through diversification when the assets combined have perfectly positively correlated returns. The portfolio standard deviation of 0.08 in this situation is the same as the weighted average of the standard deviations of the individual assets.

For $\rho_{1,2} = +0.2$

$$\rho = \sqrt{(0.5)^2(0.08)^2 + (0.5)^2(0.08)^2 + (2)(0.5)(0.5)(0.2)(0.08)(0.08)}$$
$$= \sqrt{0.0016 + 0.0016 + 0.00064} = \sqrt{0.00384} = 0.062$$

Risk reduction does occur through diversification when the assets combined are not perfectly positively correlated. With a low positive correlation of 0.2, the portfolio risk is reduced from 0.08 to 0.062. Figure 4-5 shows the extent of risk reduction through diversification when there are different degrees of correlation between Project E and Project F.

Correlation Coefficient (ρ)	Portfolio Risk (σ_p)	
+1.0	0.080	**FIGURE 4-5**
+0.5	0.069	Risk reduction through diversification for a portfolio containing Project E and Project F at various degrees of correlation
0.0	0.057	
−0.5	0.040	
−1.0	0.000	

D. Computing the portfolio standard deviation becomes more complex as the size of the portfolio increases.

Methods are available for computing the standard deviation of a portfolio with more than two assets. These methods are complex and require numerous calculations and hence are not demonstrated here.

4-5. Capital Asset Pricing Model

The capital asset pricing model (CAPM) provides a general framework for analyzing risk-return relationships for all types of assets. In evaluating these relationships, CAPM does not use *total risk*, which is measured by standard deviation, as a risk measure, but only one part of total risk called *systematic risk*. CAPM is one of the major developments in modern financial theory. The discussion here focuses on risk-return relations involving common stock, but CAPM is also applied to capital budgeting decisions as discussed in Chapter 13.

A. *Total risk* **may be be separated into two major components: systematic and unsystematic risk.**

1. **Unsystematic risk**, also called *company risk* or *diversifiable risk*, is that part of a security's risk caused by factors unique to a particular firm. Unsystematic risk can be diversified away because it represents essentially random events. Negative events affecting one firm can be offset by positive events affecting another firm. Sources of unsystematic risk include:

   - Strikes
   - Company management
   - Marketing strategies
   - Operating and financial leverage

2. **Systematic risk**, also called *market risk* or *nondiversifiable risk*, is that part of a security's risk caused by factors affecting the market as a whole. Systematic risk cannot be eliminated by diversification because it affects all firms simultaneously. Some firms are more sensitive than others to factors that affect systematic risk. Systematic risk is therefore the only relevant risk. Factors affecting systematic risk include:

   - Inflation
   - Interest rates
   - Business cycles
   - Fiscal and monetary policies

Figure 4-6 shows the effect of diversification on both types of risk. As the number of stocks increases, the diversifying effect of each additional stock on unsystematic risk diminishes.

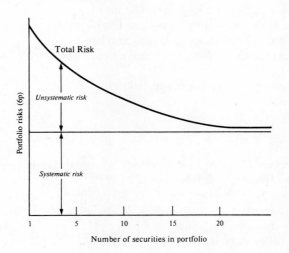

FIGURE 4-6   Effect of diversification on unsystematic and systematic risk

B. Systematic risk is measured by a stock's *beta coefficient, b.*

Beta is a measure of the sensitivity of a security's return relative to the returns of a broad-based market portfolio of securities. *Beta* is defined mathematically as the ratio of the covariance of returns of security, *i*, and market portfolio, *m*, to the variance of returns of the market portfolio. **Covariance** is an absolute statistical measure of the extent to which two variables, such as securities returns, move together. As shown in Equation 4-2, variance is the standard deviation squared. Equation 4-8 gives the formula for an individual security's beta.

$$\text{Beta}_i = b_i = \frac{\text{Covariance }(r_i, r_m)}{\text{Variance}_m}$$

$$= \frac{\rho_{im}\sigma_i\sigma_m}{\sigma_m^2} \tag{4-8}$$

where ρ_{im} = correlation coefficient between security, i, and the market portfolio, m

σ_i = standard deviation of security, i

σ_m = standard deviation of the market portfolio, m

σ_m^2 = variance of the market portfolio, m

1. Beta is computed by regressing a security's returns against the returns of a broad-based market index, such as the Standard & Poor's 500 Stock Composite Index or Value Line Index. The slope of the regression line, also called the **characteristics line**, is an estimate of the security's beta. Betas are computed and published by services such as Value Line and Merrill Lynch. Equation 4-9 is the regression equation for determining beta. Further details and explanation of regression analysis may be found in any standard statistics textbook.

REGRESSION EQUATION FOR BETA $r_i = a_i + b_i r_m + e_i$ **(4-9)**

where r_i = required return on security, i

a_i = intercept that equals the risk-free rate, r_f

b_i = beta coefficient of security, i

r_m = required return on the market portfolio

e_i = random error term that reflects the unsystematic risk of security, i

2. A security's or portfolio's beta is interpreted relative to the market beta of 1.0. A beta may be positive or negative. The returns of a security with a *positive* beta move in the same direction as the return of the market. The returns of a security with a *negative* beta move in the opposite direction of the market. Negative betas are uncommon.

• If b > 1.0, the security is more volatile or risky than the market.
• If b = 1.0, the security has the same volatility or risk as the market.
• If b < 1.0, the security is less volatile or risky than the market.
• If b = 0.0, the security is uncorrelated with market movements and is riskless.

EXAMPLE 4-12: The betas of four common stocks are given below:

Stock	1	2	3	4
b_i	2.0	0.5	0.0	−1.0

If market returns increase by 10 percent and only the effect of systematic risk is considered, the stock returns would be affected as follows:
Stock 1 is twice as volatile as the market and should provide a 2.0 percent change in its systematic return for each 1.0 percent change in the market. Thus, if market returns increase by 10 percent, Stock 1's returns should increase by 20.0 percent (2.0 × 10 percent).
Stock 2 is half as risky as the market and therefore its return should increase by 5.0 percent (0.5 × 10 percent).
Stock 3 is unaffected by the market and provides no market-related change in return because it has no market-related risk.
Stock 4 has the same risk as the market but moves in the opposite direction. Stock 4's return should decrease by 10.0 percent (−1.0 × 10 percent).

C. A portfolio's beta is the weighted average of the betas of its individual securities.

Equation 4-10 is the formula for the portfolio beta.

PORTFOLIO BETA $b_p = \sum_{i=1}^{n} w_i b_i$ **(4-10)**

where w_i = the weight of security, i, in the portfolio

b_i = the beta coefficient of security, i

n = the number of securities in the portfolio

EXAMPLE 4-13: The following amounts are invested in the four stocks given in Example 4-12.

Security	Investment	w_i	b_i
1	$25,000	0.5	2.0
2	10,000	0.2	0.5
3	10,000	0.2	0.0
4	5,000	0.1	−1.0
Total	$50,000	1.0	

Using Equation 4-10, the portfolio beta is:

$$b_p = (0.5)(2.0) + (0.2)(0.5) + (0.2)(0.0) + (0.1)(-1.0)$$
$$= 1.0$$

D. The capital asset pricing model expresses risk-return relationships using beta as the relevant risk measure.

CAPM states that the required rate of return on a risky asset consists of the risk-free rate plus a premium for systematic risk. Equation 4-11 presents the formula for the capital asset pricing model.

CAPITAL ASSET PRICING MODEL $\qquad r_i = r_f + b_i(r_m - r_f)$ $\qquad$ **(4-11)**

where $\qquad r_i$ = required (or expected) return on security, *i*

$\qquad r_f$ = expected risk-free rate of return

$\qquad r_m$ = expected return on the market portfolio

$\qquad b_i$ = beta coefficient of security, *i*

1. The **risk-free rate of return**, r_f, is the return required on a security having no systematic risk and is generally measured by the yield on short-term U.S. Treasury securities such as Treasury bills.

   - The risk-free rate consists of two components: a *real* rate that excludes any inflationary expectations, and an *inflation premium* that equals the expected inflationary rate.
   - The risk-free rate changes in the same direction and by the same amount as the inflation premium changes. Since the risk-free rate is part of a security's required rate of return, a change in inflationary expections will also increase the required return on all securities, r_m.

2. The **risk premium**, $b_i(r_m - r_f)$, is the return required in excess of the risk-free rate and is due to systematic risk. Part of the risk premium is the **market risk premium** $(r_m - r_f)$, which is the additional return expected for holding a market portfolio of "average" riskiness (b = 1.0). The risk premium for a specific security will differ from the market risk premium if the individual security's beta does not equal 1.0.

EXAMPLE 4-14: Referring to Example 4-12, the betas of Stock 1 and Stock 2 are 2.0 and 0.5, respectively. The risk-free rate is 8 percent and the expected return on the market is 14 percent.

Using Equation 4-11, the required rates of return and risk premiums are:

Stock 1	Stock 2
$r_1 = 0.08 + (2.0)(0.14 - 0.08)$	$r_2 = 0.08 + (0.5)(0.14 - 0.08)$
$= 0.08 + 0.12$	$= 0.08 + 0.03$
$= 0.20$ or 20 percent	$= 0.11$ or 11 percent

Stock 1 requires a 20 percent return and has a high risk premium of 12 percent. Stock 2 requires an 11 percent return and has a low risk premium of 3 percent. The risk premiums are high or low relative to the market risk premium of 6 percent (14 percent − 8 percent), which represents the risk premium on average risk stocks.

E. The capital asset pricing model is expressed graphically by the security market line (SML).

The security market line represents the linear relationship between a security's required rate of return and its risk as measured by beta. The slope of the SML is the market risk premium ($r_m - r_f$) and is constant. For example, an increase in inflationary expectations will cause the SML to shift upward, but the slope will remain constant. This is because both components of the market risk premium, namely r_m and r_f, will increase by the same amount and thus keep the slope constant. However, the slope of the SML will change if investors become more *risk-averse* and thus require a higher return for a given level of risk. Figure 4-7 illustrates the security market line and the risk-return tradeoff of Stock 1 and Stock 2.

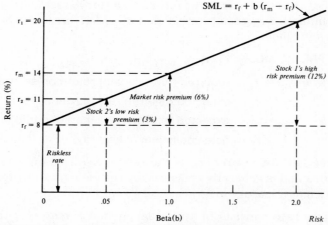

FIGURE 4-7   The security market line (SML)

F. CAPM can be used to calculate a market-based hurdle rate for evaluation purposes.

A **hurdle rate** is the minimum rate of return required for a project to be accepted. If an asset's expected rate of return equals or exceeds the required return (falls on or above the SML), as computed by CAPM, the asset is accepted; otherwise it is rejected. In equilibrium, the required return of an asset or security equals its expected return.

EXAMPLE 4-15: Example 4-14 shows that Stock 1 and Stock 2 have required rates of return of 20 percent and 11 percent, respectively. Assume the expected return for Stock 1 is 18 percent and for Stock 2 is 15 percent. Should the investments be acquired based on the SML?

Figure 4-8 on the following page shows that Stock 2's return is above the SML and should be acquired because its higher expected return more than compensates for its additional risk. Stock 1 is rejected because it provides less expected return for its risk than is required.

G. The capital asset pricing model is based on restrictive assumptions about investor behavior and the securities market.

1. Assumptions about investor behavior include:

   • Investors are risk-averse and expect to be rewarded for taking risks.
   • Investors act rationally and prefer a security with the highest return for a given

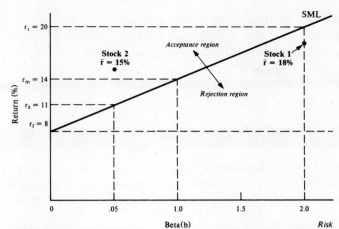

FIGURE 4-8 Using the security market line (SML) to select securities

level of risk, or the lowest risk for a given level of return.

- Investors make their decisions based on a single time horizon. That is, investors view the asset's risk and return characteristics for the same time period, such as a year.
- Investors share the same expectations about the risk and return characteristics of securities.

2. Assumptions about the securities market include:

- All investors can borrow or lend in unlimited amounts at the risk-free rate.
- Financial markets are frictionless in that there are no taxes or transactions costs.
- All assets are perfectly divisible and perfectly liquid.
- Information is freely available to all investors.

Some of these assumptions do not reflect reality. Although extensive testing of the CAPM has produced mixed results, the findings generally show that expected returns and perceived risk are related and that the market is dominated by risk-averse investors.

RAISE YOUR GRADES

Can you explain...?

☑ the meaning of risk
☑ the difference between objective and subjective probabilities
☑ the difference between a discrete and a continuous probability distribution
☑ why riskiness increases with time
☑ the meaning of the expected value of returns
☑ the difference between an absolute and a relative risk measure
☑ the characteristics of a normal curve
☑ the three risk preference categories of decision makers
☑ the meaning of an efficient portfolio
☑ what correlation coefficients of $+1$, -1, and 0 indicate
☑ how diversification can reduce portfolio risk
☑ the difference between systematic and unsystematic risk
☑ how a security's beta is computed
☑ what a beta > 1, a beta $= 1$, and a beta < 1 indicate
☑ the difference between standard deviation and beta as risk measures

☑ the formula for the capital asset pricing model
☑ common measures of the risk-free rate and market portfolio
☑ the assumptions underlying the capital asset pricing model

SUMMARY

1. Risk is the variability of an asset's future returns. When only one return is possible, there is no risk. When more than one return is possible, the asset is risky.
2. The riskiness of an outcome may be described using either objective or subjective probabilities.
3. A probability distribution shows possible outcomes with a probability assigned to each outcome.
4. An asset's probability distribution is used to compute an asset's expected value of return and risk.
5. The expected value of return of a single asset is the weighted average of the returns, with the weights being the probabilities of each return.
6. The risk of a single asset is measured by its standard deviation or coefficient of variation. The standard deviation measures the variability of outcomes around the expected value and is an absolute measure of risk. The coefficient of variation is the ratio of the standard deviation to the expected value and is a relative measure of risk.
7. A normal probability distribution is used to determine the probability of a particular outcome and is a symmetrical, bell-shaped curve.
8. Decision makers may be classified into three categories according to their risk preferences: risk-averse, risk-neutral, and risk-taking. Financial theory assumes that decision makers are risk-averse.
9. The expected return from a portfolio of two or more assets is the weighted average of expected returns from the individual assets in the portfolio.
10. Portfolio risk is measured by the portfolio standard deviation. Portfolio risk is influenced by diversification. Risk reduction is achieved through diversification whenever the returns of the assets combined in a portfolio are not perfectly positively correlated. Correlation measures the tendency of two variables to move together.
11. Total risk of a security may be separated into two components: systematic risk and unsystematic risk.
12. Systematic risk is that part of a security's risk caused by factors affecting the market as a whole. Systematic risk is undiversifiable and is measured by beta.
13. Unsystematic risk is that part of a security's risk caused by factors unique to a particular firm or industry. Unsystematic risk is diversifiable.
14. The capital asset pricing model (CAPM) provides a general framework for analyzing risk and return relationships for all assets.
15. CAPM expresses risk-return relationships using beta as the relevant measure of risk. CAPM separates an asset's return into a risk-free rate of return and a risk premium.
16. The security market line is a graphic representation of the CAPM and represents the risk-return relationship as linear. A change in the expected return for the market portfolio would change the slope of the SML.

RAPID REVIEW

True or False

1. Risk is the variability of an asset's past returns. [Section 4-1A]
2. Probabilities range from −1 to +1. [Section 4-1B]

3. A probability distribution contains possible outcomes for a particular event with a probability assigned to each outcome. [Section 4-1C]

4. A subjective probability is based on the decision maker's opinion. [Section 4-1C]

5. A bar chart is an example of a discrete probability distribution. [Section 4-1C]

6. The tighter the dispersion around an expected value, the less the risk. [Section 4-1C & 4-2B]

7. A asset's riskiness is not related to the length of time it is held into the future. [Section 4-1D]

8. Expected value is the weighted average of the probability distribution of possible returns. [Section 4-2A]

9. The standard deviation is a relative risk measure. [Section 4-2B]

10. The coefficient of variation is determined by dividing the expected value by the standard deviation. [Section 4-2C]

11. The lower the coefficient of variation, the less the risk. [Section 4-2C]

12. For a normal distribution, about 68 percent of the outcomes should fall within ± 1 standard deviation of the mean. [Section 4-2D]

13. Most investors are risk neutral. [Section 4-3B]

14. The expected return from a portfolio is the weighted average of the expected returns from the individual assets. [Section 4-4A]

15. A correlation coefficient of -1 indicates a lack of relationship. [Section 4-4B]

16. The more positively correlated the returns of securities in a portfolio, the greater their effect on diversification. [Section 4-4B]

17. The standard deviation of a portfolio is always the weighted average of the standard deviations of the individual assets. [Section 4-4B]

18. The total risk of a security equals systematic risk plus unsystematic risk. [Section 4-5A]

19. Systematic risk can be diversified away by adding more securities to a portfolio. [Section 4-5A]

20. Beta measures the sensitivity of a security's return relative to returns of the market portfolio. [Section 4-5B]

21. The market portfolio has a beta of zero. [Section 4-5B]

22. Betas are generally negative. [Section 4-5B]

23. A stock with a beta of 1.5 is riskier than a stock with a beta of 1.3. [Section 4-5B]

24. A portfolio beta is the weighted average of the individual securities' betas. [Section 4-5C]

25. The capital asset pricing model (CAPM) expresses a risk-return relationship using the standard deviation as the appropriate measure of risk. [Section 4-5D]

26. The required rate of return consists of a risk-free rate plus a risk premium. [Section 4-5D]

27. A common proxy for the risk-free rate is the return on the Standard & Poor's Stock Composite Index. [Section 4-5D]

28. The security market line (SML) is a graphic representation of a linear risk-return relationship. [Section 4-5E]

29. Assets plotting above the security market line should be accepted based on their risk-return characteristics. [Section 4-5F]

30. CAPM assumes that investors are risk-averse and act rationally. [Section 4-5G]

Multiple Choice

31. A high-risk stock may be characterized as having a probability distribution of returns that is

    (*a*) relatively flat
    (*b*) relatively peaked
    (*c*) upward sloping
    (*d*) downward sloping

    [Section 4-1C]

32. An absolute measure of risk is:

    (*a*) coefficient of variation
    (*b*) correlation coefficient
    (*c*) standard deviation
    (*d*) expected value

    [Section 4-2B]

33. If a project has a return distribution with an expected value of $2,000 and a coefficient of variation 0.20, its standard deviation is:

    (*a*) $400
    (*b*) $1,000
    (*c*) $2,000
    (*d*) $10,000

    [Section 4-2C]

34. A decision maker who is willing to invest not more than $8,000 in an investment that has an expected value of $10,000 may be described as:

    (*a*) a risk taker
    (*b*) a risk averter
    (*c*) risk neutral
    (*d*) reckless

    [Section 4-3B]

35. In a two-asset portfolio, the least beneficial effect of diversification is achieved if the assets' correlation coefficient is:

    (*a*) +1.0
    (*b*) 0
    (*c*) −0.5
    (*d*) −1.0

    [Section 4-4B]

36. You are thinking about investing in General Electric (GE) common stock. Which of the following examples of risk *cannot* be diversified away?

    (*a*) Death of key GE company executive
    (*b*) Potential strike of GE employees
    (*c*) Product liability suit against GE
    (*d*) Increase in the rate of inflation

    [Section 4-5A]

37. Which of the following has a beta of 1.0?

    (*a*) A risk-free asset
    (*b*) High-risk common stocks
    (*c*) The market portfolio (index)
    (*d*) None of the above

    [Sections 4-5B]

38. A firm whose common stock has a beta of less than 1.0 indicates that the stock has

(*a*) no risk
(*b*) below average risk
(*c*) average risk
(*d*) above average risk

[Section 4-5B]

39. If the risk-free rate is 10 percent and the expected return on the market portfolio is 16 percent, a security with a beta of 1.5 should have a required rate of return using the CAPM of

(*a*) 10 percent
(*b*) 16 percent
(*c*) 19 percent
(*d*) 26 percent

[Section 4-5D]

40. All of the following are CAPM assumptions *except:*

(*a*) Information is freely available to all investors
(*b*) Investors are risk-averse
(*c*) Investors have a single time horizon
(*d*) Investors have different expectations about the risk and return characteristics of assets

[Section 4-5G]

Answers

True and False

1. False	11. True	21. False	
2. False	12. True	22. False	
3. True	13. False	23. True	
4. True	14. True	24. True	
5. True	15. False	25. False	
6. True	16. False	26. True	
7. False	17. False	27. False	
8. True	18. True	28. True	
9. False	19. False	29. True	
10. False	20. True	30. True	

Multiple Choice

31. a	
32. c	
33. a	
34. b	
35. a	
36. d	
37. c	
38. b	
39. c	
40. d	

SOLVED PROBLEMS

PROBLEM 4-1: You are considering purchasing two stocks. A brokerage firm has provided estimated returns for the next year on these two stocks:

Stock A		Stock B	
Probability	Return (%)	Probability	Return (%)
0.05	−10	0.10	10
0.20	5	0.20	15
0.25	10	0.40	20
0.35	15	0.20	25
0.15	25	0.10	30

(a) Construct bar charts for Stock A and Stock B.
(b) Determine whether the probability distributions are symmetrical or skewed.
(c) Calculate the range of returns for each stock.
(d) Evaluate the riskiness of the stocks based on the data provided and the answers to parts (a) through (c) above.

Answer:

(a) The bar charts for Stock A and Stock B are shown below:

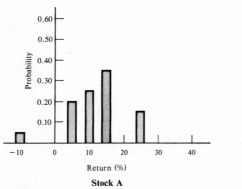

Stock A

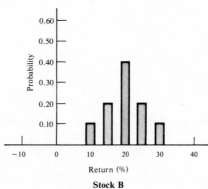

Stock B

(b) Stock A's probability distribution is skewed to the left and Stock B's probability distribution is symmetrical.
(c) Stock A's range of returns is 35 percentage points [25 − (−10)] and Stock B's range of returns is 20 percentage points [30 − 10].
(d) Stock A is riskier than Stock B because Stock A has a wider range of returns and a flatter probability distribution.   **[Section 4-1C]**

PROBLEM 4-2: Referring to Problem 4-1, what is the expected value of the returns for Stock A and Stock B?

Anwer: Using Equation 4-1, the expected value of the returns for each stock is:

Stock A

$$\bar{r}_A = (0.5)(-0.10) + (0.20)(0.05) + (0.25)(0.10) + (0.35)(0.15) + (0.15)(0.25)$$
$$= 0.12 \text{ or } 12 \text{ percent}$$
$$\bar{r}_B = (0.10)(0.10) + (0.20)(0.15) + (0.40) + (0.20) + (0.20)(0.25) + (0.10)(0.30)$$
$$= 0.20 \text{ or } 20 \text{ percent} \qquad\qquad \textbf{[Section 4-2A]}$$

PROBLEM 4-3: Ivison Yachts, Inc. plans to introduce a new design called the Caribbean Queen. The expected returns depend on the degree of market acceptance of the new yacht.

Market Acceptance	Probability	Expected Returns (%)
Very Weak	0.1	0
Weak	0.2	10
Moderate	0.4	20
Strong	0.2	30
Very Strong	0.1	40

(a) Calculate the expected value of the returns.
(b) Calculate the standard deviation of the returns.
(c) Calculate the coefficient of variation of the returns and interpret its meaning.

Answer:

(*a*) The calculation of the expected value in Equation 4-1 can be set up in tabular form.

i	p_i	r_i (%)	$p_i r_i$ (%)
1	0.1	0	0
2	0.2	10	2.0
3	0.4	20	8.0
4	0.2	30	6.0
5	0.1	40	4.0
			$\bar{r} = $ 20.0 percent

[Section 4-2A]

(*b*) The calculation of the standard deviation using Equation 4-3 can also be set up in tabular form. The square root of the variance, σ^2, of 120 percent is 10.95 percent (rounded).

i	r_i (%)	$\bar{r}$ (%)	r_i (%) $- \bar{r}$ (%)	$(r_i - \bar{r})^2$ (%)	p_i	$p_i(r_i - \bar{r})^2$ (%)
1	0	20	-20	400	0.1	40.0
2	10	20	-10	100	0.2	20.0
3	20	20	0	0	0.4	0
4	30	20	10	100	0.2	20.0
5	40	20	20	400	0.1	40.0
					$\sigma^2 = $	120.0

$$= \sqrt{120.0} = 10.95 \text{ percent} \qquad \textbf{[Section 4-2B]}$$

(*c*) Using Equation 4-4, the coefficient of variation is:

$$\text{cv} = \frac{10.95}{20.00} = 0.55$$

A coefficient of variation of 0.55 means that there is 0.55 percent risk for every 1 percent of return. **[Section 4-2C]**

PROBLEM 4-4: Brenner Enterprises is evaluating two projects whose returns are normally distributed. These projects have the following characteristics:

	Project X/9	Project X/10
Net investment..	$ 5,000	$25,000
Expected return ($\bar{r}$)	10,000	50,000
Standard deviation (σ)	2,000	10,000
Coefficient of variation (cv)...........................	0.20	0.20

(*a*) What is the ranking of the two projects based on their standard deviations and coefficients of variation?
(*b*) Which is the more appropriate risk measure in the situation—standard deviation or coefficients of variation?

Answer:

(*a*) Project X/10 is riskier than Project X/9 when ranked by their standard deviations. However, the two projects are equally risky when ranked by their coefficients of variation.
(*b*) In this situation, the coefficient of variation is the more appropriate risk measure because the projects have different net investments and expected values. Thus, a relative measure of risk (coefficient of variation) is needed rather than an absolute measure (standard deviation). **[Sections 4-2B & C]**

PROBLEM 4-5: Referring to Problem 4-4, Project X/9 has an expected value of $10,000 and a standard deviation of $2,000. Answer the following questions about Project X/9.

(a) What is the range of returns within ± 1 standard deviation of the expected value (mean)? Within ± 2 standard deviations?

(b) What percentage of the returns should fall within ± 1 and ± 2 standard deviations of the mean?

Answer:

(a) The ranges for Project X/9 are shown below:

Expected Value	Standard Deviation	Range
$10,000	± 1	$8,000 — $12,000
$10,000	± 2	$6,000 — $14,000

(b) Approximately 68 percent of the returns should lie between ± 1 standard deviation of the expected value and about 95 percent within ± 2 standard deviations.

[Section 4-2D]

PROBLEM 4-6: Referring again to Project X/9 in Problem 4-4, answer the following questions.

(a) What is the probability that the return will be greater than $13,000?

(b) What is the probability that the return will be between $5,000 and $13,000?

Answer:

(a) Calculating the probability that the return will exceed $13,000 requires three steps. First, compute the z value using Equation 4-5 as follows:

$$z = \frac{\$13,000 - \$10,000}{\$2,000} = 1.5$$

Next, find $\Pr(0 < z < 1.5)$ in Appendix E, which is 0.4332 or 43.32 percent. This probability is the chance of getting a return between the expected return of $10,000 and a return of $13,000. Finally, the probability of getting a return greater than $13,000 must be calculated. Remember that in a normal distribution, 50 percent of the outcomes lies on each side of the expected value. The probability of receiving a return of more than $13,000 is 0.0668 (0.5000 − 0.4332) or 6.68 percent.

(b) Determining the probability of a return falling between $5,000 and $13,000 requires several additional steps. First, determine the z value for a return between $5,000 and $10,000 using Equation 4-5:

$$z = \frac{\$5,000 - \$10,000}{\$2,000} = -2.50$$

Next, find $\Pr(-2.50 < z < 0)$ in Appendix E, which is 0.4938 or 49.38 percent. (Appendix E applies to either positive or negative z values.) Finally, the probability of a return between $5,000 and $13,000 is obtained by adding the probability of a return between $5,000 and $10,000, or 0.4938, and the probability of a return between $10,000 and $13,000, or 0.4332. This produces a probability of 0.9270 (0.4938 + 0.4332) or 92.70 percent chance of obtaining a return between $5,000 and $13,000. **[Section 4-2D]**

PROBLEM 4-7: You plan to form a portfolio of two stocks, Banana Computers and Discount Food Stores, and are considering two different options involving the weight of each stock in your portfolio. You estimate the correlation coefficient of the returns between Banana Computers and Discount Food Stores to be $\rho_{1,2} = +0.5$. Other characteristics of the two stocks are shown on the following page.

	Banana Computers (%)	Discount Food Stores (%)
Expected return (r_i)...........................	24	8
Standard deviation (σ_i)	16	2
Weight of each stock in the portfolio (w_i)		
Plan A	60	40
Plan B	20	80

(*a*) Compute the expected portfolio return and portfolio standard deviation for both Plan A and Plan B.

(*b*) Discuss the results.

Answer:

(*a*) Using Equation 4-6, the expected portfolio return for each plan is:

Plan A	Plan B
$\bar{r}_p = (0.6)(0.24) + (0.4)(0.08)$	$\bar{r}_p = (0.2)(0.24) + (0.8)(0.08)$
$= 0.176$ or 17.6 percent	$= 0.112$ or 11.2 percent

Using Equation 4-7, the portfolio standard deviation for each option is:

Plan A

$$\sigma_p = \sqrt{(0.6)^2(0.16)^2 + (0.4)^2(0.02)^2 + (2)(0.6)(0.4)(0.5)(0.16)(0.02)}$$
$$= \sqrt{0.00922 + 0.00006 + 0.00077} = \sqrt{0.01005} = 0.10025 \text{ or } 10.025 \text{ percent}$$

Plan B

$$\sigma_p = \sqrt{(0.2)^2(0.16)^2 + (0.8)^2(0.02)^2 + (2)(0.2)(0.8)(0.5)(0.16)(0.02)}$$
$$= \sqrt{0.00102 + 0.00026 + 0.00051} = \sqrt{0.00179} = 0.04231 \text{ or } 4.231 \text{ percent}$$

[Sections 4-4A & B]

(*b*) As shown in Plan B, both the expected portfolio return and portfolio standard deviation decrease as a greater proportion of the portfolio is invested in Discount Food Stores. Thus, the influence of Banana Computer's higher expected risk and return are replaced in the portfolio by Discount Food Stores' lower expected risk and return.

[Section 4-4C]

PROBLEM 4-8: Referring to the data and your results in Problem 4-7 for Plan A, do the following:

(*a*) Calculate the portfolio standard deviation when $\rho_{1,2} = +0.1$ and $\rho_{1,2} = -0.4$.

(*b*) Describe what happens to the portfolio's risk as the correlation coefficient of returns between the two stocks moves from positive to negative.

Answer:

(*a*) Using Equation 4-7, the portfolio standard deviation is:

Plan A when $\rho_{1,2} = +0.1$

$$\sigma_p = \sqrt{(0.6)^2(0.16)^2 + (0.4)^2(0.02)^2 + (2)(0.6)(0.4)(0.1)(0.16)(0.02)}$$
$$= \sqrt{0.00922 + 0.00006 + 0.00015} = \sqrt{0.00943} = 0.09711 \text{ or } 9.711 \text{ percent}$$

Plan A when $\rho_{1,2} = -0.4$

$$\sigma_p = \sqrt{(0.6)^2(0.16)^2 + (0.4)^2(0.02)^2 + (2)(0.6)(0.4)(-0.4)(0.16)(0.02)}$$
$$= \sqrt{0.00922 + 0.00006 - 0.00061} = \sqrt{0.00867} = 0.09311 \text{ or } 9.311 \text{ percent}$$

(b) The portfolio's risk becomes smaller as the correlation coefficient between the two securities becomes less positive, zero, or more negative. As shown above, the portfolio standard deviation for Plan A is 9.711 when $\rho_{1,2} = +0.1$, but decreases to 9.311 percent when $\rho_{1,2} = -0.4$. **[Sections 4-4B & C]**

PROBLEM 4-9: Referring to Problem 4-7, you decide to invest $10,000 in the two stocks using Plan A. That is, you invest 60 percent in Banana Computers and 40 percent in Discount Food Stores. The betas of Banana Computers and Discount Food Stores are 1.6 and 0.8, respectively. What is the portfolio beta?

Answer: Using Equation 4-10, the portfolio beta is:

$$b_p = (0.6)(1.6) + (0.4)(0.8) = 0.96 + 0.32 = 1.28 \qquad \textbf{[Section 4-5C]}$$

PROBLEM 4-10: The common stock of Diversified Industries has an estimated beta of 1.2. The risk-free rate is 7 percent and the expected return on the market is 12 percent.

(a) What is the required rate of return for Diversified Industries using the capital asset pricing model (CAPM)?
(b) What is the market risk premium?

Answer:

(a) Using Equation 4-11, the required rate of return is:

$$r_i = 0.07 + (1.2)(0.12 - 0.07) = 0.13 \text{ or } 13 \text{ percent}$$

(b) The market risk premium is the return on the market portfolio (r_m) less the risk-free rate (r_f).

$$r_m - r_f = 0.12 - 0.07 = 0.05 \text{ or } 5 \text{ percent} \qquad \textbf{[Section 4-5D]}$$

PROBLEM 4-11: Referring to Problem 4-10, the risk-free rate of 7 percent includes an inflation premium of 4 percent. If the inflationary expectations of investors increase to 6 percent, what would happen to the required rate of return for Diversified's common stock?

Answer: The risk-free rate consists of a real rate and an inflation premium. If the inflation premium increased from 4 to 6 percent, the risk-free rate would increase from 7 to 9 percent. Inflation would also lead investors to expect a higher return on the market portfolio which would increase the return on the market portfolio, r_m, from 12 to 14 percent. Using Equation 4-11, the required rate of return under the new inflationary expectations would be:

$$r_i = 0.09 + (1.2)(0.14 - 0.09) = 0.15 \text{ or } 15 \text{ percent}$$

Thus, inflationary expectations would increase the required return for Diversified Industries and other common stocks. **[Section 4-5D]**

PROBLEM 4-12: Kumar Securities plans to purchase equal amounts of four of the following stocks for one of its clients. The client already holds a highly diversified portfolio. The risk-free rate of return is estimated at 8 percent and the expected market return at 14 percent.

Stock	1	2	3	4	5	6
Beta$_i$	1.5	1.0	0.8	2.0	0.3	1.2

(a) What is the risk premium on each security?
(b) What four stocks should be selected if the client wants the lowest risk portfolio?
(c) What is the required rate of return on the four-stock portfolio selected? Assume an equal investment in each stock.

Answer:

(*a*) The risk premiums are shown below:

Stock	Risk Premium $b_i(r_m - r_f)$
1	$(1.5)(0.14 - 0.08) = 0.09$ or 9 percent
2	$(1.0)(0.14 - 0.08) = 0.06$ or 6 percent
3	$(0.8)(0.14 - 0.08) = 0.048$ or 4.8 percent
4	$(2.0)(0.14 - 0.08) = 0.12$ or 12 percent
5	$(0.3)(0.14 - 0.08) = 0.018$ or 1.8 percent
6	$(1.2)(0.14 - 0.08) = 0.072$ or 7.2 percent

(*b*) The four stocks that provide the lowest risk portfolio are those with the lowest betas and therefore the lowest risk premiums, namely stocks 2, 3, 5, and 6.

(*c*) The required rate of return on the portfolio of stocks 2, 3, 5, and 6 is determined in two steps. First, assuming equal weights of 25 percent for each stock, the portfolio's beta is found by substituting these weights and the stock's beta into Equation 4-10.

$$b_p = (0.25)(1.0) + (0.25)(0.8) + (0.25)(0.3) + (0.25)(1.2) = 0.825$$

Next, using the capital asset pricing model in Equation 4-11 produces the required rate of return.

$$r_p = 0.08 + (0.825)(0.14 - 0.08)$$
$$= 0.1295 \text{ or } 12.95 \text{ percent}$$

[Sections 4-5C and D]

5 VALUATION

THIS CHAPTER IS ABOUT

- ☑ **Concepts of Value**
- ☑ **Basic Valuation Model**
- ☑ **Bond Valuation**
- ☑ **Yield to Maturity**
- ☑ **Preferred Stock Valuation**
- ☑ **Common Stock Valuation**

Valuation is the process of estimating the worth of an asset. The valuation of *real assets*, such as plant and equipment, is the subject of capital budgeting, which is discussed in Chapters 12 and 13. The valuation of *financial assets*, such as stocks and bonds, is called **security valuation** and is the subject of this chapter.

Keep in mind that the terms *value* and *price* of securities are used interchangeably in this chapter when valuing corporate securities. The concepts of the time value of money and risk and return presented in Chapters 3 and 4, respectively, are used to determine the value of financial assets. The financial manager is concerned with security valuation because investor buying and selling determines the market value of a corporation's securities. In order to maximize the value of a firm's common stock, financial decisions must be made that enhance the desirability of a firm's common stock to investors.

5-1. Concepts of Value

The term *value* is used in different ways depending on whether the entire firm or individual assets are being valued. These different types of value include the following:

A. *Going-concern value* **is the value of a firm as an operating business.**

This concept of value focuses on the firm's ability to generate future sales and cash flows rather than upon its balance sheet assets. Going-concern value is an important consideration when one firm wishes to acquire or take over another.

B. *Liquidating value* **is the amount that a firm would realize by selling its assets and paying off its liabilities.**

Liquidating value is of concern to both creditors and owners of firms facing potential bankruptcy.

C. *Book value* **is the accounting value of an asset or a firm.**

Book value is based on historical data shown on the firm's balance sheet and hence may not reflect an asset's current value or replacement value. Book value is frequently used in computing financial ratios. For example, the book value per share of common stock is equal to the firm's net worth (the stockholders' equity section of the balance sheet) divided by the number of common shares outstanding.

D. *Market value* **is the price for which an asset can be sold.**

The market value or price of an asset may be higher or lower than an asset's book value. For example, firms typically sell inventories for prices above their book values. The market value of some assets, such as a share of stock that is frequently traded, is readily determined. However, the market value of other assets, such as a specific parcel of land or a building, may be difficult to establish because these assets are infrequently traded or may not be readily marketable.

E. *Instrinsic value*, **also called** *fair value* **or** *capitalized value*, **is the present value of all of an asset's expected future returns (cash flows) when discounted at the investor's required rate of return.**

The required rate of return or the *capitalization rate* on an asset is a function of the uncertainty, or risk, associated with the returns from the asset. Intrinsic value may be interpreted as the maximum price that an investor would pay for a financial asset and still achieve the required rate of return. Intrinsic value provides a useful measure of valuing financial assets because these assets provide a claim against future cash flows. In a marketplace in which all investors are assumed to have the same accurate information with respect to securities, called an **efficient market**, the intrinsic value of a security is equal to its market value. However, inefficiencies in the market may cause the intrinsic value and market value of a security to differ.

5-2. Basic Valuation Model

A. A *valuation model* **attempts to isolate significant factors affecting security prices and rates of return.**

As shown in Equation 5-1, the basic valuation model is an intrinsic value model. This model shows that the amount of the expected returns, their timing, and their riskiness are factors that affect the price of a security. The value of a security is directly related to the amount of expected cash flows and is inversely related to the length of time over which they occur and to the amount of risk. With certain modifications, the basic valuation model may be used to value bonds, preferred stock, and common stock. These three financial assets are discussed in Chapter 20, but their valuation is discussed below.

BASIC VALUATION MODEL
$$P_0 = \sum_{t=1}^{n} \frac{C_t}{(1 + k)^t}$$
(5-1)

where
P_0 = Present value or price of the asset at time zero
C_t = Expected return (cash flow) in period t
k = Investor's required rate of return
n = Length of the holding period
t = Time period

B. The basic valuation model involves two major risk-return assumptions.

1. The model assumes that returns in the form of cash flows, C_t, are represented by a *point estimate* or single value for a particular time period, t, rather than a probability distribution. For financial assets, cash flows may be in the form of interest and dividend payments, the value of a bond when it matures, and/or the price of a security if it is sold.
2. The model assumes that the various risks associated with these cash flows are reflected in the investor's required rate of return, k.

5-3. Bond Valuation

A **bond** is a long-term debt security in which the issuer promises to pay a series of periodic interest payments in addition to returning the principal at maturity. Most corporate bonds have the following characteristics: an initial maturity of 10 to 30 years; a $1,000 principal, called the **par value** or *face value*, paid at maturity; and fixed semiannual interest payments. Annual interest payments equal the bond's **coupon rate**, or stated rate of interest, on the bond's par value multiplied by its par value. (Some bonds, called **zero coupon bonds**, do not pay interest, only the principal at maturity.)

Bond valuation is a relatively straightforward process since the cash flows (interest payments and/or principal repayment) are specified in the bond contract or **indenture**. A bond's **current yield** is calculated by dividing the annual interest payment by the bond's current market price. The intrinsic value of a bond is the present value of the contractual payments that its issuer is required to make, discounted at the required rate of return.

A. The intrinsic value or market price of a bond fluctuates in response to changes in the investor's required rate of return.

The required rate of return, or discount rate, on corporate bonds includes a risk-free rate plus a risk premium. (These concepts are discussed in Chapter 4.) Two factors affecting the investor's required rate of return for bonds are interest rate risk and purchasing power risk. **Interest rate risk** is the risk that interest rates will increase in the future, while **purchasing power risk** is the risk of future inflation.

B. There is an inverse relationship between changes in risk and bond prices.

An increase in either interest rate risk or purchasing power risk will cause the prices of outstanding bonds to fall, while a decrease in these risks will cause bond prices to rise. However, the prices of shorter-term bonds are less sensitive to changes in interest rates than long-term bonds because of the time value of money. That is, the longer the maturity of the bond, the greater will be its change in price in response to a given change in the market interest rate. The relationship between interest rates and bond value is outlined by the following facts:

1. If the current market interest rate (the investor's required rate of return) equals the coupon rate, a bond's selling price, P_0, will equal its par value, M.
2. If the current market interest rate is more than the coupon rate, a bond's selling price will be less than its par value. Such a bond is said to sell at a *discount*, which equals $M - P_0$. Investors are not willing to pay par value because the bond pays less interest than newly issued bonds with similar characteristics.
3. If the current market interest rate is less than the coupon rate, a bond's selling price will be more than its par value. Such a bond sells at a *premium*, which equals $P_0 - M$. Investors are willing to pay more than par value for these bonds because of the higher returns.

C. If a bond sells at a discount (premium), its value is less (more) when interest is paid semiannually than when it is paid annually.

The intrinsic value of a bond with annual interest payments is shown in Equations 5-2 and 5-3. Although interest on corporate bonds is typically paid semiannually, it is less complicated to show an initial bond valuation model in which annual interest payments are assumed.

BOND VALUATION MODEL WITH ANNUAL INTEREST

$$P_0 = \sum_{t=1}^{n} \frac{I}{(1 + k_d)} + \frac{M}{(1 + k_d)^n} \qquad (5\text{-}2)$$

Equation 5-2 may be simplified further as follows:

$$P_0 = I(\text{PVIFA}_{k_d, n}) + M(\text{PVIF}_{k_d, n}) \qquad (5\text{-}3)$$

where P_0 = Present value or price of a bond at time zero

I = Annual interest payment

M = Par or principal payment required in period n

k_d = Investor's required rate of return on bonds

n = Length of the holding period

t = Time period

PVIFA = Present value interest factor of an annuity (Appendix D)

PVIF = Present value interest factor of a single amount (Appendix C)

EXAMPLE 5-1: An Olympic Oil Company bond has a 10 percent coupon rate and a par value of $1,000. Interest is paid annually and the bond matures in 10 years. The required rate of return is 10 percent.

(a) Substituting the values I = $100 (0.10 × $1,000), M = $1,000, k_d = 10 and n = 10 in Equation 5-3 results in an intrinsic value of $1,000.50.

$$P_0 = (\$100)(\text{PVIFA}_{0.10,10}) + (\$1,000)(\text{PVIF}_{0.10,10})$$
$$= (\$100)(6.145) + (\$1,000)(0.386) = \$614.50 + 386.00 = \$1,000.50$$

(b) The bond would sell exactly for its par value because its coupon rate is equal to the required rate of return. The computed value of $1,000.50 is slightly greater than $1,000 due to rounding errors in computing the present values using Appendices C and D.

EXAMPLE 5-2: Referring to data in Example 5-1, assume that the required interest changes to 8 percent and 12 percent. Under each interest rate scenario, Olympic Oil has the following questions:

(a) What is the value of the bond?
(b) Will the bond sell at a discount, at par, or at a premium? Why?

Management concludes the following:

(a) Using Equation 5-3, the value of the bond for each required rate of interest is shown below:

For k_d = 8 percent

$$P_0 = (\$100)(\text{PVIFA}_{0.08,10}) + (\$1,000)(\text{PVIF}_{0.08,10})$$
$$= (\$100)(6.710) + (\$1,000)(0.463) = \$671.00 + 463.00 = \$1,134.00$$

For k_d = 12 percent

$$P_0 = (\$100)(\text{PVIFA}_{0.12,10}) + (\$1,000)(\text{PVIF}_{0.12,10})$$
$$= (\$100)(5.650) + (\$1,000)(0.322) = \$565.00 + 322.00 = \$887.00$$

(b) If the interest rate falls to 8 percent, the bond price would rise and would sell for a premium of $134 ($1,134 − $1,000) because the required rate of interest is less than the coupon rate. If the interest rate rises to 12 percent, the price of the Olympic Oil Company bond would fall and the bond would sell at a *discount* of $113 ($1,000 − $887). This is because the 12 percent required rate of return is greater than the 10 percent coupon rate.

The intrinsic value of a bond with semiannual interest is shown in Equations 5-4 and 5-5. In Equations 5-4 and 5-5 the annual interest rate, I, is converted to semiannual interest, $I/2$, and the annual required rate of return, k_d, is converted to semiannual return, $k_d/2$, by dividing by 2. The number of years to maturity, n, is multiplied by 2 to obtain the number of six-month periods, $2n$.

BOND VALUATION MODEL WITH SEMIANNUAL INTEREST

$$P_0 = \sum_{t=1}^{2n} \frac{I/2}{(1 + k_d/2)^t} + \frac{M}{(1 + k_d/2)^{2n}} \tag{5-4}$$

$$P_0 = (I/2)(\text{PVIFA}_{k_d/2,\,2n}) + M(\text{PVIF}_{k_d/2,\,2n}) \tag{5-5}$$

EXAMPLE 5-3: Recall the Olympic Oil Company bond in Examples 5-1 and 5-2. The following questions have arisen with respect to required rates of return of 8, 10, and 12 percent.

(a) What is the value of the bond if interest is paid semiannually?
(b) What is the relationship among the bond values when interest is paid annually and semiannually under each interest rate scenario?

Using Equation 5-5, the bond values for each required rate of return are shown below:

For k_d = 8 percent

$$P_0 = (\$100/2)(PVIFA_{0.08/2,(2)(10)}) + (\$1,000)(PVIF_{0.08/2,(2)(10)})$$
$$= (\$50)(13,590) + (\$1,000)(0.456) = \$679.50 + 456.00 = \$1,135.50$$

For k_d = 10 percent

$$P_0 = (\$100/2)(PVIFA_{0.10/2,(2)(10)}) + (\$1,000)(PVIF_{0.10/2,(2)(10)})$$
$$= (\$50)(12.462) + (\$1,000)(0.377) = \$623.10 + 377.00 = \$1,000.10$$

For k_d = 12 percent

$$P_0 = (\$100/2)(PVIFA_{0.12/2,(2)(10)}) + (\$1,000)(PVIF_{0.12/2,(2)(10)})$$
$$= (\$50)(11.470) + (\$1,000)(0.312) = \$573.50 + 312.00 = \$885.50$$

A comparison of the bond values using both semiannual and annual interest payments for the three required rates of return is shown in Figure 5-1. In this example, the bond's value is $1.50 higher with semiannual than with annual interest payments when the bond sells at a premium. However, the bond's value is $1.50 lower with semiannual than with annual interest payments when the bond sells at a discount. Thus, no difference in value results between semiannual and annual interest payments when the required rate of return and the coupon rate are the same. Increasing the frequency of compounding accentuates the interest rate differences.

Required Rate of Return, k_d (%)	Selling Status of the Bond	Bond Value with Interest Paid		Difference in Value [(1) − (2)]
		Semiannually (1)	Annually (2)	
8	Premium	$1,135.50	$1,134.00	1.50
10	Par value	1,000.10*	1,000.50*	*
12	Discount	885.50	887.00	−1.50

* Bond values should be exactly $1,000 with the difference in value due to rounding errors in the present value tables in Appendices C and D.

FIGURE 5-1   Bond values for various required rates of return for an Olympic Oil Company bond with a 10-year maturity, 10 percent coupon, and $1,000 par value.

5-4. Yield to Maturity

The yield to maturity, *YTM*, is the rate of return, k_d, earned on a bond held until maturity. In other words, the YTM is the discount rate that equates the present value of all interest payments plus the repayment of principal from a bond with the present bond price. The YTM may be calculated by solving for k_d, using Equations 5-2 or 5-4 or their alternate forms, Equations 5-3 or 5-5, depending on whether interest is paid annually or semiannually. This computation implicitly assumes that all interest payments are reinvested over the remaining life of the bond at a rate of return equal to its YTM. The YTM may be calculated with the present value tables in Appendices C and D using a trial-and-error approach. Different rates, k_d, are substituted into the appropriate equations until the discounted cash flows, I and M, exactly equal the present value, P_0, of the bond. (For a bond with specific maturity, the procedure for finding the YTM is exactly the same as finding the internal rate of return *(IRR)* for capital budgeting projects discussed in Chapter 13.)

An approximation for YTM may be calculated using Equation 5-6, in which the annual interest payment, I, plus the annual bond discount or premium amortization, $(M - P_0)/n$, is divided by the average investment, $(M + P_0)/2$. The term $(M - P_0)$ is positive if the bond is selling at a discount and is negative if the bond is selling at a premium.

APPROXIMATE YIELD TO MATURITY
$$\text{YTM} = \frac{I + (M - P_0)/n}{(M + P_0)/2} \tag{5-6}$$

EXAMPLE 5-4: A corporate bond with a par value of $1,000 and a coupon rate of 10 percent matures in eight years. The price of the bond is $1,114.70. Using both Equation 5-3 and Equation 5-6 with annual interest payments, the yield to maturity would be computed as follows:

(a) Because the bond is selling at a premium, the YTM must be less than the 10 percent coupon rate. Using a trial-and-error approach, appropriate present value interest factors for a 9 percent rate are substituted into Equation 5-3. The calculated value of $1,055.50 is below the current selling price of $1,114.70, which indicates that an even lower rate is needed.

For $k_d = 9$ percent

$$P_0 = (\$100)(\text{PVIFA}_{0.09,8}) + (\$1,000)(\text{PVIF}_{0.09,8})$$
$$= (\$100)(5.535) + (\$1,000)(0.502) = \$553.50 + 502.00 = \$1,055.50$$

Using a second rate of 7 percent produces a value of $1,179.10, which is above the current selling price of $1,114.70. Thus, a higher rate is needed.

For $k_d = 7$ percent

$$P_0 = (\$100)(\text{PVIFA}_{0.07,8}) + (\$1,000)(\text{PVIF}_{0.07,8})$$
$$= (\$100)(5.971) + (\$1,000)(0.582) = \$597.10 + 582.00 = \$1,179.10$$

Using a third rate of 8 percent produces a price exactly equal to the current market price. Hence, the YTM is exactly 8 percent. In this problem, the exact YTM of 8 percent is slightly below the approximate YTM of 8.1 percent.

For $k_d = 8$ percent

$$P_0 = (\$100)(\text{PVIFA}_{0.08,8}) + (\$1,000)(\text{PVIF}_{0.08,8})$$
$$= (\$100)(5.747) + (\$1,000)(0.540) = \$574.70 + 540.00 = \$1,114.70$$

(b) Using Equation 5-6, the approximate yield to maturity is found by substituting $I = \$100$, $M = \$1,000$, and $P_0 = \$1,114.70$ as follows:

$$\text{Approximate yield to maturity} = \frac{\$100 + (\$1,000 - \$1,114.70)/8}{(\$1,000 + \$1,114.70)/2} = \frac{\$100 - \$14.34}{\$1,057.35}$$

$$= \frac{\$85.66}{\$1,057.35} = 0.081 \text{ or } 8.1 \text{ percent}$$

5-5. Preferred Stock Valuation

Preferred stock is stock that has a claim against income and assets before common stock but after debt. Preferred stock is often considered a hybrid security because it possesses characteristics of both debt and equity. For example, preferred stock is similar to debt in that both securities generally have fixed payments. Preferred stock typically pays regular fixed cash dividends on a quarterly basis. Preferred stock is similar to equity in that most preferred issues have no maturity. There are exceptions, however, to both of these general characteristics.

A. Preferred stock valuation is relatively simple if the firm pays fixed dividends at the end of each year.

If this condition holds, then the stream of dividend payments can be treated as a perpetuity and be discounted by the investor's required rate of return on a preferred stock issue. (A *perpetuity* is an annuity with an infinite life span.) This rate depends on the risk that the firm may not be able to meet its dividend payments. Investors normally require a higher rate of return on preferred stock than on bonds because preferred stock is riskier. This is because bond holders have priority over preferred stockholders in their claims to both income and assets. Thus, the value of a share of preferred stock, P_0, is the sum of the present values of future dividends discounted at the investor's required rate of return.

B. The intrinsic value of preferred stock can be calculated by capitalizing a perpetual stream of dividends, assuming for simplicity that each dividend payment is made annually.

PREFERRED STOCK
VALUATION MODEL
$$P_0 = \sum_{t=1}^{\infty} \frac{D_p}{(1 + k_p)^t} \tag{5-7}$$

Equation 5-7 can be simplified into the following valuation model:

$$P_0 = \frac{D_p}{k_p} \tag{5-8}$$

where
D_p = Per share cash dividend paid on a perpetuity

k_p = Investor's required rate of return on preferred stock

∞ = Sign for infinity

EXAMPLE 5-5: United Electric and Power Company has an issue of preferred stock outstanding that pays a yearly dividend of $5.40. Investors require a 12 percent return on this preferred stock. Its intrinsic value can be found by substituting D_p = $5.40 and k_p = 0.12 in Equation 5-8:

$$P_0 = \frac{\$5.40}{0.12} = \$45.00$$

5-6. Common Stock Valuation

Common stock is stock held by the owners of the firm. Common stock valuation is complicated by the uncertainty of future returns. These returns may be in the form of cash dividend payments and/or changes in the stock's price (gains or losses) over the holding period. Dividends are uncertain because there is no legal requirement to pay them unless they are declared. Furthermore, common stock dividends may increase, remain constant, or decrease. Future share prices are also uncertain. Thus, stocks are generally riskier than bonds because the cash flows must be estimated. Although there are numerous common stock valuation models, the following discussion focuses on models that assume varying **holding periods** (the length of time that an investor expects to own or hold a security) and rates of dividend growth.

A. Common stock valuation models may be classified as finite-period and infinite-period dividend valuation models.

1. A *finite-period dividend valuation model* is one in which an investor plans to purchase a common stock and hold it for a specific length of time. For example, the

holding period may be for one or more periods. During the holding period, the investor expects to receive cash dividends and to sell the stock for a price at the end of the holding period. Corporations generally make quarterly dividend payments on common stock. Equation 5-9 is the finite-period stock valuation model.

FINITE-PERIOD STOCK VALUATION MODEL

$$P_0 = \sum_{t=1}^{n} \frac{D_t}{(1 + k_s)} + \frac{P_n}{(1 + k_s)^n}$$

(5-9)

where D_t = Per share cash dividend paid on common stock in period t

P_n = Per share price of common stock in period n

k_s = Investor's required rate of return on common stock

EXAMPLE 5-6: An investor plans to buy common stock of Maryland Farms and to sell it at the end of one year. The investor expects Maryland Farms to pay a $2.60 cash dividend and to sell for $25.00 at the end of the year. If the investor's required rate of return is 15 percent, the value of the stock to this investor would be computed as shown below. Substituting D_1 = $2.60, P_1 = $25.00, and k_s = 0.15 in Equation 5-9 indicates that the investor should pay no more than $24.00 per share for a share of Maryland Farms common stock to realize an expected return of 15 percent.

$$P_0 = \frac{\$2.60}{1 + 0.15} + \frac{\$25.00}{1 + 0.15} = \frac{\$27.60}{1.15} = \$24.00$$

2. An *infinite-period stock valuation model* assumes that an investor plans to purchase a common stock and hold it indefinitely. Hence, the returns are only in the form of dividends over multiple periods. Equation 5-10 is an infinite-period stock model that shows the intrinsic value of a share of common stock is equal to the expected stream of dividends discounted at the investor's required rate of return.

INFINITE-PERIOD STOCK VALUATION MODEL

$$P_0 = \sum_{t=1}^{\infty} \frac{D_t}{(1 + k_s)^t}$$

(5-10)

B. Common stock valuation models may be classified as zero, constant, and supernormal growth dividend models.

1. A *zero growth dividend model* assumes dividends remain a fixed amount over time. Equation 5-11 is a zero growth dividend model. This valuation model is similar to the preferred stock valuation model in Equation 5-8 because both equations treat dividends as a perpetuity.

ZERO GROWTH DIVIDEND VALUATION MODEL

$$P_0 = \frac{D_p}{k_s}$$

(5-11)

EXAMPLE 5-7: Consolidated Stores expects to pay a $3.00 cash dividend at the end of the year indefinitely into the future. If investors in this stock require a 15 percent return, the value of a share of Consolidated Stores would be computed as by substituting D_p = $3.00 and k_s = 0.15 in Equation 5-11 which produces a value of $20.00.

$$P_0 = \frac{\$3.00}{0.15} = \$20.00$$

2. A *constant growth dividend model* assumes that dividends grow at a constant rate each period. Substituting $D_0(1 + g)^t$ for D_t in Equation 5-10 produces the constant growth dividend model in Equation 5-12.

CONSTANT GROWTH DIVIDEND VALUATION MODEL

$$P_0 = \sum_{t=1}^{\infty} \frac{D_0(1 + g)^t}{(1 + k_s)^t}$$

(5-12)

where D_0 = Per share dividend in the current period

g = Constant dividend growth rate

If the investor's required rate of return, k_s, is greater than the dividend growth rate, g, then Equation 5-12 can be simplified into the *Gordon constant growth model* shown in Equation 5-13. This model is the most frequently used dividend model for valuing common stock.

GORDON CONSTANT GROWTH DIVIDEND VALUATION MODEL
$$P_0 = \frac{D_1}{k_s - g} \qquad \text{(5-13)}$$

EXAMPLE 5-8: Channel, Inc. currently pays $2.00 per share in common stock dividends. The firm's dividends are expected to grow at a constant rate of 5 percent per year. Investors require a 15 percent return on Channel's common stock. D_1 is calculated by using $D_0(1 + g)^t$, which is the numerator in Equation 5-12.

$$D_1 = (\$2.00)(1 + 0.05)^1 = \$2.10$$

Substituting $D_1 = \$2.10$, $k_s = 0.15$, and $g = 0.05$ in Equation 5-13 produces a common stock value of $21.00.

$$P_0 = \frac{\$2.10}{0.15 - 0.05} = \$21.00$$

3. A *supernormal growth dividend model* assumes that dividends grow at an above-normal rate over some time period and then grow at a normal rate thereafter. This two-stage model is more flexible than the zero or constant growth rate models and can be adjusted to allow for any number of different expected growth rates. Equation 5-14 is a supernormal dividend growth model. This model states that the value of a firm's common stock equals the present value of the expected dividends during the above-normal growth period plus the present value of the stock price at the end of the above-normal growth period.

SUPERNORMAL GROWTH DIVIDEND MODEL
$$P_0 = \sum_{t=1}^{m} \frac{D_0(1 + g_s)^t}{(1 + k_s)^t} + \left[\frac{D_{m+1}}{k_s - g_n}\right]\left[\frac{1}{(1 + k_s)^m}\right] \qquad \text{(5-14)}$$

where g_s = Supernormal growth rate

           g_n = Normal growth rate

           m = Period of supernormal growth

      D_{m+1} = Dividends per share paid in period $m + 1$

EXAMPLE 5-9: Talbott Industries expects dividends to grow at a rate of 10 percent a year for the next five years and 6 percent a year thereafter. The firm's current dividend is $2.00 per share. An investor, who requires a 16 percent rate of return, would compute the value of Talbott's common stock in three steps using Equation 5-14.

Step 1. Find the present value of the dividends during the above-normal growth period.

$$P_0 = \sum_{t=1}^{5} \frac{D_0(1 + g_s)^t}{(1 + k_s)^t} = \sum_{t=1}^{5} \frac{\$2.00(1.10)^t}{(1.16)^t}$$

Year t	Dividend $\$2.00(1.10)^t = D_t$ (1)	Present Value Interest Factor $PVIF_{0.16, t}$ (2)	Present Value, D_t [(1) × (2)] (3)
1	$2.00(1.100) = $2.20	0.862	$1.90
2	2.00(1.210) = 2.42	0.743	1.80
3	2.00(1.331) = 2.66	0.641	1.71
4	2.00(1.464) = 2.93	0.552	1.62
5	2.00(1.611) = 3.22	0.476	1.53
		Total	$8.56

Step 2. Find the present value of the stock price in Year 5, $PV(P_5)$. This step involves calculating the stock value at the end of Year 5, P_5.

$$P_5 = \frac{D_{m+1}}{k_s - g_n} = \frac{D_5(1 + g_n)}{0.16 - 0.06} = \frac{(\$3.22)(1.06)}{0.10} = \frac{\$3.413}{0.10} = \$34.13$$

Next, the stock value at the end of Year 5, $P_5 = \$34.13$, is discounted back to the present at the 16 percent required rate of return, $PVIF_{0.16,5} = 0.476$.

$$PV(P_5) = P_5 \left[\frac{1}{(1 + k_e)^m} \right] = \$34.13 \left[\frac{1}{(1.16)^5} \right] = \$34.13(0.476) = \$16.25$$

Step 3. Sum the present value of the five years' dividends and the present value of the stock value in Year 5 to get the value of the stock in P_0.

$$P_0 = \$8.56 + \$16.25 = \$24.81$$

RAISE YOUR GRADES

Can you explain...?

☑ why the financial manager is concerned about security valuation
☑ who determines the value of the firm's financial assets
☑ five different types of value
☑ why intrinsic value is used to evaluate the desirability of financial assets
☑ what the basic valuation model is
☑ what characteristics of bonds simplify the calculation of intrinsic value
☑ the relationship between changes in interest rates and bond prices
☑ the conditions that cause a bond to sell at a discount, at par value, or at a premium
☑ what the meaning of yield to maturity is
☑ how to calculate a bond's yield to maturity
☑ how to calculate the intrinsic value of a preferred stock
☑ what factors complicate the valuation of common stock
☑ the difference between a limited-period and an infinite-period stock valuation model
☑ three common stock valuation models

SUMMARY

1. Valuation is the process of estimating the worth of an asset. For financial assets, such as stocks and bonds, valuation involves calculating the present value of the asset's expected future returns discounted at the investor's required rate of return. The discount or capitalization rate depends on the risk associated with the asset's returns.
2. The financial manager must understand the valuation process in order to maximize stockholder wealth so that the manager can make decisions that have a positive impact on the firm's stock price. Financial decisions may influence the firm's risk-return characteristics, which in turn are reflected in the price of its common stock.
3. The value of a firm or its assets is measured in several ways: going-concern value, liquidating value, book value, market value, and intrinsic value. Intrinsic value is a useful measure for valuing financial assets because it incorporates cash flows, the investor's required rate of return, and the time value of money.
4. The basic valuation model states that the present value of an asset is equal to the summation of all its future cash flows discounted for their respective periods at a required rate of return.

5. The value of a bond with a finite maturity is relatively straightforward because the cash flows can be readily determined. A bond's value is the present value of the stream of fixed interest payments plus the present value of the principal payments, both discounted at the investor's required rate of return. If the required rate of return is more than the bond's coupon rate, the bond will sell at a discount. If the required rate of return is less than the coupon rate, the bond will sell at a premium.

6. The yield to maturity is the rate an investor would receive if a bond were bought today and held to maturity.

7. Preferred stock valuation is relatively simple if the security has fixed payments and no maturity. Under these circumstances, the value of a share of preferred stock is the present value of its future dividends discounted at the investor's required rate of return.

8. Common stock is more difficult to value than either bonds or preferred stock because both the future dividend payments and the resale price of the stock are uncertain. If the stock is not going to be sold, then the value of a share of stock is the present value of all expected future dividends over an infinite time horizon.

9. The zero growth dividend model is a naive model that assumes dividends on common stock remain fixed over time.

10. The most commonly used model, called the constant growth model, assumes that dividends on common stock grow at a constant rate each period.

11. The supernormal growth model assumes that dividends on common stock grow at an above-normal rate over some time period and then grow at a normal rate thereafter.

RAPID REVIEW

True or False

1. Going-concern value is the accounting value of an asset on a firm's balance sheet. [Sections 5-1A]

2. Book value and market value of an asset are generally the same. [Sections 5-1D]

3. Investors may pay more than the intrinsic value for a security and still achieve their required rate of return. [Section 5-1E]

4. The basic valuation model indicates that a security's price is a function of its cash flows, their timing, and the investor's required rate of return. [Section 5-2A]

5. The annual interest paid on a bond equals the bond's coupon rate multiplied by the bond's par value. [Section 5-3]

6. Bond interest is typically paid annually. [Section 5-3]

7. The required rate of return on a financial asset equals a risk-free rate plus a risk premium. [Section 5-3A]

8. The prices of short-term bonds fluctuate more widely in response to changes in interest rates than do the prices of long-term bonds. [Section 5-3B]

9. There is an inverse relationship between the required rate of return on a bond and bond prices. [Section 5-3B]

10. If the required rate of return is greater than the coupon rate on a bond, the bond will sell at a premium. [Section 5-3B]

11. If a bond sells for $950 and its par value is $1,000, the discount is $50. [Section 5-3B]

12. Bonds selling at a premium will have a lower value with semiannual interest than with annual interest. [Section 5-3B]

13. A bond will sell for its exact par value when its coupon rate is equal to the required rate of return. [Section 5-3B]

14. The intrinsic value of a bond is the present value of the stream of periodic dividend payments plus the present value of the maturity value. [Section 5-3C]

15. Yield to maturity is the rate of return an investor will earn if a bond is held to maturity. [Section 5-4]

16. If preferred stock pays a fixed dividend and is not sold, its value may be found by capitalizing a perpetual stream of dividends. [Sections 5-5A & B]

17. The valuation of common stocks is more complicated than the valuation of either bonds or preferred stocks. [Section 5-6]

18. The returns from common stocks are generally more certain than the returns from other types of securities. [Section 5-6]

19. A holding period is the length of time that an investor expects to own or hold a security. [Section 5-6A]

20. The Gordon constant growth model, $P_0 = D_1/(k_s - g)$, requires that k_s be greater than g. [Section 5-6B]

Multiple Choice

21. The value of a firm as an operating business is called

    (a) going-concern value
    (b) liquidating value
    (c) intrinsic value
    (d) book value

    [Section 5-1A]

22. The accounting value of an asset or a firm is called

    (a) market value
    (b) book value
    (c) intrinsic value
    (d) liquidating value

    [Section 5-1C]

23. In an efficient marketplace, the market value of a security should equal its

    (a) going-concern value
    (b) liquidating value
    (c) book value
    (d) intrinsic value

    [Section 5-1E]

24. In the basic valuation model shown in Equation 5-1, the value or price of a security is influenced by all of the following *except* the

    (a) amount of expected future returns
    (b) book value of the security
    (c) timing of expected future returns
    (d) investor's required rate of return

    [Section 5-2A]

25. Bond payments on corporate bonds are typically made

    (a) monthly
    (b) quarterly
    (c) semiannually
    (d) annually

    [Section 5-3]

26. If the market interest rate is below the coupon rate, a bond will sell at

    (a) its par value
    (b) a discount
    (c) a premium
    (d) a price of $1,000

    [Section 5-3B]

27. Assuming that two bonds are similar except for their maturities, what is the sensitivity of the price movements of the shorter-term bond to a given change in the market interest rate relative to the longer-term bond?

    (*a*) More sensitive
    (*b*) Less sensitive
    (*c*) Equally sensitive
    (*d*) More information is needed to determine relative sensitivity

    [Section 5-3B]

28. The yield to maturity computation assumes that

    (*a*) all interest payments are reinvested at a rate equal to the bond's yield to maturity
    (*b*) bond interest is paid semiannually
    (*c*) the coupon rate is the same as the market interest rate
    (*d*) None of the above

    [Section 5-4]

29. If the investor's required rate of return for a particular preferred stock issue increases, then the value or price of this preferred stock should

    (*a*) increase
    (*b*) decrease
    (*c*) remain the same
    (*d*) More information is needed

    [Sections 5-5A & B]

30. The valuation of common stocks is more difficult than bonds primarily because
    (*a*) common stock generally sells at lower prices than bonds
    (*b*) there are fewer investors in common stocks than bonds
    (*c*) dividend expenses are not tax deductible whereas interest is
    (*d*) the cash flows are more uncertain for stocks than bonds

    [Section 5-6]

Answers

True and False

		Multiple Choice
1. False	11. True	21. a
2. False	12. False	22. b
3. False	13. True	23. d
4. True	14. True	24. b
5. True	15. True	25. c
6. False	16. True	26. c
7. True	17. True	27. b
8. False	18. False	28. a
9. True	19. True	29. b
10. False	20. True	30. d

SOLVED PROBLEMS

The following information applies to Problems 5-1 to 5-6. Montgomery Corporation issued 20-year bonds five years ago with a par value of $1,000. The coupon rate is 14 percent and investors require a 10 percent return on these bonds.

PROBLEM 5-1: How much interest does Montgomery Corporation pay annually on each bond?

Answer: The annual interest payment of $140 is computed by multiplying the coupon rate of 14 percent by the $1,000 par value of the bond. **[Section 5-3]**

PROBLEM 5-2: Will the bond sell at a discount, at par, or at a premium? Explain why.

Answer: The bond will sell at a premium because the required rate of return is less than the bond's coupon rate. Thus, investors are willing to pay more for this bond because it pays more interest than newly issued bonds with similar characteristics.

[Section 5-3B]

PROBLEM 5-3: Assume that interest is paid annually. Using Equation 5-3, what is the intrinsic value of the bond?

Answer: Substituting $I = \$140$, $M = \$1,000$, $PVIFA_{0.10,15} = 7.606$, and $PVIF_{0.10,15} = 0.239$ in Equation 5-3 the intrinsic value of $1,303.84.

$$P_0 = (\$140)(7.606) + (\$1,000)(0.239) = \$1,064.84 + \$239 = \$1,303.84 \quad \textbf{[Section 5-3C]}$$

PROBLEM 5-4: What is the current yield on the bond?

Answer: The current yield on this bond is 10.74 percent ($140/$1,303.84). **[Section 5-3]**

PROBLEM 5-5: Assume that interest is paid semiannually. Using Equation 5-5, what is the intrinsic value of the bond?

Answer: Substituting $I/2 = \$70$, $M = \$1,000$, $PVIFA_{0.10/2,(2)(15)} = 15.373$, and $PVIF_{0.10/2,(2)(15)} = 0.231$ in Equation 5-5, the present value of the cash flows of $1,307.11.

$$P_0 = (\$70)(15.373) + (\$1,000)(0.239) = \$1,076.11 + \$239 = \$1,315.11 \quad \textbf{[Section 5-3C]}$$

PROBLEM 5-6: What is the relationship between the intrinsic value of this bond if interest is paid semiannually and the intrinsic value if it is paid annually?

Answer: The value of the bond is greater by $11.27 ($1,315.11 − $1,303.84) with semiannual interest versus annual interest when the bond sells at a premium.

[Section 5-3C]

PROBLEM 5-7: Given below is information about three $1,000 par value bonds, each of which pays interest semiannually. The required rate of return on each bond is 10 percent.

Bond	Coupon Rate (Percent)	Maturity (Years)
A	6	10
B	10	15
C	14	20

(*a*) Without performing any calculations, determine whether each bond should sell at a discount, at its par value, or at a premium.

(*b*) What is the intrinsic value of each bond?

(*c*) How do your expectations compare with your computations?

Answer:

(*a*) Bond A should sell at a discount because the required rate of return exceeds the coupon rate. Bond B should sell at its par value of $1,000 because the required rate of return equals the coupon rate. Bond C should sell at a premium because the required rate of return is below the coupon rate.

(b) Using Equation 5-5 and the appropriate present value factors found in Appendices C and D, the intrinsic value of each bond is calculated as follows:

For Bond A where I/2 = $30, $k_d/2$ = 5 percent, and 2n = 20

$$P_0 = (\$30)(12.462) + (\$1,000)(0.377) = \$373.86 + \$377 = \$750.86$$

For Bond B where I/2 = $50, $k_d/2$ = 5 percent, and 2n = 30

$$P_0 = (\$50)(15.373) + (\$1,000)(0.231) = \$768.65 + \$231 = \$999.65$$

For Bond C where I/2 = $70, $k_d/2$ = 5 percent, and 2n = 40

$$P_0 = (\$70)(17.159) + (\$1,000)(0.142) = \$1,201.13 + \$142 = \$1,343.13$$

(c) Bond A should sell at a discount of $249.14 ($1,000 − $750.86). Bond B's calculated value differs slightly from its $1,000 par value due to rounding in Appendices C and D. Bond C should sell at a premium of $343.13 ($1,343.13 − $1,000). Thus, the expectations and calculations agree. **[Sections 5-3B & C]**

PROBLEM 5-8: Montana Power and Light has two $1,000 par value bonds outstanding. Bond X matures in five years and Bond Y matures in 15 years. Both bonds pay $80 interest annually and currently sell at their par value. Thus, the current required rate of return is 8 percent.

(a) Which bond should show the greater price change in response to an increase in the required rate of return?
(b) What is the intrinsic value of each bond if the required rate of return is 9 percent?
(c) Compare the price changes in the two bonds when the required rate of return changes to 9 percent.

Answer:

(a) Bond Y should have the greater price sensitivity to a change in the required rate of return because of its longer maturity. That is, the present value of future cash flows is more affected by changes in discount rates than less distant cash flows.
(b) Using Equation 5-3, the intrinsic value of each bond is as follows:

For Bond X when I = $80, k_d = 9 percent, and n = 5

$$P_0 = (\$80)(3.890) + (\$1,000)(0.650) = \$311.20 + \$650 = \$961.20$$

For Bond Y when I = $80, k_d = 9 percent, and n = 15

$$P_0 = (\$80)(8.060) + (\$1,000)(0.275) = \$644.80 + \$275 = \$919.80$$

(c) Each bond sold for its par value of $1,000 before the change in the required rate of return. Bond Y would decline in value by $80.20 ($1,000.00 − $919.80) compared to a $38.80 ($1,000.00 − $961.20) decline for Bond X. **[Sections 5-3B & C]**

PROBLEM 5-9: A $1,000 par value bond matures in 18 years, carries a 12 percent coupon, and currently is quoted at $1,165. Interest is paid annually. Using a trial-and-error process, calculate the bond's yield to maturity to the nearest whole percent.

Answer: The yield to maturity of this bond is determined by substituting present value interest factors for different discount rates (Appendices C and D) in Equation 5-3 until a price of $1,165 is found. The yield to maturity is less than 12 percent because the bond sells at a premium. The end result of this trial-and-error process is a YTM of 10 percent as shown below.

For I = $120, k_d = 10 percent, and n = 18

$$P_0 = (\$120)(8.201) + (\$1,000)(0.180) = \$984.12 + \$180.00 = \$1,164.12 \quad \textbf{[Section 5-4]}$$

PROBLEM 5-10: Referring to Problem 5-9, what is the bond's approximate yield to maturity using Equation 5-6?

Answer: The approximate yield to maturity is found by substituting $I = \$120$, $M = \$1,000$, $P_0 = \$1,165$, and $n = 18$ in Equation 5-6 as follows:

$$\text{Approximate YTM} = \frac{\$120 + (\$1,000 - \$1,165)/18}{(\$1,000 - \$1,165)/2} = \frac{\$120 - 9.17}{\$1,082.50}$$

$$= \frac{\$110.83}{\$1,082.50} = 0.1024 = 10.24 \text{ percent}$$

[Section 5-4]

PROBLEM 5-11: Standard Telephone Company has a preferred stock that pays a \$4.50 annual dividend. What is the value of this preferred stock to investors requiring an 8 percent, a 10 percent, and a 12 percent return, respectively?

Answer: Substituting $D_p = \$4.50$ and the appropriate k_p in Equation 5-8 gives the following values:

Required Rates of Return

8 Percent	10 Percent	12 Percent
$P_0 = \dfrac{\$4.50}{0.08} = \$56.25$	$P_0 = \dfrac{\$4.50}{0.10} = \$45.00$	$P_0 = \dfrac{\$4.50}{0.12} = \$37.50$

[Section 5-5B]

PROBLEM 5-12: A preferred stock pays an annual dividend of \$6.75 and has a current market price of \$75.25. What is the required rate of return on this preferred stock?

Answer: The required rate of return is calculated by modifying and solving Equation 5-8 as follows:

$$P_0 = \frac{D_p}{k_p}$$

Solve for k_p:

$$k_p = \frac{D_p}{P_0} = \frac{\$6.75}{\$75.25} = 8.97 \text{ percent}$$

[Section 5-5B]

PROBLEM 5-13: Cabin John Corporation's earnings and dividends have been growing at an annual rate of 12 percent for the past 10 years and are expected to continue growing at this rate for the next three years. The firm's last dividend was \$2.50. A share of the firm's common stock is expected to sell for \$68.00 at the end of three years. At what price should Cabin John's common stock sell if investors require a 9 percent return?

Answer: Using Equation 5-9 for the finite-period stock valuation model, the present value of the stream of dividends and the stock's expected selling price at the end of year 3 is \$60.42.

Year, t	Dividend $\$2.50(1.12)^t = D_t$ (1)	Present Value Interest Factor $PVIF_{0.09,t}$ (2)	Present Value, D_t [(1) × (2)] (3)
1	\$2.50(1.120) = \$2.80	0.917	\$ 2.57
2	2.50(1.254) = 3.14	0.842	2.64
3	2.50(1.405) = 3.51	0.772	2.71
			\$ 7.92
3 Common Stock Price = \$68.00		0.772	52.50
		Total =	\$60.42

[Section 5-6A]

PROBLEM 5-14: Ross Enterprises has paid $2.60 in annual dividends on its common stock for the past eight years and expects to maintain this amount for the foreseeable future. If an investor requires a 13 percent return on this stock, how much would she be willing to pay for a share?

Answer: Substituting $D_p = \$2.50$ and $k_s = 0.13$ into the zero growth dividend valuation model in Equation 5-11, the current value of $20.00.

$$P_0 = \frac{\$2.60}{0.13} = \$20.00 \qquad \textbf{[Section 5-6B]}$$

PROBLEM 5-15: Common stock dividends of Fitness Industries have been growing at an annual rate of 10 percent. The current dividend per share is $1.20. If an investor requires a 15 percent return on the stock, what is the current value of 100 shares of Fitness Industries under each of the following conditions?

(*a*) Dividends are expected to continue growing at a constant rate of 10 percent.
(*b*) The dividend growth rate is expected to decrease to 8.5 percent and to remain constant at that level.
(*c*) The dividend growth rate is expected to increase to 12.5 percent and to remain constant at that level.

Answer: Using the Gordon constant growth model shown in Equation 5-13, the current value of a share of Fitness Industries is:

(*a*) For $D_1 = \$1.32\ (\$1.20 \times 1.10)$, $k_s = 0.15$, and $g = 0.10$

$$P_0 = \frac{\$1.32}{0.15 - 0.10} = \$26.40$$

(*b*) For $D_1 = \$1.30\ (\$1.20 \times 1.085)$, $k_s = 0.15$, and $g = 0.085$

$$P_0 = \frac{\$1.30}{0.15 - 0.085} = \$20.00$$

(*c*) For $D_1 = \$1.35\ (\$1.20 \times 1.125)$, $k_s = 0.15$, and $g = 0.125$

$$P_0 = \frac{\$1.35}{0.15 - 0.125} = \$54.00 \qquad \textbf{[Section 5-6B]}$$

PROBLEM 5-16: Standard Building Products currently pays a $0.90 dividend per share on its common stock. Its dividends are expected to grow at a rate of 8 percent a year for the next four years and to continue to grow thereafter at a rate of 5 percent. What is the value of a share of Standard Building Products' common stock if investors require a 14 percent rate of return?

Answer: Equation 5-14 for a supernormal growth dividend model is used to determine the value of a share of Standard Building Products. The first step is to calculate the present value of the dividends during the four-year supernormal growth period.

Year t	Dividend $\$0.90(1.08)^t = D_t$ (1)	Present Value Interest Factor $PVIF_{0.14, t}$ (2)	Present Value, D_t [(1) × (2)] (3)
1	$0.90(1.080) = $0.97	0.877	$0.85
2	0.90(1.166) = 1.05	0.769	0.81
3	0.90(1.260) = 1.13	0.675	0.76
4	0.90(1.360) = 1.22	0.592	0.72
			Total = $3.14

The second step is to calculate the stock value at the end of year 4, P_4, as follows:

$$P_4 = \frac{D_{m+1}}{k_s - g_n} = \frac{D_4(1 + g_n)}{0.14 - 0.05} = \frac{(\$1.22)(1.05)}{0.09} = \frac{\$1.28}{0.09} = \$14.23$$

Next, the stock value at the end of Year 4, P_4, is discounted back to the present at the 14 percent required rate of return, where $PVIF_{0.14,4} = 0.592$.

$$PV(P_4) = P_4\left[\frac{1}{(1 + k_s)^m}\right] = \$14.23\left[\frac{1}{(1.14)^4}\right] = \$14.23(0.592) = \$8.42$$

Finally, the present value of the first four years' dividends and the present value of the stock value in year 4, $PV(P_4)$, are summed to get the stock value, P_0.

$$P_0 = \$3.14 + \$8.42 = \$11.56 \qquad \text{[Section 5-6B]}$$

6 ANALYZING FINANCIAL STATEMENTS

THIS CHAPTER IS ABOUT

☑ **Financial Analysis Overview**
☑ **Basic Financial Statements**
☑ **Ratio Analysis**
☑ **Common-size Statements**
☑ **Comparative Financial Analysis**

6-1. Financial Analysis Overview

Financial analysis is the judgmental process of evaluating a firm's past financial performance and its future prospects. The process requires the application of common sense and judgment in addition to analytical techniques, and typically involves analyzing and interpreting the firm's financial statements and other financial data. Financial analysis helps users understand the numbers presented in statements and serves as a basis for financial decision making. There are many prospective users of the firm's financial data: creditors, owners, management, and others, including customers, suppliers, labor unions, regulators, and competitors. This chapter, however, focuses on financial analysis from management's perspective.

A. Financial analysis consists of three major stages.

1. *Preparation*. Several preparatory steps are needed in order to conduct a financial analysis. The steps include establishing the objectives of the analysis and assembling the financial statements and other financial data. Objectives depend on the perspective of the financial statement user and the questions to be answered by the analyst. For example, management analyzes financial statements to help in planning and decision making. The analysis provides answers to such questions as:
   - How has the firm performed in the past?
   - What are the firm's strengths and weaknesses?
   - What changes are needed to improve future performance?

   To answer these and other questions, management gathers data from several sources. Common sources provided by a firm are the annual report and Form 10-K.
   - An *annual report* contains basic financial statements and other information about the firm's current and future prospects.
   - *Form 10-K* is a more detailed annual report filed with the Securities and Exchange Commission (SEC) by firms that sell securities to the public.

   Other sources outside of the firm include:
   - *Moody's Manuals*, Moody's Investor Service, Inc.
   - *Corporation Records* and *Earnings Forecaster*, Standard & Poor's Corporation.
   - *The Value Line Investment Survey*, Value Line, Inc.
   - *The Wall Street Journal*, *Barrons*, *Business Week*, *Forbes*, and *Fortune*.

2. *Computation and interpretation.* Once the objectives of the analysis are determined and the financial data gathered, various tools and techniques are used to gain a basic understanding of the firm's condition and performance. The most frequently used techniques in analyzing financial statements are ratio analysis and common-size statements.
   - *Ratio analysis* converts dollar amounts in financial statements to ratios.
   - *Common-size statements* express individual statement accounts as percentages of a base amount.

   These techniques are discussed in Section 6-3 and Section 6-4.

3. *Evaluation.* This final stage is used to determine the meaningfulness of the analysis and to develop conclusions and recommendations. Evaluation usually begins by comparing the firm's ratios and common-size statements to appropriate standards or benchmarks. (This is the purpose of *comparative financial analysis*, which is discussed in Section 6-5.) Management then forms conclusions about the firm's performance based on the evaluation, develops answers to questions posed in the first step of the analysis, and makes specific recommendations.

B. Financial analysis has several limitations.

There are eight basic limitations to financial analysis:

1. *Financial statements deal only in numerical or measurable terms.* Financial analysis helps provide some understanding behind the numbers, but the evaluation of a firm is not limited to numbers. It also involves qualitative considerations such as the quality of management and the firm's product or service mix.

2. *Differences in operating and accounting practices make comparisons difficult.* The accounting procedures differ among firms in reporting such items as inventory, depreciation, pension fund contributions, mergers and acquisitions. The comparisons are only valid if the same accounting procedures are used.

3. *Appropriate industry comparisons may not exist.* Firms, especially large ones, often span several different industry groups. The more diverse a firm's operations, the more difficult it generally is to find a single industry standard of comparison. Also, new industries may not yet have generated standards.

4. *Industry averages may be inadequate standards of comparison.* Favorable comparison to an industry average does not necessarily signify adequate performance. For example, a firm's profitability may be poor, but still exceed the industry average if the industry's profitability is low. A better basis of comparison may be the performance of industry leaders.

5. *Management may influence ratios by taking short-run actions prior to preparing the financial statements.* Management can engage in *window dressing* by using certain techniques to make the financial statements look better.

6. *Several definitions exist for some common ratios.* When comparing a firm's ratios to an industry average, the ratios must be computed in the same manner to avoid distortion.

7. *Inflation may distort financial ratios.* Financial statements are based on historical costs and fail to account for inflation. Inflation may lead to phantom profits primarily because net sales are stated in currents dollars, and assets, such as inventory and fixed assets, at historical cost. For example, in a period of rapidly rising inflation, the first in-first out (FIFO) inventory costing method overstates profits because the least expensive inventory is charged off against sales. However, current value and constant dollar accounting methods may be used to counteract this problem.

8. *Financial ratios may be misinterpreted.* Ratios provide little useful information by themselves but must be combined with other tools and information to gain meaning. The meaningfulness of financial ratios really depends on the skill and insight of the analyst. Ratios do not identify the causes of the firm's financial health but they may serve as "red flags" that alert the analyst to trouble spots.

6-2. Basic Financial Statements

Financial statement analysis focuses primarily on the balance sheet and the income statement. However, data from other statements, such as the statement of retained earnings and statement of changes in financial position, may also be used.

A. The *balance sheet* shows a firm's financial condition at a specific point in time.

The balance sheet is a financial "snapshot" of a firm taken at the end of a reporting period. As shown in Figure 6-1 the balance sheet is divided into two parts: one contains assets and the other contains the claims against assets. These claims are divided into liabilities and stockholders' equity, also called *owners' equity, shareholders' equity,* and *net worth.*

Eagle Manufacturing Company
Comparative Balance Sheet
December 31, 19x7 and 19x8
(in thousands of dollars)

Assets	19x8	19x7
Current assets		
Cash	$ 2,500	$ 3,000
Marketable securities................................	1,000	1,300
Accounts receivable...................................	16,000	12,000
Inventories	20,500	18,700
Total current assets	$40,000	$35,000
Fixed assets		
Land and buildings	$28,700	$24,200
Machinery and equipment	31,600	29,000
Total fixed assets	$60,300	$53,200
Less accumulated depreciation	18,300	17,200
Net fixed assets.......................................	$42,000	$36,000
Total assets	$82,000	$71,000
Liabilities and Stockholders' Equity		
Current liabilities		
Accounts payable......................................	$ 7,200	$ 6,000
Notes payable—10% bank	5,500	7,000
Accrued liabilities	900	700
Current maturity of long-term debt.....................	3,000	3,000
Other liabilities.......................................	1,400	1,200
Total current liabilities	$18,000	$17,900
Long-term liabilities		
Long-term debt—12% mortgage bonds	27,000	30,000
Total liabilities	$45,000	$47,900
Stockholders' Equity		
Common stock—$5 par, 2,000,000 shares authorized; 1,300,000 shares outstanding in 19x8 and 1,000,000 shares outstanding in 19x7	6,500	5,000
Capital in excess of par..............................	14,000	5,350
Retained earnings.....................................	16,500	12,750
Total stockholders' equity	$37,000	$23,100
Total liabilities and stockholders' equity	$82,000	$71,000

FIGURE 6-1   Eagle Manufacturing Company Balance Sheet

Each part always balances the other as shown by the **accounting equation: assets = liabilities + stockholders' equity**. Figure 6-1 shows a comparative balance sheet for Eagle Manufacturing Company.

1. **Assets** represent resources that the company has control over, that may provide future benefit, and that can be objectively valued. Assets may be classified as current or fixed.

   • *Current assets* are items that normally become cash or are consumed/sold within one year. Current assets include cash, marketable securities, accounts receivable, and inventory.
   • *Fixed assets* are assets with a useful life of more than one year. Fixed assets include property, plant, and equipment.

2. **Liabilities** are claims by nonowners against the assets. Liabilities are divided into current liabilities and long-term liabilities.

   • *Current liabilities* are those accounts usually paid within one year. Examples include accounts payable, short-term notes payable, and accruals or existing obligations that have not been paid.
   • *Long-term liabilities* are items usually paid within a period greater than one year, such as bonds.

3. **Stockholders' equity** is the claim by owners against the assets. Equity includes direct investments by the firm's owners plus undistributed profits (retained earnings).

B. **The *income statement* shows the results of the firm's operations over a given period of time.**

The income statement summarizes a firm's revenues and expenses over a reporting period, such as one year. The difference between the revenues and expenses is a firm's profit or loss, which is often called the *bottom line*. Figure 6-2 presents a comparative income statement for Eagle Manufacturing Company.

Eagle Manufacturing Company
Income Statement
For the Years Ended December 31, 19x7 and 19x8
(in thousands of dollars)

	19x8	19x7
Net sales	$120,000	$110,000
Cost of goods sold	90,000	83,000
Gross profit	$ 30,000	$ 27,000
Operating expenses		
Selling	5,000	4,800
General and administrative	8,000	7,600
Depreciation	1,100	800
Lease payments	1,650	1,600
Earnings before interest and taxes (EBIT)	$ 14,250	$ 12,200
Interest expense		
Interest on bank notes	550	700
Interest on other debt	3,600	3,960
Earnings before taxes	$ 10,100	$ 7,540
Taxes (34%)	3,434	2,564
Net income	$ 6,666	$ 4,976

FIGURE 6-2 Eagle Manufacturing Company Income Statement

1. **Revenues** are inflows of assets resulting from the sale of goods and services.
2. **Expenses** are costs incurred to produce revenues.

C. **The *statement of retained earnings* reports the amount of profits reinvested in the firm.**

Profits not paid out in dividends are recorded as **retained earnings** on the balance sheet. Retained earnings accumulate over the firm's life but do not represent cash or funds allotted for any other purpose. Figure 6-3 is a statement of retained earnings for Eagle Manufacturing Company.

Eagle Manufacturing Company
Statement of Retained Earnings
December 31, 19x8
(in thousands of dollars)

Retained earnings—January 1	$12,750
Net income	6,666
Total	$19,416
Less cash dividends	
Common stock—$2.00 per share	2,600
Retained earnings—December 31	$16,816

FIGURE 6-3 Eagle Manufacturing Company Statement of Retained Earnings

D. **The *statement of changes in financial position* (SCFP), also called a *funds flow statement* or *sources and uses of funds statement*, shows a firm's financing and investing activities over a specific reporting period.**

The SCFP highlights changes in the firm's financial position from one period to the next. This statement may be prepared on a *cash basis* or a *net working capital basis*. The basic difference between the two methods is that the cash basis provides more detail for purposes of financial analysis. Figure 6-4 on page 93 is a statement of changes in financial position for Eagle Manufacturing Company on a net working capital basis. Preparation of this statement begins by developing a **schedule of changes in net working capital accounts**, which shows the increase or decrease in net working capital for the period. **Net working capital** equals current assets minus current liabilities. Figure 6-4 also indicates that a firm's sources less its uses of funds for a specific period always equal the net increase or decrease in funds.

1. Sources of funds include:

   • Decrease in assets
   • Increase in liabilities
   • Increase in stockholders' equity
   • Depreciation and other noncash charges
   • Net income

2. Uses of funds include:

   • Increase in assets
   • Decrease in liabilities
   • Decrease in stockholders' equity
   • Cash dividends
   • Net loss

Eagle Manufacturing Company
Statement of Changes in Financial Position
For the Year Ended December 31, 19x8
(in thousands of dollars)

Sources of Funds

Sources provided from operations:

Net Income..	$ 6,666
Add: Depreciation	1,100
Funds provided from operations...	$ 7,766
Issuance of common stock	9,834
Total sources of funds..	$17,600

Uses of Funds

Purchase of land and buildings...	$ 4,500
Purchase of machinery and equipment....................................	2,600
Reclassification of long-term debt to current debt......................	3,000
Payment of common stock dividends	2,600
Total uses of funds...	$12,700
Increase in net working capital	$ 4,900

Schedule of Changes in Working Capital Accounts

Increase (decrease) in current assets

Cash..	$ (500)
Marketable securities...	(300)
Accounts receivable	4,000
Inventories	1,800
Increase in net current assets	$ 5,000

Increase (decrease) in current liabilities

Accounts payable...	$ 1,200
Notes payable	(1,500)
Accrued liabilities	200
Other liabilities	200
Increase in net current liabilities...................................	$ 100
Increase in net working capital	$ 4,900

FIGURE 6-4 Eagle Manufacturing Company Statement of Changes in Financial
Position—Working Capital Basis

6-3. Ratio Analysis

Ratio analysis is perhaps the most commonly used tool in financial statement analysis. **Ratio analysis** standardizes financial data by converting dollar figures in the financial statements into ratios. A **financial ratio** is a mathematical relationship among several numbers usually stated in the form of percentages or times. Ratios are easy to compute and serve as yardsticks of a firm's financial condition or performance. These yardsticks or financial flags are meaningful only when compared with other information, such as an industry standard or trend. Usually a group of ratios is needed to analyze a firm's overall performance. Ratios are classified into five major categories: liquidity, asset management, debt management, profitability, and market/book. Figure 6-5, page 94, lists ratios from each of these five categories.

Equation	Ratio	Formula
	Liquidity ratios	
(6-1)	Current ratio	$\dfrac{\text{Current assets}}{\text{Current liabilities}}$
(6-2)	Quick ratio	$\dfrac{\text{Quick assets}}{\text{Current liabilities}}$
	Asset management ratios	
(6-3)	Accounts receivable turnover	$\dfrac{\text{Net sales}}{\text{Accounts receivable}}$
(6-4)	Average collection period	$\dfrac{\text{365 days}}{\text{Accounts receivable turnover}}$
(6-5)	Inventory turnover	$\dfrac{\text{Cost of goods sold}}{\text{Inventory}}$
(6-6)	Fixed asset turnover	$\dfrac{\text{Net sales}}{\text{Net fixed assets}}$
(6-7)	Total asset turnover	$\dfrac{\text{Net sales}}{\text{Total assets}}$
	Debt management ratios	
(6-8)	Debt ratio	$\dfrac{\text{Total liabilities}}{\text{Total assets}}$
(6-9)	Debt-equity ratio	$\dfrac{\text{Total liabilities}}{\text{Stockholders' equity}}$
(6-10)	Times-interest-earned ratio	$\dfrac{\text{EBIT}}{\text{Interest expense}}$
(6-11)	Fixed-charge-coverage ratio	$\dfrac{\text{EBIT + lease payments}}{\text{Interest + lease payments} + (\text{principal payment} + \text{pfd. stock div.})/(1 - \text{tax rate})}$
	Profitability ratios	
(6-12)	Gross profit margin	$\dfrac{\text{Gross profit}}{\text{Net sales}}$
(6-13)	Operating profit margin	$\dfrac{\text{EBIT}}{\text{Net sales}}$
(6-14)	Net profit margin	$\dfrac{\text{Net income}}{\text{Net sales}}$
(6-15)	Return on investment	$\dfrac{\text{Net income}}{\text{Total assets}}$
(6-16)	DuPont formula return on investment	$\dfrac{\text{Net income}}{\text{Net sales}} \times \dfrac{\text{Net sales}}{\text{Total assets}}$
(6-17)	Return on equity	$\dfrac{\text{Net income}}{\text{Stockholders' equity}}$

FIGURE 6-5   Summary of financial ratios

Equation	Ratio	Formula
(6-18)	Modified DuPont formula return on equity	$$\dfrac{\text{Return on investment}}{1 - \text{debt ratio}}$$
	Market/book ratios	
(6-19)	Earnings per share	$$\dfrac{\text{Net income} - \text{preferred stock dividends}}{\text{Average common shares outstanding}}$$
(6-20)	Price/earnings ratio	$$\dfrac{\text{Current market price per share}}{\text{Earnings per share}}$$
(6-21)	Book value per share	$$\dfrac{\text{Total stockholders' equity} - \text{preferred stock}}{\text{Common shares outstanding}}$$
(6-22)	Dividends per share	$$\dfrac{\text{Total cash dividends on common shares}}{\text{Common shares outstanding}}$$
(6-23)	Dividend payout	$$\dfrac{\text{Cash dividends per share}}{\text{Earnings per share}}$$
(6-24)	Dividend yield	$$\dfrac{\text{Cash dividends per share}}{\text{Current market price per share}}$$

FIGURE 6-5 (Continued)

A. *Liquidity ratios* **measure a firm's ability to meet short-term obligations.**

Liquidity ratios, such as the current ratio and quick ratio, measure the degree to which a firm's current assets are sufficient to pay current liabilities.

1. The **current ratio** measures a firm's ability to satisfy the claims of short-term creditors by using only current assets. Equation 6-1 shows that the current ratio is computed by dividing current assets by current liabilities. A low ratio suggests that a firm may have difficulty paying its bills, whereas a high ratio indicates that a firm may be sacrificing some return because too much financial capital is tied up in current assets. The quality of this ratio depends on the composition and timing of the firm's current assets and current liabilities. If the firm has a large portion of its current assets in accounts receivable and inventories, it must convert them into cash before paying its bills.

$$\text{Current ratio} = \frac{\text{Current assets}}{\text{Current liabilities}} \qquad \textbf{(6-1)}$$

EXAMPLE 6-1: Using the information in Figure 6-1, calculate and interpret the meaning of Eagle Manufacturing Company's current ratio for 19x8. The industry average is 2.0 times.

$$\text{Current ratio} = \frac{\$40{,}000}{\$18{,}000} = 2.22 \text{ times}$$

The current ratio of 2.22 means that Eagle has $2.22 in current assets for every dollar in current liabilities. This ratio slightly exceeds the industry average, but Eagle still may or may not be able to pay its debts when they are due.

2. The **quick ratio** measures short-term liquidity by removing the least liquid current assets, such as inventories and prepaid items (including prepaid insurance or prepaid interest), from current ratio calculations. The quick ratio, sometimes called the

acid-test ratio, is a more rigorous test of liquidity than the current ratio because it considers only quick assets as available to meet maturing current liabilities. **Quick assets** are cash, marketable securities, and accounts receivable. Equation 6-2 shows that the quick ratio is computed by dividing quick assets by current liabilities.

$$\text{Quick ratio} = \frac{\text{Quick assets}}{\text{Current liabilities}} \qquad (6\text{-}2)$$

EXAMPLE 6-2: Calculate and interpret Eagle Manufacturing Company's quick ratio for 19x8. The industry average is 1.25 times.

$$\text{Quick ratio} = \frac{\$19{,}500}{\$18{,}000} = 1.08 \text{ times}$$

The quick ratio of 1.08 times indicates that Eagle has $1.08 in quick assets for every dollar in current liabilities. Because Eagle has no prepaid items, the ratio suggests that the firm has more inventories than the industry average. This does not necessarily mean that Eagle has a problem because industry averages are not magic numbers. The financial analyst must go behind the numbers to determine why a discrepancy exists.

B. *Asset management ratios* **measure how effectively a firm manages its assets.**

Asset management ratios, or *activity ratios*, usually compare sales with the level of investment in various asset accounts. These comparisons help analysts determine how well a firm utilizes its funds. Asset management ratios include the average collection period and various turnover ratios involving accounts receivable, inventories, fixed assets, and total assets.

1. **Accounts receivable turnover** indicates how many times accounts receivable are collected during a year. A high accounts receivable turnover usually suggests efficiency in converting receivables into cash but it could also mean that a firm has a restrictive credit policy. That is, a firm may provide customers with a short time period to pay their accounts receivable, such as 10 days. Equation 6-3 shows that the accounts receivable turnover is computed by dividing net sales by accounts receivable. Technically, only credit sales should be used in the numerator because accounts receivable arise only from credit sales, not net sales which may also include cash sales. Financial statements rarely report credit sales. Hence, the use of net sales tends to overstate the actual accounts receivable turnover ratio.

$$\text{Accounts receivable turnover} = \frac{\text{Net sales}}{\text{Accounts receivable}} \qquad (6\text{-}3)$$

EXAMPLE 6-3: Compute and interpret the accounts receivable turnover for Eagle Manufacturing for 19x8. The industry average is 10.40 times.

$$\text{Accounts receivable turnover} = \frac{\$120{,}000}{\$16{,}000} = 7.50 \text{ times}$$

Eagle's accounts receivable turnover of 7.50 times is considerably below the industry average. This may suggest a problem in sales being too low, accounts receivables being too high, or both. A ratio lower than the industry average may also suggest that Eagle is granting more liberal credit terms than other companies.

2. The **average collection period** indicates how many days a firm takes to convert receivables into cash. The ratio is used to evaluate credit and collection policies. If the average collection period considerably exceeds a firm's credit terms, this may indicate that a firm is not effective in collecting its accounts receivable or that it may be giving credit to marginal customers. A long collection period reduces the liquidity of receivables and affects a firm's ability to meet short-term maturing obligations. A short collection period may indicate that credit and collection

policies are too restrictive. Equation 6-4 shows that the average collection period is computed by dividing 365 by the accounts receivable turnover (Equation 6-3). Some analysts use 360 days instead of 365 in computing this ratio.

$$\text{Average collection period} = \frac{365 \text{ days}}{\text{Accounts receivable turnover}} \tag{6-4}$$

EXAMPLE 6-4: Compute and interpret the average collection period for Eagle Manufacturing for 19x8. The company grants 30-day credit terms and the industry average is 35 days.

$$\text{Average collection period} = \frac{365 \text{ days}}{7.50 \text{ times}} = 48.67 \text{ days}$$

Eagle extends 30-day credit terms but takes about 49 days to collect. The lengthy collection period suggests that a potential problem exists in either managing credit or collecting accounts.

3. **Inventory turnover** measures the efficiency of the firm in managing and selling inventory. High inventory turnover generally indicates superior selling practices and improved liquidity and profitability because less money is tied up in inventory. However, high inventory turnover can also signal problems, such as lost sales due to insufficient inventory. Low turnover may suggest that a firm carries either excess or obsolete inventory. Low inventory turnover may also result from stockpiling in anticipation of a strike or price increase.

   The type of industry is important in assessing inventory turnover. For example, a grocery store would have a high inventory turnover relative to an airplane manufacturer. Equation 6-5 shows that inventory turnover is calculated by dividing cost of goods sold by inventory.

$$\text{Inventory turnover} = \frac{\text{Cost of goods sold}}{\text{Inventory}} \tag{6-5}$$

Inventory turnover can be computed in several other ways. For example, sales is sometimes used in the numerator rather than cost of goods sold. This second approach is inferior because it mixes two types of figures. Sales are usually stated in terms of markups on the cost of goods sold, whereas inventory is stated at cost. Another approach uses average inventory in the denominator instead of ending inventory. Average inventory is usually computed by adding the beginning and ending inventories for the year and dividing by 2. This approach is appropriate if a company does not have highly seasonal sales. Otherwise, average monthly inventory should be used.

EXAMPLE 6-5: Compute and interpret the inventory turnover for Eagle Manufacturing for 19x8. The industry average is 6.00 times.

$$\text{Inventory turnover} = \frac{\$90,000}{\$20,500} = 4.39 \text{ times}$$

Eagle's inventory turnover of 4.39 is below the industry average of 6.0 times. Eagle may have a larger investment of inventory relative to sales than similar firms in its industry. A high inventory level may concern Eagle because the investment in inventory must be financed.

4. **Fixed asset turnover** indicates management's efficiency in managing fixed assets. A high fixed asset turnover ratio generally suggests that fixed assets are being used productively. A low ratio may indicate overinvestment in fixed assets, low sales, or both. A firm's fixed asset turnover ratio is affected by several factors, including the cost of the assets, the time elapsed since their acquisition, the depreciation

methods used, and the extent to which a firm leases rather than owns its fixed assets. Equation 6-6 shows that fixed asset turnover is computed by dividing net sales by net fixed assets.

$$\text{Fixed asset turnover} = \frac{\text{Net sales}}{\text{Net fixed assets}} \qquad (6\text{-}6)$$

EXAMPLE 6-6: Compute and interpret the fixed asset turnover ratio for Eagle Manufacturing for 19x8. The industry average is 3.50 times.

$$\text{Fixed asset turnover} = \frac{\$120,000}{\$42,000} = 2.86 \text{ times}$$

A fixed asset turnover ratio of 2.86 times means that Eagle generated $2.86 in net sales for every dollar in fixed assets, which is below the industry average. Because of the shortcomings of this ratio, the analyst should perform further analysis before concluding that Eagle is not using its fixed assets to the same capacity as other firms in the industry. For example, the analyst should see if Eagle's depreciation methods are identical with other firms. The use of different cost recovery (depreciation) methods will affect the fixed asset turnover ratio.

5. **Total asset turnover** measures the management's efficiency in managing total assets to generate sales. This ratio indicates the sales dollars generated per dollar of investment in assets. A high ratio suggests greater efficiency in using assets to produce sales. The total asset turnover ratio is a composite of all of the other asset management ratios. Equation 6-7 shows that total asset turnover is computed by dividing net sales by total assets.

$$\text{Total asset turnover} = \frac{\text{Net sales}}{\text{Total assets}} \qquad (6\text{-}7)$$

EXAMPLE 6-7: Calculate and interpret the total asset turnover ratio for Eagle Manufacturing for 19x8. The industry average is 2.00 times.

$$\text{Total asset turnover} = \frac{\$120,000}{\$82,000} = 1.46 \text{ times}$$

A total asset turnover ratio of 1.46 times means that Eagle generates $1.46 in net sales for every dollar of total assets. Eagle is not generating sufficient sales for the size of its investment in assets. This result is not surprising because Eagle's other turnover ratios, namely accounts receivable, inventory, and fixed assets, are also below the industry average. Eagle should take steps to increase sales, dispose of some of its investment in assets, or both.

C. *Debt management ratios*, also called *solvency* or *leverage ratios*, show the extent to which a firm uses debt to finance investments and its ability to meet interest charges and other fixed payments.

Financial leverage is the extent to which a firm uses debt financing. As the percentage of debt financing increases, a firm becomes more highly leveraged. The amount of financial leverage concerns both creditors and owners because it affects the riskiness of the firm. Creditors experience more risk as financial leverage increases because an increase in debt requires the commitment of more funds to pay interest and repay principal. The failure to meet these obligations could force a firm into bankruptcy. A highly leveraged firm may also find additional debt financing more difficult and expensive.

Although leverage implies risk, it also provides owners with the opportunity to enhance their return and maintain control. *Favorable leverage* magnifies the owners' rate of return. It occurs when the firm earns more on borrowed funds than it pays in interest. However, leverage is a double-edged sword. *Unfavorable leverage* reduces the owners' rate of return and occurs when the cost of debt exceeds the firm's rate of return on assets. Owners also maintain control because using debt avoids the sale of new stock.

There are two basic types of debt management ratios—financial leverage ratios, such as the debt ratio and the debt-equity ratio; and coverage ratios, such as times interest earned and fixed charge coverage ratios.

1. The **debt ratio** measures the percentage of total assets financed by debt. The higher the ratio, the more of a firm's assets are provided by creditors relative to owners. Creditors prefer a low or moderate debt ratio because it provides more protection in case a firm experiences financial problems. Equation 6-8 shows that the debt ratio is determined by dividing total liabilities by total assets.

$$\text{Debt ratio} = \frac{\text{Total liabilities}}{\text{Total assets}} \qquad \text{(6-8)}$$

EXAMPLE 6-8: Compute and interpret the debt ratio for Eagle Manufacturing for 19x8. The industry average is 45.00 percent.

$$\text{Debt ratio} = \frac{\$45,000}{\$82,000} = 0.5488 = 54.88 \text{ percent}$$

Eagle's debt ratio of 54.88 percent indicates that creditors have supplied about 55 cents of every dollar in assets. With a higher debt ratio than the industry average, Eagle may experience some difficulty in raising additional debt. Future creditors may require a higher rate of return to compensate for the higher risk associated with the firm's having leverage greater than the industry average.

2. The **debt-equity ratio** expresses the relationship between the amount of a firm's total assets financed by creditors (debt) and owners (equity). The debt-equity ratio is similar to the debt ratio but, as Equation 6-9 shows, is computed by dividing total liabilities by stockholders' equity. Sometimes long-term debt is used rather than total liabilities in order to express debt in the form of permanent financing.

$$\text{Debt-equity ratio} = \frac{\text{Total liabilities}}{\text{Stockholders' equity}} \qquad \text{(6-9)}$$

EXAMPLE 6-9: Compute and interpret the debt-equity ratio for Eagle Manufacturing for 19x8. The industry average is 81.81 percent.

$$\text{Debt-equity ratio} = \frac{\$45,000}{\$37,000} = 1.2162 = 121.62 \text{ percent}$$

Eagle's debt-equity ratio indicates that creditors provided about $1.22 in financing for every dollar contributed by owners. Eagle has more financial leverage than average for the industry and consequently may have greater financing charges.

3. **Times interest earned** measures a firm's ability to meet its interest payments from operating profit. A high ratio indicates that a firm has a cushion in covering interest expenses. That is, earnings could decline somewhat without jeopardizing the firm's ability to make interest payments. A low ratio suggests that creditors are more at risk in receiving interest due. Consequently, the firm may face difficulty in raising additional financing through debt. As Equation 6-10 shows, times interest earned is determined by dividing earnings before interest and taxes (EBIT) by interest expense.

$$\text{Times-interest-earned ratio} = \frac{\text{EBIT}}{\text{Interest expense}} \qquad \text{(6-10)}$$

EXAMPLE 6-10: Calculate and interpret the times-interest-earned ratio for Eagle Manufacturing for 19x8. The industry average is 5.50 times.

$$\text{Times-interest-earned ratio} = \frac{\$14,250}{\$4,150} = 3.43 \text{ times}$$

Eagle earns 3.43 times more than its interest charges. Its times-interest-earned ratio is below the industry average, again showing that Eagle is making extensive use of credit to finance its operations. The company may also have problems in obtaining additional debt financing in the future because Eagle is more risky than similar firms.

4. **Fixed-charge-coverage ratio** is a broad measure of the firm's ability to meet the total of other fixed obligations and interest payments. These other fixed charges typically include lease payments, principal payments on debt, and preferred stock dividends. A firm's fixed charges are examined on a before-tax basis. Because interest payments and lease payments are made on a before-tax basis, no adjustments are necessary. However, a tax adjustment is necessary because principal payments and preferred stock dividends are not tax deductible and are paid from after-tax earnings. The after-tax payments are divided by $(1 - t)$, where t is the marginal tax rate, to convert the payments to a before-tax basis.

   The fixed-charge-coverage ratio is also a risk measure. Creditors and preferred stockholders view a firm as more risky the lower the ratio. With a low ratio, a firm may be unable to meet its fixed obligations if earnings decline and may be forced into bankruptcy. A high ratio suggests a larger cushion of protection in the event of a worsening financial position. Equation 6-11 shows that the fixed-charge-coverage ratio is calculated by dividing earnings before interest and taxes (EBIT) plus lease payments by total fixed charges. Principal payments and preferred stock dividends are adjusted to a pre-tax basis by dividing by 1 minus the income tax rate, t.

$$\text{Fixed-charge-coverage ratio} = \frac{\text{EBIT} + \text{lease payments}}{\text{Interest} + \text{lease payments} + (\text{principal payments} + \text{preferred stock dividends})/(1 - t)} \quad \text{(6-11)}$$

EXAMPLE 6-11: Calculate and interpret the fixed-charge-coverage ratio for Eagle Manufacturing for 19x8. The industry average is 2.50 times.

$$\text{Fixed-charge-coverage ratio} = \frac{\$14,250 + \$1,650}{\$4,150 + \$1,650 + (\$3,000)/(1 - 0.34)}$$

$$= \frac{\$15,900}{\$10,345} = 1.54 \text{ times}$$

Eagle is able to cover its fixed charges only 1.54 times compared with the industry average of 2.50 times. This low ratio gives creditors a small margin of safety in case Eagle experiences lower earnings. Eagle does not have any preferred stockholders, but the firm did repay part of its long-term debt during the accounting period.

D. *Profitability ratios* measure the earning power of a firm.

Because profitability ratios show the combined effect of many management decisions, they are used to evaluate overall management effectiveness. Specifically, they indicate how effectively a firm's management generates profits on sales, total assets, and owners' equity. Five of the most common profitability ratios are gross profit margin, operating profit margin, net profit margin, return on assets, and return on equity. In computing these ratios, the terms *profits*, *earnings*, and *income* may be used interchangeably.

1. **Gross profit margin** indicates the percentage of each sales dollar remaining after deducting the cost of goods sold. This ratio indicates management's effectiveness in

pricing, generating sales, and controlling production costs. Equation 6-12 shows that gross profit margin is determined by dividing gross profit by net sales.

$$\text{Gross profit margin} = \frac{\text{Gross profit}}{\text{Net sales}} \qquad \textbf{(6-12)}$$

EXAMPLE 6-12: Calculate and interpret the gross profit margin for Eagle Manufacturing for 19x8. The industry average is 26.00 percent.

$$\text{Gross profit margin} = \frac{\$30,000}{\$120,000} = 25.00 \text{ percent}$$

A gross profit margin of 25.00 percent means that 25 cents remain from each dollar of sales after deducting cost of goods sold. Eagle's gross profit margin is only slightly lower than the industry average, suggesting that the firm's pricing policies and production costs may be similar to other companies in its industry.

2. **Operating profit margin** indicates the percentage of each sales dollar remaining after deducting both cost of goods sold and operating expenses. Operating profit margin represents the profits earned on a firm's ordinary business activities before deducting interest and taxes. The ratio serves as a measure of overall operating efficiency. Equation 6-13 shows that operating profit margin is determined by dividing earnings before interest and taxes by net sales.

$$\text{Operating profit margin} = \frac{\text{EBIT}}{\text{Net sales}} \qquad \textbf{(6-13)}$$

EXAMPLE 6-13: Calculate and interpret the operating profit margin for Eagle Manufacturing for 19x8. The industry average is 15.50 percent.

$$\text{Operating profit margin} = \frac{\$14,250}{\$120,000} = 11.88 \text{ percent}$$

Eagle's operating profit margin of 11.88 percent means that Eagle generates slightly less than 12 cents in operating profit per dollar of net sales. The ratio is below the industry average, indicating that Eagle may have higher operating costs and perhaps lower selling prices relative to the average firm in its industry.

3. **Net profit margin** measures the percentage of each sales dollar remaining after deducting all expenses. Equation 6-14 shows that net profit margin on sales is determined by dividing net income by sales.

$$\text{Net profit margin} = \frac{\text{Net income}}{\text{Net sales}} \qquad \textbf{(6-14)}$$

EXAMPLE 6-14: Calculate and interpret the net profit margin on sales for Eagle Manufacturing for 19x8. The industry average is 6.00 percent.

$$\text{Net profit margin} = \frac{\$6,666}{\$120,000} = 5.56 \text{ percent}$$

Eagle's profit margin of 5.56 percent indicates that for every dollar in sales the firm generates slightly more than 5 cents in profits. This ratio is slightly below the industry average of 6 percent, suggesting that the firm's sales are too low, expenses too high, or both.

4. **Return on investment** (ROI), also called *return on assets* (ROA), measures the overall effectiveness of management in generating profits from its total investment in assets. Firms generally seek a high return on assets. As Equation 6-15 shows, return on investment is the ratio of net income to total assets. Sometimes analysts

use average total assets (the sum of beginning and ending total assets for the period divided by 2) in Equation 6-15, instead of using simply the ending total assets for the period.

$$\text{Return on investment} = \frac{\text{Net income}}{\text{Total assets}} \qquad \text{(6-15)}$$

Return on investment can also be calculated using the DuPont formula. The **DuPont formula** (Equation 6-16) shows that return on investment consists of two components—net profit margin (Equation 6-14) and total asset turnover (Equation 6-7). The contribution of each of these components to ROI differs among industries.

$$\text{DuPont formula return on investment} = \frac{\text{Net}}{\text{profit margin}} \times \frac{\text{Total}}{\text{asset turnover}}$$

$$= \frac{\text{Net income}}{\text{Net sales}} \times \frac{\text{Net sales}}{\text{Total assets}} \qquad \text{(6-16)}$$

EXAMPLE 6-15: Calculate and interpret the return on investment for Eagle Manufacturing for 19x8. The industry average is 12.00 percent (profit margin of 6.00 percent × total asset turnover of 2.00).

$$\text{Return on investment} = \frac{\$6,666}{\$82,000} = 8.13 \text{ percent*}$$

$$\text{DuPont formula return on investment} = \frac{\$6,666}{\$120,000} \times \frac{\$120,000}{\$82,000}$$

$$= 5.56 \text{ percent} \times 1.46 \text{ times} = 8.12 \text{ percent*}$$

* There is a slight difference between the two ROI calculations due to rounding.

Eagle's ROI of 8.13 percent is substantially below the industry average. The DuPont formula shows that Eagle is deficient in both profit margin and total asset turnover relative to the industry. To improve its profit margin, Eagle should increase its sales relative to its costs or reduce costs relative to sales.

5. **Return on equity** (ROE) measures the rate of return realized by a firm's stockholders on their investment and serves as an indicator of management performance. A high ROE is generally associated with effective management performance and a low ROE with ineffective performance. However, a high ROE may also indicate that a firm is more risky due to higher leverage. Likewise, a low ROE may indicate more conservative financing. As Equation 6-17 shows, return on equity is calculated by dividing net income by stockholders' equity.

$$\text{Return on equity} = \frac{\text{Net income}}{\text{Stockholders' equity}} \qquad \text{(6-17)}$$

Return on equity can also be calculated using the **modified DuPont formula**, which shows how financial leverage affects return on equity. With only equity financing, a firm's ROI would equal its ROE. The use of debt provides stockholders with the opportunity to increase their ROE. If financial leverage is favorable, any return that exceeds the interest payments will accrue to the stockholders and magnify their return. Equation 6-18 shows the relationship between ROE, ROI (Equation 6-15) and leverage (Equation 6-8).

$$\text{Modified DuPont formula return on equity} = \frac{\text{Return on investment}}{1 - \text{debt ratio}} \qquad \text{(6-18)}$$

EXAMPLE 6-16: Calculate and interpret the return on equity for Eagle Manufacturing for 19x8. The industry average is 21.82 percent [ROI of 12 percent divided by $(1-0.45)$].

$$\text{Return on equity} = \frac{\$6,666}{\$37,000} = 18.02 \text{ percent}$$

$$\text{Modified DuPont formula return on equity} = \frac{8.13}{(1 - 0.5488)} = \frac{8.13}{0.4512} = 18.02 \text{ percent}$$

Eagle's ROE of 18.02 percent is below the industry's 21.82 percent average, but not as far below as the return on investment. The difference results from Eagle's greater use of favorable financial leverage.

E. *Market ratios* **are ratios used primarily for investment decisions and long-range planning.**

There are four market ratios of particular interest to investors: earnings per share, the price/earnings ratio, the dividend payout ratio, and dividend yield.

1. **Earnings per share** (EPS) is the dollar amount earned on a share of stock during the reporting period. It provides a measure of overall performance and is an indicator of the possible amount of dividends that may be expected. Equation 6-19 shows that earnings per share is calculated by dividing the net income less preferred stock dividends by the average number of common shares outstanding. Technically, the *average number of common shares outstanding* is a weighted average with the weights determined by the length of time the shares are outstanding. If a company has convertible securities, warrants, stock options, or other contracts (Chapter 20) that permit the number of shares of common stock outstanding to be increased in future periods, more than one measure of EPS should be reported. This measure, called **fully diluted earnings per share**, is calculated in most introductory accounting textbooks.

$$\text{Earnings per share} = \frac{\text{Net income} - \text{preferred stock dividends}}{\text{Average common shares outstanding}} \quad \textbf{(6-19)}$$

EXAMPLE 6-17: Calculate and interpret the earnings per share for Eagle Manufacturing for 19x8. Eagle had 1,300,000 shares outstanding for all of 19x8. The average EPS for the industry average is $5.50.

$$\text{Earnings per share} = \frac{\$6,666}{1,300*} = \$5.13$$

* The shares are stated in thousands as is net income.

Since Eagle Manufacturing has no preferred stock in its capital structure, the earnings available to common stockholders equals the firm's net income. Eagle's EPS of $5.13 is below the industry average of $5.50. However, numerous accounting practices can affect a firm's EPS.

2. **Price/earnings ratio** (P/E) expresses the multiple that the market places on a firm's earnings per share. A high P/E multiple often reflects the market's perception of the firm's growth prospects. Thus, if investors believe that a firm's future earnings potential is good, they may be willing to pay a higher price for the stock and thus boost its P/E multiple. Equation 6-20 shows that the P/E ratio is computed by dividing the current market price per share by earnings per share.

$$\text{Price/earnings ratio} = \frac{\text{Current market price per share}}{\text{Earnings per share}} \quad \textbf{(6-20)}$$

EXAMPLE 6-18: Calculate and interpret the price/earnings ratio for Eagle Manufacturing for 19x8. The firm's year-end market price of common stock is $35.00 per share. The P/E ratio for the industry is 12.00 times ($66.00/$5.50).

$$\text{Price/earnings ratio} = \frac{\$35.00}{\$5.13} = 6.82 \text{ times}$$

Eagle's P/E ratio shows that the market is willing to pay about $7 dollars for every dollar in earnings. However, the market is willing to pay $12 for every dollar in earnings for other firms in the industry. Eagle's lower P/E suggests that investors do not value Eagle Manufacturing as highly as other firms, perhaps because its growth potential in earnings is not perceived to be as great as other firms.

3. **Book value per share** is the value of each share of common stock based on the firm's accounting records. Equation 16-21 shows that book value per share is computed by subtracting the book value of preferred stock from total stockholders' equity and then dividing by the number of common shares outstanding.

$$\text{Book value per share} = \frac{\text{Total stockholders' equity} - \text{preferred stock}}{\text{Common shares outstanding}} \qquad \text{(6-21)}$$

EXAMPLE 6-19: Calculate and interpret the book value per share for Eagle Manufacturing for 19x8. Based on Figure 6-1, Eagle has total stockholders' equity of $37,000,000, no preferred stock, and 1,300,000 shares outstanding. The book value per share for the industry is $46.50.

$$\text{Book value per share} = \frac{\$37,000}{1,300} = \$28.46$$

Eagle's book value is $28.46 per share, which is considerably lower than the industry average of $46.50 per share.

4. **Dividends per share** is the dollar amount of dividends paid on a share of common stock during the reporting period. Equation 6-22 shows the formula for calculating dividends per share.

$$\text{Dividends per share} = \frac{\text{Total cash dividends on common shares}}{\text{Common shares outstanding}} \qquad \text{(6-22)}$$

EXAMPLE 6-20: Calculate and interpret the dividends per share for Eagle Manufacturing for 19x8. Figure 6-3 shows that total cash dividends on common shares are $2,600,000 and Figure 6-1 indicates that 1,300,000 common shares are outstanding during 19x8. Dividends per share for the industry are $1.10.

$$\text{Dividends per share} = \frac{\$2,600}{1,300} = \$2.00$$

Eagle pays $2.00 in dividends for each share of common stock outstanding, which is more than the industry average of $1.10.

5. **Dividend payout** shows the percentage of earnings paid to shareholders. As Equation 6-23 indicates, dividend payout is determined by dividing dividends per share by earnings per share.

$$\text{Dividend payout} = \frac{\text{Cash dividends per share}}{\text{Earnings per share}} \qquad \text{(6-23)}$$

EXAMPLE 6-21: Calculate and interpret the dividend payout for Eagle Manufacturing for 19x8. Eagle paid $2.00 per share in dividends and had earnings per share of $5.13. The industry's average dividend payout ratio is 20 percent ($1.10/$5.50).

$$\text{Dividend payout} = \frac{\$2.00}{\$5.13} = 0.3899 \text{ or } 38.99 \text{ percent}$$

Eagle paid nearly 39 percent of its earnings in dividends compared with 20 percent for the industry. The firm's higher payout ratio may reflect lower growth opportunities than the average for other firms in its industry.

6. **Dividend yield** shows the rate earned by shareholders from dividends relative to the current price of the stock. Dividend yield is part of a stock's total return. Another portion of a stock's total return is the price appreciation on the stock. Equation 6-24 indicates that dividend yield is calculated by dividing cash dividends per share by the current market price per share of the common stock.

$$\text{Dividend yield} = \frac{\text{Cash dividends per share}}{\text{Current market price per share}} \qquad \text{(6-24)}$$

EXAMPLE 6-22: Calculate and interpret the dividend yield for Eagle Manufacturing for 19x8. Dividends per share are $2.00 and the market price per share is $35.00. The dividend yield for the industry is 1.67 percent ($1.10/$66.00).

$$\text{Dividend yield} = \frac{\$2.00}{\$35.00} = 0.0571 \text{ or } 5.71 \text{ percent}$$

Eagle's dividend yield of 5.71 percent is considerably above the industry average of 1.67 percent. The higher dividend yield may reflect fewer investment opportunities on the part of Eagle relative to the industry as a whole.

6-4. Common-size Statements

Common-size statements express individual balance sheet and income statement accounts as percentages of a base total. This method of analysis can be used to interpret financial statements between companies and over time. Common-size statements are also used to analyze the internal structure of a firm.

(*a*) The *common-size income statement* expresses each item on the income statement as a percentage of net sales.

EXAMPLE 6-23: Calculate and interpret the common-size income statement for Eagle Manufacturing for 19x7 and 19x8.

Figure 6-6 presents the common-size income statement for Eagle Manufacturing. This statement reveals trends in the income statement accounts. Eagle's profit margin (net

Eagle Manufacturing Company
Common-Size Income Statement
For the Years Ended December 31, 19x7 and 19x8

	19x8 Percent	19x7 Percent
Net sales	100.0	100.0
Cost of goods sold	75.0	75.5
Gross profit	25.0	24.5
Operating expenses		
Selling	4.2	4.4
General and administrative	6.7	6.9
Depreciation	0.9	0.7
Lease payments	1.4	1.5
Earnings before interest and taxes (EBIT)*	11.9	11.1
Interest expense		
Interest on bank notes	0.5	0.6
Interest on other debt	3.0	3.6
Earnings before taxes	8.4	6.9
Taxes (34%)	2.9	2.3
Net income*	5.5	4.6

* *Does not add up exactly due to rounding.*

FIGURE 6-6 Eagle Manufacturing Company Common-Size Income Statements

income/sales) increased from 4.6 percent in 19x7 to 5.6 percent in 19x8, but it is still slightly below the industry average. The increased profit margin is attributable to changes in both revenue and expense accounts. For example, cost of goods sold decreased slightly as a percent of net sales, suggesting that Eagle either raised prices, cut the costs of the goods produced, or both. Figure 6-2 shows that Eagle experienced an absolute dollar increase in selling, general, and administrative expenses, but Figure 6-6 indicates that on a percentage of net sales basis these accounts declined.

(b) The *common-size balance sheet* expresses each item on the balance sheet as a percentage of total assets.

Eagle Manufacturing Company
Common-Size Balance Sheet
December 31, 19x7 and 19x8

	19x8 Percent	19x7 Percent
Assets		
Current assets		
Cash	3.0	4.2
Marketable securities	1.2	1.8
Accounts receivable	19.5	16.9
Investories	25.0	26.3
Total current assets	48.7	49.2
Fixed assets		
Land and buildings	35.0	34.1
Machinery and equipment	38.5	40.8
Total fixed assets	73.5	74.9
Less accumulated depreciation	22.3	24.2
Net fixed assets	51.2	50.7
Total assets*	99.9	99.9
Liabilities and Stockholders' Equity		
Current liabilities		
Accounts payable	8.8	8.5
Notes payable—10% bank	6.7	9.9
Accrued liabilities	1.1	1.0
Current maturity of long-term debt	3.7	4.2
Other liabilities	1.7	1.7
Total current liabilities	22.0	25.3
Long-term liabilities		
Long-term debt—12% mortgage bonds	32.9	42.3
Total liabilities	54.9	67.6
Stockholders' Equity		
Common stock—$5 par, 2,000,000 shares authorized; 1,300,000 shares outstanding in 19x8 and 1,000,000 shares outstanding in 19x7	7.9	7.0
Capital in excess of par	16.7	7.5
Retained earnings	20.5	18.0
Total stockholders' equity	45.1	32.5
Total liabilities and stockholders' equity*	100.0	100.10

* Does not come out to exactly 100 percent due to rounding.

FIGURE 6-7   Eagle Manufacturing Company Common-Size Balance Sheet

EXAMPLE 6-24: Calculate and interpret the common-size balance sheet for Eagle Manufacturing for 19x7 and 19x8.

Figure 6-7 shows the common-size balance sheet for Eagle Manufacturing. The results show only minor changes in both the composition of the assets and current liabilities from one year to the other. The largest percentage shifts occur in the long-term debt and equity accounts. During the year, the firm paid off some of its long-term debt ($3,000 in long-term debt was reclassified as current debt), issued new common stock, and reinvested some of its earnings.

6-5. Comparative Financial Analysis

Ratios and common-size statements gain meaning through comparative financial analysis, which relates the firm's performance to appropriate standards or benchmarks.

A. There are three major standards of comparison: management goals, historical standards, and industry standards.

1. *Management goals* are set in advance for specific ratios or financial statement accounts and serve as a basis for evaluating actual performance.
2. *Historical standards* are used to compare current performance to past trends within the same firm.
3. *Industry standards* are used to compare a firm's financial condition to that of the industry.

B. Two approaches are used to make comparisons of financial statements: cross-sectional analysis and time-series analysis.

1. **Cross-sectional analysis** evaluates a firm's financial condition at a specific point in time. With cross-sectional analysis, a firm generally compares its own financial performance against a cross-section of similar firms in the same industry. When a firm compares its own financial ratios to industry averages, the assumption is implicitly made that the industry average is correct. Industry comparisons provide a relative rather than an absolute measure of performance. For example, a firm may be performing better than the industry on a specific ratio, but the industry average may be abnormally low. Comparing ratios to other firms requires that the ratios be computed in the same way. Otherwise, the comparisons may be meaningless.

EXAMPLE 6-25: A comparative financial analysis of Eagle's ratios is shown in Figure 6-8. Eagle's liquidity appears to be reasonably good and improving, but its ability to meet short-term maturing obligations may be affected by excessive inventories. The asset management ratios indicate that Eagle is not managing its assets very effectively. Using a higher level of assets to produce sales reduces profits. Eagle's average collection period considerably exceeds its own credit terms and the average for other firms in the industry. The firm has more debt than comparable firms, which makes Eagle more risky, but debt management ratios have improved from 19x7 to 19x8. Eagle's level of debt results in high interest charges which may affect Eagle's future borrowing power. Eagle seems to be doing a reasonable job in managing its cost of goods sold but other operating and interest expenses are depressing its profitability. The overall financial condition of Eagle is improving in some areas but is still weak.

Ratio	Calculation 19x8	Calculation 19x7	Industry Averages*	Evaluation	
Liquidity ratios					
Current ratio	2.22x	1.96x	2.00x	Improved	Good
Quick ratio	1.08x	0.91x	1.25x	Improved	Fair
Asset management ratios					
Accounts receivable turnover	7.50x	9.17x	10.40x	Worsened	Poor
Average collection period	48.67 days	39.82 days	35.00 days	Worsened	Poor
Inventory turnover	4.39x	4.44x	6.00x	Worsened	Poor
Fixed asset turnover	2.86x	3.06x	3.50x	Worsened	Poor
Total asset turnover	1.46x	1.55x	2.00x	Worsened	Poor
Debt management ratios					
Debt ratio	54.88%	67.47%	45.00%	Improved	Poor
Debt-equity ratio	121.62%	207.36%	81.81%	Improved	Poor
Times-interest-earned	3.43x	2.62x	5.50x	Improved	Poor
Fixed-charge-coverage	1.54x	1.28x	2.50x	Improved	Poor
Profitability ratios					
Gross profit margin	25.00%	24.55%	26.00%	Improved	Fair
Operating profit margin	11.88%	11.09%	15.50%	Improved	Poor
Net profit margin	5.56%	4.52%	6.00%	Improved	Fair
Return on investment	8.13%	7.01%	12.00%	Improved	Poor
Return on equity	18.02%	21.54%	21.82%	Worsened	Poor
Market/book ratios					
Earnings per share	$5.13	$4.98	$5.50	Improved	Fair
Price/earnings ratio	6.82x	6.02x	12.00x	Improved	Poor
Book value per share	$28.46	$23.10	$46.50	Improved	Poor
Dividends per share	$2.00	2.00	$1.10	Same	Good
Dividend payout	38.99%	40.16%	20.00%	Worsened	Good
Dividend yield	5.71%	6.67%	1.67%	Worsened	Good

* Industry averages are assumed to remain constant for 19x7 and 19x8.

FIGURE 6-8   Cross-sectional analysis of Eagle Manufacturing Company

2. **Time-series analysis**, or *trend analysis*, measures a firm's performance over time. Time-series analysis is often used to identify trends. Sometimes ratios are plotted on a graph to help show these trends.

EXAMPLE 6-26: Eagle Manufacturing Company's current ratios for a five-year period and comparable industry averages are presented below.

Current Ratio	19x4	19x5	19x6	19x7	19x8
Eagle Manufacturing	3.20x	2.60x	2.40x	1.96x	2.22x
Industry Average	2.60x	2.20x	2.05x	2.00x	2.00x

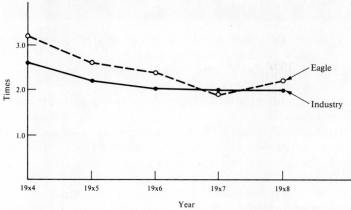

FIGURE 6-9   Time-series analysis of Eagle Manufacturing Company's current ratio versus the industry average

A trend analysis in Figure 6-9 of Eagle's current ratios shows that its liquidity position declined more rapidly than the industry average. But in 19x8 Eagle experienced an increase in liquidity relative to the industry.

C. Sources of comparative financial data include:

1. Dun and Bradstreet's *Key Business Ratios* provides 14 key ratios for about 125 industries, based on their financial statements.
2. Robert Morris Associates' *Annual Statement Studies* present financial ratios and common-size statements separated into four categories of firm size for over 330 lines of business.
3. Prentice-Hall's *Almanac of Business and Industrial Financial Ratios* is a comprehensive source of industry ratios.
4. The Federal Trade Commission and the Securities and Exchange Commission jointly publish the *Quarterly Financial Report for Manufacturing Corporations*, which contains balance sheet and income statement data of various manufacturing companies listed according to industry group and size of firm.

RAISE YOUR GRADES

Can you explain...?

☑ the meaning and purpose of financial analysis
☑ the three major stages in financial analysis
☑ the two most frequently used tools in financial analysis
☑ the limitations of financial analysis
☑ the four basic financial statements
☑ how financial ratios are used
☑ the five major categories of financial ratios
☑ how to compute and interpret financial ratios
☑ the DuPont formula
☑ how common-size statements are used
☑ how to construct a common-size balance sheet and income statement
☑ how cross-sectional analysis and time-series analysis differ
☑ several sources of comparative financial data

SUMMARY

1. Financial analysis is the judgmental process of analyzing and interpreting a firm's financial statements and other financial data.
2. Financial analysis consists of three major steps: preparation, computation and interpretation, and evaluation.
3. The mostly frequently used tools of financial statement analysis are ratio analysis and common-size statements.
4. Financial statement analysis involves several limitations such as the reliability of accounting data, the problem of determining and using appropriate industry averages, and the difficulty of interpreting financial ratios.
5. The balance sheet and the income statement are the most frequently used financial statements, but financial analysis also relies upon the statement of retained earnings and the statement of changes in financial position.
6. Ratio analysis is the major tool in financial analysis. Ratios are used as financial yardsticks to evaluate past, present, and projected future performance.
7. Ratios are classified into five major categories: liquidity, asset management, debt management, profitability, and market/book ratios.
8. Liquidity ratios measure a firm's ability to meet short-term obligations. Liquidity ratios include the current ratio and the quick ratio.
9. Asset management ratios measure how effectively a firm manages its assets. Asset management ratios include the average collection period and various turnover ratios involving accounts receivable, inventories, fixed assets, and total assets.
10. Debt management ratios show the extent to which a firm uses debt to finance investments and its ability to meet interest charges and other fixed payments. Debt management ratios include financial leverage ratios such as the debt ratio and the debt-equity ratio, and coverage ratios such as the times-interest-earned ratio and the fixed-charge-coverage ratio.
11. Profitability ratios measure a firm's earning power. Profitability ratios include gross profit margin, operating profit margin, net profit margin, return on investment, and return on equity.
12. Market/book ratios are used for investment purposes and long-range planning.
13. The Dupont formula highlights the relationship between net profit margin and total asset turnover in determining return on investments.
14. Common-size statements allows the comparison of firms with different levels of net sales and total assets by expressing relationships in percentages.
15. A common-size balance sheet is constructed by expressing each account on the balance sheet as a percentage of total assets. A common-size income statement expresses each account as a percentage of net sales.
16. Comparative financial analysis measures a firm's performance relative to standards such as management goals, historical standards, and industry standards.
17. Cross-sectional analysis evaluates a firm's performance at a specific point in time.
18. Time-series analysis evaluates a firm's performance over time.
19. Sources of comparative financial data include Dun and Bradstreet, Robert Morris Associates, and the Federal Trade Commission.

RAPID REVIEW

True or False

1. Financial statement analysis involves little judgment on the part of analysts when industry comparisons are available. [Section 6-1]
2. The first step in financial analysis is computing financial ratios. [Section 6-1A]
3. Form 10-K is a document issued by the Federal Trade Commission containing key business ratios for numerous industries. [Section 6-1A]

4. Valid comparative financial analysis depends on the availability of data for appropriately defined industries. [Section 6-1A]

5. Different accounting procedures may affect ratio comparisons between individual companies and industry averages. [Section 6-1B]

6. Some ratios can be computed in several ways. [Section 6-1B]

7. A balance sheet shows the results of a firm's operations over a period of time. [Section 6-2A]

8. An income statement shows a firm's financial condition at a specific point in time. [Section 6-2B]

9. The statement of changes in financial position summarizes a firm's financing and investing activities for a specific period and explains the change in financial position from one period to the next. [Section 6-2D]

10. A decrease in accounts receivable is a source of funds. [Section 6-2D]

11. An increase in notes payable is a use of funds. [Section 6-2D]

12. Financial ratios serve as yardsticks to evaluate a firm's performance. [Section 6-3]

13. Liquidity ratios measure a firm's ability to meet long-term obligations. [Section 6-3A]

14. A firm with a high current ratio may have trouble paying its bills when they become due. [Section 6-3A]

15. A quick ratio of 2.0 times indicates that a firm's current assets are twice as much as its current liabilities. [Section 6-3A]

16. The quick ratio is a more rigorous test of short-term solvency than is the current ratio. [Section 6-3A]

17. A firm's average collection period is influenced by its credit and collection policies. [Section 6-3B]

18. A good measure of inventory turnover ratio is sales divided by inventory. [Section 6-3B]

19. Financial leverage is the extent to which a firm uses debt financing. [Section 6-3C]

20. Creditors tend to favor a firm with high financial leverage. [Section 6-3C]

21. A debt-equity ratio greater than 1.0 indicates that a firm finances more of its assets through owners than creditors. [Section 6-3C]

22. The times-interest-earned ratio is a broader measure of a firm's coverage capabilities than the fixed-charge-coverage ratio. [Section 6-3C]

23. Creditors view a firm as more risky when the fixed-charge-coverage ratio increases. [Section 6-3C]

24. A net profit margin of 10 percent indicates that a firm generates 10 cents in net income for every dollar of total assets. [Section 6-3D]

25. The Dupont formula shows that return on investment is a function of net profit margin and fixed asset turnover. [Section 6-3D]

26. A firm's return on equity exceeds its return on investment under conditions of favorable leverage. [Section 6-3D]

27. Common-size statements are used to evaluate trends and to make industry comparisons. [Section 6-4]

28. A common-size balance sheet states each asset, liability, and stockholders' equity account as a percentage of total assets. [Section 6-4A]

29. Time-series analysis measures a firm's financial ratios over time. [Section 6-5B]

30. Dun and Bradstreet and Robert Morris Associates publish ratios of industry averages. [Section 6-5C]

Multiple Choice

31. Which of the following is a use of funds?

    (*a*) An increase in an asset account
    (*b*) A net increase in stockholders' equity
    (*c*) Depreciation
    (*d*) Net income

[Section 6-2D]

32. Liquidity ratios are computed using information from the

    (*a*) balance sheet
    (*b*) income statement
    (*c*) statement of changes in financial position
    (*d*) Both a and b

[Section 6-3A]

33. Which of the following statements is *false*?

    (*a*) Financial leverage concerns only owners
    (*b*) Financial leverage provides owners with the opportunity to increase their rate of return
    (*c*) High financial leverage may increase the cost of obtaining additional debt financing
    (*d*) Financial leverage affects the riskiness of a firm

[Section 6-3C]

34. Which type of ratio measures the earning power of a firm?

    (*a*) Liquidity
    (*b*) Asset management
    (*c*) Debt management
    (*d*) Profitability

[Section 6-3D]

35. Which of the following are used in comparative financial analysis as standards?

    (*a*) Historical standards
    (*b*) Company goals
    (*c*) Industry averages
    (*d*) All of the above

[Section 6-5B]

Answers

True and False

1. False	11. False	21. False
2. False	12. True	22. False
3. False	13. False	23. False
4. True	14. True	24. False
5. True	15. False	25. False
6. True	16. True	26. True
7. False	17. True	27. True
8. False	18. False	28. True
9. True	19. True	29. True
10. True	20. False	30. True

Multiple Choice

31. a
32. a
33. a
34. d
35. d

SOLVED PROBLEMS

PROBLEM 6-1: Classify the following items as sources or uses of funds.

Item	$	Item	$
(a) Cash	+ 5,000	(e) Net income	+ 50,000
(b) Inventories	− 20,000	(f) Repurchase of stock	+ 100,000
(c) Accounts payable	− 8,000	(g) Equipment	+ 15,000
(d) Cash dividends paid	+ 2,000	(h) Long-term debt	+ 10,000

Answer:

(a) Use	(e) Source
(b) Source	(f) Use
(c) Use	(g) Use
(d) Use	(h) Source

[Section 6-2D]

PROBLEM 6-2: Nance Corporation's current assets, inventories, and current liabilities for a four-year period are as follows:

Item	19x6	19x7	19x8	19x9
Current assets	$20,000	$22,400	$25,600	$28,100
Inventories	8,200	10,000	12,500	14,000
Current liabilities	10,000	10,200	10,700	11,000

(a) Calculate the firm's current and quick ratios for each year.
(b) Discuss the firm's liquidity position over the four-year period.

Answer:

(a) The current and quick ratios are calculated using Equation 6-1 and 6-2, respectively, and are as follows:

Ratio	19x6	19x7	19x8	19x9
Current	2.00x	2.20x	2.39x	2.55x
Quick	1.18x	1.22x	1.22x	1.28x

(b) Both the current and quick ratios improved over the four-year period. The current ratio increased to a greater extent than the quick ratio due to the buildup in inventories. **[Section 6-3A]**

PROBLEM 6-3: Leete Enterprises has current assets of $60,000 and current liabilities of $30,000. What immediate impact (increase, decrease, or no effect) would each transaction have on the firm's current ratio?

(a) Collect $5,000 of accounts receivable in cash.
(b) Purchase $10,000 of inventories on short-term credit.
(c) Sell $30,000 of common stock for cash.
(d) Sell $15,000 of fixed assets for cash.

Answer: Substituting $60,000 in current assets and $30,000 in current liabilities in Equation 6-1 gives a current ratio of 2.00 times ($60,000/$30,000).

(a) The current ratio remains unchanged because the decrease in accounts receivable and the increase in cash both affect current assets and thus offset one another.

(*b*) The current ratio decreases to 1.75 times ($70,000/$40,000) because current assets (inventories) and current liabilities (accounts payable) each increase by $10,000.

(*c*) The current ratio increases to 3.00 times ($90,000/$30,000). Current assets (cash) increase by $30,000 but current liabilities do not change because common stock is part of the stockholders' equity portion of the balance sheet.

(*d*) The current ratio increases to 2.50 times ($75,000/$30,000) because current assets increase by $15,000. **[Sections 6-2A and 6-3A]**

PROBLEM 6-4: Complete the balance sheet of Kittell Company based on the following financial data:

Net sales.....	$ 750,000
Total asset turnover.....	3.00 times
Fixed asset turnover	5.00 times
Accounts receivable turnover	18.75 times
Quick ratio	2.00 times

Kittell Company
Balance Sheet

Cash	(a)	Accounts payable	(f)
Accounts receivable.....	(b)	Long-term debt.....	100,000
Inventories	(c)	Common stock	75,000
Net fixed assets	(d)	Retained earnings.....	50,000
		Total liabilities and	
Total assets.....	(e)	stockholders' equity	(g)

Answer: The balance sheet for Kittell Company is shown below:

Kittell Company
Balance Sheet

Cash	10,000	Accounts payable	$ 25,000
Accounts receivable.....	40,000	Long-term debt.....	100,000
Inventories	50,000	Common stock	75,000
Net fixed assets	150,000	Retained earnings.....	50,000
		Total liabilities and	
Total assets.....	$250,000	stockholders' equity.....	$250,000

Total assets (e) are found by using Equation 6-7 and solving for total assets as follows:

$$\text{Total asset turnover} = \frac{\text{Net sales}}{\text{Total assets}}$$

$$3.00 = \frac{\$750,000}{\text{Total assets}}$$

$$\text{Total assets} = \frac{\$750,000}{3.00} = \$250,000$$

According to the accounting equation: assets = liabilities + stockholders' equity. Since total assets = $250,000, liabilities + stockholders' equity (g) = $250,000. Accounts payable (f) is found by subtracting long-term debt, common stock, and retained earnings from total liabilities and stockholders' equity. Thus, accounts payable = $25,000 [$250,000 − ($100,000 + $75,000 + $50,000)].

Net fixed assets (d) are found using Equation 6-6 and solving for fixed assets as follows:

$$\text{Fixed asset turnover} = \frac{\text{Net sales}}{\text{Net fixed assets}}$$

$$5.00 = \frac{\$750,000}{\text{Net fixed assets}}$$

$$\text{Net fixed assets} = \frac{\$750,000}{5.00}$$

$$= \$150,000$$

Accounts receivable (b) is found using Equation 6-3 and solving for accounts receivable as follows:

$$\text{Accounts receivable turnover} = \frac{\text{Net sales}}{\text{Accounts receivable}}$$

$$18.75 = \frac{\$750,000}{\text{Accounts receivable}}$$

$$\text{Accounts receivable} = \frac{\$750,000}{18.75}$$

$$= \$40,000$$

Cash (a) is found using Equation 6-2 and solving for cash as follows. The only current liabilities are accounts payable of $25,000.

$$\text{Quick ratio} = \frac{\text{Quick assets}}{\text{Current liabilities}}$$

$$2.00 = \frac{\text{Cash} + \$40,000}{\$25,000}$$

$$\text{Cash} + \$40,000 = (2.00)(\$25,000) = \$50,000$$

$$\text{Cash} = \$50,000 - \$40,000 = \$10,000$$

Inventories (c) are found by subtracting cash, accounts receivable, and net fixed assets from total assets. Thus, inventories = $50,000 [$250,000 − ($10,000 + $40,000 + $150,000)].

[Sections 6-2A, 6-3A and 6-3B]

PROBLEM 6-5: Sugarman Enterprises paid a $2.50 per share dividend on 100,000 shares of common stock and $4.00 per share dividend on 25,000 shares of preferred stock. Net income for the year was $850,000. The current market price of the common stock is $52.50.

(a) Calculate the earnings per share of common stock.
(b) Calculate the firm's price/earnings ratio.
(c) Calculate the dividend payout ratio of common stock.
(d) Calculate the dividend yield of common stock.

Answer:

(a) Substituting net income = $850,000, preferred stock dividends = $100,000 ($4.00 × 25,000 shares), and average number of common shares outstanding = 100,000 in Equation 6-19, the earnings per share is $7.50.

$$\text{Earnings per share} = \frac{\$850,000 - \$100,000}{100,000}$$

$$= \$7.50$$

(b) Substituting the current market price = $52.50 and the earnings per share of $7.50 in Equation 6-20, the a price/earnings ratio is 7.00 times.

$$\text{Price/earnings ratio} = \frac{\$52.50}{\$7.50}$$

$$= 7.00 \text{ times}$$

(c) Substituting the dividends per share of common stock = $2.50 and the earnings per share = $7.50 in Equation 6-22, the a dividend payout is 33.33 percent.

$$\text{Dividend payout} = \frac{\$2.50}{\$7.50}$$

$$= 0.3333 \text{ or } 33.33 \text{ percent}$$

(d) Substituting the dividends per share of common stock = $2.50 and the current market price of the common stock = $52.50 in Equation 6-23, the a dividend yield is 4.76 percent.

$$\text{Dividend yield} = \frac{\$2.50}{\$52.50}$$

$$= 0.0476 \text{ or } 4.76 \text{ percent}$$

[Section 6-3E]

Use the following data when answering Problems 6-6 through 6-14.

Weitzel Printing, Inc.
Balance Sheet
December 31, 19x7 and 19x8
(in thousands of dollars)

	19x8	19x7
Assets		
Cash	$ 3,000	$ 4,500
Accounts receivable	13,000	8,000
Inventories	6,500	5,000
Prepaid expenses	1,000	1,200
Total current assets	$23,500	$18,700
Net plant and equipment	31,000	25,000
Total assets	$54,500	$43,700
Liabilities and Stockholders' Equity		
Accounts payable	$ 4,500	$ 3,600
Notes payable	3,700	3,500
Accrued payables	2,000	2,300
Total current liabilities	$10,200	$ 9,400
Long-term debt	16,000	8,500
Total liabilities	$26,200	$17,900
Common stock	20,000	20,000
Retained earnings	8,300	5,800
Total stockholders' equity	$28,300	$25,800
Total liabilities and stockholders' equity	$54,500	$43,700

Weitzel Printing, Inc.
Income Statement
For the Years Ended December 31, 19x7 and 19x8
(in thousands of dollars)

	19x8	19x7
Net sales	$80,000	$70,000
Cost of goods sold	57,000	52,000
Gross profit	$23,000	$18,000
Operating expenses		
Selling	3,000	3,100
General and administrative	5,400	4,900
Depreciation	5,100	3,800
Earnings before interest and taxes (EBIT)	$ 9,500	$ 6,200
Interest expense	2,000	1,200
Earnings before taxes	$ 7,500	$ 5,000
Taxes (34%)	2,550	1,700
Net income	$ 4,950	$ 3,300

Ratio	Industry Average
Current ratio	2.5 times
Quick ratio	1.3 times
Accounts receivable turnover	10.2 times
Average collection period	35.3 days
Inventory turnover	6.8 times
Fixed asset turnover	4.0 times
Total asset turnover	2.1 times
Debt ratio	40.0 percent
Debt-equity ratio	66.7 percent
Times interest earned	5.8 percent
Net profit margin	5.0 percent
Return on investment	10.5 percent
Return on equity	17.5 percent

PROBLEM 6-6: Calculate the liquidity ratios of Weitzel Printing for 19x8 and compare them to the industry averages. Does this analysis suggest any problems?

Answer:

$$\text{Current ratio} = \frac{\text{Current assets}}{\text{Current liabilities}} = \frac{\$23,500}{\$10,200} = 2.30 \text{ times}$$

$$\text{Quick ratio} = \frac{\text{Quick assets}}{\text{Current liabilities}} = \frac{\$16,000}{\$10,200} = 1.60 \text{ times}$$

Weitzel's overall liquidity position is good. Its current ratio is slightly below the industry average but its quick ratio is slightly above average. The quick ratio suggests that Weitzel has more quick assets and/or fewer inventories and prepaid expenses than the industry.

[Section 6-3A]

PROBLEM 6-7: Calculate Weitzel's asset management ratios for 19x8 and compare them to the industry averages. Use a 365-day year to calculate the industry average for the average collection period. Does the analysis suggest any strengths or weaknesses?

Answer:

$$\text{Accounts receivable turnover} = \frac{\text{Net sales}}{\text{Accounts receivable}} = \frac{\$80,000}{\$13,000} = 6.2 \text{ times}$$

$$\text{Average collection period} = \frac{365 \text{ days}}{\text{Accounts receivable turnover}} = \frac{365}{6.2} = 58.9 \text{ days}$$

$$\text{Inventory turnover} = \frac{\text{Cost of goods sold}}{\text{Inventory}} = \frac{\$57,000}{\$6,500} = 8.8 \text{ times}$$

$$\text{Fixed asset turnover} = \frac{\text{Net sales}}{\text{Net fixed assets}} = \frac{\$80,000}{\$31,000} = 2.6 \text{ times}$$

$$\text{Total asset turnover} = \frac{\text{Net sales}}{\text{Total assets}} = \frac{\$80,000}{\$54,500} = 1.5 \text{ times}$$

Weitzel appears to be turning over its accounts receivable far less often than the industry average. Consequently, its average collection period exceeds the industry average by over 23 days. These ratios may signal problems in generating sales, extending credit, or collecting receivables. Weitzel's inventory turnover is higher than the industry average, which could indicate effectiveness in managing inventory. On the other hand, a low ending inventory could affect Weitzel's ability to produce sales. The firm's relatively low fixed asset turnover suggests that Weitzel's investment in fixed assets is high relative to its sales. Its total fixed asset turnover is also below the industry average, which may suggest that its sales are too low, total assets too high, or both. Without obtaining additional data about Weitzel's operations, it is difficult to draw strong conclusions regarding its asset management.   **[Section 6-3B]**

PROBLEM 6-8: How might the following factors affect your ratio analysis when comparing Weitzel's asset management ratios with industry averages?

(a) Weitzel extends 45-day credit terms versus 30-day terms for the industry; credit sales are 90 percent of total sales for Weitzel and 70 percent for the industry.
(b) Weitzel has a pronounced seasonal sales pattern which makes its accounts receivable at their highest and inventories at their lowest in December. The sales pattern for the printing industry as a whole is far more stable.
(c) Weitzel's fixed assets are relatively new compared with other firms in the printing industry.

Answer:

(a) Based on credit sales, Weitzel's average collection period exceeds the industry average by 15 days. However, Weitzel provides credit terms which are also 15 days longer than the industry average. Both Weitzel and the industry appear to have some problems in collecting accounts receivables, but Weitzel's difficulties do not appear to be nearly as severe as suggested in Problem 6-7.

AVERAGE COLLECTION PERIOD ADJUSTED FOR CREDIT SALES

	Weitzel	Industry
Average collection period / Percentage of credit sales	$\frac{58.9}{0.9} = 65.4 \text{ days}$	$\frac{35.3}{0.7} = 50.4 \text{ days}$
Credit terms difference	45.0 days	30.0 days
	20.4 days	20.4 days

(*b*) A pronounced seasonal sales pattern would distort some of Weitzel's asset management ratios. Because the ratios are computed based on year-end amounts, Weitzel's accounts receivable turnover would be understated, its average collection period overstated, and its inventory turnover overstated relative to the industry. Total asset turnover would also be affected. Using monthly averages rather than year-end figures would reduce the impact of seasonal variations in the turnover ratios.

(*c*) The value of Weitzel's fixed assets is relatively high because they are new and have not been subject to much depreciation. Thus, its fixed asset turnover ratio is relatively low compared with the industry average.   **[Section 6-3B]**

PROBLEM 6-9: Calculate Weitzel's leverage ratios for 19x8, except the fixed-charge-coverage ratio, and compare them to the average for other firms in its industry. How risky is Weitzel compared with the industry in terms of financial leverage?

Answer:

$$\text{Debt ratio} = \frac{\text{Total liabilities}}{\text{Total assets}} = \frac{\$26,200}{\$54,500} = 48.1 \text{ percent}$$

$$\text{Debt-equity ratio} = \frac{\text{Total liabilities}}{\text{Stockholders' equity}} = \frac{\$26,200}{\$28,300} = 92.6 \text{ percent}$$

$$\text{Times-interest-earned ratio} = \frac{\text{EBIT}}{\text{Interest expense}} = \frac{\$9,500}{\$2,000} = 4.8 \text{ times}$$

Weitzel's financial leverage exceeds the industry average. Thus, Weitzel may be viewed as more risky than the average firm. Its times-interest-earned ratio is less than the industry average which also indicates higher riskiness.   **[Section 6-3C]**

PROBLEM 6-10: Calculate Weitzel's profitability ratios for 19x8 including net profit margin, ROI, and ROE. Compare them to the average firm in its industry. What do these profitability ratios indicate?

Answer:

$$\text{Net profit margin} = \frac{\text{Net income}}{\text{Net sales}} = \frac{\$4,950}{\$80,000} = 6.2 \text{ percent}$$

$$\text{Return on investment} = \frac{\text{Net income}}{\text{Total assets}} = \frac{\$4,950}{\$54,500} = 9.1 \text{ percent}$$

$$\text{Return on equity} = \frac{\text{Net income}}{\text{Stockholders' equity}} = \frac{\$4,950}{\$28,300} = 17.5 \text{ percent}$$

Weitzel's net profit margin of 6.2 percent is higher than the industry average of 5.0 percent, and its return on investment is below the industry average. However, its return on equity is comparable to the industry average.   **[Section 6-3E]**

PROBLEM 6-11: Use the DuPont formula to determine if Weitzel's lower return on investment is primarily due to items on the balance sheet or income statement.

Answer:

$$\text{DuPont formula return on investment} = \text{Net profit margin} \times \text{Total asset turnover}$$
$$\text{Weitzel} = 6.2 \times 1.5 = 9.3 \text{ percent}$$
$$\text{Industry} = 5.0 \times 2.1 = 10.5 \text{ percent}$$

Weitzel's relatively low total asset turnover ratio indicates that it carries more assets relative to sales than the average firm in its industry. Its net profit margin exceeds the industry average. Thus, the balance sheet, not the income statement, accounts for its lower return on investment. **[Section 6-3D]**

PROBLEM 6-12: Construct Weitzel's common-size balance sheet for both 19x7 and 19x8 and identify major trends.

Answer:

Weitzel Printing, Inc.
Common-size Balance Sheet
December 31, 19x7 and 19x8

	19x8 Percent	19x7 Percent
Assets		
Cash	5.5	10.3
Accounts receivable	23.9	18.3
Inventories	11.9	11.4
Prepaid expenses	1.8	2.7
Total current assets	43.1	42.7
Net plant and equipment	56.9	57.2
Total assets*	100.0	99.9
Liabilities and Stockholders' Equity		
Accounts payable	8.3	8.2
Notes payable	6.8	8.0
Accrued payables	3.7	5.3
Total current liabilities	18.8	21.5
Long-term debt	29.4	19.5
Total liabilities	48.2	41.0
Common stock	36.7	45.8
Retained earnings	15.2	13.3
Total stockholders' equity	52.1	59.1
Total liabilities and stockholders' equity*	100.1	100.1

* Does not add up exactly to 100 due to rounding.

The common-size balance sheets reveal several major changes in the composition of the balance sheet accounts. On the assets side, the percentage held in cash decreased while accounts receivable increased. The composition of Weitzel's financial structure shifted toward a large percentage of debt financing, especially long-term debt. **[Section 6-4A]**

PROBLEM 6-13: Construct Weitzel's common-size income statement for both 19x7 and 19x8 and identify major trends.

Answer:

Weitzel Printing, Inc.
Common-Size Income Statement
For the Years Ended December 31, 19x7 and 19x8

	19x8 Percent	19x7 Percent
Net sales	100.0	100.0
Cost of goods sold	71.3	74.3
Gross profit	28.8*	25.7
Operating expenses		
Selling	3.8	4.4
General and administrative	6.8	7.0
Depreciation	6.4	5.4
Earning before interest and taxes	11.9*	8.9
Interest expense	2.5	1.7
Earnings before taxes	9.4	7.1
Taxes (34%)	3.2	2.4
Net income	6.2	4.7

* Some totals may not come out exactly due to rounding.

Weitzel's net profit margin improved in 19x8 primarily due to decreases in cost of goods sold and selling expenses relative to sales. Interest expenses increased due to the larger amount of debt. **[Section 3-4B]**

PROBLEM 6-14: Based on the following ratios for Weitzel Printing, Inc. and its industry averages, perform a trend analysis of the return on investment and the return on equity using the Dupont formulas. Discuss the underlying causes of the trends.

Ratio	19x5	19x6	19x7	19x8
Weitzel Printing, Inc.				
Net profit margin	3.8%	4.0%	4.7%	6.2%
Total asset turnover	1.9x	1.8x	1.6x	1.5x
Debt ratio	38.0%	38.8%	41.0%	48.1%
Industry Averages				
Net profit margin	5.5%	5.3%	5.2%	5.0%
Total asset turnover	1.8x	1.9x	2.0x	2.1x
Debt ratio	37.2%	37.0%	39.3%	40.0%

Answer: Based on the DuPont formulas in Equations 6-16 and 6-18, the return on investment (ROI) and return on equity (ROE) are summarized below.

Ratio	19x5	19x6	19x7	19x8
Weitzel Printing, Inc.				
Return on investment	7.2%	7.2%	7.5%	9.1%
Return on equity	11.6%	11.8%	12.8%	17.5%
Industry Averages				
Return on investment	9.9%	10.1%	10.4%	10.5%
Return on equity	15.8%	16.0%	17.1%	17.5%

Weitzel's ROI remained below the industry average throughout the entire period. Weitzel's profit margin steadily increased while its total asset turnover decreased. The improvement in Weitzel's ROI in 19x8 resulted from the increase in its net profit margin, which outweighed the decline in its total asset turnover. The trends for the industry averages regarding profit margin and total asset turnover are the opposite of Weitzel's trends. The industry averages show a gradual increase in ROI.

Weitzel's ROE remained below the industry average throughout the entire period, except for 19x8. Weitzel's increase in ROE for 19x8 resulted from increases in both ROI and financial leverage. Weitzel's debt ratio increased throughout the period and remained above the industry average. The industry's ROE increased throughout the entire period.

[Section 6-5B]

7 BREAKEVEN ANALYSIS AND LEVERAGE

7-1. Breakeven Analysis

Breakeven analysis, broadly known as *cost-volume-profit analysis*, examines the relationships among a firm's sales, costs, and profits at various output levels. This chapter focuses primarily on *operating breakeven analysis*, which includes only sales revenues, operating costs, and operating profits.

A. Breakeven analysis is based on several simplifying assumptions.

Simplifying assumptions make breakeven analysis easy to use, but they also limit the analysis to some extent. However, the assumptions make the technique more realistic in the short run of one year or less.

1. *Assumption of linearity*. Breakeven analysis assumes that the behavior of revenues and costs is linear over the relevant range of output levels. The *relevant range* is the range of activity in which selling prices and fixed costs remain constant and variable costs are proportional to sales volume. Within the relevant range, volume is the only factor affecting costs. Factors which lower costs, such as greater efficiency and productivity, are assumed to be unchanged. In practice, major changes may occur over the long run in selling prices and costs which may invalidate the assumption of linearity.

2. *Assumption of accurate estimates*. Breakeven analysis assumes that costs and revenues can be accurately estimated at each level of output. In practice, these factors are always subject to uncertainty, but can be more accurately estimated within a short timeframe.

3. *Assumption of cost classification appropriateness*. Breakeven analysis assumes that all costs can be divided into fixed and variable components.

   - **Fixed costs** are expenditures that do not vary as volume changes. Examples include lease and rental payments, insurance, depreciation, and management salaries. These costs must be paid regardless of the sales level.
   - **Variable costs** are expenditures that vary directly with the level of volume. Examples include raw materials and direct labor costs.

   In practice, all costs are variable over time. Also, there are more than two cost categories. Some costs, called **semivariable costs**, are partly fixed and partly variable. Breakeven analysis assumes that semivariable costs can be separated into fixed and variable components. Semivariable costs sometimes increase in a stepwise manner as output increases. For example, sales commissions may be fixed over a volume range but may increase to higher levels over higher volume ranges. Figure 7-1 shows the relationship between various types of costs and the level of sales volume.

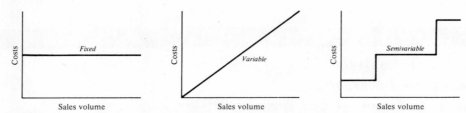

FIGURE 7-1   The relationships between types of cost and sales volume

4. *Assumption of constant sales mix*. Breakeven analysis assumes that the sales mix is maintained as total volume changes. Thus, the firm produces and sells either a single product or constant mix of different products. In practice, sales mix often changes over time.

B.   Breakeven analysis has four major applications.

The name breakeven analysis implies the point at which a firm "breaks even," that is, the sales volume where revenues equal costs. The term is somewhat misleading because breakeven analysis is used for other purposes besides determining the breakeven output of a firm. For example, it can also be used to examine the effects of changes in sales, operating costs, operating profits (earnings before interest and taxes or EBIT), income (either before-tax or after-tax), and earnings per share.

1. *Evaluation of new products*. Breakeven analysis may be used to determine the level of sales required for a new product to breakeven or to earn a specified operating profit.
2. *Analysis of a modernization, automation, or expansion program*. Breakeven analysis enables decision makers to analyze the cost of modernization or expansion on a firm's profitability. The effect of substituting fixed for variable costs through automation can be analyzed through breakeven analysis.
3. *Examination of pricing decisions*. Breakeven analysis helps decision makers assess the impact of changing selling prices on a firm's output level and its operating profit.
4. *Determination of sales/target profit*. Breakeven analysis is used to determine the output needed to obtain a target operating profit. Firms are interested in making profits, not just breaking even. Breakeven analysis can be used to determine the sales volume required to reach specific profit goals.

C.   The *operating breakeven point* is the level of sales where neither operating profits nor losses are incurred.

At the breakeven point, sales revenue exactly covers all fixed and variable operating costs. The result is an operating profit or EBIT equal to zero. The breakeven point may be determined using algebraic or graphic methods.

1. The *algebraic method* expresses the breakeven point as a formula. The breakeven point formula is stated in either units (Equation 7-1) or dollar sales volume (Equation 7-2).

OPERATING BREAKEVEN POINT IN UNITS

$$Q_b = \frac{F}{p - v}$$

(7-1)

where Q_b = operating breakeven point in units

F = fixed operating costs

p = selling price per unit

v = variable operating costs per unit

The difference between the selling price per unit and the variable operating costs per unit, $(p - v)$, is called the **contribution margin**. The contribution margin shows how much each unit of output contributes to fixed operating costs coverage and operating profit.

OPERATING BREAKEVEN POINT IN DOLLAR SALES
$$S_b = \frac{F}{1 - (v/p)}$$
(7-2)

where S_b = operating breakeven point in dollar sales

v/p = variable cost per dollar of sales

Breakeven analysis assumes that both price (p) and variable cost per unit (v) are constant within the relevant range. Thus, the variable cost ratio (v/p) is also constant for any level of sales. Equation 7-2 can also be used for multiproduct firms, assuming that the product mix does not change.

EXAMPLE 7-1: Taylor Publishing Company is conducting an analysis of a proposed new textbook. Taylor estimates that fixed costs will be $100,000 and the variable cost per unit will be $30. Taylor plans to sell the book for $40.

Using Equation 7-1, the operating breakeven point is 10,000 books.

$$Q_b = \frac{\$100,000}{\$40 - \$30} = 10,000 \text{ units}$$

Each book sold contributes $10 ($40 − $30) to covering the fixed operating costs. Selling 10,000 books, each having a $10 contribution margin, generates the $100,000 needed to cover fixed operating costs.

EXAMPLE 7-2: *Recall the data in Example 7-1.* Based on Equation 7-2, Taylor Publishing would have to sell $400,000 worth of books to reach its operating breakeven point. For every book sold, the variable costs represent 75 percent ($30/$40) of sales. For a single product, the breakeven point can also be determined by multiplying the selling price per unit by the breakeven point in units. ($40 × 10,000 = $400,000).

$$S_b = \frac{\$100,000}{1 - (\$30/\$40)} = \frac{\$100,000}{0.25} = \$400,000$$

Equation 7-3 shows the formula for the target profit point in units.

TARGET PROFIT POINT IN UNITS
$$Q_{tp} = \frac{F + TP}{p - v}$$
(7-3)

where Q_{tp} = quantity in units to achieve target operating profit

TP = target operating profit

EXAMPLE 7-3: *Recall the data in Example 7-1.* Based on Equation 7-3, Taylor Publishing has to sell 15,000 books to achieve its target operating profit goal of $50,000. Figure 7-2 shows that the difference between total revenues and total costs ($600,000 − $550,000) is $50,000 at 15,000 units.

$$Q_{tp} = \frac{\$100,000 + \$50,000}{\$40 - \$30} = 15,000 \text{ units}$$

2. The *graphic method* provides a visual representation of the breakeven point using a breakeven chart. A breakeven chart is plotted with dollar revenues and costs on the

vertical axis and units sold on the horizontal axis. The operating breakeven point is determined by following three steps.

- *Draw the total revenue (TR) line.* Select any two levels of volume. Determine total revenues at each volume level by multiplying the quantity of units sold (Q) by the selling price per unit (p). Plot these two points and connect them with a straight line. The total revenue line begins at the origin where zero units sold produces zero revenues.
- *Draw the total cost (TC) line.* Select any two levels of volume. Determine total costs at each volume level by adding fixed plus variable costs. Plot these two points and connect them with a straight line. The total cost line begins on the vertical axis at the level of fixed costs since fixed costs are incurred when zero units are sold.
- *Determine the point where the TR and TC lines intersect.* Draw a perpendicular line from this point to the horizontal axis to find the operating breakeven point in units (Q_b). Draw a straight line from the point of intersection to the vertical axis to find the breakeven point in dollar sales volume (S_b). Output levels below the breakeven point result in an *operating loss, TR < TC,* and output levels above the breakeven point result in an *operating profit, TR > TC.*

EXAMPLE 7-4: To draw a breakeven chart using the information provided in Example 7-1, two levels of output—0 and 15,000 units—are arbitrarily selected to determine the total revenue and total cost lines. Total revenues equal \$0 at 0 units and \$600,000 (\$40 × 15,000) at 15,000 units. Total costs equal \$100,000 (fixed costs) at 0 units and \$550,000 [\$50,000 + (15,000 × \$30,000)] at 15,000 units. The total revenue and total cost lines are plotted and intersect at 10,000 units and \$400,000 sales volume. Figure 7-2 shows the breakeven chart.

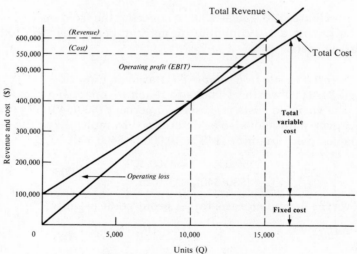

FIGURE 7-2   Linear breakeven analysis chart for Taylor Publishing Company

D. There are three variations of breakeven analysis.

The three variations of breakeven analysis are cash, nonlinear, and overall breakeven analyses.

1. **Cash breakeven analysis** is used to determine cost-profit-volume relationships based on cash receipts and payments. Not all revenues and costs used in breakeven analysis involve cash. For example, operating costs may include noncash outlays such as depreciation. The cash breakeven point subtracts noncash expenses from operating expenses. Thus, the **cash breakeven point** is the number of units sold where operating cash revenues exactly cover all operating cash expenses. The cash

breakeven point will be lower than the operating breakeven point. Equation 7-4 shows the cash breakeven point.

CASH BREAKEVEN POINT IN UNITS

$$Q_{cb} = \frac{F - N}{p - v}$$

(7-4)

where Q_{cb} = cash breakeven point in units

N = noncash outlays

EXAMPLE 7-5: *Recall the data in Example 7-1.* Taylor Publishing Company expects to have $10,000 in noncash outlays for depreciation.

Based on Equation 7-4, Taylor's cash breakeven point is computed as 9,000 units, 1,000 units fewer than its breakeven point on a noncash basis.

$$Q_{cb} = \frac{\$100,000 - \$10,000}{\$40 - \$30} = 9,000 \text{ units}$$

2. **Nonlinear breakeven analysis** involves nonlinear revenue and cost functions. The breakeven analysis technique can be adapted to more realistic assumptions than those considered so far. For example, nonlinear breakeven analysis does not assume that a firm's selling price per unit and variable cost per unit are independent of sales volume. In practice, firms often lower their selling price to generate more sales. This results in a curvilinear total revenue function. Variable cost per unit frequently declines over some range due to economies of scale and then increases as a firm approaches capacity. Changing variable costs per unit produces a curved total cost function. As Figure 7-3 shows, nonlinear breakeven analysis may result in several breakeven points, at output level Q_1 and Q_3. Output below Q_1 and above Q_3 results in operating losses. Operating profits occur between the range Q_1 and Q_3. Total operating profits are maximized within the profit range at the point of maximum distance between the total revenue and total cost curves, at output level Q_2.

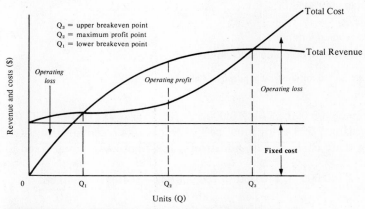

FIGURE 7-3 Nonlinear breakeven analysis chart

3. **Overall breakeven analysis** determines the level of sales where neither profits nor losses are incurred after considering all costs, not just operating costs. A firm usually incurs both operating costs and financing costs. For example, financing costs include interest on debt and preferred stock dividends. Unlike interest payments, preferred stock dividend payments are not tax deductible. Thus, a dollar of dividends is more costly than a dollar of interest. To make interest and dividends comparable on a pre-tax basis, preferred stock dividends must be divided by $(1 - t)$, where t is the marginal income tax rate. Figure 7-4 lists the various costs in a revised income statement format. Equation 7-5 shows the level of units that must be sold to cover all fixed costs.

Q_p = Sales revenue
$-Q_v$ = $-$Variable operating costs
$-F$ = $-$Fixed operating costs
EBIT = Operating profits
$-I$ = $-$Interest expense (fixed financing cost)
EBT = Earnings before taxes
$-t$ = $-$Income taxes (variable cost)
NI = Net income
$-D_p$ = $-$Preferred stock dividends (fixed financing cost)
EAC = Earnings available to common stockholders

FIGURE 7-4   Components of a revised income statement

OVERALL BREAKEVEN POINT IN UNITS

$$Q_{ob} = \frac{F + I + [D_p/(1 - t)]}{p - v} \qquad (7\text{-}5)$$

where Q_{ob} = overall breakeven point in units
I = interest expense
D_{ps} = preferred stock dividends
t = marginal income tax rate

EXAMPLE 7-6: Look at the data below. Recall that p = \$40 and v = \$30.

	15,000 Units
Sales revenue (\$40 × 15,000 units)..	\$600,000
—Variable operating costs (\$30 × 15,000 units)	450,000
—Fixed operating costs	100,000
EBIT	\$ 50,000
—Interest expense...	10,000
Earnings before taxes...	\$ 40,000
—Income taxes (40%)*...	16,000
Net income...	\$ 24,000
—Preferred stock dividends..	4,000
Earnings available to common stockholders.................................	\$ 20,000

* A 40 percent tax rate is used for illustrative purposes only.

Substituting F = \$100,000, I = \$10,000, $D_p/(1 - t)$ = (\$4,000)(1 − 0.40), p = \$40, and v = \$30, in Equation 7-5, Taylor must sell 11,667 books to cover all costs: 10,000 books to cover fixed operating costs and an additional 1,667 books to cover fixed financing costs.

$$Q_{ob} = \frac{\$100,000 + \$10,000 + [\$4,000/(1 - 0.40)]}{\$40 - \$30} = \frac{\$116,667}{\$10} = 11,667$$

7-2. Concept of Leverage

Leverage involves a multiplier effect. The leverage concept is very general because it applies to many other disciplines besides finance. Leverage simply measures the relationship between two variables. A change in one variable (independent variable) results in a change in another variable (dependent variable). With an actual lever, a small push on one end may result in a large lift of the other (the *multiplier effect*). In this context, **leverage** is defined as the percentage change in the dependent variable divided by the percentage change in the independent variable.

In finance, leverage is used to describe the ability of fixed costs to magnify returns; that is, fixed costs allow a firm to magnify small changes into large ones. For example, the existence of fixed costs permits a change in sales (independent variable) to be magnified into a relatively large change in returns (dependent variable).

A. Leverage is produced by the fixed costs on using assets and sustaining liabilities.

There are two types of fixed costs.

1. Fixed *operating* costs are fixed costs incurred in conducting a firm's normal business activities. Fixed operating costs often result from using fixed assets in operations. One such operating cost is depreciation. A firm with a high proportion of fixed assets will also have high fixed operating costs. Using fixed operating costs in operations results in **operating leverage**. Operating leverage is determined by the mix of assets.

2. Fixed *financing* costs are contractual obligations that a firm undertakes in financing its operations. The amount of fixed financing costs depends on the mix of debt and common stock equity. The main sources of fixed financing costs are interest on debt and dividends on preferred stock. Leases also represent a source of fixed financing costs for many firms. Using funds with a fixed cost in operations results in **financial leverage**. Hence, financial leverage is determined by how a firm finances its assets.

B. Firms have some control over their mix of fixed and variable costs.

By determining the composition of its assets and how they are financed, management is able to influence its leverage.

EXAMPLE 7-7: Taylor Publishing Company is attempting to reduce variable costs through increased automation by purchasing new labor-saving machines. The increase in fixed assets results in higher fixed operating costs such as depreciation. Financing the new machines through debt increases fixed capital costs by the amount of the additional interest expense. Thus, leverage increases as fixed operating costs and/or fixed financing costs become a larger proportion of a firm's total costs.

C. Higher leverage increases a firm's potential return but also increases the risk associated with achieving this return.

Firms use leverage in an attempt to earn returns in excess of the fixed costs. The multiplier effect through which leverage works, however, can magnify returns in both directions. Just as a change in leverage, if successful, can increase returns, it can reduce returns if it fails. Changes in leverage also alter a firm's risk. In this case, *risk* refers to the degree of uncertainty associated with a firm's ability to meet fixed obligations. Fixed costs must be met regardless of the level of operations or sales.

7-3. Operating Leverage and Business Risk

Operating leverage is the variability of operating profit, given a change in sales. Operating leverage is caused by the presence of fixed operating costs such as depreciation, salaries, and utilities. The use of operating leverage magnifies fluctuations in operating profit (earnings before interest and taxes or EBIT). As sales increase, fixed costs remain constant over a range of output, but profits—or reductions in losses depending on the sale level—increase. The greater the fixed operating costs relative to variable operating costs, the more variable the EBIT. Once high fixed cost firms reach their operating breakeven point, their profits grow rapidly. The multiplier effect resulting from using fixed operating costs is called the **degree of operating leverage**. Figure 7-5, page 130, shows the components of operating leverage.

Q_p = Sales revenue
$-Q_v$ = $-$Variable operating costs
$\underline{-F}$ = $\underline{-Fixed\ operating\ costs}$
EBIT = Operating profits

FIGURE 7-5 Components of operating leverage, using a revised income statement format

A. **The *degree of operating leverage (DOL)* is the percentage change in EBIT that results from a given percentage change in sales.**

The degree of operating leverage is computed in two ways.

1. Equation 7-6 computes the DOL using a percentage change formula which requires two different values for sales and EBIT. The sales level, Q, where DOL is measured must be specified because DOL differs at each sales level.

$$DOL\ at\ Q = \frac{Percentage\ change\ in\ EBIT}{Percentage\ change\ in\ sales}$$

$$= \frac{\dfrac{\triangle EBIT}{EBIT}}{\dfrac{\triangle Sales}{Sales}} \tag{7-6}$$

where Q = sales (units of output) where DOL is measured

$\triangle$ EBIT = change in EBIT

$\triangle$ Sales = change in sales

EXAMPLE 7-8: Use the information provided below to calculate Taylor Publishing Company's degree of operating leverage when 15,000 books are sold.

	15,000 units	16,500 units
Sales	$600,000	$660,000
$-$Variable operating costs	450,000	495,000
$-$Fixed operating costs	100,000	100,000
EBIT	$ 50,000	$ 65,000

Using Equation 7-6, the DOL equals 3.0, which means that each 1 percent change in sales volume results in a 3 percent change in EBIT. As shown below, a 10 percent increase in sales produces a 30 percent (3.0 × 10 percent) increase in EBIT. Similarly, a 10 percent decrease in sales results in a 30 percent decrease in EBIT.

$$DOL\ at\ 15,000\ units = \frac{\left(\dfrac{\$65,000 - \$50,000}{\$50,000}\right)}{\left(\dfrac{\$660,000 - \$600,000}{\$600,000}\right)} = \frac{0.30}{0.10} = 3.0$$

	15,000 Units (1)	16,500 Units (2)	Percentage Change [(2) − (1)]/(1)	
Sales	$600,000	$660,000	+10%	
$-$Variable operating costs	450,000	495,000		$DOL = \dfrac{30\%}{10\%} = 3.0$
$-$Fixed operating costs	100,000	100,000		
EBIT	$ 50,000	$ 65,000	+30%	

2. Equation 7-7 provides a more direct way to calculate DOL using the variables defined in Section 7-1 on breakeven analysis.

$$\text{DOL at Q} = \frac{\text{Sales} - \text{Variable costs}}{\text{EBIT}}$$

$$= \frac{Q(p - v)}{Q(p - v) - F} \quad \text{(7-7)}$$

EXAMPLE 7-9: Use Equation 7-7 to calculate Taylor Publishing Company's degree of operating leverage when 15,000 books are sold. As defined in Example 7-1, $p = \$40$, $v = \$30$, and $F = \$100,000$.

$$\text{DOL at 15,000 units} = \frac{(15,000)(\$40 - \$30)}{(15,000)(\$40 - \$30) - \$100,000}$$

$$= \frac{\$150,000}{\$50,000} = 3.0$$

The DOL at 15,000 units is 3.0, which is the same as that obtained using Equation 7-6. Figure 7-6 illustrates the relationship between breakeven analysis and operating leverage for Taylor Publishing Company.

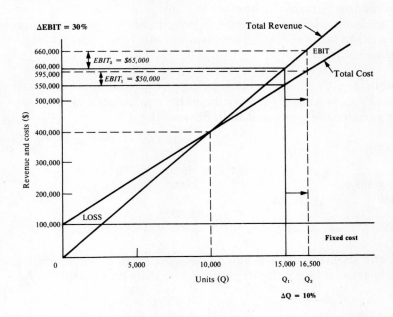

FIGURE 7-6
Relationship between breakeven analysis and operating leverage for Taylor Publishing Company

B. The degree of operating leverage has several properties. Some of these properties are shown in Figure 7-7.

1. DOL changes when measured at different base sales levels (Q).
2. DOL is negative below and positive above the operating breakeven point. A positive DOL indicates the percentage increase in operating profits that occurs from a 1 percent increase in output. A negative DOL indicates the percentage decrease in operating losses that results from a 1 percent increase in output.
3. DOL is undefined at the operating breakeven point. The denominator (EBIT) of Equation 7-7 is zero at the operating breakeven point. An undefined value is produced when a positive number is divided by zero.
4. DOL becomes a larger absolute number as base sales approach the operating breakeven point.
5. Positive and negative changes in sales of equal magnitude from the same base sales level result in equal degrees of operating leverage change. This is because the concept of leverage is linear.

Base Sales Level (Q)	Degree of Operating Leverage (DOL)
0	0
1,000	− 0.11
3,000	− 0.43
5,000	− 1.00
7,000	− 2.33
9,000	− 9.00
10,000*	Undefined
11,000	+11.00
13,000	+ 4.33
15,000	+ 3.00
17,000	+ 2.43
19,000	+ 2.11

* Operating breakeven point

FIGURE 7-7
DOL at different base sales levels for Taylor Publishing Company

C. The degree of operating leverage is affected by cost structure.

Firms may alter their DOL by changing the relationship between fixed and variable operating costs. For example, a firm may employ labor-saving equipment which increases fixed costs and reduces variable labor costs per unit. This tradeoff between fixed and variable costs produces a larger contribution margin. Such a cost structure increases DOL, which results in large operating profits when sales are high and large operating losses when sales are low.

EXAMPLE 7-10: Taylor Publishing Company is considering two production processes with different cost structures. Process A involves less automated equipment and thus has lower fixed costs and higher variable costs per unit than Process B.

	Process A	Process B
Selling price per unit	$ 40.00	$ 40.00
Variable operating costs per unit	30.00	25.00
Contribution margin per unit	10.00	15.00
Total fixed costs	100,000	180,000
Operating breakeven point.......................	10,000 units	12,000 units

Figure 7-8 shows the EBIT and DOL for various sales levels. At sales of 15,000 units, Process A is more attractive because it offers slightly higher operating profits (EBIT). As

Process A	Units	Sales	Operating Costs	EBIT	DOL
	5,000	$200,000	$250,000	$−50,000	−1.00
	10,000	400,000	400,000	0	undefined
	12,000	480,000	460,000	20,000	6.00
	15,000	600,000	550,000	50,000	3.00
	20,000	800,000	700,000	100,000	2.00

Process B	Units	Sales	Operating Costs	EBIT	DOL
	5,000	$200,000	$305,000	$−105,000	−0.71
	10,000	400,000	430,000	− 30,000	−5.00
	12,000	480,000	480,000	0	undefined
	15,000	600,000	555,000	45,000	5.00
	20,000	800,000	680,000	120,000	2.50

FIGURE 7-8 Impact of different cost structures on EBIT and DOL for Taylor Publishing Company

sales increase, Process B becomes more attractive due to higher operating leverage. At 20,000 units, Process B provides $20,000 more operating profits than Process A.

D. *Business risk* is the variability or uncertainty of operating profits.

Business risk, also called **operating risk**, is the risk of being unable to cover fixed operating costs. Firms with highly unpredictable operating profits (EBIT) have high business risk whereas firms with highly predicatable operating profits have low business risk. Factors influencing the uncertainty of EBIT include unexpected variations in sales, selling prices, variable costs, and the level of fixed costs relative to sales. Increases in operating fixed costs also increase the risk of being unable to cover them. Generally, the higher the variability of each of these factors, the higher the business risk.

Firms have partial control over business risk. Even though business risk is influenced by a firm's industry characteristics and other factors, firms do have some control over factors such as the mix of fixed costs and variable costs which also affect the firm's business risk.

EXAMPLE 7-11: *Recall the information in Example 7-10 and Figure 7-8.* Holding other factors constant, the higher the operating leverage, the higher the business risk. Process B requires higher fixed costs and lower variable costs than Process A. If Taylor Publishing adopts Process B, its operating breakeven point increases from 10,000 units to 12,000 units. The higher breakeven point increases the risk that Taylor Publishing will be unable to cover its fixed operating costs. Process B also results in greater variability in EBIT due to its higher DOL. Thus, Taylor's business risk is increased if Process B is chosen.

7-4. Financial Leverage and Financial Risk

Financial leverage is the variability in earnings per share, given a change in operating profits. It is caused by the presence of fixed financial costs, such as interest payments and preferred stock dividends, in the firm's cost structure. When a firm incurs fixed financing costs, a change in EBIT is magnified into a larger change in earnings per share (EPS). **Earnings per share** is the amount earned on each share of common stock outstanding. Earnings per share is calculated by dividing the earnings available for common stockholders by the average number of shares of common stock outstanding. The multiplier effect resulting from using debt with fixed financing costs is called the **degree of financial leverage**. Figure 7-9 shows the components of financial leverage.

$$
\begin{aligned}
\text{EBIT} &= \text{Operating profits} \\
-\text{I} &= -\text{Interest expense (fixed financing cost)} \\
\hline
\text{EBT} &= \text{Earnings before taxes} \\
-\text{t} &= -\text{Income taxes (variable cost)} \\
\hline
\text{NI} &= \text{Net income} \\
-\text{D}_p &= -\text{Preferred stock dividends (fixed financing cost)} \\
\hline
\text{EAC} &= \text{Earnings available to common stockholders} \\
\text{n} &= \text{Shares of common stock outstanding} \\
\text{EPS} &= \text{Earnings per share (EAC/n)}
\end{aligned}
$$

FIGURE 7-9   Components of financial leverage, using a revised income statement format

A. The *degree of financial leverage (DFL)* is the percentage change in earnings per share (EPS) that results from a given percentage change in earnings before interest and taxes (EBIT). The degree of financial leverage is computed in two ways.

1. Equation 7-8 computes the DFL using a percentage change formula which requires two different values for EBIT and EPS. The EBIT point, Q, where DFL is measured must be specified because DFL differs at each EBIT level.

$$\text{DFL at Q} = \frac{\text{Percentage change in EPS}}{\text{Percentage change in EBIT}}$$

$$= \frac{\dfrac{\triangle \text{EPS}}{\text{EPS}}}{\dfrac{\triangle \text{EBIT}}{\text{EBIT}}} \tag{7-8}$$

where Q = EBIT (units of output) where DFL is measured

$\triangle$ EPS = change in EPS

$\triangle$ EBIT = change in EBIT

EXAMPLE 7-12: Use the information provided below to calculate Taylor Publishing Company's degree of financial leverage where EBIT is $50,000 for 15,000 units sold.

	15,000 Units	16,500 Units
Sales revenue	$600,000	$660,000
—Variable operating costs	450,000	495,000
—Fixed operating costs	100,000	100,000
EBIT	$ 50,000	$ 65,000
—Interest expense	10,000	10,000
Earnings before taxes	$ 40,000	$ 55,000
—Income taxes (40%)*	16,000	22,000
Net income	$ 24,000	$ 33,000
—Preferred stock dividends	4,000	4,000
Earnings available to common stockholders	$ 20,000	$ 29,000
Shares of common stock	20,000	20,000
Earnings per share	$1.00	$1.45

* A 40 percent tax rate is used for illustrative purposes only.

$$\text{DFL at \$50,000 EBIT} = \frac{\left(\dfrac{\$1.45 - \$1.00}{\$1.00}\right)}{\left(\dfrac{\$65,000 - \$50,000}{\$50,000}\right)} = \frac{0.45}{0.30} = 1.5$$

Using Equation 7-8, the DFL equals 1.5 which means that each 1 percent change in EBIT results in a 1.5 percent change in EPS. As shown below, a 30 percent increase in EBIT produces a 45 percent (1.5 × 30 percent) increase in EPS. Similarly, a 30 percent decrease in EBIT results in a 45 percent decrease in EPS.

	15,000 Units (1)	16,500 Units (2)	Percentage Change [(2) − (1)]/(1)	
Sales Revenue	$600,000	$660,000	+10%	DOL =
—Variable operating costs .	450,000	495,000		
—Fixed operating costs	100,000	100,000		$\dfrac{30\%}{10\%}$ = 3.0
EBIT	$ 50,000	$ 65,000	+30%	
—Interest expense	10,000	10,000		
Earnings before taxes	$ 40,000	$ 55,000		DCL =
—Income taxes (40%)	16,000	22,000		$\dfrac{45\%}{10\%}$ = 4.5
Net income.	$ 24,000	$ 33,000		DFL =
—Preferred stock dividends	4,000	4,000		
Earnings available to common stockholders. . . .	$ 20,000	$ 29,000		$\dfrac{45\%}{30\%}$ = 1.5
Shares of common stock . . .	20,000	20,000		
Earnings per share.	$1.00	$1.45	+45%	

2. Equation 7-9 is another way to calculate DFL.

$$\text{DFL at Q} = \frac{\text{EBIT}}{\text{EBIT} - \text{Fixed financing costs}}$$

$$= \frac{Q(p - v) - F}{Q(p - v) - F - I - [D_p/(1 - t)]} \qquad \text{(7-9)}$$

where I = interest expense

D_p = preferred stock dividends

t = marginal income tax rate

EXAMPLE 7-13: Taylor Publishing Company's EBIT equals $50,000. As defined in Example 7-1, $Q = 15,000$, $p = \$40$, $v = \$30$, and $F = \$100,000$. As shown in Example 7-12, $I = 10,000$, $D_p = \$4,000$, and $t = 40$ percent.

At an EBIT of $50,000, the DFL is 1.5, which is the same result obtained using Equation 7-8. Figure 7-10 illustrates financial leverage for Taylor Publishing Company.

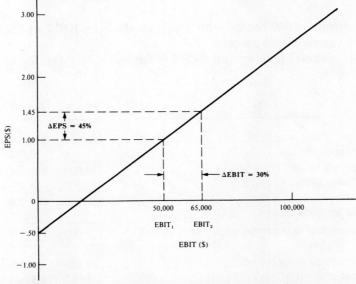

FIGURE 7-10   Illustration of financial leverage for Taylor Publishing Company

$$\text{DFL at \$50,000 EBIT} = \frac{(15,000)(\$40 - \$30) - \$100,000}{(\$15,000)(\$40 - \$30) - \$100,000 - \$10,000 - [\$4,000/(1 - 0.40)]}$$

$$= \frac{\$50,000}{\$33,333} = 1.5$$

B. The degree of financial leverage has several properties.

Five properties of DFL are:

1. DFL changes when measured at different base EBIT levels.
2. A DFL greater than 1.0 indicates financial leverage.
3. Positive and negative changes in EBIT of equal magnitude from the same base EBIT level result in equal degrees of change in financial leverage.
4. Financial leverage is favorable when a firm earns more on invested funds than it pays in related financing costs.
5. Financial leverage is unfavorable when a firm earns less on invested funds than it pays in related financing costs.

C. Capital structure is affected by the degree of financial leverage.

Capital structure consists of all permanent sources of capital available to a firm, such as permanent debt, preferred stock, and common stock. Firms may alter their DFL by changing the mix of permanent sources of capital. For example, increasing the proportion of debt and preferred stock in a firm's capital structure also increases its fixed financing costs. This change in capital structure increases DFL, which results in large increases in EPS when EBIT is high and large decreases in EPS when EBIT is low.

EXAMPLE 7-14: Taylor Publishing Company must raise $365,000 to finance its operations. The firm is considering three financing plans to raise the money. The company can issue common stock at $10 per share, obtain 8 percent debt financing, or issue 10 percent preferred stock at $50 per share. (Previous examples are based on Plan B.)

	Plan A	Plan B	Plan C
Common stock	$365,000	$200,000	$115,000
Debt	0	125,000	250,000
Preferred stock	0	40,000	0

Taylor expects to sell 15,000 books, which will produce an EBIT of $50,000. The firm's marginal income tax rate is 40 percent.

The impact of financial leverage on EPS for Taylor Publishing for each of the three plans is shown below:

	Plan A	Plan B	Plan C
EBIT	$50,000	$50,000	$50,000
− Interest expense	0	10,000	20,000
Earnings before taxes	$50,000	$40,000	$30,000
− Income taxes (40%)	20,000	16,000	12,000
Net income	$30,000	$24,000	$18,000
− Preferred stock dividend	0	4,000	0
Earnings available to common stockholders (EAC)	$30,000	$20,000	$18,000
Shares of common stock (n)	36,500	20,000	11,500
Earnings per share (EAC/n)	$0.82	$1.00	$1.57
DFL	1.00	1.50	1.67

The DFL for each plan is found using Equation 7-9.

$$DFL_A = \frac{\$50,000}{\$50,000 - \$0} = 1.00$$

$$DFL_B = \frac{\$50,000}{\$50,000 - \$10,000 - [\$4,000/(1 - 0.40)]} = 1.50$$

$$DFL_C = \frac{\$50,000}{\$50,000 - \$20,000} = 1.67$$

Plan A has no financial leverage because only common stock is used. Without financial leverage, a 1 percent change in EBIT produces a proportional 1 percent increase in EPS. This is indicated by a DFL of 1.00 for Plan A. Plan B uses financial leverage to magnify EPS. At an EBIT of $50,000, a 1 percent change in EBIT produces a 1.50 percent change in EPS for Plan B. Plan C has more financial leverage than Plan B as indicated by the higher amount of fixed financing costs, $20,000 for Plan C versus $14,000 for Plan B. At an EBIT of $50,000, a 1 percent change in EBIT produces a 1.67 percent change in EPS for Plan C. Figure 7-11 shows that as a plan's fixed financing costs rise, its DFL increases. Hence, financing plans with higher DFLs have steeper slopes as plotted in Figure 7-11.

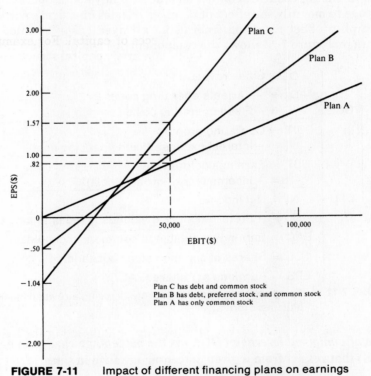

FIGURE 7-11   Impact of different financing plans on earnings per share for Taylor Publishing Company

D. *Financial risk* is the variability or uncertainty of earnings per share.

Financial risk is also the risk of being unable to cover fixed financing costs. Firms with highly unpredictable EPS have high financial risk whereas firms with highly predictable EPS have low financial risk. Firms have direct control over financial risk through the mix of debt and equity in their capital structure.

1. Financial leverage increases the variability of a firm's EPS and the risk of being unable to cover financing costs. Generally, the higher a firm's DFL, the greater its financial risk.

2. Changes in income tax rates may affect a firm's financial leverage. For example, lower tax rates increase both a firm's EPS and DFL, while higher tax rates have the opposite effect.

EXAMPLE 7-15: Using the information in Example 7-14 and Figure 7-11, how does the financial leverage associated with the three financing plans affect the financial risk for Taylor Publishing Company?

Holding other factors constant, the higher the financial leverage, the higher the financial risk. Plan A has no financial risk because it has no fixed financing costs. Plan B and Plan C have increasing degrees of financial leverage because of increasing fixed financing costs. Plan C results in a greater variability in EPS, due to its higher DFL, and a greater possibility of being unable to meet fixed financial costs if EBIT decreases. Thus, Taylor Publishing will assume more financial risk by adopting Plan C.

7-5. Combined Leverage and Overall Risk

Combined leverage is variability of EPS, given a change in sales. Combined leverage is not a distinct type of leverage, but measures total leverage due to both fixed operating costs and fixed financing costs. Combined leverage employs both operating leverage and financial leverage to magnify the effect of changes in sales on a firm's earnings per share. The joint multiplier effect resulting from using all fixed costs is called the degree of combined leverage. Figure 7-12 shows the components of combined leverage.

$$
\text{DCL}\left\{
\begin{array}{l}
\text{DOL}\left\{
\begin{array}{ll}
Q_p = & \text{Sales revenue} \\
-Q_v = & -\text{Variable operating costs} \\
-F = & -\text{Fixed operating costs} \\
\hline
\text{EBIT} = & \text{Operating profits} \\
\end{array}
\right. \\
\text{DFL}\left\{
\begin{array}{ll}
-I = & -\text{Interest expense (fixed financing cost)} \\
\hline
\text{EBT} = & \text{Earnings before taxes} \\
-t = & -\text{Income taxes (variable cost)} \\
\hline
\text{NI} = & \text{Net income} \\
-D_p = & -\text{Preferred stock dividends (fixed financing cost)} \\
\hline
\text{EAC} = & \text{Earnings available to common stockholders} \\
n = & \text{Shares of common stock outstanding} \\
\end{array}
\right. \\
\text{EPS} = \text{Earnings per share (EAC/n)}
\end{array}
\right.
$$

FIGURE 7-12   Components of combined leverage, using a revised income statement format

A. The *degree of combined leverage (DCL)* is the percentage change in earnings per share (EPS) that results from a given percentage change in sales.

The degree of combined leverage is computed in three ways.

1. Equation 7-10 computes the DCL using a percentage change formula which requires two different values for sales and EPS. The DCL is computed at a specific sales level, Q.

$$
\text{DCL at Q} = \frac{\text{Percentage change in EPS}}{\text{Percentage change in sales}}
$$

$$
= \frac{\dfrac{\triangle \text{EPS}}{\text{EPS}}}{\dfrac{\triangle \text{Sales}}{\text{Sales}}} \tag{7-10}
$$

where   Q = sales (units of output) where DCL is measured

$\triangle$EPS = change in EPS

$\triangle$Sales = change in sales

EXAMPLE 7-16: Use the information in Example 7-12 to calculate Taylor Publishing Company's degree of combined leverage when 15,000 books are sold.

Using Equation 7-10, the DCL equals 4.5 which means that each 1 percent change in sales volume results in a 4.5 percent change in EPS. As shown below, a 10 percent increase in sales produces a 45 percent (4.5 × 10 percent) increase in EPS.

$$\text{DCL at 15,000 units} = \frac{\left(\dfrac{\$1.45 - \$1.00}{\$1.00}\right)}{\left(\dfrac{\$660,000 - \$600,000}{\$600,000}\right)} = \frac{0.45}{0.10} = 4.5$$

2. Equation 7-11 is a second way to calculate DCL. The equation shows that the degree of combined leverage (DCL) is the product of the degree of operating leverage (DOL) and the degree of financial leverage (DFL).

$$\text{DCL at Q} = \text{DOL at Q} \times \text{DFL at Q} \qquad \textbf{(7-11)}$$

EXAMPLE 7-17: Using the information provided in Examples 7-8 and 7-12 and Equation 7-11, the combined leverage for Taylor Publishing Company at 15,000 units is calculated as follows:

$$\text{DCL at 15,000 units} = 3.0 \times 1.5 = 4.5$$

3. Equation 7-12 provides a third way to calculate DFL. This method simply substitutes Equation 7-7 and Equation 7-9 into Equation 7-11 to obtain the DCL.

$$\text{DCL at Q} = \frac{Q(p - v)}{Q(p - v) - F} \times \frac{Q(p - v) - F}{Q(p - v) - F - I - [D_p/(1 - t)]}$$

$$= \frac{Q(p - v)}{Q(p - v) - F - I - [D_p/(1 - t)]} \qquad \textbf{(7-12)}$$

EXAMPLE 7-18: Recall that $p = \$40$, $v = \$30$, and $F = \$100,000$, $I = \$10,000$, $D_p = \$4,000$, and $t = 40$ percent. Using Equation 7-12, the DCL at 15,000 units is 4.5, which is the same as that obtained using Equation 7-10 and Equation 7-11.

$$\text{DCL at 15,000 units} = \frac{(15,000)(\$40 - \$30)}{(15,000)(\$40 - \$30) - \$100,000 - \$10,000 - [\$4,000/(1 - 0.40)]}$$

$$= \frac{\$150,000}{\$33,333} = 4.5$$

B. *Overall risk* **is the variability or uncertainty in EPS resulting from both business and financial risk.**

Overall risk is also the risk of being unable to cover total costs. Generally, a firm's overall risk can be measured by the degree of combined leverage. Factors that influence business risk and financial risk combine to affect total risk. A firm's total risk is affected by its level of fixed operating and fixed financing costs. As fixed costs rise, the risk associated with covering these costs also increases. The ultimate risk of being unable to meet these costs is bankruptcy.

C. Firms may influence their overall risk by trading off business and financial leverage.

Equation 7-11 shows that DCL is a function of DOL and DFL. A firm may use different degrees of operating leverage and financial leverage to achieve a desired level of overall leverage and hence overall risk. For example, a firm with a high DOL may limit its overall risk by reducing fixed financing costs. This can be accomplished by decreasing the proportion of debt and preferred stock in its capital structure, which reduces DFL.

Firms are limited in the amount of leverage they can use to increase EPS. As a firm's overall riskiness increases, investors require higher rates of return to compensate for the higher risk. Thus, the cost of debt and preferred stock increases as risk increases, which tends to offset the gains achieved from using leverage.

RAISE YOUR GRADES

Can you explain . . . ?

☑ the meaning of breakeven analysis
☑ some assumptions and weaknesses of breakeven analysis
☑ the difference between fixed costs and variable costs
☑ the applications of breakeven analysis
☑ how to find the operating breakeven point
☑ what is meant by the term contribution margin
☑ how to construct a breakeven chart
☑ what is meant by cash breakeven analysis
☑ how to determine the overall breakeven point
☑ what is meant by the term *leverage*
☑ the difference between fixed operating costs and fixed financing costs
☑ why leverage involves a risk-return tradeoff
☑ the meaning of operating leverage
☑ how to determine the degree of operating leverage
☑ the relationship between operating leverage and business risk
☑ what is meant by the term *financial leverage*
☑ how to determine the degree of financial leverage
☑ how capital structure affects financial leverage
☑ the relationship between financial leverage and financial risk
☑ the meaning of the term *combined leverage*
☑ how to determine the degree of combined leverage
☑ the relationship between combined leverage and overall risk

SUMMARY

1. Breakeven analysis examines the relationships among a firm's sales, costs, and profits at various output levels.
2. Breakeven analysis is a useful planning and analysis tool, especially for a short time horizon, provided its assumptions are not ignored. The chief assumptions involve linearity, the accuracy of estimates, the accuracy of classifying costs, and the applicability to multiproduct firms.
3. Breakeven analysis separates costs into fixed costs that remain constant as sales volume changes and variable costs that have a direct relationship to sales volume.
4. Breakeven analysis is used to evaluate new products, to analyze modernization,

automation, and expansion programs, to examine pricing decisions, and to determine sales needed to reach a target profit.

5. The operating breakeven point is found by dividing fixed operating costs by the contribution margin, which is the difference between a product's price and variable cost per unit. The operating breakeven point is shown graphically on a breakeven chart at the point where the total operating revenue line intersects the total operating cost line.

6. Breakeven analysis can be modified to provide a cash breakeven point and an overall breakeven point. The simplifying assumptions underlying breakeven analysis can also be changed to produce more realistic nonlinear breakeven analysis.

7. Leverage involves a multiplier effect in which a change in an independent variable (such as sales) causes a greater change in a dependent variable (such as earnings per share).

8. Leverage is caused by the presence of fixed costs among a firm's overall costs. Operating leverage is created by fixed operating costs such as depreciation; financial leverage by fixed financing costs such as interest on debt and preferred stock dividends. Combining both operating leverage and financial leverage creates combined leverage.

9. Changes in fixed costs create different degrees of leverage which alter a firm's risk-return profile. Increasing fixed costs magnifies the potential return to stockholders but also increases the possibility that a firm may be unable to cover the fixed costs.

10. Operating leverage is the variability of operating profit, given a change in sales, and is measured by the degree of operating leverage (DOL).

11. The degree of operating leverage is the percentage change in earnings before interest and taxes (EBIT) divided by the percentage change in sales at a specific sales level. The greater the fixed operating costs, the more variable a firm's EBIT and the higher the DOL.

12. Business risk, which is the variability or uncertainty of EBIT, is affected by operating leverage and other factors. Holding these other factors constant, business risk changes in the same direction as operating leverage changes.

13. Financial leverage is the variability in earnings per share (EPS), given a change in operating profit, and is measured by the degree of financial leverage (DFL).

14. The degree of financial leverage is the percentage change in EPS divided by the percentage change in EBIT. The greater the fixed financial costs, the more variable a firm's EPS and the higher the DFL.

15. Financial risk, which is the variability of EPS, is affected by financial leverage and other factors. Holding these other factors constant, financial risk changes in the same direction as financial leverage changes.

16. Combined leverage is the variability in EPS, given a change in sales, and is measured by the degree of combined leverage (DCL).

17. The degree of combined leverage is the percentage change in EPS divided by the percentage change in sales. Operationally, DCL is obtained by multiplying DOL by DFL. The greater total fixed costs, the more variable a firm's EPS and the higher the DCL.

18. Overall risk is the variability or uncertainty in EPS resulting from both business and financial risk. The degree of combined leverage (DCL) provides a measure of a firm's overall risk. A firm may influence its overall risk by controlling the factors that affect risk, such as its level of fixed costs.

RAPID REVIEW

True or False

1. Breakeven analysis is also called cost-volume-profit analysis. [Section 7-1]

2. Breakeven analysis separates costs into three types: fixed, variable, and semivariable. [Section 7-1A]

3. Fixed costs remain constant over all output ranges. [Section 7-1A]

4. Variable costs vary indirectly with production output. [Section 7-1A]

5. Linear breakeven analysis assumes that both selling price and fixed cost per unit remain constant over the relevant range of output. [Section 7-1A]

6. Breakeven analysis assumes that a multiproduct firm maintains a constant product and sales mix. [Section 7-1A]

7. Breakeven analysis is most applicable using a long-term planning horizon. [Section 7-1A]

8. Breakeven analysis can be used to determine the impact that changing the selling price has on profits. [Section 7-1B]

9. The operating breakeven point is determined by dividing fixed operating costs by the contribution margin per unit. [Section 7-1C]

10. A firm's earnings before interest and taxes (EBIT) is zero at the operating breakeven point. [Section 7-1C]

11. A breakeven chart is plotted with dollar revenues and costs on the horizontal axis and units sold on the vertical axis. [Section 7-1C]

12. The total cost line passes through the origin on an operating breakeven chart when sales are zero. [Section 7-1C]

13. Total operating revenues equal total operating costs at the breakeven point. [Section 7-1C]

14. The cash breakeven point is lower than the operating breakeven point if a firm has noncash outlays. [Section 7-1D]

15. Nonlinear breakeven analysis may result in more than one breakeven point. [Section 7-1D]

16. Leverage involves a multiplier effect which describes the ability of fixed costs to magnify returns. [Section 7-2]

17. Fixed financing costs involve interest expense and common stock dividends. [Section 7-2A]

18. Changes in leverage alter a firm's returns but have no effect on the variability of returns. [Section 7-2C]

19. Operating leverage measures fluctuations in earnings per share (EPS) resulting from interest charges. [Section 7-3]

20. A degree of operating leverage (DOL) of 3.0 indicates that a 1 percent increase in EBIT produces a 3 percent increase in sales. [Section 7-3A]

21. The degree of operating leverage (DOL) changes when measured at different levels of sales. [Section 7-3B]

22. The degree of operating leverage (DOL) gets smaller as the base sales level approaches the operating breakeven point. [Section 7-3B]

23. Business risk is the variability or uncertainty of operating profits. [Section 7-3D]

24. Operating leverage effects business risk. [Section 7-3D]

25. Financial leverage is caused by the presence of fixed financing costs. [Section 7-4]

26. The greater the degree of financial leverage (DFL), the greater the sensitivity of EPS to a change in EBIT. [Section 7-4B]

27. Financial risk refers to the risk of being unable to cover fixed financial costs. [Section 7-4D]

28. Combined leverage refers to a firm's ability to use fixed costs to magnify the effect of changes in sales on earnings per share. [Section 7-5]

29. The degree of combined leverage (DCL) may be obtained by adding the degree of operating leverage (DOL) to the degree of financial leverage (DFL). [Section 7-5A]

30. Overall risk is the risk associated with a firm's ability to cover fixed operating and fixed financing costs. [Section 7-5B]

Multiple Choice

31. Fixed costs include all of the following except:

    (*a*) interest expense
    (*b*) direct labor
    (*c*) rent
    (*d*) depreciation

    [Section 7-1A]

32. Potential applications of breakeven analysis include:

    (*a*) evaluating new products
    (*b*) pricing policy decisions
    (*c*) examining the effect of automation
    (*d*) All of the above

    [Section 7-1B]

33. Business risk is influenced by all of the following except:

    (*a*) product demand
    (*b*) uncertainty of selling prices
    (*c*) financial leverage
    (*d*) operating cost structure of the firm

    [Section 7-3B]

34. All of the following are properties of financial leverage except:

    (*a*) The degree of financial leverage changes when measured at different base EBIT levels
    (*b*) Financial leverage applies only to positive changes in EBIT
    (*c*) A degree of financial leverage greater than 1.0 indicates favorable financial leverage.
    (*d*) Financial leverage is favorable when a firm earns more on invested funds than it pays for the related financing costs

    [Section 7-4B]

35. The degree of combined leverage indicates:

    (*a*) the percentage change in sales that results from a percentage change in EPS
    (*b*) the percentage change in EBIT that results from a percentage change in sales
    (*c*) the percentage change in EPS that results from a percentage change in EBIT
    (*d*) the percentage change in EPS that results from a percentage change in sales

    [Section 7-5A]

Answers

True and False

			Multiple Choice
1. True	11. False	21. True	31. b
2. False	12. False	22. False	32. d
3. False	13. True	23. True	33. c
4. False	14. True	24. True	34. b
5. True	15. True	25. True	35. d
6. True	16. True	26. True	
7. False	17. False	27. True	
8. True	18. False	28. True	
9. True	19. False	29. False	
10. True	20. False	30. True	

SOLVED PROBLEMS

PROBLEM 7-1: Segal Associates offers training courses to the general public. The firm is considering offering a new one-day course in Time Management. It estimates that its fixed costs will be $4,000 and its variable costs will be $50 per participant. Segal Associates plans to charge each participant $250.

(*a*) What is the contribution margin? Explain what it means.
(*b*) What is the operating breakeven point?
(*c*) How many participants must attend the course in order for Segal Associates to achieve a target operating profit of $2,000?

Answer:

(*a*) The contribution margin of $200 is calculated by subtracting the variable cost per unit of $50 from the price per unit of $250. Thus, each participant will contribute $200 to covering the firm's operating fixed costs. After the firm's fixed costs are completely covered (the firm has reached its operating breakeven point), each participant will contribute $200 towards the firm's operating profits.

(*b*) Substituting F = $4,000, p = $250, and v = $50 in Equation 7-1, the operating breakeven point is:

$$Q_b = \frac{\$4,000}{\$250 - \$50} = 20 \text{ participants}$$

(*c*) Substituting F = $4,000, TP = $2,000, p = $250, and v = $50 in Equation 7-3, the target profit point in units is:

$$Q_{tp} = \frac{\$4,000 + \$2,000}{\$250 - \$50} = 30 \text{ participants} \qquad \textbf{[Section 7-1C]}$$

PROBLEM 7-2: Referring to Problem 7-1, Segal Associates is considering two pricing strategies for its proposed Time Management course. Strategy A involves a charge of $250 per participant and Strategy B involves a charge of $350 per participant. If the firm charges $250 per participant it expects to attract 40 participants; if it charges $350 it expects only 25 participants. Fixed costs remain at $4,000 and variable costs at $50 per participant. If the firm's goal is to make as much operating profit as possible, what pricing strategy should it follow?

Answer: Using the revised income statement format shown in Figure 7-4, the operating profits under each strategy are as follows:

	Strategy A ($250 per person)	Strategy B ($350 per person)
Sales revenue	$10,000	$8,750
—Variable operating costs	2,000	1,250
—Fixed operating costs	4,000	4,000
Operating profits (EBIT)	$ 4,000	$3,500

Segal Associates should charge the lower price of $250 because it results in $500 ($4,000 − $3,500) more operating profits.   **[Section 7-1D]**

PROBLEM 7-3: Elegant Tie Company is planning to introduce a new line of ties with a college emblem. The firm expects to sell 16,000 ties to various colleges and universities for $10 each. Fixed costs are $35,000, variable costs are $6 per tie, and interest expenses are $5,000. At a production level of 16,000, the firm's projected operating profits (EBIT) are $29,000.

(a) What is the overall breakeven point in units?
(b) What is the degree of operating leverage?
(c) What is the degree of financial leverage?
(d) What is the degree of combined leverage?

Answer:

(a) Substituting $F = \$35,000$, $I = \$5,000$, $p = \$10.00$, and $v = \$6.00$ in Equation 7-5, the overall breakeven point is:

$$Q_{ob} = \frac{\$35,000 + \$5,000}{\$10 - \$6} = \frac{\$40,000}{\$4} = 10,000 \text{ ties} \qquad \textbf{[Section 7-1D]}$$

(b) Substituting $Q = 16,000$, $p = \$10.00$, $v = \$6.00$, and $F = \$35,000$ in Equation 7-7, the degree of operating leverage is 2.21

$$\text{DOL at 16,000 units} = \frac{(16,000)(\$10.00 - \$6.00)}{(16,000)(\$10 - \$6) - \$35,000}$$

$$= \frac{\$64,000}{\$29,000} = 2.21 \qquad \textbf{[Section 7-3A]}$$

(c) Substituting $Q = 16,000$, $p = \$10.00$, $v = \$6.00$, $F = \$35,000$, and $I = \$5,000$ in Equation 7-9, the degree of financial leverage is 1.21.

$$\text{DFL at \$29,000 EBIT} = \frac{(16,000)(\$10 - \$6) - \$35,000}{(16,000)(\$10 - \$6) - \$35,000 - \$5,000}$$

$$= \frac{\$29,000}{\$24,000} = 1.21 \qquad \textbf{[Section 7-4A]}$$

(d) Substituting the results shown in "b" and "c" above in Equation 7-12 produces a degree of combined leverage of 2.67.

$$\text{DCL at 16,000 units} = \frac{(16,000)(\$10 - \$6)}{(16,000)(\$10 - \$6) - \$35,000 - \$5,000}$$

$$= \frac{\$64,000}{\$24,000} = 2.67 \qquad \textbf{[Section 7-5A]}$$

Use the following data when answering Problems 7-4 through 7-13:

Farrelly Enterprises has fixed operating costs of $500,000, variable operating costs per unit of $20, and a selling price of $40. The firm's capital structure consists of a $600,000 loan at 10 percent interest, 10,000 shares of preferred stock paying an annual dividend of $3 per share, and 50,000 shares of common stock outstanding. Farrelly has a 34 percent tax rate.

PROBLEM 7-4: Calculate Farrelly's operating breakeven point in units and in dollar sales.

Answer: Substituting $F = \$500,000$, $p = \$40$, and $v = \$20$ in Equation 7-1, the operating breakeven point in units is:

$$Q_b = \frac{F}{p - v} = \frac{\$500,000}{\$40 - \$20} = 25,000 \text{ units}$$

Using Equation 7-2, the operating breakeven point in dollar sales is:

$$S_b = \frac{F}{1 - (v/p)} = \frac{\$500,000}{1 - (\$20/\$40)} = \$1,000,000 \qquad \textbf{[Section 7-1C]}$$

PROBLEM 7-5: Determine the total operating profit or loss at sales levels of 10,000 units, 25,000 units, and 40,000 units.

Answer: Using the revised income statement format shown in Figure 7-4, the operating profit or loss is:

	10,000 Units	25,000 Units	40,000 Units
Sales revenue	$400,000	$1,000,000	$1,600,000
Variable operating costs	200,000	500,000	800,000
Fixed operating costs	500,000	500,000	500,000
Operating profit (EBIT)	($300,000)	0	$ 300,000

[Section 7-1C]

PROBLEM 7-6: Draw a breakeven chart for Farrelly Enterprises and label all parts.

Answer: Figure 7-13 is the breakeven chart for Farrelly Enterprises. The total revenue (*TR*) line is drawn by plotting sales revenue at the levels shown in Problem 7-5 and connecting these values with a straight line. The total cost (*TC*) line is drawn in a similar fashion. The variable and fixed costs are added to get total cost and are then plotted. The intersection of *TR* and *TC* is the breakeven point. **[Section 7-1C]**

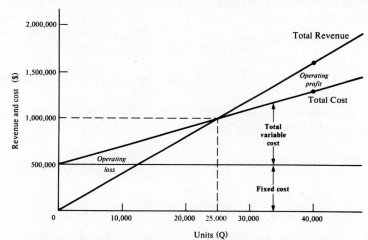

FIGURE 7-13   Linear breakeven analysis chart for Farrelly Enterprises

PROBLEM 7-7: Farrelly expects to earn $400,000 in operating profits during the next year. Calculate the target breakeven point in units and in dollar sales.

Answer: Using Equation 7-3, the target profit breakeven point in units is:

$$Q_{tp} = \frac{F + TP}{p - v} = \frac{\$500,000 + \$400,000}{\$40 - \$20} = 45,000 \text{ units}$$

The target profit breakeven point in dollar sales is obtained by multiplying the selling price per unit by the target profit breakeven point in units, $40 × 45,000 units = $1,800,000. **[Section 7-1C]**

PROBLEM 7-8: Suppose that $100,000 in fixed costs represents noncash outlays such as depreciation. Compute Farrelly's cash breakeven point in units and sales volume. How does the cash breakeven point compare with the operating breakeven point in Problem 7-4?

Answer: Using Equation 7-4, the cash breakeven point is:

$$Q_{cb} = \frac{F - N}{p - v} = \frac{\$500,000 - \$100,000}{\$40 - \$20} = 20,000 \text{ units}$$

The cash breakeven point in dollar sales is $40 × 20,000 units = $800,000. The cash breakeven point is lower than the operating breakeven point by 5,000 units, or $200,000.

[Section 7-1D]

PROBLEM 7-9: Determine the overall breakeven point in units and dollar sales.

Answer: Using Equation 7-5, the overall breakeven point is:

$$Q_{ob} = \frac{F + I + [D_{ps}/(1 - t)]}{p - v}$$

$$= \frac{\$500,000 + \$60,000 + [\$30,000/(1 - 0.34)]}{\$40 - \$20} = 30,273 \text{ units}$$

The overall breakeven point in dollar sales is $40 × 30,273 units = $1,210,920.

[Section 7-1D]

PROBLEM 7-10: Suppose Farrelly believes that the current price of $40 per unit is too high as competition increases. What effect will lowering the price to $36 per unit have on the firm's overall breakeven point? (Assume a $36 selling price for this problem only.)

Answer: Farrelly's overall breakeven point increases from 30,273 units to 37,841 units.

$$Q_{ob} = \frac{\$500,000 + 60,000 + [\$30,000/(1 - 0.34)]}{\$36 - \$20} = 37,841 \text{ units}$$

[Section 7-1D]

PROBLEM 7-11: Assume that the selling price remains at $40 per share and the base sales level is 40,000 units.

(a) Prepare an income statement showing the percentage change in EBIT if sales increase by 10 percent or decline by 10 percent.
(b) Compute Farrelly's degree of operating leverage (DOL) at 40,000 units using the percentage change formula, Equation 7-6.
(c) Indicate the properties of DOL illustrated in this example.

Answer:

(a) A 10 percent change in sales results in a 26.7 per change in EBIT as shown below:

Units	△Sales = −10.0% 36,000	40,000	△Sales = +10.0% 44,000
Sales revenue	$1,440,000	$1,600,000	$1,760,000
Variable operating costs	720,000	800,000	880,000
Fixed operating costs	500,000	500,000	500,000
Operating profit (EBIT)	$ 220,000	$ 300,000	$ 380,000
	△EBIT = −26.7%		△EBIT = +26.7%

[Section 7-1D]

(b) Using Equation 7-6, the DOL at 40,000 units is 2.67 which indicates that a 10 percent change in sales produces a 26.7 percent change in EBIT.

$$\text{DOL at 40,000 units} = \frac{\dfrac{\triangle\text{EBIT}}{\text{EBIT}}}{\dfrac{\triangle\text{Sales}}{\text{Sales}}}$$

$$\triangle\text{Sales} = -10\% \qquad\qquad \triangle\text{Sales} = +10\%$$

$$\text{DOL} = \frac{\left(\dfrac{\$80,000}{\$300,000}\right)}{\left(\dfrac{\$160,000}{\$1,600,000}\right)} = 2.67 \qquad \text{DOL} = \frac{\left(\dfrac{-\$80,000}{\$300,000}\right)}{\left(\dfrac{-\$160,000}{\$1,600,000}\right)} = 2.67$$

[Section 7-3B]

(c) This example shows that positive and negative changes in sales of equal magnitude from the same base sales level result in equal degrees of operating leverage. Another property shown is that DOL is positive above the operating breakeven point of 25,000 units.   [Section 7-3A]

PROBLEM 7-12: Farrelly expects to sell 45,000 units when the selling price is $40 per unit. The firm's EBIT is $400,000 when 45,000 units are sold.

(a) Calculate the degree of operating leverage.
(b) Calculate the degree of financial leverage.
(c) Calculate the degree of combined leverage.

Answer:

(a) Using Equation 7-7, the DOL is 2.25.

$$\text{DOL at 45,000 units} = \frac{Q(p - v)}{Q(p - v) - F}$$

$$= \frac{(45,000)(\$40 - \$20)}{(45,000)(\$40 - \$20) - \$500,000} = 2.25$$

[Section 7-3A]

(b) Using Equation 7-9, the DFL is 1.36.

$$\frac{\text{DFL at}}{\$400,000 \text{ EBIT}} = \frac{Q(p - v) - F}{Q(p - v) - I - [D_p/(1 - t)]}$$

$$= \frac{(45,000)(\$40 - \$20) - \$500,000}{(45,000)(\$40 - \$20) - \$500,000 - \$60,000 - [\$30,000/(1 - 0.34)]}$$

$$= 1.36$$

[Section 7-4A]

(c) Using Equation 7-11, the DCL is 3.06.

$$\text{DCL at 45,000 units} = \text{DOL} \times \text{DFL}$$

$$= 2.25 \times 1.36 = 3.06 \qquad \text{[Section 7-5A]}$$

PROBLEM 7-13: Farrelly is considering changing its capital structure by adding $300,000 in financing. Plan A involves obtaining new debt at a before-tax cost of 12 percent and Plan B involves issuing 5,000 shares of new common stock at $60 per share. The firm expects to sell 45,000 units at $40 per unit.

(a) Determine the earnings per share (EPS) under each financing alternative.
(b) Calculate the overall breakeven point under each plan.
(c) Calculate the degree of financial leverage (DFL) under each plan.
(d) Evaluate the attractiveness of each plan in terms of risk and return.

Answer:

(a) Using the format shown in Figure 7-4, the EPS under the additional debt financing plan is $3.41 versus $3.53 for the common stock financing.

	Plan A Debt	Plan B Common Stock
Sales revenue	$1,800,000	$1,800,000
—Variable operating costs	900,000	900,000
—Fixed operating costs	500,000	500,000
Operating profit (EBIT)	$ 400,000	$ 400,000
—Interest expense		
Old (10%)	60,000	60,000
New (12%)	36,000	0
Earnings before taxes	$ 304,000	$ 340,000
—Income taxes (34%)	103,360	115,600
Net income	$ 200,640	$ 224,000
—Preferred stock dividends	30,000	30,000
Earnings available to common stockholders (EAC)	$ 170,640	$ 194,400
Shares of common stock (n)	50,000	55,000
Earnings per share (EAC/n)	$3.41	$3.53

[Section 7-1D]

(*b*) Using Equation 7-5, the overall breakeven point with additional debt financing is 32,073 units versus 30,273 units with the common stock alternative.

$$\text{Q}_{ob} \text{ for Plan A} \atop \text{at 45,000 units} = \frac{\$500,000 + \$96,000 + [\$30,000/(1 - 0.34)]}{\$40 - \$20} = 32,073 \text{ units}$$

$$\text{Q}_{ob} \text{ for Plan B} \atop \text{at 45,000 units} = \frac{\$500,000 + \$60,000 + [\$30,000/(1 - 0.34)]}{\$40 - \$20} = 30,273 \text{ units}$$

[Section 7-1D]

(*c*) Using Equation 7-9, the DFL is 1.55 with debt financing and 1.36 with common stock financing.

$$\text{DFL for Plan A} \atop \text{at \$400,000 EBIT} = \frac{(45,000)(\$40 - \$20) - \$500,000}{(45,000)(\$40 - \$20) - \$500,000 - \$96,000 - [\$30,000/(1 - 0.34)]}$$

$$= 1.55$$

$$\text{DFL for Plan B} \atop \text{at \$400,000 EBIT} = \frac{(45,000)(\$40 - \$20) - \$500,000}{(45,000)(\$40 - \$20) - \$500,000 - \$60,000 - [\$30,000/(1 - 0.34)]}$$

$$= 1.36$$

[Section 7-4A]

(*d*) At estimated sales of 45,000 units, the common stock financing plan offers a higher return than the debt financing plan as indicated by its higher EPS, $3.53 versus $3.41. The debt financing plan is the riskier of the two because it has a higher overall breakeven point and a higher DFL. Holding other factors constant, new debt financing becomes more attractive as sales increase. However, the common stock plan provides higher return and lower risk when the sales level is 45,000 units.   **[Section 7-4A]**

8 FINANCIAL PLANNING, FORECASTING, AND BUDGETING

THIS CHAPTER IS ABOUT

- ☑ **Financial Planning**
- ☑ **Financial Forecasting**
- ☑ **Budgeting**
- ☑ **The Cash Budget**
- ☑ **Pro Forma Statements**

8-1. Financial Planning

Financial planning is the development of a set of plans for the orderly acquisition and utilization of capital. Financial planning is a key element of a firm's success because it provides a guide to its financial future. Through financial planning, a firm determines where it will obtain funds and how they will be used. Financial planning involves coordinating a firm's financial activities in order to maximize shareholder wealth.

A. The financial planning process consists of five major steps.

Figure 8-1 on page 151 illustrates the steps in the financial planning process. They are:

1. *Set corporate goals.* The starting point of financial planning is establishing long-range goals. Financial goals are "ends" the firm wants to achieve that are financially oriented. The overriding goal of the firm should be maximization of stockholders' wealth.

2. *Develop long-term financial plans.* Long-term financial plans reflect not only what a firm expects to achieve in the long run, but also general guidelines on how to get there. Financial forecasts serve as inputs to long-term financial plans. Because of the long-term nature of these plans, usually two to ten years, they are somewhat tentative and are revised as new information becomes available. These plans focus on such areas as implementing proposed capital expenditure programs, raising additional financing, and acquiring new products or businesses or divesting old ones.

3. *Develop short-term financial plans.* Short-term financial plans reflect a firm's expected short-run financial outcomes and activities and generally cover a one- or two-year period. Sales forecasts also serve as inputs in developing short-term financial plans. These plans provide greater detail and focus more on cash flows than long-term financial plans.

4. *Develop individual budgets.* Once management determines a plan of action for the future, these plans are incorporated into budgets. A **budget** is a financial expression of management's plans. Budgets specify the resources required to achieve specific results and serve as performance standards against which operations are compared, evaluated, and adjusted. Numerous individual budgets are prepared, including sales, production, selling expense, and administrative budgets.

5. *Develop a consolidated budget.* Individual budgets are then combined to form a single consolidated budget. This is used in turn to prepare projected cash budgets and pro forma financial statements. These documents reflect the firm's expectations in terms of cash flows, profitability, and financial condition.

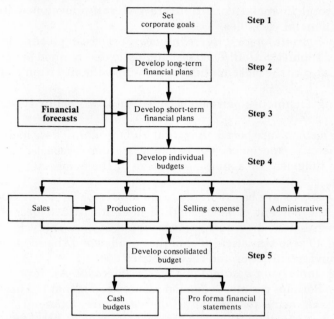

FIGURE 8-1   Steps in the financial planning process.

B. Planning, budgeting, and forecasting are interrelated.

Planning, budgeting, and forecasting are related, but different, processes. Before budgets are developed, managers set goals and develop plans. Budgets specify the financial resources needed to carry out plans. Hence, budgeting is part of the planning process. Forecasts indicate what the firm expects to happen, while goals represent what a firm wants to happen. Forecasts do not plan for a result, but predict something such as the level of inflation or interest rates. Forecasting is needed to do planning and budgeting but it is not the same thing.

8-2. Financial Forecasting

Financial forecasting is the process of projecting or estimating some future financial event or condition of a firm. It serves as the basis for establishing budgets, estimating future financial needs, and monitoring a firm's financial affairs. Forecasting is an important part of a financial manager's job, but making reliable forecasts is difficult.

The forecasting process generally begins with the sales forecast. A **sales forecast** is an estimate of a firm's sales for a specified future period. Sales forecasts are key inputs for many of a firm's activities, such as production scheduling, plant design, inventory management, personnel planning, and financial planning and budgeting. However, forecasting sales is difficult because future sales depend on many factors both internal and external to the firm. Internal factors include the firm's pricing policy, production capacity, advertising and other promotion, product/service characteristics, and sales force quality. External factors include competition, industry conditions, and overall economic conditions. Internal factors are generally within management's control, but external factors are not. It is difficult to forecast the behavior of things over which there is no control.

A. Forecasting involves three basic steps.

1. *Identify the individual financial variables to forecast.* The forecasting process begins by determining which variables to forecast. Sales is usually the first variable forecasted because it is the most important element in financial planning. Forecasts of a firm's total financial condition are generally developed from forecasts of individual financial variables.

2. *Apply the appropriate forecasting techniques.* Forecasting techniques vary widely in their level of sophistication. The most sophisticated method is not necessarily the best. It must also be the most applicable to the specific situation and the needs of the manager.

   Forecasting techniques can be classified into two major types, subjective and objective.

   - *Subjective methods* are based on insight and opinion. These methods make use of the forecaster's experience. For example, a sales forecast may be based on the subjective judgment of a single executive or the composite view of many sales managers.

   - *Objective methods* are based on facts and analyses. These methods include trend forecasts, the percent of sales method, and statistical forecasting techniques such as regression, moving averages, input-output analysis, and exponential smoothing. (These statistical techniques are beyond the scope of this book, but may be found in statistics and econometrics books.)

3. *Examine the underlying assumptions of the forecasts.* All forecasts are based on assumptions. Perhaps the most common assumption is that the firm's past financial condition is an accurate predictor of its future financial condition. If the assumptions are not valid, then the forecasts may be of little value. The financial manager should examine the reasonableness of the assumptions and determine the forecast's sensitivity to changes in the assumptions. If changing an assumption has little impact on the forecast, then this assumption is not critical. The financial manager should also adjust the forecast to reflect internal and external factors that may not have been taken into account by the forecasting method.

B. *Trend forecasts* project historical values of a single variable into the future.

Trend forecasts are based on historical data about an individual financial variable. A trend forecast can be made by using statistical methods, averaging past historical relationships, or by plotting values of some relevant variable on a scatter diagram and then drawing a trend line. A **trend line** is the line that best fits the overall data. Trend lines may be linear (straight line) or nonlinear (curved line). A trend line which passes through the origin denotes a constant ratio between the variables. Trend forecasts ignore possible changes in factors which may invalidate the assumption that past trends will continue into the future.

EXAMPLE 8-1: Jennings Industries wishes to forecast future sales based on the historical sales given below.

Year	Sales *(in thousands of dollars)*
19x1	$20,300
19x2	25,000
19x3	28,700
19x4	26,000
19x5	30,100
19x6	36,300
19x7	38,100
19x8	40,000

Using the trend line shown in Figure 8-2, Jennings' sales are estimated to be approximately $43,000,000 in 19x9. A linear trend line best fits the data.

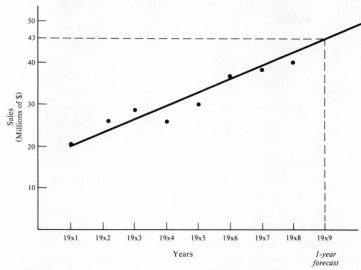

FIGURE 8-2   Trend analysis for Jennings Industries.

C. *Percent of sales forecasts* **are forecasts based on the relationship between sales and some other financial variable.**

Forecasts of one variable (the *forecast variable*) are often based on a forecast for another variable (the *base variable*). Sales are the most common base for forecasts using ratios because most financial variables are related to sales over the long run. In the short run, some variables, such as fixed assets and fixed costs, are independent of sales.

There are four important traits to a percent of sales forecast.

1. A percent of sales forecast for an individual financial variable involves three steps:
   • *Estimating the ratio between the forecast variable and sales.* Historical data and subjective judgment are frequently used to estimate the relationship between the two variables.
   • *Forecasting sales.*
   • *Forecasting the variable using Equation 8-1.*

PERCENT OF SALES FORECAST FOR A SINGLE VARIABLE $\dfrac{\text{Forecast}}{\text{variable}} = \text{Ratio} \times \dfrac{\text{Sales}}{\text{forecast}}$ **(8-1)**

EXAMPLE 8-2: *Recall the sales forecast in Example 8-1.* Jennings Industries wishes to forecast its inventory level for 19x9. Past relationships between sales and inventory show a tendency for higher sales to require higher inventories. The ratio of inventory to sales is estimated to be 2.5 percent. Substituting a ratio of inventory to sales of 0.025 and a sales forecast of $43,000,000 in Equation 8-1 the expected inventory level is

Inventory forecast = 0.025 × $43,000,000 = $1,075,000

2. The percent of sales method is useful for short-term forecasting. The percent of sales method assumes that the relationships between the forecast variable and sales remain constant. The assumption of constant relationships is generally more realistic in the short term.

EXAMPLE 8-3: Refer to the following data for Jennings Industries.

	Year	Inventory	Sales
		(in thousands of dollars)	
Historical	19x1	$620	$20,300
	19x2	720	25,000
	19x3	810	28,700
	19x4	860	26,000
	19x5	880	30,100
	19x6	950	36,300
	19x7	950	38,100
	19x8	1,000	40,000
Forecast	1-year	?	43,000
	5-year	?	60,000

(*a*) The relationship is not constant between inventory and sales because inventory has generally decreased as a percent of sales over time. Figure 8-3 shows a trend which represents the average past relationship between inventory and sales. A constant inventory-to-sales ratio would be indicated if the trend line went through the origin. That is, inventory would be zero when sales are zero.

Year	Sales/Inventory (%)
19x1	3.1
19x2	2.9
19x3	2.8
19x4	3.3
19x5	2.9
19x6	2.6
19x7	2.5
19x8	2.5

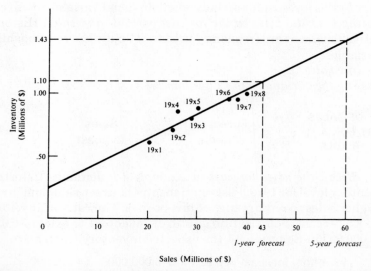

FIGURE 8-3   Relationship between inventory and sales for Jennings Industries.

(*b*) Inventory forecasts using the percent of sales and trend forecast methods are as follows (assume a 2.5 percent inventory-to-sales ratio when using the percent of sales method):

Inventory Forecasts for Jennings Industries

Percent of sales method
1-year forecast $1,075,000 = 0.025 × $43,000,000
5-year forecast $1,500,000 = 0.025 × $60,000,000

Trend forecasts (using Figure 8-3)
1-year forecast $1,100,000 at forecast sales of $43,000,000
5-year forecast $1,430,000 at forecast sales of $60,000,000

(c) For the one-year forecasts, the results of the two methods are reasonably close and differ by only $25,000. For the five-year forecasts, the discrepancy between the forecasts widens to $70,000. In this example, trends forecasts are more appropriate because the assumption that inventory is a constant percent of sales does not hold.

3. The percent of sales method may be used to forecast external financing requirements. The percent of sales method permits a firm to forecast the amount of external financing needed to support a sales increase. The method assumes that specific balance sheet accounts change directly with sales and remain a fixed percentage of sales.

- On the assets side, current assets including cash, accounts receivable, and inventory generally increase spontaneously with increases in sales. Fixed assets are generally independent of sales unless a firm is operating at full capacity, in which case fixed assets must also increase to support a higher sales level.
- On the liabilities and stockholders' equity side, current liabilities including accounts payable, notes payable, and accrued wages and taxes generally increase spontaneously with sales. Retained earnings may also increase, but not in direct proportion to increases in sales. Permanent sources of capital, such as bonds, preferred stock, and common stock, do not increase spontaneously with increases in sales.

Equation 8-2 shows the procedure for determining the required amount of external financing using the percent of sales method.

$$\begin{matrix} \text{External funds} \\ \text{needed} \end{matrix} = \begin{matrix} \text{Increase in} \\ \text{assets} \end{matrix} - \begin{matrix} \text{Increase in} \\ \text{liabilities} \end{matrix} - \begin{matrix} \text{Increase in} \\ \text{retained earnings} \end{matrix}$$

$$= \frac{A}{S}(\triangle S) - \frac{L}{S}(\triangle S) - (PM)(PS)(1 - d) \qquad \textbf{(8-2)}$$

where
$\dfrac{A}{S}$ = assets that increase spontaneously with sales as a percentage of current sales

$\dfrac{L}{S}$ = liabilities that increase spontaneously with sales as a percentage of current sales

$\triangle S$ = change in sales

PM = profit margin on sales

PS = projected sales

d = dividend payout ratio (the percentage of earnings paid out in dividends)

EXAMPLE 8-4: Jennings Industries wants to forecast its external financing requirements for 19x9. The firm's current sales are $40,000,000. Next year Jennings expects to increase sales by $3,000,000, earn a profit margin on sales of 5 percent, and pay 50 percent of its earnings out in dividends. The firm has sufficient capacity to increase sales to $43,000,000 without acquiring additional fixed assets. Jennings believes that all current assets and only accounts payable vary directly with sales.

Jennings Industries
Balance Sheet
December 31, 19x8
(in thousands of dollars)

Cash	$ 750	Accounts payable	$ 1,350
Accounts receivable	2,250	Other current liabilities	150
Inventory	1,000	Total current liabilities	$ 1,500
Total current assets	$ 4,000		
Fixed assets	15,000		
Less accumulated		Long-term debt (10%)	6,000
depreciation	5,000	Common stock	5,000
Net fixed assets	10,000	Retained earnings	1,500
Total assets	$14,000	Total liabilities and equity	$14,000

The balance sheet items which vary directly with sales are shown below as a percentage of $40,000,000 in current sales.

Jennings Industries
Balance Sheet
December 31, 19x8
(as a percentage of sales)

Cash	1.875	Accounts payable	3.375
Accounts receivable	5.625	Other current liabilities	n.a.*
Inventory	2.500	Total current liabilities	3.375
Total current assets	10.000	Long-term debt	n.a.
		Common stock	n.a.
Fixed assets	n.a.	Retained earnings	n.a.
Total assets	10.000	Total liabilities and equity	3.375

* n.a. = not applicable

The following figures are inserted in Equation 8-2: $A/S = 0.10$, $L/S = 0.03375$, $\triangle S = \$3,000,000$, $PM = 0.05$, $PS = \$43,000,000$, and $d = 0.50$.

$$\text{External funds needed} = (0.10)(\$3,000,000) - (0.03375)(\$3,000,000)$$
$$- (0.05)(\$43,000,000)(1 - 0.50)$$
$$= \$300,000 - \$101,250 - \$1,075,000 = -\$876,250$$

The negative balance shows that Jennings does not need any external funds to finance a $3,000,000 increase in sales. In fact, the firm has $876,250 in additional funds available.

4. The percent of sales method may be used to forecast income statements and balance sheets. The percent of sales method begins with a sales forecast. Income statement or balance sheet accounts that vary proportionately with sales are usually estimated based on historical relationships. These percentages are multiplied by estimated sales and then are adjusted to account for expected future events and trends. Items that do not vary directly with sales are also estimated and used to forecast future financial statements. The major advantage of the percent of sales method of forecasting is that it is simple to use.

EXAMPLE 8-5: The management of Jennings Industries wants to forecast its income statement for the year ending December 31, 19x9, assuming:

1. Sales are forecast to be $43,000,000.
2. Items varying directly with sales are:

   • Cost of goods sold at 66 percent of sales.
   • Other operating expenses at 20 percent of sales.

3. Items not varying directly with sales are:
   - Total depreciation expense, estimated to be $1,120,000.
   - Interest expense, which remains unchanged from 19x8 at $600,000.
4. An income tax rate of 50 percent. (This assumption is for tax purposes only.)
5. A dividend payout ratio of 50 percent. The **dividend payout ratio** is the percentage of earnings distributed to stockholders in the form of dividends.

The forecasted income statement using the percent of sales method would appear as follows:

Jennings Industries
Forecasted Income Statement
For the Year Ending December 31, 19x9
(in thousands of dollars)

Net sales...	$43,000
Cost of goods sold (0.66 × $43,000).......................	28,380
Gross profit...	$14,620
Other operating expenses (0.20 × $43,000)...............	8,600
Depreciation..	1,120
Earnings before interest and taxes.........................	$ 4,900
Interest expense (0.10 × $6,000)...........................	600
Earnings before taxes..	$ 4,300
Income taxes (0.50)*...	2,150
Net income (0.05 × $43,000)................................	$ 2,150
Dividends (0.05)...	1,075
Additions to retained earnings..............................	$ 1,075

A 50 percent tax rate is used for illustrative purposes only.

EXAMPLE 8-6: The management for Jennings Industries wants to forecast the balance sheet for the year ending December 31, 19x9 using the assumptions in Example 8-4 and the additions to retained earnings of $1,075,000. If the assets do not equal the liabilities and stockholders' equity, they plan to "plug in" additional available or required funds as needed to balance the statement.

The forecasted balance sheet for Jennings would appear as shown below. The plug-in figure of $1,996,250 (rounded to $1,996,000) represents the $876,250 in additional available funds, using Equation 8-1 in Example 8-4, plus $1,120,000 in depreciation as a noncash outlay.

Jennings Industries
Forecasted Balance Sheet
December 31, 19x9
(in thousands of dollars)

Cash...........................	$ 806	Accounts payable................	$ 1,450
Accounts receivable.............	2,419	Other current liabilities..........	150
Inventory.......................	1,075	Total current liabilities........	$ 1,601
Total current assets...........	$ 4,300		
Fixed assets.............. 15,000			
Less accumulated			
depreciation........... 6,120		Long-term debt (10%)...........	6,000
Net fixed assets.................	8,880	Common stock..................	5,000
Additional available funds.......	1,996	Retained earnings...............	2,575
Total assets..................	$15,176	Total liabilities and equity.....	$15,176

8-3. Budgeting

Budgeting is the process of formulating a written statement that details the firm's financial plans in numerical terms for a limited future period. The written statement is called a **budget**. Budgeting is an integral part of the overall financial planning process. Once management determines its future plans, these plans are incorporated into a budget.

A. A budget is used for three major purposes: planning, coordination, and control.

1. *Planning.* Budgeting forces managers to anticipate and prepare for changing conditions. Budgets are explicit expressions of management plans.
2. *Coordination.* Budgeting helps managers to coordinate their efforts. In doing so, they must determine the relationship between their departments and the firm as a whole. The budgetary process also identifies conflicting goals and interests. This helps resolve differences which could cause less efficient allocation of a firm's resources.
3. *Control.* Budgets serve as standards against which actual results are compared and evaluated. Monitoring differences between actual and budgeted amounts helps managers measure performance and alerts them to matters which need corrective action. Budgets are indispensable tools for effectively administrating a financial plan.

B. Budgets are classified into three types: operational, financial, and capital.

1. *Operational budgets* reflect a firm's short-term financial plans and relate directly to operating activities involving revenues and expenses. Examples of different types of operating budgets include the sales budget, the production budget, the selling expense budget, and the administrative budget.

   - The *sales budget* is a financial plan involving the expected dollar volume of a firm's products and services. The sales budget is the first budget prepared and serves as the basis for the firm's budgeting activities in other areas. This budget is usually prepared by the marketing department.
   - The *production budget* shows the amount and timing of the funds required to produce a firm's products. This type of budget includes raw materials, direct labor, purchases, and manufacturing overhead incurred in the production process. The production budget is usually prepared by the manufacturing department.
   - The *selling expense budget* contains the various costs of advertising and selling a firm's products or services.
   - The *administrative budget* reflects the other expenses incurred in a firm's overall operation, such as general office and executive staff expenses.

   These and other individual operational budgets are combined to form a firm's overall operating budget as a *pro forma (projected) income statement*, which estimates a firm's revenues, costs, and profitability for the planning period.

2. *Financial budgets* show how a firm's operations are affected by financing and investing activities. The major financial budgets are the cash budget, pro forma balance sheet, and pro forma statement of changes in financial position.
3. *Capital budgets* are projected expenditures on long-term projects. These projects are planned additions to a firm's fixed assets such as the acquisition of land, buildings, and equipment that are usually expected to be placed in service during the next year. Thus, the capital budget also affects the operating and financial budgets of that year.

8-4. The Cash Budget

The **cash budget** is a projection of cash receipts and cash disbursements over some future time period. The cash budget is used to anticipate fluctuations in the level of cash and to forecast the firm's future financial needs (cash surpluses and cash shortages). If a firm's ending cash balance exceeds a minimum cash balance, the surplus funds can be invested to increase a firm's return. The cash budget also serves as an early warning of potential cash problems. If a cash shortage is projected, the financial manager has time to make financing arrangements in order to ensure timely payments to creditors and others. Finally, the cash budget is used as a control mechanism to examine variances between actual and budgeted cash flows.

A. Preparing a cash budget involves six steps.

1. *Select the time horizon.* The **time horizon** is the planning period covered by a cash budget. The time horizon depends on management needs. Cash budgets are usually developed on a monthly basis, but firms with more volatile cash flows may prepare weekly or daily cash budgets.
2. *Forecast sales.* The sales forecast is the cornerstone of the cash budget because it is used to estimate many variables contained in the cash budget. The accuracy of a cash budget depends largely on the accuracy of the sales forecast.
3. *Estimate cash receipts.* **Cash receipts** are the cash inflows expected during the period. A separate schedule is usually prepared to determine total cash receipts. Cash receipts result from:

   - Cash sales
   - Collections of accounts receivable
   - Other items not directly related to sales, including interest received, dividends received, proceeds from the sale of assets such as equipment, and proceeds from the sale of stocks and bonds.

4. *Estimate cash disbursements.* **Cash disbursements** are the cash outflows expected during the period. A separate schedule is generally prepared to determine total cash disbursements. Items requiring cash disbursements include:

   - Current cash purchases
   - Accounts payable resulting from purchases in prior periods
   - Direct labor
   - Factory overhead
   - Other operating items such as utilities and leases, selling expenses, and general and administrative expenses
   - Capital expenditures
   - Taxes
   - Interest
   - Dividends

5. *Compute the net cash flow.* The **net cash flow** is the difference between the cash receipts and the cash disbursements for the period.
6. *Develop a cash summary.* A **cash summary** shows whether the firm requires additional financing or has excess cash over a specific time horizon. As Figure 8-4 illustrates, a cash summary is determined by:

   - Adding the beginning cash to the firm's net cash flow to get the ending cash balance for a period.
   - Subtracting the minimum cash balance from the ending cash to determine the cash surplus or cash shortage. The **minimum cash balance** is the desired amount of cash a firm wants to have on hand during any period. This balance depends largely on the certainty of a firm's environment. Firms in more volatile environments with more uncertain cash flows generally maintain higher minimum cash balances than do firms in more stable environments. A *cash surplus* occurs when the ending cash exceeds the minimum cash balance. A *cash shortage* occurs when the ending cash is less than the minimum cash balance.

	Period 1	Period 2	$\cdots$	Period n
Cash receipts	_____	_____	$\cdots$	_____
—Cash disbursements	_____	_____	$\cdots$	_____
Net cash flow	_____	_____	$\cdots$	_____
+Beginning cash	_____	_____	$\cdots$	_____
Ending cash	_____	_____	$\cdots$	_____
—Minimum cash balance	_____	_____	$\cdots$	_____
Cash surplus	_____	_____	$\cdots$	_____
Cash shortage	_____	_____	$\cdots$	_____

Cash Summary { Net cash flow, +Beginning cash, Ending cash, —Minimum cash balance, Cash surplus, Cash shortage }

FIGURE 8-4   The general format of a cash budget.

Figure 8-4 shows the general format of a cash budget.

B. The cash budget typically contains three major sections: cash receipts, cash disbursements, and cash summary.

Some cash budgets also contain a financing section which details the expected amount of borrowing and repayment of debt during the budget period.

EXAMPLE 8-7: Jennings Industries' management wants to develop and interpret cash budgets for January, February, and March 19x9, based on the following assumptions:

Cash receipts

1. Sales are $3,000,000 in December 19x8 and $3,200,000 per month in January through March 19x9. These sales are 25 percent in cash and 75 percent on credit. Credit sales represent accounts receivable which are collected during the month following the sale. Bad debts are negligible.

Cash disbursements

2. Monthly purchases are 50 percent of sales. Ten percent of purchases are cash and 90 percent are credit. Credit purchases represent accounts payable which are paid in the month following the purchase.
3. Direct labor is 5 percent of sales and factory overhead is 6 percent of sales. Other operating costs are 20 percent of sales and include selling, general, and administrative expenses. These costs are paid during the month in which they are incurred. Depreciation is not included as an operating cost because it is a noncash outlay.
4. The capital budget requires a payment of $1,000,000 in March to purchase new equipment.
5. Quarterly income tax payments are estimated to be $687,000 and are made in March.
6. Dividend payments are estimated to be $344,000 and are paid in March.
7. The beginning cash balance is $750,000, but the firm wants to maintain a minimum cash balance of $800,000 throughout the quarter.

Figure 8-5 shows the monthly cash budgets for Jennings Industries for the first quarter of 19x9. The firm has cash surpluses in January and February and a cash shortage in March. Additional plans are needed to invest unnecessary idle cash and to acquire funds to cover cash deficiencies.

Jennings Industries
Cash Budget for the First Quarter of 19x9
(in thousands of dollars) } Step 1

Schedule A—Cash Receipts

Sales Forecast	December $3,000	January $3,200	February $3,200	March $3,200 } Step 2
Cash sales (25%)	$ 750	$ 800	$ 800	$ 800 ⎫
Collection of accounts receivable				
1-month lag		2,250	2,400	2,400 ⎬ Step 3
Total cash receipts....................		$3,050	$3,200	$3,200 ⎭

Schedule B—Cash Disbursements

Purchases (50% of sales).................	$1,500	$1,600	$1,600	$1,600 ⎫
Payments to suppliers:				
Cash purchases (10%)	150	160	160	160
Payment of accounts payable,				
1-month lag		1,350	1,440	1,440
Direct labor................................		160	160	160
Factory overhead.........................		192	192	192 ⎬ Step 4
Other operating costs.....................		640	640	640
Capital expenditure.......................				1,000
Income tax payment				687
Other cash outlays				
Dividend payments.....................				344
Total cash disbursements		$2,502	$2,592	$4,623 ⎭

Cash Budget

Total cash receipts		$3,050	$3,200	$3,200 ⎫
−Total cash disbursements		2,502	2,592	4,623 ⎬ Step 5
Net cash flow.............................		$ 548	$ 608	($1,423) ⎭
+Beginning cash.........................		750	1,298	1,906 ⎫
Ending cash		$1,298	$1,906	$ 483
−Minimum cash balance.................		800	800	800 ⎬ Step 6
Cash surplus		$ 498	$1,106	0
Cash shortage............................		0	0	$ 317 ⎭

FIGURE 8-5   Cash budget for Jennings Industries during the first quarter of 19x9.

8-5. Pro Forma Statements

The major difference between pro forma statements and actual financial statements is timing. Pro forma statements, also called **budgeted** or **forecasted statements**, forecast future events whereas actual financial statements concern past events. Pro forma statements serve as important planning and control tools. For example, pro forma statements provide explicit information about management's forecasts of the future. By comparing the pro forma statements to the actual results at the end of the period, management can determine whether it met, exceeded, or failed to meet its goals.

A. Preparing pro forma statements involves three major steps.

1. *Select the time horizon.* As with cash budgets, the time horizon is the time period for which the pro forma statements are prepared. The time horizon chosen depends on the purpose of the analysis.

2. *Develop estimates.* Pro forma income statements provide estimates of various revenues and expenses, and pro forma balance sheets provide estimates of assets, liabilities, and stockholders' equity. The financial manager sometimes prepares multiple sets of pro forma statements using a different set of assumptions for each. This approach, called **sensitivity analysis**, allows managers to evaluate the sensitivity of their forecasts to changes in specific assumptions. For example, projects can be based on a pessimistic, a most-likely, or an optimistic sales forecast. The methods used for forecasting these amounts are the same as discussed previously and involve both qualitative and quantitative approaches.

3. *Construct the pro forma statements.* Pro forma statements can be developed indirectly using the cash budget as a base or directly using the percent of sales method. The percent of sales method for preparing pro formas is a short-cut approach discussed in Section 8-2C. A longer approach for pro forma statement preparation is based on the cash budget plus supplementary information. This longer approach is discussed below.

B. The *pro forma income statement* is a forecast of a firm's revenues, expenses, and profits or losses over the time horizon.

1. A cash budget provides much of the information needed to develop a pro forma income statement. Both statements are prepared for the same time horizon.

2. Pro forma income statements exclude some information contained in a cash budget. Income statements are generally prepared on an accrual basis rather than on a cash basis. The *accrual basis* recognizes revenues as they are earned and expenses as they are incurred, which is usually not when cash changes hands. Excluded items include cash receipts from financing sources such as the sale of stocks and bonds, and cash disbursements for capital expenditures such as plant and equipment.

3. Supplementary information is needed to prepare a pro forma income statement. Information not provided in a cash budget but required for the pro forma income statement includes:

   - Depreciation expense, which is a noncash outlay.
   - Income tax rate.
   - Inventory levels. Cost of goods sold is the cost of inventory sold and is not usually the same as payments for inventory acquired. The difference between beginning and ending inventory levels for the period affects the cost of goods sold.

EXAMPLE 8-8: *Refer to the data in Example 8-7 and Figure 8-5.* Jennings' management wants to determine the total cost of goods sold during the first quarter of 19x9, under the following conditions:

(a) Beginning and ending inventory are $1,000,000.
(b) Ending inventory is greater than beginning inventory by $200,000.
(c) Ending inventory is less than beginning inventory by $200,000. Depreciation relating to the manufacturing function is possible to inventory, but depreciation relating to selling, general, and administrative expenses is not. Total depreciation for the first quarter is $450,000 of which 50 percent is applied to cost of goods sold.

Figure 8-6 shows the effect of changing inventory levels on the cost of goods sold. Selling less inventory than was produced during the period increases ending inventory and decreases the cost of goods sold used in the income statement. Selling more inventory than was produced has the opposite effect; ending inventory decreases and cost of goods sold increases. These results also show that cost of goods sold may include depreciation which is not included in the cash budget.

Jennings Industries
Cost of Goods Manufactured and Sold
For the Quarter Ended March 31, 19x9
(in thousands of dollars)

	Ending Inventory		
Cost of goods manufactured and sold	20% Decrease	Remains the same	20% Increase
Beginning inventory	$1,000	$1,000	$1,000
+Cost of goods manufactured			
Purchases (direct materials)	4,800	4,800	4,800
Direct labor	480	480	480
Factory overhead	576	576	576
Depreciation	225	225	225
=Cost of goods available for sale	$7,081	$7,081	$7,081
−Ending inventory	800	1,000	1,200
=Cost of goods sold	$6,281	$6,081	$5,881

FIGURE 8-6   Impact of changing inventory levels on the cost of goods sold for
Jennings Industries for the quarter ended March 31, 19x9.

EXAMPLE 8-9: *Recall the data in Example 8-7 and Example 8-8.* In constructing monthly pro forma income statements for the entire first quarter of 19x9, Jennings assumes the following:

(*a*) Beginning and ending inventory levels are $1,000,000 for each month.
(*b*) Cost of goods sold is $2,027,000 per month including $75,000 depreciation per month.
(*c*) Additional depreciation of $75,000 per month is applied to non-manufacturing functions.
(*d*) The tax rate is 50 percent.

Jennings' pro forma income statements are shown in Figure 8-7.

Jennings Industries
Pro Forma Income Statements
For the First Quarter 19x9
(in thousands of dollars)

	January	February	March	Total
Net sales	$3,200	$3,200	$3,200	$9,600
Cost of goods sold	2,027	2,027	2,027	6,081
Gross profit	$1,173	$1,173	$1,173	$3,519
Other operating expenses	640	640	640	1,920
Depreciation	75	75	75	225
Earnings before taxes	$ 458	$ 458	$ 458	$1,374
Income taxes (50%)*	229	229	229	687
Net income	$ 229	$ 229	$ 229	$ 687
Dividends	0	0	344	344
Addition to retained earnings	$ 229	$ 229	($ 115)	$ 343

* *A 50 percent tax rate is used for illustrative purposes only.*

FIGURE 8-7   Pro forma income statements for Jennings Industries for the first
quarter 19x9.

C. The *pro forma balance sheet* **is a forecast of a firm's assets, liabilities, and stockholders' equity at the end of the period.**

A pro forma balance sheet can be developed based on a cash budget, a pro forma income statement, the beginning balance sheet, and supplementary data. Balance sheet accounts can be forecast using Equation 8-3.

$$\text{Forecast ending balance} = \text{Beginning balance} + \text{Inflows} - \text{Outflows} \qquad \textbf{(8-3)}$$

The beginning balance for a specific account is known and any inflows or outflows concerning the account are forecasts. The specific accounts used in Equation 8-3 depend on which type of ending balance is being forecast.

EXAMPLE 8-10: Using data in Figure 8-5, forecast the ending balance for accounts payable for the end of the first quarter 19x9 for Jennings Industries. Total purchases for the quarter are $4,800,000 and total payments are $4,710,000. Based on the balance sheet of December 31, 19x8 shown in Example 8-4, the beginning accounts payable is $1,350,000.

Equation 8-3 is used to forecast the ending accounts payable as follows:

$$\begin{matrix} \text{Ending} \\ \text{accounts payable} \end{matrix} = \begin{matrix} \text{Beginning} \\ \text{accounts payable} \end{matrix} + \begin{matrix} \text{Total} \\ \text{purchases} \end{matrix} - \begin{matrix} \text{Total} \\ \text{payments} \end{matrix}$$

$$\$1,440,000 = \$1,350,000 + \$4,800,000 - \$4,710,000$$

The ending accounts payable is the amount owed on credit purchases at the end of the quarter.

EXAMPLE 8-11: Use data from Figure 8-5 through Figure 8-7 to construct a pro forma balance sheet for March 31, 19x9 for Jennings Industries. The beginning balance sheet for December 31, 19x8, is shown in Example 8-4.

The pro forma balance sheet for March 31, 19x9 is shown in Figure 8-8.   The balance sheet accounts are determined as follows:

(a) *Cash* is assumed to be the minimum cash balance of $800,000. The actual ending cash is $483,000, with the remaining $317,000 assumed to be borrowed in the form of notes payable.

(b) *Accounts receivable* is the credit sales for March of $2,400,000 (0.75 × $3,200,000).

(c) *Inventory* is assumed to be $1,000,000.

(d) *Net fixed assets* is the beginning net fixed assets plus capital expenditures less depreciation, $10,000,000 + $1,000,000 − $450,000 = $10,550,000. The depreciation includes the $225,000 in depreciation related to the manufacturing function included in cost of goods sold, and $225,000 in depreciation related to selling, general, and administrative expenses which is shown separately in the pro forma income statement.

Jennings Industries
Pro Forma Balance Sheet
March 31, 19x9
(in thousands of dollars)

Cash	$ 800	Accounts payable	$ 1,440
Accounts receivable.............	2,400	Notes payable...................	317
Inventory.......................	1,000	Other current liabilities..........	150
Total current assets	$ 4,200	Total current liabilities...........	$ 1,907
Fixed assets.............. 16,000			
Less accumulated		Long-term debt (10%)	6,000
depreciation 5,450		Common stock	5,000
Net fixed assets	10,550	Retained earnings.............	1,843
Total assets...................	$14,750	Total liabilities and equity	$14,750

FIGURE 8-8   Pro forma balance sheet for Jennings Industries for the quarter ended March 31, 19x9.

(e) *Accounts payable* is the credit purchases made in March of $1,440,000 (0.90 × $1,600,000.)

(f) *Notes payable* of $317,000 is the amount of borrowing needed to maintain the minimum cash balance $800,000.

(g) *Other current liabilities* are assumed to be $1,500,000.

(h) *Long-term bonds* and *common stock* remain constant.

(i) *Retained earnings* is the beginning retained earnings plus net income less dividend payments, $1,500,000 + $687,000 − $344,000 = $1,843,000.

D. The *pro forma statement of changes in financial position* shows a firm's predicted sources and uses of funds during a future time period.

This statement, often called a *pro forma funds flow statement*, is also used to estimate a firm's financial requirements and to determine the best way to meet these requirements. The funds flow statement is prepared last and is developed by determining the changes in successive balance sheets and classifying them as either a source or use of funds. Decreases in assets and increases in liabilities and stockholders' equity are *sources* of funds; increases in assets and decreases in liabilities and stockholders' equity are *uses* of funds. Noncash expense items, such as depreciation, are considered sources of funds. A change in retained earnings is generally divided into two accounts: net income (source) or net loss (use) and dividends (use). This statement is further divided into long-term sources and uses and short-term or working capital sources and uses. **Working capital** is a firm's current assets.

EXAMPLE 8-12: Jennings Industries uses the following information to develop a pro forma funds flow statement for the period ending March 31, 19x9:

Jennings Industries
Pro Forma Comparative Balance Sheet
For the Quarter Ended March 31, 19x9
(in thousands of dollars)

	December 31 19x8	March 31 19x9	Change
Assets			
Cash	$ 750	$ 800	+$ 50
Accounts receivable	2,250	2,400	+ 150
Inventory	1,000	1,000	0
Total current assets	$ 4,000	$ 4,200	+$ 200
Fixed assets	15,000	16,000	+ 1,000
Less accumulated depreciation	5,000	5,450	+ 450
Net fixed assets	$10,000	$10,550	+$ 500
Total assets	$14,000	$14,750	+$ 750
Liabilities and equity			
Accounts payable	$ 1,350	$ 1,440	+$ 90
Notes payable	0	317	+ 317
Other current liabilities	150	150	0
Total current liabilities	$ 1,500	$ 1,807	+$ 407
Long-term debt (10%)	6,000	6,000	0
Common stock	5,000	5,000	0
Retained earnings	1,500	1,843	+$ 343*
Total liabilities and equity	$14,000	$14,750	+$ 750

* Jennings' net income was $687, of which it paid $344 in dividends. The addition to retained earnings was $343 ($687 − $344).

The pro forma funds flow statement for Jennings Industries is shown in Figure 8-9. The results show that the major sources of funds are expected to be from net income and depreciation. Plant expansion and dividends are expected to be the major uses. The firm's working capital position is expected to decrease and additional funds will be needed to maintain the minimum cash balance of $800,000. These funds are expected to come from $317,000 in notes payable.

Jennings Industires
Pro Forma Funds Flow Statement
For the Quarter Ended March 31, 19x9
(in thousands of dollars)

Sources of funds

From operations

Net income	$ 687
Depreciation	450
Total sources of funds	$1,137

Use of funds

Capital expenditure for plant	$1,000
Dividend payments	344
Total uses of funds	$1,344
Net decrease in working capital	$ 207

Changes in components of working capital

Increase (decrease) in current assets

Cash	$ 50
Accounts receivable	150
Total increase in current assets	$ 200

Increase (decrease) in current liabilities

Accounts payable	$ 90
Notes payable	317
Total increase in current liabilities	$ 407
Net decrease in working capital	$ 207

FIGURE 8-9   Pro forma funds flow statement for Jennings Industries for the quarter ended March 31, 19x9.

RAISE YOUR GRADES

Can you explain...?

☑ the meaning of financial planning
☑ the five steps in the financial planning process
☑ the relationships among planning, budgeting, and forecasting
☑ the meaning of financial forecasting
☑ why accurate sales forecasts are important
☑ the three steps in financial forecasting
☑ how trend forecasts and the percent of sales method differ
☑ several uses of the percent of sales method
☑ the meaning of budgeting
☑ the benefits of budgets
☑ three major types of budgets
☑ the purpose of a cash budget
☑ how to prepare a cash budget

☑ what pro forma statements are
☑ how to prepare pro forma statements
☑ how funds flow statements are used in financial planning

SUMMARY

1. Financial planning is the development of a set of plans for the orderly acquisition and utilization of capital.
2. The financial planning process involves five steps.
   - Set corporate goals.
   - Develop long-term financial plans.
   - Develop short-term financial plans.
   - Prepare individual budgets.
   - Develop a consolidated budget.
3. Planning, budgeting, and forecasting are interrelated. Financial plans are management's way of preparing for an uncertain future, and budgets are financial expressions of management plans. Forecasts are used as inputs for a firm's plans and budgets.
4. Financial forecasting is the process of projecting or estimating some future financial event or condition of a firm.
5. Accurate sales forecasts are critical because they are key inputs to a firm's overall planning and budgeting.
6. Forecasting involves three basic steps:
   - Identify the individual financial variables to forecast.
   - Apply the appropriate forecasting techniques.
   - Examine the underlying assumptions of the forecast.
7. Forecasting techniques are classified into subjective methods and objective methods. Subjective methods are based on insight and opinion; objective methods on facts and analyses. Forecasts generally incorporate both methods.
8. Trend forecasts project historical values of a single variable into the future using a trend line. The percent of sales method makes forecasts assuming a constant relationship between sales and another financial variable.
9. The percent of sales method is used to forecast short-term external financial requirements and to develop pro forma financial statements.
10. Budgeting is the process of formulating a budget for a limited future period.
11. Budgets are useful as planning, coordinating, and controlling mechanisms.
12. Budgets are classified into three types: operating, financial, and capital budgets.
13. Cash budgets are projections of cash receipts and disbursements over some future time period. They are used to anticipate fluctuations in a firm's level of cash and to predict periods of cash surpluses and cash shortages.
14. A cash budget is prepared by following six steps:
    - Select the time horizon.
    - Forecast sales.
    - Estimate cash receipts.
    - Estimate cash disbursements.
    - Compute the net cash flow.
    - Develop a cash summary.
15. Pro forma statements are projected or budgeted financial statements. They can be prepared using the percent of sales method or after constructing a cash budget.
16. A pro forma funds flow statement is used to predict a firm's sources and uses of funds during a future time period and to estimate financial requirements.

RAPID REVIEW

True or False

1. Financial planning is the process of projecting or estimating some future financial event or condition of a firm. [Section 8-1]

2. The first step in the financial planning process is to develop long-term financial plans. [Section 8-1A]

3. A sales forecast is a key ingredient in a firm's financial planning. [Section 8-2]

4. Examples of subjective methods of forecasting include trend forecasts and the percent of sales method. [Section 8-2A]

5. The most sophisticated forecasting technique is generally the most appropriate. [Section 8-2A]

6. Trend forecasts project historical values of a single variable into the future. [Section 8-2B]

7. The most common base for forecasts using ratios is sales. [Section 8-2C]

8. The percent of sales method is most appropriate in making long-term forecasts. [Section 8-2C]

9. All balance sheet items typically remain a constant percent of sales, at least in the short-term. [Section 8-2C]

10. Key outputs of a firm's financial plans are budgets. [Section 8-3]

11. Capital budgets express a firm's short-term financial plans. [Section 8-3B]

12. The cash budget includes cash receipts, but no cash disbursements. [Sections 8-4A & B]

13. The ideal time horizon for a cash budget is six months. [Section 8-4A]

14. The cash budget relies heavily on the sales forecast as an input. [Section 8-4A]

15. Depreciation is included as a cash outflow in a cash budget. [Section 8-4B]

16. Pro forma statements report a firm's actual performance during previous reporting periods. [Section 8-5]

17. Sensitivity analysis can be used to evaluate the impact of a changing specific assumption on pro forma statements. [Section 8-5A]

18. The pro forma income statement indicates a firm's financial condition at the end of the budget period. [Section 8-5B]

19. A pro forma balance sheet can be developed solely from data contained in a firm's cash budget, provided that both statements are prepared for the same time period. [Section 8-5C]

20. A pro forma funds flow statement can be used to determine a firm's future financial requirements. [Section 8-5D]

Multiple Choice

21. Budgets are used by the firm in
    (a) planning its financial and operating activities
    (b) coordinating activities within the firm
    (c) controlling the financial plan
    (d) All of the above
    [Section 8-3A]

22. All of the following are operating budgets except
    (a) sales budget
    (b) production budget
    (c) cash budget
    (d) administrative budget
    [Section 8-3B]

23. The first step in preparing a cash budget is to:

(*a*) forecast sales
(*b*) estimate cash receipts
(*c*) estimate cash disbursements
(*d*) select the time horizon

[Section 8-4A]

24. What information not contained in a cash budget is needed to prepare a pro forma income statement?

(*a*) Sales
(*b*) Dividends
(*c*) Inventory levels
(*d*) Tax payments

[Section 8-5B]

25. Which statement is usually prepared last?

(*a*) Cash budget
(*b*) Pro forma funds flow statement
(*c*) Pro forma income statement
(*d*) Pro forma balance sheet

[Section 8-5D]

Answers

True and False				*Multiple Choice*
1. False	6. True	11. False	16. False	21. d
2. False	7. True	12. False	17. True	22. c
3. True	8. False	13. False	18. False	23. d
4. False	9. False	14. True	19. False	24. c
5. False	10. True	15. False	20. True	25. b

SOLVED PROBLEMS

PROBLEM 8-1: When using the percent of sales method to forecast the amount of external funds needed, which of the following balance sheet items typically vary directly with sales?

(*a*) Preferred stock
(*b*) Cash
(*c*) Accounts payable
(*d*) Accounts receivable
(*e*) Long-term bonds

(*f*) Common stock
(*g*) Inventory
(*h*) Dividends
(*i*) Accrued wages and salaries
(*j*) Taxes payable

Answer: The balance sheet items that vary directly with sales are: (*b*), (*c*), (*d*), (*g*), (*i*), and (*j*).
[Section 8-2C]

Problems 8-2 through 8-4 refer to Hampton Sportswear.

PROBLEM 8-2: Hampton Sportswear manufactures various types of athletic and sports clothing. Prepare forecasts for Hampton Sportswear based on the methods indicated:

(*a*) Sales have increased at an average rate of 6 percent per year for the past five years. Last year sales amounted to $5,000,000. Use a trend forecast to project next year's sales.

(*b*) The relationship between sales and cost of goods sold is shown below. Apply a graphical approach to forecast cost of goods sold in 19x6 based on the sales forecast obtained in part (*a*) above.

Year	Sales	Cost of Goods Sold
19x1	$4,000,000	$3,000,000
19x2	4,200,000	3,100,000
19x3	4,500,000	3,300,000
19x4	4,700,000	3,400,000
19x5	5,000,000	3,500,000

(*c*) Other operating expenses for 19x6 are expected to remain a constant percent of 19x5 sales. Other operating expenses amounted to $500,000 in 19x5. Use the percent of sales method to forecast other operating expenses for 19x6.

Answer:

(*a*) Sales for 19x6 are expected to be $5,300,000 (1.06 × $5,000,000).
(*b*) Cost of goods sold is forecast to be $3,700,000 in 19x6.

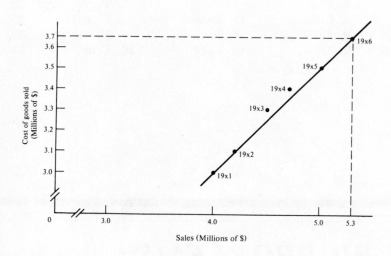

(*c*) Other operating expenses are forecast to be $530,000 in 19x6.

$$\frac{\text{Other operating expenses (19x5)}}{\text{Sales (19x5)}} = \frac{\$500,000}{\$5,000,000} = 0.10 \text{ or } 10 \text{ percent}$$

Using Equation 8-1, the forecast of other operating expenses is:

$$0.10 \times \$5,300,000 = \$530,000 \quad \textbf{[Sections 8-2B and 8-2C]}$$

PROBLEM 8-3: Based on the information in Problem 8-2 and the following assumptions, prepare a pro forma income statement dated December 31, 19x6 for Hampton Sportswear. Assume depreciation of $200,000, interest payments of $120,000, and a 34 percent tax rate.

Answer: Hampton's pro forma income statement is shown below.

Hampton Sportswear
Pro Forma Income Statement
For the Year Ending December 31, 19x6
(in thousands of dollars)

Net sales..	$5,300
Cost of goods sold	3,700
Gross profit	$1,600
Other operating expenses	530
Depreciation...	200
Earnings before interest and taxes	$ 870
Interest expense	120
Earnings before taxes...	$ 750
Income taxes (34%)	255
Net income...	$ 495

[Section 8-5B]

PROBLEM 8-4: Reliable Appliances wants to determine whether it needs any external financing during the next year. The company forecasts that sales will increase from $450,000 to $600,000. Reliable expects to achieve a 10 percent after-tax profit margin and to pay out 20 percent of its earnings in dividends. Based on historical relationships, assets which are related directly to sales are expected to increase by 60 cents for each dollar increase in sales. Spontaneously generated liabilities are expected to increase by 20 cents for each additional dollar of sales. Determine the amount of additional funds needed, if any.

Answer: Substituting $A/S = 0.60$, $L/S = 0.20$, $\triangle S = \$150,000$, $PM = 0.10$, and $d = 0.20$ in Equation 8-2, the amount of external funds needed is:

External funds needed $= (0.60)(\$150,000) - (0.20)(\$150,000) - (0.10)(\$600,000)(1 - 0.20)$

$$= \$90,000 - \$30,000 - \$48,000 = \$12,000 \qquad \textbf{[Section 8-2C]}$$

PROBLEM 8-5: Use the percent of sales method to prepare a pro forma balance sheet dated December 31, 19x6 for Hampton Sportswear. Does Hampton require any additional financing? Assume the following:

- Sales are forecast to be $5,300,000 in 19x6.
- The percentage of sales for accounts which vary directly with sales is:

Account	Percent
Cash	5
Accounts receivable	10
Inventory	20
Net fixed assets	50
Accounts payable	12
Accruals	6

- Other current liabilities are $200,000.
- Long-term debt is $1,000,000.
- Common stock is $1,500,000.
- The beginning retained earnings are $400,000.
- Net income is $495,000.
- Dividend payout ratio is 30 percent.

Answer: The pro forma balance sheet is determined by multiplying each percent of sales by net sales to get specific accounts. Other accounts not varying directly with sales are inserted into the balance sheet. The ending retained earnings are the beginning retained earnings plus net income minus dividends, $400,000 + $495,000 − ($495,000)(0.30) = $746,500. The results show that Hampton needs $104,500 in additional financing. The pro forma balance sheet for Hampton Sportswear is shown below.

Hampton Sportswear
Pro Forma Balance Sheet
December 31, 19x6
(in thousands of dollars)

Cash	$ 265	Accounts payable	$ 636
Accounts receivable	530	Accruals	318
Inventory	1,060	Other current liabilities	200
Total current assets	$1,855	Total current liabilities	$1,154
		Long-term debt (12%)	1,000
		Common stock	1,500
		Retained earnings	746.5
Net fixed assets	2,650	Additional financing needed	104.5
Total assets	$4,505	Total liabilities and equity	$4,505

[Section 8-2C]

Problem 8-6 through Problem 8-12 refer to Karadbil Company.

PROBLEM 8-6: Forecast the monthly cash receipts for October through December 19x4 for Karadbil Company, based on the following information:

(*a*) Actual and estimated sales are in thousands of dollars.

Actual		Estimated	
July	$10,000	October	$10,000
August	8,000	November	12,000
September	7,000	December	15,000
		January	9,000

(*b*) Sales are 20 percent cash sales; 50 percent of monthly sales are collected one month after the sale, and the remaining 30 percent are collected two months after the sale. There are no bad debts.

Answer: The cash receipts summary is shown below:

Cash Receipts Summary (in thousands of dollars)

	July	August	September	October	November	December
Sales	$10,000	$8,000	$7,000	$10,000	$12,000	$15,000
Collections:						
Present month (20%)	$2,000	$1,600	$1,400	$2,000	$2,400	$ 3,000
1-month lag (50%)		5,000	4,000	3,500	5,000	6,000
2-month lag (30%)			3,000	2,400	2,100	3,000
Total cash receipts		$6,600	$8,400	$7,900	$9,500	$12,000

[Sections 8-4A & B]

PROBLEM 8-7: Forecast the monthly cash disbursements from October through December 19x4 for Karadbil Company, based on the following information:

(*a*) Purchases are 40 percent of sales and are made one month preceding the sales date.
(*b*) Forty percent of the purchases are paid during the month of the purchase and the remaining 60 percent are paid one month after the purchase.
(*c*) Wages and salaries are $1,000,000 per month plus 5 percent of sales.
(*d*) Rent is $1,200,000 per month.
(*e*) Other operating expenses are $800,000 per month.
(*f*) Interest expense is $60,000 per month on $6,000,000 of 12 percent notes payable.
(*g*) Income taxes of $2,500,000 are paid in December.

Answer: The cash disbursements summary is shown below.

Cash Disbursements Summary (in thousands of dollars)

	September	October	November	December	January
Sales	$ 7,000	$10,000	$12,000	$15,000	$ 9,000
Purchases: 40% of next month's sales	4,000	4,800	6,000	3,600	
Payments:					
Present month (40%)	$ 1,600	$ 1,920	$ 2,400	$ 1,440	$ 3,600
1-month lag (60%)		2,400	2,880	3,600	2,160
Wages and salaries		1,500	1,600	1,750	
Rent		1,200	1,200	1,200	
Other operating expenses...........		800	800	800	
Interest expense		60	60	60	
Income taxes.......................				2,500	
Total cash disbursements.........		$ 7,880	$ 8,940	$11,350	$ 5,760

[Sections 8-4A & B]

PROBLEM 8-8: Prepare monthly cash budgets for Karadbil Company from October to December 19x4. Use the cash receipts summary shown in Problem 8-6, the cash disbursements summary shown in Problem 8-7, and the following information:

(*a*) The beginning cash balance on October 1 is $2,000,000.
(*b*) A minimum cash balance of $2,500,000 is desired throughout the period.

Answer: The cash budget is shown on page 174. Karadbil is expected to have a cash shortage during October, but cash surpluses in November and December. In order for Karadbil to maintain its minimum cash balance of $2,500,000, the firm will need to borrow $480,000 in October. The cash surpluses of $80,000 in November and $730,000 in December may be placed in some form of marketable security, which is an interest-earning, short-term instrument.

An alternate cash summary which highlights the borrowing and repaying debt and investing surplus cash in marketable securities is shown below. The net cash flow is derived from the Karadbil's cash budget.

Karadbil Company
Cash Budget
For the Fourth Quarter of 19x4
(in thousands of dollars)

	October	November	December
Total cash receipts.....................	$ 7,900	$ 9,500	$12,000
−Total cash disbursements............	7,880	8,940	11,350
Net cash flow	$ 20	$ 560	$ 650
+Beginning cash	2,000	2,020*	2,580*
Ending cash............................	$ 2,020	$ 2,580	$ 3,230
−Minimum cash balance	2,500	2,500	2,500
Cash surplus...........................	0	$ 80	$ 730
Cash shortage	$ 480	0	0

Karadbil Company
Alternate Cash Summary
For the Fourth Quarter of 19x4
(in thousands of dollars)

	October	November	December
Net cash flow	$ 20	$ 560	$ 650
+Beginning cash	2,000	2,500*	$ 2,500*
+Marketable securities................	0	0	80
−Minimum cash balance	2,500	2,500	2,500
Borrowing required	$ 480	$ 0	$ 0
Cash surplus...........................	0	560	730
Use of cash surplus			
Repay debt	0	480	0
Invest in marketable securities.......	0	80	730
Total borrowing required...............	$ 480	0	0

* There are differences between the beginning cash balance for November and December in the cash budget and the alternate cash summary. In the alternate cash summary, the minimum cash balance of $2,500 is maintained by borrowing to meet this minimum, or by using any cash surplus to repay existing short-term debt or to invest in marketable securities.

[Sections 5-4A & B]

PROBLEM 8-9: Use data from Problem 8-6 and Problem 8-7 to determine the cost of goods sold for Karadbil Company for the three-month period October through December 19x4. Assume the firm has a beginning inventory of $10,000,000 but projects an ending inventory of $7,750,000 on December 31. Depreciation is $500,000 per month.

Answer: Karadbil's cost of goods sold is $26,600,000.

Karadbil Company
Cost of Goods Manufactured and Sold
For the Quarter Ending December 31, 19x4
(in thousands of dollars)

Cost of goods manufactured and sold	
Beginning inventory—October 1...	$10,000
+Cost of goods manufactured	
Purchases (direct materials)..	14,400
Wages and salaries (direct labor).....................................	4,850
Rent (factory overhead)...	3,600
Depreciation...	1,500
=Cost of goods available for sale.......................................	$34,350
=Ending inventory...	7,750
=Cost of goods sold	$26,600

[Section 8-5B]

PROBLEM 8-10: Prepare a pro forma income statement for Karadbil Company for the quarter ended December 31, 19x4. Use the cash budget prepared in Problem 8-8 and the cost of goods sold shown in Problem 8-9. The firm's income tax rate is 34 percent.

Answer: The pro forma income statement is shown below.

Karadbil Company
Pro Forma Income Statement
For the Quarter Ending December 31, 19x4
(in thousands of dollars)

Net sales..	$37,000
Cost of goods sold	26,600
Gross profit	$10,400
Other operating expenses	2,400
Earnings before interest and taxes	$ 8,000
Interest	180
Earnings before taxes...	$ 7,820
Income taxes (40%)	2,659
Net income..	$ 5,161

[Section 8-5B]

PROBLEM 8-11: The balance sheet for Karadbil Company for September 30, 19x4 is shown below. During each of the next three months the firm plans to maintain a $2,500,000 minimum cash balance. Karadbil pays no dividends. Based on this information and the information provided in Problem 8-8 through Problem 8-10, construct a pro forma balance sheet for Karadbil Company for December 31, 19x4.

Karadbil Company
Balance Sheet
September 30, 19x4
(in thousands of dollars)

Cash	$ 2,000	Accounts payable	$ 2,400
Accounts receivable.............	8,000	Notes payable (12%)	6,000
Inventory.......................	10,000	Accrued income taxes payable ..	500
Total current assets	$20,000	Total current liabilities	$ 8,900
		Common stock	45,000
Net fixed assets	50,000	Retained earnings.............	16,100
Total assets	$70,000	Total liabilities and equity	$70,000

Answer: The pro forma balance sheet for Karadbil Company is shown below.

- The ending cash balance is $3,230,000.
- Accounts receivable of $15,600,000 consists of 30 percent of the sales in November (0.30 × $12,000,000 = $3,600,000) plus 80 percent of the sales in December (0.80 × $15,000,000 = $12,000,000).
- Ending inventory is $7,750,000 as shown in Problem 8-9.
- Net fixed assets is the beginning fixed assets less the depreciation for the quarter ($50,000,000 − $1,500,000 = $48,500,000).
- Accounts payable represent 60 percent of the purchases in December (0.60 × $3,600,000 = $2,160,000).
- Notes payable remain at $6,000,000.
- Accrued income taxes payable are the beginning accrued income taxes payable plus this quarter's accrued income taxes less estimated taxes paid ($500,000 + $2,659,000 − $2,500,000 = $659,000).
- Common stock remains unchanged at $45,000,000.
- Retained earnings are the beginning retained earnings plus net income minus cash dividends ($16,100,000 + $5,161,000 − 0 = $21,261,000).

Karadbil Company
Pro Forma Balance Sheet
December 31, 19x4
(in thousands of dollars)

Cash	$ 3,230	Accounts payable	$ 2,160
Accounts receivable	15,600	Notes payable (12%)	6,000
Inventory	7,750	Accrued income taxes	659
Total current assets	$26,580	Total current liabilities	$ 8,819
		Common stock	45,000
Net fixed assets	48,500	Retained earnings	21,261
Total assets	$75,080	Total liabilities and equity	$75,080

[Section 8-5C]

PROBLEM 8-12: Prepare a pro forma funds flow statement for Karadbil Company for the quarter ending December 31, 19x4. Discuss the major sources and uses of funds during the quarter.

Karadbil Company
Pro Forma Funds Flow Statement
For the Quarter Ending December 31, 19x4
(in thousands of dollars)

Sources of funds

From operations

Net income	$ 5,161
Depreciation	1,500
Total sources of funds	$ 6,661

Uses of funds

Net increase in working capital	$ 6,499

(Continues)

Karadbil Company
Pro Forma Funds Flow Statement
For the Quarter Ending December 31, 19x4
(in thousands of dollars)

Changes in components of working capital

Increase (decrease) in current assets

Cash	$ 1,230
Accounts receivable	7,600
Inventory	(2,250)
Total increase in current assets	$ 6,580
Increase (decrease) in current liabilities	
Accounts payable	($ 240)
Accrued income taxes	159
Total decrease in current liabilities	($ 81)
Net increase in working capital	$ 6,499

[Section 8-5D]

EXAMINATION I (CHAPTERS 1–8)

True-False

1. The emphasis of financial management has remained constant over time.
2. The primary goal of the firm is the maximization of earnings per share.
3. The sole proprietorship is the dominant form of business organization in the U.S. in terms of asset size and sales volume.
4. According to the Tax Reform Act of 1986, the maximum corporate tax rate on taxable income is 34 percent.
5. All other factors being equal, an ordinary annuity will earn less than an annuity due.
6. As time and/or interest rates increase, present value interest factors (PVIFs) decrease.
7. Present value interest factors of an annuity (PVIFAs) are smaller than the number of periods of the annuity, n.
8. Risk reduction of a portfolio increases as the correlation coefficients of its assets decrease.
9. The capital asset pricing model (CAPM) considers systematic risk as the only relevant risk.
10. Systematic risk is measured by a stock's coefficient of variation.
11. Increased interest rate risk will cause a fall in the price of outstanding bonds.
12. The constant growth model assumes the growth rate is less than the required rate of return.
13. The first step in financial statement analysis is to apply the appropriate financial tools and techniques, such as ratio analysis.
14. The current ratio is used to evaluate a firm's liquidity.
15. Profitability ratios show the extent to which a firm uses debt to finance investments.
16. The DuPont formula shows that return on investment is calculated by multiplying net profit margin and fixed asset turnover.
17. Output levels below the operating breakeven point will result in operating losses.
18. The degree of financial leverage is the percentage change in earnings before interest and taxes (EBIT) that results from a given percentage change in sales.
19. The accuracy of a cash budget depends primarily on the accuracy of the sales forecast.
20. A pro forma statement is a projection of future financial statements.

Multiple Choice

1. A major function of the financial manager of a large corporation is

   (a) reconciling bank statements.
   (b) determining the best financing mix for the firm.
   (c) preparing the corporate tax returns.
   (d) coordinating the annual audit.

2. Profit maximization does not adequately describe the goal of the firm because it

   (a) ignores risk.
   (b) ignores the distribution of return.
   (c) lacks a time dimension.
   (d) All of the above.

3. The form of business in which ownership is most easily transferred is the

    (*a*) sole proprietorship.
    (*b*) limited partnership.
    (*c*) publicly held corporation.
    (*d*) general partnership.

4. The true owners of a corporation are the

    (*a*) debt holders.
    (*b*) common stockholders.
    (*c*) managers of the firm.
    (*d*) board of directors of the firm.

5. Compound interest is paid on the
    (*a*) principal.
    (*b*) total accumulated interest.
    (*c*) future value.
    (*d*) Both a and b

6. The formula for compound value is

    (*a*) $FV_n = (1 + i)/PV$.
    (*b*) $FV_n = PV(1 + i)^n$.
    (*c*) $FV_n = PV/(1 + i)^n$.
    (*d*) $FV_n = PV(1 - i)^n$.

7. In the formula $FV_n = PV[1 + (i/m)]^{mn}$, the letter m refers to

    (*a*) the number of years that money is invested.
    (*b*) the number of times per year interest is compounded.
    (*c*) the effective rate of interest.
    (*d*) the nominal rate of interest.

8. The rate of interest used to find present values is usually called the

    (*a*) discount rate.
    (*b*) amortized rate.
    (*c*) simple rate.
    (*d*) compound rate.

9. In comparing two projects that are distributed normally with identical expected returns, the project which has the smaller standard deviation of its expected returns

    (*a*) has a flatter probability distribution.
    (*b*) has a more skewed probability distribution.
    (*c*) is less risky.
    (*d*) has a bigger range of returns.

10. Which of the following is the best measure to use in comparing the riskiness of two projects with different expected returns?

    (*a*) Standard deviation
    (*b*) Variance
    (*c*) Correlation coefficient
    (*d*) Coefficient of variation

11. In finance, investors are generally assumed to be

    (*a*) risk averters.
    (*b*) risk neutral.
    (*c*) risk takers.
    (*d*) None of the above

12. An efficient portfolio provides the

    (*a*) highest return for a given amount of risk.
    (*b*) least risk for a given level of return.

(c) highest possible return and the least amount of risk.

(d) Either a or b.

13. Going-concern value is an important consideration when

    (a) computing financial ratios.

    (b) facing bankruptcy.

    (c) considering the takeover of a firm.

    (d) preparing the corporate financial statements.

14. The value of a security is _____ related to the amount of the expected cash flows and _____ related to the amount of risk.

    (a) directly; inversely

    (b) inversely; directly

    (c) directly; directly

    (d) inversely; inversely

15. The basic valuation model assumes

    (a) returns are represented by a probability distribution.

    (b) risks associated with cash flows are reflected in the investor's required rate of return.

    (c) relevant cash flows do not include the maturity value of bonds.

    (d) relevant cash flows include interest, but not dividends.

16. In a common-size income statement, each account is expressed as a percentage of

    (a) net sales.

    (b) net income.

    (c) cost of goods sold.

    (d) total assets.

17. When calculating the operating breakeven point in units, which of the following must be known?

    (a) Total interest expense

    (b) Variable cost per dollar of sales

    (c) Selling price per unit

    (d) Dollar level of sales

18. Overall breakeven analysis determines the level of sales where neither profits nor losses are incurred after considering

    (a) future expenses for replacing outdated equipment.

    (b) inflation effects.

    (c) common stock dividends.

    (d) operating and financing costs.

19. The percent of sales method of forecasting

    (a) will give exactly the same results as the trend forecast method in the long run.

    (b) is used primarily to forecast the statement of changes in financial position.

    (c) can be used to predict the amount of external funds needed in the future.

    (d) None of the above

20. A cash summary

    (a) is the amount in the cash account at the end of the year.

    (b) is part of the statement of retained earnings.

    (c) determines whether a cash surplus or cash shortage is expected for a particular future period.

    (d) requires that the minimum cash balance be added to the ending cash balance.

Fill In The Blank

1. The three major functions of the financial manager are _____, _____ and _____.

2. The theoretical goal of the financial manager is to _____.

3. In trying to meet the goal of the firm, the financial manager makes decisions involving a set of _____ tradeoffs.

4. The _____ form of business organization is easily formed, but it has the disadvantage of _____ for all business debts.

5. The _____ tax rate is the rate paid on each added dollar of taxable income.

6. A(n) _____ is a stream of equal payments made at regular time intervals.

7. The required rate of return is also known as the _____ rate.

8. An annuity with an infinite life is called a _____.

9. _____ is the variability of an asset's future returns.

10. Total risk is separated into _____ and _____ risk.

11. If the common stock returns of a company are _____ volatile than the market, the beta would be _____ than 1.0.

12. At zero risk the interest rate level is called the _____ rate of return.

13. The slope of the security market line (SML) will _____ if investors become more risk-averse.

14. A bond's _____ is calculated by dividing the annual interest payment by the bond's current market price.

15. _____ is the discount rate that equates the present value of all interest payments plus the repayment of principal from a bond with the present bond price.

16. The current ratio is an example of a(n) _____ ratio.

17. A common-size balance sheet expresses each item on the balance sheet as a percentage of total _____.

18. Breakeven analysis assumes that the sales mix is _____.

19. Whenever a firm uses resources that have _____ costs, it is employing leverage.

20. The _____ is a projection of cash receipts and cash disbursements over some future time period.

Problems

1. You invest $5,000 in a project in which you expect to earn 8 percent compounded annually for the next five years. How much will you have at the end of five years if your expectations are met?

2. The Johnsons plan to retire in 25 years. When they retire, the Johnsons expect to need a minimum of $75,000 a year. They plan to live long lives, and would like to leave the principal of their investment untouched to enable them to leave an endowment to their alma mater. How much would they need to invest as a lump sum today in order to achieve their goal? Ignore taxes and assume the Johnsons can make 8 percent on their investment.

3. Modern Appliance Store borrows $200,000 for five years at a cost of 9 percent. All payments are made at the end of the year. What is the annual payment?

4. Stock A has an expected return of 12 percent and Stock B has an expected return of 18 percent. The standard deviations of their expected returns are 3 percent and 4.5 percent, respectively. Which stock is riskier?

5. Diversified Industries uses the capital asset pricing model to evaluate investment projects. Project A has a beta of 1.5. The risk-free rate is 6 percent and the expected return on the market portfolio is 12 percent. The expected return on Project A is 18 percent.

   (*a*) What is the required rate of return on this project?

   (*b*) Should the project be accepted?

6. You are evaluating two securities of Ogling Optical. The preferred stock is selling for $20 per share and pays $1 per share annual dividends. Ogling's bonds mature in 20 years, are selling for $900, and pay annual interest of $60. Assume you would hold the preferred stock indefinitely and that you would hold the bond to maturity. Which investment will give you the better rate of return?

7. The following comparative financial information is for Fred's Grocery and Alyce's Supermarket. Calculate the current ratio, debt ratio, net profit margin, and return on equity for both and evaluate them with respect to each other and to the industry averages.

Ratio	Industry Averages
Current ratio	1.30 times
Debt ratio	0.37 percent
Net profit margin	3.53 percent
Return on equity	4.99 percent

Income Statement	Fred's	Alyce's
Net sales	$240,000	$300,000
Cost of goods sold	110,000	155,000
Gross profit	$130,000	$145,000
Operating expenses	116,000	119,000
Earnings before interest and taxes	$ 14,000	$ 26,000
Interest Expense	4,000	6,000
Earnings before taxes	$ 10,000	$ 20,000
Taxes (15%)	1,500	3,000
Net income	$ 8,500	$ 17,000

Balance Sheet	Fred's	Alyce's
Current assets	$150,000	$200,000
Fixed assets	70,000	85,000
Total assets	$220,000	$285,000
Current liabilities	$ 90,000	$ 95,000
Long-term liabilities	40,000	60,000
Total liabilities	$130,000	$155,000
Stockholders' equity	$ 90,000	$130,000
Total liabilities and stockholders' equity	$220,000	$285,000

8. Modern Crafts is considering branching out into the woodworking business in order to make video tape storage racks. The firm expects that the fixed costs of the new business will be $100,000 and the labor and supplies will amount to $4 per rack produced. The firm plans to sell the racks for $20 each. What is the firm's operating breakeven point in units and in dollar sales?

ANSWERS TO EXAMINATION I

True-False

1. False [Section 1-2]
2. False [Sections 1-3A & C]
3. False [Section 2-1C]

4. True [Section 2-2A]
5. True [Section 3-3B]
6. True [Section 3-4B]

7. True [Section 3-5B]
8. True [Section 4-4B]
9. True [Section 4-5]
10. False [Section 4-5C]
11. True [Section 5-3B]
12. True [Section 5-6B]
13. False [Section 6-1A]

14. True [Section 6-3A]
15. False [Section 6-3D]
16. False [Section 6-3D]
17. True [Section 7-1C]
18. False [Section 7-4A]
19. True [Section 8-4A]
20. True [Section 8-5]

Multiple Choice

1. b [Section 1-1]
2. d [Section 1-3C]
3. c [Section 2-1C]
4. b [Section 2-1C]
5. d [Section 3-2B]
6. b [Section 3-2C]
7. b [Section 3-2E]
8. a [Section 3-4]
9. c [Section 4-2B]
10. d [Section 4-2C]

11. a [Section 4-3B]
12. d [Section 4-4]
13. c [Section 5-1A]
14. a [Section 5-2A]
15. b [Section 5-2B]
16. a [Section 6-4B]
17. c [Section 7-1C]
18. d [Section 7-1D]
19. c [Section 8-2C]
20. c [Section 8-4A]

Fill In The Blank

1. financial analysis and planning, acquisition of funds, utilization of funds [Sections 1-1A and 1-1C]
2. maximize stockholder wealth [Section 1-3A]
3. risk-return [Section 1-3C]
4. sole proprietorship, unlimited liability [Section 2-1A]
5. marginal [Section 2-2A]
6. annuity [Section 3-3B]
7. discount [Section 3-4]
8. perpetuity [Section 3-6]
9. Risk [Section 4-1]
10. systematic, unsystematic [Section 4-5A]
11. more (less), greater (less) [Section 4-5C]
12. risk-free [Section 4-5E]
13. increase [Section 4-5F]
14. current yield [Section 5-3]
15. Yield to maturity [Section 5-4]
16. liquidity [Section 6-3A]
17. assets [Section 6-4A]
18. constant [Section 7-1A]
19. fixed [Section 7-2A]
20. cash budget [Section 8-4]

Problems

1. Substituting PV = \$5,000 and $FVIF_{0.08,5} = 1.469$ (Appendix A) in Equation 3-2, the investment would be worth:

$$FV_5 = (\$5,000)(1.469) = \$7,345 \qquad \textbf{[Section 3-2D]}$$

2. The first step in this problem is to calculate the amount which would be needed 25 years from now in order to provide a perpetuity with payments of \$75,000. Substituting $A = \$75,000$ and $i = 0.08$ in Equation 3-13, the present value of a perpetuity is:

$$PV = \frac{\$75,000}{0.08} = \$937,500$$

The next step is to discount \$937,500 to the present at a rate of 8 percent to determine how much must be invested today. Substituting $FV_{25} = \$937,500$ and $PVIF_{0.08,25} = 0.146$ (Appendix C) in Equation 3-9, the present value is:

$$PV = (\$937,500)(0.146) = \$136,875 \quad \textbf{[Sections 3-4B and 3-6]}$$

3. Substituting $PV_5 = \$200,000$ and $PVIFA_{0.09,5} = 3.890$ (Appendix D) in Equation 3-16, the loan amortization payment is:

$$A = \frac{\$200,000}{3.890} = \$51,413.88 \qquad \textbf{[Section 3-9]}$$

4. Using Equation 4-4, the coefficient of variation is used to determine the relative risk of each stock.

$$CV_A = \frac{0.03}{0.12} = 0.25 \qquad CV_B = \frac{0.045}{0.180} = 0.25$$

Since the stocks have identical coefficients of variation, they are equally risky.

[Section 4-2C]

5. This problem uses the capital asset pricing model.

   (*a*) Substituting $r_f = 0.06$, $b_a = 1.5$, and $r_m = 0.12$ in Equation 4-11, the required rate of return is:

$$r_a = 0.06 + (1.5)(0.12 - 0.06) = 0.15 \text{ or } 15 \text{ percent}$$

   (*b*) Diversified Industries should accept the project because the expected rate of return exceeds the required rate of return. **[Sections 4-5E and 4-5G]**

6. The preferred stock valuation model is used to determine its rate of return. Rearranging Equation 5-8 as $k_p = D_p/P_0$ and substituting $D_p = \$1$ and $P_0 = \$20$ in its new form, the dividend yield on the preferred stock is:

$$k_p = \frac{\$1.50}{\$20} = 0.075 \text{ or } 7.5 \text{ percent}$$

The approximate yield to maturity (YTM) formula is used to calculate the rate of return on a bond held to maturity. Substituting $I = \$60$, $M = \$1,000$, $P_0 = \$900$, and $n = 20$ in Equation 5-6, the approximate yield to maturity is:

$$YTM = \frac{\$60 + (\$1,000 - \$900)/20}{(\$1,000 + \$900)/2} = \frac{\$60 + \$5}{\$950} = 0.0684 \text{ or } 6.84 \text{ percent}$$

The preferred stock offers a higher rate of return but it is also more risky than the bond. **[Sections 5-4 & 5-5A & B]**

7. Equations 6-1, 6-8, 6-14, and 6-17 are used to compute the following ratios for the two food store chains.

Ratio	Fred's	Alyce's	Industry
Current ratio (times)	1.67	2.11	1.30
Debt ratio (%)	59.09	54.39	37.00
Net profit margin (%)	3.54	5.67	3.53
Return on equity (%)	9.44	13.08	4.99

Each of these ratios is higher than the industry average. Both chains have more debt than the industry average and are more liquid and profitable. Alyce's Supermarkets outperforms Fred's Groceries, as measured by net profit margin and return on equity, and has a lower percentage of debt outstanding. **[Section 6-3]**

8. Substituting $F = \$100,000$, $p = \$20$, and $v = \$4$ in Equation 7-1, the operating breakeven point in units is:

$$Q_b = \frac{\$100,000}{\$20 - \$4} = 6{,}250 \text{ units}$$

Substituting these same values in Equation 7-2, the operating breakeven point in dollar sales is:

$$S_b = \frac{\$100,000}{1 - (\$4/\$20)} = \$125,000 \qquad \textbf{[Section 7-1C]}$$

9 AN OVERVIEW OF WORKING CAPITAL MANAGEMENT

THIS CHAPTER IS ABOUT

☑ **Nature of Working Capital and Its Management**
☑ **Risk-return Tradeoffs**
☑ **Working Capital Management Strategies**

9-1. Nature of Working Capital and Its Management

Working capital is the firm's total investment in current assets. **Current assets** are assets that are likely to be converted into cash, sold, exchanged or expensed in the normal course of business, usually within one year. Working capital management includes the administration of each current asset account such as cash, marketable securities, accounts receivable, and inventory.

A. *Working capital management* **concerns decisions about a firm's current assets and current liabilities.**

These decisions are required to plan and control the flow of dollars among various working capital accounts and other balance sheet accounts to ensure adequate liquidity for the firm. Working capital management decisions are also required to establish and monitor appropriate levels in each working capital account to enhance the firm's profitability. Working capital management involves decisions about how these assets are financed.

B. *Net working capital* **is the difference between the firm's current assets and current liabilities.**

Current liabilities are debts and other obligations coming that fall due within one year. Working capital management also includes the administration of each current liability account.

C. **The firm's net working capital is directly related to its current ratio.**

1. If current assets exceed current liabilities, net working capital is positive and the current ratio is greater than one. In this situation, net working capital is that portion of current assets which must be financed with long-term debt and equity.
2. If current assets equal current liabilities, net working capital is zero and the current ratio is one.
3. If current assets are less than current liabilities, net working capital is negative and the current ratio is less than one. In the latter situations, there is no long-term financing of current assets.

EXAMPLE 9-1: Holmberg Manufacturing Company has the following balance sheet as of December 31, 19x7.

Holmberg Manufacturing Company
Balance Sheet
December 31, 19x7
(in thousands of dollars)

Cash..	$ 3,000
Marketable securities	1,000
Accounts receivable	6,000
Inventory...	10,000
Total current assets..	$20,000
Net fixed assets	50,000
Total assets..	$70,000
Current liabilities	$15,000
Long-term liabilities..	20,000
Total liabilities...	$35,000
Stockholders' equity	35,000
Total liabilities and equity..	$70,000

(a) Holmberg's working capital is the firm's current assets of $20,000,000.

(b) Holmberg's net working capital is the firm's current assets less its current liabilities.

$$\text{Net working capital} = \text{Current assets} - \text{Current liabilities}$$
$$= \$20,000,000 - \$15,000,000 = \$5,000,000$$

(c) Holmberg's current ratio is 1.33 times, which indicates that part of its current assets are financed by long-term debt and equity.

$$\text{Current ratio} = \frac{\text{Current assets}}{\text{Current liabilities}} = \frac{\$20,000,000}{\$15,000,000} = 1.33 \text{ times}$$

D. Working capital management is important for several reasons.

1. *Working capital comprises a large portion of the firm's total assets.* Although the level of working capital varies widely among different industries, firms in manufacturing and retailing industries often keep more than half of their total assets in current assets.

2. *Working capital represents those assets that are most manageable.* The financial manager has considerable control in managing the level of current assets and current liabilities.

3. *Working capital management consumes the largest portion of the financial manager's time.* The financial manager devotes more time to daily operational decisions involving working capital management than any other area.

4. *Working capital management directly affects the firm's long-term growth and survival.* This is due to the fact that higher levels of working capital are needed to support production and sales growth.

5. *Working capital management directly affects the firm's liquidity and profitability.* An appropriate mix of working capital components is needed to maintain a firm's liquidity. **Liquidity** is the ability to convert an asset into cash without significant loss. Without sufficient liquidity, a firm may be unable to pay its liabilities as they become due. The amount of working capital also affects a firm's profitability because current assets must be financed and financing costs money.

E. The goal of working capital management is to maintain the optimal level of net working capital that maximizes shareholder wealth.

There is no single working capital policy that is optimal for all firms or for any single firm in all situations. The optimal working capital policy is difficult to develop in practice because not all factors are within management's control. Factors affecting a firm's working capital position are listed on page 188.

1. *The kind of firm.* Working capital requirements differ greatly among manufacturing, retailing, and service organizations. For example, retailing firms have a high proportion of total assets in the current category because they earn their return from current assets such as inventory.
2. *The volume of sales.* More current assets, such as accounts receivable and inventories, are needed to support a higher level of sales.
3. *The variability of cash flows.* The greater the fluctuations in the firm's cash inflows and outflows, the greater the level of net working capital required.
4. *The length of the operating cycle.* The **operating cycle** or **cash cycle** is the length of time cash is tied up in a firm's operating process. For example, the operating cycle of a manufacturing firm is the length of time required to purchase raw materials on credit, produce and sell a product, collect the sales receipts, and repay the credit. Shortening the operating cycle reduces the amount of time funds are tied up in working capital and thus lowers the level of working capital required.

9-2. Risk-return Tradeoffs

Determining the firm's optimal investment in working capital involves a tradeoff between liquidity and profitability. Increasing working capital improves the firm's liquidity and lowers risk but also increases financing costs which may in turn weaken profits. In this context, **return** means return on equity (ROE), while **risk** is the probability of technical insolvency (the inability to pay obligations as they become due). The financial manager's responsibility is to minimize the costs associated with working capital without jeopardizing liquidity or disrupting operations.

A. Decisions involving risk-return tradeoffs in working capital management are based on several assumptions.

1. Fixed assets remain constant and are financed by previously acquired capital. Thus, working capital management does not include decisions about fixed assets.
2. Current assets earn a lower rate of return than fixed assets. The earning power of assets depends on the type of firm. Manufacturing firms earn less on their current assets than on fixed assets because the fixed assets enable these firms to generate products for sale. For retailing firms, however, the earning assets are current assets and the assumption does not hold.
3. Current liabilities are generally a cheaper form of financing than long-term liabilities. Short-term interest rates are usually lower than long-term rates. When this is true the yield curve is upward sloping. A **yield curve**, or *term structure of interest rates*, describes the relationship between interest rates and debt maturities over time. Under some conditions, short-term interest rates exceed long-term rates, and a downward-sloping or an *inverted yield curve* results. Figure 9-1 illustrates both upward- and downward-sloping yield curves.

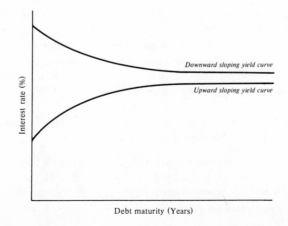

FIGURE 9-1
Upward and downward sloping yield curves.

B. The general level of interest rates is influenced by numerous factors.

Interest is the cost of using money. It is expressed as a rate per period of time, usually one year. Factors which influence interest rate levels include supply and demand, Federal Reserve policy, and business cycles. Three main theories are used to explain the shape of yield curves: expectations, liquidity preference, and market segmentation. All three theories have some merit, but no single theory fully describes the term structure of interest rates.

1. *Expectations theory* states that long-term interest rates are a function of the expected future short-term interest rates. Upward-sloping yield curves result when short-term rates are expected to rise in the future. Downward-sloping yield curves result when short-term rates are expected to decline.

2. *Liquidity preference theory* asserts that long-term debt will yield more than short-term debt. This theory is based on the risk preferences of both borrowers and lenders. Borrowers generally prefer long-term debt because short-term debt increases the risk of having to refund the debt under adverse conditions. Firms are thus willing to pay a higher interest rate for long-term debt. Lenders generally prefer to lend short-term because of the greater risk involved in lending long-term. They are willing to accept lower yields on short-term debt because it enables them to take full advantage of possible future rate increases. The pressures of supply and demand caused by the liquidity preferences of borrowers and lenders produce a traditional upward-sloping yield curve.

3. *Market segmentation theory* states that securities markets are segmented by maturity. Some borrowers require short-term funds while others need long-term funds. Different lenders are also inclined toward either short- or long-term lending. The shape of the yield curve depends on the supply and demand for funds by these different sectors. For example, if more short-term funds are available relative to demand than long-term funds, the yield curve will slope upward. This is because lenders will be able to demand and to get a higher return from long-term borrowers than short-term borrowers because of the relatively short supply of long-term funds. Conversely, a strong demand for short-term funds when their supply is low relative to the supply and demand for long-term funds results in a downward-sloping yield curve.

9-3. Working Capital Management Strategies

Effective working capital management requires a set of strategies to manage the level, composition, and financing of a firm's current assets. Decisions should be analyzed simultaneously to determine their joint impact on return and risk.

A. Working capital management strategies are classified by their risk-return characteristics.

Figure 9-2 shows various strategies for managing working capital.

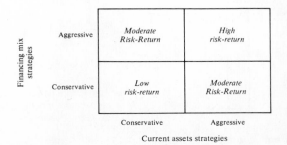

FIGURE 9-2
Risk-return tradeoffs using alternative working capital management strategies.

1. *Conservative strategies* are low-risk, low-return approaches to working capital management. Conservative strategies include holding liquid assets, especially cash and marketable securities, in excess of expected needs and minimizing the amount of short-term financing used to finance them.
2. *Aggressive strategies* are high-risk, high-return approaches to working capital management. Aggressive strategies include minimizing the amount of liquid assets and maximizing the amount of short-term debt used to finance them.
3. *Moderate strategies* are moderate-risk, moderate-return approaches to working capital management. Most firms follow moderate strategies in which they use intermediate levels of both current assets and current liabilities. The *matching* or *hedging approach* matches the maturity of the source of funds to the length of time the funds are needed. This strategy finances short-term needs with short-term sources and long-term needs with long-term sources. An alternative strategy is to offset an aggressive current liabilities strategy with a conservative current asset strategy to provide an overall strategy having moderate risk-return characteristics.

B. Current asset strategies concern both the level and composition of a firm's working capital.

1. Risk and return are both lowered as the level of working capital is increased. This conservative current asset strategy is a low-risk, low-return approach to managing working capital. A high level of current assets, especially in the form of cash and marketable securities, reduces the risk of technical insolvency because liquidity will be in excess of expected needs. Return is also reduced because it costs more to maintain a high level of working capital. Yet, maintaining the same level of current assets while changing their composition from more liquid cash and marketable securities to less liquid accounts receivable and inventory will increase both profitability and risk.
2. Risk and return are both increased as the level of working capital is decreased. This aggressive current asset strategy provides high-risk and high-return. Risk associated with a firm's ability to pay its liabilities as they mature increases. A firm's return also increases because less money is tied up in assets with low earning power.

C. Financing mix strategies concern the financing of a firm's working capital.

Assets can be divided into two categories. **Permanent assets** consist of fixed assets plus the portion of a firm's current assets that remain unchanged over the year. **Fluctuating assets** are current assets that vary over the year due to seasonal or cyclical needs. Figure 9-3 illustrates a firm's typical financing needs over time. A firm's

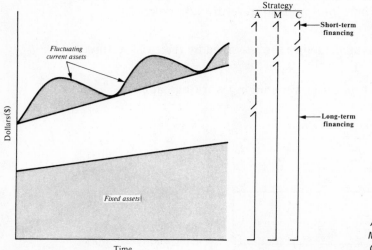

FIGURE 9-3   Financing mix under alternative working capital management strategies.

risk-return characteristics are influenced by whether current assets are financed through current liabilities or long-term debt and equity.

1. Risk and return are both increased as the proportion of short-term debt is increased. A firm using this aggressive current liabilities strategy borrows heavily on a short-term basis. Short-term debt is used to finance all of a firm's fluctuating assets plus some of its permanent current assets, and the firm increases its risk of being unable to repay or replace the debt as it matures. Risk is also increased because short-term interest rates are more volatile than long-term rates. The expected rate of return increases due to the lower cost associated with short-term financing.
2. Risk and return are both lowered as the proportion of short-term debt is decreased. This conservative strategy substitutes long-term financing for short-term borrowing. Only part of a firm's fluctuating assets are financed with short-term debt and the remainder with long-term capital. The risk of being unable to repay or replace short-term debt is reduced because of the lower amount of current liabilities. Profitability is also reduced because of the higher cost of long-term financing.

EXAMPLE 9-2: Holmberg Manufacturing Company is considering three working capital management strategies for the coming year: (1) a conservative strategy requiring a large investment in current assets, $30,000,000, and a small amount of short-term debt, $5,000,000; (2) a moderate strategy using both a moderate amount of current assets, $20,000,000, and short-term debt, $15,000,000; and (3) an aggressive strategy having a small investment in current assets, $10,000,000, and a large amount of short-term debt, $25,000,000. Fixed assets are to remain at $50,000,000 throughout the year. The firm's capital structure requires total liabilities to be 50 percent of total assets. Interest rates are expected to be 8 percent on short-term debt and 12 percent on long-term debt. The firm expects to earn 20 percent before interest and taxes (EBIT) on $80,000,000 in sales. The firm has a 34 percent tax rate.

The risk-return impact of these three strategies is shown below. The return on equity increases from 18.8 percent to 29.5 percent as the working capital strategy becomes more risky. Both the net working capital and current ratio decrease as the working capital management strategy becomes riskier.

	Strategy		
	Conservative	Moderate	Aggressive
Balance Sheet	(in thousands of dollars)		
Current assets (CA)	$30,000	$20,000	$10,000
Fixed assets.....................	50,000	50,000	50,000
Total assets	$80,000	$70,000	$60,000
Current liabilities (CL) (8%)	$ 5,000	$15,000	$25,000
Long-term liabilities (12%)	35,000	20,000	5,000
Total liabilities	$40,000	$35,000	$30,000
Stockholders' equity (SE)	40,000	35,000	30,000
Total liabilities and equity	$80,000	$70,000	$60,000
Forecasted sales	$80,000	$80,000	$80,000
EBIT (20% of sales)	16,000	16,000	16,000
Interest expenses			
Short-term (8%)...............	400⎤	1,200⎤	2,000⎤
Long-term (12%)..............	4,200⎦ 4,600	2,400⎦ 3,600	600⎦ 2,600
Earnings before taxes	$11,400	$12,400	$13,400
Taxes (34%)	3,876	4,216	4,556
Net income (NI)..................	$ 7,524	$ 8,184	$ 8,444
Return on equity (NI/SE).........	18.8 percent	23.4 percent	29.5 percent
Net working capital (CA − CL) ..	$25,000	$ 5,000	($15,000)
Current ratio (CA/CL)	6.0 times	1.3 times	0.4 times

RAISE YOUR GRADES

Can you explain ...?

☑ the meaning of working capital management
☑ the difference between working capital and net working capital
☑ why working capital is important
☑ the goal of working capital management
☑ several factors influencing a firm's working capital policy
☑ why working capital management involves risk-return tradeoffs
☑ the difference between conservative, aggressive, and moderate strategies of working capital management
☑ how current asset strategies involve risk-return tradeoffs
☑ how financing-mix strategies involve risk-return tradeoffs
☑ the meaning of a yield curve
☑ several theories involving the shape of a yield curve

SUMMARY

1. Working capital represents a firm's investment in current assets. Net working capital is current assets minus current liabilities.
2. Working capital management is the management of a firm's current assets and current liabilities.
3. Working capital management is important because of its impact on reaching the goal of the firm. Working capital management affects not only a firm's short-term liquidity and profitability but also its long-term growth and survival. The manageability of working capital enables the manager to contribute to shareholder wealth maximization.
4. The goal of working capital management is to maintain the optimal level of net working capital in order to maximize shareholder wealth.
5. There is no single working capital policy that is optimal for all firms. An optimal working capital policy is influenced by numerous factors, including the kind of firm, the volume and variability of sales, and the length of a firm's operating cycle.
6. Working capital management involves risk-return tradeoffs because the level, composition, and financing of working capital always affect both a firm's risk and its profitability. Decisions involving these risk-return tradeoffs should be examined simultaneously to determine their joint impact on risk and profitability.
7. Risk-return tradeoffs are used to categorize working capital management strategies. Conservative strategies are characterized by low risk, low return; aggressive strategies by high risk, high return; and moderate strategies by moderate risk, moderate return.
8. Risk and profitability are both affected by the level of working capital. Too little working capital increases the risk of being unable to meet maturing obligations, but increases expected profitability. Too much working capital reduces profitability because it costs money to carry excess working capital, but it also reduces risk.
9. Risk and profitability are both increased as the proportion of short-term debt to finance working capital is increased. Similarly, risk and profitability are both decreased as the proportion of short-term debt is decreased.
10. A yield curve shows the structure of interest rates by plotting on a graph the yield of all bonds of the same quality with maturities ranging from the shortest to the longest available.
11. Several theories are used to explain the shape of a yield curve: expectations theory, liquidity preference theory, and market segmentations theory.

RAPID REVIEW

True or False

1. Working capital management concerns decisions about all of a firm's assets. [Section 9-1A]

2. Net working capital equals working capital less current liabilities. [Section 9-1B]

3. A firm with a current ratio greater than one has positive net working capital. [Section 9-1C]

4. Net working capital is that portion of a firm's current assets financed with long-term funds. [Section 9-1C]

5. Working capital management uses only a small portion of the financial manager's time. [Section 9-1D]

6. Liquidity is the ability to convert an asset into cash without significant loss. [Section 9-1D]

7. The goal of working capital management is to maintain the optimal level of net working capital. [Section 9-1E]

8. The greater the stability of cash flows, the higher the requirement for net working capital. [Section 9-1E]

9. Lengthening the cash cycle increases a firm's required level of working capital. [Section 9-1E]

10. Technical insolvency is the inability of a firm to pay its obligations as they come due. [Section 9-2]

11. Short-term interest rates are generally higher than long-term interest rates. [Section 9-2A]

12. The traditional yield curve is upward sloping. [Section 9-2A]

13. Expectations theory can be used only to explain upward sloping yield curves. [Section 9-2B]

14. The hedging approach is an example of an aggressive working capital management strategy. [Section 9-3A]

15. Long-term financing is used to finance current assets under the hedging approach. [Section 9-3A]

16. Maintaining a high level of current assets in the form of marketable securities reduces the probability of technical insolvency. [Section 9-3B]

17. A higher level of working capital increases the firm's profitability. [Section 9-3B]

18. The term *permanent assets* refers only to fixed assets such as machinery, buildings, and equipment. [Section 9-3C]

19. Using short-term debt to finance permanent assets increases the risk of insolvency. [Section 9-3C]

20. Financing fluctuating current assets with long-term financing is a conservative strategy. [Section 9-3C]

Multiple Choice

21. Net working capital is a firm's:

    (a) current assets
    (b) current liabilities
    (c) current assets less current liabilities
    (d) total assets less total liabilities

    [Section 9-1B]

22. Working capital is important for all the following reasons *except* that is:

    (a) consists of a large portion of a firm's total assets
    (b) affects a firm's liquidity and profitability
    (c) consumes a small portion of the financial manager's time
    (d) consists of those assets that are most manageable

    [Section 9-1D]

23. The optimal level of working capital depends on all of the following factors *except* the:

    (a) kind of firm
    (b) stability of dividends
    (c) variability of cash flows
    (d) length of the cash cycle

    [Section 9-1E]

24. Which of the following assumptions does not underlie risk-return tradeoffs in managing working capital?

    (a) Fixed assets remain constant
    (b) Current assets are less profitable than fixed assets
    (c) The yield curve is downward sloping
    (d) Short-term financing is less expensive than long-term financing

    [Section 9-2A]

25. Which of the following theories explains only upward-sloping yield curves?

    (a) Expectations theory
    (b) Liquidity preference theory
    (c) Market segmentation theory
    (d) None of the above

    [Section 9-2B]

26. A firm following an aggressive working capital strategy would:

    (a) hold substantial amounts of liquid assets
    (b) minimize the amount of short-term financing
    (c) finance fluctuating assets with long-term financing
    (d) minimize the amount of funds held in liquid assets

    [Section 9-3A]

27. Conservative working capital management strategies involve:

    (a) low risk, low return
    (b) low risk, high return
    (c) high risk, high return
    (d) moderate risk, moderate return

    [Section 9-3A]

28. According to the hedging approach, working capital should be financed with:

    (a) spontaneously generated funds
    (b) short-term financing
    (c) short-term and long-term financing
    (d) long-term financing

    [Section 9-3A]

29. The probability of technical insolvency is reduced by:

    (a) financing permanent assets with short-term debt
    (b) financing fluctuating assets with long-term debt

(c) maintaining a high level of liquid assets
(d) Both b and c

[Sections 9-3B & C]

30. Which of the following actions would increase risk?

(a) Increase the level of working capital
(b) Change the composition of working capital to include more liquid assets
(c) Increase the amount of short-term borrowing
(d) Increase the amount of equity financing

[Section 9-3C]

Answers

True or False

		Multiple Choice
1. False	11. False	21. c
2. True	12. True	22. c
3. True	13. False	23. b
4. True	14. False	24. c
5. False	15. False	25. b
6. True	16. True	26. d
7. True	17. False	27. a
8. False	18. False	28. b
9. True	19. True	29. d
10. True	20. True	30. c

SOLVED PROBLEMS

Use the following information about Sunset Patio Company to solve Problems 9-1 through 9-5.

The Sunset Patio Company has the following balance sheets as of December 31, 19x6 and 19x7.

	19x7	19x6
Cash	$ 2,000	$ 1,500
Marketable securities	3,000	2,000
Accounts receivable	3,500	2,500
Inventory	3,500	4,000
Prepaid expenses	500	500
Total current assets	$12,500	$10,500
Net fixed assets	60,000	60,000
Total assets	$72,500	$70,500
Accounts payable	$ 1,000	$ 6,000
Notes payable	4,000	2,000
Total current liabilities	$ 5,000	$ 8,000
Long-term debt	10,000	10,000
Total liabilities	$15,000	$18,000
Common stock	15,000	15,000
Additional paid-in capital	20,000	20,000
Retained earnings	22,500	17,500
Total stockholders' equity	$57,500	$52,500
Total liabilities and equity	$72,500	$70,500

PROBLEM 9-1: Determine the working capital for each year.

Answer: Sunset Patio Company's working capital equals its current assets which are $10,500 for 19x6 and $12,500 for 19x7. **[Section 9-1]**

PROBLEM 9-2: Calculate the net working capital each year.

Answer: Sunset Patio Company's net working capital (current assets—current liabilities) for 19x6 and 19x7 is:

Year	Current Assets	−	Current Liabilities	= Net Working Capital
19x6	$10,500	−	$8,000	= $2,500
19x7	$12,500	−	$5,000	= $7,500

[Section 9-1A]

PROBLEM 9-3: Calculate the current ratio for each year.

Answer: Sunset Patio Company's current ratio (current assets/current liabilities) for 19x6 and 19x7 is:

Year	Current Ratio
19x6	$10,500/$8,000 = 1.31 times
19x7	$12,500/$5,000 = 2.50 times

PROBLEM 9-4: Has the composition of Sunset Patio Company's current assets become more or less liquid?

Answer: A percentage (common-size) statement of Sunset Patio Company's current assets for 19x6 and 19x7 is shown below.

	19x7 (Percent)	19x6 (Percent)
Cash	16.0	14.3
Marketable securities	24.0	19.0
Accounts receivable	28.0	23.8
Inventory	28.0	38.1
Prepaid expenses	4.0	4.8
Total current assets	100.0	100.0

The composition of the current assets has become more liquid. The percentage of current assets held in the most liquid assets (cash and marketable securities) increased from 33.3 percent in 19x6 to 40.0 percent in 19x7. **[Sections 9-1D]**

PROBLEM 9-5: Has the overall liquidity of Sunset Patio Company improved?

Answer: Based on the increase in the firm's current ratio and the shift in the composition of current assets, the liquidity position of Sunset Patio Company has improved from 19x6 to 19x7. **[Sections 9-3A-C]**

Problems 9-6 through 9-13 refer to DiBacco Manufacturing Company. Use the following information to solve Problem 9-6 and Problem 9-7.

DiBacco Manufacturing Company
Balance Sheet
December 31, 19x7

Cash	$ 20,000	Current liabilities* (10%)........	$ 200,000
Marketable securities	30,000	Long-term liabilities (15%)	300,000
Accounts receivable.............	150,000	Total liabilities	$ 500,000
Inventory.......................	200,000		
Total current assets	$ 400,000		
Net fixed assets	600,000	Stockholders' equity.............	$ 500,000
Total assets...................	$1,000,000	Total liabilities and equity	$1,000,000

* *Assume that all current liabilities are in the form of short-term debt.*

During 19x7 the firm's earnings before interest and taxes were 20 percent of $800,000 in sales. The income tax rate is 34 percent.

PROBLEM 9-6: Determine the level of working capital, net working capital, and current ratio.

Answer:

$$\text{Working Capital} = \$400,000$$
$$\text{Net Working Capital} = \$400,000 - \$200,000 = \$200,000$$
$$\text{Current Ratio} = \$400,000 \div \$200,000 = 2 \text{ times}$$

[Sections 9-1A through 9-1C]

PROBLEM 9-7: Calculate the return on equity (net income/stockholders' equity).

Answer: DiBacco's return on equity is 12.5 percent ($62,700/$500,000).

DiBacco Manufacturing Company
Income Statement
For the Year Ended December 31, 19x7

Net sales...	$800,000
EBIT (20% of sales)	160,000
Less: Interest expense	
Short-term debt (10%)	20,000
Long-term debt (15%)	45,000
Earnings before taxes...	$ 95,000
Less: Income taxes (34%)...	32,300
Net income...	$ 62,700

[Section 9-2]

Use the following information about DiBacco Manufacturing Company to solve Problem 9-8 and Problem 9-9.

DiBacco Manufacturing Company decides to examine its working capital policy. In addition to its current strategy of maintaining current assets at 50 percent of sales, DiBacco is considering two other strategies based on current assets at 30 or 70 percent of next year's sales. Projected net sales and fixed assets for next year are $1,000,000 and $600,000, respectively. DiBacco plans to maintain its existing capital structure of 50 percent debt and 50 percent equity. Current liabilities are to be 40 percent of projected total liabilities.

PROBLEM 9-8: Calculate DiBacco's net working capital and current ratio under each of the three strategies.

Answer: The net working capital and current ratios for each strategy are shown below.

	Strategies Current Assets as a Percent of Sales		
	30%	50%	70%
Current assets (CA)	$300,000	$ 500,000	$ 700,000
Fixed assets	600,000	600,000	600,000
Total assets.........................	$900,000	$1,100,000	$1,300,000
Current liabilities (CL)*	$180,000	$ 200,000	$ 260,000
Long-term liabilities....................	270,000	330,000	390,000
Total liabilities......................	$450,000	$ 550,000	$ 650,000
Stockholders' equity (SE)...............	450,000	550,000	650,000
Total liabilities and equity...............	$900,000	$1,100,000	$1,300,000
Net working capital (CA − CL)	$120,000	$ 300,000	$ 440,000
Current ratio (CA/CL)	1.7 times	2.5 times	2.7 times

* Assume that all current liabilities are in the form of short-term debt.

[Section 9-1B & C]

PROBLEM 9-9: Explain what effect these strategies would have on DiBacco's liquidity.

Answers: The firm's liquidity position, as measured by the amount of net working capital and current ratio, improves when current assets are a higher percentage of sales.

[Section 9-1D]

Refer to Problem 9-7 and the following information for DiBacco Manufacturing Company to solve Problems 9-10 through 9-11.

DiBacco Manufacturing Company expects its earnings before interest and taxes in 19x8 to be 18 percent of $1,000,000 in sales. Interest rates are projected to remain at 10 percent for short-term debt and 15 percent for long-term debt. The firm's tax rate will be 34 percent.

PROBLEM 9-10: What is DiBacco's rate of return on equity for each of the three strategies?

Answer: The rate of return on equity for each strategy is shown below.

	Strategies Current Assets as a Percent of Sales		
	30%	50%	70%
Net sales................................	$1,000,000	$1,000,000	$1,000,000
EBIT (18% of sales).....................	180,000	180,000	180,000
Interest expense			
Short-term debt (10%).................	18,000	20,000	26,000
Long-term debt (15%)	40,500	49,500	58,500
Earnings before taxes...................	$ 121,500	$ 110,500	$ 95,500
Income taxes (34%).....................	41,310	37,570	32,470
Net income.............................	$ 80,190	$ 72,930	$ 63,030
Return on equity (NI/SE)	17.8%	13.0%	9.7%

[Section 9-3A]

PROBLEM 9-11: Describe the relationship between DiBacco's liquidity and profitability.

Answer: DiBacco's profitability decreases as liquidity increases. For example, the firm's liquidity (current ratio = 2.7 times) is the highest but profitability (ROE = 9.7 percent) is the lowest when current assets are 70 percent of sales.   **[Section 9-2]**

Use the following information for DiBacco Manufacturing Company to solve Problem 9-12 and Problem 9-13.

DiBacco Manufacturing Company wants to determine the impact of changing the financing mix when using an aggressive current asset strategy of having current assets at 30 percent of sales. Earnings before interest and taxes are expected to be $180,000. Short-term interest rates are 10 percent and long-term rates are 15 percent. The firm's tax rate is 34 percent. DiBacco wants to maintain a mix of 50 percent debt and 50 percent equity under conservative, hedging, and aggressive financing strategies as shown below:

DiBacco Manufacturing Company
Pro Forma Balance Sheet
December 31, 19x8

	Financing-Mix Strategies		
	Conservative	Hedging	Aggressive
Current assets (CA)	$300,000	$300,000	$300,000
Fixed assets	600,000	600,000	600,000
Total assets..........................	$900,000	$900,000	$900,000
Current liabilities (CL) (10%)............	$100,000	$300,000	$450,000
Long-term liabilities (15%)..............	350,000	150,000	0
Total liabilities........................	$450,000	$450,000	$450,000
Stockholders' equity (SE)................	450,000	450,000	450,000
Total liabilities and equity.............	$900,000	$900,000	$900,000

PROBLEM 9-12: Show the expected return on equity, net working capital, and current ratio for each proposed strategy.

Answer: The return on equity, net working capital, and current ratio for each strategy are shown below.

	Financing-Mix Strategies		
	Conservative	Hedging	Aggressive
EBIT	$180,000	$180,000	$180,000
Interest expenses			
Short-term (10%).....................	10,000	30,000	45,000
Long-term (15%)	52,500	22,500	0
Earnings before taxes...................	$117,500	$127,500	$135,000
Income taxes (34%)....................	39,950	43,350	45,900
Net income (NI)	$ 77,550	$ 84,150	$ 89,100
Return on equity (NI/SE)	17.2%	18.7%	19.8%
Net working capital (CA-CL).............	$200,000	0	($150,000)
Current ratio (CA/CL)	3.0 times	1.0 times	0.7 times

[Sections 9-1B & C]

PROBLEM 9-13: Describe the risk-return tradeoffs of these three policies.

Answer: Combining an aggressive current asset strategy with an aggressive financing-mix strategy produces the highest return on equity. Higher potential profitability is accompanied by greater risk in the form of lower liquidity. DiBacco may be unable to meet required payments due to its relatively low level of working capital. In fact, the firm's net working capital is negative under this aggressive financing-mix strategy.

[Sections 9-3A through 9-3C]

10 MANAGING CASH AND MARKETABLE SECURITIES

THIS CHAPTER IS ABOUT

☑ **Managing Cash**
☑ **Float**
☑ **Accelerating Collections**
☑ **Slowing Disbursements**
☑ **Determining Appropriate Cash Balances**
☑ **Investing Idle Cash**
☑ **Types of Marketable Securities**

10-1. Managing Cash

Cash management is the process of managing a firm's liquid assets. **Liquid assets** consist of cash and assets easily converted into cash, such as marketable securities. **Cash** is the amount of currency the firm has on hand, checks, and bank balances. Cash is the firm's most liquid asset. **Marketable securities** are generally short-term investment instruments used by the firm to earn a return on temporarily idle funds. Marketable securities represent *near cash* because they can be readily converted into cash.

A. The goal of cash management is to determine the target cash balance required to maintain liquidity while minimizing the total costs related to the investment in cash.

Cash management requires making risk-return tradeoffs. Excessive cash balances involve unnecessary costs that reduce profitability. Inadequate cash balances increase the risk of being unable to meet required payments because of possible cash shortages. Thus, cash management involves having the optimum amount of liquid assets on hand at the appropriate time.

B. There are four reasons for holding liquid assets.

1. *Transactions balances* are cash balances needed to meet expected cash flows. Transactions balances are necessary to conduct normal business activities and arise from the non-synchronization of cash inflows and outflows. The firm's need for transactions balances is reduced by the availability of commercial credit.
2. *Precautionary balances* are cash balances needed to meet unexpected cash flows. Precautionary balances provide a cushion against the uncertain cash flows due to seasonal or cyclical operations or unexpected problems. These balances are usually held in temporary interest-bearing investments.
3. *Compensating balances* are cash balances needed to compensate banks for providing loans and services. Some banks require firms to maintain a certain amount of money in their checking accounts in lieu of explicit payments to the lending bank. The bank then lends this money to earn a return for the services provided to the firm.

4. *Speculative balances* are cash balances needed to take advantage of profit-making activities. Liquid assets are sometimes held for opportunities requiring funds on short notice. This speculative motive is the least important reason for holding liquid assets.

C. Cash management involves three major decision areas.

All three major decision areas are incorporated into the firm's cash budget. These areas are as follows:

1. *Managing collections and disbursements.* This step involves minimizing idle cash balances by accelerating receipts and slowing disbursements. Management can control many factors that cause time lags in cash flows, but some factors are beyond its control.
2. *Determining appropriate cash balances.* This decision involves determining the minimum levels of cash needed to provide liquidity while minimizing the total costs of holding an investment in cash. Several approaches including mathematical models are available for determining the firm's optimal cash balances.
3. *Investing idle cash.* This step concerns developing strategies for managing marketable securities and selecting appropriate short-term investment instruments.

10-2. Float

Managing collections and disbursements requires a thorough understanding of float. **Float** is an amount of money represented by checks outstanding and in process of collection. It is measured in dollar-days. Thus, $5 million in float can be $1 million for five days, $5 million for one day, or any combination of amount and time that produces $5 million dollar-days. **Float time** is the time lag or delay between the moment of disbursement of funds on the part of the customer and the moment of receipt of funds on the part of the firm (seller). This time lag, also called **checkbook float**, results in a difference between the firm's cash balance as shown on the bank's books and the amount shown on the firm's own books.

A. There are two major types of float.

1. **Negative or collection float** is money received by the firm from its customers. **Collection float time** is the length of time between when a customer's check is mailed to the firm and when the money becomes available to the firm. A firm with negative float has an excess of *book* cash balances over *bank net collected* cash balances.

   Collection float consists of three separate elements.
   * **Mail float**—the time required for a check to move by mail from the customer (debtor) to the firm (creditor).
   * **Processing float**—the time required by the receiving firm to process and deposit a check with its bank for collection after receipt.
   * **Clearing time float**—the time required for the bank to clear a check.

   Collection float represents a foregone investment opportunity because these funds are not available to a firm until the buyers' checks clear. Thus, firms like to have a small collection float. Effective cash management attempts to reduce negative float by accelerating collections.

EXAMPLE 10-1: Marshak Enterprises receives average cash receipts of $25,000 per day. Six days are usually required from the time a check is mailed to the time that the money is available for use by the firm.

Marshak Enterprises' average collection float is $150,000 ($25,000 × 6 days). Thus, the firm's cash balance as shown on the bank's books would be $150,000 less than the amount shown on the firm's own books. The collection time float is six days.

2. **Positive or disbursement float** is money paid by the firm to its employees, suppliers, creditors, and others. **Disbursement float time** is the length of time during which the firm can continue to use funds that have been disbursed to, but not yet collected by, other parties. A firm with positive float has an excess of bank net collected cash balances over the balances shown on its own books. Positive float benefits the firm because it can earn a return on the delayed payment. Thus, firms like to have a large disbursement float. Effective cash management attempts to increase positive float by showing disbursements.

EXAMPLE 10-2: Marshak Enterprises writes $20,000 in checks each day. On average, it takes five days from the time the firm sends the checks to the time the cash leaves the firm's bank account.

Marshak Enterprises' disbursement float is $100,000 ($20,000 × 5 days). Thus, the firm's bank account averages $100,000 more than the balances recorded on its own checkbook. The disbursement time float is five days.

B. The development of electronic funds transfer systems (EFTS) has greatly reduced float.

Electronic funds transfer systems refer to the use of computers and other electronic devices to speed the transfer of funds and other financial data. Thus, various EFTS can be used to reduce both collection and disbursement float. For example, the use of electronic transfers between financial institutions through an *automated clearinghouse* (a computer facility linked by wire and computer tape to all the financial institutions served by the clearinghouse) has increased the speed and accuracy of clearing checks and other cash items.

10-3. Accelerating Collections

The objective of accelerating collections is to increase the speed of payment receipt without incurring excessive costs. The major purpose of speeding collections is to free cash in order to reduce the firm's total financing requirement.

A. There are several ways to expedite collections.

1. *Bill promptly and accurately*. The time consumed in the process of preparing invoices may be reduced through more efficient clerical procedures and better trained personnel.
2. *Send invoices from a location near the buyer*. Decentralized billing locations may reduce the time required for the customers to receive invoices if the firm's business is geographically disbursed.
3. *Use concentration banking*. Concentration banking involves the use of decentralized collections centers and local banks to speed up collection of payments. The purpose of concentration banking is to accelerate the flow of funds by instructing customers to remit payments to strategic collection centers. The payments are then deposited in the collection center's local bank. Surplus funds are transferred from these local bank accounts to *concentration accounts* or centralized bank accounts.
4. *Use a lockbox system*. A **lockbox** is a special post office box in the customers' local area to which customers are instructed to send their payments. A local bank picks up the checks, clears them in the local area, and notifies the firm of daily balances. The purpose of a lockbox collection system is to eliminate processing float. A lockbox system can also reduce the firm's internal processing costs because the bank handles the clerical work. The profitability of a lockbox system depends on the geographical dispersion of customers, the size of a typical payment, and the earnings rate on the released funds.
5. *Change the paying behavior of customers*. A firm may encourage its customers to pay sooner by using letters, telephone calls, or personal visits and by supplying self-addressed envelopes in which to pay their bills. The use of economic incentives,

such as cash discounts, may also encourage customers to pay bills faster. A **cash discount** is a reduction in price in exchange for the early payment.

6. *Use wire transfers.* A **wire transfer** is a means of electronically sending money between banks through the Federal Reserve System or a private bank wire system. Wire transfers eliminate mailing and check-clearing time associated with other funds transfer methods and are often used to transfer funds from collection banks to the concentration bank. Thus, the faster the firm deposits checks with its bank, the sooner they can be processed and cleared.

7. *Use depository transfer checks.* A **depository transfer check** is an unsigned, nonnegotiable check drawn against the bank of deposit with the purpose of concentrating funds. Depository transfer checks are also used to transfer funds from local collection center banks to the concentration bank in a timely manner. The depository check transfer process is slower than the wire transfer process but it is also less expensive. Depository transfer checks must clear through the banking system and thus do not eliminate mail or clearing float.

B. Accelerating collections reduces float and results in potential savings for the firm.

Accelerating collections benefits the firm because it can earn a return on the early collection of cash. Adopting methods to accelerate collections generally involves some costs. Hence, the return earned or benefits achieved from reducing collection float must exceed the cost. Equation 10-1 provides a way of calculating the annual pretax benefit of reducing collection float.

$$\begin{matrix} \text{Annual pretax} \\ \text{benefit of reducing} \\ \text{collection float} \end{matrix} = \begin{matrix} \text{Days reduction} \\ \text{in float time} \end{matrix} \times \begin{matrix} \text{Average daily} \\ \text{collections} \end{matrix} \times \begin{matrix} \text{Expected} \\ \text{return} \end{matrix} \qquad \textbf{(10-1)}$$

EXAMPLE 10-3: Owens Industries is planning to use a lockbox system which is expected to reduce the firm's collection float from six days to four days. The lockbox system will cost the firm $1,000 per month. The firm's average daily collections are $60,000. Investment opportunities of similar risk provide an expected return of 15 percent. Management is faced with the following questions:

(a) What is the dollar reduction in collection float by implementing the lockbox system?

(b) What is the annual pretax benefit of reducing the total collection float from 6 days to 4 days?

(c) What is the maximum amount that the firm should be willing to pay for the lockbox arrangement annually?

(d) Should Owens Industries use the lockbox system?

Owens' management reached the following conclusions:

(a) By implementing the lockbox system, collection float will be reduced by $120,000 (2 days × $60,000).

(b) Substituting the reduction in float time = 2 days, average daily collections = $60,000, and expected return = 15 percent in Equation 10-1 indicates that Owens will be able to earn an additional $18,000 by reducing the collection float.

$$\begin{matrix} \text{Annual pretax benefit of} \\ \text{reducing collection float} \end{matrix} = (2 \text{ days})(\$60,000)(0.15) = \$18,000$$

(c) The cost of the lockbox arrangement is $12,000 (12 months × $1,000 per month) and the savings is $18,000. The maximum amount that Owens Industries should pay annually is $18,000.

(d) Owens Industries should use the lockbox system because the projected benefits exceed the costs by $6,000.

Annual pre-tax benefit.	$18,000
Annual pre-tax cost	12,000
Annual savings of the lockbox system	$ 6,000

10-4. Slowing Disbursements

The objective of slowing disbursements is to delay paying suppliers and other creditors as long as possible without jeopardizing the firm's credit standing or incurring any additional finance charges.

A. There are several ways to delay disbursements.

1. *Delay payments to suppliers.* The firm should pay its bills on time, not before or after they are due. Early payments result in lower average cash balances and thus the loss of potential returns from investing idle cash. Late payments result in lost discounts and jeopardize a firm's credit rating. Cash disbursements can be slowed by taking advantage of credit terms offered by vendors.

2. *Establish a zero balance system.* A **zero balance system** is a payment system that uses a master disbursing account to service all other disbursing accounts. Only the master account has a dollar balance. Checks written against zero balance accounts and presented to the bank for payment are covered either by the bank automatically transferring sufficient funds to cover daily payments from the master account or by receiving a daily payment from the firm by a wire transfer. A zero balance system provides centralized control over the disbursement of funds and eliminates idle cash balances.

3. *Use drafts to pay bills.* A **draft** is an order for the payment issued by one party to another party. Unlike checks, time drafts are not payable on demand. A draft must be presented to and accepted by the issuing party before payment will be made. A bank acts only as an agent in collecting the draft and in clearing and presenting drafts for final payment to the firm. The use of drafts causes some delay before the cash must be deposited to cover the drafts. This delay allows the firm to maintain smaller bank balances. These benefits, however, are offset by the higher cost of drafts relative to checks and service charges imposed by banks on firms using drafts.

4. *Match transfers with check clearings.* This is the strategy of managing disbursement float. The practice of "playing the float" allows the financial manager to increase the firm's interest earnings on investments by minimizing the balances in disbursement accounts. The firm estimates the dollar amount of the checks expected to clear on a daily basis and then transfers sufficient funds into a disbursement account. Synchronizing transfers with check clearings is often used with predictable accounts such as payroll and dividend disbursements. This procedure requires careful analysis of payment patterns and accurate forecasting. Otherwise, the firm may have insufficient funds in its checking account when checks arrive for payment.

5. *Use remote disbursements.* Remote disbursements lengthen the time it takes for a check to clear the banking system. Checks can take up to a week longer to clear a distant bank than to clear a local bank. This allows the firm to keep its money longer. One approach is to use *crisscross patterns.* Checks written for payment of goods or services in a firm's own locale are drawn against a bank in a distant part of the country to get the crisscross effect. For example, a firm in New York may issue a check drawn against a San Francisco bank to pay suppliers who are also in New York.

B. Slowing disbursements may involve opportunity costs.

An **opportunity cost** is the rate of return that funds could earn if they were invested in the best available alternative. A firm incurs an opportunity cost if it fails to take advantage of a cash discount provided by creditors. A cash discount is a reduction in price given for early payment. For example, if a supplier gives a firm credit terms of 2/10, net 30, this means that a 2 percent discount is given if the account is paid within 10 days, otherwise the entire amount is due within 30 days. Equation 10-2 shows the approximate annual percentage cost of not taking discounts.

$$\frac{\text{Cost of foregoing}}{\text{a cash discount}} = \frac{\text{discount (\%)}}{100\% - \text{discount (\%)}} \times \frac{360 \text{ days}}{\text{credit period} - \text{discount period}} \quad \textbf{(10-2)}$$

The numerator of the first ratio, discount (%), represents the cost per dollar of credit, while the denominator, 100% − discount (%), is the funds made available by not taking the discount. The second term in the equation is the number of times each year this cost is incurred. Sometimes 365 days is used instead of 360 days. (The subject of a missed discount is also discussed in Chapter 18.)

EXAMPLE 10-4: Brite Lights, Inc. buys materials from a supplier who gives credit terms of 2/10, net 30. The firm is trying to decide whether to take the discount or to pay sometime after the discount period.

Substituting the discount percent = 2 percent, the credit period = 30 days, and the discount period = 10 days in Equation 10-2, the failure to take the cash discount results in an annual opportunity cost of :

$$\frac{2\%}{100\% - 2\%} \times \frac{360}{30 - 10} = 0.3673 = 36.73 \text{ percent}$$

If possible, Brite Lights should take the cash discount because it represents a savings, but the firm should pay on the tenth day. If the firm fails to take the cash discount, it should pay the full invoice on the thirtieth day and thus take advantage of the credit for the longest possible time. The company could jeopardize its relationships with the supplier and its credit rating by paying later than the credit terms specify.

10-5. Determining Appropriate Cash Balances

Cash balances should be adequate but not excessive. Cash balances that are too high or too low are costly to the firm and reduce profitability. Thus, the appropriate cash balance involves a tradeoff between liquidity and profitability. The level of cash balances depends on numerous factors, including management's attitude toward risk and the firm's cash management policies, liquidity position, projected cash flows, and ability to borrow.

A. A firm's target cash balance is the larger of its required compensating balances or its transactions balances plus precautionary balances.

The appropriate cash level to maintain is usually the total of compensating balance requirements of banks with which the firm has accounts. When compensating balances are not required, the target cash balance reflects the transactions balances plus precautionary balances. Determining transactions and precautionary balances is difficult because of the variability and uncertainty of cash flows.

B. Cash management models are mathematical models used to determine the optimal cash balances.

Cash management may be considered as an inventory problem. Optimal cash balances may be found by using inventory-type models discussed in Chapter 11. Cash management models vary both in their complexity and usefulness. Formal models are often impractical to implement because of restrictive assumptions and costly procedures in obtaining input data. However, these formal models can provide insight and guidance into the problem of determining appropriate cash balances. They are especially useful when combined with cash budgets and pro forma financial statements.

There are two major types of cash management models.

1. *Deterministic models* assume that the firm has steady, predictable cash flows over some time period. Deterministic models, also called **cost-balancing models**, specify the optimal cash balance needed to minimize total costs. These relatively simple models generally ignore seasonal or cyclical trends and assume that the firm's cash inflows and outflows occur at a steady, predictable rate. One deterministic cash management model is the *Baumol model*. Figure 10-1 shows that under the

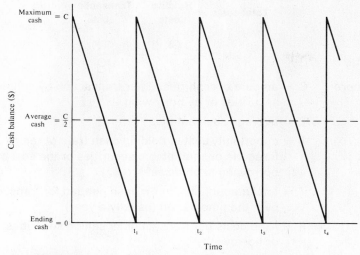

FIGURE 10-1   Baumol model of cash balances.

Baumol model the firm begins with C dollars in cash. When this amount is expended, the cash balance is replenished by selling marketable securities or by borrowing additional C dollars. Determining the optimal cash balance or optimal transaction size, C^*, involves a tradeoff between holding costs and transaction costs.

- **Holding costs** are the opportunity costs associated with holding larger than average cash balances instead of earning a return on securities or other less liquid assets. For example, holding cash balances results in the interest foregone on investments in marketable securities. Holding costs increase as cash balances increase.

- **Transaction costs** are costs associated with inadequate cash balances, such as the cost of selling securities (brokerage fees) or borrowing to raise cash (interest expenses). Transaction costs decline as cash balances increase.

Figure 10-2 indicates that combining the transaction and holding cost curves produces a U-shaped total cost curve. The optimal level of cash balances is the minimum point of the total cost curve, C^*. The optimal average cash balance is $C^*/2$. Equation 10-3 shows how holding costs and transaction costs are combined in the Baumol model to produce total costs. For simplicity, costs are expressed on a before-tax basis.

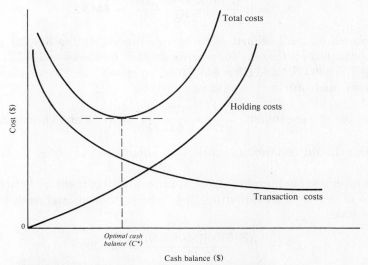

FIGURE 10-2   Determination of the optimal cash

$$\text{Total costs} = \frac{\text{Holding}}{\text{costs}} + \frac{\text{Transaction}}{\text{costs}}$$

$$= \frac{Ck}{2} + \frac{TF}{C} \qquad \text{(10-3)}$$

where
C = amount of cash raised per transaction by selling securities or by borrowing

$C/2$ = average cash balance

k = opportunity cost of holding cash (rate of return foregone on marketable securities or the cost of borrowing to hold cash)

T = total amount of net new cash needed for transactions over the time period (usually a year)

F = fixed costs per transaction of selling securities or borrowing

T/C = number of transactions during the period

Equation 10-4 is the Baumol model for determining the optimal amount of funds to transfer to the firm's cash account to minimize total costs, C^*. Equation 10-4 is derived from Equation 10-3 using either calculus or algebra.

OPTIMAL CASH BALANCES OR
OPTIMAL TRANSACTION SIZE
$$C^* = \sqrt{\frac{2FT}{k}} \qquad \text{(10-4)}$$

Equation 10-5 shows that the number of transactions needed to provide adequate cash over the period is determined by dividing the total amount of net new cash needed for transactions over the entire period, T, by the optimal amount of cash, C^*.

$$\text{Number of transactions} = \frac{T}{C^*} \qquad \text{(10-5)}$$

EXAMPLE 10-5: Lakewood Properties expects to have a steady demand for cash for the next year amounting to $800,000. The transaction cost associated with selling marketable securities or borrowing each time the firm needs to replenish its cash balances is $100. The opportunity interest rate is 8 percent per year.

(a) Substituting $F = \$100$, $T = \$800,000$, and $k = 0.08$ in Equation 10-4, the optimal level of cash balances of Lakewood Properties is:

$$C^* = \sqrt{\frac{(2)(\$100)(\$800,000)}{0.08}} = \$44,721$$

Thus, the firm should sell securities or borrow funds totaling $44,721 when its cash balances approach zero, thereby increasing its cash balances to $44,721.

(b) Substituting $T = \$800,000$ and $C^* = \$44,721$ in Equation 10-5, the approximate number of transactions made during the year is:

$$\text{Number of transactions} = \frac{T}{C^*} = \frac{\$800,000}{\$44,721} = 17.89 \text{ or 18 transactions}$$

Thus, the firm should conduct a transaction about once every 20 days (360 days/18 transactions).

(c) Suppose the interest rate increases from 8 percent to 10 percent. Substituting the new interest rate of $k = 0.10$ in Equation 10-4 reduces the optimal cash balances from $44,721 to $40,000.

$$C^* = \sqrt{\frac{(2)(\$100)(\$800,000)}{0.10}} = \$40,000$$

There is an inverse relationship between the optimal cash balances, C^*, and the holding costs, k. Less cash should be held as the opportunity cost of holding cash increases.

(*d*) Now suppose transaction costs increase from $100 to $150 but the interest rate remains 8 percent. Substituting the new transaction cost of $F = \$150$ in Equation 10-4 increases the optimal level of cash balances from $44,721 to $54,772.

$$C^* = \sqrt{\frac{(2)(\$150)(\$800,000)}{0.08}} = \$54,772$$

There is a direct relationship between the optimal cash balances, C^*, and the fixed costs of making a securities trade or borrowing, F.

2. *Probabilistic models* incorporate uncertainty in the the cash inflows and outflows. The Miller-Orr model assumes that daily cash flows are random but that their distribution is approximately normal. Figure 10-3 shows how the Miller-Orr model operates over time. This model establishes an upper limit, U, and a lower limit, L, for cash balances. Marketable securities are bought if the upper limit is reached. This action reduces the cash balances to Z dollars. Marketable securities are sold if the lower control point is reached, increasing the cash balances to Z dollars. In both cases, Z is referred to as the *target cash balance* or *return point*. No action is taken when cash balances fluctuate between the upper and lower limits.

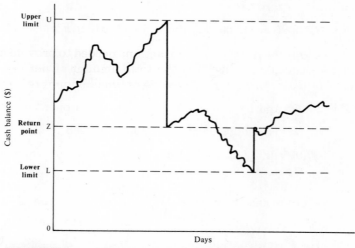

FIGURE 10-3   Miller-Orr model of cash balances.

Probabilistic models are generally more complex than deterministic models because they deal with conditions of uncertainty. Equation 10-6 shows that the Miller-Orr model incorporates not only information about holding and transaction costs but also information about the variability of cash flows.

OPTIMAL LEVEL OF CASH BALANCES
$$Z = \sqrt[3]{\frac{3F\sigma^2}{4k}} + L \qquad \text{(10-6)}$$

where Z = target cash balance or return point

F = fixed costs per transaction

σ^2 = variance of net daily cash balances (the variability in the distribution of changes in the firm's cash balances)

k = opportunity cost on a daily basis (daily interest rate on marketable securities)

L = lower limit

This model has several important implications:

- The target cash balance, Z, increases with both F and σ^2.
- The target cash balance, Z, decreases with k because holding more cash is more costly as the value of k increases.
- The target cash balance is not midway between the upper and lower limits.
- The lower limit is not necessarily zero.

Equation 10-7 shows the optimal value for the upper control limit.

OPTIMAL VALUE OF THE UPPER LIMIT
$$U = 3Z - 2L \qquad \textbf{(10-7)}$$

The average cash balance cannot be determined exactly, but can be approximated using Equation 10-8.

$$\text{Average cash balance} = \frac{4Z - L}{3} \qquad \textbf{(10-8)}$$

EXAMPLE 10-6: Biles Electronics Company's daily net cash flows fluctuate randomly and have a variance of $1,000,000. The current interest rate on marketable securities is 12 percent annually. Assume a daily compound interest rate of 0.000315 based on a 360-day year. The fixed costs of converting marketable securities into cash are $150. The firm wants to use the Miller-Orr model to direct transfers from cash to marketable securities and vice versa. The firm maintains a zero cash balance as its lower limit.

(a) Substituting $F = \$150$, $\sigma^2 = \$1,000,000$, and $k = 0.000315$ in Equation 10-6, the optimal cash balance is:

$$Z = \sqrt[3]{\frac{(3)(\$150)(\$1,000,000)}{(4)(0.000315)}} = \$7,095$$

(b) Substituting $Z = \$7,095$ and $L = \$0$ in Equation 10-7, the upper limit is:

$$H = (3)(\$7,095) - (2)(\$0) = \$21,285$$

(c) Substituting $Z = \$7,095$ and $L = \$0$ in Equation 10-8, the average cash balance is estimated to be:

$$\text{Average cash balance} = \frac{(4)(\$7,095) - \$0}{3} = \$9,460$$

10-6. Investing Idle Cash

Idle funds are typically invested in marketable securities, such as Treasury bills and commercial paper. Marketable securities are held as a substitute for cash and as a temporary investment to meet seasonal needs or to cover unpredictable financing needs. An alternative to holding excess cash in marketable securities is to use short-term borrowing as a source of needed cash balances. This strategy is generally regarded as more risky because the firm may encounter difficulties in borrowing funds or repaying loans. The firm could also invest idle funds in securities offering higher expected returns such as stocks and bonds. However, these securities are not suitable for near-cash reserves due to their risks.

A. The appropriate level of marketable securities depends on several factors.

1. *Predictability of cash flows.* Cash flow patterns are generally only partially predictable. Other factors being equal, firms with less predictable cash flows should maintain a higher level of investment in marketable securities. Although owning marketable securities does not reduce uncertainty, it does provide a source for meeting both expected and unexpected financial requirements.
2. *Transaction costs.* The ability of marketable securities to buffer against cash shortages diminishes as the cost of buying and selling these securities increases.

3. *Interest rates.* Higher interest rates on marketable securities make holding cash more costly. Consequently, investment in marketable securities generally increases as short-term interest rates rise.

B. **There are five major characteristics to consider in selecting marketable securities.**

1. **Marketability** is the ability to sell a security quickly and with the minimum possibility of loss. Marketability is of prime importance for temporary investments and is enhanced by selecting widely-held, actively traded securities.
2. **Default risk** is the risk that a debt's interest or principal will not be repaid.
3. **Maturity** is the length of time remaining before a security is due to be repaid. Maturity should be short to reduce:

   - **Credit risk**—the risk that the issuing firm's financial position will worsen.
   - **Interest rate risk**—the risk that a loss will be incurred on the sale of a security sold before the maturity date due to an increase in interest rates.
   - **Purchasing power risk**—the risk that inflation will reduce the purchasing power of the sum of money to be repaid.

4. **Rate of return** is the yield of a security. A security's return is related to its risk. Generally, highly marketable securities with short maturities and low default risk have low yields.
5. **Minimum purchase size** is the lowest size of a security which can be purchased. Minimum purchase sizes exist for certain marketable securities and generally range from $1,000 to $100,000.

10-7. Types of Marketable Securities

Money market instruments are the most suitable form of investment for idle funds. The **money market** is the market for short-term debt instruments. A **money market instrument** is a high-grade security characterized by a high degree of safety of principal and maturities of one year or less. Money market instruments are divided into two major types:

- **Discount paper**—a money market instrument which sells for less than its par or face value. The buyer receives the par value at the security's maturity. The difference between the security's purchase price and par value represents the buyer's return.
- **Interest-bearing securities**—debt instruments which pay interest based on the security's face value.

A. **A *treasury bill* is a short-term U.S. government security with a maturity of one year or less, issued at a discount from face value.**

A treasury bill, or T-bill, is often called a risk-free security. T-bills are sold through competitive bidding at weekly and monthly auctions in minimum denominations of $10,000 with original maturities of 91 days, 182 days, and 52 weeks. Treasury bills are characterized by their lack of default risk, high degree of marketability, and exemption from state income taxes. Other Treasury securities include Treasury notes (securities with maturities of 1 to 10 years) and Treasury bonds (debt instruments with maturities of 10 years or longer), which have longer maturities. These other securities are only suitable for inclusion in a firm's marketable securities portfolio as they approach their maturity dates.

B. **A *Federal agency issue* is a debt instrument issued by an agency of the federal government.**

Federal agency issues include securities issued by housing credit agencies, including Federal Home Loan Banks and the Federal National Mortgage Association (Fannie Mae), and securities issued by farm credit agencies, including Banks for Cooperatives,

Federal Intermediate Credit Banks, and Federal Land Banks. These securities are sold in both discount and interest-bearing forms. Maturities range from a few days to several years. Their yields are generally below most private sector money market instruments and only moderately above Treasury securities of comparable maturity. Agency securities have low default risk and high marketability. Federal agency issues are not general obligations of the U.S. Treasury.

C. *Commercial paper* **is a short-term, unsecured obligation with maturities ranging from 2 to 270 days, issued by banks, corporations, and other borrowers.**

Marketability for commercial paper is poor, but firms that issue paper directly are generally prepared to repurchase the paper prior to maturity. The default risk varies but is normally low. Commercial paper is usually discounted but it can be interest bearing. Generally such instruments are sold by large corporations in multiples of $100,000.

D. **A** *negotiable certificate of deposit* **(NCD) is a debt instrument issued by a bank that usually pays interest at maturity.**

The default risk varies with the issuing institution. The minimum size of NCDs is $100,000 with maturities ranging from a few weeks to several years. Yields are above T-bills and commercial paper because NCDs contain some default and interest rate risks. NCDs can be easily resold prior to maturity. U.S. dollar-denominated NCDs issued by banks abroad are called **Eurodollar CDs**.

E. **A** *banker's acceptance* **is a time draft drawn on, and accepted by, a bank.**

A banker's acceptance begins as a written demand or draft for a bank to pay a given sum at a future date. The draft becomes a banker's acceptance when a bank writes "accepted" on it. Banker's acceptances are used as a source of financing in international trade. Banker's acceptances are sold as discount paper with maturities ranging from a few weeks to 9 months. The dollar amount of a banker's acceptance depends on the size of the commercial transaction. The yields on acceptances are competitive with the returns on other money market instruments, such as commercial paper and negotiable certificates of deposit. The competitive yield reflects their relatively low default risk because as many as three parties may be liable for payment at maturity. Banker's acceptances are traded in the marketplace.

F. **A** *repurchase agreement* **is an agreement whereby a seller of securities agrees to repurchase the securities on a specified future date at an agreed upon price.**

Repurchase agreements, also called RPs or repos, are attractive to corporations because of the flexibility or maturities. RPs are commonly made for one business day although longer, tailor-made maturities are possible. There are no standard denominations for RPs. These agreements have little risk because of their short maturity and the promise of the borrower to repurchase the securities at a fixed price. The securities involved are not limited to U.S. government issues but can be any sort of security which the supplier of funds is willing to accept.

G. **A** *money market mutual fund* **is an open-ended mutual fund that invests in money market instruments.**

Money market mutual funds sell shares to investors and then pool the funds to acquire money market instruments. These funds permit small investors to participate directly in high-yielding securities that often are available only in relatively large denominations. There are no standard denominations, but the minimum initial investment is usually $1,000. The shares are highly liquid because they can be sold back to the fund at any time. Yields depend on the money market instruments held in the portfolio of the fund.

RAISE YOUR GRADES

Can you explain...?

☑ the meaning of cash management
☑ four reasons for holding liquid assets
☑ three decision areas of cash management
☑ the meaning of float
☑ how a firm can accelerate collections
☑ the difference between concentration banking and a lockbox system
☑ how a firm can slow disbursements
☑ the tradeoff involved in determining the minimum cash balances
☑ the appropriate level of minimum cash balances
☑ the difference between deterministic and probabilistic cash management models
☑ factors affecting the appropriate level of marketable securities
☑ the criteria for selecting marketable securities
☑ different types of marketable securities

SUMMARY

1. Cash management is the process of managing a firm's liquid assets, which consist of cash and marketable securities.
2. Cash is the amount of currency a firm has on hand plus checks and bank balances.
3. Marketable securities are short-term investment instruments used to provide a return on temporarily idle funds.
4. A firm holds liquid asset balances to conduct transactions, for precautionary purposes, to compensate its banks for providing loans and services, and for speculative motives.
5. Cash management involves three decision areas: managing collections and disbursements, determining appropriate cash balances, and investing idle cash. All of these areas are incorporated into the firm's cash budget.
6. Float is money in the process of being collected.
7. Float time is the time lag between the moment of disbursement of funds on the part of the customer (buyer) and the receipt of funds on the part of the firm (seller). Float is classified into two types: collection (negative) float and disbursement (positive) float.
8. The primary object of accelerating collections is to hasten the receipt of payments without incurring excessive costs. Methods for reducing collection time include prompt billing, sending invoices from a location near the buyer, using concentration banking or a lockbox system, changing the paying behavior of customers, and using wire transfers or depository transfer checks.
9. The objective of controlling cash disbursements is to slow payments and to keep the firm's funds in the bank as long as possible. Techniques for slowing disbursements include delaying payments to suppliers, establishing a zero balance system, using drafts, matching transfers with check clearings, and using remote disbursements.
10. A tradeoff between liquidity and profitability is involved in determining the firm's minimum cash balances. Excessive cash balances enhance the firm's liquidity, but reduce profitability because of higher total financing costs and the opportunity costs of not investing idle cash.
11. The appropriate level of cash to maintain is the higher of the compensating balance requirements required by the firm's bank or its transactions balances plus precautionary balances. Usually the level of compensating balances dominates.
12. Cash management models are used to determine the level of optimal cash balances.

Two factors that complicate determining the optimal cash balances are variability and uncertainty of cash flows.

13. Deterministic models assume cash flow patterns are completely predictable, whereas probabilistic models assume cash flow patterns are random. These models provide some insights into the problem of cash balances, but their usefulness is limited by their restrictive assumptions and cost of implementation.

14. Idle cash balances are generally invested in marketable securities. The level of investment depends on the predictability of the firm's cash flows, transaction costs, and interest rates.

15. The primary criteria used by a firm in selecting marketable securities are marketability, default risk, maturity, rate of return, and minimum purchase size.

16. The most commonly used marketable securities are government issues, including U.S. Treasury securities and other federal agency issues. Nongovernment issues include commerical paper, negotiable certificates of deposit, bankers' acceptances, repurchase agreements, and money market mutual funds.

RAPID REVIEW

True or False

1. Liquid assets include all current assets except inventory. [Section 10-1]

2. The primary goal of cash management is to maximize the firm's return from investments in securities. [Section 10-1A]

3. Compensating balances are interest-bearing accounts which compensate firms for depositing funds in commercial banks. [Section 10-1B]

4. Funds held in precautionary balances are usually held entirely in cash. [Section 10-1B]

5. The most important reason for holding liquid assets is the speculative motive. [Section 10-1B]

6. Float is money in the process of being collected. [Section 10-2]

7. Collection float is also called negative float. [Section 10-2A]

8. Effective cash management attempts to increase negative float and decrease positive float. [Section 10-2A]

9. Use of concentration banking centralizes the firm's cash accounts. [Section 10-3A]

10. A lockbox system reduces disbursement float. [Section 10-3A]

11. The quickest way to transfer funds is by using a depository transfer check. [Section 10-3A]

12. A zero balance system provides centralized control over the disbursement of funds. [Section 10-4A]

13. Bank drafts speed up the collection of funds. [Section 10-4A]

14. The practices of remote disbursing and matching transfers with check clearings decrease disbursement float. [Section 10-4A]

15. A firm's appropriate cash balances involve a tradeoff between liquidity and profitability. [Section 10-5]

16. A firm's minimum cash balance is the smaller of its transactions balances plus precautionary balances or its total of required compensating balances. [Section 10-5A]

17. Deterministic cash management models assume that cash flows are perfectly predictable. [Section 10-5B]

18. The Baumol model aims to minimize a firm's total cost of having cash on hand. [Section 10-5B]

19. Transaction costs are costs associated with inadequate cash balances. [Section 10-5B]

20. Holding costs decrease as cash balances increase. [Section 10-5B]

21. Probabilistic cash management models assume that cash flows fluctuate randomly. [Section 10-5B]

22. The Miller-Orr model is a type of deterministic model. [Section 10-5B]

23. In the Miller-Orr model, marketable securities are sold when cash balances reach the upper control limit. [Section 10-5B]

24. The strategy of relying entirely on bank loans for short-term cash is more risky than holding marketable securities. [Section 10-6]

25. The utility of holding marketable securities diminishes as transaction costs increase. [Section 10-6A]

26. Default risk is the risk that a debt's interest or principal will not be repaid. [Section 10-6B]

27. Discount paper refers to debt instruments which pay interest on the face value of the security. [Section 10-7]

28. Treasury bills are often called risk-free securities. [Section 10-7A]

29. Repurchase agreements are used primarily to finance international trade. [Sections 10-7E & F]

30. Money market mutual funds lack liquidity because they have no secondary market. [Section 10-7G]

Multiple Choice

31. Which is *not* a purpose for a firm's holding cash?

    (*a*) To conduct normal business activities
    (*b*) To meet seasonal or unexpected cash requirements
    (*c*) To maximize the firm's earnings
    (*d*) To compensate banks for loans and services

    [Section 10-1B]

32. Collection float involves which of the following?

    (*a*) Mail float
    (*b*) Processing float
    (*c*) Clearing time float
    (*d*) All of the above

    [Section 10-2A]

33. All of the following are ways to accelerate collections *except*:

    (*a*) use a lockbox system
    (*b*) use concentration banking
    (*c*) use a zero balance system
    (*d*) use wire transfers

    [Section 10-3A]

34. All of the following are ways to slow disbursements *except*:

    (*a*) use depository transfer checks
    (*b*) use drafts
    (*c*) establish a zero balance system
    (*d*) match transfers with check clearings

    [Section 10-4A]

35. Under the Baumol model, the optimal cash balance involves a tradeoff between

    (*a*) transaction costs and holding costs
    (*b*) transaction costs and compensating balances

(c) opportunity costs and precautionary balances

(d) transaction costs and opportunity costs

[Section 10-5B]

36. The appropriate level of marketable securities depends on all of the following factors *except*:

(a) predictability of cash flows

(b) level of fixed assets

(c) transaction costs

(d) interest rates

[Section 10-6A]

37. All of the following are investment characteristics to consider when selecting marketable securities *except*:

(a) marketability

(b) default risk

(c) interest rate risk

(d) business risk

[Section 10-6B]

38. Two dimensions of marketability or liquidity are

(a) default risk and maturity

(b) speed of conversion into cash and minimum possibility of loss

(c) purchasing power risk and profit potential

(d) speed of conversion into cash and profit potential

[Section 10-6B]

39. All of the following are types of discount paper *except*

(a) Treasury bills

(b) commercial paper

(c) bankers' acceptances

(d) negotiable certificates of deposit

[Section 10-7D]

40. Which of the following consist of short-term, unsecured promissory notes generally sold by large corporations?

(a) Commercial paper

(b) Banker's acceptance

(c) Repurchase agreements

(d) Money market mutual funds

[Section 10-7C]

Answers

True or False			*Multiple Choice*
1. False	11. False	21. True	31. c
2. False	12. True	22. False	32. d
3. False	13. False	23. False	33. c
4. False	14. False	24. True	34. a
5. False	15. True	25. True	35. a
6. True	16. False	26. True	36. b
7. True	17. True	27. False	37. d
8. False	18. True	28. True	38. b
9. True	19. True	29. False	39. d
10. False	20. False	30. False	40. a

SOLVED PROBLEMS

Problem 10-1 through Problem 10-3 refer to the following information about TM Services Corporation.

The financial manager of TM Services Corporation is concerned about the firm's float. It takes on average five days for TM Services to obtain cash from its collections once a customer's check is mailed to the firm. However, it only takes four days from the time TM Services mails checks to employees, suppliers, and creditors until the checks clear the firm's bank account. The credit sales of TM Services average $50,000 per day and the firm's disbursements average $45,000 per day.

PROBLEM 10-1: How large is the firm's collection float?

Answer: The firm's average collection float is:

$$\$50,000 \times 5 \text{ days} = \$250,000 \qquad \textbf{[Section 10-2A]}$$

PROBLEM 10-2: How large is the firm's disbursement float?

Answer: The firm's average disbursement float is:

$$\$45,000 \times 4 \text{ days} = \$180,000 \qquad \textbf{[Section 10-2A]}$$

PROBLEM 10-3: If TM Services Corporation maintains a minimum cash balance of $100,000 on its own books, what will be the firm's average cash balance as shown on the bank's books?

Answer: The firm's average balance at its bank would be:

Cash balance on firm's books	$100,000
Average disbursement float	180,000
Average balance on bank's books	$280,000

Thus, TM Services Corporation has an excess of $180,000 of bank net collected balances over the balances shown on its own books. **[Section 10-2A]**

Problem 10-4 and Problem 10-5 refer to Sherman Furniture Company.

PROBLEM 10-4: Sherman Furniture Company currently has a centralized billing system in which all payments are made to a central location. The firm is considering a proposal from Second National Bank to establish a lockbox system that can shorten its accounts receivable collection period by 3 days. Credit sales for next year are estimated to be $14,600,000 and are billed on a continuous basis. Sherman forecasts that it can earn 12 percent before taxes on the released funds. The cost of the lockbox system is $10,000 for the next year.

(*a*) Determine the expected reduction in cash balances that would be realized through the adoption of a lockbox system. Use a 365-day year.

(*b*) Determine the annual pretax benefit of reducing the collection float.

(*c*) Should Sherman adopt the lockbox system?

Answer:

(a) The expected reduction in cash balances for the year is $120,000.

$$\text{Average daily collections} = \frac{\text{Annual credit sales}}{365 \text{ days}} = \frac{\$14,600,000}{365 \text{ days}} = \$40,000$$

$$\frac{\text{Reduction in}}{\text{cash balances}} = \frac{\text{Days reduction}}{\text{in float}} \times \frac{\text{Average daily}}{\text{collections}}$$

$$= 3 \times \$40,000 = \$120,000$$

(b) Using Equation 10-1, the annual pretax benefit of reducing the collection float is $14,400.

$$\text{Annual pretax benefit of reducing collection float} = (3)(\$40,000)(0.12) = \$14,400$$

(c) Yes, Sherman Furniture Company should adopt the lockbox system because the annual pretax benefit of $14,400 exceeds the $10,000 cost charged by the bank.

[Section 10-3B]

PROBLEM 10-5: Second National Bank offers Sherman Furniture Company two other options for pricing the lockbox system in lieu of paying a fixed annual charge of $10,000. With Pricing Option #2, the bank requires that Sherman keep $100,000 in a non-interest checking account as a compensating balance. With Pricing Option #3, the bank will charge $650 per month plus a $0.40 charge for each check processed. Sherman estimates that 50 checks will be processed per day. Sherman can earn 12 percent before tax on invested funds.

(a) What is the cost of each option?
(b) How do these two pricing options compare with Option #1 of paying the fixed annual charge of $10,000? Which option, if any, should Sherman Furniture Company select?

Answer:

(a) The cost per year of the lockbox system is:

Pricing Option #2

$$\text{Cost per year} = \text{Compensating balance} \times \text{expected return}$$
$$= \$100,000 \times 0.12 = \$12,000$$

Pricing Option #3

$$\text{Cost per year} = (\text{Monthly fixed charge} \times 12)$$
$$+ (\text{Checks per day} \times 365)(\text{Processing cost per check})$$
$$= (\$650 \times 12) + (50 \times 365)(\$0.40)$$
$$= \$7,800 + \$7,300 = \$15,100$$

(b) The new lockbox system is beneficial under Pricing Option #1 and Option #2, but not under Option #3. Option #1 is the most attractive because it provides the highest net benefit.

	Option #1	Option #2	Option #3
Benefit	$14,400	$14,400	$14,400
Cost	10,000	12,000	15,100
Net Benefit	$ 4,400	$ 2,400	($ 700)

[Section 10-3B]

PROBLEM 10-6: Arnell Cosmetics plans to introduce several new methods for speeding up collections and to reduce its average collection period from 32 days to 30 days. Its average collections per day are currently $150,000. Any funds freed through increased collection can earn a 14 percent return before taxes.

(*a*) How much funds will be freed by the collection speedup?

(*b*) What is the annual savings resulting from increased collections?

Answer:

(*a*) The funds freed by accelerating collections will be:

$$\$150{,}000 \times 2 \text{ days} = \$300{,}000$$

(*b*) The annual savings is:

$$\$300{,}000 \times 0.14 = \$42{,}000 \qquad \textbf{[Section 10-3B]}$$

PROBLEM 10-7: Tiny Tots Toy Company expects to have $40,150,000 in credit sales during the coming year. The firm distributes nationally but has all remittances sent to its home office in Cleveland. The firm's financial manager proposes a new collections system that will reduce float by 3 days. The released funds can be invested to earn 9 percent before taxes. Use a 365-day year.

(*a*) What is the amount of released funds?

(*b*) What is the maximum amount that the firm should be willing to pay for the proposed system?

Answer:

(*a*) The amount of the released funds is calculated by multiplying the credit sales per day times the 3-day reduction in float as follows:

$$\text{Credit sales per day} = \frac{\$40{,}150{,}000}{365 \text{ days}} = \$110{,}000$$

$$\text{Amount of released funds} = \$110{,}000 \times 3 \text{ days} = \$330{,}000$$

(*b*) Substituting the reduction in float time = 3 days, average daily collections $110,000, and expected return = 9 percent in Equation 10-1 gives an annual pretax benefit of $29,700.

$$\begin{array}{l}\text{Annual pretax benefit of} \\ \text{reducing collection float}\end{array} = (3 \text{ days})(\$110{,}000)(0.09) = \$29{,}700$$

The firm should pay no more than $29,700 to implement the proposed system.

[Section 10-3B]

PROBLEM 10-8: The financial manager of Elegant Watch Company is trying to determine whether or not to take a cash discount from one of its suppliers. The supplier offers terms of 1/15, net 30. Elegant Watch currently earns an annual return on marketable securities of 8 percent. Should the firm take the discount?

Answer: Substituting the discount = 1 percent, the credit period = 30 days, and the discount period = 15 days in Equation 10-2, the opportunity cost of foregoing the discount is:

$$\begin{array}{l}\text{Cost of foregoing} \\ \text{a cash discount}\end{array} = \frac{1\%}{100\% - 1\%} \times \frac{360}{30 - 15} = 0.2424 = 24.24 \text{ percent}$$

Elegant Watch should take the discount because the return is higher than can be earned on marketable securities.

[Section 10-4B]

Problem 10-9 and Problem 10-10 refer to Nash Tables.

PROBLEM 10-9: Nash Tables has accumulated $125,000 in excess cash which it has invested in marketable securities yielding 10 percent annually. The firm expects to use $100,000 of these marketable securities to cover net cash outflows anticipated during the next year. These net cash outflows are expected to occur evenly throughout the year. Liquidating the marketable securities involves fixed costs of $100 per transaction.

(a) Determine the optimal level of cash balances (size of withdrawal of marketable securities) using the Baumol model.
(b) What is the total costs of the cash balances? Use the optimal cash balances as the amount of cash in Equation 10-3.
(c) What is the firm's optimal average cash balances?
(d) How many times during the year will Nash have to make withdrawals from its marketable securities portfolio?

Answer:

(a) Using Equation 10-4, the optimal level of cash balances is:

$$C^* = \sqrt{\frac{(2)(\$100)(\$100,000)}{0.10}} = \$14,142$$

(b) Using Equation 10-3, the total cost for the use of cash needed for transactions is:

$$\text{Total costs} = \frac{(\$14,142)(0.10)}{2} + \frac{(\$100,000)(\$100)}{\$14,142}$$

$$= \$707 + \$707 = \$1,414$$

(c) The firm's optimal average cash balance is:

$$\text{Optimal average cash balance} = \frac{C^*}{2} = \frac{\$14,142}{2} = \$7,071$$

(d) Using Equation 10-5, Nash will make 7.07 transactions during the year by selling marketable securities to raise the cash needed.

$$\text{Number of transactions} = \frac{\$100,000}{\$14,142} = 7.07 \text{ times}$$

In practice, it is not possible for Nash to make exactly 7.07 transactions. If Nash makes 7 transactions, it will run out of cash at the end of the year. If Nash makes 8 transactions, it will have excess cash at the end of the year.   **[Section 10-5B]**

PROBLEM 10-10: Nash Tables is uncertain about the interest rate that it may be able to earn next year on marketable securities. The firm estimates that interest rates may range from 8 to 12 percent.

(a) What is the firm's optimal level of cash if interest rates are 8 percent, 10 percent, and 12 percent?
(b) What is the relationship between optimal cash balances and interest rates?

Use additional data in Problem 10-9 to solve this problem.

Answer:

(a) Using Equation 10-4, the optimal cash balances are calculated below.

8 percent interest rate

$$C^* = \sqrt{\frac{(2)(\$100)(\$100,000)}{0.08}} = \$15,811$$

10 percent interest rate

$$C^* = \sqrt{\frac{(2)(\$100)(\$100,000)}{0.10}} = \$14,142$$

12 percent interest rate

$$C^* = \sqrt{\frac{(2)(\$100)(\$100,000)}{0.12}} = \$12,910$$

(*b*) There is an inverse relationship between the optimal cash balances and the interest rates. Higher interest rates make it more expensive to hold cash balances. Thus, as interest rates increase, optimal cash balances decrease.   **[Section 10-5B]**

PROBLEM 10-11: Harris Sweater Company uses the Miller-Orr model to establish its target cash balances. The variance of the firm's daily net cash flows is $50,000. Idle cash balances are kept in marketable securities at 9 percent interest annually. The cost of transferring funds from Treasury bills into cash is $125 per transaction. Harris maintains a $5,000 minimum cash balance (lower limit) and computes its daily compound interest rate to be 0.000239, based on a 360-day year.

(*a*) What is Harris' target cash balance?
(*b*) What is the upper limit of its cash balance?
(*c*) What is the expected average cash balance?

Answer:

(*a*) Using Equation 10-6, the target cash balance is $10,810.

$$Z = \sqrt[3]{\frac{3F\sigma^2}{4k}} + L = \sqrt[3]{\frac{(3)(\$125)(\$500,000)}{(4)(0.000239)}} + \$5,000$$

$$= \$5,810 + \$5,000 = \$10,810$$

(*b*) Using Equation 10-7, the upper limit is $22,430.

$$U = 3Z - 2L = (3)(\$10,810) - (2)(\$5,000)$$

$$= \$32,430 - \$10,000 = \$22,430$$

(*c*) Using Equation 10-8, the average cash balance is $12,747.

$$\text{Average cash balance} = \frac{4Z - L}{3} = \frac{(4)(\$10,810) - \$5,000}{3} = \$12,747$$

[Section 10-5B]

11 ACCOUNTS RECEIVABLE AND INVENTORY MANAGEMENT

THIS CHAPTER IS ABOUT

- ☑ **Accounts Receivable**
- ☑ **Credit Policy**
- ☑ **Credit Analysis**
- ☑ **Inventory Management**
- ☑ **Economic Order Quantity**
- ☑ **Safety Stocks**

11-1. Accounts Receivable

Accounts receivable consists of money owed to a firm for goods or services sold on credit. This type of credit takes two basic forms.

- **Trade or commercial credit**—credit which the firm extends to other firms.
- **Consumer or retail credit**—credit which the firm extends to its final customers.

Firms offer credit in order to attract new customers and to keep current customers.

A. Granting credit affects the firm's cash cycle.

When the goods are shipped, the selling firm reduces its inventories and increases its accounts receivable. When customers pay, the firm reduces its accounts receivable and increases its cash. If customers do not pay, the selling firm eventually writes off the uncollected accounts receivable as bad debt expenses. Reducing the length of time customers take to pay accounts receivable shortens the firm's cash cycle.

B. The level of accounts receivable depends on the volume of credit sales and the average collection period.

Credit sales are noncash sales resulting from extending credit to customers. The nature of a firm's business is an important factor in determining the level of credit sales. The **average collection period** is the average number of days the firm waits, after making a credit sale, to receive the customer's cash payment. These determinants of the level of receivables are influenced both by credit policy variables that are within management's control and by economic conditions that are not within management's control.

C. Receivables are a component of a firm's working capital and represent investments.

The goal of accounts receivable management is to ensure that the firm's investment in accounts receivable is appropriate and contributes to shareholder wealth maximization. Managing accounts receivable consists of two major steps: establishing credit policy and conducting credit analysis.

11-2. Credit Policy

Credit policy is a set of guidelines for extending credit to customers. As a member of the finance department, the credit manager is primarily responsible for managing the firm's credit policy. Policy decisions involving accounts receivable are generally established by the president and vice-presidents in charge of finance, marketing, and manufacturing. A change in credit policy may affect both the firm's returns and its costs.

A. Credit policy decisions generally involve the loosening or tightening of the firm's overall credit.

1. *Loosening credit policy* is setting a less restrictive credit policy than currently exists. For example, loosening the firm's credit policy may include changes toward less rigorous credit standards, more liberal credit terms, and less aggressive collection efforts. Easing the credit policy stimulates sales and increases the investment in accounts receivable. A loose credit policy may cause some costs to rise, such as bad debt losses and opportunity costs of the added investment in accounts receivable.

2. *Tightening credit policy* is setting a more restrictive credit policy than currently exists. For example, tightening the firm's credit policy may consist of changes toward stricter credit standards, less lenient credit terms, and tougher collection efforts. Tightening the credit policy makes credit more difficult to obtain and reduces the level of both sales and accounts receivable. A tight credit policy may cause some costs to fall, such as bad debt losses and costs associated with a reduction in accounts receivable. However, other costs may rise, such as the costs of more aggressive collection efforts.

B. In theory, the firm's optimal credit policy should be one in which marginal profits on a change in credit policy equal the marginal costs.

The firm should extend its investment in accounts receivable up to the point where the expected return on the investment equals the required return. Shareholder wealth is maximized at this point. Decisions concerning the appropriate level of investment in accounts receivable are based on a tradeoff between marginal returns and marginal costs.

1. **Marginal or incremental returns** are the benefits associated with each additional dollar invested in accounts receivable. Marginal returns include the profits associated with a higher level of credit sales. Equation 11-1 shows the calculation of the return on investment from a marginal investment in accounts receivable.

$$\text{Return on marginal investment in accounts receivable (A/R)} = \frac{\text{Marginal pretax profit}}{\text{Marginal investment in A/R}} \quad \text{(11-1)}$$

2. **Marginal or incremental costs** are the costs associated with each additional dollar invested in accounts receivable. Marginal costs include the opportunity cost of the additional capital tied up in accounts receivable, the cost of administering credit and collecting receivables, and bad debt expenses. The *opportunity cost* is the required rate of return on the best alternative use of funds. Thus, the opportunity cost of funds invested in accounts receivable refers to the rate of return that the firm requires on this investment. Disagreement exists about how to measure the marginal investment in accounts receivable. Some experts use *variable cost* in measuring the opportunity cost of additional receivables investment, while others use *sales value*. The examples contained in this chapter use total sales value.

EXAMPLE 11-1: Webster Auto Parts has lost sales to competitors because of a restrictive credit policy. Management intends to liberalize its investment in accounts receivable in three stages. The firm plans to increase its investment in accounts receivable initially by $25,000 under Policy A, to add $15,000 more to accounts receivable in Policy B, and then to add $10,000 more to accounts receivable in Policy C. Each addition to accounts receivable involves greater bad debt losses because credit sales will be made to less creditworthy customers. The firm's required pretax return (or opportunity cost) on its receivables investment increases from Policy A to Policy C in order to compensate for the increased riskiness involved in extending additional credit.

	Policy A	Policy B	Policy C
Marginal pretax profits	$ 6,000	$ 3,000	$ 1,500
Marginal investment in A/R	25,000	15,000	10,000
Required pretax return	15%	20%	25%

(*a*) Using Equation 11-1, the returns on the marginal investment for the three different policies are shown below.

	Policy A	Policy B	Policy C
Return on marginal investment in A/R	$\dfrac{\$6,000}{\$25,000} = 24.0\%$	$\dfrac{\$3,000}{\$15,000} = 20.0\%$	$\dfrac{\$1,500}{\$10,000} = 15.0\%$

Webster Auto Parts should invest in accounts receivable through Policy A and Policy B because the marginal returns of 24 and 20 percent exceed or equal the required return. The additional $10,000 investment in accounts receivable provided in Policy C provides a return lower than that required and does not add to the value of the firm.

(*b*) The firm's total additional investment in accounts receivable will be $40,000, consisting of $25,000 from Policy A and an additional $15,000 from Policy B.

C. The firm's credit policy includes three major variables within the manager's control: credit standards, credit terms, and collection policies.

Credit standards are criteria and guidelines used by the firm to determine which customers get credit and how much credit each customer will get. **Credit terms** specify the repayment terms required of all customers. **Collection policies** are sets of procedures used to collect late accounts.

D. Credit standards allow the firm to exercise control over the credit quality of the accounts accepted.

Credit quality is the probability of payment. That is, the likelihood of customers paying their accounts receivable increases with their credit quality.

1. There are two common measures of credit quality: the average collection period and the bad debt loss ratio.

   - The **average collection period** is the amount of time customers take to pay the credit extended to them. An increase in the average collection period increases both the investment in accounts receivable and the cost of extending credit. Equations 11-2 and 11-3 are needed to compute the average collection period. (The average collection period is discussed further in Chapter 6.)

$$\text{Accounts receivable turnover} = \frac{\text{Net (credit) sales}}{\text{Accounts receivable}} \qquad \textbf{(11-2)}$$

$$\text{Average collection period} = \frac{365 \text{ days*}}{\text{Accounts receivable turnover}} \qquad \textbf{(11-3)}$$

* *Sometimes 360 days is used rather than 365 to simplify the calculation of the average collection period.*

EXAMPLE 11-2: Winslow Paint Company had $400,000 in credit sales during the past year and its accounts receivable averaged $40,000.

By substituting credit sales of $400,000 and accounts receivable of $40,000 in Equation 11-2, the accounts receivable turnover ratio is:

$$\text{Accounts receivable turnover} = \frac{\$400,000}{\$40,000} = 10 \text{ times}$$

Using Equation 11-3, the average collection period is:

$$\text{Average collection period} = \frac{365 \text{ days}}{10} = 36.5 \text{ days}$$

- The **bad debt loss ratio** is the proportion of the total receivables that is not paid. An increase in the bad debt loss ratio also increases the cost of extending credit. Equation 11-4 shows the bad debt loss ratio.

$$\text{Bad debt loss ratio} = \frac{\text{Bad debt expenses}}{\text{Credit sales}} \qquad \textbf{(11-4)}$$

EXAMPLE 11-3: Winslow Paint Company had $12,000 in bad debts on $400,000 in credit sales.

Substituting bad debt expenses of $12,000 and credit sales of $400,000 in Equation 11-4, the bad debt loss ratio is:

$$\text{Bad debt loss ratio} = \frac{\$12,000}{\$400,000} = 0.03 \text{ or } 3.0 \text{ percent}$$

2. Relaxing credit standards may increase the firm's sales and profits. Offering credit to more risky customers may also increase bad debt expenses, clerical and collection costs, and the opportunity cost of having more funds tied up in accounts receivable and/or inventory. Tightening credit standards may have the opposite effects. A firm operating at capacity and experiencing a sales increase may require more fixed assets. When there is idle capacity, additional profitability results from the incremental contribution margin (sales less variable costs) because fixed costs remain constant. Example 11-4 shows the effects of relaxing credit standards on marginal profits and marginal costs for Johnson Manufacturing Company.

EXAMPLE 11-4: Johnson Manufacturing Company is contemplating relaxing its credit standards in order to increase sales and to encourage more customers to purchase on credit. Credit sales are currently $500,000 but are expected to increase by $100,000. The firm has idle capacity and currently covers all of its fixed costs. The firm's variable costs are approximately 75 percent of sales. Thus, its contribution margin is 25 percent $(1 - 0.75)$ of its credit sales. The average collection period is expected to be 60 days for new customers, but existing customers are not expected to change their payment habits. The bad debt loss ratio is expected to be 3 percent of the sales to new credit customers, compared to 1 percent of the sales to current customers. The opportunity costs, on a pretax basis, of the added investment in accounts receivable are 20 percent. The owner asks the following questions (assume a 365-day year and no other changes):

(a) If the new credit standards are implemented, what will be the firm's marginal profits from the additional credit sales?
(b) What will be the additional costs associated with the new credit standards?
(c) Should Johnson Manufacturing relax its credit standards?
(d) What additional costs might Johnson Manufacturing incur by adopting the new credit standards?

Figure 11-1 presents the analysis of loosening the credit standards for Johnson Manufacturing Company.

1. Marginal profits on additional sales

    = Additional sales × Contribution margin

    = $100,000 × 0.25 = ... $25,000

2. Marginal increase in bad debt losses

    = Additional sales × Bad debt loss ratio

    = $100,000 × 0.03 = ... 3,000

3. Marginal investment in accounts receivable

    = Additional average daily sales × Average collection period

    = (Additional annual sales/365) × 60

    = ($100,000/365) × 60 = $274 × 60 = $16,440

    Opportunity cost on marginal investment in accounts receivable

    = Marginal investment in accounts receivable × Opportunity cost

    = $16,440 × 0.20 = ... 3,288

4. Net advantage (disadvantage) of liberalizing credit standards

    = Marginal profits − Marginal costs

    = 1 − (2 + 3)

    = $25,000 − ($3,000 + $3,288) = ... $18,712

FIGURE 11-1   An analysis of liberalizing credit standards for Johnson Manufacturing Company.

(a) Calculating the marginal profits on the additional credit sales involves multiplying the additional sales by the firm's contribution margin. Hence, the firm's marginal profits from relaxing its credit standards are:

MARGINAL PROFITS $100,000 × 0.25 = $25,000

(b) Calculating the marginal costs associated with the new credit policy entails determining the additional bad debts and the additional opportunity cost of the higher investment in accounts receivable. The marginal increase in bad debt losses is calculated by multiplying the additional sales by the bad debt loss ratio:

ADDITIONAL BAD DEBTS $100,000 × 0.03 = $3,000

The marginal investment in accounts receivable is determined by multiplying additional average daily sales by the average collection period [($100,000/365)(60) = $16,440]. The additional opportunity cost of the higher investment in accounts receivable is then calculated by multiplying the marginal investment in receivables by the firm's required return on the investment (opportunity cost).

OPPORTUNITY COST OF MARGINAL INVESTMENT IN A/R $16,440 × 0.20 = $3,288

(c) To determine whether the company should relax its current credit standards, it should compare its marginal profits on additional sales with the marginal costs associated with the increase in bad debt loss and the additional investment in accounts receivable.

Marginal profits	$25,000
Less: Additional bad debts...	3,000
Opportunity cost on marginal investment in A/R	3,288
Net advantage (disadvantage) of liberalizing credit standards	$18,712

Johnson Manufacturing Company should relax its credit standards because the marginal profits exceed the marginal costs.

(d) Johnson might incur additional costs from relaxing the credit terms which may include additional administration and collection costs associated with sales to less creditworthy customers. The firm may also incur costs related to an increase in inventory investment to support the new sales level.

E. Credit terms include the length of the credit period, cash discount, and cash discount period.

In trade discounts, for example, credit terms of *2/10, net 30* mean that a customer receives a two percent discount if the purchase invoice is paid within 10 days of the beginning of the credit period; otherwise, the full amount is due in 30 days. Seasonal dating on discounts may be offered to retailers and others whose sales are concentrated in a specific time period. **Seasonal datings** are special credit terms that permit discounts on payments made during the purchaser's selling season, regardless of when the goods were shipped. For example, the credit term *1/10, net 60, September 1 dating* means that the effective invoice date is September 1. A one percent discount may be taken until September 10, or the entire amount will be due October 30.

1. The **credit period** is the period over which credit is granted. Lengthening the credit period generally stimulates sales, increases the investment in accounts receivable due to a longer average collection period, and increases bad debt losses. Shortening the credit period has the opposite effects. Increases in sales have a positive effect on profits, whereas increases in accounts receivable and bad debts have a negative effect on profits.

2. A **cash discount** is a reduction in price given for early payment. Initiating or increasing the size of a cash discount usually stimulates sales, reduces the investment in accounts receivable due to a shorter average collection period, and decreases bad debt losses. Increases in profits resulting from these changes must be balanced against the cost of the cash discount. The optimal discount policy is the one in which the marginal returns and marginal costs of the cash discount exactly offset each other.

3. A **cash discount period** is the length of time a customer has to pay for a purchase and still receive the cash discount. Lengthening the cash discount period should stimulate sales and reduce bad debt losses. The net change in the average collection period is difficult to determine because of two conflicting forces affecting the firm's average collection period. Some current discount takers will pay later due to the extended discount period. This factor increases the average collection period. On the other hand, some customers, who do not now use the discount, will do so under the new policy. This second factor decreases the average collection period. Shortening the cash discount period should have the opposite effects from those described above.

EXAMPLE 11-5: Instead of liberalizing its credit standards, Johnson Manufacturing Company is considering changing its credit terms from *net 30* to *net 45*. The firm expects that this change will increase credit sales by 10 percent, from $500,000 to $550,000. The average collection period is expected to rise from 30 days to 50 days for all credit sales. The bad debt loss ratio for the new credit sales is expected to be 2 percent compared to 1 percent for old sales. Johnson's contribution margin will remain at 25 percent of sales and the pretax required rate of return on investments in receivables is 20 percent. The owner is now asking the following questions:

(a) What is the net advantage (disadvantage) in dollars of changing the credit period?
(b) Should Johnson Manufacturing adopt the new change in credit period?

The financial manager made the analyses shown on page 228.

(a) Figure 11-2 shows the analysis of the change in the credit period from net 30 to net 45. The marginal profits are $12,500 and the marginal costs, including the required return on the additional investment in accounts receivable, are only $7,850 ($1,000 + $6,850). Changing the credit period results in a net advantage of $4,650 ($12,500 − $7,850).

(b) Johnson Manufacturing should adopt the change in the credit period because the net change in returns is positive and increases the value of the firm.

1. Additional sales
   = Percent sales × Sales increase
   = $500,000 × 0.10 = $50,000

   Marginal profits on additional sales
   = Additional sales × Contribution margin
   = $50,000 × 0.25 = ... $12,500

2. Marginal increase in bad debt losses
   = Additional sales × Bad debt loss ratio
   = $50,000 × 0.02 = ... 1,000

3. New average A/R* balance
   = New average daily sales × Average collection period
   = ($550,000/365) × 50 = $1,507 × 50 = $75,350

   Current average A/R balance
   = Current average daily sales × Average collection period
   = ($500,000/365) × 30 = $1,370 × 30 = $41,100

   Marginal investment in A/R
   = New average A/R balance − Current average A/R balance
   = $75,350 − $41,100 = $34,250

   Opportunity cost of marginal investment in A/R
   = Marginal investment in A/R × Opportunity cost
   = $34,250 × 0.20 = ... 6,850

4. Net advantage (disadvantage) of changing the credit period
   = Marginal profits − Marginal costs
   = 1 − (2 + 3)
   = $12,500 − ($1,000 + $6,850) = ... $ 4,650

* A/R = accounts receivable

FIGURE 11-2 An analysis of a change in the credit period from net 30 to net 45 for Johnson Manufacturing Company.

EXAMPLE 11-6: Johnson Manufacturing Company wants to determine the effects of changing its credit terms of *net 30* to *2/10, net 30*. The new policy is expected to increase sales by 5 percent, from $500,000 to $525,000. The contribution margin on sales is 25 percent. The firm expects the average collection period to decline from 30 days to 25 days. The firm estimates that 60 percent of both current and new customers will take advantage of the new cash discount. Bad debt losses are anticipated to decrease from 1 percent of credit sales to one half of 1 percent of credit sales. The required pretax rate of return on receivables investment is 20 percent.

Figure 11-3 shows the analysis of changing the credit terms by offering a cash discount of 2/10, net 30. The net advantage of offering the discount is $3,355. Therefore, Johnson Manufacturing should initiate the cash discount because the marginal returns exceed the marginal costs by $3,355. This decision increases stockholder wealth.

1. Marginal profits on additional sales

   = Additional sales × Contribution margin

   = $25,000 × 0.25 = ... $6,250

2. Current bad debt losses

   = Current sales × Current bad debt loss ratio

   = $500,000 × 0.01 = $5,000

   New bad debt losses

   = New sales × New debt loss ratio

   = $525,000 × 0.005 = $2,625

   Reduction in bad debt losses

   = Current bad debt losses − New bad debt losses

   = $5,000 − $2,625 = ...   2,375

3. Current average A/R* balance

   = Current average daily sales × Current average collection period

   = ($500,000/365) × 30 = $1,370 × 30 = $41,100

   New average A/R balance

   = New average daily sales × New average collection period

   = ($525,000/365) × 25 = $1,438 × 25 = $35,950

   Reduction in A/R investment

   = Current average A/R balance − New average A/R balance

   = $41,100 − $35,950 = $5,150

   Earnings on funds released by reduction in A/R investment

   = Return in A/R × Required pretax rate of return

   = $5,150 × 0.20 = ...   1,030

4. Cost of cash discount

   = Annual sales × Percentage taking discount × Percentage discount

   = $525,000 × 0.60 × 0.02 =...   6,300

5. Net advantage (disadvantage) of changing credit terms

   = Marginal returns − Marginal costs

   = (1 + 2 + 3) − 4

   = ($6,250 + $2,375 + $1,030) − $6,300 = ... $3,355

* A/R = accounts receivable

FIGURE 11-3   An analysis of the change in credit terms from net 30 to 2/10, net 30 for Johnson Manufacturing Company.

F. The collection policy normally becomes an issue only after the accounts are past due.

Collection policy decisions include three steps: determining when to begin the collection efforts, selecting the appropriate collection methods, and evaluating the potential tradeoffs of increased collection expenditures.

1. *Determining when to begin the collection efforts.* This step in developing collection policy requires monitoring the status and composition of accounts receivable. Several techniques are used to monitor accounts receivable.

   • Financial ratios, such as the average collection period, are used to compare the firm's management of accounts receivable to industry averages, recent trends, and the firm's credit terms.

- An **aging schedule** is a report of how long accounts receivable have been outstanding. Figure 11-4 shows an aging schedule for Johnson Manufacturing Company.

Johnson Manufacturing Company
Aging Schedule of Accounts Receivable (A/R)

Age of A/R in Days	Outstanding A/R Dollars	Percent
0– 30	$20,550	50.0
31– 60	8,220	20.0
61– 90	6,165	15.0
91–120	4,110	10.0
over 120	2,055	5.0
Total	$41,100	100.0

FIGURE 11-4
Aging schedule for Johnson Manufacturing Company.

2. *Selecting the collection methods.* Firms usually begin their collection efforts with mild, low-cost techniques before escalating to more severe, costly methods. The continuum of collection methods from mild to severe includes the use of letters, telephone calls, personal visits, collection agencies, and legal action, in that order. Some firms may also refuse to provide additional goods or services until the customer pays past-due bills.
3. *Evaluating tradeoffs of increased collection expenditures.* Collection policy provides several tradeoffs between benefits and costs. The benefits of a tight collection policy include reduced bad debt losses and increased earnings. A restrictive collection policy shortens the average collection period and releases funds from the investment in accounts receivable. These benefits are offset by increased collection costs and lost sales. Overly aggressive collection efforts may antagonize customers and cause them to take their business elsewhere.

EXAMPLE 11-7: Johnson Manufacturing Company is considering a plan to tighten its collection policy that will cost $2,000 a year. The firm does not expect to lose any of its $500,000 in sales because of its increased collection efforts. Based on its aging schedule shown in Figure 11-4, Johnson has decided to concentrate its efforts on accounts that are at least 61 days old. As a result of its additional collection efforts, the firm expects to reduce both its average collection period from 30 days to 28 days and its bad debts loss ratio from 1 percent of sales to three-fourths of 1 percent of sales.

Figure 11-5 on page 231 shows an analysis of the proposed collection policy. The net disadvantage of tightening the collection policy is $202. Johnson should not tighten the collection policy because the marginal costs of this change exceed the marginal returns.

11-3. Credit Analysis

Credit analysis is the process of evaluating the creditworthiness of individual credit applicants. The firm uses its credit policies to analyze individual accounts. The purpose of the credit analysis is to determine the ability and willingness of applicants to repay the credit in accordance with the company's credit terms.

A. The process of conducting a credit analysis is limited by both time and cost considerations.

The firm often has only a few hours or a few days to evaluate a credit request. Delaying the decision could lead to the loss of a potential customer's order. Credit analysis also involves costs, such as the costs to acquire credit reports and to examine the customer's financial statements. The time and resources devoted to evaluating a credit

1. Current bad debt losses

   = Current sales × Current bad debt loss ratio

   = \$500,000 × 0.01 = \$5,000

   New bad debt losses

   = New sales × New bad debt loss ratio

   = \$500,000 × 0.0075 = \$3,750

   Reduction in bad debt losses

   = Current bad debt losses − New bad debt losses

   = \$5,000 − \$3,750 = ... \$1,250

2. Current average A/R* balance

   = Current average daily sales × Current average collection period

   = (\$500,000/365) × 30 = \$1,370 × 30 = \$41,100

   New average A/R balance

   = New average daily sales × New average collection period

   = (\$500,000/365) × 28 = \$1,370 × 28 = \$38,360

   Reduction in A/R investment

   = Current average A/R balance − New average A/R balance

   = \$41,100 − \$38,360 = \$2,740

   Earnings on funds released by reduction in A/R investment

   = Reduction in A/R × Required pretax rate of return

   = \$2,740 × 0.20 = ... 548

3. Cost of collection efforts 2,000

4. Net advantage (disadvantage) of tightening the collection policy

   = Marginal returns − Marginal costs

   = (1 + 2) − 3

   = (\$1,250 + \$548) − \$2,000 = ... (\$ 202)

* A/R = accounts receivable

FIGURE 11-5   An analysis of tightening the collection policy for Johnson Manufacturing Company.

applicant should be related to the potential losses that the firm may incur from making an incorrect decision.

B. Credit analysis involves three steps.

1. *Obtaining information about the credit applicant.* Information about a credit applicant is available from both the applicant and external sources.
   - *Prior experience with the customer* may serve as a valuable source of information about the applicant's creditworthiness.
   - *Financial statements* may be requested of businesses applying for credit to provide detailed information about the applicant's liquidity, profitability, and debt position.
   - *Credit reporting agencies* are national and local organizations that collect information about the financial condition and the credit standing of business firms. Dun & Bradstreet, Inc. (D&B) is the best known credit-reporting agency for business firms.
   - *Credit interchange bureaus* are local credit associations that gather and exchange information about credit customers. The Credit Interchange is a national network of local credit bureaus.

- *Banks* may provide the firm with information about their customers and may assist in obtaining information from other banks.

2. *Analyzing the credit information.* Credit analysts examine financial statements and credit reports to determine the applicant's financial strength and previous payment record. Pro forma financial statement analysis and credit-scoring systems are used to evaluate the applicant's future ability to pay. **Credit-scoring** is a numerical procedure used to examine several variables simultaneously in order to evaluate creditworthiness. A credit-scoring system is inexpensive and easy to use once developed. Regardless of which methods are used, credit analysts follow the *five Cs of credit* to guide their analysis:
   - *Character* is the applicant's ability or desire to honor the obligation.
   - *Capacity* is the applicant's ability to pay by a designated due date.
   - *Capital* is the general financial strength of the applicant.
   - *Collateral* represents the assets the applicant may offer as security for the credit.
   - *Conditions* are economic conditions beyond the applicant's control that affect the applicant's ability to pay.

3. *Making the credit decision.* The first two steps in credit analysis provide the basis for the credit decision. Judgment is a key element in the overall credit analysis process. If the applicant is granted credit, the firm usually sets a **line of credit** which is the maximum amount of credit that may be extended to the customer.

11-4. Inventory Management

Inventory management is the process of managing the investment in inventory. The goal for inventory management is to minimize the total of all associated costs in order to enhance shareholder wealth. The financial objective of minimizing the investment in inventory often conflicts with the objective of carrying sufficient inventory to meet production demands and avoid stockouts. The firm must determine the optimal level of inventory that resolves these conflicting objectives.

Inventory management is important for two reasons:

- Inventory management affects the firm's profitability. Inventory represents a sizable investment for some firms and requires tying up money.
- Errors in inventory management cannot be quickly corrected. Inventory is the firm's least liquid current asset and requires time to be converted back into cash.

A. Physical inventory management is not the direct operating responsibility of the financial manager.

The daily management of inventory is usually the responsibility of the production manager. However, inventory policy is not typically set by a single individual but by several managers with a stake in inventory management. These individuals include people from finance, marketing, manufacturing, and purchasing. The financial manager is concerned about the overall inventory level because either excess or insufficient inventory can reduce the firm's profitability.

B. Inventory is classified into three types.

Inventory functions as a buffer among the various phases of the procurement-production-sales cycle. Inventory buffers are needed to reduce the uncertainty associated with this cycle. By uncoupling the various phases of the cycle, inventory provides the firm with greater flexibility in timing the purchases of raw materials, scheduling production, and meeting unexpected demand.

1. **Raw materials** are items of input to the production process. The level of raw materials inventory is determined by several factors, including the anticipated level of production, seasonal fluctuations, reliability of suppliers, and efficiency of production operations.

2. **Work-in-process inventory** consists of items in the production process. Determinants of work-in-process inventory are the length of the production cycle and the level of current output.
3. **Finished goods** are items that have been produced but not sold. The level of finished goods is determined principally by the coordination of production and sales.

C. Overall investment in inventory is determined by three major factors.

1. *Level of sales.* The level of inventories is directly related to sales. Inventories generally increase (decrease) as sales increase (decrease).
2. *Length of the production cycle.* In general, the longer the production cycle, the larger the firm's inventory, especially work-in-process inventory.
3. *Durability and style of the product.* Lower levels of inventory are generally maintained for perishable products and items with a high probability of becoming technically obsolete or of going out of style.

11-5. Economic Order Quantity

A. The *optimal level of inventory* is that level which minimizes total inventory costs.

Excluding the actual cost of the item, inventory costs consist of ordering costs and carrying costs, which when combined represent total costs. Figure 11-6 shows the relationships among these three costs.

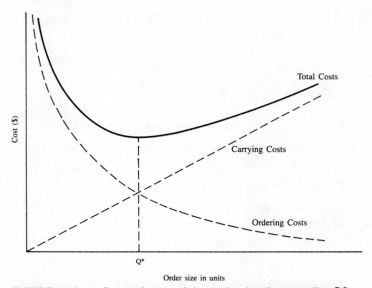

FIGURE 11-6 Determinants of the optimal order quantity, Q*

1. **Carrying costs** are the costs of holding items in inventory for a specific time period. Carrying costs include storage and handling costs, obsolescence and deterioration costs, insurance costs, taxes, and, most importantly, the opportunity cost of tying up funds in inventory. In this situation, the opportunity cost is the interest foregone, and is therefore the required rate of return on the investment in inventory. Carrying costs contain both fixed and variable components, but these costs are normally all treated as variable in simple inventory models such as the model used in this chapter. These costs are usually expressed as the variable costs per unit of holding an item of inventory. As Figure 11-6 shows, the carrying costs curve is linear and upward sloping because the carrying costs are assumed to be directly proportional to average inventory. The carrying costs are defined as the carrying cost per unit, C, multiplied by the average inventory, $Q/2$, which equals $CQ/2$.

2. **Ordering costs** are the costs of placing and receiving an order. Ordering costs include the costs of placing an order, shipping, and lost sales discounts and quantity discounts. Ordering costs contain both fixed and variable components. However, ordering costs per order are often assumed to be constant in simple inventory models, such as the model presented in this chapter. As Figure 11-6 shows, the ordering costs curve is downward sloping because the firm places fewer orders as the order size increases. Ordering costs are defined as the fixed ordering cost per order, O, multiplied by the number of orders per period, S/Q, which equals SO/Q.

3. **Total costs** are the sum of the carrying costs and the ordering costs. As Figure 11-6 shows, the total cost curve is U-shaped. This curve initially declines because ordering costs decline at a faster rate than carrying costs rise. The total cost curve eventually slopes upward as carrying costs rise faster than ordering costs decline. Thus, there is a tradeoff between ordering and carrying costs. Total costs are minimized at the lowest point on the total cost curve, Q^*. This particular point is called the **economic order quantity (EOQ)**.

- The EOQ occurs where the carrying costs and ordering costs intersect, but only when the carrying costs are strictly variable and the ordering costs are strictly fixed.
- The location of the intersection depends on whether carrying costs reflect a constant, increasing, or decreasing relationship with average inventory. (Note: Figure 10-2 shows an inventory-type model for determining the optimal cash balances. In this situation, carrying costs are assumed to be nonlinear. Thus, the optimal point in Figure 10-2 is not at the point of intersection between the carrying costs and ordering costs.)

Equation 11-5 defines total inventory costs as the sum of carrying costs and ordering costs.

$$\text{Total inventory costs} = \overbrace{\frac{CQ}{2}}^{\text{Carrying costs}} + \overbrace{\frac{SO}{Q}}^{\text{Ordering costs}} \tag{11-5}$$

C = carrying cost per unit for the period

Q = quantity ordered in units per order

S = total sales demand or usage in units for the period

O = fixed ordering cost per order

Equation 11-5 shows that the higher the order quantity, Q, the higher the total carrying costs but the lower the total ordering costs. The lower the order quantity, the lower the total carrying costs but the higher the total ordering costs.

B. The economic order quantity is an inventory control model used to determine the order quantity that minimizes the total inventory costs.

The EOQ is the value of Q that minimizes the total inventory costs given in Equation 11-5. This value of Q may be found by using either calculus or algebra. Equation 11-6 presents the economic order quantity.

ECONOMIC ORDER QUANTITY (EOQ)
$$Q^* = \sqrt{\frac{2SO}{C}} \tag{11-6}$$

Once the EOQ is determined, the optimal length of one inventory cycle, T^*, and the optimal number of orders may be computed. An **inventory cycle** is the time between placements of successive orders of an item. Equation 11-7 shows that the optimal length of one inventory cycle is the economic order quantity, Q^*, divided by the average daily demand. **Average daily demand** is the usage of inventory per day and is determined by dividing sales, *S*, by the time period being analyzed. For example, the average daily demand for a year is *S/365*.

OPTIMAL LENGTH OF AN INVENTORY CYCLE

$$T^* = \frac{Q^*}{\text{Average daily demand}}$$

(11-7)

Equation 11-8 shows the optimal number of orders to be placed.

OPTIMAL NUMBER OF ORDERS

$$N^* = \frac{S}{Q^*} \quad \text{or} \quad \frac{\text{Time period}}{T^*}$$

(11-8)

1. The firm's EOQ is affected by changing variables in the basic EOQ model shown in Equation 11-6.

   - The larger the sales per period, *S*, or ordering costs per order, *O*, the larger the EOQ.
   - The larger the inventory carrying cost, *C*, the smaller the EOQ.

2. The basic EOQ model is a deterministic model because of its simplifying assumptions. These assumptions may be relaxed to produce more realistic probabilistic EOQ models. (Note: Deterministic and probabilistic models are discussed in Section 10-5.) The assumptions of deterministic EOQ models are as follows:

   - Demand or usage, *S*, is known with certainty.
   - Demand or usage is constant throughout the time period.
   - Ordering costs, *O*, are fixed regardless of the size of the order.
   - Carrying costs per unit, *C*, are constant over the time period.
   - Inventory orders are filled without delay.
   - No quantity discounts are available.
   - No additional inventory is carried to guard against changes in sales or delivery.

EXAMPLE 11-8: Super Screens, Inc. sells wide-screen television sets through several retail outlets located in metropolitan Washington, D.C. The firm wants to determine the number of wide screens it should order at a time to minimize the total annual inventory cost. Annual demand is estimated at 1,000 units and is expected to be spread evenly throughout the year. Each set costs the company $500 and the annual carrying costs are 15 percent of the cost of inventory, or $75 per set. The cost of placing and receiving an order is $60.

(*a*) Substituting *S* = 1,000, *O* = $60, and *C* = $75 in Equation 11-6, the economic order quantity is:

$$Q^* = \sqrt{\frac{(2)(1,000)(\$60)}{\$75}} = \sqrt{1,600} = 40 \text{ sets}$$

(*b*) Substituting *C* = $75, *Q** = 40, *S* = 1,000, and *O* = $60 in Equation 11-5, the minimum total inventory costs are:

$$\text{Total inventory costs} = \frac{(\$75)(40)}{2} + \frac{(1,000)(\$60)}{40} = \$3,000$$

(*c*) The average inventory, *Q*/2*, is 20 (40/2).

(*d*) Substituting *Q** = 40 and average daily demand = 2.74 (1,000/365) in Equation 11-7 gives the optimal length of one inventory cycle for Super Screens of 14.6 days. Thus, the firm should place an order about every 15 days.

$$T^* = \frac{40}{1000/365} = \frac{40}{2.74} = 14.6 \text{ days}$$

Figure 11-7 shows the inventory position of Super Screens, Inc. without safety stocks.

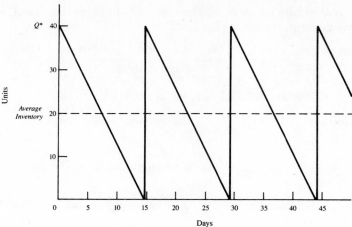

FIGURE 11-7   Inventory position of Super Screens, Inc. without safety stocks or lead times.

(e) Substituting $S = 1,000$ and $Q^* = 40$ in the first form of Equation 11-8, or time period $= 365$ and $T^* = 14.6$ in the second form of Equation 11-8, shows that Super Screens, Inc. should place 25 orders per year.

$$\text{N*} = \frac{1,000}{40} = 25 \text{ orders per year} \quad \text{or} \quad \frac{365}{14.6} = 25 \text{ orders per year}$$

11-6. Safety Stocks

Safety stocks are additional inventories carried to meet unexpected demand and unanticipated delays in shipping or production. The assumptions of the basic EOQ model do not necessarily apply in practice. For example, firms do face uncertainty about sales volume, production rates, and delivery times. These uncertainties may lead to an inventory shortage. Probabilistic inventory control models consider these uncertainties.

A. The amount of safety stocks is determined by the uncertainty of inventory demand, the uncertainty of delivery times, stockout costs and carrying costs.

1. **Lead or delivery time** is the time between order placement and receipt.
2. **Stockouts** are inventory shortages. Stockouts result in several types of costs. Raw materials and work-in-process stockouts may result in costly production delays. Finished goods stockouts may cause the firm to lose a specific sale and may damage its reputation, resulting in many lost sales. The level of safety stock involves a tradeoff between stockout costs and additional inventory carrying costs.

   • The optimal level of safety stock increases with stockout costs, the uncertainty of demand, and the probability of delays in receiving shipments.
   • The optimal safety stock decreases with the cost of carrying additional inventory.

B. A *reorder point* is the level of inventory at which an order is placed to replenish an item.

Equation 11-9 shows that the reorder point, Q_r, for a firm maintaining safety stocks is: safety stocks, SS, plus the average daily demand, multiplied by the lead time, n.

REORDER POINT WITH SAFETY STOCK $$Q_r = SS + \left(\frac{S}{\text{time period}} \times n \right)$$ **(11-9)**

Equation 11-10 shows that the firm's average inventory, Q_a, is: economic order quantity divided by 2, $Q^*/2$, plus safety stocks, SS.

AVERAGE INVENTORY WITH SAFETY STOCKS

$$Q_a = \frac{Q^*}{2} + SS$$

(11-10)

EXAMPLE 11-9: Super Screens, Inc. keeps a safety stock of 10 wide-screen television sets. The average lead time between placing and receiving an order is 4 days.

(a) Substituting $SS = 10$, $S = 1,000$, time period $= 365$ days, and $n = 4$ in Equation 11-9 indicates that Super Screens, Inc. should reorder when the inventory level reaches 21 sets.

$$Q_r = 10 + \left(\frac{1,000}{365} \times 4\right) = 10 + (2.74)(4) = 21 \text{ sets}$$

(b) Substituting $Q^* = 40$ and $SS = 21$ in Equation 11-10 indicates that the firm's average inventory with safety stocks is 30 sets.

$$Q_a = \frac{40}{2} + 10 = 30 \text{ sets}$$

Figure 11-8 shows the inventory position for Super Screens, Inc. with safety stocks and lead times.

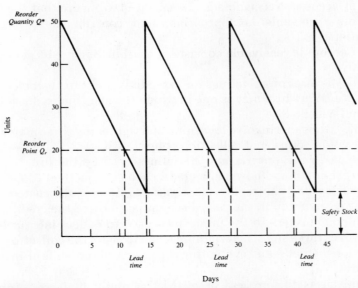

FIGURE 11-8   Inventory position of Super Screens, Inc. with safety stocks and lead times.

RAISE YOUR GRADES

Can you explain...?

☑ the two major steps in accounts receivable management
☑ what credit policy is
☑ the three credit policy variables
☑ how a firm can loosen and tighten its credit policy
☑ what credit standards are
☑ what credit terms are
☑ three variables that constitute credit terms
☑ the meaning of collection policy
☑ the three steps in making credit policy decisions

☑ what credit analysis is
☑ the three steps of credit analysis
☑ the five Cs of credit
☑ why inventory management is important
☑ three types of inventory
☑ three major factors determining the investment in inventory
☑ the difference between carrying costs and ordering costs
☑ how to calculate the economic order quantity
☑ what safety stocks are
☑ how to calculate the reorder point

SUMMARY

1. Accounts receivable consists of money owed to a firm for goods and services sold on credit.
2. The goal of accounts receivable management is to ensure that the firm's investment in accounts receivable is appropriate and contributes to shareholder wealth maximization.
3. Managing accounts receivable consists of establishing credit policy and conducting credit analysis.
4. Credit policy is a set of guidelines for extending credit to customers.
5. A firm's optimal credit policy is one in which the marginal costs of the change equal its marginal benefits.
6. Credit policy decisions involve loosening and tightening three major variables: credit standards, credit terms, and collection policy.
7. Credit standards are criteria and guidelines used by the firm to determine which customers get credit and how much credit each customer gets.
8. Credit terms specify the repayment terms required of all customers. Credit terms include the cash discount, the cash discount period, and the credit period.
9. Collection policy refers to the procedures used to collect late accounts. Collection policy involves three steps: determining when to begin the collection efforts, selecting the collection methods, and evaluating the potential tradeoffs of increased collection expenditures.
10. Credit analysis is the process of evaluating individual credit applicants. Credit analysis involves three steps: obtaining information about the credit applicant, analyzing the credit information, and making the credit decision.
11. The five Cs of credit are character, capacity, capital, collateral, and conditions. These factors are used to screen credit applicants.
12. Inventory management is the process of managing the investment in inventory. Inventory management is important because it affects the firm's profitability and errors cannot be quickly corrected.
13. Inventory is classified as raw materials, work-in-process, or finished goods.
14. The investment in inventory depends on the level of sales, the length of the production cycle, and the durability and style of the product.
15. The optimal level of inventory involves a tradeoff between carrying costs and ordering costs. Carrying costs are the costs of holding items in inventory for a specific time period. Ordering costs are costs of placing and receiving an order. The sum of these two costs is the total inventory cost.
16. The economic order quantity is the order quantity that minimizes total inventory costs.
17. Safety stock is additional inventory carried to meet unexpected demand and unanticipated delays in shipping or production. Safety stock provides a buffer or protection against these uncertainties.

RAPID REVIEW

True or False

1. Accounts receivable is an asset representing sales of goods or services on credit. [Section 11-1]

2. The goal of accounts receivable management is to maximize sales by controlling the firm's credit policy. [Section 11-1C]

3. Trade credit is credit which the firm extends to other firms. [Section 11-1]

4. Loosening credit policy includes relaxing credit standards, lengthening credit terms, and reducing collection efforts. [Section 11-2A]

5. Tightening credit policy will decrease the investment in accounts receivable. [Section 11-2A]

6. The bad debt loss ratio is calculated by dividing bad debt expenses by total sales. [Section 11-2D]

7. Credit terms of 2/10, net 30 mean a 10 percent discount for cash on delivery and a 2 percent discount for payment within 30 days. [Section 11-2E]

8. Lengthening the credit period is likely to reduce sales. [Section 11-2E]

9. One method of monitoring collection efforts is an aging schedule of accounts receivable. [Section 11-2F]

10. Credit scoring is a numerical procedure used to examine the creditworthiness of a credit applicant. [Section 11-3B]

11. The goal of inventory management is to minimize the investment in inventories. [Section 11-4]

12. The financial manager is primarily responsible for daily inventory management. [Section 11-4A]

13. Work-in-process inventories generally increase as the production cycle lengthens. [Section 11-4B]

14. The optimal level of inventory is the level which minimizes carrying costs. [Section 11-5A]

15. Total carrying costs increase directly with the level of inventories. [Section 11-5A]

16. Summing carrying costs plus ordering costs at different inventory levels produces a U-shaped total cost curve. [Section 11-5A]

17. The optimal ordering quantity in the EOQ model occurs at the point where the sum of carrying costs and ordering costs are minimized. [Section 11-5B]

18. The optimal length of the inventory cycle increases as the EOQ increases. [Section 11-5B]

19. The EOQ increases directly with usage per period. [Section 11-5B]

20. The EOQ changes inversely with ordering costs per order. [Section 11-5B]

21. The basic EOQ model assumes that demand or usage fluctuates randomly throughout the time period. [Section 11-5B]

22. Use of the basic EOQ model guards against stockouts. [Section 11-6]

23. The level of safety stock increases with the degree of uncertainty about the demand for inventory and the delivery time. [Section 11-6A]

24. The optimal level of safety stock involves a tradeoff between stockout costs and additional ordering costs. [Section 11-6A]

25. The reorder point increases as the lead time increases. [Section 11-6B]

Multiple Choice

26. Tightening credit policy is expected to

    (a) stimulate sales
    (b) increase costs associated with accounts receivable

(c) reduce the investment in accounts receivable
(d) increase the length of the cash cycle

[Section 11-2A]

27. Loosening credit policy can be achieved by

(a) shortening the credit period
(b) offering a cash discount
(c) using strict credit standards
(d) employing collection agencies

[Section 11-2A]

28. A firm's credit policy usually includes establishing

(a) credit standards
(b) credit terms
(c) collection policy
(d) all of the above

[Section 11-2C]

29. Credit standards of a firm are

(a) the repayment terms required by customers
(b) the set of procedures used to collect late accounts
(c) the length of the credit period and the cash discount offered
(d) the guidelines used by a firm to determine who will get credit

[Section 11-2C]

30. All the following are among the Cs of credit *except*

(a) character
(b) capacity
(c) contacts
(d) collateral

[Section 11-3B]

31. The investment in inventory is determined by all of the following factors *except*

(a) level of sales
(b) capital structure of the firm
(c) length of the production cycle
(d) durability of the product

[Section 11-4C]

32. Carrying costs include all of the following *except*

(a) shipping costs
(b) storage costs
(c) obsolescence
(d) opportunity costs

[Section 11-5A]

33. The basic EOQ model determines the optimal inventory level at which

(a) total revenue is maximized
(b) carrying costs are minimized
(c) total inventory costs are minimized
(d) inventory is minimized

[Section 11-5B]

34. Assumptions of the EOQ include all except

(a) uniform demand
(b) constant ordering costs

(c) constant carrying costs per unit

(d) uncertain demand

[Section 11-5B]

35. The optimal level of safety stock involves a tradeoff between

(a) stockout costs and carrying costs

(b) ordering costs and carrying costs

(c) delivery costs and carrying costs

(d) ordering costs and stockout costs

[Section 11-6A]

Answers

True or False

1. True	11. False	21. False
2. False	12. False	22. False
3. True	13. True	23. True
4. True	14. False	24. False
5. True	15. True	25. True
6. False	16. True	
7. False	17. True	
8. False	18. True	
9. True	19. True	
10. True	20. True	

Multiple Choice

26. c
27. b
28. d
29. d
30. c
31. b
32. a
33. c
34. d
35. a

SOLVED PROBLEMS

PROBLEM 11-1: Rainbow Paint Company's annual credit sales to retail stores are $4,000,000 and are spread evenly throughout the year. The firm's accounts receivable average $500,000. Assume a 365-day year.

(a) Calculate the accounts receivable turnover.

(b) Calculate the average collection period.

Answer:

(a) Substituting credit sales of $4,000,000 and accounts receivable of $500,000 in Equation 11-2, the accounts receivable turnover is:

$$\text{Accounts receivable turnover} = \frac{\$4,000,000}{500,000} = 8 \text{ times}$$

(b) Using Equation 11-3, the average collection period is:

$$\text{Average collection period} = \frac{365}{8} = 45.6 \text{ days} \qquad \textbf{[Section 11-2B]}$$

PROBLEM 11-2: Harrington Manufacturing Company has $5,000,000 in credit sales and bad debt expenses of $125,000. What is the firm's bad debt loss ratio?

Answer: Substituting bad debt expenses of $125,000 and credit sales of $5,000,000 in Equation 11-4, the bad debt loss ratio is:

$$\text{Bad debt loss ratio} = \frac{\$125,000}{\$5,000,000} = 0.025 \text{ or } 2.5 \text{ percent}$$

[Section 11-2D]

PROBLEM 11-3: Davis Supply Company sells on terms of "net 45." Its annual credit sales are $912,500 and its accounts receivable average 15 days overdue. Assume a 365-day year. What is Davis Supply Company's investment in receivables?

Answer: The firm's average daily sales are its annual (credit) sales divided by 365 days.

$$\text{Average daily sales} = \frac{\$912,500}{365 \text{ days}} = \$2,500$$

The average collection period is the credit period plus the average days past the due date.

$$\text{Average collection period} = 45 + 15 = 60 \text{ days}$$

The average investment in accounts receivable is determined by multiplying the average daily sales by the average collection period.

$$\text{Investment in accounts receivable} = \$2,500 \times 60 = \$150,000$$

[Section 11-2D]

Use the following information on Tudor Products, Inc. to solve Problems 11-4 through 11-6. Tudor Products, Inc. has credit sales of $600,000 and an average collection period of 25 days. The firm's variable cost ratio is 80 percent. The opportunity cost of funds invested in accounts receivable is 15 percent. Assume a 365-day year.

PROBLEM 11-4: What is the accounts receivable turnover for Tudor Products, Inc.?

Answer: The accounts receivable turnover is calculated by dividing 365 days by the average collection period of 25 days.

$$\text{Accounts receivable turnover} = \frac{365}{25} = 14.6 \text{ times}$$

[Section 11-2D]

PROBLEM 11-5: What is the average investment in accounts receivable for Tudor Products, Inc.?

Answer: The average investment in accounts receivable is calculated by dividing credit sales by the accounts receivable turnover.

$$\text{Average investment in accounts receivable} = \frac{\$600,000}{14.6} = \$41,096 \text{ (rounded)}$$

This method uses the total sales value of the accounts receivable. [As discussed in Section 11-2B, the dollar cost—variable cost or total cost—is sometimes used as the relevant measure of the amount of funds tied up in accounts receivable. Using only variable cost as the relevant measure, the investment in accounts receivable would be $32,877 ($41,096 × 0.80).]

[Section 11-2D]

PROBLEM 11-6: What is Tudor Products' opportunity cost of investing in accounts receivable?

Answer: The opportunity cost is calculated by multiplying the average investment in accounts receivable by the required rate of return.

$$\text{Opportunity cost of investment in accounts receivable} \quad \$41,096 \times 0.15 = \$6,164 \text{ (rounded)}$$

[Sections 11-2B & D]

PROBLEM 11-7: Butler Manufacturing Company's current sales are all on credit and amount to $750,000 a year. The firm has fixed costs of $100,000 and variable costs of 85 percent of sales. Butler has excess capacity which would permit it to expand sales without incurring additional fixed costs. One means of expanding sales is to grant credit of net 90 days to applicants who have been turned down in the past. The credit manager has prepared several estimates for each of three risk classes of applicants.

Risk Class	Total Sales	Additional Sales	Bad Debt Loss Ratio	Required Pretax Rate of Return
A	$800,000	$50,000	5%	20%
B	840,000	40,000	8	24
C	860,000	20,000	12	30

(*a*) What is the marginal pretax profits for each risk class?

(*b*) Which risk classes, if any, should Butler Manufacturing accept as new credit customers?

Answer:

(*a*) The marginal pretax profits for each risk class are shown below.

	Risk Class		
	A	B	C

1. Marginal profits on additional sales
   = Additional sales × Contribution margin
   = Additional sales × 0.15* $7,500 $6,000 $3,000

2. Marginal increase in bad debt losses
   = Additional sales × Bad debt loss ratio 2,500 3,200 2,400

3. Marginal investment in A/R
   = (Additional sales/365) × 90

A	B	C
$12,329	$9,863	$4,932

   Opportunity cost of marginal investment in A/R
   = Marginal investment in A/R × Opportunity cost 2,466 2,367 1,480

4. Net change in pretax profits
   = Marginal profits − Marginal costs
   = 1 − (2 + 3) $2,534 $ 433 ($ 880)

* *The contribution margin of 0.15 is calculated by subtracting the variable cost percentage from 1.00 or (1.00 − 0.85 = 0.15).*

(*b*) Butler Manufacturing Company should accept risk classes A and B because the marginal pretax profits exceed the marginal costs.

[Section 11-2D]

PROBLEM 11-8: Brenner Auto Supply is not satisfied with its present credit policy. A proposal under consideration is to change the credit terms from 1/10, net 30 to 2/10, net 30. The firm's current average collection period is 42 days but it is expected to decline to 38 days. The percentage of credit customers who take the discount is expected to increase from 45 percent to 60 percent under the new policy. Credit sales are anticipated to remain at $400,000 with a contribution margin of 25 percent. The bad debt losses are forecasted to decrease from 3.0 percent of credit sales to 2.5 percent. The firm's opportunity cost for investing in additional receivables is 18 percent. Should Brenner Auto Supply adopt this change in policy?

Answer: Brenner Auto Supply should not adopt the change in the discount rate because the change results in a net disadvantage of $211.

1. Marginal profits on additional sales

   = Additional sales × Contribution margin

   = $0 × 0.25 = ... $ 0

2. Current bad debt losses

   = Current sales × Current bad debt loss ratio

   = $400,000 × 0.03 = $12,000

   New bad debt losses

   = New sales × New bad debt loss ratio

   = $400,000 × 0.025 = $10,000

   Reduction in bad debt losses

   = Current bad debt losses − New bad debt losses

   = $12,000 − $10,000 = ...   2,000

3. Current average A/R balance

   = Current average daily sales × Current average collection period

   = ($400,000/365) × 42 = $1,096 × 42 = $46,032

   New average A/R balance

   = (New average daily sales × New average collection period)

   = ($400,000/365) × 38 = $1,906 × 38 = $41,648

   Reduction in A/R investment

   = Current average A/R balance − New average A/R balance

   = $46,032 − $41,648 = $4,384

   Earnings on funds released by reduction in A/R investment

   = Reduction in A/R × Required pretax rate of return

   = $4,384 × 0.18 = ...   789

4. Cost of current cash discount

   = Current sales × Current percentage taking discount
      × Current percentage discount

   = $400,000 × 0.45 × 0.01 = $1,800

   Cost of new cash discount

   = New sales × New percentage taking discount × New percentage
      discount

   = $400,000 × 0.60 × 0.02 = $4,800

   Cost of increase in cash discount

   = Cost of new cash discount − Cost of current cash discount

   = $4,800 − $1,800 = ...   3,000

5. Net advantage/disadvantage of changing credit terms

   = Marginal returns − Marginal costs

   = (1 + 2 + 3) − 4

   = ($0 + $2,000 + $789) − $3,000 = ...   (\$ 211)

[Section 11-2E]

PROBLEM 11-9: LAB Industries is considering hiring a new collection agent for its credit department. The salary for the new agent will be $25,000. As a result of increased collection efforts, the firm expects to lower bad debt losses from 3.0 percent to 2.5 percent and to reduce the average collection period from 35 days to 30 days. Hiring the new agent is not expected to change sales from its current level of $8,000,000. The firm's required pretax return from an investment in accounts receivable is 18 percent.

(a) What is the effect of hiring the new collection agent on the pretax profits of LAB Industries?

(b) Should the new agent be hired?

Answer:

(a) LAB Industries will realize a net advantage of $34,726 by hiring the new collection agent.

1. Current bad debt losses

   = Current sales × Current bad debt loss ratio

   = $8,000,000 × 0.03 = $240,000

   New bad debt losses

   = New sales × New bad debt loss ratio

   = $8,000,000 × 0.025 = $200,000

   Reduction in bad debt losses

   = Current bad debt losses − New bad debt losses

   = $240,000 − $200,000 =... $40,000

2. Current average A/R balance

   = Current average daily sales × Average collection period

   = ($8,000,000/365) × 35 = $21,918 × 35 = $767,130

   New average A/R balance

   = New average daily sales × Average collection period

   = ($8,000,000/365) × 30 = $21,918 × 30 = $657,540

   Reduction in A/R investment

   = Current average A/R balance − New average A/R balance

   = $767,130 − $657,540 = $109,590

   Earnings on funds released by reduction in A/R investment

   = Reduction in A/R × Required pretax rate of return

   = $109,590 × 0.18 = ... 19,726

3. Cost of collection efforts 25,000

4. Net advantage (disadvantage) of hiring the collection agent

   = Marginal returns − Marginal costs

   = (1 + 2) − 3

   = ($40,000 + $19,726) − $25,000 =...................................... $34,726

(b) LAB Industries should hire the new agent because the marginal returns greatly exceed the marginal costs.   **[Section 11-2F]**

PROBLEM 11-10: Tastee Ice Cream distributes 12,000 gallons of ice cream each month from its central storage facility. Monthly carrying costs are $0.10 per gallon and ordering costs are $50 per order. Ignore potential stockout costs and assume a 30-day month.

(a) What is the economic order quantity for the ice cream?

(b) What is the average inventory?

(c) What is the total inventory cost for the month?

(d) What is the optimal length of the inventory cycle?

(e) How many orders will be placed per month?

Answer:

(a) Substituting $S = 12{,}000$, $O = \$50$, and $C = \$0.10$ in Equation 11-6, the economic order quantity is:

$$Q^* = \sqrt{\frac{(2)(12{,}000)(\$50)}{\$0.10}} = 3{,}464 \text{ gallons}$$

(b) The average inventory is determined by dividing the economic order quantity, Q^*, by 2 as follows:

$$\text{Average inventory} = \frac{3{,}464}{2} = 1{,}732 \text{ gallons}$$

(c) Substituting $C = \$0.10$, $Q^* = 3{,}464$, $S = 12{,}000$, and $O = \$50$ in Equation 11-5, the total inventory costs for the month is:

$$\text{Total inventory costs} = \frac{(\$0.10)(3{,}464)}{2} + \frac{(12{,}000)(\$50)}{3{,}464} = \$346 \text{ per month}$$

(d) Substituting $Q^* = 3{,}464$ and average daily demand $= 12{,}000/30$ days in Equation 11-7, the optimal length of the inventory cycle is:

$$T^* = \frac{3{,}464}{12{,}000/30 \text{ days}} = 8.66 \text{ days}$$

(e) Substituting $S = 12{,}000$ and $Q^* = 3{,}464$ in the first form of Equation 11-8, the number of orders per month is:

$$N^* = \frac{12{,}000}{3{,}464} = 3.5 \text{ orders per month}$$

Substituting time period $= 30$ and $T^* = 8.66$ in the second form of Equation 11-8 produces the same result.

$$N^* = \frac{30}{8.66} = 3.5 \text{ orders per month}$$

[Sections 11-5A & B]

PROBLEM 11-11: Wholesale Tire Company sells 36,000 tires annually. Annual carrying costs are $5 per tire and the ordering costs are $100 per order. The firm has decided to maintain a safety stock of one month's sales or 3,000 tires. The delivery time per order is 5 days. Assume a 365-day year.

(a) What is the economic order quantity?
(b) What is the average inventory?
(c) How many orders should be placed each year?
(d) What is the total inventory cost?
(e) What is the reorder point?

Answer:

(a) Substituting $S = 36{,}000$, $O = \$100$, and $C = \$5$ in Equation 11-6, the economic order quantity is:

$$Q^* = \sqrt{\frac{(2)(36{,}000)(\$100)}{\$5}} = 1{,}200 \text{ tires}$$

(b) Substituting the economic order quantity, $Q^* = 1{,}200$, and $SS = 3{,}000$ in Equation 11-10, the average inventory is:

$$\text{Average inventory} = \frac{1{,}200}{2} + 3{,}000 = 3{,}600 \text{ tires}$$

(c) Substituting $S = 36,000$ and $Q^* = 1,200$ in Equation 11-8 indicates that the Wholesale Tire Company will make 30 orders per year or about one order every 12 days (365 days/30 orders per year = 12.17 days).

$$N^* = \frac{36,000}{1,200} = 30 \text{ orders per year}$$

(d) Wholesale Tire's total inventory cost is found by multiplying the average inventory, 3,600 tires, by the carrying cost per unit, $5, and then adding the product of the orders per year, 30, multiplied by the ordering costs per order, $100.

$$\text{Total inventory costs} = (3,600)(\$5) + (30)(\$100) = \$21,000$$

(e) Substituting $SS = 3,000$, $S = 36,000$, time period $= 365$, and $n = 5$ in Equation 11-9 indicates that Wholesale Tire should reorder when the inventory reaches 3,493 tires.

$$Q_r = 3,000 + \left(\frac{36,000}{365} \times 5\right) = 3,493 \text{ tires}$$

[Section 11-6B]

12 FUNDAMENTALS OF CAPITAL BUDGETING

THIS CHAPTER IS ABOUT

☑ **Corporate Capital Budgeting**
☑ **Capital Budgeting Process**
☑ **Generating Project Proposals**
☑ **Estimating Cash Flows**
☑ **Evaluating Project Proposals**
☑ **Selecting Projects**
☑ **Implementing and Reviewing Projects**

12-1. Corporate Capital Budgeting

Capital budgeting is the process of analyzing investment opportunities and making long-term investment decisions. There are numerous types of investment decisions that involve capital expenditures. A **capital expenditure** is an outlay whose benefits are expected to extend beyond one year. There are several different types of cash outlays that may be classified as capital expenditures and evaluated using the framework of capital budgeting. These long-term investments include the purchase of fixed assets, such as land, buildings, and equipment; expenditures for an advertising campaign, a research and development program, and employee education and training; a bond refunding analysis; a lease-versus-buy analysis; and a merger and acquisition evaluation. Chapters 12 and 13 focus on capital outlays involving fixed assets.

Capital expenditures are important to the firm because they often require substantial expenditures that affect the firm's future profitability and direction. These expenditures have long-term effects and, once made, are not easily reversed. Sound capital investment decisions can lead to higher earnings and stock prices which help the firm achieve its goal of maximizing shareholder wealth.

12-2. Capital Budgeting Process

The capital budgeting process is a system of interrelated steps for making long-term investment decisions. As Figure 12-1 on page 249 shows, the process is influenced by the firm's business strategy and information requirements.

A. Capital budgeting decisions logically flow from the firm's business strategy.

Business strategy is the plan by which the firm hopes to achieve its goals in a changing environment. Because meeting some of these goals requires capital expenditures, business strategy often necessitates the capital budgeting process. Potential investment projects must pass a strategic test of acceptability or compatibility with a firm's business strategy. All strategically acceptable project proposals must then survive an economic appraisal as well as other qualitative considerations.

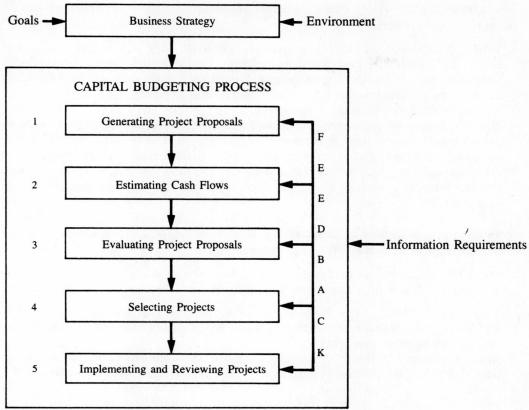

FIGURE 12-1   Integrating business strategy with the capital
budgeting process.

B. The capital budgeting process requires gathering and analyzing information.

Capital budgeting is a dynamic process because the firm's changing environment may affect the desirability of current or proposed investments. Information is needed throughout the entire capital budgeting process to ensure that the process is operating effectively. The information gathered and analyzed includes not only new information but also feedback on previous activities. For example, effective record keeping is essential in evaluating the accuracy of past estimates of revenue increases or cost savings. Information used in the capital budgeting process may include a project's expected costs and benefits, forecasts of the economic environment, market research studies, actions of competitors, and regulatory decisions.

C. The capital budgeting process involves five major steps.

1. Generating project proposals.
2. Estimating cash flows.
3. Evaluating project proposals.
4. Selecting projects.
5. Implementing and reviewing projects.

Each of these steps is examined in a separate section of this chapter.

12-3. Generating Project Proposals

The first step in the capital budgeting process is generating project proposals for the capital investment. Although ideas for capital expenditures come from many sources, both inside and outside the firm, good proposals do not just appear. In most firms, systematic procedures are established to assist in generating proposals.

A. **Two approaches are widely used to generate proposals: the top-down approach and the bottom-up approach.**

1. Under a *top-down approach*, proposals originate with top management and information is filtered down to the lower levels. Project recommendations typically come from senior-level managers and involve strategic decisions. *Strategic decisions* are non routine and involve major resources, such as plant expansion or entry into a new market. They also require the authority to approve large capital outlays.

2. Under a *bottom-up approach*, proposals originate from below and are reported to senior levels. Lower-level managers make proposals that require only *operating decisions* which are routine in nature and involve little capital, such as expenditures for office equipment. *Administrative decisions* are made by middle managers and involve projects requiring moderate resources, such as replacing manufacturing equipment.

B. **Investment proposals may be classified into four distinct types: expansion, replacement, modernization, and safety or environmental.**

Broad policy decisions are made which assign funds to each of these categories. The most common types of investment decisions involve expansion or replacement projects.

1. *Expansion projects* involve investments to increase existing capacity or to make new products or to enter new markets.
2. *Replacement projects* involve replacing worn-out or obsolete facilities or equipment with new ones. Replacement often benefits the firm through lower operating costs.
3. *Modernization projects* require expenditures to upgrade or to improve existing fixed assets. For example, modernization may involve rebuilding or overhauling an existing machine or adding air conditioning to a facility.
4. *Safety or environmental projects* require expenditures necessary to meet the requirements of government, labor unions, or insurance companies. Examples include pollution control and ventilation. These are often called *mandatory* or *nonrevenue-producing projects*.

12-4. Estimating Cash Flows

The second step in the capital budgeting process is estimating cash flows. Net cash flow is the difference between inflows and outflows of cash that result from a firm undertaking a project. Deriving accurate estimates of cash flows is the most important and most difficult step in the entire capital budgeting process.

Estimating cash flows is important because no later step in the process can overcome inaccurate or unreliable information generated by this step. In a dynamic business environment characterized by uncertainty, projecting the cash flows of a particular product is also difficult. Although past experience may help the financial manager identify factors that affect cash flows of some projects, historical data may not be available on other projects. For example, estimating the cash flows of a totally new product over its useful life may be based on assumptions that represent little more than educated guesses.

A. Cash flows differ from accounting profit.

Accounting income is not necessarily based on actual cash receipts or payments. In fact, the Tax Reform Act of 1986 provides that certain taxpayers, including most corporations, must use the accrual method of accounting for federal income tax purposes. Under the **accrual basis**, revenue is recognized as it is earned, and expenses are recognized as they are incurred, not when cash changes hands. Also, certain noncash items, including depreciation and amortization, are treated as expenses. Although depreciation expense permits the firm to reduce its tax burden, no actual payment of cash is involved. Future cash flows are emphasized over future accounting profits because cash flows are oriented toward valuation and the goal of shareholder wealth maximization.

B. Only incremental after-tax cash flows are relevant.

Incremental after-tax cash flows include all changes in the firm's cash inflows and cash outflows that result from undertaking an investment project. Cash flows that are not attributable to the investment are not relevant. Cash flows that occur before the investment decision are **sunk costs.** Sunk costs are not relevant because they are unrecoverable costs and do not change with the acceptance or rejection of the project. For example, the costs of past engineering studies have no impact on whether a firm should continue drilling for oil because these costs have already been incurred.

Costs (interest expenses) associated with financing a project involve actual cash outflows but are excluded from the project's cash flows. The financial flows are incorporated into the firm's **cost of capital** or *required rate of return,* which is the discount rate used for evaluating projects. To deduct financing charges as cash outflows and then to discount these flows by the cost of capital would result in a double counting of these costs.

C. Cash flows of a project fall into three categories: net investment, net operating cash flows, and net terminal cash flow.

1. **Net investment** is the net initial cash outlay needed to acquire a specific investment project. Most capital projects require a significant initial outlay before they generate cash inflows. The net investment is calculated by subtracting any initial cash inflows that occur in placing an asset into service from the amount of the initial cash outflows required by the project. The net investment is assumed to occur at Time Period Zero although the cash inflows and cash outflows constituting the net investment may occur at several points of time. Figure 12-2 provides a general format for computing the net investment.

> Purchase price of new asset
> + Installation and transportation costs
> + Additional net working capital
> − Proceeds from sale of old asset
> ± Tax effects on disposal of old asset
>   and/or the purchase of new one
> _____
> Net investment

FIGURE 12-2   Format for calculating net investment.

- The *initial cash outflows* include the purchase price of the new asset, outlays for installation and transportation, additional net working capital, and any other cost incurred to put the asset into service. (Net working capital is the excess of additional current assets over increased current liabilities required to support the project.) Expansion projects normally require increases in net working capital whereas replacement projects do not.
- The *initial cash inflows* include the proceeds from the disposal of existing assets if the investment proposal involves replacing an existing asset with a new asset. The tax impact of selling a depreciable asset can produce an increase or a decrease in the firm's federal income tax liability.
- The effects of the sale of an existing asset on the net investment in a new asset depend on the selling price, its original cost, and the current book value. Based on the Tax Reform Act of 1986, the rules for determining the tax impact of selling plant and equipment are summarized on page 252. (Further details involving the tax treatment of the sale of plant and equipment are discussed in Chapter 2.)

TRANSACTION	TAX EFFECT
Sale of plant or equipment at its book value	None
Sale of plant or equipment at *less* than its book value	(Selling Price − Book Value) × Marginal Tax Rate
Sale of plant or equipment at *more* than its book value but *less than* or *equal* to its original cost*	(Selling Price − Book Value) × Marginal Tax Rate
Sale of plant or equipment at more than its original cost**	(Original Cost − Book Value) × Marginal Tax Rate plus (Selling Price − Original Cost) × Capital Gains Rate

* *Any amounts received on a sale of a plant or equipment up to the original cost is treated as ordinary income since it is merely a recapture of depreciation.*

** *Net Schedule 1231 gains must be offset against net Schedule 1231 losses. Any remaining 1231 gain is a long-term capital gain which is taxed at regular rates.*

EXAMPLE 12-1: Cao Electronics purchases a new machine to replace an outmoded model. The new machine has an installed cost of $60,000. The existing asset originally cost $40,000 and has a current book value of $12,000. The firm's marginal tax rate on ordinary income is 34 percent. The firm has no other gains or losses from the sale of plant and equipment during the year.

(a) If the old machine is sold for $12,000, no taxes result from the sale of the existing machine because there is neither a gain nor a loss on the sale. The net investment in the new machine is:

Installed cost of new machine	$60,000
− Proceeds from sale of old machine	12,000
Net investment	$48,000

(b) If the old machine is sold for $8,000, the sale of the existing asset is treated as an operating loss of $4,000 ($12,000 − $8,000). This loss can be deducted in full from ordinary income, which results in a tax savings of $1,360 (0.34 × $4,000). The net investment in the new machine is:

Installed cost of new machine	$60,000
− Proceeds from sale of old machine	8,000
− Tax savings on sale of old machine	1,360
Net investment	$50,640

(c) The corporation experiences a gain of $18,000 if the old machine is sold for $30,000 ($30,000 − $12,000). This gain is treated as a recapture of depreciation. Using a 34 percent tax rate, the firm would pay $6,120 (0.34 × $18,000) in additional federal income taxes. The net investment in the new machine is:

Installed cost of new machine	$60,000
− Proceeds from sale of old machine	30,000
+ Tax on recaptured depreciation	6,120
Net investment	$36,120

(d) Cao Electronics has a total gain of $38,000 if the old machine is sold for $50,000 ($50,000 − $12,000). Although this gain is split into $28,000 ($40,000 − $12,000) of recaptured depreciation and $10,000 ($50,000 − $40,000) of long-term capital gain, the entire $38,000 is taxed at ordinary rates. The corporation incurs an increase in its tax liability of $12,920 (0.34 × $38,000). The net investment in the new machine is:

Installed cost of new machine	$60,000
− Proceeds from sale of old machine	50,000
+ Tax on sale of old machine	12,920
Net investment	$22,920

EXAMPLE 12-2: Edelman Enterprises plans to add a new machine to increase production capacity. The machine costs $18,000 plus $2,000 for installation and transportation costs and requires $4,000 in additional working capital.

This expansion involves both initial cash inflows and initial cash outflows but it does not include any cash flows associated with the disposal of an old asset. Using the format shown in Figure 12-2, the net investment is:

Purchase price of new machine	$18,000
+ Installation and transportation costs.....................................	2,000
+ Additional net working capital	4,000
Net investment..	$24,000

The depreciable basis (Section 2-2B) of the machine is:

Purchase price of new machine	$18,000
+ Installation and transportation...	2,000
Depreciable basis...	$20,000

2. **Net operating cash flows** are the incremental changes in a firm's cash flows that result from investing in a project. Net operating cash flows may vary over the project's life, and the timing of these varying flows may also vary during the year. However, operating cash flows are generally assumed to occur at the end of a given year. Figure 12-3 presents an income statement format for computing the net operating cash flows. This figure shows that various incremental cash outflows (operating expenses and taxes) and noncash outlays (depreciation expenses) are subtracted from incremental inflows (revenues) to obtain net income. Because depreciation expenses do not represent an actual outlay of funds during the accounting period but are used in computing taxable income, the amount of depreciation is added back to net income to get operating cash flows. Depreciation expenses are relevant only to the extent that they lower taxable income and result in tax savings. Thus, the amount of funds actually received from operations is understated on the income statement by the amount of depreciation expenses.

Revenues (cash)
 — Operating expenses (cash)
 — Depreciation expenses (noncash)

Taxable income*
 — Income taxes (cash)

Net Income
 + Depreciation expenses (noncash)

Net operating cash flows

 * *Excludes interest expenses.*

FIGURE 12-3
Format for calculating net operating cash flows over a project's life.

There are two methods of determining the expected net operating cash flows. Equation 12-1 defines operating cash flows as incremental net income plus incremental depreciation. This formula corresponds to the format illustrated in Figure 12-3 for calculating net operating cash flows.

$$\text{Net operating cash flow} = (\triangle R - \triangle OC - \triangle D)(1 - T) + \triangle D \qquad \textbf{(12-1)}$$

where $\triangle$ = Delta (Greek symbol for change)
   $\triangle R$ = Incremental revenues
   $\triangle OC$ = Incremental operating costs
   $\triangle D$ = Incremental depreciation and other noncash charges
   T = Tax rate (%)

Equation 12-2 presents an alternate method for computing net operating cash flows that highlights the depreciation tax savings (depreciation expense × tax rate).

$$\text{Net operating cash flows} = (\triangle R - \triangle OC)(1 - t) + \triangle TD \qquad \textbf{(12-2)}$$

where $\quad \triangle TD = $ Incremental depreciation tax savings ($\triangle D \times t$)

Both methods give the same results.

EXAMPLE 12-3. Referring to Example 12-2, the new machine which Edelman Enterprises plans to acquire for a net investment of $24,000 is expected to produce additional annual sales of $10,000 with additional annual operating expenses of $4,000. The project's expected life is 10 years. The firm plans to use the Accelerated Cost Recovery System (ACRS) rules for the 7-year property class. The company's marginal tax rate is 34 percent.

Using the format shown in Figure 12-3, the net operating cash flows for Years 1-3 and 10 for this expansion problem are:

	Year 1	Year 2	Year 3	Year 10
Cash revenues	$10,000	$10,000	$10,000	$10,000
− Cash operating costs	4,000	4,000	4,000	4,000
− Depreciation expenses	2,856	4,898	3,498	0
Taxable income	$ 3,144	$ 1,102	$ 2,502	$ 6,000
− Income taxes (34%)*	1,069	375	851	2,040
Net income	$ 2,075	$ 727	$ 1,615	$ 3,960
+ Depreciation expenses	2,856	4,898	3,498	0
Net operating cash flows	$ 4,931	$ 5,625	$ 5,149	$ 3,960

* Figures are rounded to the nearest dollar.

The amount of depreciation is determined below:

Recovery Year	Depreciation Rate* (1)	Depreciable Basis (2)	Depreciation Amount [(1) × (2)]
1	.1428	$20,000	$2,856
2	.2449	20,000	4,898
3	.1749	20,000	3,498

* The rates are found in Figure 2-2 for 7-year ACRS class.

The same procedure is followed to compute net operating cash flows for Years 4 through 9.

EXAMPLE 12-4: Early in 1988, Clark Company (CC) purchased a Model X-10 machine. Several months later, the firm's management learned that a Model X-11 machine was available which provides greater production capacity and efficiency. Both machines are in the 7-year ACRS class and have estimated lives of 10 years. Management has developed the following information about the two machines:

	Model X-11	Model X-10
Installed cost	$600,000	$500,000
Annual cash revenues	800,000	600,000
Annual cash operating expenses	500,000	400,000
Depreciation—Year 1	85,680*	71,400**

* (0.1428 × $600,000) = $85,680
** (0.1428 × $500,000) = $71,400

Depreciation percentages are found in Figure 2-2.

The firm's marginal tax rate is 34 percent. Using the format shown in Figure 12-3, the incremental after-tax net cash flows for Year 1 are:

Year 1	Model X-11 (1)	Model X-10 (2)	Incremental [(1) − (2)]
Cash revenues.............................	$800,000	$600,000	$200,000
− Cash operating expenses	500,000	400,000	− 100,000
− Depreciation expenses..................	85,680	71,400	− 14,280
Taxable income	$214,320	$128,600	$ 85,720
− Income taxes (34%).....................	72,869	43,724	− 29,145
Net income.................................	$141,451	$ 84,876	$ 56,575
+ Depreciation expenses..................	85,680	71,400	+ 14,280
Net operating cash flows	$227,131	$156,276	$ 70,855

Net operating cash flows for the remaining nine years of these projects are calculated in a similar fashion. There are no depreciation expenses after Year 8 because the assets are fully depreciated.

3. **Net terminal cash flow** is the net cash flow resulting from ending a project. The financial manager must decide when the project will be terminated. At the end of the final year, the firm receives cash inflows in the form of salvage value on the sale of the asset plus the release of any working capital as a result of the termination. Net working capital is a cash inflow because it is assumed to be liquidated and returned to the firm as cash. No tax consequences are associated with changes in net working capital.

The terminal cash inflows are reduced by any removal costs. Because the removal costs are an operating expense, the taxes on the sale of the asset are determined after subtracting removal costs. As discussed earlier in this section, the tax effects of the sale of an asset depend on the price received, its original cost, and the current book value. Figure 12-4 gives the format for calculating terminal cash flow.

Salvage value
− Removal costs
Salvage value before taxes
+ Income taxes
Net salvage value
+ Release of net working capital
Terminal cash flow

FIGURE 12-4
Format for calculating
terminal cash flow.

EXAMPLE 12-5: Referring to the new machine in Examples 12-2 and 12-3, Edelman Enterprises expects to sell the machine at the end of ten years for $2,500 with removal costs of $500. The asset is fully depreciated and the tax rate is 34 percent. The $4,000 in net working capital released is considered a cash inflow.

Using the format showing in Figure 12-4, the terminal cash flow is:

Salvage value......	$2,500
− Removal costs	500
Salvage value before taxes......	$2,000
− Income taxes (34%)......	680
Net salvage value	$1,320
+ Release of net working capital......	4,000
Terminal cash flow......	$5,320

D. Cash flows follow two patterns: *conventional* and *nonconventional*.

1. A **conventional cash flow** is a time series of net cash flows that contains only one change in sign. The following pattern of one net outflow (−) followed by three net inflows (+) is a conventional cash flow because there is only one change in sign: −, +, +, +.

2. A **nonconventional cash flow** is a time series of net cash flows that contains more than one change in sign. The following represents a nonconventional cash flow: −, +, +, −. This pattern is nonconventional because the sign changes twice. Investment projects with nonconventional cash flows may produce contradictory evaluations. Techniques for dealing with this problem are found in specialized capital budgeting texts.

12-5. Evaluating Project Proposals

After the cash flows are projected, the third step in the capital budgeting process is evaluating project proposals. Capital investments are evaluated under *certainty* or *risk*. Under certainty, the exact values associated with the investment, such as the cash flows and the required rate of return, are known in advance. In practice, few financial variables are known in advance with absolute certainty. Under risk, variables required for evaluating investment proposals are not certain and involve a margin of error. There are numerous techniques that may be used to evaluate both individual and multiple projects under conditions of certainty and risk. Most of these techniques employ time value of money concepts in order to account for a project's cash flows over time. Various techniques for assessing the economic value of investment projects are discussed in Chapter 13.

12-6. Selecting Projects

The fourth step in the capital budgeting process is selecting projects. In theory, the firm should invest in new projects up to the point where the rate of return from the last project is equal to the firm's marginal cost of capital. In practice, other factors may influence the selection process.

The final selection of projects depends on three major factors: project type, availability of funds, and decision criteria.

1. Capital expenditure decisions may be classified as independent and mutually exclusive. An **independent project** is one having a distinct function. Acceptance or rejection of an independent project does not necessarily preclude other projects from consideration. For example, a firm may wish to construct a new building and to install a computer system. Both projects could be adopted provided that each meets the firm's investment criteria and sufficient funds are available.

   A **mutually exclusive project** is an alternate way of performing the same function as other projects under consideration. Acceptance of a mutually exclusive project eliminates the other alternatives from further consideration. For example, a firm is considering building a new plant in one of four possible locations. Selecting one location eliminates the need for the other three plant sites.

2. The availability of funds affects capital budgeting decisions. *Unlimited funds* allow a firm to operate with no constraints on its capital expenditures. A firm with no capital constraints should accept all projects that meet its selection criteria. **Capital rationing** occurs when a firm places an upper limit on its capital expenditures. This limit on the size of the total capital budget is often self-imposed. The dominant cause of a budget constraint is a debt limit imposed by internal management. If there is an absolute limit on the amount of debt financing, expenditures will be cut back under two conditions: internally generated funds are too small to make up the deficit, or the firm is unwilling to undertake equity financing. Under capital rationing, a firm may not maximize shareholder wealth because it may reject *profitable projects* (projects

whose expected rate of return exceeds the required rate of return). A firm that rations funds should allocate the funds in a way that maximizes long-run return within the budget contraints.

3. Decision criteria are established to rank projects and to provide a cutoff point for capital expenditures. Frequently there are more proposals for projects than the firm is able or willing to finance. Ranking techniques are used to select the best subset of acceptable projects from a larger set that cannot be fully funded. Projects are often ranked according to a prescribed *hurdle rate* or minimum acceptable rate of return. Hurdle rates reflect the project's riskiness; common measures include the firm's *cost of capital* (the required rate of return of investors who provide funds to the firm), *opportunity cost* (the rate of return on the firm's best alternative investment available), or some risk-adjusted rate.

Capital budgeting techniques provide a useful quantitative basis for project selection. However, other factors in addition to the economic appraisal of an investment must be considered. Qualitative factors, such as personal preferences of decision makers, ethics, and social responsibility, also serve as inputs in the selection process.

Once the final projects are selected they must be combined into a **capital budget**, which is a plan of expenditures for fixed assets.

12-7. Implementing and Reviewing Projects

The fifth and final step in the capital budgeting process is implementing and reviewing accepted projects. The decision to accept or reject a proposed project must be communicated to its originator and to others in the firm. Acceptable projects must then be implemented in a timely and efficient manner. The *implementation stage* involves developing formal procedures for authorizing the expenditures of funds for capital projects. The *review stage* involves analyzing projects that have been adopted in order to determine if they should be continued, modified, or terminated. The financial manager works with managers in other departments to compile systematic records on the uses of funds. The exercise of *expenditure control* helps to ensure that costs remain within the budgeted amounts. If cost overruns occur, corporate managers must decide upon the appropriate action to take regarding the project. For example, managers may decide to abandon a project if it no longer contributes to shareholder wealth.

After a project is completed, a *post-audit* is conducted in which comparisons are made between earlier estimates and actual data. Review of past decisions may provide a basis for improving management's ability to evaluate subsequent investment alternatives.

RAISE YOUR GRADES

Can you explain...?

☑ what capital budgeting is
☑ the relationship between business strategy and the capital budgeting process
☑ the five steps in the capital budgeting process
☑ four different types of investment proposals
☑ how cash flow differ from accounting profit
☑ why only incremental after-tax cash flows are relevant in making capital budgeting decisions
☑ the three categories of cash flows in an investment project
☑ the difference between conventional and nonconventional cash flow patterns
☑ how evaluating project proposals differs under certainty and risk
☑ the difference between independent and mutually exclusive projects

☑ how capital rationing affects selecting projects
☑ what a hurdle rate is
☑ the purpose of a post-audit

SUMMARY

1. Capital budgeting is the process of analyzing investment opportunities and making long-term investment decisions.
2. Capital investments have a long-term impact on the performance of the firm.
3. Project proposals logically flow from the firm's business strategy.
4. There are five steps in the capital budgeting process: generating project proposals, estimating cash flows, evaluating project proposals, selecting projects, and implementing and reviewing projects.
5. Project proposals are generated from either a top-down or bottom-up approach.
6. There are four primary types of capital investment projects: expansion, replacement, modernization, and safety or environmental.
7. Cash flow is the net of inflows and outflows of cash that results from a firm undertaking a project.
8. Cash flow differs from accounting profit.
9. Cash flows for a particular project are measured on an incremental, after-tax basis and consider both direct and indirect effects of the project.
10. A project's cash flows consist of net investment, net operating cash flows, and net terminal cash flow.
11. Net investment is the net initial cash outlay needed to place a project in service.
12. Net operating cash flows are the incremental changes in a firm's operating cash flows that result from investing in a project. Net operating cash flows are the earnings after taxes plus depreciation and other noncash charges over the life of the project.
13. Net terminal cash flow is the net cash flow resulting from ending a project.
14. Cash flows follow conventional or nonconventional patterns.
15. Capital investments are evaluated under certainty or risk.
16. Capital investment projects are classified as independent or mutually exclusive.
17. Capital rationing occurs when a firm places an upper limit on its capital expenditures.
18. Capital rationing is normally not consistent with shareholder wealth maximization because profitable projects may be rejected.
19. Decision criteria are used to rank projects and to provide a cutoff point for capital expenditures.
20. Project selection involves both quantitative and qualitative factors.
21. The post-audit provides information useful to improving the capital budgeting process.

RAPID REVIEW

True or False

1. Capital budgeting procedures only apply to decisions involving fixed assets. [Section 12-1]
2. One reason for the importance of capital budgeting decisions is that they often involve substantial expenditures. [Section 12-1]
3. A capital budgeting project should be compatible with the firm's business strategy before it is accepted. [Section 12-2A]
4. Project proposals may be generated using either a top-down or a bottom-up approach. [Section 12-3A]

5. Expansion projects are typically nonrevenue-producing projects. [Section 12-3B]

6. Another name for cash flow is accounting profit. [Section 12-4A]

7. Cash flows are generally evaluated on a before-tax basis when making capital budgeting decisions. [Section 12-4B]

8. The costs associated with financing a project, such as interest expenses, are generally included in the project's cash flows. [Section 12-4B]

9. Installation costs of a new asset are included in determining the net investment of a project. [Section 12-4C]

10. Changes in net working capital are relevant cash flows that are normally associated with expansion projects. [Section 12-4C]

11. The cash flow associated with the sale of an old asset, including its effect on taxes, is considered in determining the net investment of a replacement project. [Section 12-4C]

12. The sale of an old machine for its book value has no impact on corporate taxes. [Section 12-4C]

13. A recapture of depreciation resulting from the sale of an old asset is treated as as ordinary income for tax purposes. [Section 12-4C]

14. The sale of a depreciable asset for more than its original cost is, in effect, taxed at ordinary tax rates. [Section 14-4C]

15. The only items relevant to determining net operating cash flows are cash items such as revenues, expenses, and taxes. [Section 12-4C]

16. Depreciation expense is relevant in computing cash flows only to the extent that it lowers taxable income and results in a tax saving. [Section 12-4C]

17. The release of any net working capital upon terminating a project is treated as ordinary income and is taxed accordingly. [Section 12-4C]

18. A pattern of conventional cash flows contains only one change in sign. [Section 12-4D]

19. When projects are evaluated under certainty, their exact cash flows are assumed to be known. [Section 12-5]

20. Acceptance of a mutually exclusive project eliminates the alternative proposals from further consideration. [Section 12-6A]

21. Capital rationing occurs when limited profitable investment projects are available and must be rationed among investors. [Section 12-6A]

22. Capital rationing leads to the maximization of shareholder wealth. [Section 12-6A]

23. A hurdle rate is the minimum acceptable rate of return on a project. [Section 12-6A]

24. The selection of investment projects is influenced by both quantitative and qualitative factors. [Section 12-6A]

25. The post-audit may improve management's ability to evaluate future investment alternatives. [Section 12-7]

Multiple Choice

26. A capital budgeting project that involves an expenditure to upgrade or to improve existing fixed assets is called a(n)

    (*a*) expansion project
    (*b*) replacement project
    (*c*) modernization project
    (*d*) safety or environmental project

    [Section 12-3B]

27. The most important step in the capital budgeting process is:

    (*a*) generating project proposals
    (*b*) estimating cash flows

(c) evaluating project proposals

(d) implementing and reviewing projects

[Section 12-4]

28. The difference between cash inflows and cash outflows is called

(a) net income after taxes

(b) total cash flow

(c) net cash flow

() cash flow

[Section 12-4]

29. Which of the following is *not* considered a relevant cash flow in determining whether or not to continue with an oil drilling project?

(a) Past engineering studies associated with the project

(b) Cost of new drilling equipment

(c) Potential revenues from striking oil

(d) Labor costs associated with the drilling

[Section 12-4B]

30. The net investment of a replacement project does not include the

(a) purchase price of the new asset

(b) installation costs of the new asset

(c) interest expense of the funds used

(d) proceeds from the sale of the old asset

[Sections 12-4B & C]

31. The sale of an asset for less than its book value results in

(a) no tax effects

(b) a loss used to offset ordinary operating income

(c) a recapture of depreciation

(d) a long-term capital gain

[Section 12-4C]

32. Which of the following is a noncash outlay associated with an investment project?

(a) Interest expenses

(b) Corporate federal income taxes

(c) Operating expenses such as labor and material

(d) Depreciation expenses

[Section 12-4C]

33. A project's net operating cash flow can be calculated as

(a) net income before taxes

(b) net income after taxes

(c) net income after taxes plus depreciation expenses and other noncash charges

(d) net income after taxes minus interest expenses

[Section 12-4C]

34. Which of the following is *not* considered in the calculation of a project's net operating cash flow?

(a) Depreciation tax shield

(b) Increased dividends if new common stock is used to finance a project

(c) Increased principal payments if new debt is used to finance a project

(d) Both b and c

[Section 12-4B]

35. Which of the following is included in a project's terminal cash flow?

(*a*) After-tax salvage value of a project
(*b*) Released working capital
(*c*) Before-tax salvage value of a project
(*d*) Both a and b

[Section 12-4C]

Answers

True or False

1. False	11. True	21. False	
2. True	12. True	22. False	
3. True	13. True	23. True	
4. True	14. True	24. True	
5. False	15. False	25. True	
6. False	16. True		
7. False	17. False		
8. False	18. True		
9. True	19. True		
10. True	20. True		

Multiple Choice

26. c	
27. b	
28. c	
29. a	
30. c	
31. b	
32. d	
33. c	
34. d	
35. d	

SOLVED PROBLEMS

Problems 12-1 through 12-3 refer to Losey Rackets, Inc.

PROBLEM 12-1: Losey Rackets, Inc. is considering the purchase of a new piece of equipment to meet the increased demand for its Model XL-4 tennis racket. The equipment costs $100,000 plus $5,000 for installation and shipping. The resulting increased production is expected to require additional net working capital of $25,000. What is the net investment that Losey Rackets, Inc. will make on the new equipment?

Answer: Using the form shown in Figure 12-2, the net investment is:

Cost of new equipment..	$100,000
+ Installation and shipping costs	5,000
Total cost of new equipment...	$105,000
+ Increase in net working capital	25,000
Net investment..	$130,000

[Section 12-4C]

PROBLEM 12-2: Referring to Problem 12-1, the new equipment that Losey Rackets, Inc. will purchase would be depreciated using the Accelerated Cost Recovery System (ACRS) and is considered 7-year class property. This equipment is expected to enable the firm to expand sales by $80,000 per year with an increase in cash operating expenses amounting to 60 percent of the increase in sales. The firm's marginal tax rate is 34 percent.

(*a*) What is the depreciable basis of the new equipment?
(*b*) What are the annual depreciation charges for the first three years?
(*c*) What is the annual net operating cash flows for the first three years?

Answer:

(*a*) The depreciable basis is $105,000 ($100,000 + $5,000).

(*b*) The annual depreciation charge is calculated below:

Recovery Year	Depreciation Rate* (1)	Depreciable Basis (2)	Depreciation Amount** [(1) × (2)]
1	.1428	$105,000	$14,994
2	.2449	105,000	25,715
3	.1749	105,000	18,365

* The rates are found in Figure 2-2 for 7-year ACRS class property.
** Rounded to the nearest dollar.

(*c*) The annual net operating cash flows are determined using the format shown in Figure 12-3.

	Year 1	Year 2	Year 3
Cash revenues	$80,000	$80,000	$80,000
− Cash operating expenses (0.60 × $80,000)	48,000	48,000	48,000
− Depreciation expenses	14,994	25,715	18,365
Taxable income	$17,006	$ 6,285	$13,635
− Income taxes (34%)	5,782	2,137	4,636
Net income	$11,224	$ 4,148	$ 8,999
+ Depreciation expenses	14,994	25,715	18,365
Net operating cash flows	$26,218	$29,863	$27,364

[Section 12-4C]

PROBLEM 12-3: Losey Rackets, Inc. estimates that the equipment's salvage value will be $10,000 at the end of its 10-year life. There will be no removal costs. The company expects to release its $25,000 in additional net working capital. If the firm's marginal tax rate is 34 percent, what is the terminal cash flow?

Answer: Using the format shown in Figure 12-4, the terminal cash flow is:

Salvage value	$10,000
− Income taxes (34%)	3,400
Net salvage value	$ 6,600
+ Release of net working capital	25,000
Terminal cash flow	$31,600

[Section 12-4C]

Use the following information to solve Problems 12-4 through 12-6.

The finance department has prepared the following information about an ACRS investment project with a 7-year life.

Purchase price of the new machine	$200,000
Installation and transportation costs	5,000
Increase in accounts receivable	25,000
Increase in inventory	10,000
Increase in accounts payable	15,000
Feasibility study prepared and paid for last year	6,000
Incremental cash sales per year	300,000
Incremental cash operating expenses (labor and materials) per year	160,000

Fixed overhead	50,000
Increase in interest expense per year	20,000
Expected salvage value in Year 12	75,000
Marginal tax rate.	34%

PROBLEM 12-4: What is the net investment at time period zero?

Answer: The net investment at time period zero will consist of the following:

Purchase price of the new machine		$200,000
+ Installation and transportation costs.		5,000
+ Additional net working capital.		
+ Increase in accounts receivable.	$25,000	
+ Increase in inventory.	10,000	
− Increase in accounts payable	15,000	20,000
Net investment.		$225,000

The cost of the feasibility study is an unrecoverable cost (sunk cost) associated with a previous decision. It should not be allocated to a new project under consideration and it has no bearing on the decision at this point in time. **[Sections 12-4B & C]**

PROBLEM 12-5: What items should be considered in computing the net operating cash flows over the project's life?

Answer: The following items are used to compute the net operating cash flows: incremental cash sales, incremental cash operating expenses, depreciation expenses, and taxes. Fixed overhead expenses generally should not be deducted from the project's receipts to determine its net operating cash flows. These fixed costs are not a relevant cash flow because they will remain the same whether the investment project is accepted or rejected. The increase in interest expenses associated with financing the investment is a cash outflow. However, financing charges are included in the firm's cost of capital, not in its operating cash flows. **[Section 12-4C]**

PROBLEM 12-6: What is the terminal cash flow in Year 12 if the machine is sold for its expected salvage value of $75,000?

Answer: Using the format in Figure 12-4, the investment's terminal cash flow in Year 3 is:

Salvage value.	$75,000
− Income taxes (34%).	25,500
After-tax salvage value.	$49,500
+ Release of net working capital	20,000
Terminal cash flow.	$69,500

The salvage value is viewed as a recapture of depreciation and, as such, is taxed at the firm's marginal tax rate. The recovery of working capital is not taxable.

[Section 12-4C]

Use the following information to solve Problems 12-7 and 12-8.

Jinco Industries is considering replacing a machine that it purchased three years ago for $100,000. The current book value of the existing machine is $43,740. The new machine costs $130,000 plus $5,000 in installation costs. The firm's marginal tax rate is 34 percent.

PROBLEM 12-7: What are the after-tax cash flow effects if the old machine is sold for the following prices?

(a) $43,740
(b) $30,000
(c) $90,000
(d) $120,000

Answer:

(*a*) There are no tax effects if the machine is sold for its book value.

(*b*) There is a loss of $13,740 ($43,740 − $30,000) if the machine is sold for less than its book value. This loss results in the following tax saving:

Tax saving = 0.34 × $13,740 = $4,672

(*c*) There is a gain if the asset is sold for an amount equal to or less than its original cost. This gain is $46,260 ($90,000 − $43,740), and is a recapture of depreciation which is treated as ordinary income.

Tax liability = 0.34 × $46,260 = $15,728

(*d*) There is a gain of $76,260 ($120,000 − $43,740) if the machine is sold for $120,000. This gain is split into a recapture of depreciation of $56,260 ($100,000 − $43,740) and a long-term capital gain of $20,000 ($120,000 − $100,000). If there are no capital losses to offset the capital gains, the total gain is taxed at 34 percent.

Tax liability = 0.34 × $76,260 = $25,928

[Section 12-4C]

PROBLEM 12-8: What is the net investment in the new machine if the old machine is sold at each of the four prices specified in Problem 12-7?

Answer: Using the format shown in Figure 12-3, the net investment of the replacement is:

	Old Machine Sold for			
	$43,740	$30,000	$90,000	$120,000
Purchase price of new machine..........	$130,000	$130,000	$130,000	$130,000
+ Installation costs.....................	5,000	5,000	5,000	5,000
− Proceeds from sale of old machine ...	43,740	30,000	90,000	120,000
− Taxes savings on loss from sale of old machine	0	4,672		
+ Tax liability on gain from sale of old machine			15,728	25,928
Net investment	$ 91,260	$100,328	$ 60,728	$ 40,928

[Section 12-4C]

PROBLEM 12-9: Traynor Corporation adopted a new investment project that resulted in the following incremental increases for the first year of the project's operation:

Cash revenues..	$50,000
Cash operating expenses	20,000
Depreciation expenses...	5,000

The firm's marginal tax rate is 34 percent. Calculate the firm's net operating cash flow using both Equations 12-1 and 12-2.

Answer: Substituting $\triangle R$ = $50,000, $\triangle OC$ = $20,000, $\triangle D$ = $5,000, and T = 0.34 in Equation 12-1, the net operating cash flows are:

Net operating cash flows = ($50,000 − $20,000 − $5,000)(1 − 0.34) + $5,000

= $16,500 + $5,000 = $21,500

Using Equation 12-2, in which $\triangle TD$ = $1,700 (0.34 × $5,000), the net operating cash flow is:

Net operating cash flows = ($50,000 − $20,000)(1 − 0.34) + $1,700

= $19,800 + $1,700 = $21,500

[Section 12-4C]

PROBLEM 12-10: Shen Manufacturing Company is considering replacing an old assembly machine with a more modern one. The old machine originally cost $35,000 and is fully depreciated. This machine is expected to remain operational for five more years. A buyer has agreed to pay $5,000 for the old machine and to remove it. The installed cost of the new machine is $60,000. The firm plans to depreciate the new machine over a 7-year period under ACRS. The purchase of the new machine is expected to increase sales from $70,000 to $85,000 and to reduce operating costs from $30,000 to $25,000 each year for the next 10 years. The increased sales require $3,000 of additional net working capital, which is assumed to occur in time period zero. The firm's income tax rate is 34 percent.

(a) What is the net investment in the new machine?

(b) What is the incremental cash flow for the first year that the new machine is placed in service?

Answer:

(a) Using the format shown in Figure 12-2, the net investment is:

Installed cost of new machine...	$60,000
+ Additional net working capital	3,000
− Proceeds from sale of old machine.......................................	5,000
+ Taxes on gain from sale of old machine (0.34 × $5,000)	1,700
Net investment..	$59,700

(b) Using the format shown in Figure 12-3, the incremental operating cash flows for the first year of the investment are:

Year 1	New Assembler (1)	Old Assembler (2)	Incremental [(1) − (2)]
Cash revenues......................	$85,000	$70,000	$15,000
− Cash operating expenses*	25,000	30,000	+ 5,000
− Depreciation expenses**	8,568	0	− 8,568
Taxable income....................	$51,432	$40,000	$11,432
− Income taxes (34%).............	17,487	13,600	− 3,887
Net income	$33,945	$26,400	$ 7,545
+ Depreciation expenses..........	8,568	0	+ 8,568
Net operating cash flows...........	$42,513	$26,400	$16,113

* The lower cash operating costs of the new assembler represent a savings. Thus, a negative cash operating expense represents a positive incremental cash flow.

** First year depreciation = 0.1428 × $60,000 = $8,568

13 CAPITAL BUDGETING TECHNIQUES UNDER CERTAINTY AND RISK

THIS CHAPTER IS ABOUT

☑ **Capital Budgeting under Certainty**
☑ **Selection Problems**
☑ **Capital Budgeting under Risk**

The preceding chapter provided the necessary background for a discussion of capital budgeting techniques. This chapter examines several methods that may be used to evaluate and to select projects. The capital budgeting techniques are applied under two conditions: certainty and risk.

13-1. Capital Budgeting under Certainty

When capital budgeting is done under *certainty*, the decision maker knows in advance the future values of all the information affecting the decision. For example, certainty prevails when the future contains only one possible net cash flow in any single year. Capital budgeting techniques under certainty may be divided into two major categories: unsophisticated and sophisticated. (All capital expenditures in this section are assumed to involve single, independent projects having conventional cash flow patterns and unlimited funds. Decision making under other conditions is discussed in Section 13-2.)

A. *Unsophisticated techniques* **do not consider some of the important factors in the asset-selection process, such as the time value of money and the cost of capital.**

Unsophisticated capital budgeting techniques include the accounting rate of return (ARR) and the payback period (PB).

1. The **accounting rate of return** (ARR) is a measure of a project's profitability from a conventional accounting standpoint. There are numerous ways to compute the ARR, but one way is to divide a project's average annual net income by its average net investment. *Average annual net income* is found by summing the expected net incomes over the project's life and dividing by the total number of periods in the life of the project. *Average net investment* is assumed to be one-half of the net investment. (Since most firms use the Accelerated Cost Recovery System to depreciate assets over their normal recovery periods, the actual average net investment will be lower than one half of the net investment). Equation 13-1 presents a common method of computing a project's ARR.

$$\text{Accounting rate of return} = \frac{\text{Average annual net income}}{\text{Average net investment}} \quad \text{(13-1)}$$

- The *decision rule* is to accept a project if the ARR is equal to or greater than the target ARR set by the firm; otherwise, the project is rejected. In ranking projects having the same target ARR, the project with the higher ARR should be chosen because it is more profitable.

- The *advantages* of using the ARR are that it is understandable, easy to calculate, and considers profitability.
- The *disadvantages* of using the ARR are that it uses accounting income rather than cash flows, ignores the time value of money, assumes the net investment is written off at a constant rate, and provides no objective criterion for decision making that will maximize shareholder wealth.

EXAMPLE 13-1: James Corporation is considering an investment in Project A based on the following information:

Project A	
Net investment	$12,000
Annual net income	2,000
Estimated life	5 years
Target ARR	25%

The average annual net income is $2,000 ($10,000/5 years) and the average net investment is $6,000 ($12,000/2). Substituting these values in Equation 13-1, the accounting rate of return is:

$$\text{Accounting rate of return} = \frac{\$2,000}{\$6,000} = 0.333 \text{ or } 33.3 \text{ percent}$$

James Corporation should accept the investment because the actual ARR of 33.3 percent is greater than the target ARR of 25 percent.

2. The **payback period** (PB) is the length of time required for a project's cumulative net cash inflows to equal its net investment. Thus, the payback measures the time required for a project to break even. If the expected annual net cash inflows are *equal* (annuity form), the payback is computed by dividing the net investment by the annual net cash inflows as shown in Equation 13-2.

PAYBACK PERIOD WITH EQUAL CASH INFLOWS $\dfrac{NI}{NCF}$ (13-2)

$$\text{where} \quad NI = \text{net investment}$$
$$NCF = \text{annual net cash inflows}$$

If the expected cash inflows are unequal, the payback is calculated by determining the length of time required for cumulative net cash inflows to equal the net investment as shown in Equation 13-3.

PAYBACK PERIOD WITH UNEQUAL CASH FLOWS $\sum_{t=1}^{PB} NCF_t = NI$ (13-3)

$$\text{where} \quad PB = \text{payback period to be determined}$$
$$NCF_t = \text{annual net cash inflow in period } t$$

- The *decision rule* is to accept a project if its computed payback period is equal to or less than the maximum payback period set by the firm; otherwise, the project is rejected. The time period that is acceptable as a payback period is a policy decision made by the firm. In two ranking projects having the same maximum allowable payback, the project with the shorter payback period should be chosen because it pays for itself more quickly.
- The *advantages* of using the payback are that it is easy to understand, calculate, and interpret; provides a measure of liquidity (measures the time required for a project to recover the initial investment); and provides a crude measure of risk (projects with shorter payback periods are considered less risky).
- The *disadvantages* of using the payback are that it ignores the time value of money; does not measure the profitability of an investment because it ignores

cash flows beyond the payback period; biases capital budgeting decisions in favor of short-term projects and against long-term projects; and provides no objective criterion for decision making that will maximize shareholder wealth.

EXAMPLE 13-2: The information provided below pertains to Project A of the James Corporation. The maximum payback period set by the firm is three years.

Project A

Net investment	$12,000
Annual net cash inflows	5,000
Estimated life	5 years

Substituting the net investment of $12,000 and annual net cash inflows of $5,000 in Equation 13-2, the payback period is:

$$\text{Payback period with equal cash flows} = \frac{\$12,000}{\$5,000} = 2.4 \text{ years}$$

For the purpose of simplicity, the net cash inflows are assumed to occur at the end of each year. If this assumption is strictly followed, Project A would require three years of cash flows before it earns its net investment because there would be no cash flows during the year. In practice, cash flows generally occur throughout the year. Thus, if cash flows are reasonably constant during the year, it is reasonable to use 2.4 years, rather than three years, as the payback period.

Project A should be accepted because the computed payback period of 2.4 years is less than the maximum payback of three years.

EXAMPLE 13-3: James Corporation is evaluating two other projects with the following cash flows:

Cash Flows

Year	Project B	Project C
0	($10,000)	($10,000)
1	2,000	5,000
2	3,000	4,000
3	4,000	1,000
4	5,000	
5	7,000	

(*a*) Using the process shown in Equation 13-3, the payback period for each project is computed below.

	Project B		Project C	
Year	Net Cash Inflows	Cumulative Net Cash Inflows	Net Cash Inflows	Cumulative Net Cash Inflows
1	$2,000	$ 2,000	$5,000	$ 5,000
2	3,000	5,000	4,000	9,000
3	4,000	9,000	1,000	10,000
4	5,000	14,000		
5	7,000	21,000		

$$\text{Payback}_B = 3 + \frac{\$1,000}{\$5,000} = 3.2 \text{ years} \qquad \text{Payback}_C = 3 \text{ years}$$

Project B's cumulative net cash inflows show that the project pays for itself between three and four years. A total of $9,000 is recovered during the first three years and the remaining $1,000 during the fourth year. It takes 0.2 years ($1,000/$5,000) to earn the additional $1,000. Hence, Project B's payback period is 3.2 years. In three years, Project C's cumulative net cash inflows exactly equal its net investment of $10,000.

(b) James Company should accept Project C over Project B because it has a shorter payback and pays for itself within the allowable maximum payback period of three years.

(c) The payback period does not measure profitability because it ignores Project B's cash flows after the payback period. From a profitability perspective, Project B is more attractive than Project C. The payback also does not recognize the time values of the cash flows. Thus, use of the payback period may lead to incorrect accept-reject decisions when investment alternatives are evaluated on the basis of their time-adjusted profitability.

B. *Sophisticated techniques* **consider such important financial factors as the time value of money and cash flow in the project-selection process.**

These techniques, also called *discounted cash flow techniques*, include net present value (NPV), profitability index (PI), and internal rate of return (IRR).

1. The **net present value** (NPV) is the sum of the present values of a project's net cash flows (net operating cash flows plus net terminal cash flows minus its net investment). The cash flows are discounted at the firm's *cost of capital*, which is used as the minimum acceptable rate of return for investment projects of average risk. The NPV model implicitly assumes that the project's net operating cash inflows are reinvested at a rate equal to the firm's cost of capital (discount rate). This model provides an *absolute measure* of a project's worth because it measures the total present value of dollar return. Equation 13-4 presents the formula for computing a project's net present value.

$$\text{Net Present Value} = \text{PV of NCF}_t - \text{NI}$$

$$= \sum_{t=1}^{n} \frac{\text{NCF}_t}{(1 + k)^t} - \text{NI} \qquad \textbf{(13-4)}$$

where NCF_t = net cash flows in period t

         NI = net investment

         k = marginal cost of capital used as a discount rate

         n = life of the project in years

(The procedure for computing the present value of cash flows is discussed further in Chapter 3).

- The *decision rule* is to accept the project if its NPV is equal to or greater than zero; otherwise, the project is rejected. If a project's NPV is equal to or greater than zero, the firm will earn a return equal to or greater than its cost of capital. In ranking projects having similar sizes, lives, and cash flow patterns, the project with the higher positive NPV should be chosen because it maximizes shareholder wealth.
- The *advantages* of using the NPV are that it considers the magnitude and timing of cash flows, provides an objective criterion for decision making which maximizes shareholder wealth, and is the most conceptually correct capital budgeting approach.
- The *disadvantages* of using the NPV are that it is more difficult to compute than unsophisticated methods and its meaning is difficult to interpret because the NPV does not provide a measure of a project's actual rate of return.

EXAMPLE 13-4: In Example 13-2, Project A has a net investment of $12,000 and annual net cash inflows of $5,000 for five years. Management wants to calculate Project A's net present value using a 16 percent discount rate.

The annual net cash inflows of \$5,000 for five years are an annuity. The NPV is calculated by multiplying \$5,000 by the present value interest factor of an annuity for five years discounted at 16 percent, $\text{PVIFA}_{0.16,5} = 3.274$ (Appendix D), and then subtracting the net investment.

Years	Cash Inflows (1)	$\text{PVIFA}_{0.16,5}$ (2)	Present Value [(1) × (2)]
1–5	\$5,000	3.274	\$16,370

Present value of cash inflows	\$16,370
− Net investment	12,000
Net present value	\$ 4,370

Project A should be accepted because its NPV is positive.

2. The **profitability index** (PI) is the ratio of the sum of the present values of a project's net cash flows divided by its net investment. The profitability index, sometimes called the *benefit/cost ratio*, uses the same information as the NPV method and measures the present value of the return for each dollar of net investment. That is, the PI indicates the increase in the value of the firm created by each dollar invested in the project. Hence, the PI is a *relative measure* of a project's profitability whereas NPV is an absolute measure of the total present value of dollar return. Equation 13-5 is the formula for computing the profitability index.

PROFITABILITY INDEX $$\text{PI} = \frac{\text{PV of NCF}_t}{\text{NI}} = \frac{\displaystyle\sum_{t=1}^{n} \frac{\text{NCF}_t}{(1 + k)^t}}{\text{NI}} \tag{13-5}$$

- The *decision rule* is to accept the project if its PI is equal to or greater than one; otherwise, the project is rejected. A project whose PI is equal to or greater than one will maintain or enhance the wealth of the owners as reflected in the share price of the firm's common stock.
- The *advantages* of using the PI are that it considers the magnitude and timing of cash flows, provides an objective criterion for decision making which maximizes shareholder wealth, and provides a relative measure of return per dollar of net investment.
- The *disadvantage* of using the PI is that conflict may arise with the NPV when dealing with mutually exclusive investments.

EXAMPLE 13-5: *Refer to the information provided in Example 13-4 for Project A. By substituting the present value of the NCF = \$16,370 and the NI = \$12,000 in Equation 13-5, the PI is:*

$$\text{Profitability index} = \frac{\$16,370}{\$12,000} = 1.36$$

Because Project A returns \$1.36 in present value for each dollar invested, it should be accepted.

3. The **internal rate of return** (IRR) is the discount rate that equates the present value of a project's net cash inflows to its net investment. Using the IRR as a discount rate produces a zero NPV. It is possible to obtain multiple IRRs for projects with nonconventional cash flow patterns.

The IRR is the most widely used capital budgeting technique. Firms often prefer the IRR for several reasons: the outcome is expressed as a percentage, the IRR can be easily compared to the cost of capital, and it separates the financing and project-selection decisions. This model implicitly assumes that all net operating cash flows are reinvested at a rate equal to the project's IRR. The IRR is the *actual* rate of return that a project earns when cash flows and the time value of money are considered, and is stated as a percentage rate. Equations 13-6 and 13-7 may be used to calculate the IRR.

INTERNAL RATE OF RETURN

$$\text{PV of NCF}_t = \text{NI} = \sum_{t=1}^{n} \frac{\text{NCF}_t}{(1 - \text{IRR})^t} = \text{NI} \tag{13-6}$$

$$\textit{or } \text{PV of NCF}_t - \text{NI} = 0 = \sum_{t=1}^{n} \frac{\text{NCF}_t}{(1 - \text{IRR})^t} - \text{NI} = 0 \tag{13-7}$$

Different procedures are available for calculating a project's IRR depending on whether or not its cash flows are in annuity form.

- When the net cash inflows are an annuity, calculating the IRR is relatively simple First, a present value interest factor of an annuity, $PVIFA_{i,n}$, for the project's annual net cash inflows is computed using Equation 13-8.

$$PVIFA_{i,n} = \frac{\text{NI}}{\text{NCF}} \tag{13-8}$$

This step produces the same number as the payback period for equal cash flows shown in Equation 13-2. Then, using Appendix D, the life of the project, n, and the interest factor, i, closest to the computed PVIFA are found. This interest factor approximates the IRR.

- When the net cash inflows are unequal, calculating the IRR involves trial and error. (However, most financial calculators have a program to compute IRR.) First, the project's NPV is computed using the firm's cost of capital. Then, by trying higher rates if the NPV is positive, or lower rates if the NPV is negative, a rate can be found that equates the NPV to zero.
- The *decision rule* is to accept the project if its IRR is equal to or greater than the firm's cost of capital, k. Otherwise, the project is rejected. In ranking two projects with the same net investment, the project with the higher IRR is preferred.
- The *advantages* of using the IRR are that it is easy to interpret, considers the magnitude and timing of cash flows, and provides an objective criterion for decision making which maximizes shareholder wealth.
- The *disadvantages* of using the IRR are that it can be tedious to compute, especially with uneven net cash inflows; assumes reinvestment of cash inflows at an often unrealistic rate; and can produce multiple IRRs with nonconventional cash flow patterns.

EXAMPLE 13-6: *Refer to the information provided in Example 13-4 for Project A.*

(*a*) Equation 13-8 is used to find the IRR of Project A, which has equal annual cash flows:

$$PVIFA_{i,5} = \frac{\$12,000}{\$5,000} = 2.4$$

Using Appendix D, a PVIFA of 2.4 for 5 years equals a discount rate between 28 and 32 percent.

The trial-and-error approach (which *must* be used with *unequal* cash flows) may also be used to get the IRR. Following the steps of this approach, an arbitrary discount rate of 16 percent for 5 years is used to get a PVIFA of 3.274 and an NPV = $4,370 [(3.274 × $5,000) − $12,000]. Since the IRR is supposed to give a zero NPV, a higher rate is used. Using a 32 percent discount rate gives a PVIFA of 2.345 and negative NPV of −$275 [(2.345 × $5,000) − $12,000]. Hence, a lower discount rate is needed. Using a 28 percent rate produces a positive NPV of $660 [(2.532 × $5,000) − $12,000]. Hence, the true IRR is bracketed between 28 and 32 percent.

(*b*) The project should be accepted because the IRR is greater than the firm's 16 percent cost of capital.

- A more exact IRR is found using **interpolation**, which is a mathematical technique for finding fractional values when only whole percentages are used in time value of money tables. Equation 13-9 is the formula for finding the interpolated interest rate once the IRR is bracketed between two discount rates. Equation 13-9 only approximates the true IRR, because it assumes that there is a linear relationship between interest rates when the relationship is really curvilinear.

$$\text{Interpolated discount rate} = i_1 + \left(\frac{NPV_1}{NPV_1 - NPV_h} \right)(i_h - i_1) \qquad \textbf{(13-9)}$$

$$
\begin{aligned}
\textit{where} \quad i &= \text{interpolated discount rate} \\
i_1 &= \text{discount rate in Appendix C just lower than } i \\
i_h &= \text{discount rate in Appendix C just higher than } i \\
NPV_1 &= \text{net present value at interest rate } i_1 \\
NPV_h &= \text{net present value at interest rate } i_n
\end{aligned}
$$

EXAMPLE 13-7: *Refer to the information in Example 13-6.* Substituting $i_1 = 0.28$, $i_h = 0.32$, $NPV_1 = \$660$, and $NPV_h = -\$275$ in Equation 13-9, the interpolated interest rate is:

$$i = 0.28 + \left(\frac{\$660}{\$660 - (-\$275)} \right)(0.32 - 0.28)$$

$$= 0.28 + (0.71)(0.04) = 0.308 \text{ or } 30.8 \text{ percent}$$

Project A's IRR lies 0.71 percent of the way between the $i_1 = 28$ percent and $i_h = 32$ percent. This fraction is multiplied by the four percentage point difference between 28 and 32 percent to give 2.8 percent, which is added to 28 percent to get an IRR of 30.8 percent.

13-2. Selection Problems

The selection of the appropriate decision rules depends on the practices of the firm and the circumstances surrounding the decision. There are three types of capital budgeting decisions: accept-reject decisions, mutually exclusive project decisions, and capital rationing decisions.

A. An *accept-reject decision* occurs when an individual project is accepted or rejected without regard to any other investment alternatives.

As long as a firm has unlimited funds and only independent projects, all projects meeting the minimum investment criteria should be accepted. Independent projects are those for which the acceptance of one does not automatically eliminate the others from further consideration. Using sophisticated capital budgeting techniques, such as NPV, PI, and IRR, to evaluate single, independent projects with conventional cash flow patterns always leads to identical accept-reject decisions and the maximization of shareholder wealth. The accept-reject decision rules for capital budgeting techniques under certainty have already been stated.

B. *Mutually exclusive projects* are competing investment proposals that will perform the same function or task.

The acceptance of one of these projects eliminates the others from further consideration.

1. The ranking of mutually exclusive projects may conflict based on accept-reject decision rules. There are four major causes for conflicting rankings among mutually exclusive projects using sophisticated capital budgeting techniques.

- The projects have different expected lives.
- The projects have substantially different net investments (size disparity).
- The projects have different timings of cash flows.
- Discounted cash flow techniques have different reinvestment rate assumptions.

2. The NPV is, theoretically, the superior technique when conflicting rankings occur. The NPV method provides correct rankings of mutually exclusive investment projects, whereas other discounted cash flow techniques sometimes do not. The NPV method implicitly assumes that the operating cash flows generated by the project are reinvested at the firm's cost of capital, which approximates the opportunity cost for reinvestment. The IRR method assumes reinvestment at the IRR, which may be an unrealistic rate. Thus, the NPV method assumes that the net operating cash flows for any of the competing alternatives can be reinvested at the same rate, whereas the IRR method uses different reinvestment rates for each competing alternative. NPV does not suffer from the weaknesses of either the IRR or PI and leads to maximizing shareholder wealth. Yet, the IRR is more widely employed in practice because decision makers find the IRR easier to visualize and interpret (except when a project has multiple IRRs).

C. *Capital rationing* **exists when the firm is unable or unwilling to finance all acceptable capital projects.**

Under capital rationing, a firm may place constraints on the total size of its capital budget during a given time period. For example, rationing capital may be employed to increase the firm's ability to accept future projects that are possibly better than those currently available. A major implication of capital rationing is that the firm may not be able to maximize shareholder wealth. However, within its capital budget constraint, the firm's objective is to select the group of projects that will provide the most benefit to the firm. This generally means accepting those projects that provide the highest overall net present value within the budget constraint.

There are numerous approaches to selecting projects under capital rationing. The appropriate decision rule in project selection under capital rationing is to select the set of projects that has the highest combined NPV and costs no more than the budget constraint. Some approaches involve ranking. For example, projects may be ranked initially by their IRRs or PIs and then the combination of projects providing the highest overall NPV within the budget constraint is determined. The portion of the firm's capital budget not invested in projects may be used for other purposes, such as buying marketable securities. Other approaches to solving capital budgeting are available that use mathematical programming techniques, but these techniques are beyond the scope of this book.

EXAMPLE 13-8: The financial manager of Selman Corporation has the following information about two mutually exclusive projects.

	Net Cash Flows	
Year	Project B	Project C
0	($20,000)	($20,000)
1	14,000	1,500
2	8,000	8,000
3	1,500	20,000

	Project B	Rank	Project C	Rank
Net present value*	$2,284	2	$3,002	1
Profitability index*	1.11	2	1.15	1
Internal rate of return	18.9 percent	1	16.1 percent	2

* The discount rate used for both projects is 10 percent.

(a) The conflict among the methods of ranking Projects B and C results from different cash flow patterns and reinvestment assumptions associated with each evaluation technique. When using a 10 percent discount rate, Project B has a higher IRR than Project C, while Project C has a higher NPV and PI than Project B. The IRR method favors Project B with its high net operating cash flows early in its life because this technique assumes that cash flows are reinvested at Project B's higher rate. The NPV assumes reinvestment at the 10 percent cost of capital, which places a smaller penalty on Project C's net operating cash inflows that are received later in its life than Project B's cash flows.

Figure 13-1 shows the NPV profiles for Projects B and C and illustrates the way different reinvestment rate assumptions cause potential conflicts in rankings between the NPV and IRR. Below the point where the two NPV profiles cross, called the *crossover point*, a conflict in ranking the projects exists between the NPV and IRR methods. Above this point, no conflict in ranking exists. Thus, below a discount rate of approximately 13 percent (12.95 percent), Project C has a higher NPV than B, but Project B has a higher IRR than C. Above a discount rate of approximately 13 percent, there is no conflict in ranking and Project B is preferred.

(b) Project C should be accepted because it provides a higher absolute return for the same net investment when using the firm's cost of capital as a discount rate.

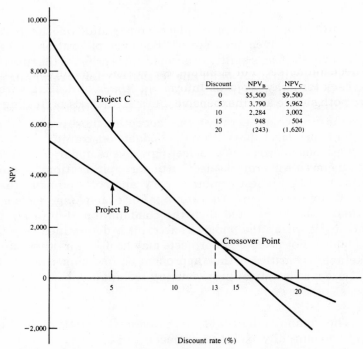

Discount	NPV_B	NPV_C
0	$5,500	$9,500
5	3,790	5,962
10	2,284	3,002
15	948	504
20	(243)	(1,620)

FIGURE 13-1   Net present value profiles of mutually exclusive Projects B and C.

EXAMPLE 13-9: Jennings Instrument Company has allocated $1,000,000 for capital expenditures for the year. The firm is considering six independent projects. Its minimum required rate of return (cost of capital) on these projects is 12 percent.

Project	Net Investment	IRR	Rank	PI	Rank	NPV at 12%	Rank
D	$500,000	25%	1	1.48	1	$240,000	2
E	300,000	18	2	1.30	4	90,000	3
F	200,000	17	3	1.38	3	75,000	4
G	700,000	15	4	1.43	2	300,000	1
H	100,000	12	5	1.00	5	0	5
I	600,000	8	6	0.88	6	(100,000)	6
Total	$2,400,000						

Jennings must decide which combination of projects provides the highest overall NPV. Projects D, E, F, G and H are all feasible projects because they meet the minimum decision criterion for each capital budgeting technique. However, Jennings Instrument Company cannot accept all five projects because their total cost of $2,400,000 exceeds the capital budget of $1,000,000. Ranking the projects by their IRRs leads to acceptance of Projects D, E, and F, involving an expenditure of $1,000,000 and a total NPV of $405,000. Ranking the projects by their PIs suggests that Project D should be accepted, followed by Projects G, F, E, and H. Projects D and G cannot both be accepted because this combination would involve a budget of $1,200,000, which would exceed the total budget by $200,000 ($1,200,000 − $1,000,000). Acceptance of Projects D, E, and F would lead to the highest total NPV of $405,000.

13-3. Capital Budgeting under Risk

Up to this point, the discussion of capital budgeting techniques has assumed that the project's cash flows were known with certainty. In reality, there are few capital budgeting projects in which certainty exists. Using the basic concepts of risk presented in Chapter 4, risk may be incorporated into evaluating capital budgeting projects in both informal and formal ways. These approaches cannot remove risk, but they can provide a means of dealing with it in a rational manner.

Informal approaches to risk adjustment are based on the decision maker's subjective evaluation of the project's risk. The decision rules using informal techniques are often internal to the decision maker. For example, the decision maker may require a shorter than normal payback for risky projects. Informal methods of dealing with risk are used because they are both simple and inexpensive. Formal methods of dealing with risk may also involve subjective judgment, but they attempt to provide more precise methods of accounting for risk. Formal methods involve two steps: risk estimation and risk measurement. Only formal methods of estimating and measuring risk are discussed below.

A. *Risk estimation* **is the process of determining the degree of risk associated with a capital budgeting project.**

   In order to adjust for risk, the project's risk must first be estimated and compared with the risk of other projects. Processes used to estimate risk are sensitivity analysis, simulation analysis, and beta estimation.

   1. **Sensitivity analysis** is the process of changing one or more variables to determine how sensitive a project's returns are to these changes. By asking "what if" questions, the decision maker is able to identify relevant variables affecting the final outcome. For example, sensitivity analysis enables the decision maker to assess the effect of changes in one or more of the inputs on a project's NPV. Once these variables are identified, the decision maker can investigate the variables more carefully in order to improve his/her ability to predict them.
   2. **Simulation analysis** is a statistically based approach for dealing with risk that provides information about the variability of a project's returns. Performing a simulation analysis requires estimating a probability distribution for each input variable of a project's cash flows, such as revenues and costs, and then combining these inputs into a mathematical model to compute the project's NPV. Random values are selected for each input variable based on the variable's probability distribution. The process is repeated many times until a probability distribution of the project's expected NPV is developed. From this distribution of returns, the decision maker is able to determine the expected value of the return and the probability of achieving a specific return. Thus, simulation analysis helps improve the decision maker's perception of the project's risk. Simulation analysis usually requires the use of computers and can be expensive.
   3. **Beta estimation** is an approach to risk measurement that involves the concepts of the capital asset pricing model (CAPM). In a capital budgeting context, beta is a

measure of the systematic risk of a project. If the beta of the project can be determined, then the project's riskiness can be treated in a manner similar to common stock. However, problems often exist in estimating the beta for nonsecurity types of investments, such as a capital budgeting project. For example, many capital budgeting projects are unique and have no historical returns from which to estimate beta. It is also impractical to determine the beta of an individual project because the assumptions of CAPM are completely violated in the world of real corporate assets. (The capital asset pricing model is discussed in Chapter 4.)

B. *Risk adjustment* is the process of adjusting a capital budgeting project for its degree of riskiness.

Once the risk present in a project is estimated, the decision maker may apply several techniques for recognizing the different levels of risk present in capital budgeting projects. Common approaches for making risk adjustment are the risk-adjusted discount rate and the certainty equivalent method to determine the project's net present value.

1. The **risk-adjusted net present value method** (NPV_r) adjusts for risk by varying the rate used to discount cash flows. Thus, the required rate of return reflects the project's riskiness. The risk-adjusted discount rate consists of three parts: risk-free rate, premium for the firm's normal risk, and an adjustment for risk above or below the firm's normal risk. Equation 13-10 is the formula for the risk-adjusted discount rate.

   RISK ADJUSTED DISCOUNT RATE $\qquad k' = r_f + r_p + r_a$ $\hfill$ (13-10)

   where $\quad r_f$ = risk-free rate

   $\qquad\quad r_p$ = premium for the firm's normal risk

   $\qquad\quad r_a$ = adjustment for a project's risk above or below the firm's normal risk

   - The appropriate risk-adjusted discount rate method follows specific guidelines in determining the net present value of a project. Projects whose returns are certain are discounted at the risk-free rate, $k' = r_f$, because they have no risk. Projects of average riskiness are discounted at the firm's cost of capital, $k' = r_f + r_p$, because this figure reflects the normal risk faced by the firm. Projects having greater than normal risk are discounted at a rate in excess of the cost of capital, $k' = r_f + r_p + r_a$. Projects having less than normal risk are discounted at a rate between the risk-free rate and the cost of capital, $k' = r_f + r_p - r_a$. Once the risk-adjusted discount rate is determined, it is used in the denominator of the net present value formula. Equation 13-11 is the formula for the risk-adjusted net present value.

   $$NPV_r = \text{PV of } NCF_t - NI$$

   RISK-ADJUSTED NET PRESENT VALUE $$= \sum_{t=1}^{n} \frac{NCF_t}{(1 + k')^t} - NI \qquad (13\text{-}11)$$

   where $\quad NCF_t$ = expected net cash flows in period t

   $\qquad\quad NI$ = net investment

   $\qquad\quad k'$ = risk-adjusted discount rate

   $\qquad\quad n$ = life of the project in years

   - The *decision rule* is to accept a project if the NPV_r is equal to or greater than zero; otherwise, the project is rejected. In ranking projects, the project with the highest NPV_r is preferred.
   - The *advantages* of using the NPV_r are that it is easy to understand and widely used.

- The *disadvantages* of using the NPV_r are that it is difficult to determine the appropriate risk-adjusted discount rate for each project or risk class, it uses a constant discount rate over the entire life of the project, and it combines the various risk components into a single rate.

EXAMPLE 13-10: Seldin Manufacturing, Inc. is evaluating two independent projects, Projects J and K. The firm determines that Project J is of average riskiness and Project K has greater than normal risk.

	Project J	Project K
Net investment...	$2,000	$2,000
Expected net cash flows in years 1–3........................	1,000	1,000
Risk adjusted discount rate	0.15	0.24

(a) The NPV_r of Project J is found by multiplying the NCF = $1,000 by the $PVIFA_{0.15,3}$ = 2.283 (Appendix D) and then subtracting the NI = $2,000.

Project J

Year	Cash Inflows (1)	$PVIFA_{0.15,3}$ (2)	Present Value [(1) × (2)]
1–3	$1,000	2.283	$2,283

Present value of cash inflows	$2,283
− Net investment	2,000
Risk adjusted net present value	$ 283

The NPV_r of Project K is found in a similar manner except that the $PVIFA_{0.24,3}$ = 1.981.

Project K

Year	Cash Inflows (1)	$PVIFA_{0.24,3}$ (2)	Present Value [(1) × (2)]
1–3	$1,000	1.981	$1,981

Present value of cash inflows	$1,981
− Net investment	2,000
Risk adjusted net present value	($ 19)

(b) Project J should be accepted because its NPV_r is positive while Project K should be rejected because it has a negative NPV_r.

2. The **certainty equivalent net present value method** (NPV_{ce}) adjusts for risk by modifying a project's risky cash flows. This approach incorporates the decision maker's utility preferences for risk versus return directly into the capital budgeting decision. In this approach, the key to the risk-adjustment process is converting risky cash flows into an equivalent risk-free factor by having the decision maker assign a certainty equivalent coefficient to each period's cash flows. A **certainty equivalent coefficient** for time period t, α_t (pronounced alpha sub t), is the ratio of the amount of cash that the decision maker would require with certainty in place of a risky cash flow. Equation 13-12 is the formula for the certainty equivalent coefficient during time period t.

CERTAINTY EQUIVALENT COEFFICIENT
$$\alpha_t = \frac{\text{Certain amount}}{\text{Risky amount}}$$
(13-12)

- The certainty equivalent coefficient ranges in value from 0 to 1.0 and varies inversely with risk. The more risky the decision maker views the cash flows, the lower the certainty equivalent coefficient. If $\alpha_t = 1.0$, the decision maker associates no risk with a project's cash flows. The certainty equivalent coefficients assigned to a project's cash flows generally decline as the length of a project increases, because risk increases with the length of a project.

EXAMPLE 13-11: Referring to information in Example 13-10, Project J's expected net cash flows are $1,000 a year for three years. In place of these risky cash flows, the decision maker is willing to accept with certainty $900 in year 1, $800 in year 2, and $700 in year 3. Substituting these certain amounts for time period t_1, t_2, and t_3, respectively, and the risky amount of $1,000 in Equation 13-12 gives the following certainty equivalent factors:

$$\alpha_1 = \frac{\$900}{\$1,000} = 0.9 \qquad \alpha_2 = \frac{\$800}{\$1,000} = 0.8 \qquad \alpha_3 = \frac{\$700}{\$1,000} = 0.7$$

- The CE method adjusts for risk in the numerator of the NPV formula. Since this method compensates for risk entirely by adjusting the cash flows downward, the cash flows are discounted at the risk-free rate to determine the NPV_{ce}. Equation 13-13 is the formula for certainty equivalent net present value.

CERTAINTY EQUIVALENT NET PRESENT VALUE

$$NPV_{ce} = PV \text{ of } NCF_t - \alpha_0 NI$$

$$= \sum_{t=1}^{n} \frac{\alpha_t NCF_t}{(1 + r^f)^t} - \alpha_0 NI \qquad \text{(13-13)}$$

where r_f = risk-free rate
α_t = certainty equivalent in period t = 1 through n
α_0 = certainty equivalent coefficient in period 0

- The decision rule is to accept a project if the NPV_{ce} is equal to or greater than zero; otherwise, the project should be rejected.
- The advantages of the NPV_{ce} are that it adjusts for the risk of each period's cash flows, it incorporates the decision maker's utility preferences directly into the analysis, and it is conceptually superior to the risk-adjusted net present value approach because it recognizes the various components of risk.
- The disadvantages of using the NPV_{ce} are that it is not widely used and involves subjectivity in determining the certainty equivalent coefficients.

EXAMPLE 13-12: Referring to information in Example 13-10, Projects J and K have expected net cash flows of $1,000 for three years and an initial investment of $2,000. The risk-free rate is 9 percent. The certainty equivalent coefficients for each project are shown below.

Year	α_t	Project J	Project K
1	α_1	0.9	0.8
2	α_2	0.8	0.6
3	α_3	0.7	0.4

Substituting the appropriate values in Equation 13-13 and using Appendix C for the PVIF of 9 percent, the certainty equivalent net present values for Project J and Project K are:

Project J

Year	α_t (1)	Cash Inflows (2)	$PVIF_{0.09,t}$ (3)	Present Value [(1) × (2) × (3)]
1	0.9	$1,000	0.917	$ 825
2	0.8	1,000	0.842	674
3	0.7	1,000	0.772	540
PV of net cash inflows				$2,039
− Net investment				2,000
Certainty equivalent net present value				$ 39

Project K

Year	α_t (1)	Cash Inflows (2)	$PVIF_{0.09,t}$ (3)	Present Value [(1) × (2) × (3)]
1	0.8	$1,000	0.917	$ 734
2	0.6	1,000	0.842	505
3	0.4	1,000	0.772	309
PV of net cash inflows				$1,548
− Net investment				2,000
Certainty equivalent net present value				($ 452)

Project J should be accepted because its NPV_{ce} is positive, while Project K should be rejected because it has a negative NPV_{ce}.

RAISE YOUR GRADES

Can you explain...?

☑ the differences between capital budgeting under certainty and risk
☑ how sophisticated and unsophisticated capital budgeting techniques differ
☑ five capital budgeting techniques under certainty
☑ the advantages and disadvantages of the accounting rate of return and the payback method
☑ the advantages and disadvantages of the net present value, profitability index, and internal rate of return
☑ what the decision rules are for the net present value, profitability index, and internal rate of return
☑ why the net present value is theoretically the most correct method for selecting projects
☑ how to interpolate
☑ what is meant by an accept-reject decision
☑ the difference between independent and mutually exclusive projects
☑ the reasons conflicts may occur in the ranking of mutually exclusive projects when using the discounted cash flow techniques

☑ the reinvestment rate assumptions of the net present value and internal rate of return techniques

☑ what capital rationing is

☑ how capital rationing affects project selection

☑ the meaning of sensitivity analysis and simulation analysis

☑ why estimating beta for capital budgeting projects is difficult

☑ two capital budgeting techniques that adjust for risk under conditions of uncertainty

☑ how the risk-adjusted discount rate method differs from the certainty equivalent approach

☑ how to compute a certainty equivalent coefficient

SUMMARY

1. Capital investments are evaluated under either certainty or risk. Under certainty the decision maker knows in advance the exact values of all variables affecting the decision, but under risk the decision maker can only estimate these values.

2. Unsophisticated techniques of capital budgeting ignore important factors in the asset selection process such as the time value of money, whereas sophisticated techniques do not.

3. Five major capital budgeting evaluation techniques used under conditions of certainty are accounting rate of return, payback period, net present value, profitability index, and internal rate of return.

4. The accounting rate of return is the ratio of the average annual net income to the average net investment. Major weaknesses of this technique are that it uses net income instead of cash flows and ignores the time value of money.

5. The payback period is the length of time required for a project to pay for itself. This method uses cash flows but ignores the time value of money.

6. The net present value is calculated by subtracting the net investment from the present value of a project's net cash flows, discounted at the firm's cost of capital. The net present value is considered theoretically superior to other capital budgeting methods in maximizing shareholder wealth.

7. The profitability index is the present value of the net cash flows divided by the net investment associated with a project. This index is a relative measure of the return per dollar of investment.

8. The internal rate of return is the discount rate that gives a net present value of zero. This method is the most frequently used capital budgeting technique in practice.

9. An independent project is acceptable if it meets any of the following decision criteria: its NPV is equal to or greater than zero; its PI is equal to or greater than 1.0; and its IRR is equal to or greater than the firm's cost of capital. Otherwise, the project is rejected.

10. Interpolation is a mathematical technique for finding fractional values when only whole percentages are used in time value of money tables.

11. An accept-reject decision occurs when an individual project is accepted or rejected without regard to any other investment alternative.

12. Capital budgeting techniques under certainty give the same accept-reject decisions for independent projects, but conflicts in project ranking may arise with mutually exclusive projects.

13. Conflicts in rankings are caused by projects having different expected lives, net investments, cash flow patterns, and/or evaluation methods with different reinvestment rate assumptions.

14. The reinvestment rate assumption of the firm's cost of capital used in the net present value method is more realistic than the reinvestment rate assumption of the internal rate of return used in the internal rate of return method.

15. Capital rationing limits the size of the capital budget for a specific time period. Several methods are available for selecting projects under capital rationing, such as ranking projects by their IRRs or PIs and selecting the combination of projects providing the highest overall NPV.

16. Both informal and formal methods are available for taking risk into account in a capital budgeting project. Informal methods are based largely on the decision maker's subjective judgment, whereas formal methods tend to make the process of estimating risk explicit.

17. The riskiness of a capital budgeting project may be estimated using sensitivity analysis, simulation analysis, and beta estimation.

18. Sensitivity analysis enables the decision maker to determine the impact on the project's return when changing a particular variable.

19. Simulation analysis is a statistical technique that provides a probability distribution of a project's returns and generally requires the use of a computer.

20. Beta estimation involves the use of the capital asset pricing model to estimate a project's risk. In practice, CAPM is difficult to apply to non security investments.

21. Two risk adjustment methods are the risk-adjusted discount rate method and the certainty equivalent method.

22. The risk-adjusted discount rate approach alters the discount rate to reflect a project's riskiness. Projects with above-average risk are discounted at a rate higher than the firm's cost of capital.

23. The certainty equivalent method adjusts for risk by modifying a project's risky cash flows and then discounting them by the risk-free rate.

RAPID REVIEW

True or False?

1. The accounting rate of return is considered a sophisticated capital budgeting technique. [Section 13-1A]

2. The accounting rate of return compares a project's average cash flows to the net investment. [Section 13-1A]

3. The payback method considers the time value of money. [Section 13-1A]

4. The payback method ignores cash flows beyond the payback period. [Section 13-1A]

5. Sophisticated capital budgeting techniques consider the time value of money. [Section 13-1B]

6. The net present value of a project can never be negative. [Section 13-1B]

7. The profitability index is a relative measure of a project's profitability. [Section 13-1B]

8. Using a project's internal rate of return as a discount rate produces a net present value equal to zero. [Section 13-1B]

9. The internal rate of return method is the most widely used capital budgeting technique. [Section 13-1B]

10. Projects with nonconventional cash flow patterns may have more than a single internal rate of return. [Section 13-1B]

11. A project is independent if its acceptance precludes the acceptance of other projects. [Section 13-2A]

12. Discounted cash flow techniques give the same accept-reject decision for independent projects with conventional cash flows. [Section 13-2A]

13. Ranking mutually exclusive projects by sophisticated capital budgeting techniques may result in conflicting accept-reject decisions. [Section 13-2B]

14. The internal rate of return technique implicitly assumes that a project's cash inflows can be reinvested at the firm's marginal cost of capital. [Section 13-2B]

15. Capital rationing occurs when a firm is unable or unwilling to finance all acceptable investment projects. [Section 13-2C]

16. Capital rationing may result in a sub-optimal investment policy. [Section 13-2C]

17. Under capital rationing, ranking projects by their IRRs and PIs always leads to identical projects being selected. [Section 13-2C]

18. Sensitivity analysis enables the decision maker to identify how relevant variables affect a project by asking "what if" questions. [Section 13-3A]

19. Performing a simulation analysis often requires the use of a computer. [Section 13-3A]

20. Estimating the beta of most individual capital budgeting projects is relatively easy. [Section 13-3A]

21. Using the risk-adjusted discount rate method, the higher a project's risk the lower the discount rate used. [Section 13-3B]

22. The risk-adjusted discount rate method adjusts for risk in the numerator of the net present value formula. [Section 13-3B]

23. A certainty equivalent coefficient represents the ratio between an amount of cash received with certainty to some risky amount. [Section 13-3B]

24. The higher the certainty equivalent coefficient, the more risky the expected cash flow. [Section 13-3B]

25. The appropriate discount rate to use in the certainty equivalent method is the firm's marginal cost of capital. [Section 13-3B]

Multiple Choice

26. The accounting rate of return method has the following weakness(es)

    (a) ignores the time value of money
    (b) uses accounting income rather than cash flows
    (c) assumes the net investment is written off at a constant rate
    (d) All of the above

    [Section 13-1A]

27. The payback method

    (a) considers the time value of money
    (b) measures a project's profitability
    (c) uses cash flows
    (d) uses the cost of capital as the discount rate

    [Section 13-1A]

28. A independent project is acceptable if its net present value is

    (a) less than zero
    (b) zero
    (c) more than zero
    (d) Both b and c

    [Section 13-1B]

29. An investment project that has a profitability index greater than one

    (a) should be accepted
    (b) should be rejected
    (c) enhances the wealth of the firm's owners
    (d) Both a and c

    [Section 13-1B]

30. The IRR and NPV ranking may differ on mutually exclusive projects because

    (a) the projects have different expected lives
    (b) the reinvestment rate assumptions of IRR and NPV differ

(c) the projects have different cash flow patterns

(d) Any or all of these

[Section 13-2B]

31. The best capital budgeting technique to use when evaluating mutually exclusive projects is the

(a) payback method

(b) net present value method

(c) profitability index method

(d) internal rate of return method

[Section 13-2B]

32. When plotting the NPV profiles of two mutually exclusive projects, a conflict occurs in ranking using the NPV and IRR methods

(a) below the crossover point

(b) at the crossover point

(c) above the crossover point

(d) Both b and c

[Section 13-2B]

33. Under capital rationing the appropriate decision rule is to

(a) select the set of projects having the highest combined NPV that does not exceed the budget constraint

(b) select the set of projects having the highest combined IRR that does not exceed the budget constraint

(c) select all projects having a profitability index greater than one

(d) select all projects having NPVs greater than zero

[Section 13-2C]

34. The risk-adjusted discount method

(a) adjusts the project's expected net cash flows to certainty

(b) adjusts the discount rate

(c) uses the firm's cost of capital as the discount rate for all projects

(d) None of these

[Section 13-3B]

35. The certainty equivalent coefficient indicating the lowest level of risk is

(a) 1.0

(b) 0.5

(c) 0

(d) −1.0

[Section 13-3B]

Answers

True or False

1. False	11. False	21. False
2. False	12. True	22. False
3. False	13. True	23. True
4. True	14. False	24. False
5. True	15. True	25. False
6. False	16. True	
7. True	17. False	
8. True	18. True	
9. True	19. True	
10. True	20. False	

Multiple Choice

26. d
27. c
28. d
29. d
30. d
31. b
32. a
33. a
34. b
35. a

SOLVED PROBLEMS

PROBLEM 13-1: The Alty Corporation is considering a capital expenditure involving a net investment of $30,000. The project has an estimated life of five years and is expected to generate after-tax profits of $4,000 per year for the first three years and $6,000 per year for the remaining two years. The project has no expected salvage value. The firm requires an accounting rate of return of at least 18 percent.

(a) What is the accounting rate of return for this project? Assume straight-line depreciation.
(b) Should the project be accepted?

Answer:

(a) Using Equation 13-1 requires determining the average annual net income and the average net investment as follows:

Year	Net Income
1	$ 4,000
2	4,000
3	4,000
4	6,000
5	6,000
Total	$24,000

$$\text{Average annual net income} = \frac{24,000}{5} = \$4,800$$

$$\text{Average net investment} = \frac{\$30,000}{2} = \$15,000$$

$$\text{Accounting rate of return} = \frac{\$4,800}{\$15,000} = 0.32 \text{ or } 32 \text{ percent}$$

(b) The project should be accepted because the ARR of 32 percent exceeds the target rate of 18 percent. **[Section 13-1A]**

Use the following information to solve Problems 13-2 and 13-3.

Brenner Company plans to make a $200,000 net investment in new equipment that is expected to generate the following cash inflows:

Year	Cash Inflows
1	$ 50,000
2	50,000
3	50,000
4	75,000
5	100,000

PROBLEM 13-2: What is the payback period of the new equipment? If the maximum acceptable payback period is three years, should the new equipment be accepted?

Answer: The payback period for unequal cash flows is computed as follows:

Year	Net Cash Inflows	Cumulative Net Cash Inflows
1	$ 50,000	$ 50,000
2	50,000	100,000
3	50,000	150,000
4	75,000	225,000
5	100,000	325,000

Since the net investment is $200,000, the new equipment pays for itself between three and four years. A total of $150,000 is recovered during the first three years plus an additional $75,000 during the fourth year. Assuming that the net cash inflows occur at a constant rate during the year, it will take approximately 0.67 years ($50,000/$75,000) to earn the additional $50,000. Hence, the payback is about 3.67 years. The new equipment should be rejected because the payback period exceeds the maximum acceptable payback of three years. **[Section 13-1A]**

PROBLEM 13-3: What is the net present value of the new equipment if the firm's cost of capital is 20 percent? Should the equipment be purchased?

Answer: The present value of the cash inflows is found by multiplying each year's cash inflows by the 12 percent present value interest factor (Appendix C) and then summing these amounts. The $200,000 net investment is then subtracted from the total of the present values of the cash inflows to obtain the NPV.

Year	Cash Inflows (1)	$PVIF_{0.12,t}$ (2)	Present Value [(1) × (2)]
1	$ 50,000	0.893	$ 44,650
2	50,000	0.797	39,850
3	50,000	0.712	35,600
4	75,000	0.636	47,700
5	100,000	0.567	56,700
Present value of cash inflows			$224,500
− Net investment			200,000
Net present value			$ 24,500

The new equipment should be accepted because the net present value is positive. Hence, accepting the project will increase stockholder wealth. **[Section 13-1B]**

PROBLEM 13-4: Biles Manufacturing Company is considering replacing an old machine with a new one. The incremental net investment is $40,000 and incremental net annual cash inflows are $13,000 for the next five years. The average annual net income is $5,000 a year for five years. The machine has no salvage value. Calculate the following:

(*a*) Accounting rate of return
(*b*) Payback period
(*c*) Net present value assuming a 15 percent cost of capital
(*d*) Profitability index
(*e*) Internal rate of return

If Biles Manufacturing has a target accounting rate of return of 25 percent, a maximum payback of four years, and a 15 percent cost of capital, should the firm undertake the project? Explain your reasoning.

Answer:

(a) Using Equation 13-1, the accounting rate of return is found as follows:

$$\text{Average annual net income} = \$5,000$$

$$\text{Average net investment} = \frac{\$40,000}{2} = \$20,000$$

$$\text{Accounting rate of return} = \frac{\$5,000}{\$20,000} = 0.250 \text{ or } 25.0 \text{ percent}$$

(b) Using Equation 13-2, the payback period with equal cash flows is:

$$\text{Payback period} = \frac{\text{Net investment}}{\text{Annual net cash inflows}} = \frac{\$40,000}{\$13,000} = 3.08 \text{ years}$$

(c) Using Equation 13-4, the net present value is:

Years	Cash Inflows (1)	$\text{PVIFA}_{0.15,5}$ (2)	Present Value [(1) × (2)]
1–5	$13,000	3.352	$43,576
− Net investment			40,000
Net present value			$ 3,576

(d) By substituting the present value of the net cash inflows = \$43,576 and the net investment = \$40,000 in Equation 13-5, the profitability index is:

$$\text{Profitability index} = \frac{\$43,576}{\$40,000} = 1.09$$

(e) Equation 13-8 is used to find the $\text{PVIFA}_{i,5}$, as follows:

$$\text{PVIFA}_{i,5} = \frac{\$40,000}{\$13,000} = 3.08$$

A $\text{PVIFA}_{i,5} = 3.08$ (Appendix D) represents a discount rate between 18 to 19 percent.

18 percent discount factor

Years	Cash Inflows (1)	$\text{PVIFA}_{0.18,5}$ (2)	Present Value [(1) × (2)]
1–5	$13,000	3.127	$40,651
− Net investment			40,000
Net present value			$ 651

19 percent discount factor

Years	Cash Inflows (1)	$\text{PVIFA}_{0.19,5}$ (2)	Present Value [(1) × (2)]
1–5	$13,000	3.058	$39,754
− Net investment			40,000
Net present value			($ 246)

Using Equation 13-9, the interpolated interest rate is:

$$i = 0.18 + \left(\frac{\$651}{\$651 - (-\$246)} \right)(0.19 - 0.18)$$

$$= 0.18 + (0.0073)(0.01)$$
$$= 0.1873 \text{ or } 18.73 \text{ percent}$$

The old machine should be replaced because the incremental cash flows resulting from acceptance of the new machine meet all the decision criteria.

Technique	Actual	Decision Criterion	Decision
ARR	25.0 percent	Target 25 percent	Accept
PB	3.08 years	Maximum 4 years	Accept
NPV	$3,576	At least zero	Accept
PI	1.09	At least one	Accept
IRR	18.73 percent	15 percent	Accept

[Section 13-1A & B]

Use the following information to solve Problems 13-5 through 13-8.

Duggan Paint Company is considering two mutually exclusive investment projects involving paint-mixing machines. Each machine has the following expected net cash flows:

	Net Cash Flows	
Year	Machine X	Machine Y
0	($40,000)	($40,000)
1	$30,000	$14,000
2	12,000	14,000
3	12,000	14,000
4	4,000	14,000

PROBLEM 13-5: Calculate each project's payback period. Which paint-mixing machine is preferred, using the payback method?

Answer: Machine X has unequal cash inflows and pays for itself in approximately 1.8 years. Using Equation 13-3, Machine X provides $30,000 in cash flows by the end of the first year and takes 0.8 years ($10,000/$12,000) to earn the remaining $10,000. Machine Y has equal cash inflows and, using Equation 13-2, its payback is approximately 2.9 years ($40,000/14,000). The shorter payback period of Machine X makes it preferable to Machine Y.   **[Section 13-1A]**

PROBLEM 13-6: Calculate each project's net present value assuming a 12 percent cost of capital. Which machine is preferred, using the NPV method?

Answer: Because Machine X has unequal cash inflows, Appendix C is used to get the $PVIF_{0.12,t}$ for each year.

Machine X

Year	Cash Inflows (1)	$PVIF_{0.12,t}$ (2)	Present Value [(1) × (2)]
1	$30,000	0.893	$26,790
2	12,000	0.797	9,564
3	12,000	0.712	8,544
4	4,000	0.636	2,544
Present value of cash inflows			$47,442
— Net investment			40,000
Net present value			$ 7,442

Because the net cash inflows are in annuity form, Appendix D is used to get the $PVIFA_{0.12,4}$ for Machine Y.

Machine Y

Year	Cash Inflows (1)	$\text{PVIFA}_{0.12,4}$ (2)	Present Value [(1) × (2)]
1–4	$14,000	3.037	$42,518
− Net investment			40,000
Net present value			$ 2,518

Machine X has a higher positive NPV and is again preferred over Machine Y.

[Section 13-1B]

PROBLEM 13-7: Calculate each project's internal rate of return to the nearest percentage. Which project is preferred, using the IRR method?

Answer: A trial-and-error approach is required to find Machine X's IRR because it has unequal net cash inflows. Using the firm's 12 percent cost of capital as a discount rate produces a positive NPV. Thus, a higher rate is needed to equate the NPV to zero. This rate is slightly less than 24 percent.

Machine X

Year	Cash Inflows (1)	$\text{PVIF}_{0.24,t}$ (2)	Present Value [(1) × (2)]
1	$30,000	0.806	$24,180
2	12,000	0.650	7,800
3	12,000	0.524	6,288
4	4,000	0.423	1,692
Present value of cash inflows			$39,960
− Net investment			40,000
Net present value			($ 40)

Because Machine Y's net cash inflows are in annuity form, the trial-and-error approach is not required. Instead, Equation 13-8 is used to find the ratio of the net investment to the annual net cash inflows, which defines the present value interest factor of an annuity $(\text{PVIFA}_{i,n})$ that equates the net investment with the annual net cash inflows.

$$\text{PVIFA}_{i,4} = \frac{\$40,000}{\$14,000} = 2.857$$

Appendix D is used to find the closest interest factor to $\text{PVIFA}_{i,4} = 2.857$. In this case, 2.857 falls between 2.914 ($i = 14$ percent) and 2.855 ($i = 15$ percent). Therefore, the $\overline{\text{IRR}}$ of Machine Y is somewhere between 14 percent and 15 percent, but closer to 15 percent. Machine X has a higher IRR than Machine Y and thus should be selected.

[Section 13-1B]

PROBLEM 13-8: Is there a conflict in ranking the project using the three methods? If so, why?

Answer: The rankings of Machine X and Machine Y for each of the three evaluation techniques are shown below:

	Machine X	Rank	Machine Y	Rank
Payback period	1.8 years	1	2.9 years	2
Net present value	$7,442	1	$2,518	2
Internal rate of return	24 percent	1	15 percent	2

There is no conflict in rankings among the three methods. Machine X is preferred using all three methods.

[Sections 13-1A & B]

PROBLEM 13-9: Krell, Inc. is considering two mutually exclusive projects with the following cash flows:

	Cash Flows	
Year	Project A	Project B
0	($50,000)	($ 50,000)
1	15,989	0
2	15,989	0
3	15,989	0
4	15,989	0
5	15,989	$100,000

The firm's minimum required rate of return on these projects is 10 percent.

(*a*) What is net present value of each project?
(*b*) What is the internal rate of return to the nearest percentage of each project?
(*c*) Which project should Krell, Inc. select?

Answer:

(*a*) The cash inflows of Project A are in annuity form. The $PVIFA_{0.10,5} = 3.791$ is found in Appendix D.

Project A

Years	Cash Inflows (1)	$PVIFA_{0.10,5}$ (2)	Present Value [(1) × (2)]
1–5	$15,989	3.791	$60,614
− Net investment			50,000
Net present value			$10,614

Project B's only cash inflow occurs in Year five. The $PVIF_{0.10,5} = 0.621$ is found in Appendix C.

Project B

Year	Cash Inflows (1)	$PVIF_{0.10,5}$ (2)	Present Value [(1) × (2)]
5	$100,000	0.621	$62,100
− Net investment			50,000
Net present value			$12,100

(*b*) The IRR for Project A is found by using Equation 13-8.

$$PVIFA_{1,5} = \frac{\$50,000}{\$15,989} = 3.127$$

Appendix D is then used to find the interest rate closest to a $PVIFA_{i,5} = 3.127$. In this situation, the rate is 18 percent.

The IRR for Project B is found by calculating the ratio of the net investment to the net cash inflow for Year 5.

$$PVIF_{i,5} = \frac{\$50,000}{\$100,000} = 0.500$$

Appendix C is then used to find the interest rate closest to a $PVIF_{i,5} = 0.500$. In this case, 0.500 falls between 0.519 ($i = 14$ percent) and 0.497 ($i = 15$ percent). Thus, the IRR for Project B is closer to 15 percent.

(c) There is a conflict in ranking between the NPV and IRR methods, as shown below:

	Project A	Rank	Project B	Rank
Net present value	$10,614	2	$12,100	1
Internal rate of return	18 percent	1	15 percent	2

This conflict in ranking is caused by the different cash flow patterns of the two projects and the implied reinvestment rate assumptions of the NPV and IRR methods. Project A's cash inflows remain stable, whereas Project B's cash inflows occur only in Year 5. Project B should be accepted because it has the higher absolute return (NPV) than Project A and thus maximizes shareholder wealth. **[Sections 13-1B]**

PROBLEM 13-10: Holmberg Machine Company has eight investment projects under consideration, all with positive NPVs and PIs. Management has placed a constraint of $5,000,000 on its total capital budget for the year.

Project	Net Investment	NPV	PI
A	$2,000,000	$400,000	1.20
B	2,500,000	350,000	1.14
C	4,000,000	500,000	1.13
D	1,500,000	450,000	1.30
E	3,000,000	150,000	1.05
F	4,500,000	700,000	1.16
G	500,000	200,000	1.40
H	1,000,000	450,000	1.45
Total	$19,000,000		

Rank the projects by their PIs. Which set of projects should be selected to provide the highest aggregate NPV if the firm's funds are rationed to $5,000,000?

Answer: The projects are ranked in descending order according to their PIs, as follows:

Project	Net Investment	NPV	PI	Rank	Decision
H	$1,000,000	$450,000	1.45	1	Accept
G	500,000	200,000	1.40	2	Accept
D	1,500,000	450,000	1.30	3	Accept
A	2,000,000	400,000	1.20	4	Accept
Total	$5,000,000	$1,500,000			Cutoff point
F	4,500,000	700,000	1.16	5	Reject
B	2,500,000	350,000	1.14	6	Reject
C	4,000,000	500,000	1.13	7	Reject
E	3,000,000	150,000	1.05	8	Reject

If the funds are rationed to $5,000,000, then the combination of Projects H, G, D, and A should be selected. These four projects cost $5,000,000 and will provide the highest aggregate NPV of $1,500,000. **[Section 13-2C]**

PROBLEM 13-11: Karadbil Toy Company plans to introduce a new board game. In order to manufacture the new game, the firm must purchase specialized equipment requiring a net investment of $100,000. The game is expected to produce annual net operating cash inflows of $30,000 for the next four years. The machine is also expected to have an after-tax salvage value of $10,000. Because this investment project has above-normal risk, the financial manager plans to discount the cash flows at 20 percent, instead of the firm's 14 percent cost of capital. The risk-free rate is 8 percent.

(a) What is the above-normal risk adjustment assigned to this project by management?
(b) What is the risk-adjusted net present value of the project?
(c) Should the project be undertaken?
(d) If the equipment's after-tax salvage value is more risky than the net operating cash inflows, how could this be taken into account in the discounting process? How would the risky nature of the after-tax salvage value affect the project's risk-adjusted net present value?

Answer:

(a) Equation 13-10 shows that the risk-adjusted discount rate consists of three components: the risk-free rate, r_f, the premium for the firm's normal risk, r_p, and an adjustment for above or below the firm's normal risk, r_a. The firm's cost of capital represents investment projects of average riskiness and thus consists of the first two components, $r_f + r_p$. Hence, the adjustment that the firm is assigning for above-normal risk is 6 percentage points as shown below:

$$k' = r_f + r_p + r_a, \quad \text{therefore,} \quad r_a = k' - (r_f + r_p)$$

$$r_a = 0.20 - (0.08 + 0.06) = 0.06 \quad \text{or} \quad 6.0 \text{ percentage points}$$

(b) The net operating cash inflows are an annuity and are discounted by a risk-adjusted factor of $PVIFA_{0.20,4} = 2.589$ (Appendix D). The after-tax salvage value occurs in Year 4 and is discounted by a $PVIF_{0.20,4} = 0.482$ (Appendix C). Using Equation 13-11, the NPV of the new equipment is computed as follows:

Year	Cash Inflows (1)	$PVIF_{0.20,t}$ (2)	Present Value [(1) × (2)]
1–4	$30,000	2.589	$ 77,670
4	10,000	0.482	4,820
PV of net cash inflows			$ 82,490
− Net investment			100,000
Net present value			($ 11,510)

(c) The project should not be undertaken because it has a negative risk-adjusted net present value. Thus, the project does not provide a sufficient return to compensate the firm for its riskiness.

(d) If the equipment's after-tax salvage value were more risky than the net operating cash inflows, a higher discount rate than 20 percent could be used. Using a higher rate to discount the after-tax salvage value would reduce the risk-adjusted net present value further and result in greater expected losses. **[Section 13-3B]**

PROBLEM 13-12: Mass Manufacturing Company has decided to use the certainty equivalent technique to evaluate two mutually exclusive projects. The expected net cash flows, NCF_t, and certainty equivalent coefficients, α_t, for the two projects are given below.

Year	Project X-10 NCF$_t$	α_t	Project X-20 NCF$_t$	α_t
0	($50,000)	1.00	($50,000)	1.00
1	20,000	0.90	30,000	0.80
2	20,000	0.90	30,000	0.70
3	20,000	0.80	25,000	0.60
4	20,000	0.80	25,000	0.60
5	20,000	0.80	15,000	0.40
6	20,000	0.70	10,000	0.20

The firm's cost of capital is 15 percent and the risk-free rate is 7 percent. Which project should be selected, using the certainty equivalent approach?

Answer: Using Equation 13-13 and Appendix C, the certainty equivalent net present values, NPV_{ce}, for Project X-10 and Project X-20 are as follows:

Project X-10

Year	α_t (1)	Cash Inflows (2)	$PVIF_{0.07,t}$ (3)	Present Value [(1) × (2) × (3)]
1	0.9	$20,000	0.935	$16,830
2	0.9	20,000	0.873	15,714
3	0.8	20,000	0.816	13,056
4	0.8	20,000	0.763	12,208
5	0.8	20,000	0.713	11,408
6	0.7	20,000	0.666	9,324
PV of net cash inflows				$78,540
— Net investment				50,000
NPV_{ce}				$28,540

Project X-20

Year	α_t (1)	Cash Inflows (2)	$PVIF_{0.07,t}$ (3)	Present Value [(1) × (2) × (3)]
1	0.8	$30,000	0.935	$22,440
2	0.7	30,000	0.873	18,333
3	0.6	25,000	0.816	12,240
4	0.6	25,000	0.763	11,445
5	0.4	15,000	0.713	4,278
6	0.2	10,000	0.666	1,332
PV of net cash inflows				$70,068
— Net investment				50,000
NPV_{ce}				$20,068

Because the NPV_{ce} of Project X-10 is positive and exceeds that of Project X-20, Project X-10 should be accepted.   **[Section 13-3B]**

EXAMINATION II (Chapters 9–13)

True-False

1. When current assets exceed current liabilities, some current assets must be financed with long-term debt or equity.
2. The goal of working capital management is to minimize the level of net working capital.
3. The liquidity preference theory states that both borrowers and lenders have risk preferences which determine that short-term debt will yield more than long-term debt.
4. An aggressive working capital strategy involves minimizing both the amount of liquid assets and the short-term debt used to finance them.
5. One way of accelerating collections is to use a lockbox system.
6. The appropriate level of cash balances is the one which minimizes transaction costs.
7. Commercial paper is a short-term, unsecured source of funds generally sold by small firms.
8. Banker's acceptances are used primarily to finance specific international transactions.
9. Tightening credit standards is generally expected to increase sales.
10. Holding other factors constant the level of accounts receivable increases as the collection period lengthens.
11. A credit term of 2/10, net 45 gives a 2 percent discount, if the bill is paid within 45 days.
12. The longer a firm's production cycle, the smaller its inventory requirement.
13. The process of evaluating and selecting long-term investments is referred to as capital budgeting.
14. The first step in the capital budgeting process is to estimate the cash flows.
15. Depreciation is a tax shield because it shields the firm from paying taxes by lowering taxable income.
16. Net terminal cash flow is the net cash flow resulting from ending a project.
17. The payback method considers the time value of money in the analysis of investment projects.
18. The decision rule for the net present value method is to accept a project if its NPV is equal to or greater than one.
19. The ranking of mutually exclusive projects using discounted cash flow techniques may conflict because of a size disparity between the net investments of the projects.
20. The risk-adjusted net present value method is based on the concept that investors require a higher rate of return for riskier projects.

Multiple Choice

1. Current assets less current liabilities is defined as

    (a) working capital.
    (b) current ratio.
    (c) net working capital.
    (d) liquidity.

2. Which of the following affects a firm's working capital position?

   (a) Type of firm
   (b) Volume of sales
   (c) Length of the operating cycle
   (d) All of the above

3. The liquidity preference theory can be used to explain

   (a) upward-sloping yield curves.
   (b) downward-sloping yield curves.
   (c) Both a and b
   (d) Neither a nor b

4. According to the hedging approach, plant and equipment should be financed with

   (a) short-term bank loans.
   (b) commercial paper.
   (c) long-term funds.
   (d) None of the above

5. Which of the following provides a cushion against uncertain seasonal cash flows?

   (a) Transactions balances
   (b) Precautionary balances
   (c) Compensating balances
   (d) Speculative balances

6. Which of the following is a method used to slow disbursements?

   (a) Wire transfer
   (b) Depository transfer check
   (c) Lockbox system
   (d) Zero balance system

7. The determination of an optimal cash balance involves minimizing the total cost of

   (a) transaction balances and precautionary balances.
   (b) transaction costs and holding costs.
   (c) speculative balances and precautionary balances.
   (d) transaction balances.

8. Which of the following is generally considered to be the safest short-term investment?

   (a) Certificates of deposit with a savings and loan
   (b) Federal agency issues
   (c) Treasury bills
   (d) Commercial paper

9. Tightening the credit policy of a firm may involve

   (a) less rigorous credit standards.
   (b) a longer credit period.
   (c) more aggressive collection methods.
   (d) an increased level of sales.

10. The five Cs of credit are used to guide a firm's selection of

    (a) credit terms.
    (b) collection policy.
    (c) cash discount period.
    (d) credit customers.

11. The optimal level of inventory minimizes

    (a) stock shortages.
    (b) order numbers.

(c) carrying costs.

(d) total inventory costs.

12. The economic order quantity (EOQ) increases when which of the following increases?

   (a) Sales

   (b) Ordering costs

   (c) Carrying costs

   (d) Both a and b

13. Which type of projects are commonly revenue-producing projects?

   (a) Replacement projects

   (b) Expansion projects

   (c) Modernization projects

   (d) Both a and b

14. The calculation of net investment may include all but one of the following:

   (a) cost of a new asset

   (b) sale of an old asset that is being replaced

   (c) additional net working capital

   (d) depreciation on the new asset

15. All of the following are included in net operating cash flows *except*:

   (a) incremental revenues

   (b) incremental operating expenses

   (c) interest expenses

   (d) depreciation expense

16. Net operating cash flows and net income differ by the amount of

   (a) accumulated depreciation.

   (b) salvage value.

   (c) taxes paid.

   (d) depreciation expense.

17. A major shortcoming of the payback period is that it

   (a) does not consider cash flows beyond the payback period.

   (b) provides no objective criterion for decision making that will maximize shareholder wealth.

   (c) is difficult to understand and interpret.

   (d) Both a and b

18. The discount rate used in the net present value (NPV) method is the firm's

   (a) marginal tax rate.

   (b) weighted average cost of capital.

   (c) profit margin on sales.

   (d) before-tax cost of debt.

19. Accepting a project with a negative net present value (NPV) should

   (a) decrease the value of the firm.

   (b) increase the value of the firm.

   (c) have no impact on the value of the firm.

   (d) decrease the assets of the firm.

20. The risk-adjusted discount method incorporates risk into the capital budgeting process by

   (a) discounting all projects by the risk-free rate.

   (b) discounting all projects by the firm's cost of capital, regardless of risk.

   (c) assigning risky projects higher discount rates than normal projects.

   (d) assigning risky projects lower discount rates than normal projects.

Fill In The Blanks

1. The _____ theory says that the shape of yield curve depends on the supply and demand for funds by different sectors of the market.

2. _____ financing strategies use the lowest proportion of long-term financing.

3. The _____ approach matches the maturity of the source of funds with the time they are needed.

4. A high level of current assets will _____ the risk of technical insolvency.

5. _____ is a firm's most liquid asset.

6. The time lag between the moment a buyer disburses funds and the moment the seller receives them is called _____.

7. A method of speeding collections which has customers remitting to decentralized collection centers and banks is called _____.

8. _____ is the risk that a debt's interest or principal will not be repaid.

9. A report of how long accounts receivable have been outstanding is called a(n) _____.

10. The best known credit reporting agency for business firms is _____.

11. The lowest point on the inventory total cost curve is called the _____.

12. Additional inventories carried to meet unexpected demand are called _____.

13. Corporate financial statements are prepared using the _____ method of accounting for tax purposes.

14. Unrecoverable costs, also called _____, are not relevant in the investment decision-making process.

15. Projects that compete with each other in such a way that the selection of one precludes all the others in the group are called _____ projects.

16. _____ occurs when a firm places an upper limit on its capital expenditures.

17. The _____ is the present value of the net cash flows divided by the net investment.

18. The _____ is the discount rate that equates the present value of the net cash inflows from a project to its net investment.

19. A risk estimation technique that uses a series of "what if" calculations under varying assumptions is called _____.

20. The _____ method adjusts for risk by modifying a project's risky cash flows.

Problems

1. The Sunset Patio Company has the following current asset and liability accounts as of December 31, 19x8 and 19x9.

    (a) Calculate the firm's working capital for each years.
    (b) Calculate net working capital for each years.
    (c) Calculate current ratios for each years.
    (d) Has the firm's overall liquidity improved?
    (e) What has happened to the riskiness of Sunset Patio's net working capital position?

	19x9	19x8
Cash...	$ 1,000	1,000
Marketable securities..................................	1,500	2,000
Accounts receivable	3,500	2,500
Inventory	6,500	4,500
Total current assets	$12,500	$10,500
Accounts payable.....................................	$ 6,000	$ 4,000
Notes payable	2,000	1,000
Total current liabilities...............................	$ 8,000	$ 5,000

2. Lang Company is considering using a lockbox system to speed up collections. The lockbox would reduce collection float from five days to three days. The lockbox will cost the firm $15,000 per year before taxes. Collections average $80,000 per day and idle cash can earn 8 percent. Should Lang Company use the lockbox system?

3. Ringold Company's total cash needs over the next two years are $2,000,000 per year with usage at a constant rate. The fixed costs of each transaction are $150 and the average interest rate on marketable securities is 9.5 percent. Use the Baumol model to answer the following questions:

   (a) What is Ringold Company's optimal cash balance?
   (b) How many transactions per year are implied by this optimal cash balance level?

4. C & G Heating and Refrigeration must order furnaces from its supplier by the half truck load (six furnaces). The annual demand is 240 furnaces with each furnace costing $1,000. Carrying costs are $30 per furnace and ordering costs are $25 per order.

   (a) What is the economic order quantity?
   (b) What will the average inventory be?
   (c) How often will C + G need to order?

5. Metro Trucking Company plans to replace two old trucks with newer models. The old trucks originally cost $60,000 and have a current book value of $20,000. The old trucks can be sold for $7,500 each. The two new trucks cost $75,000. The firm's marginal tax rate is 34 percent. What is the net investment of the new trucks?

6. Mineral Springs Company is considering a new bottling machine that will cost $120,000 installed and will be depreciated as 7-year ACRS class property. This machine is expected to increase the firm's annual revenues by $100,000 and its annual operating costs by $30,000. Mineral Springs Company is in the 34 percent tax bracket. What are the expected net after-tax cash flows for the new equipment during its first year of operation?

7. Centerville Industries is considering the purchase of new equipment costing $300,000 with an estimated life of 10 years. Annual net cash flows of the equipment is $75,000.

   (a) What is the payback period for the new equipment?
   (b) If the maximum payback is 3 years, should the new equipment be purchased?

8. Talco, Inc. is considering a project with a $40,000 net investment and net operating cash inflows of $11,652 each year for the next five years. The firm uses a 10 percent discount rate for projects with similar risk.

   (a) What is the project's net present value?
   (b) What is its profitability index?
   (c) What is its internal rate of return?
   (d) Should the project be accepted assuming that funds are available?

Answer to Examination II

True-False

1. True [Section 9-1C]
2. False [Section 9-1E]
3. False [Section 9-2B]
4. False [Section 9-3A]
5. True [Section 10-3A]
6. False [Section 10-5B]
7. False [Section 10-7C]
8. True [Section 10-7E]
9. False [Section 11-2A]
10. True [Section 11-2D]
11. False [Section 11-2E]
12. False [Section 11-4C]
13. True [Section 12-1]
14. False [Section 12-3]
15. True [Section 12-4B]
16. True [Section 12-4C]
17. False [Section 13-1A]
18. False [Section 13-1B]
19. True [Section 13-2B]
20. True [Section 13-3B]

Multiple Choice

1. c [Section 9-1B]
2. d [Section 9-1E]
3. a [Section 9-2B]
4. c [Section 9-3A]
5. b [Section 10-1A]
6. d [Section 10-4A]
7. b [Section 10-5B]
8. c [Section 10-7A]
9. c [Section 11-2A]
10. d [Section 11-3B]
11. d [Section 11-5A]
12. d [Section 11-5B]
13. d [Section 12-3B]
14. d [Section 12-4C]
15. c [Section 12-4C]
16. d [Section 12-4C]
17. d [Section 13-1A]
18. b [Section 13-1B]
19. a [Section 13-1B]
20. c [Section 13-3B]

Fill In The Blanks

1. market segmentation [Section 9-2B]
2. Aggressive [Section 9-3A]
3. hedging [Section 9-3A]
4. lower [Section 9-3B]
5. Cash [Section 10-1]
6. float [Section 10-2]
7. concentration banking [Section 10-3A]
8. Default risk [Section 10-6B]
9. aging schedule [Section 11-2F]
10. Dun & Bradstreet, Inc. [Section 11-3B]
11. economic order quantity (EOQ) [Section 11-5A]
12. safety stocks [Section 11-6]
13. accrual [Section 12-4A]
14. sunk costs [Section 12-4B]
15. mutually exclusive [Section 12-6]
16. Capital rationing [Section 12-6]
17. profitability index [Section 13-1B]
18. internal rate of return [Section 13-1B]
19. sensitivity analysis [Section 13-1A]
20. certainty equivalent [Section 13-3B]

Problems

1. Sunset Patio Company has experienced the following changes:

   (a) Working capital equals the firm's total current assets.

   Working capital for 19x8 = $10,500

   Working capital for 19x9 = $12,500

(*b*) Net working capital equals current assets less current liabilities.

$$\text{Net working capital for 19x8} = \$10{,}500 - \$5{,}000 = \$5{,}500$$
$$\text{Net working capital for 19x9} = \$12{,}500 - \$8{,}000 = \$4{,}500$$

(*c*) The current ratio is current assets divided by current liabilities.

$$\text{Current ratio 19x8} = \$10{,}500/\$5{,}000 = 2.10 \text{ times}$$
$$\text{Current ratio 19x9} = \$12{,}500/\$8{,}000 = 1.56 \text{ times}$$

(*d*) Based on Sunset Patio's current ratio, the firm's liquidity has declined. There is also a shift in the composition of current assets, from more liquid (cash and marketable securities) to less liquid (accounts receivable and inventory) current assets.

(*e*) The riskiness of the firm's net working capital position has increased because the firm is less liquid in 19x9 than in 19x8.　　　**[Section 9-1A through 9-1C]**

2. The lockbox system would save two days in collection float and free up $160,000 (2 × $80,000). Using Equation 10-1, the annual pretax benefit of reducing collection float is:

$$\begin{array}{l}\text{Annual pre-tax benefit of}\\ \text{reducing collection float}\end{array} = (2)(\$80{,}000)(0.08) = \$12{,}800$$

The annual pre-tax cost of the lockbox is $15,000. Thus, the lockbox should not be used because the cost exceed its expected benefit.

Annual pre-tax benefit	$12,800
Annual pre-tax cost	15,000
Annual loss	($ 2,200)

[Section 10-3B]

3. Ringold Company cash position is as follows:

(*a*) Substituting $F = \$150$, $T = \$2{,}000{,}000$, and $k = 0.095$ in Equation 10-4, the optimal level of cash balance, C^*, is:

$$C^* = \sqrt{\frac{(2)(\$150)(\$2{,}000{,}000)}{0.095}} = \$79{,}472$$

(*b*) Substituting $T = \$2{,}000{,}000$ and $C^* = \$79{,}472$ in Equation 10-5, the number of transactions per year is:

$$\begin{array}{l}\text{Number of}\\ \text{transactions}\end{array} = \frac{\$2{,}000{,}000}{\$79{,}472} = 25.17 \text{ or approximately 25} \qquad \textbf{[Section 10-5B]}$$

4. Computations for C & G Heating and Refrigeration are shown below.

(*a*) Substituting $S = 240$, $O = \$25$, and $C = \$30$ in Equation 11-6, the EOQ is:

$$\text{EOQ} = Q^* = \sqrt{\frac{(2)(240)(\$25)}{\$30}} = \sqrt{\frac{12{,}000}{30}} = 20$$

Because C & G must order half truckloads of six furnaces, it must order 24 furnaces.

(*b*) The average inventory, $Q/2$, is 12 (24/2).

(*c*) Substituting $S = 240$ and $Q = 24$ in Equation 11-8, the optimal number of orders, N^*, is:

$$N^* = \frac{240}{24} = 10 \qquad\qquad \textbf{[Section 11-5B]}$$

5. The proceeds from the sale of the old trucks reduces the investment in the new trucks. Because the old trucks are sold for less than their book value, the difference of $5,000 ($20,000 − $15,000) is treated as an operating loss and results in a tax savings of $1,700

$(0.34 \times \$5,000)$. Thus, the net investment in the new trucks is:

Cost of new trucks	$75,000
—Proceeds from sale of old trucks	15,000
—Tax savings on sale of old trucks	1,700
Net investment	$58,300

[Section 12-4C]

6. The net operating cash flows for Year 1 are as follows:

Cash revenues	$100,000
—Cash operating expenses	30,000
—Depreciation expenses*	17,136
Taxable income	$ 52,864
—Income taxes (34%)	17,974
Net income	$ 34,890
+Depreciation expenses	17,136
Net operating cash flows	$ 52,026

* Depreciation expense $= (0.1428)(\$120,000) = \$17,136$

[Section 12-4C]

7. The calculation for Centerville Industries follows:

   (a) Substituting net investment $= \$300,000$ and annual net cash inflows $= \$75,000$ in Equation 13-2, the payback period is:

   $$\text{Payback period} = \frac{\$300,000}{\$75,000} = 4.0 \text{ years}$$

   (b) The project should be rejected because the computed payback period of 4.0 years is greater than the maximum payback of 3 years. **[Section 13-1A]**

8. The calculations for Talco Inc. are as follows:

   (a) NPV $= (3.791)(\$11,652) - \$40,000$
   $\qquad = \$44,173 - \$40,000 = \$4,173$
   (b) PI $= \$44,173/\$40,000 = 1.104$
   (c) $\$40,000/\$11,652 = 3.433$
   Using Appendix D for a $\text{PVIFA}_{i,5} = 3.433$ gives an $i = 14$ percent.
   (d) The project should be accepted because it meets the decision criteria for acceptance for each evaluation method. That is, the NPV is positive, the PI exceeds 1, and the IRR exceeds the required rate of return.

14 COST OF CAPITAL

THIS CHAPTER IS ABOUT

☑ **Concept of the Cost of Capital**
☑ **Specific Costs of Capital**
☑ **Weighted Average Cost of Capital**
☑ **Weighted Marginal Cost of Capital**

14-1. Concept of the Cost of Capital

The cost of capital may be defined in several ways. **Cost of capital** is the rate that the firm has to pay, explicitly or implicitly, to investors for its capital. **Capital** represents the funds used to finance the firm's assets and operations. The cost of capital is also the minimum rate of return required by suppliers of the firm's capital. Finally, the cost of capital may be viewed as the minimum required rate of return that the firm must earn on new investments in order to maintain the market value of its common stock. Holding risk constant, projects with returns above the firm's cost of capital should increase its value and vice versa.

A. The cost of capital is a central concept in financial management because it provides a way of linking the investment and financing decisions of the firm.

That is, capital budgeting and cost of capital are interrelated because the cost of capital cannot be determined unless the size of the capital budget is known, and the size of the capital budget cannot be determined unless the cost of capital is known.

B. Financial managers use estimates of the firm's cost of capital primarily to help identify the discount rate to be used in evaluating capital budgeting projects.

These estimates are also used to help establish the firm's optimal capital structure. This chapter focuses on using the cost of capital to make capital budgeting decisions. Because making capital budgeting decisions hinges on the cost of new capital, attention is placed on determining the marginal costs of new funds to be raised during the planning period, not the historical costs of existing capital.

14-2. Specific Costs of Capital

The cost of capital for any particular capital source or security issue is called the **specific** (*individual or component*) **cost of capital**. There is some debate over which components are used to calculate the firm's cost of capital and how the specific costs are measured. Only permanent short-term and long-term sources of financing should be in the firm's cost of capital. These sources may include a portion of the firm's interest-bearing short-term debt and all long-term debt, preferred stock, and common equity (retained earnings and common stock). However, only long-term sources of funds are examined here to calculate the cost of capital because short-term debt is seldom used as a part of the firm's permanent financing for capital projects.

A. There are no free sources of permanent financing.

The specific cost of each component is the minimum rate of return required by the suppliers of the capital. Different costs occur because of the varying degrees of risk associated with each source of financing. The higher the risk of a particular component, the higher the return required by investors and the higher the cost to the firm. Generally, the most expensive cost of capital is new common stock (external equity), followed by retained earnings (internal equity), preferred stock, and debt.

The letter k followed by a subscript is used to identify the specific cost of capital. For example, k_d is the cost of debt. These costs are calculated on an after-tax basis and are expressed as an annual percentage. Only the cost of debt must be adjusted for taxes because the costs of the other sources are paid from after-tax cash flows. Specific costs of capital vary over time due to numerous factors, including changes in the risk characteristics of the firm, the marketability of the securities, capital market conditions, and the supply and demand for funds.

B. Most of the techniques used to measure specific costs of capital are based on capital asset pricing and valuation models.

Investor security valuation and corporate cost of capital are two sides of the same coin. These valuation models are directly applicable to *existing securities*, but must be modified for *newly issued securities* to reflect flotation costs and the risk premium associated with raising new capital. **Flotation costs**, f, are any costs associated with selling the new securities, including commissions paid to those selling the securities; the costs of printing, advertising, registration with government agencies; and discounts required to induce investors to buy (underpricing). Although the values resulting from the cost of capital equations appear to be precise, they are only approximations due to the estimates and assumptions that underlie them. Thus, the process of measuring specific costs of capital is difficult and results in rough approximations.

C. The *cost of debt* is the minimum rate of return required by suppliers of debt.

Although firms use various types of debt, such as bonds, term loans, and leasing, only the cost of bonds is discussed here because the cost of other types of debt is generally determined by the lender. The relevant specific cost of debt is the after-tax cost of new debt. Computing the cost of a new bond issue requires three steps.

1. *Determine the net proceeds from the sale of each bond.* Bonds have a par or face value, but the receipts from a bond issue are seldom equal to the issue's total par value because of flotation costs. Flotation costs reduce the net receipts of each bond sold and increase the bond's cost to the firm. Thus, the net proceeds of a bond issue, NP_d, are the market price minus flotation costs, $P_d - f$.

2. *Compute the before-tax cost of the bond.* If flotation costs are ignored and the bond sells at par, the before-tax cost of the bond is simply its *coupon rate*, which is the interest rate paid on the bond's par value. If these conditions do not hold, then either Equation 14-1 or Equation 14-2 may be used to determine the before-tax cost of the bond. (These two equations are modified forms of Equation 5-2 and Equation 5-3 in Chapter 5). Equation 14-1 shows that the before-tax cost of a debt issue is the rate of return, k_d, that equates the present value of the future interest payments and principal repayment with the net proceeds from the sale of the bond. (For the purpose of simplicity, annual interest payments are assumed and the tax savings on amortized flotation expenses are ignored).

$$NP_d = \sum_{t=1}^{n} \frac{I}{(1 + k_d)^t} + \frac{P_n}{(1 + k_d)^n} \tag{14-1}$$

Equation 14-1 may be simplified as follows:

$$NP_d = I(PVIFA_{k_d,n}) + P_n(PVIF_{k_d,n})$$

(14-2)

where	NP_d	=	net proceeds from the sale of the bond, $P_d - f$
	I	=	annual interest payment in dollars
	P_n	=	par or principal repayment required in period n
	k_d	=	before-tax cost of a new bond issue
	n	=	length of the holding period of the bond in years
	t	=	time period in years
	PVIFA	=	present value interest factor of an annuity (Appendix D)
	PVIF	=	present value interest factor of a single amount (Appendix C)

The before-tax cost of a new bond issue may also be approximated by calculating the issuer's *cost to maturity*, as shown in Equation 14-3. (The term *cost to maturity* means the same as *yield to maturity*, which is discussed in Chapter 5.)

APPROXIMATE BEFORE-TAX COST OF NEW DEBT
$$k_{d'} = \frac{I + (P_n - NP_d)/n}{(P_n + NP_d)/2}$$
(14-3)

The first term in the numerator of Equation 14-3 represents the annual interest; the second term in the numerator is the annual amortization of flotation costs and any premium or discount; and the denominator is the average amount borrowed.

3. *Compute the after-tax cost of debt.* Since interest charges are tax deductible, a tax adjustment is required. Equation 14-4 shows that the after-tax cost of debt, k_{dt}, is obtained by multiplying the before-tax cost of debt calculated in Equations 14-1 through 14-3 by $(1 - T)$, where T is the firm's marginal tax rate. Thus, the firm's after-tax cost of debt, k_{dt}, is always less than its before-tax cost of debt, k_d, for any marginal tax rate greater than zero.

AFTER-TAX COST OF DEBT
$$k_{dt} = k_d(1 - T)$$
(14-4)

where T = marginal tax rate

If the financial manager wants to measure the cost of existing debt, the current market price of the outstanding bond, P_d, would be substituted for the net proceeds, NP_d, in Equations 14-1 through 14-3. The resulting before-tax cost would then be substituted into Equation 14-4 in order to obtain the after-tax cost of existing debt. In practice, financial managers sometimes ignore flotation costs in computing the cost of either existing or new debt. When this is the case, the specific cost of debt is approximated simply by substituting the bond's coupon rate as k_d in Equation 14-4 and solving for k_{dt}.

EXAMPLE 14-1: Nickels Pipe Company plans to issue 25-year bonds with a face value of $4,000,000. Each bond has a par value of $1,000 and carries a coupon rate of 9.5 percent. However, the bond is expected to sell for 98 percent of par value. The flotation costs are estimated to be approximately $26 per bond and the firm's marginal tax rate is 34 percent. (Assume that interest payments are made annually.) Management wants to calculate the net proceeds per bond, the before-tax cost of this bond issue, the after-tax cost of the bond issue's flotation costs.

(*a*) The selling price of the bond is $980 (0.98 × $1,000). The net proceeds per bond are calculated by subtracting the $26 flotation cost from the bond's $980 selling price.

$$NP_d = \$980 - \$26 = \$954$$

(b) Substituting $NP_d = \$954$, $I = \$95$ ($0.095 \times \$1,000$), $P_n = \$1,000$, and $n = 25$ in Equation 14-1 the before-tax cost of debt, k_d is found using trial and errors as follows:

$$\$954 = \sum_{t=1}^{25} \frac{\$95}{(1 + k_d)^t} + \frac{\$1,000}{(1 + k_d)^{25}}$$

$$k_d = 10.00 \text{ percent}$$

Equation 14-2 may be used to find the present value factors that equate:

$$\$954 = (\$95)(PVIFA_{i,n}) + \$1,000(PVIF_{i,n})$$

For i or $k_d = 10.00$ percent

$$\$954 = (\$95)(PVIFA_{0.10,25}) + (\$1,000)(PVIF_{0.10,25})$$
$$= (\$95)(9.077) + (\$1,000)(0.092) = \$962.32 + \$92.00 = \$1,054.32$$

Using Equation 14-3, the approximate before-tax cost of debt is:

$$k_d' = \frac{\$95 + (\$1,000 - \$954)/25}{(\$1,000 + \$954)/2} = \frac{\$96.84}{\$977.00}$$

$$= 0.0991 \text{ or } 9.91 \text{ percent}$$

In this situation, the specific before-tax cost of debt, $k_d = 10.00$, is higher than the approximate before-tax cost of debt, $k_{d'} = 9.91$ percent.

(c) Substituting $k_d = 10$ percent and $T = 0.34$ in Equation 14-4, the after-tax cost of new debt is:

$$k_{dt} = (10.00)(1 - 0.34) = 6.60 \text{ percent}$$

Substituting $k_d' = 9.91$ percent and $T = 0.34$ in Equation 14-4, the approximate after-tax cost of new debt is:

$$k_{dt}' = (9.91)(1 - 0.34) = 6.54 \text{ percent}$$

D. The *cost of preferred stock*, k_P, is the minimum rate of return required by preferred stock investors to purchase a firm's preferred stock.

Preferred stock is a part of a firm's permanent financing mix but is infrequently issued. Preferred stock is a hybrid security that has characteristics of both *debt* and *equity*. Most preferred stocks have fixed dividend payments and no stated maturity dates. Dividend payments on preferred stock are made after interest payments on debt but before dividend payments on common stock. Thus, both the riskiness of preferred stock to investors and the resulting cost of issuing preferred stock fall somewhere between debt and common stock.

Equation 14-5 shows that the component cost of new preferred stock is computed by dividing the annual preferred stock dividend payment, D_p, by the net proceeds per share to the firm from the sale of the preferred stock, NP_p. The net proceeds represent the amount of money the firm receives per share after subtracting any flotation costs required to market the preferred stock, $P_p - f$. Equation 14-5 approximates the cost of preferred stock because it ignores the fact that dividends are usually paid quarterly. Unlike interest payments on bonds, preferred stock dividends are not a tax-deductible expense. Thus, no tax adjustment is needed to adjust the cost of preferred stock downward because the before-tax and after-tax cost of preferred stock are the same. (Equation 14-5 is derived from Equation 5-7 in Chapter 5.)

COST OF NEW PREFERRED STOCK
$$k_p = \frac{D_p}{NP_p}$$
(14-5)

where D_p = annual dividend per share on preferred stock
NP_p = net proceeds from the sale of preferred stock, $P_p - f$

The cost of existing preferred stock is determined by substituting the current market price of a share of preferred stock, P_p, in the denominator of Equation 14-5 in lieu of NP_p.

EXAMPLE 14-2: Nickels Pipe Company plans to sell preferred stock for its par value of $25.00 per share. The issue is expected to pay quarterly dividends of $0.60 per share and to have flotation costs of 3 percent of the par value or $1.50 (0.03 × $25.00). Substituting D_p = $2.40 (4 × $0.60), NP_p = $23.50 ($25.00 − $1.50) in Equation 14-5, the cost of preferred stock is:

$$k_p = \frac{\$2.40}{\$23.50} = 0.1021 \text{ or } 10.21 \text{ percent}$$

E. The *cost of common equity* is the rate of return required by stockholders to purchase a firm's common stock.

The cost of common equity capital is more difficult to measure than the costs of bonds or preferred stock because common equity does not represent a contractual obligation to make specific payments. Firms raise equity capital internally through retained earnings and externally through the sale of new common stock. The costs of these two sources of common equity are similar but not equal. The cost of new common stock is higher than the cost of retained earnings because selling new common stock involves flotation costs, which reduce the net proceeds to the firm. Thus, firms will use the lower-cost retained earnings before they issue new common stock.

1. The **cost of retained earnings**, k_r, is the rate of return stockholders require on the firm's existing common stock. *Retained earnings* are the portion of after-tax profits that the firm reinvests in itself. The cost of retained earnings is difficult to measure because retained earnings do not have market prices. However, retained earnings are not a free form of financing because there is an opportunity cost for retaining profits in a business. This *opportunity cost* represents the minimum rate of return that the firm's stockholders could earn on alternative investments of comparable risk.

   There are several ways to measure the cost of retained earnings: the Gordon constant growth model, the capital asset pricing model (CAPM), the generalized risk premium approach, and the earnings-price ratio. These techniques are appropriate for calculating the cost of new or additional retained earnings only if the funds are used to acquire assets equal in risk to the firm's existing assets and if there is no significant change in the firm's degree of financial leverage. All of these methods are subject to error when used in practice.

   - The *Gordon constant growth model* assumes that dividends grow perpetually at a constant annual rate, g. For stocks that do not pay dividends, the Gordon model cannot be used directly to determine the cost of equity capital. Equation 14-6 shows that the after-tax cost of retained earnings consists of the stock's dividend yield, D_1/P_0, plus the dividend growth rate, g. Estimates of g are usually based on historical growth rates, if earnings and dividend growth rates have been relatively stable in the past, or on analysts' forecasts. Since dividends are not a tax-deductible expense, there is no need to make an after-tax adjustment to the cost of retained earnings. (Equation 14-6 is derived from Equation 5-13 in Chapter 5.)

GORDON CONSTANT GROWTH MODEL FOR RETAINED EARNINGS
$$k_r = \frac{D_1}{P_0} + g \tag{14-6}$$

where D_1 = dividends to be received during Year 1, $D_0(1 + g)$
P_0 = current market price of the firm's common stock
g = annual constant dividend growth rate

EXAMPLE 14-3: Nickels Pipe Company's common stock is currently selling for $45.00 per share. The firm's expected dividend for the coming year is $3.60, and its expected dividend growth rate is 5 percent. Using the Gordon constant growth model, the cost of retained earnings is 13 percent. This may be found by substituting $D_1 = \$3.60$, $P_0 = \$45.00$, and $g = 0.05$ in Equation 14-6.

$$k_r = \frac{\$3.60}{\$45.00} + 0.05 = 0.08 + 0.05 = 0.13 \text{ or } 13.00 \text{ percent}$$

- The *capital asset pricing model (CAPM)* can also be used to estimate the cost of retained earnings. As discussed in Chapter 4, CAPM is a sophisticated model of the relationship return and risk. CAPM is based on several restrictive and unrealistic assumptions but it is still used in practice. Equation 14-7 shows that the cost of retained earnings is equal to a risk-free rate of return, r_f, plus a risk premium, $b_i(r_m - r_f)$.

CAPITAL ASSET PRICING MODEL
$$k_r = r_f + b_i(r_m - r_f) \tag{14-7}$$

where r_f = risk-free rate of return
r_m = expected return on the market portfolio
b_i = beta coefficient of common stock i.

All of the parameters of the model (r_f, r_m, and b_i) must be accurately estimated if the model is to provide a reasonable measure of the cost of retained earnings.

EXAMPLE 14-4: Nickels Pipe Company estimates that the risk-free rate, as measured by the return on a short-term Treasury security, is 6 percent; the rate of return on the market portfolio, as measured by the Standard and Poor's 500 Stock Index, is 12 percent; and the firm's beta on its common stock is 1.2. Using the CAPM approach, the cost of retained earnings would be 13.2 percent. This is found by substituting $r_f = 0.06$, $r_m = 0.12$, and $b_i = 1.2$ in Equation 14-7:

$$k_r = 0.06 + (1.2)(0.12 - 0.06) = 0.06 + 0.072$$
$$= 0.1320 \text{ or } 13.20 \text{ percent}$$

- The *generalized risk premium approach* is a subjective method used to estimate the required rate of return on retained earnings. Equation 14-8 shows that the required rate of return is equal to some base rate, k_d, plus a risk premium, r_p. The base rate is often the rate on Treasury bonds or the rate on the firm's own bonds. The risk premium is based on a judgmental estimate but commonly averages between 1 to 5 percentage points above the base rate. However, risk premiums are not stable over time.

GENERALIZED RISK PREMIUM METHOD
$$k_r = k_d + r_p \tag{14-8}$$

where k_d = base rate of long-term bonds
r_p = risk premium

EXAMPLE 14-5: Nickels Pipe Company's long-term bond rate is 9.5 percent. The firms management estimates that its cost of equity should require a 3 percentage point risk premium above the cost of its own bonds. Using the generalized risk premium approach, the cost of retained earnings would be 12.5 percent. This is found by substituting $k_d = 0.095$ and $r_p = 0.03$ in Equation 14-8:

$$k_r = 0.095 + 0.03 = 0.1250 \text{ or } 12.50 \text{ percent}$$

- The *earnings-price ratio* is a simplistic technique used to estimate the cost of retained earnings, which is based on the *inverse* of the firm's price-earnings ratio. The earnings-price ratio is easy to compute because it is based on readily available information, but there is little economic logic to support the use of the earnings-price ratio to measure the cost of retained earnings. For example, this technique is unsuitable for a firm that is operating at a loss because it would generate a negative cost of retained earnings. Equation 14-9 shows that the earnings-price ratio is found by dividing the current earnings per share, E, by the current market price of the firm's common stock, P_o.

EARNINGS-PRICE RATIO $$k_r = \frac{E}{P_0} \qquad \text{(14-9)}$$

where E = current earnings per share
P_0 = current market price of common stock

EXAMPLE 14-6: Nickels Pipe Company had earnings per share for the past year of $6.50, and the firm's common stock is currently priced at $45.00. Using the earnings-price ratio method, the cost of retained earnings would be 14.44 percent. This is found by substituting $E = \$6.50$ and $P_o = \$45.00$ in Equation 14-9:

$$k_r = \frac{\$6.50}{\$45.00} = 0.1444 \text{ or } 14.44 \text{ percent}$$

• The results of the various methods used to compute the cost of retained earnings may differ. For example, the four methods of computing the cost of retained earnings for Nickels Pipe Company produce the following results:

Method	Estimated Cost %
Gordon constant growth model	13.00
Capital asset pricing model	13.20
Bond yield plus risk premium approach	12.50
Earnings-price ratio	14.44

The financial manager must exercise judgment in determining which, if any, of these costs to use. If substantial differences occur, further analysis is required in order to select the estimated cost that seems to have the most merit. Finance is not an exact science and thus requires the use of considerable judgment.

2. The **cost of new common stock**, k_s, is higher than the cost of retained earnings, k_r, because the cost of a new issue must be adjusted for flotation costs. These flotation costs include both underpricing and an underwriting fee. *Underpricing* occurs when new common stock sells below the current market price of outstanding common stock, P_0, in order to attract investors and to compensate for the dilution of ownership that will take place. An *underwriting fee* is paid for marketing the new issue. Equation 14-10 modifies the Gordon model shown in Equation 14-6 to include the additional flotation costs associated with a new stock issue.

**GORDON CONSTANT
GROWTH MODEL FOR
NEW COMMON STOCK** $$k_s = \frac{D_1}{NP_s} + g \qquad \text{(14-10)}$$

where NP_s = net proceeds of the new common stock issue, $P_0 - f$

The cost of existing common stock, k'_s, is the same as the cost of retained earnings, k_r; thus, $k'_s = k_r$. No adjustment is made for flotation costs in determining either the cost of existing common stock or the cost of retained earnings.

EXAMPLE 14-7: Nickels Pipe Company's common stock has a current market price of $45.00 and an expected dividend growth rate of 5 percent. The firm is expected to pay $3.60 per share in common stock dividends during the next year. The sale of new common stock involves underpricing of $1.00 per share and an underwriting fee of $0.80 per share. By substituting $D_1 = \$3.60$, $NP_s = \$43.20$ [$45.00 - (\$1.00 + \$0.80)$], and $g = 0.05$ in Equation 14-10, the cost of new common stock is:

$$k_s = \frac{\$3.60}{\$43.20} + 0.05 = 0.0833 + 0.05 = 0.1333 \text{ or } 13.33 \text{ percent}$$

14-3. Weighted Average Cost of Capital

Once the specific cost of capital of each permanent financing source is measured, the firm's weighted average cost of capital (WACC), k_a, can be determined. The weighted average cost of capital, also called the *overall* or *composite cost of capital*, is the weighted cost of all long-term capital sources, where each specific cost of capital is weighted by its relative importance in the firm's total capital. A WACC can be computed for either the firm's existing financing or new financing. The cost of capital acquired by the firm in earlier periods is not relevant for current decision making because it represents a historical or sunk cost. Thus, only the WACC for new financing is calculated below.

A. **The weighted average cost of capital is computed by multiplying the specific cost of each type of capital by its proportion (weight) in the firm's capital structure and summing the weighted values.**

The sum of the weights must equal 1.0 because all permanent capital structure components must be taken into account when computing the WACC. Equation 14-11 summarizes the process of find the WACC.

WEIGHTED AVERAGE COST OF CAPITAL
$$\text{WACC} = k_a = \sum_{i=1}^{n} w_i k_i \qquad \textbf{(14-11)}$$

where
w_i = percentage of total permanent capital represented by capital source i
k_i = after-tax cost of each new specific cost of capital
n = number of types of new capital

B. **There are two major weighting schemes used in computing the weighted average cost of capital: historical weights and target weights.**

1. *Historical weights* are based on a firm's existing capital structure. Firms that believe their existing capital structure is optimal should use historical weights. An optimal capital structure is the combination of debt and equity that simultaneously maximizes the firm's market value and minimizes its weighted average cost of capital. (Optimal capital structure is discussed in Chapter 15.) There are two types of historical weights: book value weights and market value weights.

   • *Book value weights* measure the actual proportion of each type of permanent capital in the firm's structure based on accounting values shown on the firm's balance sheet. Book value weights are easy to compute and remain relatively stable over time because they do not depend on market prices. However, book value weights may misstate the WACC because they ignore the changing market values of bonds and equity over time. Thus, book value weights may not provide a cost of capital that is useful for evaluating current strategies.

EXAMPLE 14-8: Nickels Pipe Company's existing capital structure and specific costs of new capital, based on the computations in Section 14-2, are shown below.

Source of Capital	Book Value	Specific Cost %
Bonds ($1,000 par, 9.5% coupon)	$15,000,000	6.60
Preferred stock (200,000 shares at $25 par)	5,000,000	10.21
Common stock (1,000,000 shares at $20 par)	20,000,000	13.33
Retained earnings	10,000,000	13.00
Total	$50,000,000	

The capital cost weights are calculated by dividing the book value of a specific component by the total book value of all components.

$$w_d = \frac{\$15,000,000}{\$50,000,000} = 0.30 \qquad w_p = \frac{\$5,000,000}{\$50,000,000} = 0.10$$

$$w_s = \frac{\$20,000,000}{\$50,000,000} = 0.40 \qquad w_r = \frac{\$10,000,000}{\$50,000,000} = 0.20$$

If Nickels Pipe Company obtains new capital in book value proportions, the firm's WACC may be found by substituting the book value weights and specific costs of capital in Equation 14-11:

$$\text{WACC} = (0.30)(0.0660) + (0.10)(0.1021) + (0.40)(0.1333) + (0.20)(0.1300)$$
$$= 0.0198 + 0.0102 + 0.0533 + 0.0260 = 0.1093 \text{ or } 10.93 \text{ percent}$$

- *Market value weights* measure the actual proportion of each type of permanent capital in the firm's structure at current market prices. Market value weights are, theoretically, superior to book value weights because they provide current estimates of investors' required rates of return. However, market value weights are less stable than book value weights in computing cost of capital because market prices change frequently.

EXAMPLE 14-9: In addition to the data provided in Example 14–8, assume that the security market prices of Nickels Pipe Company are:

$$\text{Bonds} = \$980 \text{ per bond}$$
$$\text{Preferred stock} = \$25 \text{ per share}$$
$$\text{Common stock} = \$45 \text{ per share}$$

The market value of each financing source is found by multiplying the number of securities outstanding by its current market price per share. There are 15,000 ($15,000,000/$1,000) bonds outstanding.

Source of Capital	Number of Securities (1)	Market Price (2)	Market Value (1) × (2)
Bonds	15,000	$980	$14,700,000
Preferred stock	200,000	25	5,000,000
Common stock	1,000,000	45	45,000,000
Total			$64,700,000

The capital cost weights are calculated by dividing the market value of a specific component by the total market value of all sources of capital. However, retained earnings do not have a separate market value because their value is impounded into the common stock. In order to compute the WACC, the common stock's market value of $45,000,000 is divided between common stock and retained earnings in proportion to the sum of their book values. In this situation, the proportions are two-thirds ($20,000,000/$30,000,000) for common stock and one-third ($10,000,000/$30,000,000) for retained earnings. Thus, two-thirds of common stock market value, or $30,000,000, is allocated to common stock; and one-third, or $15,000,000, is allocated to retained earnings.

$$w_d = \frac{\$14,700,000}{\$64,700,000} = 0.227 \qquad w_p = \frac{\$5,000,000}{\$64,700,000} = 0.077$$

$$w_s = \frac{\$30,000,000}{\$64,700,000} = 0.464 \qquad w_r = \frac{\$15,000,000}{\$64,700,000} = 0.232$$

If the firm obtains new capital in market value proportions, the WACC is found by substituting the market value weights and specific costs of capital into Equation 14-11:

$$WACC = (0.227)(0.0660) + (0.077)(0.1021) + (0.464)(0.1333) + (0.232)(0.13)$$
$$= 0.0150 + 0.0079 + 0.0619 + 0.0302 = 0.1150 \text{ or } 11.50 \text{ percent}$$

2. *Target weights* are based on a firm's desired capital structure. Firms using target weights establish these proportions on the basis of the optimal capital structure they wish to achieve. Consequently, the firm raises additional funds so as to remain constantly on target with its optimal capital structure. Because target weights are not necessarily the same as historical weights, the WACC may vary using different weighting schemes. The theoretically preferred approach is to use target weights based on market values. If these weights are used, the stock price will be maximized and the cost of capital simultaneously will be minimized.

EXAMPLE 14-10: In addition to the data provided in Examples 14-8 and 14-9, Nickels Pipe Company has determined that its optimal capital structure is 40 percent bonds, 10 percent preferred stock, and 50 percent common equity. The firm wants to maintain this optimal capital structure in raising future long-term capital. The firm expects to have sufficient retained earnings so that it can use the cost of retained earnings as the common equity cost component. If Nickels Pipe Company raises new capital in target proportions, the firm's WACC can be found by substituting the target weights and specific costs of capital in Equation 14-11:

$$WACC = (0.40)(0.0660) + (0.10)(0.1021) + (0.50)(0.1300)$$
$$= 0.0264 + 0.0102 + 0.0650 = 0.1016 \text{ or } 10.16 \text{ percent}$$

14-4. Weighted Marginal Cost of Capital

The **marginal cost of capital** (MCC) is the cost of obtaining the next dollar of new capital. If more than one type of new financing is used, the cost of capital is called the **weighted marginal cost of capital** (WMCC). Calculating a firm's WMCC is a straightforward process when retained earnings provide all the new financing or when the specific costs of capital of the additional financing are constant. However, the specific costs of capital rise as more new financing is required, thereby causing breaks in the firm's WMCC. These increasing costs occur because (1) flotation costs cause the cost of new equity to be higher than the cost of retained earnings, and (2) suppliers of capital require higher rates of return on debt, preferred stock, and common stock to compensate for the increased risk introduced by incurring more new financing. Thus, the WMCC is an average cost of the funds raised over a specific range of new financing. A schedule or graph that relates the firm's cost of capital to different levels of new financing is called a **weighted marginal cost of capital (WMCC) schedule**.

A. There are five steps in developing a WMCC schedule.

1. Determine the percentage composition of the new financing.
2. Calculate the specific cost of capital associated with each amount of capital raised.
3. Calculate the range of total new financing at which the cost of the new components change. The levels at which a specific cost of capital increases are called **break points**. Equation 14-12 is used to calculate the break point for each financing source.

BREAK POINT $$BP_i = \frac{TF_i}{w_i}$$ (14-12)

where BP_i = break point for financing source i

TF_i = total amount of lower cost financing from source i at the break point

w_i = percentage of total permanent capital represented by capital source i

4. Calculate the WMCC for each range of total new financing.
5. Construct or plot the WMCC schedule. At each break point, the firm's WMCC schedule shifts upward.

EXAMPLE 14-11: Nickels Pipe Company wants to determine its WMCC schedule.

Source of Capital	Target Weight %	Range of New Financing (in millions)	Specific Cost %
Debt	40	Up to $4	6.60
		$4 up to $6	7.00
		$6 up to $8	8.00
Preferred stock	10	Up to $1	10.21
		$1 up to $2	11.00
Common equity	50	Up to $2	13.00
		$2 up to $5	13.33
		$5 up to $8	15.00

Determining the WMCC schedule requires completing the five steps previously discussed.

Steps 1 and **2** are given in the problem.

Step 3 involves calculating the break points for each source of capital and the resulting ranges of total new financing. Figure 14-1 shows that the firm's WMCC breaks or shifts at $4,000,000, $10,000,000, $15,000,000, and $20,000,000 of total new financing. For example, the firm can raise up to $4,000,000 before its retained earnings are exhausted as the common equity portion of its target capital structure and new, higher-cost common stock must be sold.

Source of Capital	Range of New Financing (in millions)	Specific Cost (%)	Break Point	Range of Total New Financing (in millions)
Debt	Up to $4	6.60	$4/0.40 = $10	Up to $10
	$4 up to $6	7.00	$6/0.40 = $15	$10 up to $15
	$6 up to $8	8.00	$8/0.40 = $20	$15 up to $20
Preferred stock	Up to $1	10.21	$1/0.10 = $10	Up to $10
	$1 up to $2	11.00	$2/0.10 = $20	$10 up to $20
Common equity	Up to $2	13.00	$2/0.50 = $4	Up to $4
	$2 up to $5	13.33	$5/0.50 = $10	$4 up to $10
	$5 up to $10	15.00	$10/0.50 = $20	$10 up to $20

FIGURE 14-1 Determination of the break points and range of total new financing for Nickels Pipe Company.

Step 4 involves calculating the WMCC over the ranges of total new financing between increasing break points. Figure 14-2 shows the WMCC for each range of total new financing.

Range of Total New Financing (in millions)	Weighted Marginal Cost of Capital (WMCC)
Up to $4	$WMCC_1 = (0.40)(0.0660) + (0.10)(0.1021) + (0.50)(0.1300)$ $= 0.0264 + 0.0102 + 0.0650 = 0.1016$ or 10.16 percent
$4 up to $10	$WMCC_2 = (0.40)(0.0660) + (0.10)(0.1021) + (0.50)(0.1333)$ $= 0.0264 + 0.0102 + 0.0667 = 0.1033$ or 10.33 percent
$10 to up $15	$WMCC_3 = (0.40)(0.0700) + (0.10)(0.1100) + (0.50)(0.1500)$ $= 0.0280 + 0.0110 + 0.0750 = 0.1140$ or 11.40 percent
$15 up to $20	$WMCC_4 = (0.40)(0.0800) + (0.10)(0.1100) + (0.50)(0.1500)$ $= 0.0320 + 0.0110 + 0.0750 = 0.1180$ or 11.80 percent

FIGURE 14-2 WMCC for ranges of total new financing for Nickels Pipe Company.

Step 5 is plotting the WMCC schedule as shown in Figure 14-3.

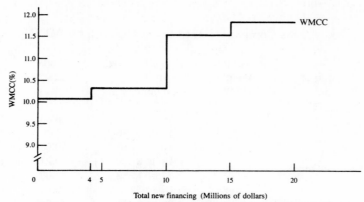

FIGURE 14-3   Weighted marginal cost of capital (WMCC) as a function of total new financing.

B. The firm's WMCC is used in conjunction with its available investment opportunities to select acceptable capital budgeting projects.

The firm's capital budgeting projects are placed in an **investment opportunities schedule** (IOS) in descending order, according to each project's internal rate of return (IRR). By combining its IOS and WMCC schedules, the financial manager can determine both the firm's optimal capital budget and cost of capital that should be used in evaluating capital budgeting projects.

1. An **optimal capital budget** is the level of capital investment that maximizes the value of the firm. The optimal capital budget is determined at the intersection of the IOS and WMCC schedules. That is, the firm should accept projects up to the point where the project's marginal return just equals its WMCC.
2. The cost of capital used in the capital budgeting process is also determined at the intersection of the IOS and WMCC schedules. The **intersection rate** is used to discount project cash flows in finding net present values or calculating profitability indexes, and as the hurdle rate when evaluating internal rates of return. By using this intersection rate, the firm will make correct accept/reject decisions, and its level of financing and investment will be optimal. Technically, this intersection rate is suitable only for those capital budgeting projects that typify the firm's overall or average risk. The discount rate should be risk-adjusted downward for projects that are less risky than the firm's average risk and upward for projects which are more risky than the firm's average risk.

EXAMPLE 14-12: Nickels Pipe Company is contemplating five independent investment projects. The investment opportunities schedule is shown below.

Project	Internal Rate of Return %	Initial Investment (in millions)	Cumulative Investment (in millions)
A	18	$5	$ 5
B	16	6	11
C	12	3	14
D	10	4	18
E	8	2	20

Figure 14-4 combines the IOS schedule and WMCC schedule (Example 14-11) for Nickels Pipe Company. To achieve its optimal capital budget, the firm should accept Projects A, B, and C because their IRRs are greater than or equal to the cost of capital that would be used to finance them. Projects D and E should be rejected because their IRRs are less than their costs of capital. The optimal capital budget of $14,000,000, which is the cumulative investment for Projects A, B, and C, is determined by the intersection of the IOS and WMCC schedules. The discount rate used in the capital budgeting process is 11.40 percent.

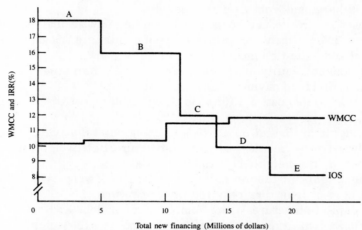

FIGURE 14-4   Using the IOS and WMCC schedules to select projects.

RAISE YOUR GRADES

Can you explain...?

☑ what the cost of capital is
☑ the major uses of the cost of capital
☑ why the cost of capital is most appropriately measured on an after-tax basis
☑ what flotation costs are
☑ how to calculate the specific costs of debt, preferred stock, and common equity
☑ why it is more difficult to measure the cost of common equity than the cost of other forms of long-term financing
☑ how to calculate the weighted average cost of capital
☑ the differences between historical weights and target weights in calculating the weighted average cost of capital
☑ why market value weights are theoretically superior to book value weights
☑ what the marginal cost of capital is
☑ the steps in developing a firm's weighted marginal cost of capital schedule
☑ the reasons that breaks occur in a firm's weighted marginal cost of capital schedule
☑ how to derive the break points in the weighted marginal cost of capital schedule
☑ what an investment opportunities schedule is
☑ what an optimal capital budget is

SUMMARY

1. The cost of capital is the minimum rate of return required by suppliers of capital to the firm.
2. The cost of capital is used to evaluate capital budgeting projects and to establish the firm's optimal capital structure.
3. The specific costs of capital are measured on an after-tax basis in order to be consistent. Only the cost of debt must be adjusted for taxes because the costs of other types of capital are paid from after-tax cash flows.
4. Flotation costs are any costs associated with selling new securities.
5. The techniques used to measure specific costs of capital are based on the capital asset pricing model and valuation models.
6. The costs of common equity are more difficult to find than other forms of long-term capital because dividend payments are not contractual.
7. The weighted average cost of capital is the weighted cost of all long-term capital sources.
8. Historical weights are based on a firm's existing capital structure, whereas target weights are based on a firm's desired capital structure. Both weighting schemes may be used in computing the weighted average cost of capital.
9. Market value weights are theoretically superior to book weights because they provide current estimates of investors' required rates of return.
10. An optimal capital structure is the combination of debt and equity that simultaneously maximizes the firm's market value and minimizes the weighted average cost of capital.
11. The marginal cost of capital is the cost of obtaining the next dollar of new capital.
12. A weighted marginal cost of capital schedule shows the relationship between the weighted cost of each dollar raised and the total new financing.
13. A break in the weighted marginal cost of capital (WMCC) schedule occurs any time any component cost changes.
14. An investment opportunities schedule (IOS) is obtained by plotting the returns expected from proposed capital budgeting projects against the cumulative investment required.
15. An optimal capital budget is the level of capital investment that maximizes the value of the firm.
16. Both the cost of capital used in the capital budgeting process and the optimal capital budget occur at the point where the firm's investment opportunities schedule and weighted marginal cost of capital schedule intersect.

RAPID REVIEW

True or False
1. The cost of capital is the minimum rate of return required by the investors supplying the funds. [Section 14-1]
2. If a firm earns a return exactly equal to its cost of capital, then the market price of its common stock should be unchanged. [Section 14-1]
3. There are no free sources of permanent financing. [Section 14-2]
4. The after-tax cost of debt is generally more expensive than the cost of common equity. [Section 14-2]
5. Flotation costs increase the cost of issuing new securities. [Section 14-2]
6. The after-tax cost of debt is lower than its before-tax cost because of the tax deductibility of interest payments. [Section 14-2A]
7. The cost of preferred stock is equal to the rate of return required by preferred stockholders multiplied by (1 − tax rate). [Section 14-2B]

8. The cost of common equity is easier to measure than the cost of other forms of long-term financing. [Section 14-2C]

9. The cost of retained earnings represents an opportunity cost to the firm's common stockholders. [Section 14-2C]

10. The Gordon constant growth model is used to determine the cost of equity capital for firms that do not pay dividends on their common stock. [Section 14-2C]

11. The capital asset pricing model and dividend valuation model are used to calculate the cost of debt. [Section 14-2C]

12. Underpricing can increase the cost of new common stock. [Section 14-2C]

13. The cost of existing common stock is the same as the cost of retained earnings. [Section 14-2C]

14. The cost of capital acquired by the firm in earlier periods is the relevant cost to use for current decision making. [Section 14-3]

15. The weighted average cost of capital is the sum of each specific cost of capital divided by the total number of different types of capital. [Section 14-3A]

16. Book value weights are theoretically superior to market value weights in calculating the firm's weighted average cost of capital. [Section 14-3B]

17. The marginal cost of capital is the cost of obtaining another dollar of new capital. [Section 14-4]

18. A break point occurs in the weighted marginal cost of capital schedule any time a component cost rises. [Section 14-4A]

19. The weighted marginal cost of capital is used as the hurdle rate in evaluating capital budgeting projects. [Section 14-4B]

20. An investment opportunities schedule plots a firm's investment projects in descending order, according to each project's profitability index. [Section 14-4B]

Multiple Choice

21. The cost of capital may be used

   (*a*) to help identify the discount rate to be used in evaluating capital budgeting projects
   (*b*) to help establish the firm's optimal capital structure
   (*c*) to determine the firm's degree of operating leverage
   (*d*) Both a and b

   [Section 14-1]

22. Which of the following is generally excluded in estimating the weighted average cost of capital?

   (*a*) Short-term debt
   (*b*) Long-term debt
   (*c*) Preferred stock
   (*d*) Common equity

   [Section 14-2]

23. The source of capital that has a special tax advantage to the firm is.

   (*a*) preferred stock
   (*b*) common stock
   (*c*) debt
   (*d*) retained earnings

   [Section 14-2]

24. Which of a firm's sources of new capital has the highest after-tax cost?

(*a*) Preferred stock
(*b*) Debt
(*c*) Common stock
(*d*) Retained earnings

[Section 14-2]

25. Specific costs of capital may vary over time, due to changes in

(*a*) the supply and demand for funds
(*b*) the risk characteristics of the firm
(*c*) the marketability of the securities
(*d*) All of the above

[Section 14-2]

26. The cost of new preferred stock is equal to

(*a*) the preferred stock dividend divided by the net proceeds
(*b*) the preferred stock dividend divided by the market price
(*c*) the preferred stock dividend divided by the par value
(*d*) (1 − tax rate) multiplied by the preferred stock dividend divided by the net proceeds

[Section 14-2B]

27. When the Gordon constant growth model is used, the cost of retained earnings equals

(*a*) the current dividend plus the expected growth in sales
(*b*) the current market price plus expected growth rate in dividends
(*c*) the expected dividend yield plus the expected growth rate in dividends
(*d*) the expected dividend payout plus the expected growth rate in dividends

[Section 14-2C]

28. Which of the following approaches can be used to estimate the cost of common equity?

(*a*) The Gordon constant growth model
(*b*) The capital asset pricing model
(*c*) Generalized risk premium approach
(*d*) All of the above

[Section 14-2C]

29. In developing a weighted marginal cost of capital schedule, the levels at which a specific cost of capital increases are called:

(*a*) flotation costs
(*b*) market value weights
(*c*) break points
(*d*) target weights

[Section 14-4A]

30. Using the intersection rate of the IOS and WMCC schedules as the discount rate for all proposed capital budget projects is appropriate if:

(*a*) all the projects typify the firm's overall or average risk
(*b*) all the projects are equally risky
(*c*) all the projects have low risk
(*d*) all the projects have high risk

[Section 14-4B]

Answers

True or False		*Multiple Choice*
1. True	11. False	21. d
2. True	12. True	22. a
3. True	13. True	23. c
4. False	14. False	24. c
5. True	15. False	25. d
6. True	16. False	26. a
7. False	17. True	27. c
8. False	18. True	28. d
9. True	19. True	29. c
10. False	20. False	30. a

SOLVED PROBLEMS

PROBLEM 14-1: Powell, Inc. recently sold bonds having a $1,000 par value for $1,025. Flotation costs of $89.56 per bond reduced the net proceeds from the sale to $935.44 per bond. The bond pays $80 in annual year-end interest and matures in 10 years. If the marginal tax rate is 34 percent, what is the after-tax cost of bonds?

Answer: Substitute $NP_d = \$935.44$, $I = \$80$, $P_n = \$1,000$, and $n = 10$ in Equation 14-1 and use the trial-and-error procedure to find the after-tax cost of bonds (k_d).

$$\$935.44 = \sum_{t=1}^{10} \frac{\$80}{(1 + k_d)^t} + \frac{\$1,000}{(1 + k_d)^{10}}$$

$$k_d = 0.0900 \text{ or } 9.00 \text{ percent}$$

Substituting $k_d = 9.00$ percent and $T = 0.34$ in Equation 14-4, the after-tax cost of new debt is:

$$k_{dt} = (9.00)(1 - 0.34) = 5.94 \text{ percent}$$

[Section 14-2C]

PROBLEM 14-2: Walker Company plans to issue 10-year bonds with a par value of $1,000 that will pay $45 every 6 months. The net proceeds to the firm from the sale of each bond is $937.79. If the firm's tax rate is 34 percent, what is the after-tax cost of new debt?

Answer: Because semiannual interest is used, the interest rate must be halved, $i/2$, and the number of periods doubled, $2n$, for the present value factors. Substitute $NP_d = \$937.79$, $I = \$45$, $P_n = \$1,000$, and $n = 10$ in Equation 14-2 and use a trial-and-error procedure to find the present value factors that equate:

$$\$937.79 = (\$45)(\text{PVIFA}_{i/2,2n}) + (\$1,000)(\text{PVIF}_{i/2,2n})$$

For i or $k_d = 10.00$ percent

$$\$937.79 = (\$45)(\text{PVIFA}_{0.05,20}) + (\$1,000)(\text{PVIF}_{0.05,20})$$

$$= (\$45)(12.462) + (\$1,000)(0.377) = \$560.79 + \$377.00 = \$937.79$$

Substituting $k_d = 10.00$ percent and $T = 0.34$ in Equation 14-4, the after-tax cost of new debt is:

$$k_{dt} = (10.00)(1 - 0.34) = 6.60 \text{ percent} \qquad \textbf{[Section 14-2C]}$$

PROBLEM 14-3: Weaver Corporation is planning to sell a new 12 percent bond maturing in 15 years at $1,000 each. Each bond has a flotation charge of $30. If the firm's marginal tax rate is 34 percent, what is the approximate after-tax cost of new bonds?

Answer: Substituting I = $120 (0.12 × $1,000), P_n = $1,000, NP_d = $970 ($1,000 − $30) and n = 15 in Equation 14-3, the approximate before-tax cost of new debt is:

$$k'_d = \frac{\$120 + (\$1,000 - \$970)/15}{(\$1,000 + \$970)/2} = \frac{\$122}{\$985} = 0.1239 \text{ or } 12.39 \text{ percent}$$

Substituting k'_d = 12.39 percent and T = 0.34 in Equation 14-4, the approximate after-tax cost of new debt is:

$$k'_{dt} = (12.39)(1 - 0.34) = 8.18 \text{ percent} \qquad \textbf{[Section 14-2C]}$$

PROBLEM 14-4: Northern Utility Company has an opportunity to sell new preferred stock for $50.00 per share that pays a $4.50 annual dividend. If each share has a $2.50 flotation charge, what will be the cost of new preferred stock to the firm?

Answer: Substituting D_p = $4.50 and NP_p = $47.50 ($50.00 − $2.50) in Equation 14-5, the cost of new preferred stock is:

$$k_p = \frac{\$4.50}{\$47.50} = 0.0947 \text{ or } 9.47 \text{ percent} \qquad \textbf{[Section 14-2D]}$$

Use the following data for Textilease, Inc. to solve Problems 14-5 through 14-8.

Current market price per share	$40.00
Current dividends per share	$ 2.50
Earnings per share	$ 6.00
Flotation costs per share for sale of new common stock	$ 3.00
Beta on the firm's common stock	0.95
Expected return on the market	0.13
Risk-free rate	0.05
Interest rate on AAA bonds	0.10

Historical pattern of dividend payments

19x1	$1.98
19x2	2.08
19x3	2.23
19x4	2.36
19x5	2.50

PROBLEM 14-5: Answer the following questions regarding Textilease, Inc.

(a) What is the firm's historical growth rate in dividends?
(b) If the firm expects its growth rate to continue, what is the cost of retained earnings using the constant growth model?
(c) What is the cost of new common stock, using the constant growth model?

Answer:

(a) The compound annual growth rate ($FVIF_{i,n}$) at which dividends grew from $1.98 to $2.50 over 4 years is found using Equation 3-14.

$$FVIF_{i,4} = \frac{\text{Ending dividend}}{\text{Beginning dividend}} = \frac{\$2.50}{\$1.98} = 1.263$$

As shown in Appendix A, a $FVIF_{i,4}$ of 1.263 equals approximately 6 percent.
(b) The expected dividends to be received during 19x6, D_1, equal $2.65 (1.06 × $2.50). Substituting D_1 = $2.65, P_0 = $40.00, and g = 0.06 in Equation 14-6, the cost of

retained earnings is:

$$k_r = \frac{\$2.65}{\$40.00} + 0.06 = 0.0663 + 0.06 = 0.1263 \text{ or } 12.63 \text{ percent}$$

(*c*) The net proceeds of the new common stock, NP_s, is \$37.00 (\$40.00 − \$3.00). Substituting $D_1 = \$2.65$, $NP_s = 37.00$ and $g = 0.06$ in Equation 14-10, the cost of new common stock is:

$$k_s = \frac{\$2.65}{\$37.00} + 0.06 = 0.0716 + 0.06 = 0.1316 \text{ or } 13.16 \text{ percent}$$

[Section 14-2E]

PROBLEM 14-6: What is the cost of retained earnings for Texilease, Inc., using the capital asset pricing model (CAPM)?

Answer: Substituting $r_f = 0.05$, $b_i = 0.95$, and $r_m = 0.13$ in Equation 14-7, the estimated cost of retained earnings is:

$$k_r = 0.05 + 0.95(0.13 - 0.05) = 0.050 + 0.076$$
$$= 0.1260 \text{ or } 12.60 \text{ percent} \qquad \text{[Section 14-2E]}$$

PROBLEM 14-7: The management of Textilease, Inc. estimates that its risk premium, r_p, on common equity is 2.50 percentage points above the interest rate on AAA bonds. What is the cost of retained earnings for Textilease, Inc., using the generalized risk premium method?

Answer: Substituting $k_d = 0.10$ and $r_p = 0.025$ in Equation 14-8, the cost of retained earnings is:

$$k_r = 0.100 + 0.025 = 0.1250 \text{ or } 12.50 \text{ percent} \qquad \text{[Section 14-2E]}$$

PROBLEM 14-8: Using the earnings-price ratio, what is the cost of retained earnings for Textilease, Inc.?

Answer: Substituting $E = \$6.00$ and $P_o = \$40.00$ in Equation 14-9, the cost of retained earnings is:

$$k_r = \frac{\$6.00}{\$40.00} = 0.1500 \text{ or } 15.00 \text{ percent} \qquad \text{[Section 14-2E]}$$

PROBLEM 14-9: Peak Manufacturing Company has the following capital structure stated in book value terms:

Source of Capital	Book Value
Bonds (\$1,000 par, 8.5% coupon)	\$3,000,000
Preferred stock (25,000 shares at \$20 par)	500,000
Common stock (200,000 shares outstanding at \$1 par)	200,000
Capital in excess of par	3,800,000
Retained earnings	2,500,000
Total	\$10,000,000

The firm's bonds are currently selling for \$965 per bond, the preferred stock for \$18 per share, and the common stock for \$40 a share. What is the market value of each source of capital?

Answer: The market value of each source of capital is found as follows:

Source of Capital	Number of Securities (1)	Market Price (2)	Market Value (1) × (2)
Bonds	3,000*	$965	$2,895,000
Preferred stock	25,000	18	450,000
Common equity	200,000	40	8,000,000
Total			$11,345,000

* $3,000,000 book value/$1,000 per bond = 3,000 bonds   **[Section 14-3B]**

PROBLEM 14-10: Martin Enterprises has compiled the following information about its capital structure and estimated costs of new financing:

Source of Capital	Book Value	Market Value	After-tax Cost %
Long-term debt	$2,000,000	$1,800,000	7.00
Preferred stock	500,000	600,000	12.00
Common equity	1,500,000	3,600,000	16.00
Total	$4,000,000	$6,000,000	

The company expects to have a significant amount of retained earnings available and does not expect to sell any additional common stock.

(*a*) What is the firm's weighted average cost of capital, using book value weights?
(*b*) What is the firm's weighted average cost of capital, using market value weights?

Answer:

(*a*) The book value weights are:

$$w_d = \frac{\$2,000,000}{\$4,000,000} = 0.500 \qquad w_p = \frac{\$500,000}{\$4,000,000} = 0.125$$

$$w_s = \frac{\$1,500,000}{\$4,000,000} = 0.375$$

Substituting the books value weights and the after-tax costs of capital in Equation 14-11, the firm's weighted average cost of capital is 11.00 percent.

$$\text{WACC} = (0.500)(0.0700) + (0.125)(0.1200) + (0.375)(0.1600)$$
$$= 0.0350 + 0.0150 + 0.0600 = 0.1100 \text{ or } 11.00 \text{ percent}$$

(*b*) The market value weights are:

$$w_d = \frac{\$1,800,000}{\$6,000,000} = 0.30 \qquad w_p = \frac{\$600,000}{\$6,000,000} = 0.10$$

$$w_s = \frac{\$3,600,000}{\$6,000,000} = 0.60$$

Substituting the market value weights and the after-tax costs of capital in Equation 14-11, the firm's weighted average cost of capital is 12.90 percent.

$$\text{WACC} = (0.30)(0.0700) + (0.10)(0.1200) + (0.60)(0.1600)$$
$$= 0.0210 + 0.0120 + 0.0960 = 0.1290 \text{ or } 12.90 \text{ percent}$$

[Section 14-3B]

PROBLEM 14-11: Thomas International's current capital structure of 35 percent debt and 65 percent equity is considered to be optimal. If the firm raises additional capital in proportion its current structure, what amount of total investment can be financed by a $26,000,000 addition to retained earnings?

Answer: Substituting TF_i = $26,000,000 and w_i = 0.65 in Equation 14-12, the break point of total new investment (financing) is:

$$BP_i = \frac{\$26,000,000}{0.65} = \$40,000,000 \qquad \text{[Section 14-4A]}$$

PROBLEM 14-12: Tony Abell, vice-president of finance of United Telecommunications, Inc. (UTI), has to decide which of the following five projects should be selected.

Project	Investment Cost (in millions)	IRR %
A	$6	18.0
B	5	16.0
C	3	15.0
D	2	14.0
E	6	12.0

UTI finances all expansion with 40 percent debt and 60 percent equity. After considering flotation costs, the before-tax cost of new debt is 8 percent for the first $3,200,000 and 12 percent for any additional debt. The firm expects to have $7,200,000 in internally generated funds for investment purposes during the coming year. The firm's common stock is currently selling for $50 and its current dividend is $2.50 per share. UTI's growth rate is expected to continue at a constant rate of 10 percent per year. Flotation costs are 15 percent of the selling price of the new common stock. The corporate tax rate is 34 percent and all projects are of average risk.

(a) Calculate the after-tax cost of debt and equity for the ranges of total new financing associated with each source of capital.
(b) Determine the break points in the firm's weighted marginal cost of capital schedule.
(c) Calculate the weighted marginal cost of capital (WMCC) for each range of total new financing.
(d) Plot the firm's investment opportunities schedule (IOS) and its WMCC schedule on the same graph.
(e) Which available projects, if any, should UTI accept? Explain why.

Answer:

(a) Using Equation 14-4, the after-tax cost of debt is:

$$\begin{aligned} \textit{Up to \$3,200,000} \qquad & k_d = (8.00)(1 - 0.34) = 5.28 \text{ percent} \\ \textit{Over \$3,200,000} \qquad & k_d = (12.00)(1 - 0.34) = 7.92 \text{ percent} \end{aligned}$$

The expected dividend, D_1, is $2.75 (1.10 × $2.50). Using Equation 14-6, the cost of retained earnings is 15.50 percent.

$$\textit{Up to \$7,200,000} \qquad k_r = \frac{\$2.75}{\$50.00} + 0.10$$

$$= 0.0550 + 0.10 = 0.01550 \text{ or } 15.50 \text{ percent}$$

The flotation costs per share are $7.50 (0.15 × $50.00).

Substituting D_1 = $2.75, NP_s = $42.50 ($50.00 − $7.50), and g = 0.10 in Equation 14-10, the cost of new common stock is 16.47 percent.

$$\textit{Over \$7,200,000} \qquad k_s = \frac{\$2.75}{\$42.50} + 0.10$$

$$= 0.0647 + 0.10 = 0.1647 \text{ or } 16.47 \text{ percent}$$

[Sections 14-2A and 14-2E]

(*b*) Using Equation 14-12, the break points are:

$$\text{Break point for debt} = \frac{\$3{,}200{,}000}{0.40} = \$8{,}000{,}000$$

$$\text{Break point for equity} = \frac{\$7{,}200{,}000}{0.60} = \$12{,}000{,}000$$

Thus, debt will cost 5.28 percent up to \$8,000,000 and 7.92 percent over \$8,000,000, whereas equity will cost 15.50 percent up to \$12,000,000 and 16.47 percent over \$12,000,000.   **[Section 14-4A]**

(*c*) The WMCC for each range of total new financing is calculated using Equation 14-11, as follows:

Range of Total New Financing (in millions)	Weighted Marginal Cost of Capital (WMCC)
Up to \$8	$\text{WMCC}_1 = (0.40)(0.0528) + (0.60)(0.1550)$
	$= 0.0211 + 0.0930 = 0.1141$ or 11.41 percent
\$8 up to \$12	$\text{WMCC}_2 = (0.40)(0.0792) + (0.60)(0.1550)$
	$= 0.0317 + 0.0930 = 0.1247$ or 12.47 percent
Over \$12	$\text{WMCC}_3 = (0.40)(0.0792) + (0.60)(0.1647)$
	$= 0.0317 + 0.0988 = 0.1305$ or 13.05 percent

[Section 14-3A]

(*d*) Figure 14-5 shows the IOS and WMCC schedules.   **[Section 14-4B]**

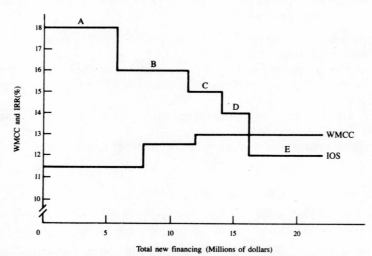

FIGURE 14-5   IOS and WMCC Telecommunications schedules for United Inc.

(*e*) UTI should adopt Projects A, B, C, and D for a total capital budget of \$16,000,000. Selecting these four projects provides an optimal capital budget that maximizes the value of the firm.   **[Section 14-4B]**

15 CAPITAL STRUCTURE

THIS CHAPTER IS ABOUT

- ☑ Concept of Capital Structure
- ☑ Capital Structure Theory
- ☑ Capital Structure Policy

15-1. Concept of Capital Structure

Capital structure is the mix of various types of debt and equity capital used by the firm. Generally, only permanent sources of capital, including permanent short-term debt, long-term debt, preferred stock, and common equity, are considered as part of a firm's capital structure. Management is concerned with changes in capital structure because of the impact on the firm's value and cost of capital. The financial manager's objective in making financing decisions is to find the particular financing mix that maximizes the total market value of the firm, which is consistent with the firm's goal of shareholder wealth maximization. This objective is referred to as the *optimal capital structure*.

15-2. Capital Structure Theory

There are numerous theories that attempt to explain how changes in financial leverage, or the use of debt, affect the value of a firm and its cost of capital. These theories address two questions: Can a firm increase shareholder wealth by replacing some of its equity with debt, and, if so, how much debt should it use? Three theories of capital structure are examined: the traditional approach, the Modigliani and Miller (MM) approach, and the contemporary approach.

The MM model without corporate taxes leads to the conclusion that there is no one optimal capital structure. Both the traditional and contemporary approaches hold that there is an optimal capital structure for each firm, but for different reasons. Empirical research on the exact relationship among leverage, value, and cost of capital has not produced definitive results. However, managers generally subscribe to the concept of an optimal capital structure.

A. The differences among the three approaches result from differing assumptions about how investors value a firm's debt and equity.

Both traditional and Modigliani and Miller (MM) theories share several common assumptions.

1. Financing occurs only through two types of capital: long-term debt and common stock.
2. The firm's investment decision is fixed, but its capital structure can be changed by issuing bonds to repurchase stock or issuing stock to retire debt.
3. There are no taxes or bankruptcy costs.

4. All earnings are paid out as dividends.
5. Net operating income, also called earnings before interest and taxes (EBIT), is constant.
6. Business risk is constant.

The MM model also assumes perfect capital markets, which implies no transaction costs and rational investor behavior. This set of assumptions holds constant all influences on firm value and cost of capital other than capital structure. These restrictive assumptions reduce the realism of the traditional and MM approach but provide a starting point for understanding the theory of capital structure. The contemporary approach relaxes some of these simplifying assumptions.

B. Given these assumptions, the impact of financial leverage on the firm can be found using several valuation and cost of capital models.

In several of the following equations, the term $(1 - T)$, where T is the corporate tax rate, is used. Taxes are irrelevant when using the traditional and MM approaches, but must be included in the contemporary theory.

1. Equations 15-1 through 15-4 are cost of capital models.
   Equation 15-1 is used to calculate the interest rate on the firm's single class of perpetual debt (bonds), k_{dt}. In a world with no taxes, $k_{dt} = k_d$.

COST OF DEBT
$$k_{dt} = \frac{I(1 - T)}{D} \tag{15-1}$$

where I = annual interest charge, $k_d D$
       D = market value of debt outstanding
       T = corporate tax rate

Equation 15-2 is used to calculate the required rate of return on the firm's common stock, k_s.

COST OF EQUITY
$$k_s = \frac{(EBIT - I)(1 - T)}{S} \tag{15-2}$$

where EBIT = earnings before interest and taxes
       S = market value of common stock outstanding

Equation 15-3 and 15-4 are alternative methods used to calculate the weighted average cost of capital, k_a.

WEIGHTED AVERAGE COST OF CAPITAL
$$k_a = w_d k_d (1 - T) + w_s k_s \tag{15-3}$$

and

$$k_a = \frac{EBIT(1 - T)}{V} \tag{15-4}$$

where w_d = market value weight of debt, D/V
       w_s = market value weight of common stock, S/V
       V = total market value of the firm, $D + S$

2. Equations 15-5 through 15-7 are valuation models.
   Equation 15-5 shows that the market value of equity is calculated by capitalizing net income by the cost of equity, k_s. *Capitalizing* is the process of converting a series of future payments into a single present value, by dividing by a discount rate called a capitalization rate.

MARKET VALUE OF EQUITY
$$S = \frac{(EBIT - I)(1 - T)}{k_s} \tag{15-5}$$

Equations 15-6 and 15-7 are alternative methods of calculating the total market value of the firm, V. The market value of debt is simply the dollar value of debt outstanding, D.

TOTAL MARKET VALUE OF THE FIRM

$$V = D + S \tag{15-6}$$

and

$$V = \frac{EBIT(1 - T)}{k_a} \tag{15-7}$$

Since EBIT is held constant, the lower the value of the weighted average cost of capital, k_a, the higher the value of the firm, V. Thus, the capital structure that maximizes the value of the firm also minimizes the weighted average cost of capital.

C. **The traditional approach to capital structure suggests that a firm can lower its weighted average cost of capital and increase its market value by the judicious use of financial leverage.**

1. This theory suggests that there is a tradeoff between cheaper debt and higher priced equity that leads to an optimal capital structure. Thus, the cost of capital and the firm's value are not independent of its capital structure. Figure 15-1A shows that as lower cost debt, k_d, is substituted for higher cost equity, k_s, the weighted average cost of capital, k_a, declines to a minimum, D/V^*, and then increases. These relationships produce a U-shaped weighted average cost of capital curve. Figure 15-1B shows that the market value of the firm first rises, reaches its peak at point D/V^* where k_a is minimized, and finally declines as leverage increases.

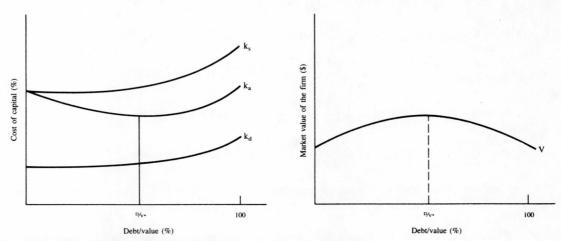

FIGURE 15-1A and 1B   Traditional approach to capital structure.

2. The traditional approach attributes the changing cost of debt and equity to changing investor attitudes toward risk. Both k_d and k_s are almost constant under "moderate" amounts of debt. However, when debt becomes excessive, both k_d and k_s increase in response to the risk.

EXAMPLE 15-1: Glazer Fitness Center (GFC) currently has no debt but is considering two plans to add leverage. Plan A involves issuing $100,000 in bonds and Plan B involves issuing $300,000 in bonds. Under both proposals, the proceeds from issuing bonds are used to retire the same amount of common stock. Data about the corporation's current and proposed capital structures are shown on page 326. Management wants to assess the impact of increasing GFC's financial leverage. Assume the traditional approach with no taxes.

		Capital Structures	
	Current	Plan A	Plan B
Cost of debt, k_d	0	0.070	0.090
Cost of equity, k_s	0.100	0.105	0.120
EBIT	$100,000	$100,000	$100,000
Debt, D	0	200,000	300,000
Interest, I	0	14,000	27,000

(a) Using Equation 15-5, the market value of equity is:

Current Capital Structure
$$S = \frac{\$100,000 - \$0}{0.100} = \$1,000,000$$

Plan A
$$S = \frac{\$100,000 - \$14,000}{0.105} = \frac{\$86,000}{0.105} = \$819,048$$

Plan B
$$S = \frac{\$100,000 - \$27,000}{0.120} = \frac{\$73,000}{0.120} = \$608,333$$

Using Equation 15-6, the market value of the firm is:

Current Capital Structure
$$V = \$0 \quad + \$1,000,000 = \$1,000,000$$

Plan A
$$V = \$200,000 + \$819,048 = \$1,019,048$$

Plan B
$$V = \$300,000 + \$608,333 = \$908,333$$

Thus, the market value of the firm is increased from $1,000,000 to $1,019,048 under Plan A but decreases to $908,333 under Plan B.

(b) Using Equation 15-4, the weighted average cost of capital is:

Current Capital Structure
$$k_a = \frac{\$100,000}{\$1,000,000} = 0.100 \text{ or } 10.0 \text{ percent}$$

Plan A
$$k_a = \frac{\$100,000}{\$1,019,048} = 0.098 \text{ or } 9.8 \text{ percent}$$

Plan B
$$k_a = \frac{\$100,000}{\$908,333} = = 0.110 \text{ or } 11.0 \text{ percent}$$

The weighted average cost of capital decreases from 10.0 percent to 9.8 percent under Plan A but increases to 11.0 percent under Plan B.

(c) Plan A is preferred over both the current capital structure and Plan B. Plan A has the highest market value and the lowest cost of capital of the three capital structures. Based on the data provided, the firm's optimal capital structure is not known. However, GFC's optimal capital structure must be less the debt/value ratio of about 33.0 percent ($300,000/$908,333) of Plan B.

D. **The Modigliani and Miller approach asserts that, in the absence of taxes and other market imperfections, both the weighted average cost of capital and the firm's value are completely unaffected by its capital structure.**

Modigliani and Miller contend that the firm's value is determined by its real assets, not by the securities it issues. Thus, capital structure is irrelevant and all capital structures are equally desirable. This theory holds under very restrictive assumptions and carries little credibility in practice. Figure 15-2A shows that, at all levels of debt, the higher cost of equity, k_s, is sufficient to exactly offset the lower cost of debt, k_d, and thus leads to a constant weighted average cost of capital, k_a. Figure 15-2B indicates that the value of the firm is independent of its financial leverage.

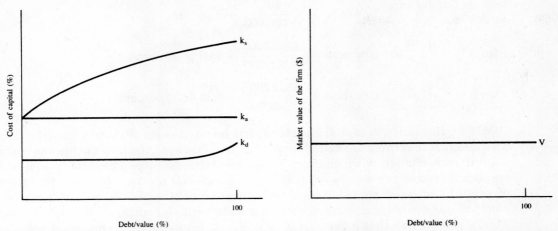

FIGURE 15-2A and 2B   Modigliani and Miller approach to capital structure without corporate taxes.

EXAMPLE 15-2: Assume the same situation as presented in Example 15-1 for Glazer Fitness Center (GFC), but use the following data:

	Current	Capital Structures Plan A	Plan B
Cost of debt, k_d	0	0.08	0.80
WACC, k_a	0.10	0.10	0.10
EBIT	$100,000	$100,000	$100,000
Debt, D	0	200,000	300,000
Interest, I	0	16,000	24,000

Management wants to assess the impact of increasing GFC's financial leverage. Assume the MM approach with no taxes.

(*a*) Since the MM approach without taxes assumes that both EBIT and k_a remain constant regardless of changes in leverage, the value of the firm cannot be altered through leverage. Substituting EBIT = $100,000 and k_a = 0.10 in Equation 15-7, the market values of the current and proposed capital structures are:

Current and Proposed Capital Structures $V = \dfrac{\$100,000}{0.10} = \$1,000,000$

(*b*) Using Equation 15-6 and solving for the market value of equity gives $S = V - D$. Thus, the market value of equity is:

Current Capital Structure   S = $1,000,000 − $0 = $1,000,000

Plan A   S = $1,000,000 − $200,000 = $800,000

Plan B   S = $1,000,000 − $300,000 = $700,000

Using Equation 15-2, the cost of equity is:

Current Capital Structure $k_s = \dfrac{\$100,000}{\$1,000,000} = 0.100$ or 10.0 percent

Plan A $k_s = \dfrac{\$100,000 - \$16,000}{\$800,000} = 0.105$ or 10.5 percent

Plan B $k_s = \dfrac{\$100,000 - \$24,000}{\$700,000} = 0.109$ or 10.9 percent

(c) The debt/value ratio is computed by dividing the market debt by the market value of the firm.

Current Capital
Structure $\text{D/V ratio} = \dfrac{\$0}{\$1,000,000} = 0 \text{ percent}$

Plan A $\text{D/V ratio} = \dfrac{\$200,000}{\$1,000,000} = 0.20 \text{ or } 20 \text{ percent}$

Plan B $\text{D/V ratio} = \dfrac{\$300,000}{\$1,000,000} = 0.30 \text{ or } 30 \text{ percent}$

MM's irrelevance to capital structure rests on an absence of market imperfections. To the extent that there are market imperfections, however, the firm's value and cost of capital may change with changes in its capital structure. The MM model with corporate income taxes shows that the use of financial leverage lowers a firm's cost of capital and raises its value because interest on debt is tax deductible. Thus, in a world of corporate income taxes, there is a substantial advantage when debt is used. Figure 15-3A shows that if the cost of debt, $k_{d(1-t)}$, is unaffected by financial leverage, then the weighted average cost of capital, k_a, declines as the firm borrows more. Figure 15-3B indicates that value is maximized with virtually 100 percent debt financing. This result is consistent with MM assumptions, but it is not observed in practice.

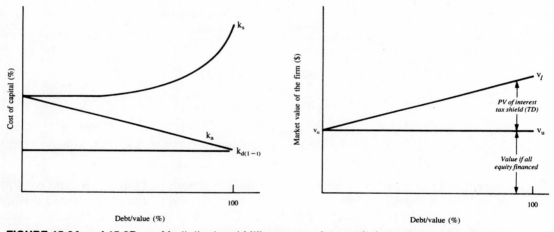

FIGURE 15-3A and 15-3B   Modigliani and Miller approach to capital structure with corporate taxes.

Equation 15-8 shows that the value of an unlevered firm with taxes, V_u, is the firm's net income divided by its cost of equity.

**VALUE OF AN UNLEVERED
FIRM WITH CORPORATE TAXES** $V_U = \dfrac{\text{EBIT}(1-T)}{k_{su}}$ (15-8)

where k_{su} = cost of equity of an unlevered firm

Equation 15-9 shows that the value of a levered firm with taxes, V_L, is the value of an unlevered firm of the same risk class, V_U, plus the present value of the interest tax shield, TD. In essence, the government pays a subsidy to the levered company to use debt.

**VALUE OF A LEVERED
FIRM WITH CORPORATE TAXES** $V_l = V_u + TD$ (15-9)

where   TD = present value of the interest tax shield

The **interest tax shield** is defined as the corporate tax rate, T, times the interest payment, which is determined by multiplying k_d times D. Equation 15-10 shows that if the debt employed by a company is permanent, the present value of the interest tax shield using the perpetuity formula is:

PRESENT VALUE OF
TAX SHIELD

$$TD = \frac{T_{k_d}D}{k_d}$$

(15-10)

EXAMPLE 15-3: Glazer Fitness Center (GFC) has earnings before interest and taxes of $100,000 and a 34 percent corporate tax rate. The firm's before-tax cost of debt is 8 percent and its cost of equity in the absence of borrowing is 10 percent. Management wants to assess the value of GFC with no leverage, with $200,000 in debt, and with $300,000 in debt. Assume an MM approach with corporate taxes.

(*a*) Substituting EBIT = $100,000, $T = 0.34$, and $k_{su} = 0.10$ in Equation 15-8, GFC's value with no leverage is:

$$V_u = \frac{(\$100,000)(1 - 0.34)}{0.10} = \frac{\$66,000}{0.10} = \$660,000$$

(*b*) Substituting $V_u = \$660,000$, $T = 0.34$, and $D = \$200,000$ in Equation 15-9, GFC's value with a $200,000 debt is:

$$V_l = \$660,000 + (0.34)(\$200,000) = \$728,000$$

GFC's value with a $300,000 debt is:

$$V_l = \$660,000 + (0.34)(\$300,000) = \$762,000$$

Due to the interest tax shelter, the firm is able to increase its value in a linear manner with more debt.

E. The *contemporary approach* to capital structure asserts that there is an optimal capital structure, or at least an optimal range of structures, for every firm.

The contemporary approach identifies several factors that can lead to an optimal capital structure for a given firm, such as tax effects (corporate and personal), financial distress, and related costs.

- *Corporate income taxes.* In the absence of personal taxes, the use of debt in the capital structure of a corporation reduces its cost of raising capital because interest on debt is tax deductible.
- *Personal taxes.* Corporate taxes are not the only taxes to consider in determining the financing mix because bondholders and stockholders must pay taxes on the returns they receive from the firm. The tax advantage associated with leverage is reduced, but not eliminated, by the personal taxes which debt and equity holders have to pay. Although it is unclear how much the corporate tax shield is offset by personal taxes, the net tax advantage of using debt is positive as long as the personal tax on stock income is less than that on debt income.
- *Financial distress and related costs.* Using debt involves costs and benefits. These costs include costs of financial distress and related costs. **Financial distress** refers to a broad spectrum of problems, ranging from relatively minor liquidity shortages to bankruptcy. **Bankruptcy** is an extreme form of financial distress involving a legal procedure to liquidate a business. The risk of bankruptcy, as well as the probability of a bankruptcy-related loss of value, increase with financial leverage. Related costs that may cause the value of the firm to decline with increases in debt include the effects of high leverage and a weak balance sheet on expected future EBIT, **agency costs** (costs arising from the separation of ownership and management when professional managers are hired), and a higher corporate interest rate at high debt levels. The inclusion of financial distress and related costs partially offsets the tax advantage and explains why firms do not finance entirely by debt. Figure 15-4, page 330, shows the net effects of financial leverage on the value of the firm.

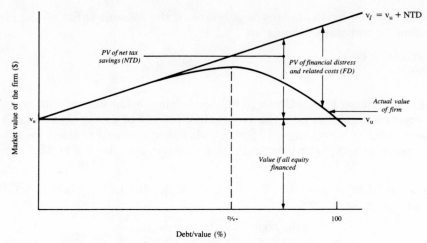

FIGURE 15-4   Net effects of leverage on the value of the firm

F. An optimal capital structure involves a tradeoff of the benefits of debt against the expected costs of financial distress and related costs.

With contemporary theory, the optimal debt level exists, at which point the marginal benefits of financial leverage equal the marginal costs. Equation 15-11 indicates the value of a levered firm, V_l, considering tax effects, financial distress, and related costs.

**VALUE OF A LEVERED FIRM
WITH TAXES, FINANCIAL
DISTRESS, AND RELATED COSTS**
$$V_l = V_u + NDT - FD$$
(15-11)

> *where*   NTD = present value of net tax savings (corporate and personal)
> FD = present value of financial distress and related costs

Figure 15-5A shows that k_a declines because of the favorable net tax treatment given debt, and then rises at relatively high degrees of financial leverage because of high bankruptcy costs and related costs. Figure 15-5B shows the value of the firm with taxes, financial distress, and related costs. It is interesting to note that Figures 15-5A and 15-5B look very similar to Figures 15-1A and 15-1B, which represent the traditional approach.

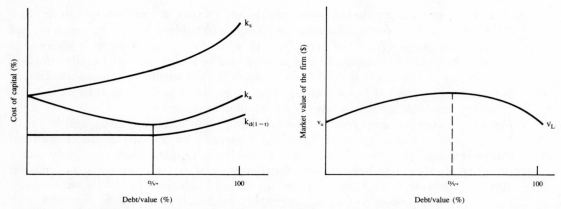

FIGURE 15-5A and 15-5B   Contemporary approach to capital structure with taxes, financial distress and related costs.

EXAMPLE 15-4: Glazer Fitness Center (GFC) is considering various levels of debt. Presently, it has no debt and has a total market value of $660,000. By issuing debt, management believes it can achieve a net tax advantage (corporate and personal combined) equal to 20 percent of the amount of the debt. However, management expects the cost of financial distress and related costs to increase at an increasing rate with leverage.

Management estimates the present value of financial distress and related costs for various levels of debt to be:

Level of Debt	Present Value of Financial Distress and Related Costs, FD
$100,000	$ 0
200,000	10,000
300,000	25,000
400,000	40,000
500,000	70,000
600,000	120,000

Using Equation 15-11, the market value of the firm is:

Level of Debt	V_u	NTD	FD	V_l
$100,000	$660,000 + (0.20)($100,000) − $ 0			= $680,000
$200,000	$660,000 + (0.20)($200,000) − $ 10,000			= $690,000
$300,000	$660,000 + (0.20)($300,000) − $ 25,000			= $695,000
$400,000	$660,000 + (0.20)($400,000) − $ 40,000			= $700,000*
$500,000	$660,000 + (0.20)($500,000) − $ 70,000			= $690,000
$600,000	$660,000 + (0.20)($600,000) − $120,000			= $660,000

* The market value of GFC is maximized with $400,000 in debt.

15-3. Capital Structure Policy

Capital structure policy involves a choice between risk and expected returns associated with the firm's financing mix. In planning its capital structure, the first major policy decision facing the firm is to determine the appropriate level of debt. Financial leverage increases the expected return on a firm's equity at the expense of increased risk. Thus, there is a tradeoff between risk and return when making capital structure decisions. The capital structure that balances risk and return to maximize the value of a firm is the **optimal capital structure**.

Although it is theoretically possible to determine a firm's optimal capital structure, financial managers cannot determine the precise percentage of debt that will maximize the market value of the firm. Thus, the final decision is somewhat subjective, but it can be based upon the best information available. In practice, financial managers use informed judgment to set a desired or **target capital structure**. This structure represents a range of values over which the firm's financial leverage varies. To the left of this range, the firm should sell debt; to the right of this range, it should sell equity. Financial managers use several analytical approaches for comparing financing alternatives.

A. *EBIT–EPS analysis* **is an analytical technique used to evaluate various capital structures in order to select the one that maximizes a firm's earnings per share (EPS).**

The EBIT–EPS analysis examines the impact of financing alternatives on EPS at different levels of EBIT. (See Chapters 6 and 7 for the calculation of EPS.) With financial leverage, EPS becomes more sensitive to changes in EBIT. The financing plans are often shown graphically on an **EBIT–EPS analysis chart**, with EBIT on the horizontal or x-axis and EPS on the vertical or y-axis. An EBIT–EPS analysis chart allows the decision maker to visualize the impact of different financing plans on EPS over a range of EBIT levels.

1. A major objective of EBIT–EPS analysis is to determine the EBIT–EPS indifference, or breakeven, points between the various financing choices. An **indifference point** is that level of EBIT where the EPS of a firm is the same, regardless which alternate capital structures are employed. At EBIT levels above the indifference point, firms with more financially levered capital structures will produce higher levels of EPS; at EBIT levels below the indifference point, firms with less financially levered capital structures will produce higher levels of EPS.
2. The indifference point between two methods of financing can be determined graphically or mathematically.

   - *Graphically*, the indifference point is found assuming two EBIT values and calculating the EPS associated with them for each financing plan. One of the points is the EPS calculated for some hypothetical level of EBIT. The second point can be the EBIT necessary to cover all fixed financial costs for a particular plan. This point, called the **financial breakeven point**, is the level of EBIT at which the firm's EPS equals zero. Thus, the financial breakeven point is the x-axis intercept of the EBIT–EPS analysis chart. Equation 15-12 shows the financial breakeven point, F_b.

FINANCIAL BREAKEVEN POINT
$$F_b = I + \frac{PD}{1 - T}$$
(15-12)

$$\begin{aligned} where \quad I \ &= \ \text{annual interest payments on outstanding debt} \\ &\quad\ \text{and proposed debt} \\ PD \ &= \ \text{preferred stock dividends} \\ T \ &= \ \text{corporate tax rate} \end{aligned}$$

In practice, however, it does not make any difference which hypothetical level of EBIT is chosen for calculating EPS since the relationship between EBIT and EPS is linear. The two points calculated for each financing plan are plotted on an EBIT–EPS analysis chart and connected with a straight line. The intersection point of these two lines is the indifference point.

   - *Mathematically*, the indifference point is found by solving for EBIT in Equation 15-13.

INDIFFERENCE POINT
$$\frac{(EBIT^* - I_1)(1 - T) - PD}{n_1} = \frac{(EBIT^* - I_2)(1 - T) - PD}{n_2}$$
(15-13)

$$\begin{aligned} where \quad EBIT^* \ &= \ \text{EBIT indifference point between the two methods of financing} \\ I_1, I_2 \ &= \ \text{total interest payments after financing for Plans 1 and 2, respectively} \\ n_1, n_2 \ &= \ \text{number of shares of common stock outstanding after financing for} \\ &\quad\ \text{Plans 1 and 2, respectively} \end{aligned}$$

EXAMPLE 15-5: Clark Equipment Company's current capital structure consists of 8 percent debt with a market value and book value of $2,000,000, and 100,000 shares of outstanding common stock with a market value of $7,500,000. The firm is considering a $3,000,000 expansion program, using one of the following financing plans:

> Plan A: Sell additional debt at 10 percent interest
> Plan B: Sell preferred stock with a 10.5 percent dividend yield
> Plan C: Sell new common stock at $75 per share

The corporate tax rate is 34 percent. Ignore flotation costs.

(a) If the expected level of EBIT after the expansion is $1,250,000, the EPS for each financing plan is calculated as follows:

	Plan A: Debt	Plan B: Preferred Stock	Plan C: Common Stock
EBIT	$1,250,000	$1,250,000	$1,250,000
— Interest on existing debt	160,000	160,000	160,000
— Interest on new debt	300,000	0	0
Earnings before taxes	$ 790,000	$1,090,000	$1,090,000
— Income taxes (34%)	268,600	370,600	370,600
Net income	$ 521,400	$ 719,400	$ 719,400
— Preferred stock dividends	0	315,000	0
Earnings available to common stockholders	$ 521,400	$ 404,400	$ 719,400
Shares of common stock	100,000	100,000	140,000
Earnings per share	$ 5.21	$ 4.04	$ 5.14

(*b*) Using Equation 15-12, the financial breakeven points are:

Plan A: $F_b = \$460,000$

Plan B: $F_b = \$160,000 + \dfrac{\$315,000}{(1 - 0.34)} = \$160,000 + \$477,273 = \$637,273$

Plan C: $F_b = \$160,000$

(*c*) Figure 15-6 is the EBIT–EPS analysis chart for the three capital structures.

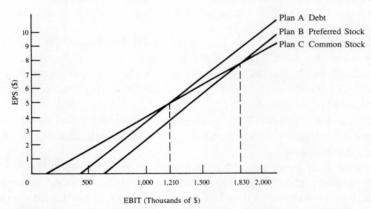

FIGURE 15-6   EBIT–EPS analysis chart for Clark Equipment Company.

(*d*) Figure 15-6 shows that there is one indifference point between debt and common stock and another between preferred stock and common stock. There is no indifference point between debt and preferred stock because debt dominates preferred stock by the same margin throughout the EBIT–EPS analysis chart. Using Equation 15-13, the indifference point between debt and common stock, with thousands of dollars omitted, is $1,210.

$$\text{EPS (debt)} = \text{EPS (common stock)}$$

$$\frac{(\text{EBIT}^* - \$460)(1 - 0.34) - \$0}{100} = \frac{(\text{EBIT}^* - \$160)(1 - 0.34) - \$0}{140}$$

$$(140)(0.66\ \text{EBIT}^* - \$303.60) = (100)(0.66\ \text{EBIT}^* - \$105.60)$$

$$92.4\ \text{EBIT}^* - \$42,504 = 66.0\ \text{EBIT}^* - \$10,560$$

$$26.4\ \text{EBIT}^* = \$31,944$$

$$\text{EBIT}^* = \$1,210 \text{ (in thousands), or } \$1,210,000$$

Similarly, the indifference point between preferred stock and common stock, with thousands of dollars omitted, is $1,830.45.

$$\text{EPS (preferred stock)} = \text{EPS (common stock)}$$

$$\frac{(\text{EBIT}^* - \$160)(1 - 0.34) - \$315}{100} = \frac{(\text{EBIT}^* - \$160)(1 - 0.34) - \$0}{140}$$

$$(140)(0.66\ \text{EBIT}^* - \$105.60 - \$315) = (100)(0.66\ \text{EBIT}^* - \$105.60)$$
$$92.4\ \text{EBIT}^* - \$58,884 = 66.0\ \text{EBIT}^* - \$10,560$$
$$26.4\ \text{EBIT}^* = \$48,324$$
$$\text{EBIT}^* = \$1,830.45 \text{ (in thousands), or } \$1,830,450$$

(e) Plan A (debt) is favored over Plan B (preferred stock) for all levels of EBIT. Plan A is favored over Plan C (common stock) when EBIT is above the indifference point of $1,210,000.

3. When using EBIT–EPS analysis, risk should be considered. EPS is useful as a performance measure but not as a criterion for financing decisions unless risk can be taken into account. There are several approaches for assessing the risks associated with financing alternatives.

- *Develop a probability distribution of the firm's EBIT.* Financial leverage magnifies the variability of EBIT.
- *Compare the intersection point of the financing alternatives with the most likely level of EBIT.* The greater the level of EBIT relative to the indifference point, the stronger the case for using the financing alternative that produces the higher EPS.
- *Determine the probability that EBIT will fall below the indifference point.* Use Equation 4-5 in Chapter 4 where $z = (\text{indifference point} - \text{expected EBIT}) \div$ standard deviation. The lower the probability of downside fluctuations in EBIT, the stronger the case can be made for using the financing alternative that produces the higher EPS.
- *Examine the financial breakeven point with each capital structure.* The higher the financial breakeven point, the greater the risk associated with a particular capital structure.
- *Compute debt management ratios with each capital structure and compare them with industry standards or with other companies having similar business risk.* Use Equations 6-8 through 6-11 in Chapter 6. The higher the financial leverage or the lower the coverage ratios, the greater the risk associated with a particular capital structure. Coverage ratios measure the margin of safety by which earnings and cash flows cover debt service.
- *Survey lenders and investment bankers on their views about an appropriate capital structure.*

EXAMPLE 15-6: Clark Equipment Company estimates its EBIT after expansion to be $1,250,000 and the standard deviation of EBIT to be $400,000 per year. (EBIT is assumed to be normally distributed.) Management is willing to accept a 20 percent chance that EBIT in any given year will be below the indifference point of $1,210,000. The average debt-equity ratio of other companies in the industry is 0.35 and the average times-interest-earned is 6 times. Using the results obtained in Example 15-5 and the data given above, examine the risk-return tradeoff between Plan A (debt financing) and Plan C (common stock financing).

(a) Substituting $r_i = \$1,210,000$, $\bar{r} = \$1,250,000$, and $\sigma = \$400,000$ in Equation 4-5, the z value is:

$$z = \frac{\$1,210,000 - \$1,250,000}{\$400,000} = \frac{-\$40,000}{\$400,000} = -0.10$$

Using Appendix E, the area under the normal curve with $z = -0.10$ is 0.0398. The probability that EBIT will be less than 0.10 standard deviations below the mean is 0.4602 (0.5000 − 0.0398). The 46.02 percent probability of being below the indifference point exceeds the 20 percent probability that the firm is willing to accept. Figure 15-6 on page 333 shows that the debt financing plan produces a higher EPS than the common stock financing plan when the expected EBIT exceeds the indifference point of $1,210,000. Since the expected EBIT is only slightly above the indifference point and the probability of EBIT falling below this point is high, the debt financing alternative is riskier than the common stock financing alternative.

(b) Using Equation 6-10, the times-interest-earned ratios (TIE) with Plan A and Plan C with an expected EBIT of $1,250,000 are:

$$\text{Plan A} \quad \text{TIE ratio} = \frac{\$1,250,000}{\$460,000} = 2.72 \text{ times}$$

$$\text{Plan C} \quad \text{TIE ratio} = \frac{\$1,250,000}{\$160,000} = 7.81 \text{ times}$$

Industry average = 6 times

Under Plan A, the firm's times-interest-earned ratio is below the industry average. Thus, debt financing is riskier than common stock financing.

(c) Plan A has a slightly higher EPS than Plan C, $5.21 versus $5.14, respectively, at the expected EBIT of $1,250,000, but debt financing is also more risky. The final choice must be based on judgment. Based on the limited information, Plan C appears more favorable than Plan A because the common stock financing alternative provides a slightly lower EPS but substantially less risk. However, other factors may mitigate against this conclusion.

4. EBIT–EPS analysis may be criticized because it does not directly consider the long-run financial consequences of certain capital structures and concentrates on the maximization of EPS rather than owner wealth. Maximizing EPS may result in such a high risk level that the cost of capital is not minimized and the firm's market value is not maximized.

B. There are numerous factors that may influence capital structure decisions.

Because of the difficulty in determining a firm's optimal or target capital structure, financial managers depend on both quantitative analysis and judgment in practice. The importance of judgmental factors varies greatly from one situation to another.

1. *Cash flow.* Analyzing the firm's cash flow ability to service fixed charges under various economic conditions is a useful approach to determine the appropriate debt level. Additional debt or preferred stock can increase the burden on cash flow, whereas the sale of stock can improve the firm's cash flow.

2. *Market conditions.* Market conditions can affect both the timing and attractiveness of different sources of financing. When either interest rates or the firm's stock price is low, the use of debt financing can be more attractive than common stock financing. When interest rates or the firm's stock price is high, the sale of stock may become more appealing.

3. *Profitability and stability.* More profitable and stable firms can more safely undertake highly levered capital structures than less profitable and stable firms.

4. *Control.* A management concerned about control may prefer to issue debt rather than common stock because the issuance of debt does not dilute ownership.
5. *Management preferences.* Managements differ regarding their attitudes toward risk in setting their capital structures. For example, a conservative management may place an internal constraint on the use of debt in order to limit the firm's risk exposure to an acceptable level.
6. *Financial flexibility.* Today's financing decision may influence the firm's future financing options. For example, undertaking too much debt may preclude using debt in the future. Thus, financial managers often reserve some borrowing capacity to allow for contingencies and to provide financial flexibility.
7. *Business risk.* The greater the business or operating risk, the less debt the firm should use.

RAISE YOUR GRADES

Can you explain . . . ?

☑ what capital structure is
☑ the financial manager's objective in making financing decisions
☑ what an optimal capital structure is
☑ the similarities and differences between the traditional, Modigliani and Miller, and contemporary approaches to capital structure
☑ how the use of debt can increase the value of the firm
☑ the impact of taxes, financial distress, and related costs on the value of a firm
☑ how a firm might go about determining its optimal or target capital structure
☑ what EBIT–EPS analysis is
☑ how to find an EBIT–EPS indifference point
☑ the major criticisms of EBIT–EPS analysis
☑ how to assess risk in making capital structure decisions
☑ factors other than wealth considerations that may influence capital structure decisions

SUMMARY

1. Capital structure is the composition of a firm's financing, which consists of its permanent sources of capital.
2. The financial manager's objective in making capital structure decisions is to find the financing mix that maximizes the market value of the firm. This structure is called the optimal capital structure.
3. The question of optimal capital structure remains an unresolved issue in finance.
4. Under idealized conditions with no income taxes, the traditional approach to capital structure suggests that there is an optimal capital structure which simultaneously maximizes the firm's market value and minimizes its weighted average cost of capital.
5. Under idealized conditions with no income taxes, the Modigliani and Miller model implies that the total market value and cost of capital are independent of a firm's capital structure.
6. Under idealized conditions with corporate income taxes, the Modigliani and Miller model concludes that leverage affects value, and that firms should be financed with virtually all debt.

7. Under relaxed assumptions, the contemporary approach suggests that there is an optimal range for the capital structure of the firm. If the firm finances outside this range, the value of the firm will decline.

8. Financial leverage increases the expected return on a firm's equity at the expense of increased risk.

9. Increased leverage reduces the firm's tax liability and increases the share of EBIT going to repayment of debt and equity owners. Personal taxes may offset some of the firm's tax deduction benefits on interest.

10. Increased leverage magnifies the probability of financial distress, reduces financial flexibility, and increases certain costs.

11. Choosing an optimal or target capital structure involves a tradeoff among opposing benefits and costs and requires the use of both analytical techniques and informed judgment.

12. A firm can analyze its capital structure by performing an EBIT–EPS analysis; assessing risk associated with various capital structures; computing debt management ratios and comparing them with industry standards; and seeking the opinion of lenders, investment analysts, and investment bankers.

13. EBIT–EPS analysis is useful for evaluating the sensitivity of EPS to changes in EBIT under various financing plans.

14. The indifference point is the EBIT level at which EPS is equal under alternate financing plans. This point may be found either graphically or mathematically.

15. EBIT–EPS analysis may be criticized because it does not directly consider the long-run financial consequences of financing alternatives and concentrates on earnings maximization rather than wealth maximization.

16. Capital structure decisions are tempered by such considerations as cash flow, market conditions, profitability and stability, control, management preferences, financial flexibility, and business risk.

RAPID REVIEW

True or False?

1. Capital structure generally includes all sources of capital used by the firm. [Section 15-1]

2. The objective of capital structure management is to maximize the firm's earnings per share. [Section 15-1]

3. An optimal capital structure is the financing mix that maximizes the market value of the firm. [Section 15-1]

4. The assumptions of the contemporary theory are more realistic than those of either the traditional or the Modigliani and Miller approaches. [Section 15-2A]

5. The traditional approach to capital structure views the market as being indifferent to leverage. [Section 15-2C]

6. According to the traditional approach to capital structure, a firm can maximize its market value by minimizing its cost of capital. [Section 15-2C]

7. The Modigliani and Miller approach without corporate taxes concludes that market value and the cost of capital are independent of the firm's capital structure. [Section 15-2D]

8. The Modigliani and Miller approach with corporate taxes leads to the conclusion that firms should use virtually 100 percent debt financing. [Section 15-2D]

9. An advantage of using debt financing is the tax deductibility of interest. [Sections 15-2D and 15-2E]

10. The contemporary approach to capital structure concludes that one capital structure is as good as any other. [Section 15-2E]

11. The presence of personal taxes tends to reduce the corporate tax advantage associated with debt. [Section 15-2E]

12. Bankruptcy costs work to the disadvantage of leverage, especially extreme leverage. [Section 15-2E]

13. The choice of a target capital structure involves a tradeoff between the benefits and costs of financial leverage. [Section 15-2F]

14. Financial risk increases as the proportion of debt in the firm's capital structure increases. [Section 15-3]

15. An EBIT–EPS analysis chart indicates the firm's optimal capital structure. [Section 15-3A]

16. At the EBIT–EPS indifference point, the EPS of alternative debt and equity financing plans are equal. [Section 15-3A]

17. The financial breakeven point is the level of EBIT for which the firm's EPS equals zero. [Section 15-3A]

18. One criticism of EBIT–EPS analysis is that it concentrates on maximizing EPS rather than shareholder wealth. [Section 15-3A]

19. One method of evaluating the riskiness of a firm's capital structure is to compare its debt management ratios with those of similar firms. [Section 15-3A]

20. Other things held constant, the greater a firm's business risk, the greater its ability to incur a higher proportion of debt in its capital structure. [Section 15-3B]

Multiple Choice

21. An optimal capital structure occurs under the:

    (a) traditional approach
    (b) Modigliani and Miller approach without corporate taxes
    (c) contemporary approach
    (d) Both a and c

    [Section 15-2]

22. The traditional approach to capital structure management assumes

    (a) no taxes
    (b) all earnings are paid out as dividends
    (c) EBIT is constant
    (d) All of the above

    [Section15-2C]

23. The Modigliani and Miller approach without corporate taxes suggests that the firm's weighted average cost of capital

    (a) remains constant as the proportion of debt changes
    (b) increases as the proportion of debt increases
    (c) decreases as the proportion of debt increases
    (d) increases as the proportion of debt decreases

    [Section 15-2D]

24. According to the Modigliani and Miller approach with corporate taxes, all of the following occur as the use of debt financing increases *except*:

    (a) cost of equity increases
    (b) cost of debt decreases
    (c) weighted average cost of capital increases
    (d) market value of the firm increases

    [Section 15-2D]

25. Which approach asserts that the value of the firm is independent of its capital structure?

(*a*) Traditional approach
(*b*) Modigliani and Miller approach without taxes
(*c*) Modigliani and Miller approach with taxes
(*d*) Contemporary approach

[Section 15-2D]

26. The contemporary approach to capital structure management recognizes

(*a*) tax effects
(*b*) bankruptcy costs
(*c*) agency costs
(*d*) All of the above

[Section 15-2E]

27. The inclusion of bankruptcy risk in firm valuation

(*a*) partially offsets the tax advantage of debt
(*b*) recognizes an upper limit to debt financing
(*c*) has no impact on the firm's value
(*d*) Both a and b

[Section 15-2E]

28. EBIT–EPS analysis is used for

(*a*) evaluating the likelihood of financial distress or bankruptcy
(*b*) determining the impact of a change in sales on EBIT
(*c*) examining EPS results of alternate financing plans at varying EBIT levels
(*d*) analyzing the variability of EBIT for each alternative financing plan

[Section 15-3A]

29. For EBIT levels beyond the indifference point,

(*a*) debt EPS increases faster than equity EPS
(*b*) equity EPS increases faster than debt EPS
(*c*) both debt EPS and equity EPS increase at the same rate
(*d*) both debt EPS and equity EPS remain constant

[Section 15-3A]

30. Everything else held constant, management may prefer debt financing to equity financing if

(*a*) dilution of control is a concern
(*b*) both interest rates and the firm's stock price are low
(*c*) the proportion of debt in the firm's capital structure is relatively low by industry standards
(*d*) All of the above

[Section 15-3B]

Answers

True or False

1. False	6. True	11. True	16. True
2. False	7. True	12. True	17. True
3. True	8. True	13. True	18. True
4. True	9. True	14. True	19. True
5. False	10. False	15. False	20. False

Multiple Choice

21. d	26. d
22. d	27. d
23. a	28. c
24. b	29. a
25. b	30. d

SOLVED PROBLEMS

Problems 15-1 through 15-3 refer to the Benet Company.

PROBLEM 15-1 Benet Company has expected earnings before interest and taxes (EBIT) of $800,000 and interest costs of $80,000. The firm's equity and debt capitalization rates are 12 percent and 8 percent, respectively. Assume no corporate income taxes.

(a) What is the market value of the firm?
(b) What is the weighted average cost of capital?

Answer:

(a) Substituting $k_d = 0.08$ and $I = \$80,000$ in Equation 15-1 and solving for D, the market value of debt is:

$$0.08 = \frac{\$80,000}{D} \quad \text{therefore} \quad D = \frac{\$80,000}{0.08} = \$1,000,000$$

Substituting EBIT = $800,000, $I = \$80,000$, and $k_s = 0.12$ in Equation 15-5, the market value of equity is:

$$S = \frac{\$800,000 - \$80,000}{0.12} = \frac{\$720,000}{0.12} = \$6,000,000$$

Substituting $D = \$1,000,000$ and $S = \$6,000,000$ in Equation 15-6, the total market value of the firm is:

$$V = \$1,000,000 + \$6,000,000 = \$7,000,000$$

(b) Substituting EBIT = $800,000 and $V = \$7,000,000$ in Equation 15-4, the weighted average cost of capital is:

$$k_a = \frac{\$800,000}{\$7,000,000} = 0.1143 \text{ or } 11.43 \text{ percent} \qquad \textbf{[Section 15-2B]}$$

PROBLEM 15-2: The Benet Company sells additional debt and uses the proceeds to purchase its common stock. The firm's total interest costs increase to $200,000 but its EBIT remains constant at $800,000. The firm's debt capitalization rate remains at 8 percent but its equity capitalization rate increases to 12.5 percent. Assume no corporate taxes.

(a) What is the total market value of the firm?
(b) What is the weighted average cost of capital?
(c) Is Benet Company operating in a world hypothesized by the traditionalists or by Modigliani and Miller?

Answer:

(a) Substituting $k_d = 0.08$ and $I = \$200,000$ in Equation 15-1 and solving for D, the market value of debt is:

$$0.08 = \frac{\$200,000}{D}, \text{ therefore } \quad D = \frac{\$200,000}{0.08} = \$2,500,000$$

Substituting EBIT = $800,000, $I = \$200,000$, and $k_s = 0.125$ in Equation 15-5, the market value of equity is:

$$S = \frac{\$800,000 - \$200,000}{0.125} = \frac{\$600,000}{0.125} = \$4,800,000$$

Substituting $D = \$2,500,000$ and $S = \$4,800,000$ in Equation 15-6, the total market value of the firm is:

$$V = \$2,500,000 + \$4,800,000 = \$7,300,000$$

(*b*) Substituting EBIT = $800,000 and V = $7,300,000 in Equation 15-4, the weighted average cost of capital is:

$$k_a = \frac{\$800,000}{\$7,300,000} = 0.1096 \text{ or } 10.96 \text{ percent}$$

(*c*) The market value of the firm, V, has increased and the weighted average cost of capital, k_a, has decreased with the use of additional debt. Thus, the firm is operating in a world as viewed by the traditionalists. **[Sections 15-2B through 15-2D]**

PROBLEM 15-3: Assume that the Benet Company described in Problems 15-1 and 15-2 exists in the Modigliani and Miller world without corporate taxes.

(*a*) What is the total market value of the firm?
(*b*) What is the weighted average cost of capital?
(*c*) What is the cost of equity, given the increase in debt capital described in Problem 15-2?

Answer:

(*a*) According to the MM approach, the market value of the firm remains unchanged at $7,000,000 with increased leverage.
(*b*) According to the MM approach, the weighted average cost of capital remains unchanged at 11.43 percent with increased leverage.
(*c*) Substituting V = $7,000,000 and D = $2,500,000 in Equation 15-6 and solving for S, the market value of common stock outstanding is:

$$\$7,000,000 = \$2,500,000 + S$$

$$\textit{therefore } S = \$7,000,000 - \$2,500,000 = \$4,500,000$$

Substituting EBIT = $800,000, I = $200,000, and S = $4,500,000 in Equation 15-2, the cost of equity is:

$$k_s = \frac{\$800,000 - \$200,000}{\$4,500,000} = 0.1333 \text{ or } 13.33 \text{ percent}$$

[Sections 15-2B and 15-2D]

Problems 15-4 and 15-5 refer to Tuttle Transfer Company.

PROBLEM 15-4: Tuttle Transfer Company is financed entirely with 400,000 shares of common stock selling at $25 per share. The firm pays 100 percent of its earnings as dividends. EBIT is expected to remain constant at $1,500,000 in the future. Ignore taxes and assume no growth.
(*a*) What is the total market value of the firm?
(*b*) What is the cost of equity?

Answer:

(*a*) Since the firm has no debt, the market value of the firm is found by multiplying the common stock selling price per share by the number of shares outstanding:

$$S = (\$25)(400,000) = \$10,000,000$$

(*b*) Substituting EBIT = $1,500,000 and S = $10,000,000 in Equation 15-2, the cost of equity is:

$$k_s = \frac{\$1,500,000}{\$10,000,000} = 0.1500 \text{ or } 15.00 \text{ percent} \qquad \textbf{[Section 15-2B]}$$

PROBLEM 15-5: The board of directors of Tuttle Transfer Company decides to retire $3,000,000 in common stock and to replace it with 10 percent long-term debt. The firm's EBIT remains at $1,500,000. According to the Modigliani and Miller approach without corporate taxes, what will be the cost of equity after refinancing?

Answer: Substituting EBIT = \$1,500,000, I = \$300,000 (0.10 × \$3,000,000), and S = \$7,000,000 (\$10,000,000 − \$3,000,000) in Equation 15-2, the cost of equity is:

$$k_s = \frac{\$1,500,000 - \$300,000}{\$7,000,000} = 0.1714 \text{ or } 17.14 \text{ percent}$$

[Sections 15-2B and 15-2D]

PROBLEM 15-6: Chavis Supply Company has a choice of capital structure A or B with the following after-tax cost of capital:

Source of Capital	Capital Structure		After-tax Cost of Capital	
	A	B	A	B
Debt	\$ 3,000,000	\$ 6,000,000	0.08	0.10
Equity	7,000,000	4,000,000	0.14	0.18
Total	\$10,000,000	\$10,000,000		

(a) What is the weighted average costs of capital for each of the capital structures?
(b) Which capital structure is less costly?

Answer:

(a) Substituting w_d = 0.30 (\$3,000,000/\$10,000,000), k_{dt} = 0.08, w_s = 0.70 (\$7,000,000/\$10,000,000), and k_s = 0.14 in Equation 15-3, the weighted average cost of capital under capital structure A is 12.2 percent.

$$k_a = (0.30)(0.08) + (0.70)(0.14) = 0.024 + 0.098$$
$$= 0.122 \text{ or } 12.2 \text{ percent}$$

Substituting w_d = 0.60 (\$6,000,000/\$10,000,000), k_{dt} = 0.10, w_s = 0.40 (\$400,000/\$10,000,000), and k_s = 0.18 in Equation 15-3, the weighted average cost of capital under capital structure B is 13.2 percent.

$$k_a = (0.60)(0.10) + (0.40)(0.18) = 0.060 + 0.072$$
$$= 0.132 \text{ or } 13.2 \text{ percent}$$

(b) Capital structure A is less costly. **[Section 15-2B]**

PROBLEM 15-7: Leete Products has earnings before interest and taxes of \$750,000 and a 34 percent corporate tax rate. The firm's before-tax cost of debt is 10 percent and its cost of equity in the absence of borrowing is 15 percent. Assume an MM approach with corporate taxes.

(a) What is the total market value of Leete Products with no leverage?
(b) What is the total market value of the firm with \$1,000,000 and \$2,000,000 in debt?

Answer:

(a) Substituting EBIT = \$750,000, T = 0.34, and k_{su} = 0.15 in Equation 15-8, the value of Leete Products with no leverage is:

$$V_u = \frac{(\$750,000)(1 - 0.34)}{0.15} = \frac{\$495,000}{0.15} = \$3,300,000$$

(b) Substituting V_u = \$3,300,000, T = 0.34, and D = \$1,000,000 in Equation 15-9, the value with \$1,000,000 in debt is:

$$V_1 = \$3,300,000 + (0.34)(\$1,000,000) = \$3,640,000$$

The total market value with $2,000,000 in debt is:

$$V_1 = \$3,300,000 + (0.34)(\$2,000,000) = \$3,980,000$$

Due to the tax shelter, the firm is able to increase its value in a linear manner with more debt.

[Sections 15-2B and 15-2D]

PROBLEM 15-8: Selman, Inc. is an unlevered firm with an expected EBIT of $2,000,000 per year and a current market value is $20,000,000. Management is considering the use of debt. Debt would be issued and used to repurchase stock, leaving the total amount of financing unchanged. Although the firm recognizes that it cannot determine its optimal capital structure exactly, it is attempting to evaluate six possible capital structures. These capital structures, along with the present value of net tax savings and present value of financial distress and related costs, are given below:

Capital Structure	Amount of Debt in Capital Structure	Present Value of Net Tax Savings	Present Value of Financial Distress and Related Costs
A	$ 2,000,000	$ 300,000	$ 0
B	4,000,000	600,000	50,000
C	8,000,000	1,200,000	125,000
D	12,000,000	1,800,000	400,000
E	14,000,000	2,100,000	1,000,000
F	18,000,000	2,700,000	2,500,000

(a) Using the contemporary approach, which capital structure would you recommend? Why?

(b) What problems exist in using the contemporary approach?

Answer:

(a) Using Equation 15-10, the market value of the firm under each capital structure is:

Capital Structure	V_u	NTD	FD	V_1
A	$20,000,000 +	$ 300,000 −	$ 0 =	$20,300,000
B	$20,000,000 +	$ 600,000 −	$ 30,000 =	$20,550,000
C	$20,000,000 +	$1,200,000 −	$ 125,000 =	$21,075,000
D	$20,000,000 +	$1,800,000 −	$ 400,000 =	$21,400,000
E	$20,000,000 +	$2,100,000 −	$1,000,000 =	$21,100,000
F	$20,000,000 +	$2,700,000 −	$2,500,000 =	$20,200,000

Capital structure *D* is preferred because it provides the greatest market value of the firm.

(b) The major problem in using the contemporary approach is estimating the various inputs. This approach is relatively easy to apply in theory but difficult to use in practice.

[Section 15-2E and 15-2F]

PROBLEM 15-9: Sampson Sporting Goods has a capital structure consisting of 500,000 shares of common stock. The firm currently has no debt or preferred stock. The firm needs to raise $8,000,000 of external financing for capital expansion purposes. Under Plan A, the project will be financed entirely with 9 percent long-term debt. Under Plan B, the firm will sell 250,000 shares of common stock. The firm's corporate tax rate is 34 percent.

(a) Calculate the financial breakeven points for Plan A and Plan B.

(b) Calculate the EBIT–EPS indifference point.

(c) Prepare an EBIT–EPS analysis chart.

(d) Calculate the expected EPS for both financing plans if EBIT is expected to be $2,750,000.

(e) Which financing plan should the company adopt? Why?

Answer:

(a) Substituting I = $720,000 (0.09 × $8,000,000) in Equation 15-12, the financial break-even point under Plan A is:

$$\text{Plan A} \quad F_b = \$720,000$$

Under Plan B, the firm does not have any fixed financial costs (interest or preferred stock dividends). Thus the financial breakeven point under Plan B is:

$$\text{Plan B} \quad F_b = \$0$$

(b) Using Equation 15-13, with thousands of dollars omitted, the EBIT–EPS indifference point is:

$$\text{EPS (debt)} = \text{EPS (common stock)}$$

$$\frac{(\text{EBIT}^* - \$720)(1 - 0.34) - \$0}{500} = \frac{(\text{EBIT}^* - \$0)(1 - 0.34) - \$0}{750}$$

$$\frac{0.66 \text{ EBIT}^* - \$475.20}{500} = \frac{0.66 \text{ EBIT}^*}{750}$$

Cross-multiplying,

$$(750)(0.66 \text{ EBIT}^* - \$475.20) = (500)(0.66 \text{ EBIT}^*)$$

$$495 \text{ EBIT}^* - \$356,400 = 330 \text{ EBIT}^*$$

$$165 \text{ EBIT}^* = \$356,400$$

$$\text{EBIT}^* = \$2,160 \text{ (in thousands), or } \$2,160,000$$

(c) Figure 15-7 shows the EBIT–EPS analysis chart.

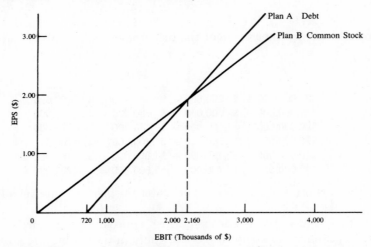

FIGURE 15-7 EBIT–EPS analysis chart for Sampson Sporting Goods.

(d) The EPS are calculated as follows:

	Plan A: Debt	Plan B: Common Stock
EBIT	$2,750,000	$2,750,000
— Interest on new debt	720,000	0
Earnings before taxes	$2,030,000	$2,750,000
— Income taxes (34%)	690,200	935,000
Net income	$1,339,800	$1,815,000
Shares of common stock	500,000	750,000
Earnings per share	$2.68	$2.42

(*e*) Sampson Sporting Goods should adopt Plan A if it can be reasonably sure that the EBIT will not drop below the indifference point. Although Plan A results in a higher EPS than Plan B, debt financing involves greater risk than common stock financing.

[Section 15-3A]

PROBLEM 15-10: Ford Manufacturing Corporation's current capital structure contains the following external financing: $20,000,000 of 11 percent bonds; 100,000 shares of preferred stock, paying $5.25 per share dividend; and 2,000,000 share of common stock. The firm is considering a major expansion plan which requires $10,000,000 in external financing. Additional funds can be raised either by selling $10,000,000 in 10 percent bonds (Plan 1) or by floating 500,000 shares of common stock (Plan 2). Management favors the sale of debt because interest rates have dropped and the firm's debt ratio is below the average for its industry. The corporate tax rate is 34 percent.

(*a*) At what EBIT level are the EPS of the financing alternatives identical?
(*b*) Does the indifference point calculated in Question (a) truly represent a point where the firm's stockholders are indifferent to the choice between debt and common stock financing? Why or why not?
(*c*) Over what range of EBIT would each structure be preferred?
(*d*) If the expected level of EBIT is $9,500,000 with a standard deviation of $1,500,000, what is the probability that EBIT will be below the indifference point? Assume that EBIT is normally distributed.
(*e*) What is the EPS for each financing alternative when EBIT is $9,500,000?
(*f*) Which structure would you recommend if EBIT is $9,500,000? Why?

Answer:

(*a*) The interest on existing debt is $2,200,000 (0.11 × $20,000,000) and the interest on the new debt is $1,000,000 (0.10 × $10,000,000). Substituting I_1 = $3,200,000, I_2 = $2,200,000, PD = $525,000 ($5.25 × 100,000), T = 0.34, n_1 = 2,000,000, and n_2 = 2,500,000 in Equation 15-13 (with thousands of dollars omitted), the EBIT–EPS indifference point is:

$$\text{EPS (debt)} = \text{EPS (common stock)}$$

$$\frac{(\text{EBIT}^* - \$3,200)(1 - 0.34) - \$525}{2,000} = \frac{(\text{EBIT}^* - \$2,200)(1 - 0.34) - \$525}{2,500}$$

$$\frac{0.66\,\text{EBIT}^* - \$2,112 - \$525}{2,000} = \frac{0.66\,\text{EBIT}^* - \$1,452 - \$525}{2,500}$$

Cross-multiplying,

$$(2,500)(0.66\,\text{EBIT}^* - \$2,637) = (2,000)(0.66\,\text{EBIT}^* - \$1,977)$$

$$1,650\,\text{EBIT}^* - \$6,592,500 = 1,320\,\text{EBIT}^* - 3,954,000$$

$$330\,\text{EBIT}^* = \$2,638,500$$

$$\text{EBIT} = \$7,995.455 \text{ (in thousands), or } \$7,995,455$$

(*b*) No. The indifference point only identifies the level of EBIT where the EPS of two financing alternatives are equal. The risk associated with the financing alternatives is not reflected by the indifference point.

(*c*) Using the maximization of EPS as the criterion, common stock financing would be favored below $7,995,455 and debt financing above $7,995,455.

(*d*) Substituting r_i = $7,995,455, $\bar{r}$ = $9,500,000, and σ = $1,500,000 in Equation 4-5, the z value is:

$$z = \frac{\$7,995,455 - \$9,500,000}{\$1,500,000} = \frac{-\$1,504,545}{\$1,500,000} = -1.00 \text{ (rounded)}$$

Using Appendix E, the area under the normal curve with a $z = -1.00$ is 0.3413. The probability that EBIT will be below the indifference point of $7,995,455 is 0.1587 (0.5000 − 0.3413), or 15.87 percent.

(e) The EPS are calculated as follows:

	Plan 1: Debt	Plan 2: Common Stock
EBIT	$9,500,000	$9,500,000
— Interest on existing debt	2,200,000	2,200,000
— Interest on new debt	1,000,000	0
Earnings before taxes	$6,300,000	$7,300,000
— Income taxes (34%)	2,142,000	2,482,000
Net income	$4,158,000	$4,818,000
— Preferred stock dividends	525,000	525,000
Earnings available to common stockholders	$3,633,000	$4,293,000
Shares of common stock	2,000,000	2,500,000
Earnings per share	$1.82	$1.72

(f) If the expected EBIT is $9,500,000, debt financing should be recommended because it provides a higher EPS than common stock financing with an acceptable level of risk. There is a 15.87 percent probability that the indifference point will not be reached.

[Section 15-3A]

16 *DIVIDEND POLICY*

THIS CHAPTER IS ABOUT

☑ **Concept of Dividend Policy**
☑ **Dividend Policy Theory**
☑ **Factors Influencing Dividend Policy**
☑ **Types of Dividend Policies**
☑ **Dividend Payment Procedures**
☑ **Stock Dividends and Stock Splits**
☑ **Stock Repurchases**
☑ **Dividend Reinvestment Plans**

16-1. Concept of Dividend Policy

Dividend policy involves the decision to pay out earnings or to retain them for re-investment in the firm. A **dividend** is a distribution of earnings to shareholders, generally paid in the form of cash or stock. The portion of after-tax earnings not paid out as dividends is called **retained earnings**. A **dividend payout ratio** is the percentage of earnings paid to shareholders in cash.

Dividend policy is important because it affects investor attitudes and the firm's financial structure, flow of funds, liquidity, growth rate, and cost of capital. The goal of dividend policy is to maximize its contribution toward increasing shareholder wealth. An optimal dividend policy strikes that balance between current dividends and future growth which maximizes the price of a firm's stock and, hence, shareholder wealth. Selecting the optimal dividend payout rate that achieves this balance is difficult for most companies because numerous factors influence dividend policy.

16-2. Dividend Policy Theory

There is considerable controversy regarding whether or not management can use dividends to influence the market value of the firm. There are two major schools of thought concerning the appropriate dividend payout rate for a corporation. One school claims that the proportion of earnings paid out in dividends is irrelevant, whereas the other believes just the opposite. Managers often believe that dividends are important in affecting the value of their firm's common stock, but academic researchers generally question the importance of the relationship between corporate dividend policy and stock prices.

A. The *dividend irrelevance* viewpoint states that in a world without taxes, transactions costs, or other market imperfections, dividend policy has no effect on the firm's market value.

   According to this view, there is no optimal dividend policy—one dividend policy is as good as any other. Thus, the shareholder is indifferent to a choice between dividends today or a claim on future earnings. The principal proponents of the dividend irrelevance view are Miller and Modigliani, who argue that the only important determinants of a company's market value are the expected level and risk of its cash flows. Thus, the value of the firm depends only on the firm's investment policy, not on the way a firm splits its earnings between dividends and reinvestment. There is agreement that, in a world of perfect capital markets, dividend policy does not affect shareholder wealth.

B. The *dividend relevance* viewpoint states that in a world with market imperfections such as taxes, flotation costs, and transaction costs, a company's dividend policy affects its market value.

However, in an uncertain world, the impact of dividend policy on stock value is not clear. Some proponents believe that the payment of dividends increases shareholder wealth, while others indicate the contrary. There are several arguments for the dividend relevance viewpoint.

1. *"Bird-in-the-hand" theory.* Because stock prices are highly variable, dividends represent a more reliable form of return than capital gains. Thus, dividends may resolve uncertainty in the minds of investors and may reduce their required rate of return on equity. The greater certainty associated with dividends may also lead investors to place a higher value on dividends than on an equivalent amount of uncertain and riskier capital gains.

2. *Informational content (or signaling) effect.* Dividend payments and dividend policy statements may impart information to investors about management's future expectations for the firm. The reaction of the market to dividend action may affect stock prices favorably or unfavorably depending on the inferences drawn by investors. For instance, a dividend increase may be interpreted by investors as a positive signal of the firm's future prospects and may be reflected in a stock price increase. Conversely, a dividend cut may indicate an unfavorable change in the earnings outlook and lead to a price decline. Reasons for a change in dividend policy should be communicated to investors to avoid confusion and misinterpretation.

3. *Clientele effect.* The clientele effect implies that investors are attracted to firms whose dividend policies meet their particular needs. Tax-exempt organizations and income-oriented investors with low income tax rates may seek out firms that pay large cash dividends. Investors seeking to minimize their taxes or who do not need cash income may prefer firms that pay no or low dividends but that offer the potential for significant growth. Thus, stockholders may place a higher value on firms whose dividend policies meet their particular needs. Opponents of this view, such as Miller and Modigliani, argue that one clientele is as good as another.

C. The *residual theory of dividends* asserts that dividends are paid out of the residual or leftover earnings remaining after profitable investment opportunities are exhausted.

Using the residual theory of dividends, a firm would retain its earnings as long as it can reinvest funds at or above the shareholders' required rate of return. Thus, the primary issue of residual theory is deciding who can best utilize the funds—the corporation or the stockholder. This theory implies that dividends are a passive decision variable and that stockholders are indifferent to the division of funds between retained earnings and dividends. However, the residual theory is incomplete because it ignores how stockholders feel about receiving dividends. Few firms strictly follow this policy because it may result in highly variable dividends, which in turn may lead to volatile stock prices and investor dissatisfaction. Using the residual theory of dividends involves four steps:

1. Determine the optimal capital budget.
2. Determine the amount of equity needed to finance the optimal capital budget.
3. Use retained earnings (internal equity) to supply this equity to the greatest extent possible.

4. Pay dividends only if more earnings are available than are needed to support the optimal capital budget.

EXAMPLE 16-1: Fisher, Inc. has an optimal capital structure of 40 percent debt and 60 percent equity. Total earnings available to common stockholders for the coming year are expected to be $1,500,000. The firm's marginal cost of capital is 14 percent. Fisher, Inc. has the following investment opportunities schedule:

Project	Investment	IRR (%)
A	$1,000,000	24
B	600,000	18
C	400,000	15
D	500,000	12
E	300,000	10

The firm's optimal capital budget consists of Projects A, B, and C because the IRR for each of these projects exceeds the firm's marginal cost of capital. These three projects require a total investment of $2,000,000, of which only $1,200,000 (0.60 × $2,000,000) is common equity. If dividends are treated as residual, the firm would pay $300,000 ($1,500,000 − $1,200,000) in dividends to maintain its optimal capital structure.

16-3. Factors Influencing Dividend Policy

Numerous factors influence a firm's choice of dividend policy. Because the relative importance of these factors changes over time and across companies, it is difficult to develop a general model for use in establishing dividend policy.

A. Corporations may face restrictions or limitations on the payment of dividends.

1. *Legal constraints.* Most states forbid corporations to pay dividends that would impair the initial capital contributions of the firm. This legal restriction is called the **capital impairment rule**. In some states *capital* is defined to include only the par value of common stock; in others, capital is more broadly defined to include both the par value of common stock and the capital in excess of par account. Other legal constraints include borrowing funds to pay dividends and paying dividends when the firm is declared legally insolvent. **Insolvency** is a situation in which either a firm's liabilities exceed its assets or it is unable to pay debts when due.

EXAMPLE 16-2: Gray Manufacturing Company has the following capital accounts on its balance sheet:

Common stock (200,000 shares outstanding at $5 par)	$1,000,000
Capital in excess of par	3,000,000
Retained earnings	2,000,000
Total stockholders' equity	$6,000,000

In states where the firm's capital is defined as the par value of its common stock, the firm could legally pay out $5,000,000 ($3,000,000 + $2,000,000) in cash dividends without impairing its capital. In states where the firm's capital includes all paid-in capital, the firm could pay out only $2,000,000 in cash dividends.

2. *Contractual constraints.* A firm may be constrained in the amount of cash dividends it pays because of restrictive provisions contained in loan agreements, bond indentures, lease contracts, and preferred stock agreements. These provisions protect or strengthen the interests of creditors and preferred stockholders.
3. *Internal constraints.* Management is constrained in paying dividends by the availability of cash. The less liquid a firm is, the less able it is to pay dividends.

B. A firm's level of investment and future growth prospects may influence its dividend policy.

Fast-growing companies usually reinvest most of their earnings, whereas more mature companies often have higher dividend payout ratios.

C. Dividend policy may be affected by the availability of external financing.

New and/or small firms often have limited access to capital markets and must rely heavily on internal funds to finance profitable projects. Consequently, they restrict their cash dividend payments. Medium-to-large size firms with good performance records have relatively easy access to capital markets and thus may adopt more liberal dividend payout policies.

D. The preferences of the owners may determine the dividend policy.

Stockholders may prefer one dividend policy over another for several reasons:
1. Shareholders attempt to match their own income needs and tax status with the magnitude and stability of the firm's level of dividends. While the payment of a cash dividend is usually taxable to the recipient, the tax burden is not equal for all recipients.
2. If management desires to maintain control, it may limit stock sales and hence retain more earnings than it normally would. Sale of new equity results in dilution of control unless the existing owners acquire a proportionate share of the new issue. Maintenance of control is particularly important for small, closely-held firms.

E. The cost of raising external equity capital may affect a firm's dividend policy.

Retained earnings or internal equity is less costly than new stock issues because no flotation costs are involved. Large corporations can generally issue common stock at a lower cost than small- and medium-size firms.

F. Other considerations in determining dividend policy are earnings and legal listing.

1. *Earnings record and prospects.* A firm with a stable record of earnings is generally more willing to maintain a higher dividend payout ratio than a firm with erratic earnings.
2. *Legal listing.* Some states have a legal list of securities in which pension funds, insurance companies, and other fiduciary institutions are permitted to invest. One of the requirements for legal listing is payment of regular cash dividends.

16-4. Types of Dividend Policies

There are many distinct dividend policies, but most policies fall into one of three categories.

A. A *stable dividend policy* is characterized by the tendency to keep a stable dollar amount of dividends per share from period to period.

Corporations tend to establish a predetermined target dividend payout ratio in which dividends are increased only after management is convinced that future earnings can support the higher dividend payment. Under this policy, dividend changes will normally lag behind earnings changes. Firms are reluctant to lower their dividend payments, even in times of financial distress. Most firms follow a relatively stable dividend policy for four reasons:
1. Many business executives believe that stable dividend policies lead to higher stock prices. The empirical evidence on the relationship between dividend policy and stock prices is inconclusive.

2. Investors may view constant or steadily increasing dividends as more certain than a fluctuating cash dividend payment.
3. There is less chance to convey erroneous informational content with a stable dividend policy. Thus, firms tend to avoid reducing the annual dividend because of the information content that a dividend cut may convey.
4. Dividend stability is required for legal listing.

EXAMPLE 16-3: Amling Products, Inc. earned $4,000,000 last year and paid $1.40 per share in dividends on 1,000,000 outstanding shares. Because of a temporary slump in the market, the firm expects to earn $3,600,000 this year. If the company maintains a stable dividend policy, it will maintain a $1.40 dividend per share, despite the expected decline in earnings.

B. A *constant dividend payout ratio policy* is one in which a firm pays out a constant percentage of earnings as dividends.

This policy is easy to administer once the firm selects the initial payout ratio. A constant dividend payout policy will cause dividends to be unstable and unpredictable, if earnings fluctuate. Few firms follow a constant dividend payout policy because stock prices may be adversely affected by highly volatile dividends.

EXAMPLE 16-4: *Refer to the data in Example 16-3.* If Amling Products, Inc. maintains a constant dividend payout ratio each year, this year's dividends per share would be computed as follows:

$$\text{Dividends last year} = (\$1.40)(1{,}000{,}000 \text{ shares}) = \$1{,}400{,}000$$

$$\text{Dividend payout ratio} = \frac{\$1{,}400{,}000}{\$4{,}000{,}000} = 0.35 \text{ or 35 percent}$$

$$\text{Dividends this year} = (0.35)(\$3{,}600{,}000) = \$1{,}260{,}000$$

$$\text{Dividends per share this year} = \frac{\$1{,}260{,}000}{1{,}000{,}000} = \$1.26$$

C. A *regular dividends plus extras policy* is one in which a firm maintains a low regular dividend plus an extra dividend, if warranted by the firm's earnings performance.

This policy represents a compromise between the previous two policies and is common among firms that experience cyclical swings in earnings. A regular dividends plus extras policy gives the firm flexibility but it leads to some uncertainty among shareholders.

16-5. Dividend Payment Procedures

The board of directors sets the firm's dividend policy but the financial manager is responsible for implementing this policy. Dividends are usually paid quarterly, if they are paid at all. There are four critical dates associated with each payment: declaration date, record date, ex-dividend date, and payment date.
1. The **declaration date** is the day on which the company's board of directors meets, decides to pay dividends, and announces the specifics of its decision, such as the amount of the dividend. The firm is legally obligated to meet the dividend payment once the dividend is declared.
2. The **record date** is the date on which a firm closes its stock transfer books and makes up a list of shareholders who are eligible to receive the declared dividend.
3. The **ex-dividend date** is the date on which the right to the most recently declared dividend no longer goes along with the sale of the stock. Because of the time needed to make bookkeeping entries when a stock is traded, the stock will sell *ex dividend* for four business days prior to the record date. Shareholders purchasing stock before this date

will receive the next dividend. Shareholders purchasing stock on or after the ex-dividend date will not receive the upcoming dividend. In theory, the stock price should drop by the amount of the dividend on the ex-dividend date.

4. The **payment date** is the date the company distributes its dividend checks to the holders of record. The payment date is usually set at 2 to 4 weeks after the record date.

EXAMPLE 16-5: At the quarterly June 1 meeting of the Filkins Company, the board of directors announces that it is going to pay a $2.50 per share dividend. The payment is to be made on July 3 to all stockholders of record as of Friday, June 12. Figure 16-1 shows the four critical dates. The ex-dividend date is four business days prior to Friday, June 12, or Monday, June 8.

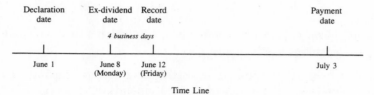

FIGURE 16-1   Critical dividend dates for Filkins Company.

16-6. Stock Dividends and Stock Splits

A stock dividend is technically a form of dividend payment, whereas a stock split is not. Stock dividends and stock splits are similar in that no cash is distributed in either case, both result in a larger number of shares outstanding, and the total net worth remains unchanged. In a practical sense, there is little difference between the two except their accounting treatment. Stock dividends and stock splits are not taxable until the shares are sold.

Theoretically, stock dividends and stock splits represent nothing more than a distribution of pieces of paper. A 100 percent stock dividend or a 2-for-1 stock split is similar in concept to exchanging a $10 bill for two $5 bills. By themselves, stock dividends and stock splits do not alter shareholder wealth. However, their psychological effects on owners is generally favorable. In some instances, the market price of the stock after a stock dividend or a stock split may be greater than the mathematical reduction that should occur, because of the favorable informational content conveyed. The announcement of the split or of a large stock dividend may indicate to investors that management is confident of continued growth which, in turn, may push the market price per share upward.

A. **A *stock dividend* is a distribution of additional shares of stock to existing stockholders on a pro rata basis.**

A stock dividend represents a form method of paying dividends. The dividend is usually expressed as a percentage of the shares held by a shareholder and is normally in the 2 to 10 percent range. A firm may use stock dividends to conserve cash, supplement cash dividends, and broaden its ownership base. One disadvantage associated with stock dividends is that they are more costly to administer than cash dividends. With a stock dividend the shareholder receives nothing of real value because it neither changes the shareholder's proportional ownership nor wealth. However, from the shareholder's perspective, the advantage is that additional stock is not taxed until sold whereas a cash dividend is declarable as income in the year it is received.

1. The accounting treatment of a stock dividend involves transferring an amount equal to the current market value of the stock dividend from retained earnings to other stockholders' equity accounts. This deduction in retained earnings is added to the common stock account at par value and the remainder is added to the account, Capital In Excess of Par. The par value of the common stock remains unchanged. Thus, the effect of a stock dividend is to capitalize a portion of the firm's retained earnings. Equation 16-1 shows the dollar amount transferred from retained earnings resulting from a stock dividend.

DOLLAR AMOUNT TRANSFERRED FROM RETAINED EARNINGS $= S \times D_s \times M$ **(16-1)**

where S =   total number of shares outstanding before the stock dividend
          D_s =   percentage of the stock dividend
          M =   original market price of common stock before the stock dividend

EXAMPLE 16-6: Lummer Corporation has the following common stockholders' equity:

Stockholders' Equity (Before Stock Dividend)

Common stock (1,000,000 shares outstanding at $5 par)	$ 5,000,000
Capital in excess of par	10,000,000
Retained earnings	35,000,000
Total stockholders' equity	$50,000,000

The corporation declares a 10 percent stock dividend, and the market price of the stock before the stock dividend is $22 per share. Substituting $S = 1,000,000$, $D_s = 0.10$, and $M = \$22$ in Equation 16-1, the dollar amount transferred from retained earnings to other stockholders' equity accounts is:

$$\text{Dollar amount transferred from retained earnings} = (1,000,000)(0.10)(\$22) = \$2,200,000$$

The number of shares outstanding is increased by 100,000 ($0.10 \times 1,000,000$). Therefore, of the $2,200,000, $500,000 ($5 par $\times$ 100,000) is added to the common stock account and the remaining $1,700,000 is added to Capital In Excess of Par.

Stockholders' Equity (After Stock Dividend)

Common stock (1,100,000 shares outstanding at $5 par)	$ 5,500,000
Capital in excess of par	11,700,000
Retained earnings	32,800,000
Total stockholders' equity	$50,000,000

2. A stock dividend causes earnings per share (EPS) to decline in proportion to the number of new shares issued. Equation 16-2 shows the calculation of the firm's EPS after a stock dividend.

$$\text{Adjusted EPS} = \frac{\text{EPS}}{1 + D_s} \qquad \textbf{(16-2)}$$

where   EPS   =   original earnings per share

EXAMPLE 16-7: Before issuing a 10 percent stock dividend, Lummer Corporation had 1,000,000 shares of common stock outstanding and total earnings available to common stockholders of $3,300,000. Thus, its EPS before the stock dividend was $3.30 ($3,300,000/1,000,000). After the stock dividend, the EPS dropped to $3.00. Substituting EPS = $3.30 and D_s = 0.10 in Equation 16-2, the adjusted EPS are:

$$\text{Adjusted EPS} = \frac{\$3.30}{1.10} = \$3.00$$

3. A stockholder's proportionate claim to the firm's net worth and earnings remains unchanged with a stock dividend. Equation 16-3 shows the calculation of a stockholder's claim to earnings.

$$\text{Stockholder's claim to earnings} = \text{Shares} \times \text{EPS} \qquad \textbf{(16-3)}$$

EXAMPLE 16-8: A stockholder originally owned 100 shares of Lummer Corporation before, and 110 shares after, a 10 percent stock dividend. The EPS were $3.30 before and $3.00 after the stock dividend. Substituting the following values in Equation 16-3, the stockholder's claim to earnings remains the same before and after the stock dividend.

	Before Stock Dividend	After Stock Dividend
Claim to earnings	100 × $3.30 = $33.00	110 × $3.00 = $33.00

4. A stock dividend results in a decrease in the market price of each share of stock in proportion to the number of new shares issued. However, shareholder wealth does not change because the increase in the number of new shares exactly offsets the decline in the share price. Equation 16-4 shows the market price of a share of common stock, adjusted for a stock dividend.

$$\text{Adjusted market price of a share of common stock} = \frac{M}{1 + D_s} \qquad \textbf{(16-4)}$$

Equation 16-5 is a formula for calculating stockholder wealth.

$$\text{Stockholder wealth} = \text{Shares} \times M \qquad \textbf{(16-5)}$$

EXAMPLE 16-9: A stockholder owned 100 shares of Lummer Corporation stock at a market price of $22 a share before the firm declared a 10 percent stock dividend.

(a) Substituting $M = \$22$ and $D_s = 0.10$ in Equation 16-4, the adjusted market price is:

$$\text{Adjusted market price of a share of common stock} = \frac{\$22.00}{1.10} = \$20.00$$

(b) Substituting the following values in Equation 16-5, the stockholder's wealth position remains unchanged before and after the stock dividend.

	Before Stock Dividend	After Stock Dividend
Stockholder wealth	(100)($22.00) = $2,200	(110)($20.00) = $2,200

B. A *stock split* is a method of increasing the number of shares of common stock outstanding without any change in the shareholders' equity or the aggregate market value at the time of the split.

The pro rata distribution of shares with a stock split is usually much higher than with a stock dividend. Directors of a corporation will authorize a split to make ownership more affordable to a broader base of investors.

1. The accounting treatment of a stock split involves increasing both the number of shares authorized and outstanding and dividing the par value of the common stock by the size of the split. When a stock split requires an increase in authorized shares and/or change in par value of the stock, the shareholders must approve an amendment of the corporate charter.

EXAMPLE 16-10: Petty Company decides its stock is selling at a high market price and declares a 2-for-1 stock split. Stockholders' equity before the stock split is shown below.

Stockholders' Equity (Before 2-for-1 Stock Split)

Common stock (5,000,000 shares outstanding at $2 par)	$10,000,000
Capital in excess of par	40,000,000
Retained earnings	20,000,000
Total stockholders' equity	$70,000,000

With a 2-for-1 stock split, the par value decreases by one-half; the number of authorized and outstanding shares doubles. No changes occur in the stockholders' equity account balances.

Stockholders' Equity (After 2-for-1 Stock Split)	
Common stock (10,000,000 shares outstanding at $1 par)	$10,000,000
Capital in excess of par	40,000,000
Retained earnings	20,000,000
Total stockholders' equity	$70,000,000

2. A *reverse stock split* is a procedure whereby a corporation reduces the number of common shares outstanding. Reverse stock splits are used to bring low-priced shares up to more desirable trading levels. The total number of shares will have the same value immediately after the reverse split, but each share will be worth more.

16-7. Stock Repurchases

A **stock repurchase** is the act of a firm buying back its own shares of common stock. Common stock reacquired by the issuing firm is known as **treasury stock**. A firm may repurchase stock directly from its stockholders through a **tender offer**, in the open market, or on a negotiated basis from holders of large blocks of shares, such as institutions.

A. There are several reasons for share repurchase.

1. Share repurchase provides an alternate means of distributing excess cash to the owners. It allows stockholders to decide whether or not to sell their share to receive cash. In theory, shareholders are indifferent to a choice between cash dividends and share repurchase, but this position may change when taxes and transaction costs are brought into the decision-making process.
2. Corporate management may acquire its own shares because it believes that they are selling at a low price. Treasury stock can be resold to raise funds, possibly at higher prices than when the shares were originally repurchased.
3. Corporate management may need additional shares for mergers and acquisitions, stock dividends, and stock option plans.
4. Firms may repurchase shares as a protective device against being taken over as a merger candidate.
5. Shares may be repurchased to alter the firm's capital structure. Share repurchase increases financial leverage as equity is reduced.
6. Share repurchase may increase the earnings per share and market price of stock by reducing the number of shares outstanding.

EXAMPLE 16-11: Brick Corporation reported the following financial data:

Earnings available to common stockholders	$2,000,000
Number of shares outstanding	1,000,000
Earnings per share ($2,000,000/1,000,000)	$2
Market price per share ($2 × 9.5)	$19
Price/earnings ratio ($19/$2)	9.5
Excess cash	$1,000,000
Expected cash dividend per share ($1,000,000/1,000,000)	$1

The firm plans to distribute $1,000,000 in excess cash to stockholders through the repurchase of outstanding shares. Shares will be repurchased through a tender offer at $1 above the current market price to induce sales.

With $1,000,000 in excess cash, the firm can purchase 50,000 shares ($1,000,000/$20). This repurchase will reduce the total shares outstanding to 950,000 (1,000,000 − 50,000) shares. The new earnings per share will rise to $2.11 ($$2,000,000/950,000). The stock price will rise to $20 (9.5 × $2.11) per share.

B. Shares repurchase has several disadvantages.

1. Stockholders may prefer cash dividends to share repurchase.
2. The reduced number of shares outstanding may decrease trading activity.
3. Share repurchase may divert funds from other investment opportunities.
4. Share repurchase may shift control of the firm to fewer owners.

16-8. Dividend Reinvestment Plans

A **dividend reinvestment plan** (DRP) is an arrangement which allows stockholders to automatically reinvest dividends in more shares of the company's stock. DRPs provide shareholders with numerous potential advantages, including convenient acquisition of additional shares, low or no transaction costs, discounts on stock purchases, and convenient recordkeeping. However, stockholders may have to pay taxes on reinvested dividends. The firm may benefit through improved shareholder goodwill, market price support for its stock, and a broaden base of investors.

There are two major types of DRPs:

1. *Regular dividend investment plan.* With a regular DRP, corporations use reinvested dividends to purchase outstanding shares. These plans are used primarily to foster stockholder goodwill. Regular DRPs do not provide new capital for the firm.
2. *New capital dividend reinvestment plan (NCDRP).* With an NCDRP, firms use reinvested dividends to purchase newly issued stock. Thus, NCDRPs serve as a means of raising new equity capital.

RAISE YOUR GRADES

Can you explain...?

☑ the concept of dividend policy
☑ the goal of corporate dividend policy
☑ two schools of thought involving the role that dividend policy plays in the determination of share value
☑ three major arguments favoring the relevance of dividend policy
☑ what is meant by the residual theory of dividends
☑ what factors influence a firm's choice of dividend policy
☑ three general types of dividend policies
☑ why managers prefer a stable dollar dividend policy to a policy of paying out a constant percentage of earnings as dividends
☑ the four relevant dates in the dividend payout procedure
☑ the similarities and differences between a stock dividend and a stock split
☑ why firms issue stock dividends and stock splits
☑ why corporations repurchase their own stock
☑ three methods of making stock repurchases
☑ the advantages to the corporation and its stockholders of dividend reinvestment plans

SUMMARY

1. Dividend policy determines the distribution of a firm's earnings between retention and dividend payments to stockholders.
2. The goal of dividend policy is to maximize its contribution toward increasing shareholder wealth.

3. An optimal dividend policy balances stockholders' need for current cash flows with the company's investment opportunities and future growth.

4. One school of thought contends that dividend policy is irrelevant in the determination of share value, while another school holds the opposite view.

5. Three major arguments favoring the relevance of dividends are the "bird-in-the-hand" theory, the informational content effect, and the clientele effect.

6. The residual theory of dividends states that a firm will pay dividends only if acceptable investment opportunities for these funds are currently unavailable.

7. Numerous factors influence a firm's choice of dividend policy, including legal, contractual, and internal constraints; investment opportunities and growth prospects; alternative sources of capital; owner considerations, including their preferences and desire for control; the cost of selling stock; the earnings record; and legal listing.

8. Some of these factors favor high dividends, while others imply a lower payout policy. Factors that may impair a firm's ability to pay dividends include restrictive covenants, the need for liquidity, rapid growth requiring new capital for expansion, limited access to the capital markets, and unstable earnings.

9. Dividend policies adopted by firms may be grouped into three general categories: a stable dividend policy, a constant dividend payout ratio policy, and a regular dividends plus extras policy.

10. Managers generally prefer a stable dollar amount of dividends because they believe that this policy leads to higher stock prices and avoids erroneous informational content.

11. The dividend payment procedure uses a declaration date, a record date, an ex-dividend date, and a payment date.

12. Both a stock dividend and a stock split are ways of distributing shares to common stockholders. In theory, they do not increase shareholder wealth. However, they can convey information to investors.

13. The only real difference between a stock dividend and a stock split is their accounting treatment.

14. Firms may issue stock dividends or splits to conserve cash, to supplement cash dividends, and to broaden the ownership base of their stock.

15. The decision to repurchase shares may be viewed as an alternative to the payment of a cash dividend.

16. Firms repurchase their own stock to increase their earnings and market price per share. Repurchased shares are also used for mergers and acquisitions, stock dividends, and stock option plans. Management may repurchase shares because they believe that their shares are currently undervalued.

17. Stock repurchases can be made directly in the marketplace, through tender offers, or on a negotiated basis from holders of large blocks of stock.

18. Corporations may use dividend reinvestment plans to improve shareholder goodwill, to provide market support for their stock, to broaden their investor base, and to raise new equity capital.

19. Dividend reinvestment plans help stockholders reinvest dividends at minimal costs.

RAPID REVIEW

True or False

1. The dividend payout ratio is the ratio of dividends per share to market price per share. [Section 16-1]

2. In a world of perfect markets, dividend policy has no effect on the firm's market value. [Section 16-2]

3. The "bird-in-the-hand" theory suggests that it is generally less risky for a stockholder to receive dividends now than to allow the firm to reinvest earnings in anticipation of receiving a higher return later. [Section 16-2B]

4. Informational effects refer to what investors infer from a dividend pattern or change in dividend policy. [Section 16-2B]

5. A consideration in establishing a firm's dividend policy is the availability of cash. [Section 16-3A]

6. Rapidly growing companies generally have lower payout ratios than slow growth firms. [Section 16-3B]

7. Firms which have limited access to the capital market tend to prefer a low dividend payout ratio. [Section 16-3C]

8. The desire for legal listing may be a determinant of a corporation's dividend policy. [Section 16-3F]

9. The residual theory of dividends provides a constant percentage of earnings as dividends. [Section 16-4B]

10. The record date is the date when the dividend is declared. [Section 16-5]

11. The ex-dividend date occurs after the record date. [Section 16-5]

12. Stock dividends are fully taxable when they are received by stockholders. [Section 16-6]

13. The major difference between a stock dividend and a stock split is their accounting treatment. [Section 16-6]

14. The effect of a stock dividend is to increase a firm's retained earnings. [Section 16-6A]

15. In theory, stock dividends should not increase the total value of shareholders' wealth. [Section 16-6A]

16. A major motive for a stock split is to decrease the market price of the stock by increasing the number of shares outstanding. [Section 16-6B]

17. A stock split involves a transfer from retained earnings to other stockholders' equity accounts. [Section 16-6B]

18. A reverse stock split is used to increase a stock's market price to a more attractive trading range. [Section 16-6B]

19. Treasury stock is common stock reacquired by the issuing firm. [Section 16-7]

20. A tender offer is a formal offer by a company to buy a specified number of its own shares. [Section 16-7]

Multiple Choice

21. What type of dividend policy pays out whatever remains after profitable investment opportunities are satisfied?

    (a) Residual dividend policy
    (b) Stable dividend policy
    (c) Constant dividend payout ratio policy
    (d) Regular dividends plus extras policy

    [Sections 16-3A through 16-3C]

22. An increase in which of the following is likely to *increase* a firm's ability to pay dividends?

    (a) Liquidity
    (b) Access to capital markets
    (c) New capital requirements for expansion
    (d) Both a and b

    [Sections 16-3A through 16-3C]

23. Which of the following factors does *not* affect a firm's dividend policy?

    (a) Restrictive covenants in the firm's loan agreements
    (b) An unstable earnings pattern

(c) Owner preferences

(d) Common stock par value

[Sections 16-3A, 16-3D, and 16-3E]

24. Which of the following is the most common dividend policy?

    (a) Residual dividend policy
    (b) Stable dividend policy
    (c) Constant dividend payout ratio policy
    (d) Regular dividends plus extras policy

    [Section 16-4A]

25. The final approval of a firm's dividend policy comes from

    (a) the president of the company
    (b) the chief financial officer
    (c) the treasurer
    (d) the board of directors

    [Section 16-5]

26. When do stockholders first learn about the amount of their next dividend?

    (a) Declaration date
    (b) Record date
    (c) Ex-dividend date
    (d) Payment date

    [Section 16-5]

27. How many business days is the ex-dividend date prior to the record date?

    (a) One
    (b) Two
    (c) Four
    (d) Five

    [Section 16-5]

28. Stock splits

    (a) reduce retained earnings
    (b) increase the common stock account
    (c) increase the number of shares of common stock outstanding
    (d) leave the par value of common stock unchanged

    [Section 16-6B]

29. What generally occurs when a firm repurchases shares from existing stockholders?

    (a) Earnings per share increase
    (b) Market price per share increases
    (c) Number of shares outstanding decreases
    (d) All of the above

    [Section 16-7A]

30. Which of the following serves as a means of raising new equity capital?

    (a) Stock dividend
    (b) Stock split
    (c) Stock repurchase
    (d) New capital dividend reinvestment plan

    [Section 16-8]

Answers

True or False		*Multiple Choice*
1. False	11. False	21. a
2. True	12. False	22. d
3. True	13. True	23. d
4. True	14. False	24. b
5. True	15. True	25. d
6. True	16. True	26. a
7. True	17. False	27. c
8. True	18. True	28. c
9. False	19. True	29. d
10. False	20. True	30. d

SOLVED PROBLEMS

PROBLEM 16-1: Last year, Finn Corporation had $3,000,000 in after-tax earnings. It also averaged 1,500,000 shares of common stock outstanding and followed a policy of paying out 20 percent of its earnings in dividends.

(*a*) What were the company's earnings per share?
(*b*) What were the company's dividends per share?

Answer:

(*a*) The earnings per share were:

$$\text{EPS} = \frac{\$3,000,000}{1,500,000} = \$2.00$$

(*b*) The dividends per share were:

$$\text{DPS} = (0.20)(\$2.00) = \$0.40 \qquad \textbf{[Section 16-1]}$$

PROBLEM 16-2: Colorfast, Inc. follows a stable dividend policy and pays out a quarterly dividend of $0.25 per share. Last year, earnings per share were $2.50. What was the dividend payout ratio?

Answer: The dividend payout is computed by dividing the yearly dividends per share by the earnings per share.

$$\text{Dividend payout ratio} = \frac{(4)(\$0.25)}{\$2.50} = 0.40 \text{ or } 40 \text{ percent} \qquad \textbf{[Section 16-1]}$$

PROBLEM 16-3: Glaser Mining Company follows a policy of financing the equity portion of investment from retained earnings and of only paying dividends if funds are available. The firm wishes to maintain a capital structure of 30 percent debt and 70 percent equity. Its current earnings are $4,000,000 and its acceptable investment projects cost $7,000,000. How much will the firm pay in cash dividends?

Answer: To maintain the capital structure, the investment must be funded as follows:

$$\text{Required debt} \quad (0.30)(\$7,000,000) = \$2,100,000$$
$$\text{Required equity} \quad (0.70)(\$7,000,000) = \$4,900,000$$

To provide the $4,900,000 in required equity, Glaser Mining must retain the entire $4,000,000 in earnings and issue new stock for the remaining $900,000. By following the current dividend policy, the company will pay no cash dividends. **[Section 16-2C]**

PROBLEM 16-4: Ridgewell Caterers, Inc. has the following equity accounts:

Common stock (1,000,000 shares outstanding at $1 par)	$1,000,000
Capital in excess of par	2,000,000
Retained earnings	500,000
Total stockholders' equity	$3,500,000

The stock is trading at $5 a share. At the company's annual meeting, some stockholders insisted that the firm should payout all of its retained earnings as dividends. The firm currently has $400,000 in cash, of which half is needed to meet the requirements of its borrowing agreements.

(*a*) What is the maximum amount of dividends that the company could pay without violating the capital impairment rule? Is paying this amount realistic?

(*b*) What is the practical limit to the payment of dividends?

Answer:

(*a*) The legal limit depends on state law. If the capital impairment provisions of state law are limited to the par value of common stock, the maximum amount of dividends is $2,500,000, which is the amount of retained earnings ($500,000) plus capital in excess of par ($2,000,000). Otherwise, the maximum amount of dividends is the retained earnings of $500,000. Neither amount is realistic because the company would not have the cash available to pay.

(*b*) In practice, the company's dividends could not exceed the amount of its excess cash of $200,000 (0.50 × $400,000), unless the company raised additional funds.

[Section 16-3A]

PROBLEM 16-5: Precision Tune currently has 800,000 shares of common stock outstanding. The company earned $3,000,000 last year and paid $1.50 per share in dividends. The company expects its earnings to increase to $3,500,000 this year but to decline the following year.

(*a*) If the company maintains a stable dollar amount of dividends per share, how large a dividend will each shareholder receive this year?

(*b*) If the company maintains a constant dividend payout ratio policy, how large a dividend will each shareholder receive this year?

Answer:

(*a*) With a stable dividend policy, Precision Tune will maintain its current $1.50 cash dividend per share.

(*b*) With a constant dividend payout ratio policy, dividends per share will be $1.75.

$$\text{Dividends last year} = (\$1.50)(800,000) = \$1,200,000$$

$$\text{Dividend payout ratio} = \frac{\$1,200,000}{\$3,000,000} = 0.40 \text{ or } 40 \text{ percent}$$

$$\text{Dividends this year} = (0.40)(\$3,500,000) = \$1,400,000$$

$$\text{Dividends per share this year} = \frac{\$1,400,000}{800,000} = \$1.75$$

[Sections 16-1, 16-4A, and 16-4B]

PROBLEM 16-6: The directors of Neri Bottling Company announced on August 27 that a quarterly dividend of $0.38 would be paid on Tuesday, September 29 to stockholders of record as of Tuesday, September 15. What is the ex-dividend date for this quarter?

Answer: The ex-dividend date is Wednesday, September 9. **[Section 16-5]**

Problems 16-7 and 16-8 use the following data.

Bonanno Pizza has the following equity accounts:

Common stock (200,000 shares outstanding at $3 par)	$ 600,000
Capital in excess of par	1,400,000
Retained earnings	4,000,000
Total stockholders' equity	$6,000,000

The company's common stock is currently selling for $30 per share.

PROBLEM 16-7: The board of directors of Bonanno Pizza approved a 20 percent stock dividend.

(*a*) What is the total dollar amount transferred from retained earnings as a result of the stock dividend?
(*b*) How many shares are added to the common stock account?
(*c*) Reconstruct the equity section of the balance sheet after the stock dividend.

Answer:

(*a*) Substituting $S = 200,000$, $D_s = 0.20$, and $M = \$30$ in Equation 16-1, the dollar amount transferred from retained earnings is:

$$\text{Dollar amount transferred from retained earnings} = (200,000)(0.20)(\$30) = \$1,200,000$$

(*b*) A total of 40,000 shares ($0.20 \times 200,000$) is added to the common stock account.
(*c*) Of the $1,200,000 transferred from retained earnings, $120,000 ($3 par $\times$ 40,000) is added to the common stock account, and $1,080,000 ($1,200,000 − $120,000) is added to the capital in excess of par account. The stockholders' equity accounts are as follows:

Common stock (240,000 shares outstanding at $3 par)	$ 720,000
Capital in excess of par	2,480,000
Retained earnings	2,800,000
Total stockholders' equity	$6,000,000

[Section 16-6A]

PROBLEM 16-8: The board of directors is planning a 3-for-1 stock split. What would be the stockholders' equity section of Bonanno Pizza after the stock split?

Answer: With a 3-for-1 stock split, the par value declines from $3 to $1, and the number of outstanding shares triples to 600,000 shares.

Common stock (600,000 shares outstanding at $1 par)	$ 600,000
Capital in excess of par	1,400,000
Retained earnings	4,000,000
Total stockholders' equity	$6,000,000

[Section 16-6B]

PROBLEM 16-9: Tracor Rustproofing had earnings of $4.20 per share this year before declaring a 5 percent stock dividend. What will be the EPS after the stock dividend?

Answer: Substituting EPS = $4.20 and $D_s = 0.05$ in Equation 16-2, the adjusted EPS will be:

$$\text{Adjusted EPS} = \frac{\$4.20}{1.05} = \$4.00 \qquad \textbf{[Section 16-6A]}$$

PROBLEM 16-10: Pettway Nursery has announced a 2 percent stock dividend. Shares currently sell for $51.

(*a*) If you owned 500 shares of Pettway Nursery, how many shares would you have after the stock dividend?

(*b*) What would the share price be immediately after the stock dividend?

(*c*) Would your wealth position change as a result of the stock dividend?

Answer:

(*a*) Your number of shares would increase to 510 (1.02 × 500).

(*b*) Substituting $M = \$51$ and $D_s = 0.02$ in Equation 16-4, the adjusted market price is:

$$\text{Adjusted market price} = \frac{\$51.00}{1.02} = \$50.00$$

(*c*) Your wealth position would theoretically not change as a result of a stock dividend.

	Before Stock Dividend	After Stock Dividend
Stockholder wealth	(500)($51) = $25,500	(510)($50) = $25,500

[Section 16-6A]

PROBLEM 16-11: Kennedy Corporation has the following financial data:

Before Repurchase	
Net earnings	$1,500,000
Shares outstanding	500,000
Earnings per share	$3
Price/earnings ratio	10
Market price per share	$30
Expected dividend	$2

The company can use $1,000,000 excess cash either to pay a $2 cash dividend per share or to repurchase 31,250 shares at $32 per share.

(*a*) What will happen to the earnings per share after the repurchase?

(*b*) What will happen to the market price of the stock, assuming that the price/earnings ratio remains constant?

(*c*) In this case, does the wealth position of the firm's shareholders differ if the firm pays dividends or repurchase stock? Ignore taxes and transaction costs.

(*d*) What assumptions underlie this analysis?

Answer:

(*a*) Earnings per share will increase to $3.20 ($1,500,000/468,750).

(*b*) The stock price will rise to $32 (10 × $3.20).

(*c*) The wealth position would remain the same for each alternative. A stockholder would receive benefits of $2 per share; either a $2 cash dividend or a $2 increase in stock price.

(*d*) This analysis assumes that shares could be purchased for exactly $32 and that the price/earnings ratio remains at 10. It also ignores tax effects and transaction costs. If the company could buy the shares for less than $32 a share, the remaining shareholders would gain. The opposite would occur if the shares were purchased for more than $32. If the price/earnings ratio rose as a result of the repurchase, the remaining shareholders would gain. If the price/earnings ratio dropped, they would lose.

[Section 16-7A]

17 FINANCIAL MARKETS AND INSTITUTIONS

THIS CHAPTER IS ABOUT

☑ **Financial Markets**
☑ **Financial Intermediaries**
☑ **Investment Bankers**
☑ **Private Placements**
☑ **Privileged Subscriptions**
☑ **Regulation of Securities Markets**

Business firms need money for many purposes, such as acquiring assets and paying debts. Most companies are unable to meet all of their funding needs internally by retaining earnings. Consequently, these firms seek outside financing by selling securities and obtaining loans.

Funds may be acquired from individuals, other businesses, and government units, but individual savers are the ultimate source of funds. Funds are transferred from suppliers (net savers) to demanders (net investors) through the financial system, including the financial markets and all financial institutions. Transfers can take place through financial intermediaries, investment bankers, private placements, and privileged subscriptions. To keep financial markets and institutions competitive and to prevent market concentration, regulations are imposed by numerous governmental bodies.

17-1. Financial Markets

A **financial market** is the mechanism through which financial assets are bought, sold, or exchanged. A financial asset is a claim against the future income and assets of the issuer. Financial assets, including money, debt securities, and equity securities, are strictly paper assets. In financial transactions, one paper asset (money) is traded for another paper asset (loans or securities). The issuer of *debt securities* agrees to pay the lender a specified amount of money at a future date, whereas the issuer of *equity securities* is selling ownership in the corporation. Debt and equity securities are financial assets from the investor's viewpoint, but are claims on assets from the issuing firm's perspective.

A. Financial markets function in three important ways to serve corporate financial management.

1. *Finance asset growth.* Corporations turn to financial markets to obtain funds for investments in various assets such as plant and equipment. They exchange their own securities for money to buy more capital assets. Without financial markets, taking advantage of investment opportunities would depend upon the amount of the firm's accrued savings.

2. *Provide a resale market.* Financial markets enable purchasers of financial assets to sell or exchange these assets whenever they wish. Without a resale market for stocks (which have no maturity) and for bonds (which have long maturities) in-

vestors would be reluctant to purchase corporate securities. This reluctance would result from the inability of purchasers to take advantage of more desirable investment opportunities as they arose and the increased risk of having to hold an asset long term.

3. *Test the value of financial assets.* The presence of financial markets enables firms desiring to sell securities to set prices by examining the market pricing of similar securities. The resale market determines the value of a firm's existing securities through buying and selling activities.

B. There are many different financial markets.

Financial markets are highly diverse but may be classified into several broad categories. One classification involves the maturity dates of the assets, and is separated into *money markets* and *capital markets*. Each of these categories is then subdivided into *primary markets* and *secondary markets*, based on whether the financial assets are initial issues or whether they have previously entered the market.

1. **Money markets** are the financial markets for short-term debt instruments. The money market is a decentralized market, but considerable money market activity occurs in New York. The primary participants in the money market are financial institutions, governmental units, and business firms. Money market instruments are characterized by a high degree of safety and maturities of one year or less. From the financial manager's perspective, key money market instruments include Treasury bills, federal agency issues, commercial paper, negotiable certificates of deposit, bankers' acceptances, repurchase agreements, and money market mutual funds. These money market instruments are discussed in Chapter 18.

2. **Capital markets** are the financial markets in which intermediate and long-term instruments are bought and sold. Capital markets are more centralized than money markets and major participants include corporations, government, and individuals. Capital market securities include both debt and equity.

   - **Debt securities** are obligations of the borrower to return the borrowed funds at a specified time and to pay interest to the lender. There are many different types of debt, such as bonds and mortgages, in the capital markets. A **bond** is a long-term promise to repay a specified dollar amount borrowed plus interest. A **mortgage** is a loan secured by real estate, such as land and buildings, that is repaid with interest in periodic installments. Intermediate and long-term debt instruments are discussed in Chapters 19 and 20, respectively.
   - **Equity securities** are ownership shares of the firm receiving the funds. There are only two major types of equity securities: common stock and preferred stock. Common stock is the security that represents ownership of the corporation. Preferred stock is a long-term equity security which usually pays a fixed dividend. Preferred stock also represents ownership to some extent, but it has some characteristics of debt. Equity securities are discussed in Chapter 20.

3. **Primary markets** are the financial markets in which newly issued securities are bought and sold for the first time. The issuing company receives the proceeds from the sales of the security, less any related costs of the issue. Most new securities are sold through either a public offering or a private placement.

   - A **public offering** is the sale of new securities to the investment public.
   - A **private placement** is the nonpublic sale of new securities or other investments directly to a limited number of investors.

   As an alternative to a public offering or a private placement, a corporation may also offer its common stock to select potential investors on a *privileged-subscription basis*. These methods of distributing corporate securities are discussed in greater detail in Sections 17-3 through 17-5.

4. **Secondary markets** are financial markets in which previously issued securities are bought and sold. Secondary markets are resale markets and are not used for

corporate fund-raising. Thus, corporations receive no money from the sale of securities in secondary markets. Secondary markets for corporate securities are either organized exchanges or over-the-counter (OTC) markets.

- **Organized exchanges** are centralized markets in which listed securities are traded. Organized security exchanges consist of two national exchanges, the New York Stock Exchange and the American Stock Exchange, both of which are located in New York, and several regional exchanges, including the Midwest, Pacific, Philadelphia, Boston, and Cincinnati exchanges. The New York Stock Exchange is the oldest and largest stock exchange in the United States. A company must be *listed* on an exchange before its securities can be traded there, but they could be traded elsewhere if the company is not listed. The requirements for listing vary among the exchanges but usually pertain to such matters as the firm's size, the number of shares outstanding, the diversity of ownership, and financial performance.

  Security exchanges have two major characteristics. First, all transactions of listed securities are conducted at a central trading facility by individuals or representatives of organizations who purchase memberships called **seats** on the exchange. Most seats are held by brokerage firms. Second, transactions are conducted in an **auction market** in which specialists facilitate trading by uniting buyers and sellers. A **specialist** is a member of an organized security exchange who specializes in certain stocks and aids the trading process by keeping an inventory of these shares. Specialists bring buyers and seller together, sometimes buying and selling from their own account in order to keep an orderly market.

EXAMPLE 17-1: Herb Stutts wants to buy 100 shares of General Products stock at the prevailing market price. He has an account with F. E. Mutton's office in Washington, D.C., with a broker named Greg Raven. To purchase the shares, Herb Stutts would place the order with his **broker**, who is hired to buy or sell securities for investors but who does not take ownership of the securities. Greg Raven would have the order sent to one of the firm's members on the New York Stock Exchange. This person, called a **floor broker**, goes to the appropriate location on the floor of the exchange where General Products stock is traded and bargains with various sellers to get the best available price. The floor broker notifies one of the firm's clerks, who sends information about the trade back to the office in Washington, D.C. Greg Raven receives this information and notifies Herb Stutts. The brokerage firm charges a **brokerage commission** on the transaction and the broker gets part of this fee.

- **Over-the-counter markets** are the markets for securities that are not listed and traded on the organized exchanges. Unlike organized security exchanges, OTC markets have no centralized trading facilities and do not operate as auction markets. Instead, OTC markets consist of **dealers**, who *make a market* in the shares of a particular firm by buying and selling from their own accounts, and from numerous brokers, who serve as agents for investors. In OTC markets, securities are traded competitively on a bid-asked basis by brokers and dealers who are connected by telephones and by a computerized telecommunications network of the National Association of Securities Dealers Automated Quotation (NASDAQ) system. Dealers quote *bid* and *asked* prices, which are available on NASDAQ, for the securities that they hold. The **bid price** is the highest price at which dealers or other prospective buyers are willing to pay for a given security and the **asked price** is the lowest price at which they will sell the security. Together, the two prices constitute a *quotation*. Dealers do not charge commissions but are compensated by the *spread* or difference between the bid and asked quote. Securities of more firms are traded in the OTC markets than the organized security exchanges, but the dollar volume of the securities traded is greater on the exchanges. Most corporate bonds and government securities are traded in the OTC markets.

17-2. Financial Intermediaries

A. Financial intermediaries are firms that facilitate the flow of funds from suppliers to demanders.

The process of acquiring funds from one party (suppliers) for the purpose of making them available to another party (demanders) is called **financial intermediation**. Intermediaries are able to lend at lower rates than individual suppliers. Financial intermediaries also provide business firms with the convenience of dealing with them as opposed to dealing directly with many individual savers. Thus, financial intermediaries are a convenient and relatively low-cost source of financing.

B. Financial intermediaries may be divided into three broad classes: depository institutions, insurance companies, and other financial intermediaries.

Within these three classes, the most important suppliers of funds to corporations are commercial banks, insurance companies, pension and trust funds, and mutual funds. The remaining depository institutions, such as savings and loan associations, mutual savings banks, and credit unions, as well as the other financial intermediaries, are important sources of financing for individuals rather than corporations.

1. A **depository institution** is a financial institution that accepts deposits and lends money. Depository institutions include commercial banks, savings and loan associations, mutual savings banks, and credit unions. Depository institutions were once among the most heavily regulated businesses in the economy. Changes in the economy, technology, competition, and consumer demand for financial services made many regulations obsolete. Legislation, such as the Depository Institutions Deregulation and Monetary Control Act of 1980 and the Garn-St. Germain Depository Institutions Act of 1982, was enacted that partially deregulated depository financial institutions. These acts reduced the distinction among depository institutions and increased their ability to compete with other financial institutions.

   - *Commercial banks* are sometimes called "financial department stores" because they provide diverse financial services. Business firms rely heavily upon commercial banks for both borrowing and lending. Commercial banks are a particularly important source of short- and intermediate-term business loans.
   - *Savings and loan associations* (S & Ls) primarily serve individual savers and residential mortgage borrowers. Business firms generally do not rely heavily on S & Ls for daily financing needs.
   - *Mutual savings banks* acquire most of their funds from individuals. Mutual savings banks generally lend or invest funds through the financial markets rather than through negotiated loans. For example, mutual savings banks invest in home mortgages and corporate bonds.
   - *Credit unions* are institutions established to provide credit to individuals who share a common bond, such as working for the same employer. Credit unions deal primarily in transfers of funds among customers.

2. An **insurance companies** collects premiums from policyholders in return for providing benefits in the event of death (life insurance) or financial losses from fire and other perils (property and casualty insurance). Insurance companies are able to accumulate large amounts of funds for investment purposes. *Life insurance companies* invest primarily in corporate bonds and mortgages and are a major source of long-term debt financing for business firms. *Property and casualty insurance companies* invest mainly in state, local, and federal government securities as well as in corporate securities.

3. Other financial intermediaries include pension funds, mutual funds, trust funds, and finance companies.

- A **pension fund** is institutions that provide income to retired and disabled persons. Pension funds may be broadly divided into private pension funds and government-sponsored pension funds. Both types of funds invest heavily in corporate stocks and bonds.
- A **mutual fund** is a type of investment company that pools money primarily from individuals to invest in securities. Mutual funds invest heavily in corporate securities.
- A **trust fund** receives donations from various sources to fund their activities. Trust funds, including charitable organizations, college endowment funds, and research foundations, place sizable amounts of money in corporate stocks and bonds.
- **Finance companies** obtain their funds by issuing securities and borrowing from commercial banks. They use their funds to make short- and intermediate-term loans to individuals and business firms.

17-3. Investment Bankers

An **investment banker** is a financial specialist who acts as an agent between buyers and sellers of new security issues. This term is a misnomer because the investment banker is neither a long-term investor nor a banker. Because most companies issue new long-term debt and equity infrequently, they rely on investment bankers to perform services for them. Although investment bankers perform many services besides handling security issues, this section focuses on public security issues.

A. The investment banker performs three major functions.

1. *Underwriting.* When an investment banker underwrites a new issue, the banker actually buys the security issue at a discount from the proposed sale price. The issuer receives a price guarantee that specifies the amount of money it will receive regardless of whether the underwriter is able to sell all of the securities. Corporations generally use the underwriting method when selling common stock. The investment banker bears the risk of being unable to sell the issue and of any price fluctuations during the time the security is being distributed. There are two ways in which investment bankers underwrite securities.

   - A **negotiated underwriting** is an arrangement in which the issuing firm and its investment banker negotiate the terms of the issue. Most large industrial corporations use negotiated underwriting.
   - **Competitive bid underwriting** is an arrangement in which the issuer sells the securities to the underwriter with the highest bid (price). Competitive bidding usually results in a higher price than a negotiated offering. This form of underwriting is required for state bond issues and many publicly regulated companies such as electric utilities.

2. *Advise and counsel.* The investment banker advises the issuer on the timing of an issue, its pricing, and the features needed for a successful sale. Investment bankers serve in other advisory capacities in areas such as mergers, acquisitions, and financial planning.
3. *Marketing.* Investment bankers have considerable expertise in selling and distributing securities. On some issues, the investment banker simply serves as a selling agent and is not an underwriter. Under this arrangement, called a **best effort arrangement**, investment bankers promise to do their best to sell an issue to the public, associated with an underwriting. The best efforts basis is generally used with low-risk firms that expect to sell their securities easily or with high-risk firms that offer securities which investment bankers do not wish to underwrite. Whether an underwriting or best effort basis is used, the investment banker must develop a distribution system for selling the issue.

B. A corporation and/or its investment banker follow several steps in issuing new securities.

The steps vary somewhat depending on whether an issue is a public offering, private placement, or privileged subscription. The mechanics of a negotiated underwriting are as follows:

1. *Select the investment banker.* The issuer interviews several investment bankers and selects one based on the investment banker's ability to conduct a successful offering.

2. *Conduct conferences.* After an investment banker is selected, the issuer and the investment banker hold a series of *pre-underwriting conferences* to determine such matters as the amount of capital to be raised, the type of security to be sold, the timing of the issue, and the terms of their agreement. The investment banker also conducts an extensive investigation of the issuer's present and future financial position. If both parties are satisfied with the terms they have reached, they sign a tentative *underwriting agreement.* This agreement contains all of the major provisions of the sale except for the price of the security and the date of sale.

3. *Syndicate the underwriting.* The investment banker may underwrite the entire issue by itself if the issue is small. For larger issues, the investment banker usually invites other investment bankers to establish an *underwriting syndicate* in order to help finance the issue, share the risk, and assure successful market distribution. The original investment banker usually serves as the syndicate's manager.

4. *Register the issue.* With some exceptions, a corporation must file a registration statement and a prospectus with the Securities and Exchange Commission (SEC) and get its approval before a public issue can be sold. A **registration statement** is a document that provides full disclosure of all material facts relating to the issue, such as the firm's background, its financial statements, and details on the proposed underwriting syndicate. The SEC review process can take as little as 20 days but the total registration process often takes several months to complete. During the 20-day waiting period, the company may distribute a condensed version of the registration statement, called a **preliminary prospectus** or **red herring**, to potential investors in order to advertise the issue. The time delay of registration for future issues may be avoided by filing a **shelf registration**. Under a shelf registration, a corporation can obtain a registration that lasts up to two years. As soon as the registration is approved by the SEC, the firm can sell its securities to the public anytime during the two-year period without delay.

5. *Form the selling group.* During the registration process, the underwriter syndicate usually forms a selling group to market the issue to the public. Syndicate members act as wholesalers of the issue who distribute part of their shares in the underwriting to other investment bankers and securities firms, who serve as retailers to the public. Figure 17-1 illustrates an underwriting syndicate and selling group distribution system.

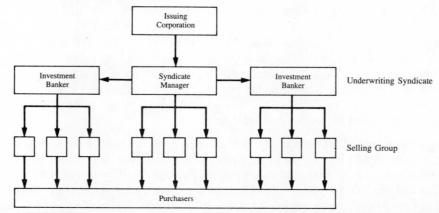

FIGURE 17-1   Underwriting syndicate and selling group for distributing a new issue

6. *Price the issue.* The *offering price* of the security, which is the price at which the security is offered to the public, is generally not set until the end of the registration period in order to have a current "feel" of the market at the time of pricing. Once the registration statement is approved by the SEC, the final prospectus, including the security price and time of sale, is printed.

7. *Sell the issue.* The issue cannot be sold until it is approved by the SEC and formally placed on the market, which is usually the day after approval. However, the selling group may publicize the issue through advertising and personal contacts before approval. Therefore, an issue may be sold out within hours of being offered for sale. If all shares are not sold immediately, the issue is *undersubscribed.* During the offering period, the syndicate manager stands ready to stabilize the resale price of the security at a level no lower than the security's offering price. This activity, known as **price-pegging**, is used to provide price support by placing orders to buy the security at a specified price. If the issue is slow to sell, the offering price may be abandoned in favor of a lower price, which may result in a loss to the underwriters.

8. *Terminate the syndicate.* After the issue is sold out, the syndication is terminated.

C. *Flotation costs* are the firm's costs of issuing new securities.

Total flotation costs of a public security issue consist of compensation to the investment banker plus other company issue expenses. The investment banker is compensated for assuming the risk of an underwriting, selling the securities to investors, and advising the issuer. Compensation for the risk-bearing is an **underwriting profit**, while compensation for the service function of selling is the **selling concession**. The investment banker may also receive an advisory fee. When combined, these fees represent the total compensation to the investment banker and are called the **underwriting spread**. Thus, the underwriting spread is the difference between the gross proceeds of a security sale and the amount that the issuer actually receives. Other costs incurred by the issuer include legal and accounting expenses, prospectus printing costs, and filing fees related to registration of the issue with the SEC. The flotation costs of issuing new securities vary widely and depend on several factors.

1. *Type of security.* Flotation costs are generally highest on common stock issues, followed by preferred stock and bonds, in that order. With common stock issues, the investment banker incurs more risk and higher marketing expenses than with either preferred stock or bonds.

2. *Quality of the security.* An issue's quality rests on the financial strength of the issuer. Low-quality issues have higher flotation costs than high-quality issues. Underwriters bear more risk and incur higher costs in selling low-quality issues and require compensation for these factors.

3. *Size of the issue.* Overall flotation costs in percentage terms generally vary inversely with issue size. Small issues are more expensive as a percentage of total funds raised than large issues because numerous issuing costs are fixed.

EXAMPLE 17-2: LeMoine Industries wishes to raise $40,000,000 from the sale of common stock. The firm and its underwriting syndicate agree to an offering price of $20 per share. The firm also agrees to pay the syndicate $0.75 per share as a risk-bearing fee, plus 1 percent of the sales proceeds to compensate the syndicate for other services rendered, such as selling the securities. The firm will incur other issuing expenses of $350,000 for the offering. From this information, we can conclude:

(*a*) LeMoine Industries must sell $2,000,000 shares in order to raise $40,000,000 at an offering price of $20 per share. The underwriters will earn a risk-bearing fee of $1,500,000 ($0.75 × 2,000,000) and other fees of $400,000 (0.01 × $40,000,000). The total compensation or underwriting spread received by the underwriters is $1,900,000.

(*b*) Assuming that the investment bankers are able to sell the common stock issue for $40,000,000, the underwriting spread is 4.75 percent ($1,900,000/$40,000,000) of the gross proceeds of the security sale.

(*c*) LeMoine Industries will receive $37,750,000, which represents the gross proceeds of the sale of $40,000,000 less the underwriting spread of $1,900,000 and other costs of $350,000.

17-4. Private Placements

A **private placement** is the direct sale of an entire issue to a limited number of investors rather than to the general public. The issue's terms and price are negotiated directly with these investors, who typically include institutional investors such as life insurance companies and pension funds. Unlike most public offerings, a private placement is a non-underwriting method of raising funds in the primary securities market. As such, private placements do not have to be registered with the SEC. Bonds and preferred stock are the type of security most frequently offered in a private placement. Although the services of an investment banker are not always required in private placements, corporations do use them for finding potential investors and for negotiating the terms of the agreement.

A. Private placements offer several advantages to the firm over public issues as a mechanism for financing.

1. *Lower flotation costs.* The issuer can save on flotation costs by eliminating underwriting costs, sales commissions, and registration expenses.
2. *Speed.* Private placements avoid the time delays involved in registration and approval by the SEC.
3. *Flexibility.* A private placement facilitates tailoring the terms and provisions of the offering to meet the issuer's specific needs. If the issuer encounters difficulties, renegotiation is easier with a private, as opposed to a public, offering because of the limited number of investors.
4. *Privacy.* A private placement does not require public disclosure of information about the issuer to the public, which could benefit competitors.

B. Private placements have several disadvantages to the issuer.

1. *Higher cost of capital.* Private investors generally require a higher rate of return because they cannot sell the securities in resale markets, since the securities are not registered. Thus, the interest rate on debt issues is generally higher and the price on equity issues is typically lower than comparable public issues.
2. *Difficulty in raising funds.* The issuing corporation may encounter difficulty in raising large amounts of funds during certain time periods because institutional investors lack the funds to invest.
3. *Restrictions.* Private placements are concentrated in the hands of relatively few investors who may exert their bargaining power to obtain concessions from a company which needs financing or experiences difficulties once the placement is made. Thus, private placements may have more restrictive provisions imposed on the issuer to protect the investors.

17-5. Privileged Subscriptions

As an alternative to a public or private offering, the corporation may use other techniques to sell securities. With a **privileged subscription**, also called a *rights offering*, a corporation gives existing shareholders an opportunity to buy new shares of its common stock before any public offering is made. Corporations may also provide plans that offer shares to managers through stock option plans, to employees through stock purchase plans, and to existing shareholders through dividend reinvestment plans. However, these latter three plans do not necessarily involve the sale of new stock.

A. A rights offering is an attempt to sell new common stock to the firm's existing stockholders by issuing rights.

A **right** is an option to buy a specified number of shares of common stock at a specified price per share over a fixed time period. In a rights offering, existing shareholders have the ability to maintain their proportionate ownership in the corporation when new issues are made. This privilege, called a **preemptive right**, is required by most states. In order to provide an incentive for stockholders to subscribe to the new issue, management sets the **subscription price** that stockholders will have to pay for each new share below the market price. Each shareholder receives one right for each share already owned. Stockholders may choose to exercise their rights, sell their rights, or let them expire.

1. The number of rights required to purchase a share of stock depends on the amount of required financing, the subscription price per share, and the number of common shares outstanding prior to the new issue. Equation 17-1 shows how to compute the number of new shares that must be sold.

$$\frac{\text{Number of new shares}}{\text{to be sold}} = \frac{\text{Amount of required financing}}{\text{Subscription price per share}} \qquad \textbf{(17-1)}$$

Equation 17-2 is the computation of the number of rights needed to buy a new share.

$$\frac{\text{Number of rights}}{\text{to buy a new share}} = \frac{\text{Number of common shares outstanding}}{\text{Number of new shares to be sold}} \qquad \textbf{(17-2)}$$

EXAMPLE 17-3: Taff Corporation plans to raise $2,500,000 through a rights offering. The firm has 400,000 shares of common stock outstanding, which currently sell for $30 per share. Management decides to set the subscription price at $25 per share.

Substituting $2,500,000 in required financing and a $25 per share subscription price in Equation 17-2 shows that Taff Corporation must sell 100,000 new shares.

$$\frac{\text{Number of new}}{\text{shares to be sold}} = \frac{\$2,500,000}{\$25} = 100,000 \text{ shares}$$

Substituting 400,000 shares outstanding and 100,000 new shares in Equation 17-2 indicates that four rights are required to purchase each new share.

$$\frac{\text{Number of rights}}{\text{to buy a new share}} = \frac{400,000}{100,000} = 4 \text{ rights}$$

2. Stock rights have value because the holder may buy common stock for less than the market price. Stock rights are negotiable instruments traded on security exchanges. The value of a right depends on the market price of the stock, the subscription price, and the number of rights needed to buy a new share. The theoretical value of a right may be computed when the stock is selling rights-on and ex-rights. When a stock trades **rights-on**, purchasers receive the rights along with the shares they purchase. Equation 17-3 shows the theoretical value of one right when the stock is selling rights-on.

VALUE OF ONE RIGHT $$R_o = \frac{M_o - S}{N + 1} \qquad \textbf{(17-3)}$$

where R_o = theoretical value of one right when stock is selling rights-on

M_o = market price of one share of stock selling rights-on

S = subscription price per share

N = number of rights required to purchase one share of stock

EXAMPLE 17-4: *Refer to Example 17-3.* Taff Corporation's stock is currently selling rights-on for $30 per share. The rights offering has a subscription price of $25 per share and requires four rights to purchase a new share of stock. Substituting the appropriate values in Equation 17-3, the theoretical value of one right is $1. A right should therefore be worth $1 in the marketplace.

$$R_o = \frac{\$30 - \$25}{4 + 1} = \$1$$

3. When a stock trades **ex-rights**, purchasers no longer receive the rights when they purchase the stock. The stock usually goes ex-rights four business days before the **date of record**, which is the date a corporation examines its shareholder records to determine who receives the rights. On the ex-rights date, the stock price is expected to drop by the value of one right because purchasers no longer receive the right as part of the purchase. Thus, the fact that the subscription price in a rights offering is lower than the market price should lead to a diluted market price of the stock when it goes ex-rights. Equation 17-4 indicates the market price of a share of stock when it goes from rights-on to ex-rights.

$$M_e = M_o - R_o \tag{17-4}$$

where M_e = market price of one share of stock selling ex-rights.

Equation 17-5 shows the the theoretical value of one right when the stock is selling ex-rights.

$$R_e = \frac{M_e - S}{N} \tag{17-5}$$

where R_e = theoretical value of one right when stock is selling ex-rights

EXAMPLE 17-5: *Refer to Examples 17-3 and 17-4.* According to Equation 17-4, the market price of Taff Corporation stock selling ex-rights is $29.

$$M_e = \$30 - \$1 = \$29$$

Substituting the $29 market price in Equation 17-5 makes the value of a right $1 when the stock is selling ex-rights. Thus, the theoretical value of one right is the same when the stock is selling either rights-on or ex-rights.

$$R_e = \frac{\$29 - \$25}{4} = \$1$$

4. A rights offering itself does not increase shareholder wealth. Theoretically, stockholders do not gain if they exercise or sell their rights, but they will suffer a loss by letting the rights expire. In actual practice, the market value of a right may differ from its theoretical value depending the behavior of market participants. The resale value of a right typically decreases as the ex-rights date approaches.
5. Rights offerings may be made directly to shareholders or through an investment banker. Most companies use the investment banker as a selling agent. The investment banker often agrees to provide a **standby underwriting** whereby shares not bought through the rights offering are purchased at a specified price by the investment banker.
6. Rights offerings have several advantages and disadvantages. The primary advantage of a rights offering to existing shareholders is that it protects them from a dilution of their investment and control. From the company's perspective, a rights offerings has lower flotation costs than a public issue and may also increase stockholder loyalty and stimulate interest in the company, which may aid future financing. Rights offerings, however, do lead to a more narrow distribution of stock and may cause losses to shareholders who fail to exercise their rights or sell them.

B. A *stock option plan* **is a method which gives managers the opportunity to purchase a certain number of shares of the firm's common stock at a specified price within a stated period of time.**

As indicated in Chapter 1, the goals of management may differ from the goals of the firm's owners. Stock option plans provide management with an incentive to act in the best long-run interest of the firm's owners by making managers stockholders.

C. A *stock purchase plan* **is a fringe benefit program that allows employees to purchase the firm's stock.**

Stock purchase plans are intended to increase employee motivation and interest in the company. Another form of stock purchase is the employee stock ownership plan (ESOP), whereby employees regularly accumulate shares and may ultimately assure control of the firm.

D. A *dividend reinvestment plan* **is an arrangement whereby existing stockholders may reinvest all or part of their cash dividends in more shares of a firm's stock.**

Some dividend reinvestment plans allow stockholders to acquire stock at a discount below the current market price and to invest additional cash to purchase shares. Dividend reinvestment plans are widely used by utilities to raise new capital.

17-6. Regulation of Securities Markets

Securities markets are regulated by both the federal government and individual states, as well as by self-regulation. Regulation of securities markets is designed to provide investors with reliable information for making sound investment decisions, to protect investors against fraudulent practices, and to ensure orderly security transactions.

A. The *Securities and Exchange Commission (SEC)* **is a federal agency that regulates both primary and secondary markets for publicly traded corporate securities.**

This regulatory power was vested in the SEC through two major legislative acts.

1. The *Securities Act of 1933* regulates the public sale of corporate securities. Except for a few exemptions, this act requires that corporations issuing new securities provide full disclosure of all relevant information regarding these securities. For example, under the the Securities Act of 1933, the firm is required to submit a registration statement and a prospectus which must be approved before a new security can be issued and sold.

2. The *Securities Exchange Act of 1934* regulates the trading of securities on secondary markets. This act was designed to protect small investors and promote market efficiency by requiring full disclosure of traded securities, monitoring insider trading, making certain trading practices illegal, and regulating brokers, dealers and security exchanges. The 1934 Act also created the Securities and Exchange Commission to administer federal securities laws.

B. States regulate the sale of securities within their boundaries.

State regulations that govern public offerings of securities within the various states, frequently called **blue sky laws**, are intended to protect investors against security fraud.

C. Self-regulation is provided by several groups.

The organized security exchanges have developed their own regulations and the *National Association of Securities Dealers* (NASD) provides self-regulation of over-the-counter markets.

RAISE YOUR GRADES

Can you explain...?

☑ the primary role of the financial system
☑ how money markets and capital markets differ
☑ how primary markets and secondary markets differ
☑ the major participants in financial markets
☑ the roles of brokers and dealers in financial markets
☑ the differences between organized security exchanges and over-the-counter markets
☑ the purpose served by financial intermediaries
☑ the three broad classes of financial intermediaries
☑ the functions of an investment banker
☑ how a negotiated underwriting and competitive bid underwriting differ
☑ the steps in selling a new public security issue
☑ the role of an investment banker in a best effort arrangement
☑ the factors influencing the flotation costs of a new issue of securities
☑ the advantages and disadvantages of a private placement
☑ what a privileged subscription is
☑ why rights have value
☑ the purposes of the Securities Act of 1933 and the Securities Exchange Act of 1934

SUMMARY

1. The financial system is a network of financial markets and institutions that channels funds from suppliers (net savers) into the hands of demanders of these funds (net investors).
2. Key participants in the financial system are individuals, businesses, governmental units, and financial institutions.
3. Corporations rely on financial markets to finance asset growth, provide a resale market for their securities, and test the value of their financial assets.
4. Financial markets may be classified into several major categories, including money or capital markets, and primary and secondary markets.
5. Money markets deal in short-term securities, whereas capital markets deal in intermediate- and long-term securities.
6. Primary markets are those in which new securities are issued; secondary markets are those in which previously issued securities are traded.
7. Within the secondary markets, existing securities are traded on organized security exchanges and over-the-counter (OTC) markets.
8. There are several organized exchanges, with the New York Stock Exchange being the largest. Exchanges are centralized marketplaces operating as auction markets. Securities not listed on the exchanges are traded in the over-the-counter markets.
9. OTC securities are not traded in a central facility, but rather through a telecommunications network linking various market participants. The stocks of most companies are traded over-the-counter but the dollar volume of trading is usually higher on the exchanges.
10. Brokers and dealers serve a vital role in financial markets. Brokers facilitate trading securities for investors but do not take ownership of the securities. Dealers buy and sell securities from their own accounts and take ownership of the securities.
11. Financial intermediaries create financial assets for suppliers and lend money to those who need it. Intermediaries provide business firms with large amounts of financing by

pooling the money of numerous savers. Financial intermediaries consist of depository institutions, insurance companies, and other intermediaries, such as pension funds and mutual funds.

12. Investment bankers assist firms in raising long-term funds in the capital markets. The investment banker bears risk and provides a source of funds by underwriting a new issue; advises and counsels the issuer; and markets and distributes the securities.

13. Two major ways of underwriting a security issue are negotiated underwriting and competitive bid underwriting. With a negotiated underwriting, the issuing firm negotiates the terms of the issue with the investment banker. With a competitive bidding arrangement, the issuer sells the securities to the underwriter who offers the highest price.

14. Selling a new public issue involves numerous steps. Often the original investment banker forms a syndicate to spread the risk of the underwriting to other investment bankers. A selling group may also be formed to facilitate the sale and distribution of the securities.

15. The cost of selling new securities consists of the underwriting spread and administrative costs. These costs vary with the type of security, its quality, and the size of the issue.

16. A firm may sell new securities through a private placement instead of a public offering. Private placements generally involve lower flotation costs and more flexibility and privacy than a public sale of securities. However, private placements may result in a higher cost of capital, control problems, and difficulty in raising funds during certain periods.

17. A corporation may use a privileged subscription or rights offering to sell common stock to select potential investors. A rights offering enables existing stockholders to purchase the firm's new shares of common stock by exercising stock rights that have been issued to them.

18. A right has value because it permits shareholders to buy new shares at a price below the market price. The shareholder may sell these rights or let them expire. Although stockholders do not necessarily gain if they exercise or sell their rights, they will suffer a loss if they let their rights expire.

19. Other ways of selling new shares of a firm's stock are through stock option plans, stock purchase plans, and dividend reinvestment plans. However, firms may also buy their own stock in the market, instead of issuing new shares, to provide stock for these plans.

20. Securities markets are regulated by the federal government, individual state governments, and self-regulation. At the federal level, the Securities Act of 1933 regulates the sale of new securities, while the Securities Exchange Act of 1934 regulates the trading of existing securities.

21. States have blue sky laws for regulating the sale of securities within their boundaries. The organized exchanges and the over-the-counter markets are also self-regulated.

RAPID REVIEW

True or False

1. The primary role of the financial system is to facilitate savings and investment in the economy. [Section 17-1]

2. Financial markets provide the mechanisms through which financial assets are bought, sold, or traded. [Section 17-1]

3. Money markets include both short-term and long-term debt securities. [Section 17-1B]

4. Capital markets are where long-term debt and equity capital are raised. [Section 17-1B]

5. Primary markets consist of organized exchanges and over-the-counter markets. [Section 17-1B]

6. An investor who resells existing securities is participating in a secondary financial market. [Section 17-1B]

7. The largest and most dominant security exchange is the American Stock Exchange. [Section 17-1B]

8. The organized security exchanges are auction markets. [Section 17-1B]

9. A dealer is hired to buy or sell securities for investors but does not take ownership of the securities. [Section 17-1B]

10. The over-the-counter markets have centralized trading facilities primarily located in New York. [Section 17-1B]

11. Financial intermediation is the process by which security dealers facilitate trading by introducing buyers to sellers. [Section 17-2]

12. Financial intermediaries channel funds from suppliers to demanders at a lower cost than could be achieved by direct lending from individual investors. [Section 17-2A]

13. The investment banker bears the risk of loss from falling stock prices during the underwriting period. [Section 17-3A]

14. With a best effort arrangement, the investment banker provides the issuer with a guarantee that the entire security will be sold at a specified price. [Section 17-3A]

15. An underwriting syndicate is formed to diversify the risk and to gain wide distribution of securities. [Section 17-3B]

16. Any attempt of underwriters to peg the price of a security during the distribution period is illegal. [Section 17-3B]

17. Once approved by the Securities and Exchange Commission, a shelf registration enables a corporation to sell its securities to the public anytime during a five-year period without delay. [Section 17-3B]

18. The underwriting spread is used partly to compensate the investment banker for assuming the risk of an underwriting. [Section 17-3C]

19. Total flotation costs are generally higher for bonds than other securities. [Section 17-3C]

20. A private offering is exempt from the registration requirements of the Securities and Exchange Commission. [Section 17-4A]

21. A rights offering allows existing shareholders to maintain their ownership position in the firm. [Section 17-5A]

22. Preemptive rights are guaranteed by the Securities Act of 1933. [Section 17-5A]

23. Each stock right enables a stockholder to purchase one new share of common stock. [Section 17-5A]

24. Stock rights generally increase shareholder wealth. [Section 17-5A]

25. The Securities Exchange Act of 1934 regulates the trading of securities in the secondary markets. [Section 17-6A]

Multiple Choice

26. Functions of financial markets include

    (a) financing asset growth
    (b) providing a resale market
    (c) testing the value of financial assets
    (d) All of the above

    [Section 17-1A]

27. Which of the following is not a capital market instrument?

    (a) Preferred stock
    (b) Mortgage
    (c) Commercial paper
    (d) Bond

    [Section 17-1B]

28. The initial public sale of a security occurs in

(*a*) primary markets
(*b*) secondary markets
(*c*) organized security exchanges
(*d*) NASDAQ

[Section 17-1B]

29. Listed securities are traded in

(*a*) primary markets
(*b*) organized security exchanges
(*c*) over-the-counter markets
(*d*) the New York Stock Exchange only

[Section 17-1B]

30. Bid and asked prices on securities are provided to investors through

(*a*) investment bankers
(*b*) the Securities and Exchange Commission
(*c*) the New York Stock Exchange
(*d*) the NASDAQ

[Section 17-1B]

31. Which of the following financial intermediaries is *not* an important supplier of funds to corporations?

(*a*) Commercial banks
(*b*) Savings and loan associations
(*c*) Insurance companies
(*d*) Pension funds

[Section 17-2B]

32. Which one of the following services is not performed by investment bankers for their clients?

(*a*) Providing advice to firms issuing securities
(*b*) Selling and distributing securities
(*c*) Underwriting new security issues
(*d*) Investing in securities for the long term

[Section 17-3A]

33. Which of the following is *not* an advantage of a private placement over a public offering?

(*a*) Greater speed of raising funds than a public offering
(*b*) Lower interest rate on debt
(*c*) Lower flotation costs
(*d*) More flexibility than a public offering

[Sections 17-4A through 17-4B]

34. All of the following are advantages of a rights offering *except* that it:

(*a*) increases the investor base of the stock
(*b*) protects existing stockholders against dilution of control
(*c*) results in lower flotation costs than a public issue
(*d*) increases loyalty among some stockholders

[Section 17-5A]

35. Blue sky laws

(*a*) regulate the activity of the over-the-counter market
(*b*) refer to provisions of the Securities Act of 1933

(*c*) pertain to state laws governing public security issues

(*d*) require a negotiated underwriting of state bond issues

[Section 17-6B]

Answers

True or False			*Multiple Choice*
1. True	11. False	21. True	26. d
2. True	12. True	22. False	27. c
3. False	13. True	23. False	28. a
4. True	14. False	24. False	29. b
5. False	15. True	25. True	30. d
6. True	16. False		31. b
7. False	17. False		32. d
8. True	18. True		33. b
9. False	19. False		34. a
10. False	20. True		35. c

SOLVED PROBLEMS

PROBLEM 17-1: An investment banker has agreed to sell an issue of 2,000,000 shares of common stock of Quality Products at an agreed-upon offering price of $40 per share. The investment banker guarantees the issuing firm a price of $38.50 per share. Other administrative expenses of the issue are $600,000.

(*a*) What is the underwriting spread associated with this offering?

(*b*) What are the total flotation costs as a percentage of the gross proceeds?

Answer:

(*a*) The underwriting spread per share is $1.50 ($40.00 − $38.50) and the total underwriting spread is $3,000,000 ($1.50 × 2,000,000). Thus, the gross proceeds from the sale are $80,000,000 ($40 × 2,000,000) with $77,000,000 ($38.50 × 2,000,000) going to Quality Products and $3,000,000 to the investment banker.

(*b*) The total flotation costs of $3,600,000 consist of the underwriting spread of $3,000,000 plus $600,000 in administrative costs. Since Quality Products raised $80,000,000, the flotation costs as a percentage of the gross proceeds are 4.5 percent ($3,600,000/$80,000,000). **[Section 17-3C]**

PROBLEM 17-2: In Problem 17-1, how would the investment banker fare if the stock were sold for only $36 per share?

Answer: If the entire 2,000,000 shares are sold for $36 per share, the gross proceeds from the sale would be $72,000,000 ($36 × 2,000,000). The investmennt banker would experience a gross loss of $5,000,000, which is the difference between the $72,000,000 gross proceeds and $77,000,000 guaranteed by Quality Products. **[Section 17-3C]**

PROBLEM 17-3: In Problem 17-1, assume that the stock issue is on a best effort arrangement instead of an underwriting. What is the investment banker's responsibility if only 1,500,000 shares are sold?

Answer: If the stock issue were on a best efforts basis, the investment banker has no responsibility for unsold securities. Compensation to the investment banker would include only the selling concession and advisory fees, not underwriting profit.

[Section 17-3C]

PROBLEM 17-4: Seckler Corporation plans to raise $20,000,000 through the sale of $1,000 par value bonds. Total flotation costs are $320,000. How many bonds must be sold at par value to net $20,000,000?

Answer: Seckler would have to sell 20,320 bonds ($20,320,000/$1,000) in order to net $20,000,000   **[Section 17-3C]**

PROBLEM 17-5: Finn Technologies has 1,000,000 shares of common stock outstanding and is contemplating a rights offering. The offering's subscription price is $10 and the current price of the stock is $12. The firm plans to raise $5,000,000.

(*a*) How many new shares must be sold to raise the $5,000,000?
(*b*) How many rights are needed to purchase one share of stock?

Answer:

(*a*) Substituting $5,000,000 in required financing and a $10 subscription price in Equation 17-1 shows that Finn Technologies must sell:

$$\frac{\text{Number of new}}{\text{shares to be sold}} = \frac{\$5,000,000}{\$10 \text{ per share}} = 500,000 \text{ shares}$$

(*b*) Finn Technologies currently has 1,000,000 shares outstanding and needs to sell 500,000 new shares. Substituting these values in Equation 17-2 indicates that two rights are needed to acquire a single new share of stock.

$$\frac{\text{Number of rights}}{\text{to buy a new share}} = \frac{1,000,000}{500,000} = 2 \text{ rights} \qquad \textbf{[Section 17-5A]}$$

PROBLEM 17-6: Using information provided in Problem 17-5, answer the following questions:

(*a*) What is the value of one right when the stock is selling rights-on?
(*b*) What is the price of the stock ex-rights?
(*c*) What is the theoretical value of the one right when the stock is selling ex-rights?

Answer:

(*a*) Substituting appropriate values into Equation 17-3 the theoretical value of one right when the stock is selling rights-on is:

$$R_o = \frac{\$12 - \$10}{2 + 1} = \$0.67$$

(*b*) Equation 17-4 shows that the rights-on stock price of $12.00 should drop by $0.67, the value of one right, to produce an ex-rights stock price of $11.33.

$$M_e = \$12.00 - \$0.67 = \$11.33$$

(*c*) According to Equation 17-5, the theoretical value of one right when Finn Technologies stock is selling ex-rights is $0.67:

$$R_e = \frac{\$11.33 - \$10.00}{2} = \$0.67 \qquad \textbf{[Section 17-5A]}$$

PROBLEM 17-7: In Problem 17-6, what is the loss in market value of a shareholder who owns 100 shares of common stock in Finn Technologies and allows the rights to expire?

Answer: Since the ex-rights price of each share of stock would theoretically drop by $0.67, a shareholder with 100 shares of Finn Technologies stock would experience a $67 ($0.67 × 100) loss in market value by allowing the rights to expire.   **[Section 17-5A]**

PROBLEM 17-8: Fallsriver, Inc. recently raised $4,000,000 by selling new common stock through a rights offering. The subscription price was $40 per share. The firm had 500,000 shares outstanding prior to the rights offering. The price of the firm's stock ex-rights dropped to $45 per share.

(*a*) What was the value of one right?
(*b*) What was the rights-on price of the stock?

Answer:

(*a*) Using Equation 17-1, Fallsriver sold 100,000 new shares to raise $4,000,000. Since the firm already had 500,000 shares outstanding, Equation 17-2 shows that five rights were needed to purchase one share of stock. The theoretical value of one right when the stock is selling ex-rights is determined by substituting the $45 ex-rights price of the common stock, the $40 subscription price, and the five rights necessary to purchase a single share of stock in Equation 17-5. Thus, the value of one right is $1.00.

$$\text{Number of new shares to be sold} = \frac{\$4,000,000}{\$40} = 100,000 \text{ shares}$$

$$\text{Number of rights to buy a new share} = \frac{500,000}{100,000} = 5 \text{ rights}$$

$$\text{Value of one right when stock is selling ex-rights} = \frac{\$45 - \$40}{5} = \$1.00$$

(*b*) The $46 rights-on price of the stock, M_o, is determined by rearranging the terms of Equation 17-4 as shown below and by solving for M_o.

Ex-rights price of common stock $\quad M_e = M_o - R_o$

Rights-on price of common stock $\quad M_o = M_e + R_o$

$$= \$45 + \$1 = \$46 \qquad \textbf{[Section 17-5A]}$$

18 SHORT-TERM FINANCING

THIS CHAPTER IS ABOUT

- ☑ **Overview of Short-term Financing**
- ☑ **Trade Credit**
- ☑ **Accruals**
- ☑ **Unsecured Bank Financing**
- ☑ **Commercial Paper**
- ☑ **Accounts Receivable Financing**
- ☑ **Inventory Financing**

18-1. Overview of Short-term Financing

Short-term financing refers to debt originally scheduled for repayment within one year. Short-term financing is used to finance all or part of the firm's working capital requirements and sometimes to meet permanent financing needs. The amount of short-term versus intermediate- and long-term financing used to provide funds to meet a firm's needs depends largely on management's risk-return strategies. However, shorter-term financing is often less expensive and more flexible than longer-term financing.

A. Short-term financing may be either unsecured or secured.

Unsecured short-term financing is an obligation without specific assets pledged as collateral. **Collateral** is the asset that the borrower pledges to a lender until a loan is repaid. The stronger the firm's overall credit rating, the more likely it will borrow on an unsecured basis. Both borrowers and lenders prefer to do business on an unsecured basis. Unsecured loans are more risky to lenders, but provide maximum flexibility to borrowers and are less costly to administer than secured loans. The lender depends on the cash-generating ability of the firm to repay the debt. However, if the lender defaults on the loan or goes into bankruptcy, the unsecured lender's chance of receiving full or partial payment is diminished because secured creditors have a prior claim to the firm's assets. Unsecured credit is found on the balance sheet under accounts payable, accruals, and notes payable.

Secured short-term financing is an obligation with specific assets pledged as collateral. Accounts receivable and inventory are the most common sources of collateral for short-term financing. The lender expects the loan to be repaid from the cash-generating ability of the borrower. However, if the borrower defaults, the lender has the legal right to seize the collateral and sell it to pay off the loan.

B. Firms obtain short-term financing from several sources.

1. *Other business firms.* Business firms provide short-term financing by giving trade credit and by purchasing commercial paper from firms in need of funds.
2. *Financial intermediaries.* Commercial banks are the primary source of unsecured

short-term loans. Banks and other financial intermediaries, such as insurance companies and pension funds, purchase commercial paper. The primary sources of secured short-term loans are commercial banks and commercial finance companies. A *commercial finance company* is a financial institution that makes loans which are secured by accounts receivables, inventories, or fixed assets.

3. *Individuals.* People are the ultimate suppliers of funds to business firms. Individuals do not supply short-term financing directly, except to small firms. Instead, savings and investments of individuals are channeled through the financial markets and financial intermediaries to business firms.

C. Sources of short-term financing may be either spontaneous or negotiated.

1. **Spontaneous sources** of short-term financing are sources that arise automatically from ordinary business transactions. Spontaneous sources do not require any special effort or negotiation on the part of the financial manager. The two major sources of spontaneous financing are accounts payable and accruals. The level of spontaneous credit is a function of the firm's operations. As sales increase, current liabilities typically increase. These liabilities finance part of the firm's asset expansion brought on by the increased sales. Management can influence the level of accounts payable and accruals to some extent to achieve inexpensive financing. The costs of spontaneous financing are generally implicit rather than explicit. The goal of managing spontaneous sources of short-term financing is to minimize their cost.

2. **Negotiated sources** of short-term financing are sources that require special effort or negotiation. The major sources of negotiated short-term credit are bank loans, commercial paper, accounts receivable loans, and inventory loans.

18-2. Trade Credit

Trade credit is short-term credit extended by suppliers of goods and services and subject to certain terms and conditions. Trade credit results when a firm acquires supplies, materials, or merchandise and does not pay for them immediately. These transactions are typically recorded on the balance sheet as accounts or notes payable by the buyer and as accounts or notes receivable by the seller. Trade credit is the primary source of short-term financing for most business firms. Manufacturers, retailers, and wholesalers make more extensive use of trade credit than do service firms. Trade credit is particularly important for small firms because they often do not qualify for financing from other sources. The major advantages of trade credit are its availability, convenience, and extremely low cost.

A. Three major types of trade credit are open accounts, notes payable, and trade acceptances.

1. An **open account** is an informal, prearranged extension of short-term credit by a supplier to a firm. A buyer is not required to sign a note indicating liability to the seller. Open accounts, better known as accounts payable, are the most common type of trade credit because of their availability and flexibility.

2. **Notes payable** are a formal type of trade credit in which the buyer signs a promissory note indicating liability to the seller. Promissory notes are sometimes used for less creditworthy buyers, including those whose accounts are overdue. The formality of promissory notes gives the lender increased power to enforce the credit.

3. **Trade acceptances** are formal agreements in which the delivery of goods is not completed until the buyer accepts a draft drawn by the seller. The seller draws a draft on the buyer ordering the buyer to pay the draft at some future date. Shipment of the goods is delayed until the buyer accepts the draft. When the draft is accepted it becomes a trade acceptance. If the firm's bank rather than the firm itself guarantees payment, the acceptance is a banker's acceptance.

B. The specific nature of an open account is determined by four factors.

These four factors are:

1. *Credit terms.* Credit terms are the conditions under which a buyer is required to repay the credit that is extended by a seller. The elements of credit terms include the length of the credit period, the cash discount, and the cash discount period. The credit period and cash discount period also require a starting date. Credit terms of *3/10, net 45 EOM* contain all of these elements. These credit terms specify that a 3 percent cash discount can be obtained if the payment is made within the first 10 days (cash discount period) from the end of the current month (starting date); otherwise, the net or full amount is due 45 days (the credit period) from the end of the month. The elements of credit terms are discussed in more detail in Chapter 11.
2. *Nature of the product.* Products with a low turnover rate often have longer credit terms than those with a high turnover rate.
3. *Seller's financial position.* A seller in a weak financial position cannot extend credit terms as favorable as a seller in a strong financial condition.
4. *Buyer's financial position.* A buyer in a weak financial position is likely to accept less favorable credit terms than a buyer in a strong financial position who has extensive credit opportunities.

C. There are normally no explicit costs of trade credit.

Credit received during the discount period is sometimes called **free trade credit**. The view that trade credit is free may be misleading. There are costs associated with trade credit, but they are not as obvious as costs of other forms of financing, such as interest charges.

1. *Hidden costs.* Suppliers of trade credit incur the costs of operating a credit department and financing account receivables. They pass these costs on to buyers in the price of the product or service. Including the cost of extending credit in the selling price makes the analysis of credit costs difficult for the buyer.
2. *Missed cash discount.* Trade credit does not have explicit cost if there is no discount offered or if the buyer pays the invoice during the discount period. However, if the terms of sale include a discount and the discount is not taken, an *opportunity cost* is incurred because the buyer foregoes an opportunity to pay less for the purchases. In essence, the discounted value is the selling price. When the buyer fails to pay within the discount period, the amount of the discount lost is the cost of not paying the discounted value until the end of the remaining portion of the discounted period. For example, a typewriter priced at $1,000 can be bought with terms *2/10, net 30*. The selling price is actually $980, since this is the amount for which the typewriter can be bought. The $20 discount is the fee the buyer pays the seller for not having to pay the $980 for another 20 days. Equation 18-1 shows the effective annual interest rate (cost) of foregoing the discount as a percentage of the discounted amount.

$$\frac{\text{Cost of foregoing}}{\text{a cash discount}} = \frac{\text{Discount } (\%)}{100\% - \text{discount } (\%)} \times \frac{360 \text{ days}}{\text{Credit period} - \text{Discount period}} \quad \text{(18-1)}$$

This equation assumes that payments are made on the last day of the credit period, and a 360-day year. Assuming a 365-day year increases the cost of foregoing a cash discount. The net credit period is the number of days between the end of the discount period and the end of the credit period.

EXAMPLE 18-1: Speedy Shoe Company receives two different credit terms from suppliers: *2/10, net 30* and *2/10, net 60*. The firm will receive a 2 percent discount if payment is made within 10 days; otherwise, full payment is required within 30 or 60 days depending on the supplier.

(a) Substituting the given values in Equation 18-1, the effective annual percentage costs of foregoing discounts of 2/10, net 30 and 2/10, net 60 are 36.73 percent and 14.69 percent, respectively.

Credit Terms: 2/10, net 30

$$\text{Cost of foregoing a cash discount} = \frac{2\%}{100\% - 2\%} \times \frac{360}{30 - 10} = 0.3673 \text{ or } 36.73 \text{ percent}$$

Credit Terms: 2/10, net 60

$$\text{Cost of foregoing a cash discount} = \frac{2\%}{100\% - 2\%} \times \frac{360}{60 - 10} = 0.1469 \text{ or } 14.69 \text{ percent}$$

(b) The cost of trade credit decreases as the net credit period increases. The *net credit period* is the number of days between the end of the discount period and the end of the credit period. This relationship assumes that the discount period remains constant.

(c) The cost of the discount missed is an opportunity cost foregone for not paying by the tenth day. Forfeiting the discount is equivalent to borrowing at an effective annual interest rate of either 36.73 percent or 14.69 percent, depending on the discount foregone and the net credit period. Thus, missing discounts can be a very expensive source of short-term financing.

D. Stretching accounts payable may involve severe consequences.

Stretching accounts payable is postponement of payment beyond the end of the credit period. Stretching payments reduces the cost of foregoing a cash discount but may damage the buying firm's credit rating and its relationships with suppliers over time. If the buying firm stretches its accounts payable too often or for too long, suppliers may refuse to extend credit and may require the buyer to pay cash before delivery (CBD) or cash on delivery (COD).

18-3. Accruals

Accruals are current liabilities for services received but for which complete payments have not been made. Accruals include wages, taxes, rent, and interest payable. Accruals are interest-free sources of financing and do not involve either implicit or explicit costs. Firms can alter the amount of accrued wages by changing the frequency of wage payments, but they have less control over other accruals.

EXAMPLE 18-2: Duggan Corporation is considering a change in its payroll period, from biweekly to monthly. The biweekly payroll is normally $200,000. Assuming wages accrue at a constant rate, the average level of the accrued wages account is currently $100,000 ($200,000/2). Duggan Corporation has an opportunity cost of 12 percent.

Equation 18-2 shows that Duggan Corporation increases the average level of accrued wages by $100,000 by changing the payroll period from every two weeks to every four weeks. Equation 18-3 shows that a $100,000 change in accruals can save the firm $12,000 a year because accruals represent a costless source of financing.

$$\text{Change in average accrued wages} = \text{Net average accrued wages} - \text{Current average accrued wages} \tag{18-2}$$

$$= \frac{\$400,000}{2} - \frac{\$200,000}{2} = \$100,000$$

$$\text{Savings by changing the payroll period} = \text{Opportunity cost} \times \text{Change in accrued wages} \tag{18-3}$$

$$= (0.12)(\$100,000) = \$12,000$$

18-4. Unsecured Bank Financing

Unsecured bank financing is the second most important source of short-term financing following trade credit. Unlike trade credit, bank loans are negotiated, rather than spontaneous, sources of funds. Commercial bank loans are used primarily for temporary needs or seasonal working capital requirements, such as financing the buildup of accounts receivable and inventory. These loans are typically self-liquidating because they are expected to be repaid when the accounts receivable and inventory are converted into cash. Unsecured bank loans appear on the firm's balance sheet under notes payable.

A. Unsecured bank financing can take three major forms.

Unsecured bank financing can be a single loan, a line of credit, and a revolving credit agreement.

1. A **single loan** is a loan for a specific amount and maturity for a specific purpose. The borrower signs a **promissory note**, which is a formal document specifying the terms and conditions of the loan. These terms and conditions include the amount borrowed, the interest rate charged, and the time of repayment. Promissory notes generally have maturities from 30 to 90 days and are repaid in a single payment. These loans may have fixed or floating interest rates.

   - A **fixed-rate note** is a note in which the rate of interest remains constant until maturity.
   - A **floating-rate note** is a note in which the rate of interest may vary over the term of the note.

2. A **line of credit** is a borrowing arrangement for a specific time period, usually one year, in which a bank places a ceiling on the total amount of credit available. A line of credit is both easy and convenient to use. The firm simply overdraws its checking account balances at the bank up to the specified limit. The interest charged is based on the size of the average outstanding loan, not the maximum size of the line of credit. Because an informal line of credit does not legally bind a bank to provide the funds, a commitment fee is not customarily charged.

3. A **revolving credit agreement** is a contractual and binding obligation by a bank to provide a specific amount of funds for a certain time period. This guaranteed line of credit normally runs from one to three years and requires a commitment fee. A **commitment fee** is a fee charged by a bank on any funds not borrowed during the commitment period. This fee is usually less than one percent of the average unused funds. A revolving credit agreement reduces the riskiness of the credit agreement from the borrower's perspective, but also increases the cost of the credit, due to the commitment fee.

B. Unsecured bank loans generally contain several provisions.

1. A **compensating balance** is a minimum or average balance that the lending bank requires the borrower to maintain in either a checking account or a time deposit. The amount of the compensating balance is normally between 10 and 20 percent of either the amount of the bank's commitment or the loan outstanding. Compensating balances increase the effective interest rate if these funds are not available to the borrower or if they are placed in low- or non-interest paying accounts. The lender gains some protection by requiring compensating balances, because these balances may be applied against the loan in the event of default. This provision is called the **right of offset**.

2. A **protective covenant** is a promise in a loan agreement to perform and/or to restrain from doing certain acts. Although these restrictions benefit the lender, they also reduce the ability of borrower to make certain decisions. The two most common protective covenants include an annual cleanup period and operating restrictions.

- The **annual cleanup period** is a continuous period of time in which the firm must be out of debt to the bank. An annual cleanup period is required to ensure that the firm is using the borrowed funds only for temporary or seasonal financing. This covenant applies specifically to lines of credit.
- **Operating restrictions** are limitations placed on a firm in conducting its business operations. These restrictions include maintaining minimum liquidity ratios, placing limits on the total amount of indebtedness, and restricting the size of dividend payments over the life of the loan.

C. The cost of unsecured bank financing is determined by several factors.

1. *Prime rate.* The **prime rate** is the interest rate charged by banks to their most creditworthy customers. The prime rate is usually the lowest interest rate charged. Sometimes during periods of intense interest rate competition a subprime rate appears. The prevailing level of the prime rate depends on changing supply-and-demand relationships for short-term funds which are in turn affected by economic conditions and Federal Reserve policy. For example, the Federal Reserve may act to restrict the money supply, which in turn puts upward pressure on interest rates.
2. *Characteristics of the borrower.* Lenders require higher interest rates as the creditworthiness of the borrower declines.
3. *Characteristics of the lender.* Several characteristics of banks may affect the interest rates they charge including their cost of funds, attitudes toward risk, lending policies, geographic location, and size. Thus, borrowers should investigate several banks when seeking a loan because interest rates vary among banks.
4. *Characteristics of the loan.* The size and length of the loan and the methods of assessing charges and repayment may affect the cost of the loan to borrowers. Banks often charge a higher rate on small loans because many of the costs of analyzing and processing a loan are fixed. For example, it does not cost the banks 10 times more to negotiate a $500,000 loan than to negotiate a $50,000 loan.

D. There are many ways to calculate interest on bank loans.

The stated or nominal interest rate is the rate quoted on a loan. This rate is not necessarily the effective interest rate. The effective interest rate on a loan is the true percentage interest cost paid to the borrower to use the funds. Equation 18-4 is the formula for determining the dollar amount of interest expense during the loan maturity period.

$$\text{Interest expense} = \frac{\text{Interest}}{\text{rate}} \times \frac{\text{Loan}}{\text{amount}} \times \frac{\text{Loan maturity}}{\text{360 days}} \qquad \textbf{(18-4)}$$

Equation 18-5 provides a general formula for calculating the before-tax effective annual interest rate for various bank loans. If an after-tax cost is needed, the effective annual interest rate would be multiplied by 1 minus the tax rate. In Equation 18-5, **usable funds** is the net amount of the loan that the firm can use after taking into consideration the amount borrowed, any interest and fees paid in advance, required compensating balances, and the firm's normal bank balance.

$$\begin{array}{l}\text{Effective annual} \\ \text{interest rate on} \\ \text{bank loans}\end{array} = \frac{\text{Interest expense} + \text{fees}}{\text{Usable funds}} \times \frac{\text{360 days}}{\text{Loan maturity}} \times 100 \qquad \textbf{(18-5)}$$

Equation 18-5 may be used to calculate the effective annual interest rates on bank loans with simple interest, discounted interest, compensating balances, and commitment fees, as well as interest rates on commercial paper.

1. A **simple interest loan** is a loan on which interest is calculated on the principal amount or unpaid balance of the loan and is paid only with the principal at maturity. No fees are generally attached to a simple interest loan and the borrower has the full amount of the funds available over the entire period. The stated and effective interest rates are identical in simple interest loans.

EXAMPLE 18-3: Hill Company is negotiating a $100,000 single payment loan at an annual stated rate of 12 percent from the First National Bank. Hill Company plans to borrow the money for three months.

To find the effective annual interest rate, Equation 18-4 is first used to determine the interest expense for three months. A 30-day month is assumed.

$$\text{Interest expense} = 0.12 \times \$100,000 \times \frac{90}{360} = \$3,000$$

Equation 18-5 yields an effective annual interest rate of 12 percent.

$$\text{Effective annual interest rate} = \frac{\$3,000}{\$100,000} \times \frac{360}{90} \times 100 = 12.00 \text{ percent}$$

2. A **discounted loan** is a loan on which the bank deducts the interest in advance and distributes the remaining amount of the loan to the borrower. The effective interest rate always exceeds the stated rate because the borrower does not receive the full loan amount with a discounted loan.

EXAMPLE 18-4: Hill Company is offered a $100,000, six-month loan from the Second National Bank, which also has a stated rate of 12 percent. The bank requires the borrower to pay the interest in advance.

To find the effective annual interest rate on the loan, Equation 18-4 is used to first find the interest expense for six months.

$$\text{Interest expense} = 0.12 \times \$100,000 \times \frac{180}{360} = \$6,000$$

The usable funds are the amount borrowed of $100,000 less the interest expense of $6,000. Substituting these values in Equation 18-5 yields an effective annual percentage cost of the discounted loan to Hill Company of 12.77 percent.

$$\text{Effective annual interest rate} = \frac{\$6,000}{\$100,000 - \$6,000} \times \frac{360}{180} \times 100 = 12.77 \text{ percent}$$

3. An **installment loan** is a loan which requires the borrower to make equal payments at regular intervals over the life of the loan. Each payment consists of both interest and principal. The effective interest rate is higher than the stated rate because the borrower only has use of the full amount of loan over a small portion of the borrowing period. Equation 18-6 only approximates the effective annual interest rate on an installment loan because it ignores the effect of compounding the interest rate.

$$\text{Effective annual interest rate on an installment loan} = \frac{2mi}{(P)(n+1)} \times 100 \qquad \textbf{(18-6)}$$

where m = number of payment periods per year
i = total interest expense on the loan
P = original principal of the loan
n = total number of loan payments

EXAMPLE 18-5: Discount Clothing is negotiating a loan of $60,000 for 6 months on an installment basis. The bank indicates that payments of $10,600 will be made at the end of each month. The stated interest rate is 12 percent per year or 1 percent a month, assuming that interest is not compounded. The total interest on the loan is $3,600. Substituting the values $m = 12$, $i = \$3,600$, $P = \$60,000$, and $n = 6$ in Equation 18-6 gives an effective annual interest rate of 20.57 percent.

$$\text{Effective annual interest rate on an installment loan} = \frac{(2)(12)(\$3,600)}{(\$60,000)(6+1)} \times 100 = 20.57 \text{ percent}$$

4. Compensating balances may raise the effective cost of borrowing if the required balance is larger than the firm's normal cash balance with the bank. Compensating balance requirements may also increase the amount of funds the firm has to borrow. Equation 18-7 shows the total amount of the loan needed to provide a specific amount of funds when compensating balances are required. If the firm already maintains compensating balances in excess of the bank's requirements, these funds may be used to reduce the amount of the loan.

$$\text{Amount of loan required with a compensating balance} = \frac{\text{Funds needed}}{1.0 - \text{Compensating balance percentage}} \qquad \textbf{(18-7)}$$

EXAMPLE 18-6: A firm needs $200,000 to buy equipment. The bank offers to lend the money for one year at 10.5 percent simple interest plus a compensating balance of 20 percent. The firm does not maintain any excess compensating balances with the bank. By substituting the given values in Equation 18-7, the firm must borrow $250,000 to have $100,000 in usable funds.

$$\text{Amount of loan required with a compensating balance} = \frac{\$200,000}{1.0 - 0.2} = \$250,000$$

The annual interest expense is $26,250 (0.105 × $250,000) and the required compensating balance is $50,000 (0.20 × $250,000). The usable funds of $200,000 ($250,000 − $50,000) are calculated by subtracting the required compensating balance from the loan amount. Substituting these values in Equation 18-5 yields an effective annual interest rate of 13.13 percent.

$$\text{Effective annual interest rate} = \frac{\$26,250}{\$250,000 - \$50,000} \times 100 = 13.13 \text{ percent}$$

5. Commitment fees increase the effective cost of a loan. Commitment fees are generally required by revolving credit agreements. The firm incurs charges both for interest on the amount borrowed and for a commitment fee on the average unused balance of the total credit available.

EXAMPLE 18-7: Bartfeld Industries has a $300,000 revolving credit agreement with its bank. The firm expects its borrowing will average $200,000 over the next year. The bank charges a commitment fee of 0.5 percent on the unused balance which is paid at the end of the loan period. The bank does not require a compensating balance but charges 15 percent interest on the borrowed funds. From this information we can find the expected effective annual interest rate on the revolving credit agreement.

The expected annual interest expense on the revolving credit is $30,000 (0.15 × $200,000). The average unused portion of the credit is expected to be $100,000 resulting in a commitment fee of $500 (0.005 × $100,000). Hence, the total cost is $30,500. The net proceeds from the loan to Bartfeld Industries are $200,000. The commitment fee is not subtracted because it is paid at the end of the loan period. Substituting these figures in Equation 18-5 yields an effective annual interest rate on the revolving credit agreement of 15.25 percent.

$$\text{Effective annual interest rate} = \frac{\$30,000 + \$500}{\$200,000} \times 100 = 15.25 \text{ percent}$$

E. The borrower should consider several factors when applying for a loan.

1. *Borrower's and lender's wants.* The borrower wants to know the specific characteristics of the loan such as compensating balances, protective covenants, flexibility in withdrawing funds, repayment schedules, and the effective interest rate. The bank is concerned with the borrower's ability to repay plus the amount, purpose, and timing of the loan.

2. *Type of information to submit.* The borrower should submit a loan application package. The extensiveness of this package depends on such factors as the existing relationship between the borrower and the lender and the size of the loan. The loan application package generally contains several parts.

- A *cover letter* describes the most relevant factors regarding the loan including its purpose, amount, and timing.
- *Historical information* about the borrower provides the bank with a means of evaluating the firm's financial condition. Information may include recent financial statements, past records of the firm's short-term borrowing, and a profile of the firm and its major officers.
- *Pro forma financial statements* that include a cash budget indicate the firm's ability to repay the loan.

18-5. Commercial Paper

As discussed in Chapter 10, business firms often invest temporary cash in commercial paper to provide both a reserve of liquidity and a return. From the buyer's perspective, commercial paper is held as marketable securities on the balance sheet. From the seller's standpoint, commercial paper is a source of short-term financing appearing on the balance sheet under notes payable. Commercial paper is an alternative to bank loans.

A. *Commercial paper* is short-term, unsecured debt issued by firms having a high credit standing.

Most commercial paper is issued in multiples of $100,000 with maturities from two to 270 days. Sale of commercial paper is typically limited to large, financially strong corporations but some medium-sized firms also issue commercial paper. Commercial paper is sold to investors both directly and through dealers.

1. In a **direct placement**, the issuer sells directly to the public. The issuer bears the risk of selling the entire issue.
2. In a **dealer-placed issue**, an investment banking group buys an entire issue and resells it at a higher price to investors. Dealers, also called *commercial paper houses*, are intermediaries who provide their services to sellers for a fee.

B. Commercial paper provides the seller with both advantages and disadvantages.

1. Commercial paper has three major advantages to the seller.

- The cost of commercial paper is normally below the prime lending rate. Unlike some banks loans, commercial paper requires no collateral, compensating balances, or protective covenants.
- The sale of commercial paper gives the issuing firm access to a wide range of credit sources including other corporations, banks, life insurance companies, and pension funds.
- Use of commercial paper avoids regulations which limit the maximum size of bank loans to a single borrower. Commercial banks are prohibited from lending an amount greater than 10 percent of their unimpaired capital and surplus to any one borrower.

2. Commercial paper has three major disadvantages to the seller.

- Commercial paper may be an unreliable source of financing. The amount of funds available in the commercial paper market depends on the excess liquidity of market participants. During conditions of tight money, firms may need to maintain backup lending agreements with banks to insure the availability of funds. The commitment fee associated with keeping these guaranteed lines of credit as backup partially offsets the lower cost of commercial paper.
- The commercial paper market is highly impersonal. Firms encountering temporary financial difficulties may not be able to replace maturing commercial paper

issues. Banks are considerably more flexible in their dealings with firms than are investors in commercial paper.

- Commercial paper usually cannot be paid off until maturity. Firms that no longer need the funds from commercial paper issues continue to incur interest costs until maturity. Issuing firms may offer to redeem their commercial paper prior to maturity but investors may refuse and continue to hold the paper until maturity.

C. Commercial paper is sold on a discount basis.

The issuing firm receives less than the face value when the paper is sold and pays the full face value when the paper matures. The effective annual interest rate on commercial paper depends on size of the discount and the maturity date of the issue. The discount rate is influenced by prevailing short-term interest rates. The borrower may also pay a placement fee if the issue is sold through commercial paper dealers. A **placement fee** is the dealer commission for arranging the sale of the issue. Equation 18-5 may be used to calculate the effective annual interest rate on commercial paper. In this formula, usable funds are defined as the face value of the issue less the interest charges and placement fee.

EXAMPLE 18-8: National Department Stores plans to issue $1,000,000 worth of commercial paper that matures in 90 days. The issue is expected to sell for $975,000. The commercial paper dealer charges a placement fee of 0.2 percent of the face value of the issue. Interest expenses are $25,000 ($1,000,000 − $975,000) and the placement fee is $2,000 (0.002 × $1,000,000). The firm's usable funds equal $973,000 ($1,000,000 − $25,000 − $2,000). Substituting these values in Equation 18-5 produces an effective annual interest rate of 11.10 percent.

$$\text{Effective annual interest rate} = \frac{\$25,000 + \$2,000}{\$973,000} \times \frac{360}{90} \times 100 = 11.10 \text{ percent}$$

18-6. Accounts Receivable Financing

Accounts receivable are one of the most frequently used sources of collateral for short-term financing because of their liquidity. Firms use two major types of accounts receivable financing: pledging and factoring.

A. *Pledging* is the use of accounts receivable as collateral for short-term loans extended by financial institutions.

There is no transfer of ownership with pledging. This method of financing receivables has several advantages, including a ready source of cash on either a temporary or continuous basis and the avoidance of negative customer reactions if the receivables are sold. However, pledging is costly and requires the firm to perform all credit and collections functions and to bear all credit risks. The pledging process is completed in four steps.

1. *Select the acceptable accounts.* The borrower conducts a credit analysis of its customers to insure that the accounts pledged are solvent. The borrower then sends invoices along with a loan request to the lender. The lender reviews the invoices and selects the accounts receivable which will be accepted as collateral.
2. *Adjust the acceptable accounts.* The lender adjusts the dollar value of the accepted receivables downward to reflect potential returns of merchandise and allowances for cash discounts.
3. *Determine the advance.* The lender advances only a percentage of the adjusted value of the accounts receivable. The percentage may vary from 50 to 90 percent depending on the lender and its evaluation of the quality of the receivables. The borrowing firm signs a promissory note and a security agreement before receiving the advance. A **security agreement** is a standardized form which indicates the specific assets pledged for the purpose of securing a loan.

4. *Collect the accounts.* The borrower normally collects payments directly from customers and then forwards these payments to the lender. The lender deducts the loan amount from the amount collected and returns the balance to the borrower.

B. Pledging has two distinct characteristics: nonnotification and recourse.

Nonnotification means that the borrower's customers are not notified that their receivables have been pledged by the firm. The buyer continues to make payments to the borrower, who forwards them to the lender. Nonnotification is usually the procedure followed when accounts receivable are pledged. If the lender requires added protection against possible fraud, the customer is notified to make payment directly to the lender.

Recourse means that the borrower is responsible for defaults on the accounts receivable pledged to the lender.

C. The stated cost of pledging is higher than the cost of an unsecured bank loan.

There are two reasons which explain the higher cost of pledging: the financially weaker position of firms which pledge accounts receivable and the lender's higher cost of administration. Loans secured by accounts receivable involve a service charge and an interest charge.

1. The **service charge** is the fee charged by the lender to cover the administrative costs. The service charge is approximately 1 to 2 percent of the amount of the pledged assets.
2. The interest charge is the fee charged on the unpaid balance of the loan. The interest charge ranges from 2 to 5 percentage points above the prime rate.

D. *Factoring* is the sale of accounts receivable to a financial institution, which manages and collects the accounts.

Factoring is not a form of secured short-term financing because it involves the sale of accounts receivable to obtain short-term funds. Thus, there is a change of ownership of receivables with factoring. The major advantage of factoring is that the purchaser of the receivables bears all the credit and collection risks. Factoring is costly and is sometimes viewed negatively by customers when their accounts are sold. However, among industries in which factoring is commonly used such as textile and clothing manufacturing, no stigma is attached to this financing method.

The factoring process differs somewhat from pledging. Under factoring, the financial institution or *factor* that purchases accounts receivable performs three functions: credit checking, lending, and risk bearing. The seller receives orders from buyers and sends them to the factoring company for a credit check. Once the factoring company selects the accounts of acceptable risk and agrees to purchase these receivables, the seller is notified and the shipment is made. The seller informs the buyer to make payment directly to the factor, who is responsible for the risk of collecting the accounts receivable. When payments are received, the factor deposits money into the firm's account either on specified payment dates or when payments are received. The factor may also make advances to the seller on uncollected accounts receivable. The maximum amount of the advance is the amount of the factored receivables less factoring commissions, interest expense, and a reserve that the factor maintains to cover any returns or allowances by customers. The factor normally holds a reserve of 5 to 10 percent of the factored receivables. The full reserve is ultimately returned to the firm, provided its customers make no returns or adjustments.

E. Factoring has two distinct characteristics directly opposite to those of pledging: notification and nonrecourse.

Notification means that the borrower's customers are notified to make payments to the lender. **Nonrecourse** means that the factor absorbs bad debts and cannot turn to the seller for payment. The factor receives title to the accounts receivable.

F. There are two major factoring costs: factoring commissions and interest on advances.

Factoring commissions are payments for credit checking, collections, and risk-taking. The commission is generally 1 to 3 percent of the factored receivables. **Interest on advances** is an interest charge made against money lent to the seller prior to collecting the accounts receivable. The factor charges an interest rate of 2 to 5 percentage points above the prime rate.

Equation 18-8 is the formula for computing the effective annual interest rate on factoring receivables. This equation assumes that the amount of the advance received is constant.

$$\text{Effective annual interest rate on factoring receivables} = \frac{\text{Net annual cost}}{\text{Average amount received}} \qquad \text{(18-8)}$$

EXAMPLE 18-9: Springer Textile Company expects to have $1,200,000 in credit sales during the year and plans to factor all of its accounts receivable. Accounts receivable are collected every 30 days and amount to $100,000 a month. Thus, $100,000 in receivables are factored each month. The factor holds a 10 percent reserve for returns and allowances, charges a 2 percent factoring commission per month, and charges 1 percent per month interest on the amount actually advanced. The interest expense is paid in advance and is computed after deducting the reserve and commission. Factoring is expected to save the company $6,000 in bad debt losses and $10,000 in administrative and clerical costs during the year.

(*a*) Assuming a 360-day year, Springer Textile Company will receive $87,120 as an advance during each monthly factoring cycle. The firm will eventually receive the $10,000 reserve less any returns and allowances for the receivables factored every month.

Average accounts receivables per month	$100,000
Less: Reserve for returns (0.10 × $100,000)	10,000
Factoring commission (0.02 × $100,000)	2,000
Funds available for advance per month prior to interest	$ 88,000
Less: Interest on advance (0.01 × $88,000)	880
Average amount received from the factor	$ 87,120

(*b*) The net annual cost of factoring receivables is $16,560.

Factoring commission per month	$ 2,000
Interest expenses per month	880
Total factoring cost per month	$ 2,880
Total factoring cost per year (12 × $2,880)	$34,560
Less: Savings in bad debt expenses per year	6,000
Savings in administrative and clerical cost	12,000
Net annual cost of factoring receivables	$16,560

Substituting this value and the amount of funds advanced by the factor in Equation 18-8 gives an effective annual interest rate of 19.01 percent.

$$\text{Effective annual interest rate} = \frac{\$16,560}{\$87,120} \times 100 = 19.01 \text{ percent}$$

G. Short-term financing through accounts receivables provides the firm with both advantages and disadvantages.

1. Accounts receivable financing has three major advantages.

   • *Additional funding source.* Accounts receivable financing provides funds that small or financially weak firms might otherwise be unable to obtain.

- *Flexibility.* Both pledging and factoring give the borrowing firm flexibility because financing is directly linked with sales.
- *Avoids certain costs.* Factoring relieves the borrower of collection and credit-risk costs because the factor assumes these responsibilities.

2. Accounts receivable financing has two major disadvantages.

- *Cost.* The stated cost of accounts receivable financing is higher than unsecured short-term financing.
- *Sacrifice of liquidity.* Pledging uses a highly liquid asset as security. Factoring sacrifices the firm's long-term liquidity to meet short-term obligations.

18-7. Inventory Financing

Firms usually use inventory financing after they have exhausted their borrowing capacity on receivables. Thus, inventory is second only to accounts receivable as the most desirable asset used for securing short-term financing. The desirability of inventory determines the percentage of funds that a lender will advance against the inventory's book value. Advances against inventory generally range from 50 to 90 percent of the inventory's book value. All inventory is not equally desirable as collateral for loans.

A. The desirability of inventory as collateral depends on several factors.

1. *Production stage of inventory.* Raw materials and finished goods are more acceptable types of inventory as security for a loan than goods in process.
2. *Physical properties.* Inventory that is nonperishable, durable, and not subject to obsolescence is considered the most appropriate as collateral. Thus, standardized or staple items of a durable nature such as lumber or major appliances represent desirable collateral.
3. *Marketability.* Inventory that can be easily liquidated at stable market prices is suitable as collateral.
4. *Identifiability.* Inventory that is readily identifiable is desirable because it helps protect the lender against possible fraud. For example, new automobiles are considered appropriate collateral because they can be identified by means of a serial number.

B. Inventory loans may be classified as to which party has control over the inventory.

In an inventory loan, the inventory may be controlled by the borrower or the lender.

1. If the borrower holds the inventory, the loan may be made under a blanket (floating) lien or a trust receipt arrangement. These inventory loans are the least expensive to administer.

- A **blanket lien** is an arrangement that gives the lender a lien against the borrower's entire inventory. A **lien** is a legal instrument that gives the lender the right to possession of a specific asset in the event that the borrower defaults. The floating lien is the least restrictive from the firm's viewpoint because the borrower is free to sell the inventory. With this arrangement, the lender cannot exercise control over the inventory and is afforded little protection against fraud. Consequently, the lender generally advances less than 50 percent of the inventory's average book value. The interest cost of a floating lien is about 3 to 5 percentage points above the prime rate.
- A **trust receipt** is a security agreement under which the borrower holds the inventory in trust for the lender. The lender may actually buy the inventory from the supplier for the borrower or may advance between 80 to 100 of the funds to purchase the inventory. The lender retains title to specific inventory items until the goods are sold. After the time of the sale, the proceeds of the sale are sent immediately to the lender. The interest charge is normally about 2 percentage

points above the prime rate and is paid only on the declining loan balance. Trust receipts used to finance automobiles, construction equipment, and appliances are called **floor planning**.

2. The inventory may be controlled by the lender. A **warehouse receipt loan** is an arrangement whereby the lender receives control of the pledged collateral. The lender hires a warehousing company to take possession of the inventory either on or off the borrower's premises. Warehouse receipt loans are generally more expensive than other secured lending arrangements because of the costs of hiring a warehousing company. The fixed costs of warehousing arrangements are relatively high, which make them unsuitable for small firms. Warehousing arrangements increase the acceptability of inventory as loan collateral and provide flexibility by linking financing to the growth in inventories. There are two principal types of warehousing arrangements: public warehouses and field warehouses.

- A **public** or **terminal warehouse** is a licensed storage facility operated by bonded managers. Under a terminal warehousing arrangement, inventory is stored in a public warehouse located near the borrower. When goods are delivered to the warehouse, the warehouse manager checks the merchandise and issues a *warehouse receipt* showing title to the goods. The lender then advances the firm funds against the warehoused merchandise. As the firm repays the loan, the lender authorizes the warehousing company to release appropriate amounts of inventory to the firm. The public warehouse arrangement is both costly and inconvenient to the borrower.
- A **field warehouse** is a warehouse operated by a warehousing company on the premises of the borrower. The procedures under field and public warehouse arrangements are quite similar but the field warehouse is the more economical method to finance inventory. A field warehouse requires public notification of the field warehousing arrangement and supervision of the field warehouse by the warehousing company. The cost of field warehousing includes a warehousing fee from 1 to 3 percent of the inventory value charged by the warehousing company and a service fee from 2 to 3 percentage points above the prime rate charged by the lender.

EXAMPLE 18-10: Becker Corporation wants to finance its $800,000 inventory using a blanket lien. Funds are needed for four months. The firm's average inventory is expected to remain constant over this period. The lender will advance 45 percent of the inventory's average book value at a cost of 12 percent. The amount of the funds advanced is $360,000 (0.45 × $800,000). The annual interest cost per year is 12 percent or 4 percent for the one-third (4 months/12 months) of the year. The interest cost of the loan is computed as follows:

Average amount of funds advanced	$360,000
Interest rate (0.12 × 0.33)	0.04
Interest cost	$ 14,400

RAISE YOUR GRADES

Can you explain...?

☑ the difference between secured and unsecured short-term financing
☑ several sources of spontaneous financing
☑ what trade credit is
☑ three major types of trade credit
☑ when trade credit is free

☑ how to determine the cost of foregoing a cash discount
☑ three forms of unsecured bank financing
☑ two provisions of unsecured bank loans
☑ determinants of the cost of unsecured bank financing
☑ why the stated interest and effective interest rate differ
☑ how to calculate the effective annual interest rate on different types of short-term financing
☑ differences between a simple interest loan, a discounted loan, and an installment loan
☑ what commercial paper is
☑ several advantages and disadvantages of using commercial paper as a source of short-term financing
☑ two types of accounts receivable financing
☑ desirable characteristics of inventory as collateral
☑ the difference between a floating lien and a trust receipt
☑ two types of warehousing arrangements

SUMMARY

1. Short-term financing refers to debt originally scheduled for repayment within one year. Short-term financing may be either unsecured or secured. Secured credit requires collateral whereas unsecured credit does not.

2. Short-term financing may be classified as spontaneous or negotiated. Spontaneous sources arise from ordinary business transactions whereas negotiated sources require special effort. Spontaneous sources include accounts payable and accruals. Negotiated short-term credit consists of bank loans, commercial paper, accounts receivable loans, and inventory loans.

3. Trade credit is short-term credit extended by suppliers of goods and services. Open accounts, notes payable, and trade acceptances are all types of trade credit but open accounts are the most widely used. Unlike the other two types of short-term trade credit, an open account is an informal arrangement.

4. Trade credit normally has no explicit costs. Trade credit does have hidden costs and missed cash discounts result in opportunity costs.

5. Stretching accounts payable, or the postponement of payment beyond the end of the credit period, may damage the firm's credit rating and its relationships with suppliers.

6. Accruals are current liabilities for services rendered but for which payments have not been made. Accruals include wages, taxes, rent, and interest payable and are spontaneous sources of short-term financing.

7. Unsecured, short-term bank financing is extended in the form of a single loan, a line of credit, or a revolving credit agreement. A line of credit is an informal borrowing agreement in which a bank agrees to extend credit up to a specific amount. Unlike a line of credit in which the bank is not legally obligated to provide the credit, a revolving credit agreement is guaranteed.

8. Unsecured bank loans often have protective covenants and require firms to maintain compensating balances. These loan requirements are intended to protect the lender.

9. The cost of unsecured bank financing is determined by the prime rate and the characteristics of the borrower, the lender, and the loan itself.

10. The stated interest rate of a loan is not necessarily the effective or true interest rate. The effective interest rate is higher than the stated rate on both discounted and installment loans. Loans requiring compensating balances and commitment fees also cause the effective rate to exceed the stated rate.

11. Commercial paper is a short-term obligation with maturities ranging from 2 to 270 days issued by banks, corporations, and other borrowers to investors with temporarily idle funds. Such instruments are unsecured and usually discounted.

12. Accounts receivable financing may be obtained through pledging or factoring. With a pledging arrangement, the firm uses accounts receivable as collateral for short-term loans. Customers are generally not notified of the pledging arrangement and the borrower continues to bear the default risk. With factoring, the firm actually sells accounts receivable to a financial institution. Customers to make payments directly to a factoring company who now bears the default risk.

13. Inventory varies in its desirability as a source of collateral for short-term financing. The desirability of inventory as collateral depends on its production stage, physical properties, marketability, and identifiability.

14. Inventory loans are classified based on the party having control over the inventory. The control over the inventory may rest with either the borrower or lender.

15. Several types of inventory loans are available. Floating liens and trust receipts leave control with the borrowing firm. These forms of financing are typically preferred because they are the least expensive to administer. Warehouse receipt loans place the control with the lender who hires a third party to oversee the inventory. Warehouse receipt arrangements are made either for public warehouses or field warehouses. A field warehouse stores inventory on the borrower's site whereas a public warehouse does not.

RAPID REVIEW

True or False

1. Short-term financing refers to debt scheduled for repayment in less than six months. [Section 18-1]

2. Both borrowers and lenders prefer to do business using secured loans. [Section 18-1A]

3. Accounts receivable and inventory are the most common sources of secured short-term financing. [Section 18-1A]

4. Commercial finance companies are the primary source of unsecured short-term loans. [Section 18-1B]

5. Both accounts payable and accruals are sources of spontaneous financing. [Section 18-1C]

6. Trade acceptances are an informal type of trade credit. [Section 18-2]

7. Trade credit appears only as an account receivable on the buyer's balance sheet. [Section 18-2]

8. Trade credit is a free source of funds when cash discounts are not offered. [Section 18-2B]

9. The cost of trade credit varies directly with the size of the missed cash discount. [Section 18-2C]

10. Accruals are interest-free sources of financing. [Section 18-3]

11. A line of credit is a legally binding agreement between a borrower and lender. [Section 18-4A]

12. A commitment fee is charged on the total amount of funds guaranteed by a revolving credit agreement. [Section 18-4A]

13. Banks generally require an annual cleanup period for a line of credit. [Section 18-4B]

14. The prime rate is the interest rate charged by banks on short-term loans to business borrowers with the highest credit rating. [Section 18-4C]

15. A discounted loan means that the borrower receives an interest rate below the prime lending rate. [Section 18-4D]

16. The stated and effective interest rates are the same on monthly installment loans. [Section 18-4D]

17. Compensating balances may increase the cost of borrowing. [Section 18-4D]

18. The cost of commercial paper is normally above the prime lending rate on bank loans. [Section 18-5B]

19. Commercial paper is a reliable source of financing for firms of all sizes. [Section 18-5B]

20. Commercial paper is sold on a discount basis. [Section 18-5C]

21. Pledging agreements are usually characterized by nonnotification and recourse. [Section 18-6B]

22. The stated cost of pledging is generally higher than the cost of an unsecured bank loan. [Section 18-6C]

23. In a factoring agreement, the title of the inventory passes to the financial institution. [Section 18-6D]

24. Factoring relieves the borrower of collection and credit-risk costs because the factor assumes these responsibilities. [Section 18-6D]

25. Inventory is the most desirable asset for securing short-term financing. [Section 18-7]

26. The control over the inventory rests with the borrowing firm using floating liens and trust receipts. [Section 18-7B]

27. Lender advances on floating liens are generally higher than on trust receipts. [Section 18-7B]

28. Under a trust receipt arrangement, the lender retains title to inventory until the goods are sold. [Section 18-7B]

29. The borrower retains control of the inventory stored under a public warehousing agreement. [Section 18-7B]

30. Inventory remains on the premises of the borrower under a field warehousing agreement. [Section 18-7B]

Multiple Choice

31. Which of the following is *not* a negotiated source of short-term financing?

   (*a*) Bank loan
   (*b*) Open account
   (*c*) Factoring
   (*d*) Warehouse receipt loan

   [Section 18-1C]

32. What happens to the cost of a foregone cash discount as the number of days between the end of the discount period and the end of the credit period increases?

   (*a*) Rises
   (*b*) Falls
   (*c*) Remains constant
   (*d*) Fluctuates erratically

   [Section 18-2C]

33. All of the following are types of trade credit *except*:

   (*a*) open accounts
   (*b*) notes payable
   (*c*) lines of credit
   (*d*) trade acceptances

   [Section 18-2A]

34. Stretching accounts payable is likely to do all of the following *except*:

(*a*) increase the cost of foregoing a cash discount
(*b*) lower the buyer's credit rating
(*c*) damage relationships with suppliers
(*d*) lead to refusal of credit by suppliers

[Section 18-2D]

35. For which type of loan is the stated interest rate equal to the effective interest rate?

(*a*) Installment loan
(*b*) Discounted loan
(*c*) Simple interest loan
(*d*) Revolving credit agreement

[Section 18-4D]

36. Small business firms are generally unable to use which of the following sources of short-term funds?

(*a*) Bank loan
(*b*) Trade credit
(*c*) Commercial paper
(*d*) Floating lien

[Section 18-5A]

37. Inventory used as collateral should generally not be highly:

(*a*) perishable
(*b*) marketable
(*c*) identifiable
(*d*) durable

[Section 18-7A]

38. Floor planning is a type of short-term financing using:

(*a*) warehouse receipts
(*b*) open account trade credit
(*c*) trust receipts
(*d*) revolving credit

[Section 18-7B]

39. Which type of inventory financing provides the least amount of security to the lender?

(*a*) Public warehousing arrangement
(*b*) Field warehousing agreement
(*c*) Trust receipts
(*d*) Blanket lien

[Section 18-7B]

40. Which of the following is *not* a form of unsecured short-term financing?

(*a*) Commercial paper
(*b*) Trade credit
(*c*) Revolving credit agreement
(*d*) Blanket lien

[Section 18-7B]

Answers

True or False

				Multiple Choice
1. False	11. False	21. True	31. b
2. False	12. False	22. True	32. b
3. True	13. True	23. True	33. c
4. False	14. True	24. True	34. a
5. True	15. False	25. False	35. c
6. True	16. False	26. True	36. c
7. False	17. True	27. False	37. a
8. False	18. False	28. True	38. c
9. True	19. False	29. False	39. d
10. True	20. True	30. True	40. d

SOLVED PROBLEMS

PROBLEM 18-1: The Bender Corporation received credit terms of 2/15, net 45 EOM on a purchase of $20,000. The supplier delivered the merchandise on August 10. The firm was short of cash and stretched its credit by paying ten days late. The supplier did not impose any penalty for late payment because Bender had always paid its bills on time in the past.

(*a*) What were the payment periods? When did Bender Corporation actually pay for the goods?

(*b*) What was the actual opportunity cost foregone by paying late?

(*c*) How does the rate in Part (b) compare to the effective annual discount rate if Bender had paid the bill on time?

Answer:

(*a*) The credit terms specified that Bender Corporation could take the cash discount until 15 days after the end of August or until September 15; otherwise, the full $200,000 was due 45 days after the end of August or by October 15. The firm actually paid the account on October 25 because it paid ten days late.

(*b*) The credit period in Equation 18-1 is extended by 10 days to reflect the late payment. The actual opportunity cost foregone by paying late was 18.37 percent.

$$\text{Cost of foregoing a cash discount} = \frac{2\%}{100\% - 2\%} \times \frac{360}{(45 + 10) - 15} = 0.1837 \text{ or } 18.37 \text{ percent}$$

(*c*) The opportunity cost of the cash discount foregone of 24.49 percent is calculated by using Equation 18-1.

$$\text{Cost of foregoing a cash discount} = \frac{2\%}{100\% - 2\%} \times \frac{360}{45 - 15} = 0.2449 \text{ or } 24.49 \text{ percent}$$

Bender Corporation lowered its opportunity costs of foregoing a cash discount from 24.49 percent to 18.37 percent by paying late. However, the firm may injure its relationship with the supplier by continuing to make late payments.

[Sections 18-2B and 18-2C]

PROBLEM 18-2: HKB, Inc. receives several different credit terms from suppliers.

Supplier	Amount	Credit Terms
X	$10,000	1/10, net 30
Y	5,000	2/15, net 45
Z	8,500	3/15, net 90

(*a*) What is the effective annual percentage cost if HKB, Inc. pays on the final due date rather than taking the cash discount from each supplier?

(*b*) What is the amount paid if each of the discounts is taken?

Answer:

(*a*) Substituting these values in Equation 18-1 yields the cost of foregoing a cash discount for each of the three suppliers as follows:

Supplier	Annual Percentage Cost
X	$\dfrac{1\%}{100\% - 1\%} \times \dfrac{360}{30 - 10} = 0.1818$ or 18.18 percent
Y	$\dfrac{2\%}{100\% - 2\%} \times \dfrac{360}{45 - 15} = 0.2449$ or 24.49 percent
Z	$\dfrac{3\%}{100\% - 3\%} \times \dfrac{360}{90 - 15} = 0.1405$ or 14.85 percent

(*b*) The amount paid on the various accounts payable is determined as follows:

$$\text{Amount paid after a cash discount} = \text{Purchase amount} \times (1 - \text{percentage discount})$$

Supplier

$$X = (\$10,000)(1 - 0.01) = \$9,900$$
$$Y = (\$5,000)(1 - 0.02) = \$4,900$$
$$Z = (\$8,500)(1 - 0.03) = \$8,245$$

[Section 18-2C]

PROBLEM 18-3: Sale Products, Inc. borrows $250,000 from the Louisiana National Bank on an unsecured basis. The bank requires a 10 percent compensation balance which is not availabe to the borrowor.

(*a*) What is the dollar amount of the compensating balance?

(*b*) How much of the loan is actually available to the firm?

Answer:

(*a*) The compensating balance is $25,000 (0.10 × $250,000).

(*b*) Sale Products has only $225,000 ($250,000 − $25,000) in usable funds.

[Section 18-4B]

PROBLEM 18-4: McConnell Sporting Equipment has obtained a $50,000 bank loan at a simple interest rate of 14 percent. The firm borrows the money for six months.

(*a*) How much interest will the firm pay?

(*b*) What is the effective annual interest cost if both the interest and principal are paid at the end of six months?

Answer:

(*a*) Using Equation 18-4, McConnell Sporting Equipment will pay $3,500 in interest for the six months.

$$\text{Interest expense} = 0.14 \times \$50,000 \times \frac{180}{360} = \$3,500$$

(*b*) Substituting the values in Equation 18-5, the effective interest rate is:

$$\text{Effective annual interest rate} = \frac{\$3,500}{\$50,000} \times \frac{360}{180} \times 100 = 14.00 \text{ percent}$$

[Section 18-4D]

PROBLEM 18-5: Refer to the information in Problem 18-4, except assume that the loan is on a discount basis.

(a) What is the amount of usable funds available to McConnell Sporting Equipment at the time of the loan?
(b) What is the effective annual interest rate?

Answer:

(a) The interest expense is subtracted from the loan amount to obtain the usable funds of $46,500 ($50,000 − $3,500).
(b) Substituting the interest expense = $3,500, usable funds = $46,500, and the loan maturity = 180 days in Equation 18-5, the effective annual interest rate is:

$$\frac{\text{Effective annual}}{\text{interest rate}} = \frac{\$3,500}{\$46,500} \times \frac{360}{180} \times 100 = 15.05 \text{ percent}$$

[Section 18-4D]

PROBLEM 18-6: Selman Products expects to borrow $450,000 from State National Bank. This discounted loan requires an average compensating balance of 10 percent and an annual interest rate of 9 percent. What is the effective annual interest rate under each of the following conditions?

(a) No existing checking account balances can be used to meet the new compensating balance requirement.
(b) Selman Products maintains $20,000 in average checking account balances that can be used to compensate the bank for the loan.
(c) Selman Products maintains $60,000 in average checking account balances that can be used to compensate the bank for the loan.

Answer:

(a) Selman Products must maintain a compensating balance of $45,000 (0.10 × $450,000) and pay annual interest expenses of $40,500 (0.09 × $450,000). The amount of usable funds of $364,500 ($450,000 − $45,000 − $40,500) is determined by subtracting both the compensating balances and the prepaid interest from the total loan amount. Substituting these values in Equation 18-5 yields an effective annual interest rate of 12.35 percent.

$$\frac{\text{Effective annual}}{\text{interest rate}} = \frac{\$45,000}{\$450,000 - \$45,000 - \$40,500} \times 100 = 12.35 \text{ percent}$$

(b) Selman Products currently maintains a $20,000 checking account balance and needs an additional $25,000 to meet the new requirement of $45,000. Thus, the firm has $384,500 ($450,000 − $25,000 − $40,500) in usable funds. Again using Equation 18-5, the effective annual interest rate is 11.70 percent.

$$\frac{\text{Effective annual}}{\text{interest rate}} = \frac{\$45,000}{\$450,000 - \$25,000 - \$40,500} \times 100 = 11.70 \text{ percent}$$

(c) Selman Products currently maintains a checking account balance of $60,000, which is larger than the required compensating balance of $45,000. Hence, the firm has $409,500 ($450,000 − $40,500) in usable funds. Substituting these values in Equation 18-5 produces an effective interest rate is 10.99 percent.

$$\frac{\text{Effective annual}}{\text{interest rate}} = \frac{\$45,000}{\$450,000 - \$40,500} \times 100 = 10.99 \text{ percent}$$

[Section 18-4D]

PROBLEM 18-7: Calvert International borrows $800,000 for nine months with an installment loan from Perpetual Bank. The loan is to be repaid in nine equal payments of $96,000 at the end of each month. What is the effective annual interest rate of the loan?

Answer: The interest expense on the loan equals the total payments less the principal amount of the loan.

$$\text{Interest expense} = (9 \times \$96{,}000) - \$800{,}000 = \$64{,}000$$

The number of payment periods per year, m, is 12 because interest is paid monthly; the number of total payments, n, is 9. Substituting these values in Equation 18-6, the effective annual interest rate is approximately:

$$\text{Effective annual interest rate on an installment loan} = \frac{(2)(12)(\$64{,}000)}{(\$800{,}000)(9+1)} \times 100 = 19.20 \text{ percent}$$

[Section 18-4D]

PROBLEM 18-8: Brooks Music Company negotiated a one-year revolving credit agreement with Nashville National Bank for $400,000 at a stated interest rate of 10 percent. The bank requires a commitment fee of $5,000 to be paid at the beginning of the loan period and a compensating balance of $40,000 to be kept in its checking account. Brooks Music has a $15,000 checking account balance that can be used to meet part of the compensating balance requirement. If Brooks Music Company borrows $400,000 for the entire year, what is the effective annual interest rate?

Answer: The annual interest charge is expected to be $40,000 (0.10 × $400,000). Adding the commitment fee to the interest charge gives a total cost of $45,000 ($40,000 + $5,000). Brooks Music will have to add $25,000 to its existing $15,000 checking account balances to reach the $40,000 required compensating balance level. The usable funds are determined by subtracting the additional compensating balances and the commitment fee paid in advance from the amount borrowed. The amount of usable funds is $370,000 ($400,000 − $25,000 − $5,000). Using Equation 18-5 shows the calculation of the effective annual interest rate is:

$$\text{Effective annual interest rate} = \frac{\$40{,}000 + \$5{,}000}{\$400{,}000 - \$25{,}000 - \$5{,}000} \times 100 = 12.16 \text{ percent}$$

[Section 18-4D]

PROBLEM 18-9: United Industries wants to issue commercial paper. The firm contacts a commercial paper dealer who agrees to sell a $20,000,000 issue of commercial paper maturing in 120 days at a 9 percent annual interest rate. The dealer charges a fee of $30,000. What is the effective annual interest rate?

Answer: Using Equation 18-4, the interest expense is:

$$\text{Interest expense} = (0.09 \times \$20{,}000{,}000) \times \frac{120}{360} = \$600{,}000$$

The total cost of the commercial paper is $630,000 ($600,000 + $30,000) and the amount of usable funds is $19,370,000 ($20,000,000 − $600,000 − $30,000). Substituting these values in Equation 18-5, the effective annual interest rate is:

$$\text{Effective annual interest rate} = \frac{\$600{,}000 + \$30{,}000}{\$20{,}000{,}000 - \$600{,}000 - \$30{,}000} \times \frac{360}{120} \times 100$$

$$= 9.76 \text{ percent}$$

[Section 18-4D]

PROBLEM 18-10: Mammoth Industries plans to issue $5,000,000 in commercial paper for 120 days. Since commercial paper is sold on a discount basis, the proceeds of the issue are expected to be $4,850,000. The placement cost is $12,500. What is the effective annual interest rate on the commercial paper?

Answer: Substituting the interest cost of $150,000 ($5,000,000 − $4,850,000), the placement fee of $12,500, usable funds of $4,837,500 ($5,000,000 − $150,000 − $12,500) and 120 days in Equation 18-5, the effective annual interest rate is:

$$\text{Effective annual interest rate} = \frac{\$150,000 + \$12,500}{\$4,837,500} \times \frac{360}{120} \times 100 = 10.08 \text{ percent}$$

[Section 18-5C]

PROBLEM 18-11: Davidson, Inc. plans to factor $200,000 per month in accounts receivable. Savings in the firm's credit and collections department will amount to $2,500 per month. Standard Finance Company offers to buy the accounts receivable on a nonrecourse basis for a 3 percent factoring commission and requires a 20 percent reserve for returns and allowances. Thus, the factor will absorb bad-debt losses which average 1 percent of credit sales. Standard Finance will advance funds at 2 percentage points over the 7 percent prime lending rate.

(a) What amount of funds can Davidson, Inc. obtain from factoring its receivables?
(b) What is the net annual cost of factoring its receivables?
(c) What is the effective annual cost of this financing arrangement?

Answer:

(a) Davidson, Inc. can raise $152,845 per month from this source of financing.

Average level of receivables per month	$200,000
Less: Reserve for returns (0.20 × $200,000)	40,000
Less: Factoring commission (0.03 × $200,000)	6,000
Funds available for advance per month	$154,000
Less: Interest on advance (0.09/12 × $154,000)	1,155
Amount of funds advanced from the factor	$152,845

(b) The net annual cost of factoring receivables is $31,860.

Factoring commission per month	$6,000
Interest expense per month	1,155
Total factoring cost per month	$7,155
Total factoring cost per year (12 × $7,155)	$85,860
Less: Savings in bad debt expenses per year (0.01)(12 × $200,000)	24,000
Less: Savings from closing credit and collections department (12 × $2,500)	30,000
Net annual cost of factoring receivables	$31,860

(c) Using Equation 18-8, the effective annual cost of factoring receivables is 20.84 percent.

$$\text{Effective annual interest rate on factoring receivables} = \frac{\$31,860}{\$152,845} = 20.84 \text{ percent}$$

[Section 18-6D]

19 INTERMEDIATE-TERM FINANCING

THIS CHAPTER IS ABOUT

☑ **Term Loans**
☑ **Equipment Financing Loans**
☑ **Leases**

Most business firms use short-, intermediate-, and long-term debt financing. These three types of debt financing have several distinguishing features of which the most obvious is the length of their initial maturity. *Short-term debt* has an initial maturity of a year or less while *intermediate-term debt* matures in from one to ten years and *long-term debt* matures in more than ten years. However, the distinction between intermediate- and long-term debt regarding their maturity is rather arbitrary. The financial manager uses short-term debt principally to finance fluctuating working capital needs and intermediate- and long-term debt to finance permanent working capital and fixed assets. Repayment of long-term debt generally comes from the borrower's net cash inflows rather than liquidation of its assets. Intermediate-term financing includes term loans, equipment financing loans, and leases.

19-1. Term Loans

A **term loan** is a business loan with a maturity of more than one year. These loans are negotiated directly between the borrower and lender and, hence, no intermediary is involved. Term lenders include commercial banks, insurance companies, commercial finance companies, pension funds, equipment suppliers, government agencies, and venture capitalists.

A. There are several major characteristics of term loans.

1. *Repayment schedule.* Term loans are usually amortized, or paid off, in equal installments over the life of the loan. Each installment includes both interest and the repayment of principal. The word amortization is derived from the French "a mortir" which means "to extinguish, or to deaden." Thus, a loan is being gradually extinguished by paying it off. Some term loans, however, require equal installments that only partially amortize the loan over its life, followed by a large lump-sum payment at maturity, known as a **balloon payment**. The calculation of the loan amortization payment, *A*, for an ordinary annuity is shown in Equation 19-1. Recall from Chapter 3 that an ordinary annuity is a payment made at the end of each period.

LOAN PAYMENT
$$A = \frac{\text{Amount of the loan}}{\text{PVIFA}_{i,n}}$$
(19-1)

where $\text{PVIFA}_{i,n}$ = Present value interest factor of an annuity at interest rate, *i*, and time period, *n*.

EXAMPLE 19-1: DKB Corporation has a 3-year term loan of $100,000 at an interest rate of 10 percent per year. The commercial bank requires the firm to make equal installments at the end of each year.

The $PVIFA_{0.10,3}$ of 2.487 is found in Appendix D by locating the intersection of 10 percent interest with three periods. Substituting these values in Equation 19-1 produces an amortization payment, rounded to the nearest dollar, of $40,209 each year for three years. It should be noted that the PVIFAs used in Appendix D are rounded to three decimal places, which may introduce some rounding errors.

LOAN PAYMENT
$$A = \frac{\$100,000}{2.487} = \$40,209$$

The debt is discharged by equal periodic payments but varying portions of each payment are applied toward principal and interest. The interest is paid first, then the remainder of the payment is used to reduce the debt. The breakdown of payments into interest portions and principal portions is called an **amortization schedule**. Each period's interest payment is determined by multiplying the interest rate, i, by the balance of the loan at the beginning of the period. The principal repayment is calculated by subtracting the interest payment for the period from the total payment for the period. The remaining balance is found by subtracting the principal repayment for the period from the period's beginning principal balance.

EXAMPLE 19-2: As shown in Example 19-1, DKB Corporation borrowed $100,000 at 10 percent and repaid the loan in three equal year-end installments of $40,209. The firm's amortization schedule is as follows:

End of Year	Beginning Balance	Loan Payment	Interest Payment [0.10 × (2)]	Principal Reduction [(3) − (4)]	Remaining Balance [(2) − (5)]
(1)	(2)	(3)	(4)	(5)	(6)
1	$100,000	40,209	$10,000	$30,209	$69,791
2	69,791	40,209	6,979	33,230	36,561
3	36,561	40,209	3,656	36,553	0*

* The actual remaining balance in this example is $8 ($36,561 − $36,553). This is due to rounding the $PVIFA_{0.10,3}$ in Appendix D when computing the loan payment, rounding the loan payment, and rounding the interest and principal payments to the nearest dollar. Without rounding, the ending balance in the third year would be exactly zero.

In Year 1, the interest payment of $10,000 shown in Column 4 is determined by multiplying the 10 percent interest rate by the $100,000 beginning balance in Column 2. The reduction in principal, $30,209, shown in Column 5, is found by subtracting the interest payment of $10,000 from the total payment of $40,209. Finally, the balance of $69,791 shown in Column 6 is calculated by subtracting the principal reduction of $30,209 from the $100,000 beginning balance. A similar process is repeated for each year.

2. *Costs.* The interest rate on a term loan may be fixed or may vary with a market index such as the prime rate. With a fixed interest rate, the installment payments remain level over the loan's duration. However, with a floating rate a change in the interest rate alters the size of the installment payments or the length of the loan and hence the loan's amortization schedule. The actual interest rate depends on various factors including the maturity and size of the loan, the financial riskiness of the borrower, and the general level of interest rates. This rate is generally higher than on short-term loans because term loans are riskier and less liquid. The cost of term loans may also be affected by commitment fees and stock purchase options, known as **equity kickers**, required by some lenders to provide compensation in addition to the interest payments.

3. *Collateral.* Term loans may be secured or unsecured. Secured term loans require collateral in the form of various types of current and/or fixed assets. For example, longer maturity term loans are frequently secured by mortgages on real estate.

4. *Covenants.* The lender incorporates covenants or provisions into the loan agreement to insure the repayment of the loan. These covenants may limit future management flexibility. The number of restrictive provisions is often determined by the financial strength of the borrower with weaker firms having more restrictions. Loan covenants may be divided into four broad categories: affirmative covenants, negative covenants, restrictive covenants, and default provisions.

   - *Affirmative covenants* require the borrowing firm to take certain actions during the term of the loan. Affirmative provisions may require the borrower to submit periodic financial statements, to carry a minimum amount of insurance and working capital, to pay taxes and other liabilities when due, and to maintain all its facilities in good working order.

   - *Negative covenants* prohibit the borrowing firm from taking certain actions without the lender's prior written approval. Typical negative covenants prohibit the borrower from engaging in mergers or consolidations and from purchasing, leasing, or liquidating fixed assets.

   - *Restrictive covenants* limit the scope of the borrower's actions. For example, restrictive covenants often place constraints on subsequent borrowing, limit cash dividends, and the amount of payments such as employees' salaries and bonuses.

   - *Default provisions* contained in an acceleration clause permit the lender to demand repayment of the entire loan immediately under certain conditions in which the borrower is considered to be in default. For example, the lender may require immediate repayment if the borrower fails to make principal and interest payments on time or if the borrower violates any of the covenants specified in the loan agreement.

B. The advantages of term loans include speed, flexibility, confidentiality, low issuance costs and the avoidance of possible nonrenewal of short-term loans.

1. *Speed.* Term loans may be executed quickly through private negotiations. These loans do not require registration with the Securities and Exchange Commission and thus avoid the associated time delay.

2. *Flexibility.* Direct negotiation enables the borrower to tailor the loan to meet specific needs and enhances the ability of the borrower to modify the terms of the loan agreement at a later date.

3. *Confidentiality.* Financial information about the borrower and terms of the loan is not made public.

4. *Low issuance costs.* Term loans involve direct negotiation which is less costly than a public offering of debt.

5. *Avoids possible nonrenewal of short-term loans.* The longer maturity of term loans avoids the potential problem of not being able to renew short-term loans.

C. The disadvantages of term loans include covenants, collateral, overall cost, and cash drain.

1. *Covenants.* Specific provisions of the loan agreement that prohibit or restrict the firm's operations may reduce flexibility.

2. *Collateral.* Assets pledged as collateral for a term loan generally may not be used to secure other financing.

3. *Overall Cost.* Term loans may be relatively expensive depending on the interest rate and provisions for equity kickers.

4. *Cash drain.* Periodic amortization payments may place a large cash drain on the firm because each payment contains both interest and principal, whereas notes payable or bonds payable require only interest payments until maturity.

19-2. Equipment Financing Loans

An **equipment financing loan** is a loan used to finance the purchase of new equipment in which the equipment is used as collateral for the loan. These loans are usually made for less than the full market value of the pledged equipment in order to provide a margin of safety to the lender. Equipment financing loans contain covenants but they are usually less restrictive than term loans. Sources of equipment financing loans include commercial banks, equipment manufacturers, sales finance companies, insurance companies, and pension funds. Two instruments used in connection with equipment financing loans are the *conditional sales contract* and the *chattel mortgage*.

A. A *conditional sales contract* is a financing agreement in which the seller of the equipment retains the title of the equipment until all payments have been made.

Conditional sales contracts are made almost exclusively by equipment manufacturers. The buyer normally makes a down payment and agrees to pay for the equipment in installments. If the buyer defaults, the seller may repossess the equipment. The equipment appears as an asset and the loan as a liability on the borrower's balance sheet.

B. A *chattel mortgage* is a lien on personal property, which gives the lender the right to sieze and sell the equipment in the event of default on the loan by the borrower.

Chattel mortgages are commonly used by commercial banks and sales finance companies when making direct equipment financing loans. The lender files a notification of the lien with the appropriate public office in the state where the equipment is located.

19-3. Leases

A lease is a contractual agreement in which the asset's owner (*lessor*) agrees to let another party (*lessee*) use that asset in accordance with the terms of a contract. The lessor and lessee negotiate the terms of the lease contract which normally include the length of the lease, amount and frequency of lease payments, covenants, cancellation provisions, renewal and purchase options, maintenance and related cost provisions, and property improvement features. Leasing is considered a source of financing provided by the lessor to the lessee. Common lessors include manufacturers and distributors, independent leasing companies, and financial institutions such as commercial banks, life insurance companies, and pension funds. The growth in leasing is attributable largely to tax effects in which tax shelters may be transferred from the user of the asset to the supplier of the capital in such a way that both the lessor and lessee benefit. Practically any item can be leased.

A. There are two major types of leases: operating and capital.

The accounting requirements for classifying a lease as operating or capital are discussed in Section 19-3C.

1. An **operating lease**, sometimes called a *service* or *maintenance lease*, is a short-term, cancelable agreement that provides the lessee with use of an asset on a period-by-period basis. The life of the contract is significantly shorter than the economic life of the asset. However, the lessee is generally given the option to renew a lease at the expiration of the contract. An operating lease is usually cancelable before the expiration date by either the lessor or the lessee. The lessor is typically responsible for maintenance, insurance, and property taxes on the asset. The cost of the equipment is not fully amortized in an operating lease in that the lease payments are not sufficient to recover the cost of the asset from a single lessee. Operating leases are used to gain the use of a variety of assets such as office equipment, computers, and automobiles.

2. A **capital** or **financial lease**, is a long-term agreement that obligates the lessor to make payments for a predetermined time period. The characteristics of financial leases are basically the opposite of operating leases. That is, financial leases cover most of economic life of the assets, are noncancelable, provide no maintenance services except under a separate agreement, and fully amortize the cost of the leased property. Failure to make the lease payments on a capital lease may result in insolvency and bankruptcy court action. Financial leases often involve real estate, airplanes, ships, railroad cars, and specialized equipment.

B. Several types of leasing arrangements can be negotiated within the classifications of operating and capital leases.

1. A **direct lease** is a lease that is initiated when a firm acquires the use of an asset that it did not previously own. Direct leases generally involve new equipment acquired from a manufacturer, distributor, or a specialized leasing company by the lessor. The lessor then leases the property to a given lessee.

2. A **sale and leaseback** is an arrangement in which a firm sells an asset it already owns to another party and then immediately leases it back from the buyer. The lessee receives cash from the sale of the asset and continues using the asset. A sale and leaseback arrangement can be used with an operating or a capital lease.

3. In a **leveraged lease**, also known as a *third-party lease*, the lessor borrows a substantial portion of the purchase price of an asset from lenders and then leases the asset to the lessee. Lease payments are usually made directly to the lender. Leveraged leases are made on a nonrecourse basis in which the lender does not have recourse to the lessor in the event of default. Instead, the loan is guaranteed by the asset. Leveraged leases are used to provide financing for assets that require large capital outlays such as heavy equipment, airplanes, and ships. Leveraged leasing transactions are oriented toward tax savings. The lessor receives the after-tax residual value of the asset. Leveraged leasing also allows a lessee to recapture some of its lost tax benefits through a lower effective cost of financing. Thus, the lessee forfeits tax benefits of ownership in exchange for lease payments that are generally lower than normal debt service payments.

C. The accounting treatment of a lease depends on the type of lease.

Prior to 1977, leases were reported only as footnotes to the balance sheet. Thus, leasing was often called **off-balance-sheet financing** because neither the leased assets nor the liabilities under the lease contracts appeared on the lessee's balance sheet. In November 1976, the Financial Accounting Standards Board (FASB) issued Statement 13 which changed the accounting treatment of leases. Statement 13 provides two basic choices for accounting for leases depending upon the classification of the lease as *capital* or *operating*. The method of accounting for leases in turn has implications for financial statement analysis.

1. A lease for new assets is classified as a capital lease by the lessee if it meets any one of the four following conditions. If none of these conditions are satisfied, the lease is an operating lease.

- The lease transfers *ownership* of the asset from the lessor to the lessee at the end of the lease term.
- The lease gives the lessee an *option to purchase* the asset at a bargain price, which probably will be exercised. A *bargain purchase option* permits the lessee to acquire the asset at a price considerably below the expected fair value of the asset when the option is exercised. The *fair value of the leased property* is the price for which the property could be sold in an arm's-length transaction.
- The *lease term* is at least 75 percent of the estimated economic life of the asset.
- The *present value of the minimum lease payments* is at least 90 percent of the fair value of the leased property when the lease goes into effect. The minimum lease

payments include the periodic lease payments plus any residual value guaranteed by the lessee. **Guaranteed residual value** is the lessee's purchase price if the lease arrangement requires the lessee to purchase the asset at the end of the lease term. However, the minimum lease payments exclude **executory costs**, such as insurance, taxes, and maintenance, which are paid by the lessor. Equation 19-2 show the calculation of the present value of the minimum lease payments when the lease payments are made *in advance*. (That is, the lease payments are made at the beginning of a period, which is the usual arrangement.)

$$PV = (L - E)(1 + PVIFA_{i,n-1}) + GR(PVIF_{i,n}) \qquad \text{(19-2)}$$

where PV = present value of the minimum lease payments made at the beginning of the period

L = periodic lease payments

E = executory costs paid by the lessor

GR = residual value guaranteed by the lessee

$PVIFA_{i,n-1}$ = present value interest factor of an annuity at discount rate *i* for period *n* − 1

$PVIF_{i,n}$ = present value interest factor of a single amount at discount rate *i* for period *n*

EXAMPLE 19-3: On January 1, 19x5, Chisholm Manufacturing Company signed a five-year, noncancelable lease for a machine with a fair value of $65,000. The machine has a total expected economic life of five years. The lessee has an option to buy the machine at the end of five years for $10,000, which is the estimated fair market value of the machine at the end of the lease term. The lessee expects to pay annual property taxes, insurance and maintenance of $3,000. The lessee does not guarantee any residual value of the machine. Annual lease payments of $15,000 are made at the beginning of each year. The discount rate is 12 percent.

(a) From the data given, the annual lease payment is $15,000 and there is no guaranteed residual value because the lessee is not required to buy the machine. No executory costs are paid. Using Appendix D, the PVIFA at a 12 percent discount rate for 4 years is 3.037. Substituting these values in Equation 19-2 gives a present value of the minimum lease payments of $60,555.

$$PV = (\$15,000 - 0)(1 + 3.037) = (\$15,000)(4.037) = \$60,555$$

(b) There is no ownership transfer or bargain purchase option. However, the lease is classified as a capital lease because the lease term of five years exceeds 75 percent of the estimated economic life of the machine. In fact, the lease term is 100 percent of the estimated economic life of the machine. In addition, the present value of the minimum lease payments, $60,555, exceeds 90 percent of the fair value of $65,000, that is, $58,500 (0.90 × $65,000).

2. A capital lease is shown on the lessee's balance sheet as both an asset (leased property under capital leases) and a liability (obligations under capital leases).

- The initial amount in both accounts is equal to the present value of the minimum lease payments or the fair value of the leased property, whichever is lower.
- The discount rate used to compute the present value of the minimum lease payments is the *lessee's* incremental borrowing rate or the *lessor's* implicit rate of interest, whichever is less. The lessee's **incremental borrowing rate** is the cost that the lessee would have incurred to borrow the funds elsewhere. The lessor's **implicit rate of interest** is the lessor's internal rate of return on the lease transaction.

This process of showing leased property as an asset is called **capitalizing the lease**. The asset is amortized using the firm's normal depreciation method. The long-term liability account is reduced by the lease payment, an amount equal to the payment of principal on an equivalent term loan. Thus, the values of the asset account and the liability account are likely to differ after the first lease payment.

If the lease arrangement has a purchase option, the leased property is amortized over its economic life; otherwise, the lease is amortized over the lease term. In addition to making these balance sheet adjustments, additional footnotes to the financial statements are required including future minimum lease payments for the next five fiscal years.

EXAMPLE 19-4: In Example 19-3, the lease obtained by Chisholm Manufacturing Company had a fair value of $65,000 on January 1, 19x5, and a present value of minimum lease payments of $60,555. The lease payments of $15,000 are made on January 1 of each year of the lease term. The interest rate is 12 percent.

(a) The lease is capitalized at $60,555 because the present value of minimum lease payments is less than the fair value of the leased property of $65,000.

(b) The initial accounting treatment of the lease for Chisholm Manufacturing Company is shown below. At the inception of the lease, the dollar amounts of the assets and liabilities required to record the lease are equal. The $15,000 represents the lease payments due during the next year. In fact, this payment is due immediately. The $45,555 represents the present value of lease payments due beyond one year in the future.

Assets		Liabilities	
Lease property under capital leases less accumulated amortization.....	$60,555	Current obligations under capital leases...........	$15,000
		Long-term obligations under capital leases...........	45,555
Total	$60,555	Total	$60,555

(c) The amortization schedule for the lease liability is shown below. No interest is incurred during time zero because the lease payment is made at the beginning of the year on January 1, 19x5. The initial $15,000 lease payment reduces the amount on which interest is incurred during the first year to $45,555 ($60,555 − $15,000). Hence, the interest payment during the first year is $5,467 (0.12 × $45,555). This process is continued throughout the remainder of the amortization of the lease liability.

End of Year	Beginning Balance	Lease Payment	Interest Payment $[0.12 \times (2)]$	Principal Reduction $[(3) - (4)]$	Remaining Balance $[(2) - (5)]$
(1)	(2)	(3)	(4)	(5)	(6)
0	$60,555	$15,000	$ 0	$15,000	$45,555
1	45,555	15,000	5,467	9,533	36,022
2	36,022	15,000	4,323	10,677	25,345
3	25,345	15,000	3,041	11,959	13,386
4	13,386	15,000	1,606	13,394	0*

* The actual balance in this example is −$8.00 ($13,386 − $13,394), which is due to rounding errors. Without rounding, the ending balance at the end of the lease term would be exactly zero.

3. An operating lease is not capitalized and does not appear on the balance sheet. Operating leases represent off-balance-sheet financing because neither the leased assets nor the liabilities under lease contracts appear on the firm's balance sheet. Hence, traditional financial ratios can be misleading unless adjustments are made in analyzing financial statements. The operating lease expenses for the period are reported on the lessee's income statement. Obligations for operating leases appear in footnotes to the firm's financial statements and include minimum future lease payments for the next five fiscal years.

D. Lease-buy analysis involves two decisions: whether or not to acquire an asset (investment decision) and how to finance the asset (financing decision).

In general, it is not correct to accept or reject a project and then, if the project is accepted, determine how it should be financed. The reason is that, in using capital budgeting procedures, the means of financing an asset may influence whether or not the project is desirable. For example, a project, if purchased, may have a negative NPV and be rejected. The same project may have a positive NPV if leased. Thus, by not considering the means of financing, a firm may reject a profitable opportunity to lease an asset. A lease-buy analysis should be made by comparing the lease contract with straight debt financing because both require a specified series of payments. Even if debt financing is more favorable than the lease, the firm may still reject debt financing in favor of some other even more favorable type of financing such as selling stock or using retained earnings.

The basic lease-buy analysis model is based on an after-tax, incremental, present-value comparison and involves three major steps.

1. *Calculate the after-tax cash flows if the asset is leased and if it is purchased.* The procedure for determining the after-tax cash flows is shown in Figure 19-1.

Lease	Purchase
(1) Calculate the minimum lease payment, L*, using Equation 19-3: $$L = \frac{\text{Amount of the lease}}{1 + \text{PVIFA}_{i,n-1}} \quad \text{(19-3)}$$	(1) Calculate the periodic loan payment, A**, using Equation 19-1: $$A = \frac{\text{Amount of the loan}}{\text{PVIFA}_{i,n}} \quad \text{(19-1)}$$
(2) Determine other tax deductible cash outflows such as maintenance, insurance, and property taxes for each period paid by the lessee.	(2) Develop a loan amortization schedule.
(3) Determine the tax savings by multiplying the sum of the lease payment and the other tax deductible cash outflows for each period by the lessee's marginal tax rate.	(3) Find the tax deductible expense for each period, including interest, property taxes, operating expenses, and cost recovery (depreciation).
(4) Determine the after-tax cash flow if leased by subtracing tax savings from the sum of the lease payments and other cash flows.	(4) Determine the tax savings by multiplying the sum of the tax deductible expenses by the firm's marginal tax rate.
	(5) Determine the after-tax salvage value of the asset at the end of its economic life by multiplying the salvage value by 1 minus the tax rate.
	(6) Determine the after-tax cash flow if purchased by subtracting the tax savings and the after-tax salvage value from the sum of the loan payments and other cash outlays*** for the appropriate periods.

  * The lease payment provides the lessor with a certain required rate of return (implicit rate of interest) and the net cost of the asset (the amount of the lease). The net cost equals the cost of the asset less the present values of the after-tax salvage value (guaranteed residual value), depreciation tax savings, and the operating expense. The lessee does not compute the payment; typically, the lessor provides it.

  ** The amount of borrowing usually equals the total cost of the asset less any down payment.

  *** Cost recovery (depreciation) is a noncash outlay.

FIGURE 19-1   Procedure for calculating the after-tax cash flows if an asset is leased or purchased.

2. *Calculate the present value of the after-tax cash outflows if leased and if purchased.* The choice of the appropriate discount rate is a controversial issue in lease-buy analysis. There are several basic options for the rate of discount to be used including:

- the after-tax borrowing rate
- the before-tax borrowing rate
- some type of risk-adjusted rate, such as the firm's weighted average cost of capital

The choice depends on the assessment of the risk of the firm's cash flows. For example, the firm's after-tax cost of debt may be used to discount cash flows having low risk. However, a higher discount rate, such as the firm's weighted average cost of capital, may be appropriate for more risky cash flows such as the salvage value of an asset.

3. *Compare the present value of the cost of leasing with the present value of the cost of borrowing to buy.* If the present value cost of leasing is less than the present value cost of borrowing to buy, then the asset should be leased. Thus, the decision criterion is to choose the alternative having the lowest present value cost.

EXAMPLE 19-5: Kingman Corporation needs a new machine priced at $100,000 that has an expected life of six years. The firm may either lease the asset or borrow to buy. The firm's marginal tax rate is 34 percent. Kingman plans to discount all cash flows, including the asset's salvage value, at the after-tax cost of borrowing because all of the cash flows are considered to be low risk. With both alternatives, Kingman bears all maintenance, insurance, and other related costs, which are expected to be $2,000 per year.

Lease: If the machine is leased, the annual lease payments will be six equal payments of $20,000 paid in advance. The lease contract does not require the lessee to purchase the machine at the end of the lease term.

Purchase: If the machine is purchased, the firm plans to use ACRS rates for 5-year property. The machine is expected to be sold for its estimated salvage value of $5,000 at the end of six years. Kingman can finance the purchase with a 12 percent term loan requiring six equal end-of-year payments consisting of principal and interest.

(a) Figure 19-2 presents a schedule of cash flows and present value analysis for each year of the leasing alternative. Column 2 shows the annual beginning-of-year lease payments of $20,000.

End of Year (1)	Lease Payment (2)	Tax Saving [0.34 × (2)] (3)	After-Tax Cash Outflow If Leased [(2) − (3)] (4)	PVIF at 8% (5)	Present Value Cost of Leasing [(4) × (5)] (6)
0	$20,000	$ 0	$20,000	1.000	$20,000
1	20,000	6,800	13,200	0.926	12,223
2	20,000	6,800	13,200	0.857	11,312
3	20,000	6,800	13,200	0.794	10,481
4	20,000	6,800	13,200	0.735	9,702
5	20,000	6,800	13,200	0.681	8,989
		6,800	(6,800)	0.630	(4,284)
					$68,423

FIGURE 19-2   Schedule of cash flows and their present values using the leasing alternative for Kingman Corporation

In this example, it is not necessary to include maintenance, insurance, and other related costs in the lease-buy analysis because Kingman bears these costs regardless of whether the firm leases or owns the machine. Column 3 indicates that the tax savings of the lease payment is obtained at the end of the year in which each payment is made. (In reality, the delay in receiving the benefits of the lease payment tax deductibility is less than one year because tax payments are made quarterly, rather than yearly.) The after-tax cash outflow shown in Column 4 is the difference between the lease payment and the tax savings. The after-tax cost of borrowing of 8 percent shown in Column 5 is obtained by multiplying the cost of borrowing by 1 minus the tax rate [0.12 × (1 − 0.34)]. This discount rate is actually 7.92 percent, but this figure is rounded to 8 percent in order to use the present value interest factors (PVIFs) in Appendix C. Finally, the present value cost of leasing for each year is obtained by multiplying the after-tax cash outflow in Column 4 by the corresponding PVIF in Column 5. The summed result shows that the present value cost of leasing is $68,423.

Figure 19-3 presents the loan amortization schedule for Kingman Corporation. The loan payment of $24,325 (rounded) is found using Equation 19-1 in which the $100,000 amount of the loan is divided by the $PVIFA_{0.12,6}$ or 4.111 (Appendix D).

End of Year	Beginning Balance	Loan Payment	Interest Payment [0.12 × (2)]	Principal Reduction [(3) − (4)]	Remaining Balance [(2) − (5)]
(1)	(2)	(3)	(4)	(5)	(6)
1	$100,000	$24,325	$12,000	$12,325	$87,675
2	87,675	24,325	10,521	13,804	73,871
3	73,871	24,325	8,865	15,460	58,411
4	58,411	24,325	7,009	17,316	41,095
5	41,095	24,325	4,931	19,394	21,701
6	21,701	24,325	2,604	21,721	0*

* The actual balance in this example is −$20 ($21,701 − $21,721) which is due to various rounding errors.

FIGURE 19-3   Loan amortization schedule of Kingman Corporation for the borrow-to-buy alternative

LOAN PAYMENT
$$A = \frac{\$100,000}{4.111} = \$24,325$$

Figure 19-4 contains the data necessary to compute the present value cost of borrowing to buy. Column 2 and Column 3 contain the loan payment and interest payment, respectively, taken from the loan amortization schedule in Figure 19-3. Column 4 shows the ACRS depreciation. Equation 2-1 in Chapter 2 is used to compute the annual depreciation amount by multiplying the ACRS rates in Figure 2-2 for 5-year property by the depreciable basis. The tax deductible expenses shown in Column 5 are the sums of interest and ACRS depreciation. Maintenance and related costs are not included because Kingman has to pay the same costs if the asset is leased. In this example, including these costs would not affect the lease-buy decision. Column 6 indicates the taxes saved from the tax-deductible expenses. Column 7 shows the after-tax salvage value of the machine. Because the machine will be fully depreciated at the end of the sixth year, its sale for $5,000 is a recapture of depreciation, which is taxed at the firm's ordinary tax rate of 34 percent. The cash outflow shown in Column 8 is the loan payment less the tax savings and salvage value. The present value cost of owning of $70,103 is computed for Column 10 by multiplying the firm's after-tax cash outflows by the PVIFs of the firm's after-tax cost of borrowing. In this case, the salvage value is considered relatively certain and does not require a higher discount rate.

(b) Based on this analysis, leasing is preferred to owning. As shown below, leasing results in an incremental savings of $1,680 relative to owning. However, because the financial cost between leasing and borrowing to buy is small, other factors may influence the final lease-buy decision.

Present value cost of owning	$70,103
Less: Present value cost of leasing	68,423
Advantage of leasing over owning	$ 1,680

End of Year (1)	Loan Payment* (2)	Interest Payment* (3)	ACRS Depreciation** (4)	Tax-Deductible Expenses [(3) + (4)] (5)	Tax Saving [0.34 × (5)] (6)
1	$24,325	$12,000	$20,000	$32,000	$10,880
2	24,325	10,521	32,000	42,521	14,457
3	24,325	8,865	19,200	28,065	9,542
4	24,325	7,009	11,520	18,529	6,300
5	24,325	4,931	11,520	16,451	5,593
6	24,325	2,604	5,760	8,364	2,844

End of Year	After-Tax Salvage Value S[1 − 0.34] (7)	After-Tax Cash Outflow If Owned [(2) − (6) − (7)] (8)	PVIF at 8% (9)	Present Value Cost of Owning [(8) × (9)] (10)
1	$ 0	$13,445	0.926	$12,450
2	0	9,868	0.857	8,457
3	0	14,783	0.794	11,738
4	0	18,025	0.735	13,248
5	0	18,732	0.681	12,756
6	3,300	18,181	0.630	11,454
				$70,103

* From Figure 19-3.
** See Figure 2-2 for 5-year property for depreciation rates.

FIGURE 19-4   Schedule of cash flows and present value analysis of the borrowing-to-buy alternative for Kingman Corporation

E. There are many potential advantages to leasing.

1. *Flexibility*. Operating leases offer flexibility because they can be cancelled. Leases containing purchase options give the lessee the flexibility of making the purchase decision at the termination of the lease term. Lease arrangements may also contain fewer restrictive covenants than other forms of intermediate-term financing.

2. *Financing*. Leasing provides an additional source of financing for facilities and equipment to firms that have limited capital budgets. Leasing may be the only source of financing available to the small or marginally profitable firm. Generally, leasing and borrowing have similar effects on the firm's total borrowing capacity because a lease uses up a part of the debt capacity of the firm.

3. *Convenience*. Leasing is a convenient way to obtain the use of assets that are needed only temporarily.

4. *Liquidity*. Leasing may increase liquidity and conserve the availability of cash for other purposes. For example, the use of sale and leaseback arrangements may permit the firm to increase liquidity by converting existing fixed assets into cash. Leasing may further enhance liquidity if it provides 100 percent financing. To do this, the leasing arrangement must not require a deposit or advance payments since, the common practice of making lease payments in advance is in substance a down payment. However, a lessee may find it difficult to locate a lessor who is willing to completely finance and lease such an asset.

5. *Shifts the risk of obsolescence*. Leasing may allow the lessee to avoid assuming the risk of obsolescence if the lessor does not properly anticipate obsolescence costs in setting lease payments. The risk of obsolescence is generally avoided when either the lease term is shorter than the asset's life or the lease arrangement has a

cancellation clause. However, the estimated risk of obsolescence is typically factored into the lease payments.

6. *Effective depreciation of land.* Leasing allows the lessee, in effect, to depreciate land because the entire lease payment is a tax deductible expense. Land owners, on the other hand, are prohibited from depreciating their land.

7. *Tax considerations.* Leasing may provide tax advantages relative to borrowing to buy. For example, a firm may have substantial losses which preclude taking advantage of ACRS depreciation involved in owning. A lessor in a high tax bracket may be able to pass on tax benefits to the lessee through lower lease payments. However, tax effects must be examined on a case-by-case basis. In some cases, leases can offer net tax advantages to the lessee, while in many other the lease contract tax advantages may not outweigh the tax advantages associated with owning.

F. There are many potential disadvantages to leasing.

1. *Cost.* Leasing is often more expensive than owning. For example, the lessor may have economies of scale of purchasing, lower borrowing costs, and a more favorable tax situation than the lessee.

2. *Lack of salvage value.* The lessee may not have any residual rights to the property upon the termination of the lease. The lack of salvage value is a disadvantage if the lease involves assets such as land and buildings that are expected to appreciate over the lease term. This disadvantage is reduced when the lease contains a bargain purchase option.

3. *Difficulty of property improvements.* Lease arrangements often require the lessee to obtain approval for making improvements on the leased property.

4. *Noncancelability.* Some leases cannot be cancelled while others require substantial penalties for cancellation. Thus, leases represent a fixed financial commitment even though the lessee may be unable to use the leased asset because it has become obsolete.

RAISE YOUR GRADES

Can you explain...?

☑ what a term loan is
☑ the major characteristics of a term loan
☑ how to construct an amortization schedule
☑ the differences among affirmative covenants, negative covenants, restrictive covenants, and default provisions
☑ the major advantages and disadvantages of term loans
☑ what a conditional sales contract is
☑ what a lease is
☑ the distinguishing characteristics of operating, financial, and leveraged leases
☑ how the capitalized value of a lease is computed
☑ what off-balance-sheet financing is
☑ the three major steps in conducting a lease-buy analysis
☑ what cash flows are used in evaluating leasing and borrowing to buy alternatives
☑ the appropriate discount rates to use in a lease-buy analysis
☑ the potential advantages and disadvantages of leasing as a source of financing

SUMMARY

1. Term loans and leases are sources of intermediate-term and sometimes long-term financing.

2. A term loan is a business loan with a maturity of more than one year. These loans are privately negotiated between the borrower and the lender.

3. Term loans are normally amortized in installments over the life of the loan and may include a balloon payment. These loans may have fixed or variable interest rates and may be secured or unsecured.

4. The lender incorporates covenants or provisions into the term loan agreement as safeguards against default on the loan. These covenants restrict the scope of the borrower's activities.

5. The major advantages of term loans include speed, flexibility, low issuance costs, and the avoidance of possible nonrenewal of short-term loans.

6. The disadvantages of term loans include restrictive loan provisions, the use of collateral in some cases, higher costs than short-term loans, and the cash drain from making annuity payments.

7. Equipment financing loans are a type of intermediate-term financing used to finance specific equipment purchases in which the purchased equipment serves as collateral. One type of equipment financing is a conditional sales contract which is provided by equipment manufacturers.

8. A lease is an agreement in which the owner or lessor of an asset agrees to let another party or lessee use the asset in return for specified payments.

9. The basic types of leases are operating and financial. Operating leases are cancelable, include maintenance and service in the lease payment, have a contract life shorter than the economic life of the asset, and do not fully amortize the cost of the asset.

10. Financial leases are noncancelable, do not provide maintenance, approximate the economic life of the asset, and fully amortize the cost of the asset.

11. A leveraged lease is distinguished from other lease arrangements such as a direct lease and a sale/leaseback in that it involves three parties—a lessor, a lender, and a lessee.

12. FASB Statement 13 classifies leases as either capital or operating leases depending on whether certain conditions are met. A capital lease is shown on the lessee's balance sheet as an asset and as a corresponding liability. Obligations for operating leases appear only in a footnote to the firm's statements and hence represent off-balance-sheet financing.

13. Lease-buy analysis involves a comparison of leasing with straight debt financing in order to determine which is the less costly source of financing. There are three major steps: calculating the after-tax cash flows if the asset is leased and if it is purchased; determining the present value of these cash flows; and choosing the alternative having the lowest present value cost.

14. A controversial area in lease-buy analysis is the appropriate rate to use in discounting the cash flows. The rate should reflect the riskiness of the cash flows. Cash outflows associated with both leasing and borrowing to buy are typically discounted at the lessee's after-tax cost of debt.

15. Leasing offers numerous advantages including flexibility, convenience, increased liquidity, and the effective depreciation of land. Leasing may also shift the risk of obsolescence to the lessor and may be the only source of financing available to some firms.

16. Leasing has several disadvantages. It tends to be costly and does not provide the lessee with any salvage value. Some leases are noncancelable and require the lessee to obtain the lessor's approval in order to make leasehold improvements.

RAPID REVIEW

True or False

1. A term loan is usually amortized over the life of the loan in equal installments each of which includes both interest and principal. [Section 19-1A]

2. Covenants are incorporated into the loan agreement primarily to safeguard the borrower against the lender. [Section 19-1A]

3. The inclusion of equity kickers tends to increase the overall cost of term loans. [Section 19-1A]

4. An acceleration clause, calling for immediate repayment, may be invoked if the borrower fails to make installment payments on time. [Section 19-1A]

5. Speed and flexibility are often cited as advantages of term loans. [Section 19-1B]

6. Commercial banks are the major providers of conditional sales contracts. [Section 19-2A]

7. In a conditional sales contract, the title of the equipment passes to the purchaser at the initiation of the sale. [Section 19-2A]

8. A chattel mortgage is a lien primarily on personal property, which gives the lender the right to seize and sell the personal property should the borrower default on the loan. [Section 19-2B]

9. Leasing involves the use of an asset without ownership. [Section 19-3]

10. The lessee owns the asset, which is leased to a lessor. [Section 19-3]

11. Both operating and financial leases are generally cancelable. [Section 19-3A]

12. In a direct lease, the firm acquires the use of an asset that it did not previously own. [Section 19-3B]

13. In a sale and leaseback arrangement, the lessee receives cash from the sale of the asset and continues to use it. [Section 19-3B]

14. In a leveraged lease, the lessor obtains a substantial portion of the purchase price from a third party in order to acquire an asset which it then leases to the lessee. [Section 19-3B]

15. A lease is classified as an operating lease if it has a bargain purchase option. [Section 19-3C]

16. The asset and liability accounts for a capital lease remain equal throughout the lease term on the lessee's balance sheet. [Section 19-3C]

17. Operating leases result in off-balance-sheet financing. [Section 19-3C]

18. The financing decision to lease or borrow to buy has no impact on the acceptability of a project using capital budgeting procedures. [Section 19-3D]

19. The choice of the appropriate discount rate in lease-buy analysis depends on the riskiness of the cash flows. [Section 19-3D]

20. The decision criterion in a lease-buy analysis is to select the lowest present value cost. [Section 19-3D]

Multiple Choice

21. Which of the following is not a source of intermediate-term financing?

    (a) Term loans
    (b) Leases
    (c) Equipment financing loans
    (d) Common stock

    [Section 19-1 through 19-3]

22. Which of the following is typically not a supplier of term loans?

    (*a*) Commercial bankers
    (*b*) Investment bankers
    (*c*) Insurance companies
    (*d*) Finance companies

    [Section 19-1]

23. Covenants imposed on a term loan may include:

    (*a*) affirmative covenants
    (*b*) negative covenants
    (*c*) restrictive covenants
    (*d*) all of the above

    [Section 19-1A]

24. What is the other major classification of leases besides operating leases?

    (*a*) Capital leases
    (*b*) Direct leases
    (*c*) Leveraged leases
    (*d*) Sale and leasebacks

    [Section 19-3A]

25. All of the following are characteristics of operating leases except:

    (*a*) operating leases may be cancelled before the expiration date.
    (*b*) operating leases fully amortize the cost of the asset.
    (*c*) operating leases provide maintenance and service by the lessor.
    (*d*) operating leases are shorter than the economic life of the asset.

    [Section 19-3A]

26. A third-party lease is called a(n):

    (*a*) sale and leaseback
    (*b*) direct lease
    (*c*) operating lease
    (*d*) leveraged lease

    [Section 19-3B]

27. Which of the following is *not* a condition for classifying a lease as a capital lease under FASB Statement 13?

    (*a*) The lease transfers ownership of the asset to the lessee at the end of the lease term.
    (*b*) The lease give the lessee a bargain purchase option.
    (*c*) The lease term extends for at least 90 percent of the leased asset's estimated economic life.
    (*d*) The present value of the lease payments at the beginning of the lease equals or exceeds 90 percent of the current fair market value of the asset.

    [Section 19-3C]

28. Lease-buy analysis assumes that leasing is comparable to:

    (*a*) borrowing with straight debt financing
    (*b*) selling preferred stock
    (*c*) selling common stock
    (*d*) retaining earnings

    [Section 19-3D]

29. In lease-buy analysis, all of the following are tax-deductible expenses *except*:

  (*a*) interest expenses
  (*b*) ACRS depreciation
  (*c*) maintenance expenses
  (*d*) principal repayment

[Section 19-3D]

30. *All but one* of the following are commonly noted as advantages of leasing?

  (*a*) Leasing may shift the risk of obsolescence to the lessor.
  (*b*) Leasing allows the lessee, in effect, to depreciate land.
  (*c*) Leasing provides salvage value to the lessee.
  (*d*) Leasing may provide 100 percent financing.

[Sections 19-3E & F]

Answers

True or False		*Multiple Choice*
1. True	11. False	21. d
2. False	12. True	22. b
3. True	13. True	23. d
4. True	14. True	24. a
5. True	15. False	25. b
6. False	16. False	26. d
7. False	17. True	27. c
8. True	18. False	28. a
9. True	19. True	29. d
10. False	20. True	30. c

SOLVED PROBLEMS

PROBLEM 19-1: Lewis Company plans to borrow $1,000,000 for eight years at 9 percent with a bank term loan. The bank requires repayment in a series of equal annual end-of-year installments.

(*a*) What is the annual loan payment rounded to the nearest dollar?
(*b*) How much total interest will Lewis Company pay over the life of the loan?

Answer:

(*a*) The annual loan payment, A, of $180,668 is found by substituting the amount of the loan, $1,000,000, and PVIFA$_{0.09,8}$ = 5.535 (Appendix D) in Equation 19-1.

$$A = \frac{\text{Amount of the loan}}{\text{PVIFA}_{0.09,8}} = \frac{\$1,000,000}{5.535} = \$180,668$$

(*b*) The total interest paid on the loan is approximately $445,344.

Total payments (8 × $180,668)	$1,445,344
Amount of the loan (principal)	1,000,000
Total interest.	$ 445,344

[Section 19-1A]

PROBLEM 19-2: A bank loan requires four annual end-of-year payments of $20,000. The interest rate is 14 percent. What is the face amount of the loan?

Answer: Solving this problem requires rewriting Equation 19-1 in order to determine the amount of the loan and substituting the yearly loan payment, $A = \$20,000$, and $PVIFA_{0.14} = 2.914$ (Appendix D), in the new equation as follows.

$$\text{Amount of the loan} = (A)(PVIFA_{0.14,4})$$
$$= (\$20,000)(2.914) = \$58,280 \quad \textbf{[Section 19-1A]}$$

PROBLEM 19-3: Dale City Bank has offered Arrow Drug Stores a 4-year loan in the amount of $250,000 at the rate of 10 percent per year. The loan will be repaid in four equal end-of-year payments of principal and interest. Calculate the amount of each of the end-of-year payments.

Answer: The annual loan payment, $78,864.35, is calculated by substituting the amount of the loan, $250,000, and $PVIFA_{0.10,4} = 3.170$ (Appendix D), in Equation 19-1.

$$A = \frac{\text{Amount of the loan}}{PVIFA_{0.10,4}} = \frac{\$250,000}{3.170} = \$78,864.35 \quad \textbf{[Section 19-1A]}$$

PROBLEM 19-4: Referring to Problem 19-3, do the following:

(*a*) Construct a loan amortization schedule. (Round the loan payment up to the nearest dollar.)

(*b*) Explain why the composition of the loan payment changes over time.

Answer:

End of Year	Beginning Balance	Loan Payment	Interest Payment $[0.10 \times (2)]$	Principal Reduction $[(3) - (4)]$	Remaining Balance $[(2) - (5)]$
(1)	(2)	(3)	(4)	(5)	(6)
1	$250,000	$78,864	$25,000	$53,864	$196,136
2	196,136	78,864	19,614	59,250	136,886
3	136,886	78,864	13,689	65,175	71,711
4	71,711	78,864	7,171	71,693	0*

* The actual remaining balance in Year 4 is $18 ($71, 711 − $71,693), which is due to rounding errors. Without rounding errors, the remaining balance would be exactly zero.

(*c*) Interest is based on the declining balance of the loan. Since the payments remain constant, the reduction in principal must increase. **[Section 19-1A]**

PROBLEM 19-5: Gordon Associates, Inc. obtained office equipment with a 3-year lease that required beginning-of-year payments of $6,000 each. This lease payment does not include executory costs. The lease arrangement requires the lessee to purchase the asset at an estimated fair market value of $10,000 at the end of the lease term. The economic life of the leased equipment is five years. The cost of the equipment, if purchased, was $25,000. Gordon's borrowing rate when the lease was negotiated was 11 percent. Is this an operating or a capital lease?

Answer: The lease is a capital lease because it meets two of the four criteria of FASB Statement 13. Ownership is transferred to the lessee at the end of the lease term, so the first condition is met. Gordon has an option to buy at the fair market value but not at a bargain purchase option, so the second condition is not met. The third requirement is also not met because the lease term is only 60 percent (3 years/5 years) of the estimated economic life of the asset which is less than the required 75 percent. However, the fourth criterion is fulfilled because the present value of the lease of $23,588 exceeds 90 percent of the fair market value of the machine of $22,500 (0.90 × $25,000). The present value of the lease is calculated by substituting $L = \$6,000$, $PVIFA_{0.11,2} = 1.713$ (Appendix D), $GR = \$10,000$, and $PVIF_{0.11,3} = 0.731$ (Appendix C) in Equation 19-2.

$$\text{PV of the lease} = (\$6,000)(1 + 1.713) + (\$10,000)(0.731) = \$23,588$$

[Section 19-3C]

PROBLEM 19-6: Referring to Problem 19-5, what are the initial balances of this lease on the firm's balance sheet?

Answer: The initial amount of the asset and liability accounts for a capital lease is the lesser of the present value of the minimum lease payments of $23,588 or the fair market value of the leased property of $25,000. The lease is shown under an asset account called "leased property under capital leases" for $23,588 and also under a liability account called "lease obligations under capital leases" for $23,588.   [Section 19-3C]

PROBLEM 19-7: Chez Robert Restaurant plans to lease two ovens with a fair market value of $10,000 each. The ovens will be leased for their economic life of 10 years with annual lease payments of $1,500 paid in advance. There is no bargain purchase option or guaranteed residual value. The discount rate is 10 percent. What is the present value of the minimum lease payments?

Answer: Substituting $L = \$1,500$ and $PVIFA_{0.10,9} = 5.759$ (Appendix D) in Equation 19-2 gives the present value of the minimum lease payments of $10,139.50.

$$\text{PV of the lease} = (\$1,500)(1 + 5.759) = \$10,139.50 \quad \text{[Section 19-3C]}$$

PROBLEM 19-8: Fairhurst Enterprises is contemplating leasing ten heavy-duty trucks from Nationwide Leasing with a total fair market value of $300,000. The trucks will be classified as a capital lease and will require five annual lease payments of $70,000 paid in advance. No guaranteed residual value is required. The lessor's implicit rate of interest is 13 percent and the lessee's incremental borrowing rate is 15 percent. What is the capitalized value of the lease?

Answer: The discount rate used to compute the present value of the minimum lease payments is the lessee's borrowing rate or the lessor's implicit rate of interest, whichever is lower. In this case, the lessor's implicit rate of interest of 13 percent is lower. The present value of the minimum lease payments is found by substituting $L = \$70,000$ and $PVIFA_{0.13,4} = 2.974$ (Appendix D) in Equation 19-2.

$$\text{PV} = (\$70,000)(1 + 2.974) = \$278,180$$

The lease is capitalized at $278,180 because the fair market value of the leased property of $300,000 is more than the present value of the minimum lease payments of $278,180.

[Section 19-3C]

PROBLEM 19-9: Standard Leasing Services requires a 15 percent implicit rate of return on assets that it leases out. The firm leases an asset with a net cost of $50,000 and requires seven equal lease payments paid at the beginning of each year. How much will Standard Leasing Services require as an annual lease payment?

Answer: Substituting the net cost of the leased property of $50,000 and $PVIFA_{0.15,6} = 3.784$ (Appendix D) in Equation 19-3 produces a minimum beginning-of-the-year lease payment of $10,452.

$$L = \frac{50,000}{1 + 3.784} = \$10,452 \quad \text{[Section 19-3D]}$$

Problems 19-10 through 19-13 refer to the following data:

Continental Pizza is deciding whether to lease or purchase two new light-duty trucks for delivering pizza. The firm has a marginal tax rate of 34 percent and an after-tax cost of borrowing of 10 percent. The terms of the lease and the purchase are given below.

Lease: The lease payments would be $7,000 a year to be paid at the beginning of each year for six years. The annual lease payments include a maintenance contract on the trucks over the lease's term. The lease payments would be tax deductible at the end of each year. The lease arrangement does not contain a bargain purchase option or transfer of ownership to the lessee at the end of the lease term.

Purchase: The trucks cost a total of $30,000. Continental Pizza could borrow the needed funds of $30,000 with a 6-year term loan. The loan would have a 15 percent interest rate and be repaid in six equal end-of-year payments. If the trucks are purchased, Continental Pizza would provide maintenance estimated to be $500 a year. The firm would use ACRS depreciation for 5-year property. Continental expects to be able to sell the two trucks for a total of $6,000, which is their estimated salvage value at the end of the sixth year. The firm plans to use a 20 percent rate to discount the salvage value, due to its riskiness. All other cash flows will be discounted at the 10 percent after-tax cost of borrowing rate. (Actually, the after-tax cost of borrowing is 9.90 percent [(0.15)(1 − 0.34)] but this rate is rounded to 10 percent in order to use the present value tables.

PROBLEM 19-10: Calculate the present value cost of leasing.

Answer: The lease payments include maintenance. The calculation of the present value cost of leasing is shown below:

End of Year (1)	Lease Payment (2)	Tax Saving [0.34 × (2)] (3)	After-Tax Cash Outflow If Leased [(2) − (3)] (4)	PVIF at 10% (5)	Present Value Cost of Leasing [(4) × (5)] (6)
0	$7,000	0	$7,000	1.000	$ 7,000
1	7,000	$2,380	4,620	0.909	4,200
2	7,000	2,380	4,620	0.826	3,816
3	7,000	2,380	4,620	0.751	3,470
4	7,000	2,380	4,620	0.683	3,155
5	7,000	2,380	4,620	0.621	2,869
6		2,380	(2,380)	0.564	(1,342)
					$23,168

[Section 19-3D]

PROBLEM 19-11: Calculate the amortization schedule for the loan if the trucks are purchased.

Answer: The loan payment, $A = \$7,928$ (rounded), is computed using Equation 19-1, in which the $30,000 loan amount is divided by $PVIFA_{0.15,6} = 3.784$ (Appendix D). The amortization schedule for the loan is shown below:

$$A = \frac{\$30,000}{3.784} = \$7,928$$

End of Year (1)	Beginning Balance (2)	Loan Payment (3)	Interest Payment [0.15 × (2)] (4)	Principal Reduction (5)	Remaining Balance [(2) − (5)] (6)
1	$30,000	$7,928	$4,500	$3,428	$26,572
2	26,572	7,928	3,936	3,942	22,630
3	22,630	7,928	3,394	4,534	18,096
4	18,096	7,928	2,714	5,214	12,882
5	12,882	7,928	1,932	5,996	6,886
6	6,886	7,928	1,033	6,895	0*

* The actual balance in this example is −$9 ($6,886 − $6,895) which is due to rounding errors.

[Section 19-3D]

PROBLEM 19-12: Calculate the present value cost of purchasing.

Answer: The cash flows and the present value cost of owning is shown below. In this schedule, two lines are shown for Year 6 in order to account for the salvage value, which is discounted at a 20 percent rate rather than at the 10 percent rate used for other cash outflows. The loan payment and interest payment in Columns 2 and 3, respectively, are taken from the amortization schedule in Problem 19-11. In Column 4, the ACRS depreciation rates are applied to the $30,000 cost of the trucks to get the dollar amount of ACRS depreciation. The ACRS rates are shown in Figure 2-2. Column 5 shows the annual maintenance expense of $500. The present value cost of owning is $20,598.

End of Year	Loan Payment*	Interest Payment*	ACRS Depreciation	Maintenance Expense	Tax-Deductible Expenses [(3) + (4) + (5)]
(1)	(2)	(3)	(4)	(5)	(6)
1	$7,928	$4,500	$6,000	$500	$11,000
2	$7,928	3,986	9,600	500	14,086
3	$7,928	3,394	5,760	500	9,654
4	$7,928	2,714	3,456	500	6,670
5	$7,928	1,932	3,456	500	5,888
6	$7,928	1,033	1,728	500	3,261

	Tax Saving [(0.34 × (6)]	After-Tax Salvage Value S[1 − 0.34]	After-Tax Cash Outflow If Owned [(2) − (7) − (8)]	PVIF at 10%	Present Value Cost of Owning [(9) × (10)]
	(7)	(8)	(9)	(10)	(11)
1	$3,740	$ 0	$4,188	0.909	$ 3,807
2	4,789	0	3,139	0.826	2,593
3	3,282	0	4,646	0.751	3,489
4	2,268	0	5,660	0.683	3,866
5	2,002	0	5,926	0.621	3,680
6	1,109	0	6,819	0.564	3,846
6′	0	3,960	(3,960)	0.335**	(1,327)
					$19,954

* From the amortization schedule in Problem 19-11.

** The salvage value is discounted at 20 percent in the sixth year due to its greater riskiness.

PROBLEM 19-13: Which alternative is more attractive? Why?

Answer: The leasing alternative, with a present value cost of $23,168, is higher than leasing, with a present value cost of $19,954. The firm would realize an incremental savings of $3,214 ($23,168 − $19,954) by purchasing. Other factors may influence the financial decision.

[Section 19-3D]

20 LONG-TERM FINANCING

THIS CHAPTER IS ABOUT

- ☑ **Bonds**
- ☑ **Preferred Stock**
- ☑ **Common Stock**
- ☑ **Convertible Securities**
- ☑ **Warrants**

Long-term external financing consists primarily of bonds, preferred stocks, and common stocks. Internally generated funds in the form of retained earnings also serve as a source of long-term corporate financing. The topic of retained earnings is discussed in conjunction with the firm's dividend policy in Chapter 16. In addition, term loans, equipment financing loans, and leases (discussed in Chapter 19) may be considered sources of long-term financing depending on the length of their maturities. Bonds and preferred stocks are generally classified as **fixed income securities** because they involve relatively constant distributions of interest or dividend payments. Common stock is a **variable income security** because dividends may vary.

20-1. Bonds

A bond is a long-term debt instrument in which the issuer promises to pay the bondholder specified amounts of interest and principal on predetermined dates. Bondholders are creditors to the issuing corporation and have prior claims to the firm's earnings and to its assets in the event of liquidation. Although bonds are also a major source of financing for federal, state, and local governments, the discussion in this text focuses on corporate bonds.

The following conditions favor issuing bonds.

1. Sales and earnings are relatively stable.
2. Coverage ratios and profit margins are adequate.
3. The firm's liquidity position is adequate.
4. The existing debt ratio is low.
5. Interest rates are low.
6. Indenture provisions of prior debt issues or the proposed debt issue are not too burdensome.
7. The firm's credit rating is satisfactory.
8. The firm's stock price is depressed.
9. Control considerations are important.

A. A bond has several major characteristics and provisions.

1. *Indenture*. An indenture is a legal document that contains the terms and conditions of the bond issue. It specifies such details as the type, maturity, and

amount of the bond, the annual interest rate, and various provisions and covenants similar to those contained in a term loan (Chapter 19). The Securities and Exchange Commission (SEC) approves indentures and makes sure that the various indenture provisions are met before a firm is permitted to sell the bonds to the public.

2. *Trustee.* A **trustee** is the bondholders' agent in a public debt offering. The trustee, who is appointed by the issuer before the bonds are sold, is usually the trust department of a commercial bank. Thus, there are three parties to a public issue: the issuer, the bondholders, and the trustee. The trustee certifies the bond issue, makes sure that the issuer fulfills the terms of the indenture, and represents the bondholders in the event of default.

3. *Par value.* The par value is the nominal value stated on the bond. Other terms for par value include *face value, maturity value, denomination, stated value,* and *principal amount.* A bond trades at par whenever its market value and its par value are equal. Most corporate bonds have $1,000 par values. Bond prices are quoted as a percentage of par value.

4. *Discount and premium.* A bond sells at a **premium** whenever its market value is above its par value, and at a **discount** whenever its market value is below its par value. The premium or discount is amortized over the life of the bond. The flotation costs of the bond are also amortized over the life of the bond and are a tax-deductible expense. The amortized premium is subject to ordinary income taxes while the amortized discount is a tax-deductible expense. Equation 20-1 is the formula for the annual amortized discount after taxes.

$$\text{Annual amortized discount after taxes} = \left(\frac{\text{Total discount}}{\text{Years to maturity}}\right)(1 - \text{marginal tax rate}) \qquad \textbf{(20-1)}$$

EXAMPLE 20-1: Carter Corporation issues bonds having a par value of $1,000 at 98. What this means is that each bond initially sold for $980 (0.98 × $1,000 par).

EXAMPLE 20-2: Carter Corporation issues 20,000 bonds having a par value of $1,000 at 98. The bonds pay 10 percent interest and mature in 20 years. Interest is paid semiannually. The firm's marginal tax rate is 34 percent.

The proceeds from the sale of the issue are determined by multiplying the amount received from the sale of a single bond by the 20,000 bonds sold. Underwriting costs are ignored. Thus, Carter Corporation received $19,600,000 ($980 × 20,000) from the issuance of the bonds.

The total discount is calculated by subtracting the total proceeds of the sale from the total par value. Thus, the firm sold the bonds at a discount of $400,000 ($20,000,000 − $19,600,000).

The annual amortized discount after taxes is calculated using Equation 20-1.

$$\text{Annual amortized discount after taxes} = \left(\frac{\$400,000}{20}\right)(1 - 0.34) = (\$20,000)(0.66) = \$13,200$$

5. *Maturity date.* All bonds issued in the United States have a maturity date. Maturities on long-term bonds typically range from 20 to 30 years. On most bonds the maturity occurs all at once whereas on others, called **serial bonds**, the maturity occurs in stages over time.

6. *Coupon rate.* The **coupon rate** is the stated or nominal rate of interest based on a bond's par value. Bond interest payments are typically made semiannually on corporate bonds and are tax deductible. However, **zero coupon bonds** provide all of the cash payments, both interest and principal, when they mature. Hence, these bonds do not pay periodic interest but sell at a deep discount from their par values. Most bonds pay a fixed interest rate, but the rates associated with **floating rate notes** adjust to changes in market interest rates. The coupon rate is influenced by several factors including the type, maturity, and quality of the bond.

EXAMPLE 20-3: *Refer to data in Example 20-2.* The total par value of Carter Corporation bonds is $20,000,000 ($1,000 × 20,000 bonds). With a coupon rate of 10 percent, total annual interest payments, *I*, are $2,000,000 (0.10 × $20,000,000) and total semiannual interest payments, *I*/2, are $1,000,000 (2,000,000/2).

7. *Points and basis points.* A **point** is the percentage change of the face value of a bond. A change of 1 percent is a move of one point. A *basis point* is the smallest measure used in quoting yields on bonds and notes. One basis point is 0.01 percent of yield. There are 100 **basis points** in each 1 percent of yield. Points and basis points are used to quote changes in bond prices and yields.

EXAMPLE 20-4: The bond quotation for Carter Corporation bonds falls from 98 to 96. The price of the bond falls by two percentage points (98 − 96) or 200 basis points (2 × 100).

8. *Call provision.* A **call provision** gives the issuer the right to repurchase the bond prior to its maturity under specified terms. The firm may decide to retire bonds to take advantage of lower interest rates, to rid itself of restrictive indenture provisions, or to reduce indebtedness. A call provision is beneficial to the issuer but detrimental to the bondholder. Thus, the issuer usually has to offer investors some enticements in order to sell a bond with a call provision. Examples of enticements or "sweeteners" include a higher-than-normal coupon rate, an agreement not to call the bond until after a specified date (**deferred call provision**), and a call premium. A **call premium** is the additional sum that a firm must pay above the bond's par value in order to repurchase a bond. The amount paid as a call premium is a tax-deductible expense to the issuing corporation. The price at which a bond may be called (the par value plus any call premium) is termed the **call price**. Call price may remain constant during the bond's life or decrease until it equals the bond's par value.

EXAMPLE 20-5: The $20,000,000 par value, 10 percent coupon, 20-year bond issue of Carter Corporation has several call provisions. The bonds cannot be called within the first five years but can be called any time thereafter. The call prices are: 110 for years 6−10, 105 for years 11−15, and 100 for years 16−20. Other costs associated with repurchasing the bond are excluded.

The total call price is calculated by multiplying the call as a percent times the total par value of the bonds. Thus, Carter Corporation must pay $22,000,000 (1.10 × $20,000,000) to repurchase the bonds during years 6−10, $21,000,000 (1.05 × $20,000,000) to repurchase the bonds during years 11−15, and $20,000,000 (1.00 × $20,000,000) to repurchase the bonds during years 16−20.

The total call premium is found by subtracting the total par value of the bonds from the total call price. Thus, the total premium is $2,000,000 during years 6−10, $1,000,000 during years 11−15, and zero during years 16−20.

9. *Conversion feature.* A **conversion feature** allows the bondholder to exchange a bond for a certain number of shares of preferred or common stock. Convertible securities are discussed in Section 20-4.

10. *Sinking fund.* A **sinking fund** is a provision which facilitates the orderly retirement of a portion of a bond issue before its maturity date. It usually requires the issuing corporation to make fixed or variable sinking fund payments at specified times. Sinking fund requirements often do not apply during the early years of a bond issue. In practice, the sinking fund requirement may be satisfied either by calling a specified dollar amount of bonds annually as determined by a lottery or by purchasing the required dollar amount of bonds on the open market. The firm will choose the redemption method that results in the greatest reduction in indebtedness for a given expenditure. If current interest rates are above the bond's coupon rate, then the current market price of the bond will be less than $1,000 and the firm should purchase the debt on the open market to meet its sinking

fund requirement. If market interest rates are below the bond's coupon rate and if the market price of the bond is above the call price, the firm should use the call procedure assuming the call premium is not too high. Regardless of the method chosen, a sinking fund is a cash drain on the firm.

EXAMPLE 20-6: The $20,000,000 par value, 20-year bond issue of Carter Corporation has a sinking fund provision. After the first four years, the firm is required to make an annual sinking fund payment of one-sixteenth of the total par value of bonds or $1,250,000 (1/16 × $20,000,000).

EXAMPLE 20-7: Carter Corporation has another bond issues whose indenture requires a sinking fund payment of $2,000,000 at the end of the current year. These bonds have a call price of 105 and a market price of 106.

The firm should call the bonds because it is less expensive to call the bonds at 105 than to purchase them in the market for 106. The firm will retire less than $2,000,000 in total par value because the bonds must be purchased at a call price which is above par.

B. Bonds may be classified according to whether or not any collateral is pledged against a bond issue.

Two major bond classifications are secured bonds and unsecured bonds.

1. **Secured bonds** are bonds backed by the pledge of collateral. *Collateral* is an asset pledged to a lender until an obligation is paid. The purpose of pledging collateral is to decrease the investment risk of the bondholder and to increase the marketability of the issue. Thus, if the issuer defaults, then the bondholder has a claim to the pledged assets prior to unsecured creditors and owners. If the bondholders' full claim is not met through the liquidation of the secured assets, they become general creditors for the remaining amount of the claim owed. There are several types of secured bonds:

    • **Mortgage bonds** are bonds backed by real property (land and buildings). Some mortgage bonds are secured by *blanket (general) mortgages* in which all or most the firm's assets serve as collateral. A corporation may sometimes use the same property to secure several bond issues. A *first-mortgage bond* gives its bondholders the first claim on secured assets. A *second-mortgage bond* gives its bondholders a secondary claim against the real property already used as security for the first-mortgage. First-mortgage bonds are sometimes called *senior debt* because they have a higher priority claim to a firm's earnings and/or assets than *junior debt*, such as second-mortgage bonds. Because of their higher degree of riskiness, second-mortgage bonds carry a higher interest rate than first-mortgage bonds.

    • **Equipment trust certificates** are bonds, usually issued by a transportation company, such as a railroad line, used to pay for new equipment. The certificates give the bondholder first claim to the equipment in case of default. A trustee holds the title of the equipment until the bond is paid off.

    • **Collateral trust bonds** are corporate debt securities backed by other securities which are usually held by a trustee.

2. **Unsecured bonds** are obligations not backed by the pledge of a specific collateral. These bonds represent a claim against the firm's earnings but not against any specific assets. The claims of unsecured bondholders are the same as those of general creditors. There are three major types of unsecured bonds:

    • **Debentures** are unsecured, long-term bonds backed only by the borrower's creditworthiness. Debentures are usually issued when the firm has a strong financial position, its property is unsuitable as collateral, or it is too weak to have other alternatives.

    • **Subordinated debentures** are unsecured bonds that rank behind other types of debt with respect to claims against earnings and assets. These bondholders still have a claim against earnings and assets ahead of preferred and common stockholders. Subordinate debentures generally are a more expensive method of financing because they expose investors to a higher degree of risk than secured bonds or debentures. However, they do not restrict the firm's ability to obtain senior debt.

- **Income bonds** are bonds that pay interest only if income is earned by the issuer. Thus, the interest is not a fixed charge, but the principal amount must be paid when due. Income bonds are sometimes used in corporate reorganizations as an alternative to bankruptcy.

C. A *bond rating* is an evaluation of the probability of a firm defaulting on a bond issue.

Bonds are often rated according to their risk and investment quality by a rating agency. An issuer may have a prospective bond issue evaluated and rated for a fee by a rating agency, such as Standard & Poor's Corporation (S&P) or Moody's Investors Service, Inc. (Moody's). As Figure 20-1 indicates, more highly rated bonds (such as Triple A bonds) are considered less risky than bonds with lower ratings (such as Single A bonds). The quality or rating of a bond is generally inversely related to the bond's interest rate or yield to maturity. That is, high-quality (high-rated) bonds have lower yields than low-quality (low-rated) bonds. Rating assignments are judgmental and are based on numerous qualitative and quantitative factors, including the firm's earnings stability and the bond's indenture provisions. A change in a bond's rating may affect the issuer's ability to raise additional long-term capital and its cost of capital.

Standard & Poor's		Moody's	
AAA	Highest grade	Aaa	Best quality
AA	High grade	Aa	High quality
A	Upper medium grade	A	Upper medium grade
BBB	Medium grade	Baa	Medium grade
BB, CCC, CC	Speculative	Ba	Have speculative elements
C	Income bond on which no interest is being paid	B	Lack characteristics of a desirable investment
		Caa	Poor; may be in default
DDD, DD, D	Bond in default; rating indicates the relative salvage value	Ca	Highly speculative; often in default
		C	Lowest grade

FIGURE 20-1   Bond ratings by Standard & Poor's and Moody's

D. There are many advantages to using bonds as a source of long-term financing.

1. *Low cost.* The after-tax cost of bonds is less than that of preferred and common stock. The lower cost of bonds is attributed to the tax deductibility of interest payments, the lower return required by bondholders relative to stockholders, and the relatively low flotation costs of bonds. Interest payments are also fixed on most bonds. Thus, bondholders do not share in any superior earnings of the firm.
2. *No dilution of control.* Bonds do not carry voting rights, and hence, current stockholders retain their proportionate voting control when bonds are issued.
3. *Less earnings dilution.* The use of bonds may dilute the firm's earnings per share less than issuing stock.

4. *Financing flexibility.* The call provision adds flexibility to the firm's financial structure by allowing it to refinance and/or retire bonds before they mature.

5. *Improved financial leverage.* A firm may increase its earnings per share through the effects of favorable financial leverage (when the borrowed funds earn more than their cost) resulting from the use of bonds.

6. *Avoid risk of using short-term debt.* The longer maturity of bonds reduces the risk associated with the firm's ability to repay old or acquire new short-term debt. Less reliance on short-term debt also leads to improved liquidity.

7. *Inflation hedge.* Interest payments and the repayment of principal become less of a burden during periods of inflation because the firm is using dollars that have less purchasing power to repay its obligations.

E. There are some limitations or disadvantages to issuing bonds from the issuer's perspective.

1. *High financial risk.* A corporation's financial risk and default risk increase when debt is used because it represents fixed commitments. The firm may be forced into bankruptcy if it fails to make interest, principal, and sinking fund payments when due. Forecasting errors may lead to overcommitments and an inability to meet these obligations. These higher risks may also increase the firm's cost of capital and lower the value of its common stock.

2. *Restricted operations.* Indenture provisions may result in less operating flexibility.

3. *Definite maturity date.* The principal amount borrowed must be repaid on a specific date whereas the proceeds from a stock issue do not.

4. *Limitation of debt in financial structure.* Lenders are reluctant to provide additional debt financing if they believe the firm is becoming too heavily leveraged.

F. A firm may wish to retire a bond before its maturity.

Corporations often retire bonds before they mature to take advantage of falling interest rates, to eliminate restrictive indenture provisions, and to change their capital structures. There are two major mechanisms for early retirement: issuing serial bonds and exercising a call privilege. Both mechanisms require foresight on the part of the issuer. One way to generate the needed funds for either process is to refund the debt. **Bond refunding** takes place when an issuer floats a new bond issue and uses the proceeds to retire previously issued bonds often bearing higher interest rates.

G. Bond refunding analysis is similar to the analysis of capital budgeting projects.

The analysis of refunding is similar to capital budgeting (Chapter 13); however, it is complicated by the tax treatment of call premiums, flotation costs, bond premiums, and bond discounts. All four are treated as ordinary expenses or income, but the timing of their tax treatments varies. Call premiums are treated as an ordinary expenses for tax purposes *in the year of the call.* Flotation costs are amortized *over the life of the bond* using a straight-line method and are treated as ordinary expenses. The unamortized portion of the flotation costs is also treated as an ordinary expense but it is deducted in the year the bond is retired. Bond premiums and bond discounts are also amortized over the life of the bond as ordinary income (premium) or expense (discount). Similar to unamortized flotation costs, all unamortized bond premiums or bond discounts are treated as ordinary income (premium) or expense (discount) in the *year of retirement.*
    A bond refunding analysis involves three major steps.

1. *Compute the initial net cash flows of the refunding decision.* The net cash outflow is the initial cash outflows minus the initial cash inflows, which include the tax savings. The new bond issue should normally be equal in value to the old bond issue.

2. *Compute the incremental annual net cash flows of the refunding decision.* The annual cash flows (savings) are calculated by subtracting the annual net cash outflows on the *new* bonds from the annual net cash outflows on the *old* bonds. The new bond issue should have a maturity equal to only the remaining life of the old bond issue.

3. *Compute the net present value (NPV) of the refunding decision.* This step is accomplished by computing the present value of the stream of future net annual cash inflows (net savings) and then subtracting from this amount the initial net cash outflow (net investment). The firm should refund the bond if the NPV is positive.

Selecting the appropriate discount rate to use in the present value analysis is controversial. Many experts believe that the after-tax cost of the new debt, not the marginal cost of capital, should be used as the discount rate because the risk is low due to the relative certainty of the cash flows.

EXAMPLE 20-8: Harris Corporation is contemplating calling $40,000,000 of 25-year bonds that were issued five years ago. The old bonds have a par value of $1,000 per bond but originally sold at a discount of $25 per bond. Thus, the initial proceeds netted the firm $39,000,000 ($975 × 40,000 bonds). The old bonds may be called at $1,100 per bond. The firm intends to sell $40,000,000 of 20-year bonds at their par value of $1,000 per bond. The new bond issue will be sold one month before the old issue is called. Thus, there will be one month of overlapping interest expense on the two issues. The firm's marginal corporate income tax rate is 34 percent. Data on the two bond issues are summarized below.

	Old Issue	New Issue
Face amount	$40,000,000	$40,000,000
Coupon rate	12 percent	10 percent
Net proceeds per bond	$975	$1,000
Life of the bond	25 years*	20 years
Call premium	10 percent	8 percent
Flotation costs	$ 600,000**	$ 750,000**

* 5 years of the life have expired
** Amortized on a straight-line basis over the life of the issue

Using the NPV approach, Harris Corporation would follow the steps below in deciding whether or not to refund the existing issue.

Step 1. Compute the initial net cash flows (net investment).

Initial cash outflows

Cost of calling old bonds ($1,100 × 40,000 bonds)	$44,000,000
Overlapping interest on old bonds [(1/12) × 0.12 × $40,000,000]	400,000
Flotation costs of new bonds	750,000
Initial cash outflows	$45,150,000

Initial cash inflows

Proceeds from new bonds	$40,000,000
Tax savings	
Call premium on old bonds (0.10 × $40,000,000 × 0.34)	1,360,000
Unamortized discount on old bonds [(20/25) × $1,000,000 × 0.34]	272,000
Unamortized flotation costs on old bonds [(20/25) × $600,000 × 0.34]	163,200
Overlapping interest on old bonds [(1/12) × 0.12 × $40,000,000 × 0.34]	136,000
Initial cash inflows	$41,931,200

Initial net cash flows (net investment)

Initial cash outflows	$45,150,000
Initial cash inflows	41,931,200
Initial net cash outflows (net investment)	$ 3,218,800

Step 2. Compute the incremental annual net cash outflows (net savings).

Annual cash outflows on old bonds

Interest expense (0.12 × $40,000,000)	$4,800,000
Less: Tax savings	
Interest expense	
(0.12 × $40,000,000 × 0.34)	1,632,000
Amortization of flotation costs	
[(1/25) × $600,000 × 0.34]	8,160
Amortization of discount	
[(1/25) × $1,000,000 × 0.34]	13,600
Annual cash outflows on old bonds......................................	$3,146,240

Annual cash outflows on new bonds

Interest expense (0.10 × $40,000,000)	$4,000,000
Less: Tax savings	
Interest expense	
(0.10 × $40,000,000 × 0.34)	1,360,000
Amortization of flotation costs	
[(1/20) × $750,000 × 0.34]	12,750
Annual cash outflows on new bonds......................................	$2,627,250

Annual incremental net cash flows (net savings)

Annual cash outflows of old bonds	$3,146,240
Annual cash outflows of new bonds	2,627,250
Annual incremental net cash flows (net savings)	$ 518,990

Step 3. Compute the net present value of the net cash flows attained in Step 1 and Step 2.
The discount rate of 7 percent is the after-tax cost of the new debt. This rate is actually 6.6 percent $[(12.0)(1 - 0.34)]$, but it rounded to 7 percent in order to use the present value table. Using Appendix D, the $PVIFA_{0.07,20} = 10.594$ is multiplied by the annual incremental net cash flows to obtain the present value. The resulting figure is subtracted from the initial net cash flows to calculate the NPV.

Present value of annual incremental net cash flows (10.594 × 518, 990)	$5,498,180
Less: Present value of net investment	3,218,800
Net present value	$2,279,380

Because the net present value of the refunding decision is positive, the issue should be refunded.

20-2. Preferred Stock

Preferred stock is a class of capital stock that pays dividends at a specified rate and that has preference over common stock in the payment of dividends and the liquidation of assets. Preferred stock is a hybrid security because it has characteristics of both debt and equity. Preferred stock provides a small amount of new financing for most corporations and is not widely used except for certain situations (mergers involving the exchange of securities and bankruptcy reorganization) and within specific industries (utilities).

The use of preferred stock is favored when the following conditions prevail:

1. Profit margins are adequate to make the use of additional leverage attractive.
2. The firm has a high debt ratio, suggesting that equity financing is needed.
3. Debt poses substantial risk.
4. Interest rates are low, lowering the cost of preferred stock.
5. Control problems exist with the issuance of common stock.

A. Preferred stock has several major features.

1. *Par value/no par value.* Par value is the face value that appears on the stock certificate. This value is rather arbitrary and is often set at relatively low amounts such as $25. Par value also represents the liquidation claim per share of preferred stock. No par preferred stock has no par value and therefore no specific per share liquidation claim.
2. *No definite maturity date.* Preferred stock is usually intended to be a permanent part of a firm's equity and has no definite maturity date. However, preferred stock sometimes carries special retirement provisions. Almost all preferred stocks have a *call feature* that gives the issuing firm the option of purchasing the stock directly from its owners, usually at a premium above its par value. Some preferred stocks have a *sinking fund* provision that requires the issuer to repurchase and retire the stock on a scheduled basis. Owners of **convertible preferred stock** have the option of exchanging their preferred stock for common stock based on specified terms and conditions.
3. *Voting rights.* Preferred stock does not ordinarily carry voting rights. Special voting procedures may take effect if the issuing firm omits its preferred dividends for a specific time period. Preferred stockholders are then permitted to elect a certain number of members to the board of directors in order to represent the preferred stockholders' interests.
4. *Dividends.* Dividends are commonly fixed and paid quarterly but are not guaranteed by the issuing firm. Some recent preferred stock issues, called *adjustable rate, variable rate,* or *floating rate preferred*, do not have a fixed dividend rate but peg dividends to an underlying index, such as one of the Treasury bill rate or other money market rates. Dividends are stated as a percentage of the par value or as a dollar amount for no par stock.
5. *Cumulative feature.* With a **cumulative** feature, all dividends in arrears must be paid before common dividends. A passed dividend on **noncumulative** preferred stock is generally lost forever. Most recent preferred stock issues are cumulative.

EXAMPLE 20-9: Regional Power Company has a no par $5 per share cumulative preferred stock that $1.25 in dividends quarterly. During the first three quarters of the year, the firm has been unable to pay preferred dividends because of insufficient income. The company has returned to profitability in the fourth quarter.

Because of the cumulative feature, Regional Power Company must pay preferred dividends totaling $5 ($3.75 in arrears plus the current $1.25 dividend) before any common dividends can be paid. If the preferred issue were noncumulative, only the current quarterly dividend of $1.25 would have to be paid.

6. *Participating feature.* Participating preferred stock entitles its holders to share in profits above and beyond the declared dividend, along with common stockholders. Most preferred stock issues are nonparticipating. Without nonparticipated preferred, the return is limited to the stipulated dividend.

EXAMPLE 20-10: Corey Company has a participating preferred stock with an annual stated dividend of $3.50. The terms of the issue specify that once the common stockholders receive $1.75 in dividends per share, the preferred holders may share equally in additional dividend payments. If the firm pays $2.00 in common dividends per share, preferred stockholders will receive a total dividend of $3.75 per share; $3.50 in regular dividends plus $0.25 in extra dividends.

7. *Protective features*. Preferred stock issues often contain covenants to assure the regular payment of preferred stock dividends and to improve the quality of preferred stock. For example, covenants may restrict the amount of common stock cash dividends, specify minimum working-capital levels, and limit the sale of securities senior to preferred stock.

B. There are several advantages to issuing preferred stocks.

1. *Favorable financial leverage*. Issuing preferred stock provides favorable financial leverage that enhances the common stockholders' return if the firm earns a rate of return on its preferred stock that is higher than its cost of capital.
2. *Financing flexibility*. Preferred stock gives the corporation the flexibility of omitting a preferred dividend in lean times without facing bankruptcy. A call provision gives the firm the flexibility of retiring the preferred issue. Preferred stock is more flexible than bonds because preferred stock has no maturity date and generally does not require a sinking fund.
3. *No dilution of control*. Due to a lack of voting rights, preferred stock does not dilute existing control of the corporation's common stockholders as long as preferred dividends are paid.
4. *No maturity*. Preferred stock does not have to be repaid.
5. *Asset preservation*. The corporation does not have to pledge assets as collateral when issuing preferred stock. Hence, assets may be preserved for use as security for debt financing.
6. *No equal participation in earnings*. Nonparticipating preferred stock is limited to a stipulated dividend.

C. There are a few disadvantages to issuing preferred stock.

1. *High cost*. Preferred stock sells at a higher cost to the company than its long-term debt because preferred dividends are not a tax-deductible expense and preferred stock is more risky to the holder than debt.
2. *Seniority of the holders' claim*. Preferred stock has preference over common stock in the payment of dividends and the liquidation of assets that may jeopardize the common shareholders' return.

20-3. Common Stock

Common stock is a form of long-term equity that represents ownership of a public corporation. Common stockholders are called *residual owners* because their claim to earnings and assets is what remains after satisfying the prior claims of various creditors and preferred stockholders. Common stockholders are the true owners of the corporation and consequently bear the ultimate risks and rewards of ownership. Stockholders carry a limited liability because their risk of potential loss is limited to their investment in the corporation's stock. Most large public corporations have widely disbursed ownership and hence managers are employed to operate the firm.

The use of common stock is favored when the following conditions prevail:

1. The firm's sales and profits fluctuate widely.
2. The market price of the firm's common stock is high.
3. The relative costs of common stock financing appear favorable.
4. The firm's financial leverage position is currently high.
5. Dilution of control is not a problem.
6. Cash flow considerations are important.

7. The corporation's ability to meet fixed income payments is questionable.
8. Debt or preferred stock would carry restrictive provisions.
9. The firm is new and lacks access to debt financing.

A. Common stock has several major features.

Some of these features involve accounting terminology which is needed to explain how common stock is recorded on the firm's balance sheet.

1. *Par value/no par value.* Common stock may be sold with or without par value. Whether or not common stock has any par value is stated in the corporation's charter. Par value of common stock is the stated value attached to a single share of stock at issuance. It has little significance except for accounting and legal purposes. If common stock is initially sold for more than its par value, the issue price in excess of par is recorded as *additional paid-in capital, capital surplus,* or *capital in excess of par.* A firm issuing no par stock may either assign a stated value or place it on the books at the price at which the stock is sold. State laws generally prohibit firms from distributing paid-in capital as dividends.

EXAMPLE 20-10: Reed Plastics Company has recently been formed. The firm issued 25,000 shares of $20 par value common stock for $30 per share. Therefore, Reed Plastics received a total of $750,000 ($30 × 25,000 shares) from the sale of common stock. Of this amount, $500,000 is credited to a capital stock account called *common stock.* The common stock account is calculated by multiplying the number of shares by the par value. The remaining $250,000 ($750,000 − $500,000) is placed in capital in excess of par account.

Common stock (25,000 shares issued and outstanding at $20 par)	$500,000
Capital in excess of par	250,000
Total stockholders' equity	$750,000

2. *Authorized, issued, and outstanding.* **Authorized shares** is the maximum number of shares that a corporation may issue without amending its charter. **Issued shares** is the number of authorized shares that have been sold. **Outstanding shares** are those shares held by the public. Both the firm's dividends per share and earnings per share are based on the outstanding shares. The number of issued shares may be greater than the number of outstanding shares because stock may be repurchased by the issuing firm. Previously issued shares that are reacquired and held by the firm are called **treasury stock.** Thus, outstanding stock is issued stock less treasury stock.

EXAMPLE 20-11: Gordon Chemical Company has 200,000 authorized shares of common stock, sells 50,000 shares, and later repurchases 10,000 shares and holds them as treasury stock.

Gordon Chemical Company could record the number of shares authorized, issued, and outstanding in several ways in the stockholders' equity section of its balance sheet.

Common stock: 200,000 shares authorized; 50,000 shares issued less 10,000 shares of treasury stock

Common stock: 200,000 shares authorized; 40,000 shares outstanding after deducting 10,000 shares in treasury stock

3. *No maturity.* Common stock has no maturity and is a permanent form of long-term financing. Although common stock is neither callable nor convertible, the firm can repurchase its shares in the secondary markets either through a brokerage firm a tender offer. A **tender offer** is a formal offer to purchase shares of a corporation.
4. *Voting rights.* Each share of common stock generally entitles the holder to vote on the selection of directors and in other matters. Stockholders unable to attend the annual meeting to vote may vote by proxy. A **proxy** is a temporary transfer of the right to vote to another party. Proxy voting is supervised by the Securities and

Exchange Commissions, but proxy solicitations are the firm's responsibility. Not all common stockholders have equal voting power. Some firms have more than one class of stock. Class A common stock typically has limited or no voting rights while Class B has full voting rights.

There are two common systems of voting: majority voting and cumulative voting.

- **Majority voting** is a voting system that entitles each shareholder to cast one vote for each share owned. Majority voting is used to indicate the common shareholders' approval or disapproval of most proposed managerial actions on which shareholders may vote. The directors receiving the majority of the votes are elected. If a group controls over 50 percent of the votes, it can elect all of the directors and prevent minority shareholders from electing any directors.

EXAMPLE 20-12: Harding Industries is in the process of electing six directors. Management backs six candidates and minority shareholders two other candidates. There are 100,000 shares outstanding and management controls 55 percent of the votes. Management can elect all six directors because it has the majority of the votes.

- **Cumulative voting** is a voting system that permits the stockholder to cast multiple votes for a single director. Cumulative voting assists minority shareholders in electing at least one director. Cumulative voting is required in some states for electing the board of directors.

EXAMPLE 20-13: Riley Company is in the process of electing four directors from a field of five candidates. The firm's charter requires cumulative voting. If a shareholder owns 100 shares of Riley Company common stock, that shareholder is entitled to cast 400 (4 × 100 shares) votes. For example, the stockholder may cast 100 votes for each of four directors or cast all 400 votes for a single director.

B. Common stockholders have numerous rights.

Stockholders' rights are specified by the state laws, the corporate charter, and the firm's bylaws. Common stockholders own the corporation and exercise their collective rights by voting. Collective and individual rights of common stockholders include:

1. The right to vote on specific issues as prescribed by the corporate charter. The issues include:

   - Electing the board of directors.
   - Selecting the firm's independent auditors.
   - Amending the corporate charter and bylaws.
   - Changing the amount of authorized stock.
   - Authorizing issuance of securities.

2. The right to proxy their vote to others.
3. The right to receive dividends, if declared by the firm's board of directors.
4. The right to share in the residual assets in the event of liquidation.
5. The right to transfer their ownership in the firm to another party.
6. The right to examine the corporation's books. In practice, this right is limited and is fulfilled when the corporation provides stockholders with quarterly and annual reports.
7. The right to share proportionately in the purchase of any new stock sold. This right, called a *preemptive right*, is limited to a minority of firms and is discussed in Chapter 17.

C. Common stock offers several advantages to the firm over bonds and preferred stock.

The advantages stem from placing minimum constraints on the firm and include:

1. *No fixed charges.* Common stock does not involve mandatory requirements to pay dividends. Thus, common stock is less risky to the firm than fixed income securities.

In practice, however, many companies follow a policy of maintaining stable dividends, and a decrease or omission in dividends may reduce the market value of the stock.

2. *No fixed maturity date.* Unlike debt, common stock is a permanent source of long-term financing. Thus, the lack of maturity eliminates future repayment obligations.

3. *Increased creditworthiness.* The sale of common stock increases the firm's ability to issue more debt because its leverage position is reduced.

4. *Potentially greater ease of sale.* Common stock may be easier to sell than debt or preferred stock especially if the firm has a rights offering or more than an optimal amount of debt in its existing capital structure.

5. *Freedom from restrictive provisions.* A new issue of common stock does not contain any of the restrictive provisions associated with debt and preferred stock financing. Thus, common stock gives the firm more financial flexibility.

D. There are several disadvantages to issuing common stock.

1. *High cost.* Both the flotation costs and the component cost of capital are higher for common stock than for either debt or preferred stock. This is because dividends are not tax-deductible and because common stock is a riskier security than either debt or preferred stock.

2. *Dilution of control and earnings.* Unless the firm has a rights offering, existing ownership and control may be diluted because new common stockholders have voting rights. A new issue of common stock may also result in a temporary reduction in earnings per share due to a greater number of outstanding shares.

3. *Loss of leverage.* By issuing common stock, the firm loses the favorable influence that financial leverage from debt or preferred stock may exert on its earnings.

20-4. Convertible Securities

A **convertible security** is a bond or preferred stock that may be converted into common stock at the option of the holder at a specified price over a specified period of time.

A. Convertible securities have several major features.

1. *Conversion price.* The conversion price is the effective price paid per share of common stock upon conversion. Equation 20-2 is the formula for the conversion price.

$$\text{Conversion price} = \frac{\text{Par value of convertible security}}{\text{Number of shares received on conversion}} \quad \text{(20-2)}$$

2. *Conversion ratio.* The conversion ratio is the number of common stock shares that may be exchanged for the convertible security. Equation 20-3 shows the calculation of the conversion ratio.

$$\text{Conversion ratio} = \frac{\text{Par value of convertible security}}{\text{Conversion price}} \quad \text{(20-3)}$$

3. *Conversion value.* The conversion value is the value of a convertible security, based on the value of the underlying shares of common stock. Equation 20-4 is the formula for conversion value.

$$\text{Conversion value} = \frac{\text{Conversion}}{\text{ratio}} \times \frac{\text{Market price of}}{\text{common stock}} \quad \text{(20-4)}$$

4. *Conversion premium.* The conversion premium is the percentage or dollar difference between the market price and conversion price of a security. The conversion premium is usually 10 to 20 percent above the market price of common stock at the

time the convertible security is issued. The amount of the premium is influenced by the expectations of the common stock's future performance.

5. *Conversion period*. The conversion period is the period during which the holder of a convertible security has the conversion option. Companies usually expect that their convertible securities will be converted into common stock within a certain time period. Conversion may be voluntary on the part of the investor, or it can be effectively forced by the issuing company by exercising the call privilege on the convertible security.

EXAMPLE 20-14: Gordon Electronics Company issued $5,000,000 of 20-year, 8 percent convertible bonds. Each $1,000 bond is convertible into 20 shares of common stock. The common stock sold at $45 per share when the convertible bonds was issued. Using Equation 20-2, the conversion price is:

$$\text{Conversion price} = \frac{\$1,000}{20} = \$50$$

Using Equation 20-3, the conversion ratio is:

$$\text{Conversion ratio} = \frac{\$1,000}{\$50} = 20$$

Thus, the bondholder will receive 20 shares of common stock upon conversion.
Using Equation 20-4, the conversion value of the security at the time of issuance is:

$$\text{Conversion value} = (20)(\$45) = \$900$$

Thus, the conversion premium at the time of issuance is $100 ($1,000 − $900), or slightly over 11 percent ($100/$900).

B. Corporations use convertible securities for several reasons.

1. *To sweeten a security offering*. A convertible issue may attract investors who otherwise may not be interested in a straight-debt or preferred stock issue. Thus, a conversion feature may add to the marketability of an issue.
2. *To shift the future capital structure*. Convertible issues permit the firm to change its capital structure without increasing total financing. Conversion results in replacing debt or preferred stock with common stocks and thus reduces the firm's debt ratios. However, no additional funds are raised by the company at the time of conversion.
3. *To provide deferred common stock financing*. Firms issue convertible securities in order to sell common stock at a higher price than the market price prevailing at the time of original issue. Convertibles also facilitate the raising of equity capital.
4. *To raise temporarily cheap funds*. The features of convertibles permit a firm to raise funds with a lower interest rate or preferred dividend rate. When convertible issues are used to finance specific projects, they provide low-cost capital during the period when earnings on assets are being developed.

20-5. Warrants

A **warrant** is an option to purchase a stated number of shares of common stock at a specified price over a given period of time. Holders of warrants do not have the rights of common stockholders until they exercise their warrants.

A. Warrants have several major features.

1. *Exercise price*. The exercise price, also called the *option price*, is the price at which the holder can purchase the issuing company's common stock upon exchange of the warrant. The exercise price normally remains constant over the life of the warrant, but it may also increase over time.

2. *Expiration date.* The expiration date is the date at which the warrant cannot be exercised and thus becomes worthless. Most warrants have limited lives, but there are some warrants with infinite lives.

3. *Detachable or nondetachable.* A **detachable warrant** is one that holders can sell separately from the bond or preferred stock. Holders of nondetachable warrants can detach them only when they exercise their option and buy stock.

4. *Theoretical value of a warrant.* The theoretical value of a warrant, also called the *minimum value,* is the lowest price for which a given warrant should sell in the marketplace. Equation 20-5 gives the theoretical value of a warrant.

THEORETICAL VALUE OF A WARRANT

$$TVW = (M - EP)(N) \tag{20-5}$$

where
TVW = theoretical value of a warrant
M = market price of common stock
EP = exercise price of a warrant
N = number of common shares that can be purchased with one warrant

EXAMPLE 20-15: Linowes, Inc. has outstanding warrants that entitle the holder to purchase four shares of common stock at $25 a share. The current market price of the common stock is $28 per share. Substituting $M = \$28$, $EP = \$25$, and $N = 4$ in Equation 20-5, the theoretical value of a warrant is:

$$TVW = (\$28 - \$25)(4) = \$12$$

5. *Warrant premium.* A **warrant premium** is the amount by which the market value of a warrant exceeds its theoretical value. Warrants generally sell at a premium over their theoretical value, due to their speculative appeal, leverage, and loss limitation. Investors are able to obtain more leverage from trading warrants than from trading the underlying stock. That is, a small percentage gain in the stock price may generate large percentage increases in the warrant price. At the same time, investors' losses are limited due to the price paid for the warrant.

Figure 20-2 shows the typical relationship between the theoretical value of a warrant and its market value. The warrant premium is largest when the stock price is at or close to its exercise price because, at this point, the opportunities for high percentage returns on investment are greatest. The size of the premium decreases as the stock price rises beyond the exercise price, because of a declining leverage impact and the increasing magnitude of potential losses.

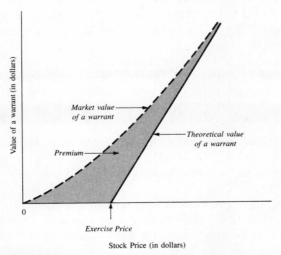

FIGURE 20-2

C. Corporations use warrants for several reasons.

1. *To sweeten fixed-income security offerings.* Companies use warrants to reduce the interest cost on debt and to avoid restrictive indenture provisions.

2. *To widen the market for the firm's debt.* Debt with warrants may attract investors who otherwise may not be interested in a straight-debt or preferred stock issue.

3. *To provide additional equity funds in the future.* Unlike convertible securities, warrants provide an influx of new equity capital to the firm. When warrants are exercised, common stock and cash increase simultaneously. At this time, new equity capital is created without the underwriting costs associated with a public issue. Thus, warrants provide a simple way for a firm to obtain needed funds.

RAISE YOUR GRADES

Can you explain...?

☑ three major sources of long-term external financing
☑ what a bond is
☑ the role of the trustee as a party to a bond issue
☑ the purpose of a call provision to the issuer
☑ the purpose of a sinking fund
☑ the difference between secured and unsecured bonds
☑ the purpose of a bond rating
☑ the advantages and disadvantages of bonds as a financing alternative
☑ the conditions favoring the use of bonds
☑ the major reasons for refunding a bond issue before maturity
☑ the steps in a bond refunding analysis
☑ in what sense preferred stock is preferred
☑ why preferred stock is called a hybrid security
☑ the conditions favoring the use of preferred stock
☑ the major features of preferred stock
☑ the advantages and disadvantages of preferred stock as a long-term financing instrument
☑ why common stock represents residual ownership in a corporation
☑ the conditions favoring the use of common stock
☑ the major features of common stock
☑ several rights of common stockholders
☑ the advantages and disadvantages of common stock as a financing instrument
☑ the similarities and differences between convertible securities and warrants

SUMMARY

1. Three major sources of long-term financing for a corporation are bonds, preferred stock, and common stock.
2. A bond is a security that carries a promise to pay interest and principal at specified dates.
3. An indenture is the agreement under which a bond is issued.
4. There are three parties to a public bond issue: the issuer, the bondholders, and the trustee. The trustee is largely responsible for enforcing the provisions of the bond indenture on behalf of the bondholders.
5. A call provision gives the issuing company the option of retiring a bond issue prior to maturity.
6. A conversion feature give bondholders the option of exchanging their bonds for shares of preferred or common stock.

7. A sinking fund is a means of facilitating the orderly retirement of bonds or preferred stock.
8. Bonds may be either secured or unsecured. Secured bonds are backed by a pledge of certain types of property whereas unsecured bonds are not secured by specific property.
9. A bond rating is a measure of a bond's quality. The higher the rating or quality of the bond, the lower the bond's risk of default and hence its interest rate.
10. The major advantages of bond financing include relatively low cost, no dilution of control, financing flexibility, financial leverage, lower risk than short-term debt, and an inflation hedge.
11. The disadvantages of bonds include increased financial and default risk, restrictions on operations, a definite maturity date, and limits of debt in the firm's financial structure.
12. Bond refunding is the process of retiring outstanding bonds. Bonds may be refunded through the sale of serial bonds or by the exercise of a call privilege.
13. Refunding often occurs when a firm redeems an existing bond issue and sells a new issue at a lower cost to take its place.
14. Bond refunding analysis uses present value techniques. The steps in a bond refunding analysis include computing the initial cash flows, the incremental annual net cash flows, and the net present value of the refunding decision.
15. Preferred stock is legally a form of equity but it occupies an intermediate position between long-term debt and common stock as a source of capital.
16. Preferred stock is a hybrid security because it has characteristics of both debt and equity.
17. Most preferred stock has a par value, no maturity, and no voting rights, and is cumulative, nonparticipating, and callable.
18. The basic advantages for the use of preferred stock financing include the ability to increase financial leverage, the flexibility of the issue, the absence of control dilution, and the preservation of assets for collateral.
19. Disadvantages of preferred stock include its relatively high cost and its preference over the common stockholders.
20. Common stock is a form of equity that is held by the true owners of the firm.
21. Common stockholders have numerous rights including voting rights, the right to dividends (if declared), the right to any remaining assets upon liquidation, the right to transfer their ownership, and the preemptive right.
22. The basic advantages of common stock stem from the fact that this source of financing places minimum constraints on the firm. Common stock gives a firm flexibility because it has no fixed charges and no maturity date.
23. Disadvantages of common stock include its high cost, potential dilution of control and earnings, and loss of leverage.
24. A convertible security is a bond or preferred stock that can be converted into common stock at the holder's option.
25. A warrant is an option to buy a stated number of shares of stock at a specified price over a given period of time.

RAPID REVIEW

True or False

1. A corporate bond is a long-term debt instrument which obligates the issuer to pay interest and principal on predetermined dates. [Section 20-1]
2. Bondholders and stockholders are both owners of a firm. [Section 20-1 and 20-3]
3. The trustee is selected by the bondholders to represent their interests. [Section 20-1A]
4. An indenture is the legal agreement which details the conditions associated with a bond issue. [Section 20-1A]

5. An 8 percent coupon rate on a $1,000 par value bond which pays interest semiannually means that the bondholder receives $80 every six months in interest. [Section 20-1A]

6. Zero coupon bonds sell at deep discounts below par value when initially issued. [Section 20-1A]

7. There are 100 basis points in each 1 percent interest. [Section 20-1A]

8. A call provision allows the firm to take advantage of rising interest rates. [Section 20-1A]

9. The presence of a sinking fund requires the gradual retirement of a bond issue prior to maturity. [Section 20-1A]

10. A mortgage bond is secured by a lien against real property. [Section 20-1B]

11. A debenture is a type of secured bond. [Section 20-1B]

12. Subordinated debentures have a lower claim on earnings and assets than debentures. [Section 20-1B]

13. The highest rating a bond can have is a Triple A. [Section 20-1C]

14. The higher a bond's quality or rating, the lower its interest rate or yield to maturity. [Section 20-1C]

15. Bondholders typically have voting rights. [Section 20-1D]

16. The bond refunding analysis involves the use of present value techniques. [Section 20-1G]

17. In making a bond refunding decision, the present value of the savings should exceed the required investment outlay. [Section 20-1G]

18. Preferred stockholders and bondholders have equal claims to earnings and assets. [Section 20-2]

19. Preferred stock has characteristics of both debt and equity. [Section 20-2]

20. Preferred stockholders have preference over common stockholders in terms of receiving dividends. [Section 20-2]

21. Default on preferred dividends may result in bankruptcy. [Section 20-2A]

22. Most preferred stock issues are both cumulative and participating. [Section 20-2A]

23. The firm's after-tax cost of preferred stock is usually less than the after-tax cost of long-term debt. [Section 20-2C]

24. Common stockholders are the residual owners of a corporation. [Section 20-3]

25. The par value of common stock represents the amount that stockholders receive in the event of liquidation. [Section 20-3A]

26. Treasury stock is the number of shares that the corporation is authorized to sell. [Section 20-3A]

27. A proxy is a revokable assignment of a common stockholder's right to vote to another party. [Section 20-3A]

28. A majority voting system entitles each shareholder to cast one vote for each share owned. [Section 20-3A]

29. A major reason why corporations use convertible securities is to sweeten a security offering. [Section 20-4B]

30. A firm receives additional equity funds when a warrant is exercised. [Section 20-5B]

Multiple Choice

31. A corporate bond's par value is usually

   (a) $100
   (b) $1,000
   (c) $5,000
   (d) Not given

   [Section 20-1A]

32. Specific collateral is required in which of the following types of financing?

(a) Preferred stock
(b) Subordinated debentures
(c) Mortgage bonds
(d) Common stock

[Section 20-1B]

33. Which of the following securities has the highest claim priority on the firm's earnings?

(a) Debentures
(b) First-mortgage bonds
(c) Income bonds
(d) Preferred stock

[Section 20-1B]

34. All of the following are possible advantages to the issuing firm of using bonds *except*:

(a) lower flotation costs than equity financing
(b) favorable impact on the firm's financial leverage
(c) fewer restrictions than common stock
(d) no dilution of voting control

[Sections 20-1D & E]

35. Which of the following is a tax-deductible expense associated with bond refunding?

(a) Flotation costs of the new bond
(b) Unamortized discount on the old bond
(c) Call premium on the old bond
(d) All of the above

[Section 20-1F]

36. The discount rate used in a bond refunding analysis is the

(a) cost of capital
(b) before-tax cost of the new bond
(c) after-tax cost of the new bond
(d) before-tax cost of the old bond

[Section 20-1F]

37. All of the following conditions favor issuing preferred stock *except*:

(a) the firm's debt position is high
(b) control considerations are important
(c) debt poses substantial risk
(d) interest rates are high

[Section 20-2]

38. In the event of bankruptcy, the holders of which of the following have the last claim on the firm's assets?

(a) Subordinated debentures
(b) Second-mortgage bonds
(c) Preferred stock
(d) Common stock

[Section 20-3]

39. Corporations use convertible securities to

(a) sweeten a security offering
(b) provide deferred common stock financing
(c) raise temporarily cheap funds
(d) All of the above

[Section 20-4B]

40. A warrant premium

    (*a*) is the difference between the market value of the warrant and its theoretical value
    (*b*) decreases as the stock price rises above the exercise price
    (*c*) is the product of the conversion ratio and the market price of the common stock
    (*d*) Both *a* and *b*

[Section 20-5A]

Answers

True or False			*Multiple Choice*
1. True	11. False	21. False	31. b
2. False	12. True	22. False	32. c
3. False	13. True	23. False	33. b
4. True	14. True	24. True	34. c
5. False	15. False	25. False	35. d
6. True	16. True	26. False	36. c
7. True	17. True	27. True	37. d
8. False	18. False	28. True	38. d
9. True	19. True	29. True	39. d
10. True	20. True	30. True	40. d

SOLVED PROBLEMS

PROBLEM 20-1: Benny's Restaurants has three bond issues outstanding. Each bond has a $1,000 par value. The firm is in the 34 percent tax bracket. The characteristics of the bonds are as follows:

Bond	Proceeds per bond	Number of bonds sold	Initial maturity	Years remaining to maturity
A	$ 960	10,000	20 years	15 years
B	$1,020	35,000	35 years	20 years
C	$1,000	5,000	30 years	18 years

    * *Excludes underwriting cost and fees.*

    (*a*) Indicate whether each bond was sold at a discount, at par, or at a premium.
    (*b*) Calculate the total discount or premium for each bond.
    (*c*) Calculate the annual amortized discount or premium for each bond.
    (*d*) Compute the annual amortized discount or premium after taxes for Bond A.
    (*e*) Compute the unamortized discount or premium for each bond.

Answer:

    (*a*) Bond A initially sold at a discount; Bond B sold at a premium; and Bond C sold at par.

    (*b*) The total discount for Bond A is $400,000 [($1,000 − $960) × 10,000 bonds]. The total premium for Bond B is $700,000 [($1,020 − $1,000) × 35,000 bonds].

    (*c*) The annual amortized discount for Bond A is $20,000 ($400,000/20 years). The annual amortized premium for Bond B is $20,000 ($700,000/35 years).

    (*d*) Substituting the appropriate values into Equation 20-1, the annual amortized discount after taxes for Bond A is:

$$\text{Annual amortized discount after taxes} = \left(\frac{\$400,000}{20}\right)(1 - 0.34) = \$13,200$$

(e) The unamortized discount for Bond A is $300,000 ($20,000 × 15 years). The unamortized premium for Bond B is $400,000 ($20,000 × 20 years). **[Section 20-1A]**

PROBLEM 20-2: Greenberg Corporation issues $2,000,000 in 25-year bonds with a coupon rate of 9 percent. The firm's tax rate is 34 percent.

(a) What is the total amount of semiannual interest paid on this bond issue before taxes?
(b) What is the after-tax cost of these semiannual interest payments?

Answer:

(a) The total amount of semiannual interest is: (0.09 × $2,000,000)/2 = $90,000.
(b) The after-tax cost of the semiannual interest payments is: $90,000 × (1 − 0.34) = $59,400. **[Section 20-1A]**

PROBLEM 20-3: Casual Shoe Manufacturers floated 5,000 bonds, each having a par value of $1,000. The bonds carry a 10.5 percent coupon rate and are currently callable at 107. What is the total amount of the call premium if all of the bonds are called?

Answer: The call premium is shown below:

Call price (5,000 bonds × $1,070)	$5,350,000
Less: Par value (5,000 bonds × $1,000)	5,000,000
Call premium	$ 350,000

[Section 20-1A]

PROBLEM 20-4: A $10,000,000 bond issue is callable at a price of 106. The par value of each bond is $1,000 and the firm's tax rate is 34 percent. What is the after-tax cost of calling the issue if all bonds are called?

Answer: The call premium on this bond is $60 per bond ($1,060 − $1,000) or 6 percent (106 − 100) of the bond's par value. A total of 10,000 bonds ($10,000,000/$1,000 par) was sold. Only the call premium is a tax-deductible expense. Thus, the after-tax cost of calling the issue can be calculated as follows:

$$[10,000 \text{ bonds} \times \$60 \times (1 - 0.34)] = \$396,000$$

or

$$[\$10,000,000 \times 0.06 \times (1 - 0.34)] = \$396,000$$

[Section 20-1A]

Use the following information for Problems 20-5 through 20-8.

Powers, Inc. has an old bond outstanding and proposes refunding it with a new bond. The characteristics of these bonds are as follows:

	Old Issue	New Issue
Total face value	$10,000,000	$10,000,000
Number of bonds	10,000	10,000
Coupon rate	15 percent	12 percent
Par value	$ 1,000	$ 1,000
Life of the bond	30 years*	20 years
Call premium	12 percent	12 percent
Flotation costs	$ 240,000**	$ 350,000**

* 10 years of the life have expired.
** Amortized on a straight-line basis over the life of the issue.

The old bond issue sold at par and the new bond issue is expected to do likewise. Powers, Inc.'s marginal tax rate is 34 percent. The overlapping interest period on the existing bonds will be two months.

PROBLEM 20-5: What are the initial net cash flows (net investment) for the bond refunding?

Answer: The following computations show that Powers, Inc. has a net investment of $1,252,600 in the refunding.

Initial cash outflows

Cost of calling old bonds ($1,120 × 10,000 bonds)	$11,200,000
Overlapping interest on old bonds [(2/12) × 0.15 × $10,000,000]	250,000
Flotation costs of new bonds	350,000
Initial cash outflows	$11,800,000

Initial cash inflows

Proceeds from new bonds.	$10,000,000
Tax savings	
Call premium on old bonds (0.12 × $10,000,000 × 0.34).	408,000
Unamortized flotation costs on old bonds [(20/30) × $240,000 × 0.34]. . . .	54,400
Overlapping interest on old bonds [(2/12) × 0.15 × $10,000,000 × 0.34] .	85,000
Initial cash inflows	$10,547,400

Initial net cash flows

Initial cash outflows	$11,800,000
Initial cash inflows	10,547,400
Initial net cash outflows (net investment)	$ 1,252,600

[Section 20-1G]

PROBLEM 20-6: What are the annual incremental net cash flows?

Answer: The following computations indicate that the annual cash flow savings are $416,200.

Annual cash outflows on old bonds

Interest expense (0.15 × $10,000,000)	$1,500,000
Less: Tax savings	
Interest expense (0.15 × $10,000,000 × 0.34)	510,000
Amortization of flotation costs [(1/30) × $240,000 × 0.34]	2,720
Annual cash outflows on old bonds.	$987,280

Annual cash outflows on new bonds

Interest expense (0.12 × $10,000,000)	$1,200,000
Less: Tax savings	
Interest expense (0.12 × $10,000,000 × 0.34)	408,000
Amortization of flotation costs [(1/20) × $350,000 × 0.34]	5,950
Annual cash outflows on new bonds.	$786,050

Annual incremental net cash flows (net savings)

Annual cash outflows of old bonds	$987,280
Annual cash outflows of new bonds	786,050
Annual incremental net cash flows (net savings)	$201,230

[Section 20-1G]

PROBLEM 20-7: What is the net present value of the net cash flows of the bond refunding?

Answer: The discount rate of 7.9 percent [12.0 × (1 − 0.34)], which is the after-tax cost of the new debt, should used to calculate the net present value. However, this discount rate is rounded to 8 percent in order to use Appendix D. The $PVIFA_{0.08,20}$ equals 9.818 and must be multiplied by the annual incremental net cash flows to obtain the present value.

Present value of net savings (9.818 × $201,230) $1,975,676
Less: Present value of net investment 1,252,600
Net present value . . . . $ 723,076

[Section 20-1F]

PROBLEM 20-8: Should the old 15 percent bonds be refunded?

Answer: The old bonds should be refunded because the present value of the future annual cash savings exceeds the net investment required to refund by $723,076.

[Section 20-1G]

PROBLEM 20-9: Thompson International, Inc. has missed its $5.00 cumulative preferred dividend for the last two years. The firm has 20,000 shares of preferred stock outstanding and 50,000 shares of common stock outstanding. During the current year, the firm earned $450,000 after taxes. What is the maximum amount of common dividends per share that Thompson International could pay from current earnings at the end of the third year?

Answer: The firm must pay a total of $300,000 ($5.00 × 20,000 shares × 3 years) in cumulative preferred dividends before any common dividends are paid. Of the $450,000 in earnings, a total of $150,000 ($450,000 − $300,000) could be paid to common stockholders in the form of cash dividends. Since there are 50,000 common shares outstanding, the maximum amount of common dividends per share is $3.00 ($150,000/50,000 shares).

[Section 20-2A]

PROBLEM 20-10: Nardini Imports has issued 70 percent of its 200,000 authorized shares. The firm has recently repurchased 10 percent of the issued shares, which it now holds as treasury stock. What is the total number of shares outstanding?

Answer: Nardini Imports has issued 140,000 shares (0.70 × 200,000 shares) and repurchased 14,000 (0.10 × 140,000) of these shares. Hence, the total number of shares outstanding is the number of issued shares less treasury stock or 126,000 shares (140,000 − 14,000).

[Section 20-3A]

PROBLEM 20-11: Flynn Metal Fabricators has 500,000 common shares authorized with a par value of $1.00 per share. The firm has sold 200,000 shares at $16 per share. Prepare the balance sheet accounts under stockholders equity.

Answer: The $3,200,000 ($16 × 200,000 shares) is recorded from the stock sale and is separated into two accounts: common stock and additional paid-in capital. The common stock account is $200,000 ($1 par × 200,000 shares) and the additional paid-in capital account is $300,000,000 ($15 × 200,000 shares). The balance sheet accounts are shown below:

Stockholders' Equity

Common stock . . . .
   (500,000 shares authorized and
   200,000 shares issued and outstanding at $1 par) . . . . $ 200,000
Additional paid-in capital. 3,000,000
   Total stockholders' equity. $3,200,000

[Section 20-3A]

PROBLEM 20-12: Hodinko Company has issued $2,000,000 in 10-year, 10 percent convertible bonds. The conversion ratio is 50. The market price of the common stock is currently $25 dollars. What is the conversion value of the convertible bonds?

Answer: Substituting the conversion ratio = 50 and the market price of common stock = $25 in Equation 20-4, the conversion value is:

$$\text{Conversion value} = (50)(\$25) = \$1{,}250$$

[Section 20-4A]

PROBLEM 20-13: WHP, Inc. has a warrant outstanding which allows the holder to purchase two shares of common stock at $35 per share. The market price of the stock is $40 per share. If the market price of the warrant is $12, what premium are investors paying?

Answer: Substituting $M = \$40$, $EP = \$35$, and $N = 2$ in Equation 20-5, the theoretical value of the warrant is $2.

$$\text{TVW} = (\$40 - \$35)(2) = \$10$$

$$\text{Warrant premium} = \$12 - \$10 = \$2$$

[Section 20-5A]

EXAMINATION III (Chapters 14–20)

True-False

1. A firm's cost of capital is measured on a before-tax basis.
2. There is no difference between the cost of a firm's retained earnings and the cost of new common stock.
3. The marginal cost of capital is the cost of obtaining another dollar of new capital.
4. The traditional approach to capital structure suggests that the firm's capital structure has no effect on its market value.
5. According to the Modigliani and Miller model without corporate taxes, a firm does not have one optimal capital structure.
6. At EBIT levels above the EBIT-EPS indifference point, more financially levered capital structures produce higher levels of EBIT.
7. The "bird-in-the-hand" theory suggests that it is generally less risky for investors to receive dividends now rather than to reinvest earnings in anticipation of higher dividends later.
8. The residual theory of dividends connects a firm's dividend policy with its level of profitable investment opportunities.
9. Stock dividends reduce a firm's retained earnings.
10. Money market instruments are generally safer than equity securities.
11. A privileged subscriptions is a mechanism for trading securities in the secondary markets.
12. In the over-the-counter market, brokers make a market in the shares of a particular firm by buying and selling from their own accounts.
13. Short-term financing must be secured.
14. Accounts payable and accruals are sources of spontaneous financing.
15. A line of credit is a more formal and binding agreement than is a revolving credit agreement.
16. The covenants in equipment financing loans are generally more restrictive than those in term loans.
17. In leveraged leases, the lessor borrows much of the money needed to purchase the asset.
18. Both operating and capital leases are shown on the lessee's balance sheet.
19. To the issuing corporation, bonds are riskier than common stock.
20. Preferred stock is generally a more costly source of financing than debt.

Multiple Choice

1. The cost of capital may be defined as
    (a) the rate that the firm has to pay to investors for its capital.
    (b) the minimum rate of return required by suppliers of the firm's capital.
    (c) the minimum required rate of return that the firm must earn on new investments in order to maintain the market value of its common stock.
    (d) All of the above

2. What source of capital provides a special tax advantage for a corporation?

   (a) Debt
   (b) Preferred stock
   (c) Common stock
   (d) Retained earnings

3. Which of the firm's sources of new capital has the highest after-tax cost?

   (a) Debt
   (b) Preferred stock
   (c) Common stock
   (d) Retained earnings

4. Which approach assumes an optimal capital structure for each firm?

   (a) Modigliani and Miller approach without taxes
   (b) Traditional approach
   (c) Contemporary approach
   (d) Both b and c

5. EBIT-EPS analysis may be criticized because it

   (a) does not directly consider risk.
   (b) concentrates on the maximization of EPS rather than shareholder wealth.
   (c) cannot be used when a firm has preferred stock financing.
   (d) Both a and b

6. Which of the following factors may influence capital structure decisions?

   (a) Level of cash flows.
   (b) Market conditions
   (c) Business risk
   (d) All of the above

7. All of the following may influence a firm's dividend policy *except*

   (a) investment opportunities.
   (b) owner preferences.
   (c) par value of common stock.
   (d) alternate sources of capital.

8. All other things held constant, what theoretically should happen to the price of a firm's common stock on the ex-dividend date?

   (a) The price of a share of stock should remain unchanged.
   (b) The price of a share of stock should drop by approximately the amount of the dividend per share.
   (c) The price of a share of stock should increase by approximately the amount of the dividend per share.
   (d) The price of a share of stock should drop by about half of the dividend per share.

9. Stock dividends and stock splits are similar in that they both

   (a) increase total shareholder wealth.
   (b) reduce retained earnings.
   (c) increase the number of shares outstanding to shareholders.
   (d) increase the proportional ownership of shareholders.

10. When an individual wishes to purchase shares of a corporation listed on the New York Stock Exchange, the person should contact a(n)

    (a) investment banker.
    (b) NASDAQ dealer.
    (c) floor broker.
    (d) stock broker.

11. A bid price is

   (*a*) the price an investment banker will guarantee a client in an underwriting.
   (*b*) the highest price at which dealers are willing to buy a security.
   (*c*) the lowest price at which dealers are willing to sell a security.
   (*d*) the original issue price in a primary market.

12. All of the following characterize private placements relative to public offerings *except*

   (*a*) Higher flotation costs
   (*b*) Greater speed
   (*c*) More privacy
   (*d*) Fewer restrictions

13. A formal agreement in which the buyer must accept a draft by the seller before receiving the purchased goods is called a(n)

   (*a*) note payable.
   (*b*) trade acceptance.
   (*c*) open account.
   (*d*) float.

14. A bank loan on which interest is deducted in advance is called a(n)

   (*a*) simple interest loan.
   (*b*) promissory note.
   (*c*) installment loan.
   (*d*) discounted loan.

15. Warehouse receipt loans

   (*a*) leave control of the inventory with the borrower.
   (*b*) have relatively high fixed costs.
   (*c*) are also called trust receipts.
   (*d*) require the borrower to have a warehousing company.

16. Which of the following would be an affirmative covenant in a term loan?

   (*a*) Requirement to submit periodic financial statements
   (*b*) Prohibition from engaging in mergers
   (*c*) Prohibition from purchasing fixed assets
   (*d*) Prohibition from leasing additional fixed assets

17. A financing agreement in which the seller retains title to the equipment until all payments are made is called a

   (*a*) conditional sales contract.
   (*b*) direct lease.
   (*c*) chattel mortgage.
   (*d*) term loan.

18. The growth in the use of leases is due largely to

   (*a*) low initiation costs.
   (*b*) tax effects.
   (*c*) aggressive lessors.
   (*d*) the lack of restrictive covenants.

19. The legal document containing the terms and conditions of a bond issue is called a(n)

   (*a*) debenture.
   (*b*) certificate of trust.
   (*c*) coupon.
   (*d*) indenture.

20. Which of the following conditions would favor issuing bonds?

   (*a*) High interest rates
   (*b*) Volatile earnings
   (*c*) High debt ratio
   (*d*) Good liquidity position

Fill In The Blanks

1. _____ is defined as the funds used to finance the firm's assets and operations.
2. An optimal capital structure is the combination of debt and equity that simultaneously maximizes the firm's market value and _____ its weighted average cost of capital.
3. The levels at which a specific cost of capital increases are called _____.
4. Modigliani and Miller's irrelevance of capital structure rests on an absence of _____.
5. An analytical technique used to evaluate alternate financing plans is _____.
6. The level of EBIT where the EPSs of two alternative capital structures are equal is called the _____.
7. Dividend payment patterns may convey _____ effects to investors about management's future expectations for the firm.
8. The _____ effect implies that investors are attracted to firms whose dividend policies meet their particular needs.
9. _____ is the act of buying back a firm's own shares of common stock.
10. _____ markets are the financial markets for short-term debt instruments.
11. A(n) _____ is a type of investment company that pools money to invest in securities.
12. Compensation which an investment banker receives for the service function of selling is called a(n) _____.
13. In an unsecured bank loan, the borrower may be required to maintain a minimum balance in a checking account called a(n) _____ balance.
14. Restrictions in a loan agreement which protect the lender are called _____.
15. _____ is the sale of accounts receivable to another party which manages and collects the accounts.
16. The breakdown of payments into interest portions and principal portions is called a(n) _____.
17. _____ leases represent off-balance-sheet financing.
18. The lease-buy analysis requires the determination of the present value of the _____ cash flows of each option.
19. Stock which has been issued and then reacquired by the firm is called _____ stock.
20. The right of existing shareholders to keep their percentage ownership by purchasing shares of a new issue is called a(n) _____ right.

Problems

1. Dallas Industries expects to pay dividends of $1.25 per share on common stock next year. The current market price of the stock is $25. The company's dividends have grown at a 5 percent compounded annual rate over the last decade. Flotation costs on

any new common stock are expected to be $1 per share. Assume that the growth rate remains constant.

    (*a*) What is the cost of the firm's retained earnings?

    (*b*) What is the cost of the firm's new common stock?

2. Kearney Computer Company has a target capital structure of 35 percent debt and 65 percent common equity. The firm's after-tax cost of individual capital components is:

Source of Capital	Specific Cost
Long-term debt	8.00%
Retained earnings	12.00
Common stock	13.00

The firm expects to retain $7,000,000 in earnings over the next year.

    (*a*) What is the firm's weighted average cost of capital before the issuance of new common stock is needed?

    (*b*) What is the total amount of investment that can be financed before new common stock is issued?

    (*c*) What is the weighted marginal cost of capital after the sale of new common stock?

3. Tri-Tex, Inc. is a new firm which needs to raise $400,000. It is considering two capital structures. One capital structure consists of 100 percent equity and involves selling 20,000 shares of common stock at $20 per share. The second structure consists of 70 percent equity and 30 percent debt. The debt may be raised by borrowing funds at a before-tax rate of 10 percent. The firm's tax rate is 34 percent.

    (*a*) What is the EBIT-EPS indifference point associated with the two financing plans?

    (*b*) If Tri-Tex's expected EBIT is $120,000, which financing plan should the firm choose?

4. You own 10,000 shares of Culnan Cosmetics, Inc. which sells for $42 per share. The firm has 500,000 shares of common stock outstanding prior to declaring a 5 percent stock dividend.

    (*a*) What should the share price be on the ex-dividend date?

    (*b*) How many shares will you own after the dividend?

    (*c*) What impact will this stock dividend have on your percentage ownership of the firm's outstanding stock?

5. Lotech Industries is planning to raise $5,000,000 through a rights offering. Management decides to set the subscription price at $50 per share. There are now 500,000 shares outstanding.

    (*a*) How many new shares will Lotech Industries have to sell?

    (*b*) How many rights are needed to buy a single share?

6. Calculate the effective interest rate on each of the loans below for $12,000. Assume a 360-day year.

    (*a*) A simple interest loan at 10 percent with all interest and principal due in one year.

    (*b*) A simple interest loan at 10 percent with all interest and principal due in one year, but which requires a $1,000 compensating balance.

    (*c*) A discounted loan which matures in one year with a 10 percent stated rate.

    (*d*) An installment loan with a stated rate of 10 percent for one year with 12 equal monthly payments.

7. Doc-in-the-Box, Inc., a walk-in medical clinic, needs to replace its existing X-ray equipment. An analysis of borrowing to buy the equipment shows that the present value cost of owning is $85,000. The firm's management believes that this cost is too high and wants to investigate another alternative. The equipment could be leased

from Med-Lease for five years for an end-of-the-year payment of $30,000. Med-Lease would provide all maintenance service. Doc-in-the-Box has a marginal tax rate of 34 percent and uses an after-tax discount rate of 8 percent to analyze the lease. Based on this information, which alternative should the firm choose?

8. Vola Tile, Inc. is planning to issue more common stock. The firm's initial and only other issue consisted of 100,000 shares, with a $25 par value, which sold for $62 per share. The firm is authorized to issue a total of 300,000 shares. If the current market price for Vola Tile is $100 per share on the date of issue, what will be shown in the stockholders equity section of the balance sheet before and after the sale of 100,000 additional shares?

Answers to Examination II

True-False

1. False [Section 14-2]
2. False [Section 14-2C]
3. True [Section 14-3]
4. False [Section 15-2C]
5. True [Section 15-2D]
6. True [Section 15-3A]
7. True [Section 16-2B]
8. True [Section 16-2C]
9. True [Section 16-6A]
10. True [Section 17-1B]
11. False [Section 17-1B]
12. False [Section 17-1B]
13. False [Section 18-1A]
14. True [Section 18-1C]
15. False [Section 18-4A]
16. False [Section 19-2]
17. True [Section 19-3B]
18. False [Section 19-3C]
19. True [Section 20-1E]
20. True [Section 20-2C]

Multiple Choice

1. d [Section 14-1]
2. a [Section 14-2A]
3. c [Section 14-2C]
4. d [Section 15-2]
5. d [Section 15-3A]
6. d [Section 15-3B]
7. c [Section 16-3B–D]
8. b [Section 16-5B]
9. c [Section 16-6A & B]
10. d [Section 17-1B]
11. b [Section 17-1B]
12. d [Section 17-4A & B]
13. b [Section 18-2A]
14. d [Section 18-4D]
15. b [Section 18-7B]
16. a [Section 19-1A]
17. a [Section 19-2A]
18. b [Section 19-3]
19. d [Section 20-1A]
20. d [Section 20-1]

Fill In The Blank

1. Capital [Section 14-1]
2. minimizes [Section 14-3A]
3. break points [Section 14-4A]
4. market imperfections [Section 15-2D]
5. EBIT-EPS analysis [Section 15-3A]
6. indifference point [Section 15-3A]
7. informational content [Section 16-2B]
8. clientele [Section 16-2B]
9. stock repurchase [Section 16-7]
10. Money [Section 17-1B]
11. Mutual funds [Section 17-2B]
12. selling concession [Section 17-3C]
13. compensating [18-4B]
14. protective covenants [Section 18-4B]
15. Factoring (Section 18-6D)
16. amortization schedule [Section 19-1A]
17. Operating [Section 19-3C]

18. after-tax [Section 19-3D]
19. treasury [Section 20-3A]
20. preemptive [Section 20-3B]

Problems

1. The computation of the cost of capital for Dallas Industries is shown below.

(a) Substituting $D_1 = \$1.25$, $P_0 = \$25.00$, and $g = 0.05$ in Equation 14-6, the cost of retained earnings is:

$$k_r = \frac{\$1.25}{\$25.00} + 0.05 = 0.05 + 0.05 = 0.10 \text{ or } 10.00 \text{ percent}$$

(b) The net proceeds of the new common stock issue, NP_c, is $24 ($25 − $1). Substituting $D_1 = \$1.25$, $NP_c = \$24.00$, and $g = 0.05$ in Equation 14-10, the cost of new common stock is:

$$k_r = \frac{\$1.25}{\$24.00} + 0.05 = 0.0521 + 0.05 = 0.1021 \text{ or } 10.21 \text{ percent}$$

[Section 14-2C]

2. Calculations for Kearney Computer Company follow.

(a) Substituting the target weights and specific costs of capital in Equation 14-11, the weighted average cost of capital (WACC) is:

$$\text{WACC} = (0.35)(0.08) + (0.65)(0.12)$$
$$= 0.028 + 0.078 = 0.106 \text{ or } 10.6 \text{ percent}$$

(b) Substituting $TF = \$7,000,000$ and $w = 0.35$ in Equation 14-12, the break point, BP, for retained earnings is:

$$\text{BP} = \frac{\$7,000,000}{0.35} = \$20,000,000$$

Thus, Kearney Computer Company can make $20,000,000 in investments before it needs to sell new common stock.

(c) The firm's weighted marginal cost of capital after the sale of common stock is:

$$\text{WMCC} = (0.35)(0.08) + (0.65)(0.13)$$
$$= 0.028 + 0.0845 = 0.1125 \text{ or } 11.25 \text{ percent}$$

[Sections 14-3A and 14-4A]

3. The calculations for Tri-Tex, Inc. follow.

(a) If the second financing alternative is used, Tri-Tex, Inc. will have $120,000 (0.30 × $400,000) in debt financing with an annual before-tax interest expense of $12,000 (0.10 × $120,000). It will also need to sell 14,000 ($280,000/$20) shares of common stock. Using equation 15-13, the EBIT-EPS indifference point is:

$$\text{EPS (debt − equity)} = \text{EPS (all equity)}$$

$$\frac{(\text{EBIT}^* - \$12,000)(1 - 0.34)}{14,000} = \frac{(\text{EBIT}^* - \$0)(1 - 0.34)}{20,000}$$

$$\frac{0.66 \text{ EBIT}^* - \$7,920}{14,000} = \frac{0.66 \text{ EBIT}^*}{20,000}$$

Cross-multiplying,

$$(20,000)(0.66 \text{ EBIT}^* - \$7,920) = (14,000)(0.66 \text{ EBIT}^*)$$
$$13,200 \text{ EBIT}^* - \$158,400,000 = 9,240 \text{ EBIT}^*$$
$$3,960 \text{ EBIT}^* = \$158,400,000$$
$$\text{EBIT}^* = \$40,000$$

(*b*) The EPS are calculated as follows:

	Debt-Equity	All Equity
EBIT	$120,000	$120,000
— Interest expense	12,000	0
Earnings before taxes	$108,000	$120,000
— Income taxes (34%)	36,720	40,800
Net Income	$ 71,280	$ 79,200
Shares of common stock	14,000	20,000
Earnings per share	$5.09	$3.96

The debt-equity capital structure is riskier and has a higher EPS than the equity capital structure. Since the expected EBIT of $120,000 is considerably higher than the indifference EBIT of $40,000, Tri-Tex, Inc. should adopt the debt-equity capital structure.   **[Section 15-3A]**

4. The calculations for Culnan Cosmetics, Inc. follow.

(*a*) Substituting $M = \$42.00$ and $D_s = 0.05$ in Equation 16-4, the adjusted market price is:

$$\text{Adjusted market price} = \frac{\$42.00}{1.05} = \$40.00$$

(*b*) You will own 10,500 (1.05 × 10,000) shares after the stock dividend.

(*c*) This stock dividend will not alter your percentage share of the firm's common stock.

$$\frac{\text{Ownership before}}{\text{stock dividend}} = \frac{10,000}{500,000} = 0.02 \text{ or } 2.00 \text{ percent}$$

$$\frac{\text{Ownership after}}{\text{stock dividend}} = \frac{10,500}{525,000} = 0.02 \text{ or } 2.00 \text{ percent}$$

[Section 16-6A]

5. The calculations for Lotech Industries follow.

(*a*) Substituting $5,000,000 in required financing and a $50 subscription price per share in Equation 17-1, the number of new shares, Lotech Industries must sell is:

$$\frac{\text{Number of new shares}}{\text{to be sold}} = \frac{\$5,000,000}{\$50} = 100,000 \text{ shares}$$

(*b*) Substituting 500,000 shares outstanding and 100,000 new shares in Equation 17-2, the number of rights needed to purchase each new share is:

$$\frac{\text{Number of rights}}{\text{to buy a new share}} = \frac{500,000}{100,000} = 5 \text{ rights}$$

[Section 17-5A]

6. Using Equation 18-4, the interest expense on each of the four loan is:

$$\text{Interest expense} = 0.10 \times \$12,000 \times \frac{360}{360} = \$1,200$$

(*a*) Using Equation 18-5, the effective interest rate on the simple interest loan is:

$$\frac{\text{Effective annual}}{\text{interest rate}} = \frac{\$1,200}{\$12,000} \times \frac{360}{360} \times 100 = 10.00 \text{ percent}$$

(*b*) Using Equation 18-5, the effective interest rate on the simple interest loan with a compensating balance is:

$$\text{Effective annual interest rate} = \frac{\$1,200}{\$12,000 - \$1,000} \times \frac{360}{360} \times 100 = 10.91 \text{ percent}$$

(*c*) Using Equation 18-5, the effective interest rate on the discounted loan is:

$$\text{Effective annual interest rate} = \frac{\$1,200}{\$12,000 - \$1,200} \times \frac{360}{360} \times 100 = 11.11 \text{ percent}$$

(*d*) Using Equation 18-6, the effective interest rate on the installment loan is:

$$\text{Effective annual interest rate on an installment loan} = \frac{(2)(12)(\$1,200)}{(\$12,000)(12 + 1)} \times 100 = 18.46 \text{ percent}$$

[Section 18-4D]

7. The present value cost of leasing is computed as follows:

End of Year (1)	Lease Payment (2)	Tax Saving [0.34 × (2)] (3)	After-tax Cash Outflow If Leased [(2) − (3)] (4)	PVIF at 8% (5)	Present Value Cost of Leasing [(4) × (5)] (6)
1	$30,000	$10,200	$19,800	0.926	$18,335
2	30,000	10,200	19,800	0.857	16,969
3	30,000	10,200	19,800	0.794	15,721
4	30,000	10,200	19,800	0.735	14,553
5	30,000	10,200	19,800	0.681	13,484
					$79,062

The present value of the cost of leasing is less expensive than the cost of owning by $5,938 ($85,000 − $79,062). Thus, Doc-in-the-Box should lease the X-ray equipment.

[Section 19-3D]

8. The first issue resulted in total proceeds of $6,200,000 ($62 × 100,000 shares), of which $3,700,000 [($62 − $25) × $100,000)] is additional capital in excess of par.

Stockholders' Equity—Before New Stock Issue

Common stock ($25 par, 300,000 shares authorized and 100,000 shares issued and outstanding)	$2,500,000
Capital in excess of par	3,700,000
Total stockholders' equity	$6,200,000

The second issue resulted in total proceeds of $10,000,000 ($100 × 100,000), of which $7,500,000 [($100 − $25) × 100,000] is additional capital in excess of par.

Stockholders' Equity—After New Stock Issue

Common stock ($25 par, 300,000 shares authorized and 200,000 shares issued and outstanding)	$ 5,000,000
Capital in excess of par	11,200,000
Total stockholders' equity	$16,200,000

[Section 20-3A]

APPENDIX A:
Future Value Interest Factor (FVIF) ($1 at i% for n Periods)

$$FVIF = (1 + i)^n \qquad FV_n = PV(FVIF_{i,n})$$

PERIOD n	1%	2%	3%	4%	5%	6%	7%	8%	9%	10%	11%	12%	13%
0	1.000	1.000	1.000	1.000	1.000	1.000	1.000	1.000	1.000	1.000	1.000	1.000	1.000
1	1.010	1.020	1.030	1.040	1.050	1.060	1.070	1.080	1.090	1.100	1.110	1.120	1.130
2	1.020	1.040	1.061	1.082	1.102	1.124	1.145	1.166	1.186	1.210	1.232	1.254	1.277
3	1.030	1.061	1.093	1.125	1.158	1.191	1.225	1.260	1.295	1.331	1.368	1.405	1.443
4	1.041	1.082	1.126	1.170	1.216	1.262	1.311	1.360	1.412	1.464	1.518	1.574	1.630
5	1.051	1.104	1.159	1.217	1.276	1.338	1.403	1.469	1.539	1.611	1.685	1.762	1.842
6	1.062	1.126	1.194	1.265	1.340	1.419	1.501	1.587	1.677	1.772	1.870	1.974	2.082
7	1.072	1.149	1.230	1.316	1.407	1.504	1.606	1.714	1.828	1.949	2.076	2.211	2.353
8	1.083	1.172	1.267	1.369	1.477	1.594	1.718	1.851	1.993	2.144	2.305	2.476	2.658
9	1.094	1.195	1.305	1.423	1.551	1.689	1.838	1.999	2.172	2.358	2.558	2.773	3.004
10	1.105	1.219	1.344	1.480	1.629	1.791	1.967	2.159	2.367	2.594	2.839	3.106	3.395
11	1.116	1.243	1.384	1.539	1.710	1.898	2.105	2.332	2.580	2.853	3.152	3.479	3.836
12	1.127	1.268	1.426	1.601	1.796	2.012	2.252	2.518	2.813	3.138	3.498	3.896	4.335
13	1.138	1.294	1.469	1.665	1.886	2.133	2.410	2.720	3.066	3.452	3.883	4.363	4.898
14	1.149	1.319	1.513	1.732	1.980	2.261	2.579	2.937	3.342	3.797	4.310	4.887	5.535
15	1.161	1.346	1.558	1.801	2.079	2.397	2.759	3.172	3.642	4.177	4.785	5.474	6.254
16	1.173	1.373	1.605	1.873	2.183	2.540	2.952	3.426	3.970	4.595	5.311	6.130	7.067
17	1.184	1.400	1.653	1.948	2.292	2.693	3.159	3.700	4.328	5.054	5.895	6.866	7.986
18	1.196	1.428	1.702	2.026	2.407	2.854	3.380	3.996	4.717	5.560	6.544	7.690	9.024
19	1.208	1.457	1.754	2.107	2.527	3.026	3.617	4.316	5.142	6.116	7.263	8.613	10.197
20	1.220	1.486	1.806	2.191	2.653	3.207	3.870	4.661	5.604	6.728	8.062	9.646	11.523
24	1.270	1.608	2.033	2.563	3.225	4.049	5.072	6.341	7.911	9.850	12.239	15.179	18.790
25	1.282	1.641	2.094	2.666	3.386	4.292	5.427	6.848	8.623	10.835	13.585	17.000	21.231
30	1.348	1.811	2.427	3.243	4.322	5.743	7.612	10.063	13.268	17.449	22.892	29.960	39.116
40	1.489	2.208	3.262	4.801	7.040	10.286	14.974	21.725	31.409	45.259	65.001	93.051	132.782
50	1.645	2.692	4.384	7.107	11.467	18.420	29.457	46.902	74.358	117.391	184.565	289.002	450.736
60	1.817	3.281	5.892	10.520	18.679	32.988	57.946	101.257	176.031	304.482	524.057	897.597	1,530.05

APPENDIX A (Continued)

$$FVIF = (1 + i)^n$$

$$FV_n = PV(FVIF_{i,n})$$

PERIOD n	14%	15%	16%	17%	18%	19%	20%	24%	28%	32%	36%	40%
0	1.000	1.000	1.000	1.000	1.000	1.000	1.000	1.000	1.000	1.000	1.000	1.000
1	1.140	1.150	1.160	1.170	1.180	1.190	1.200	1.240	1.280	1.320	1.360	1.400
2	1.300	1.322	1.346	1.369	1.392	1.416	1.440	1.538	1.638	1.742	1.850	1.960
3	1.482	1.521	1.561	1.602	1.643	1.685	1.728	1.907	2.067	2.300	2.515	2.744
4	1.689	1.749	1.811	1.874	1.939	2.005	2.074	2.364	2.684	3.036	3.421	3.842
5	1.925	2.011	2.100	2.192	2.288	2.386	2.488	2.932	3.436	4.007	4.653	5.378
6	2.195	2.313	2.436	2.565	2.700	2.840	2.986	3.635	4.398	5.290	6.328	7.530
7	2.502	2.660	2.826	3.001	3.185	3.379	3.583	4.508	5.629	6.983	8.605	10.541
8	2.853	3.059	3.278	3.511	3.759	4.021	4.300	5.590	7.206	9.217	11.703	14.758
9	3.252	3.518	3.803	4.108	4.435	4.785	5.160	6.931	9.223	12.166	15.917	20.661
10	3.707	4.046	4.411	4.807	5.234	5.695	6.192	8.594	11.806	16.060	21.647	28.925
11	4.226	4.652	5.117	5.624	6.176	6.777	7.430	10.657	15.112	21.199	29.439	40.496
12	4.818	5.350	5.926	6.580	7.288	8.064	8.916	13.215	19.343	27.983	40.037	56.694
13	5.492	6.153	6.886	7.699	8.599	9.596	10.699	16.386	24.759	36.937	54.451	79.372
14	6.261	7.076	7.988	9.007	10.147	11.420	12.839	20.319	31.961	48.757	74.053	111.120
15	7.138	8.137	9.266	10.539	11.974	13.590	15.407	25.196	40.565	64.359	100.712	155.568
16	8.137	9.358	10.748	12.330	14.129	16.172	18.488	31.243	51.923	84.954	136.969	217.795
17	9.276	10.761	12.468	14.426	16.672	19.244	22.186	38.741	66.461	112.139	186.278	304.914
18	10.575	12.375	14.463	16.879	19.673	22.901	26.623	48.039	85.071	148.023	253.338	426.879
19	12.056	14.232	16.777	19.748	23.214	27.252	31.948	59.568	108.890	195.391	344.540	597.630
20	13.743	16.367	19.461	23.106	27.393	32.429	38.338	73.864	139.380	257.916	468.574	836.683
24	23.212	28.625	35.236	43.297	53.109	65.032	79.497	174.631	374.144	783.023	1,603.00	3,214.20
25	26.462	32.919	40.874	50.658	62.669	77.388	95.396	216.542	478.905	1,033.59	2,180.08	4,499.88
30	50.950	66.212	85.850	111.065	143.371	184.675	237.376	634.820	1,645.50	4,142.07	10,143.0	24,201.4
40	188.884	267.864	378.721	533.869	750.378	1,051.67	1,469.77	5,455.91	19,426.7	66,520.8	219,562.	700,038
50	700.233	1,083.66	1,670.70	2,566.22	3,927.36	5,988.91	9,100.44	46,890.4	229,350	*	*	*
60	2,595.92	4,384.00	7,370.20	12,335.4	20,555.1	34,105.0	56,347.5	402,996	*	*	*	*

* These interest factors exceed 1,000,000.

APPENDIX B:
Future Value Interest Factor of an Annuity (FVIFA)
($1 per Period at i% per Period)

$$FVOA_n = A(FVIFA_{i,n}) \qquad FVAD_n = A(FVIFA_{i,n})(1 + i)$$

PERIOD n	1%	2%	3%	4%	5%	6%	7%	8%	9%	10%	11%	12%	13%
1	1.000	1.000	1.000	1.000	1.000	1.000	1.000	1.000	1.000	1.000	1.000	1.000	1.000
2	2.010	2.020	2.030	2.040	2.050	2.060	2.070	2.080	2.090	2.100	2.110	2.120	2.130
3	3.030	3.060	3.091	3.122	3.152	3.184	3.215	3.246	3.278	3.310	3.342	3.374	3.407
4	4.060	4.122	4.184	4.246	4.310	4.375	4.440	4.506	4.573	4.641	4.710	4.770	4.850
5	5.101	5.204	5.309	5.416	5.526	5.637	5.751	5.867	5.985	6.105	6.228	6.353	6.480
6	6.152	6.308	6.468	6.633	6.802	6.975	7.153	7.336	7.523	7.716	7.913	8.115	8.323
7	7.214	7.434	7.662	7.898	8.142	8.394	8.654	8.923	9.200	9.487	9.783	10.089	10.405
8	8.286	8.583	8.892	9.214	9.549	9.897	10.260	10.637	11.028	11.436	11.859	12.300	12.757
9	9.369	9.755	10.159	10.583	11.027	11.491	11.978	12.488	13.021	13.579	14.164	14.776	15.416
10	10.462	10.950	11.464	12.006	12.578	13.181	13.816	14.487	15.193	15.937	16.722	17.549	18.420
11	11.567	12.169	12.808	13.486	14.207	14.972	15.784	16.645	17.560	18.531	19.561	20.655	21.814
12	12.683	13.412	14.192	15.026	15.917	16.870	17.888	18.977	20.141	21.384	22.713	24.133	25.650
13	13.809	14.680	15.618	16.627	17.713	18.882	20.141	21.495	22.953	24.523	26.212	28.029	29.985
14	14.947	15.974	17.086	18.292	19.599	21.051	22.550	24.215	26.019	27.975	30.095	32.393	34.883
15	16.097	17.293	18.599	20.024	21.579	23.276	25.129	27.152	29.361	31.772	34.405	37.280	40.417
16	17.258	18.639	20.157	21.825	23.657	25.673	27.888	30.324	33.003	35.950	39.190	42.753	46.672
17	18.430	20.012	21.762	23.698	25.840	28.213	30.840	33.750	36.974	40.545	44.501	48.884	53.739
18	19.615	21.412	23.414	25.645	28.132	30.906	33.999	37.450	41.301	45.599	50.396	55.750	61.725
19	20.811	22.841	25.117	27.671	30.539	33.760	37.379	41.446	46.018	51.159	56.939	63.440	70.749
20	22.019	24.297	26.870	29.778	33.066	36.786	40.995	45.762	51.160	57.275	64.203	72.052	80.947
24	26.973	30.422	34.426	39.083	44.502	50.816	58.117	66.765	76.790	88.497	102.174	118.155	136.831
25	28.243	32.030	36.459	41.646	47.727	54.865	63.249	73.106	84.701	98.347	114.413	133.334	155.620
30	34.785	40.568	47.575	56.805	66.439	79.058	94.461	113.283	136.308	164.494	199.021	241.333	293.199
40	48.886	60.402	75.401	95.026	120.080	154.762	199.635	259.057	337.882	442.593	581.826	767.091	1,013.70
50	64.463	84.572	112.797	152.667	209.348	290.336	406.529	573.770	815.084	1,163.91	1,668.77	2,400.02	3,459.51
60	81.670	114.052	163.053	237.991	353.584	533.128	813.520	1,253.21	1,944.79	3,034.82	4,755.07	7,471.64	11,761.9

APPENDIX B (Continued)

$$FVOA_n = A(FVIFA_{i,n})$$
$$FVAD_n = A(FVIFA_{i,n})(1 + i)$$

PERIOD n	14%	15%	16%	17%	18%	19%	20%	24%	28%	32%	36%	40%
1	1.000	1.000	1.000	1.000	1.000	1.000	1.000	1.000	1.000	1.000	1.000	1.000
2	2.140	2.150	2.160	2.170	2.180	2.190	2.200	2.240	2.280	2.320	2.360	2.400
3	3.440	3.473	3.506	3.539	3.572	3.606	3.640	3.778	3.918	4.062	4.210	4.360
4	4.921	4.993	5.066	5.141	5.215	5.291	5.368	5.684	6.016	6.362	6.725	7.104
5	6.610	6.742	6.877	7.014	7.154	7.297	7.442	8.048	8.700	9.398	10.146	10.846
6	8.536	8.754	8.977	9.207	9.442	9.683	9.930	10.980	12.136	13.406	14.799	16.324
7	10.730	11.067	11.414	11.772	12.142	12.523	12.916	14.615	16.534	18.696	21.126	23.853
8	13.233	13.727	14.240	14.773	15.327	15.902	16.499	19.123	22.163	25.678	29.732	34.395
9	16.085	16.786	17.518	18.285	19.086	19.923	20.799	24.712	29.369	34.895	41.435	49.153
10	19.337	20.304	21.321	22.393	23.521	24.709	25.959	31.643	38.592	47.062	57.352	69.814
11	23.044	24.349	25.733	27.200	28.755	30.404	32.150	40.238	50.399	63.122	78.998	98.739
12	27.271	29.002	30.850	32.824	34.931	37.180	39.580	50.985	65.510	84.320	108.437	139.235
13	32.089	34.352	36.786	39.404	42.219	45.244	48.497	64.110	84.853	112.303	148.475	195.929
14	37.581	40.505	43.672	47.103	50.818	54.841	59.196	80.496	109.612	149.240	202.926	275.300
15	43.842	47.580	51.660	56.110	60.965	66.261	72.035	100.815	141.303	197.997	276.979	386.420
16	50.980	55.717	60.925	66.649	72.939	79.850	87.442	126.011	181.868	262.356	377.692	541.988
17	59.118	65.075	71.673	78.979	87.068	96.022	105.931	157.253	233.791	347.310	514.661	759.784
18	68.394	75.836	84.141	93.406	103.740	115.266	128.117	195.994	300.252	459.449	700.939	1,064.70
19	78.969	88.212	98.603	110.285	123.414	138.166	154.740	244.033	385.323	607.472	954.277	1,491.58
20	91.025	102.444	115.380	130.033	146.628	165.418	186.688	303.601	494.213	802.863	1,298.82	2,089.21
24	158.659	184.168	213.978	248.808	289.494	337.010	392.484	723.461	1,332.66	2,443.82	4,450.00	8,033.00
25	181.871	212.793	249.214	292.105	342.603	402.042	471.981	898.092	1,706.80	3,226.84	6,053.00	11,247.2
30	356.787	434.745	530.321	647.439	790.948	966.712	1,181.88	2,640.92	5,873.23	12,940.9	28,172.3	60,501.1
40	1,342.03	1,779.09	2,360.76	3,134.52	4,163.21	5,529.83	7,343.86	22,728.8	69,377.5	207,874	609,890	*
50	4,994.52	7,217.72	10,435.6	15,089.5	21,813.1	31,515.3	45,497.2	195,373	819,103	*	*	*
60	18,535.1	29,220.0	46,057.5	72,555.0	114,190	179,495	281,733	*	*	*	*	*

* These interest factors exceed 1,000,000.

APPENDIX C:

Present Value Interest Factor (PVIF) ($1 at i% for n Periods)

$$PVIF = \frac{1}{(1 + i)^n} \qquad PV = FV_n(PVIF_{i,n})$$

PERIOD n	1%	2%	3%	4%	5%	6%	7%	8%	9%	10%	11%	12%	13%
0	1.000	1.000	1.000	1.000	1.000	1.000	1.000	1.000	1.000	1.000	1.000	1.000	1.000
1	0.990	0.980	0.971	0.962	0.952	0.943	0.935	0.926	0.917	0.909	0.901	0.893	0.885
2	0.980	0.961	0.943	0.925	0.907	0.890	0.873	0.857	0.842	0.826	0.812	0.797	0.783
3	0.971	0.942	0.915	0.889	0.864	0.840	0.816	0.794	0.772	0.751	0.731	0.712	0.693
4	0.961	0.924	0.889	0.855	0.823	0.792	0.763	0.735	0.708	0.683	0.659	0.636	0.613
5	0.951	0.906	0.863	0.822	0.784	0.747	0.713	0.681	0.650	0.621	0.593	0.567	0.543
6	0.942	0.888	0.838	0.790	0.746	0.705	0.666	0.630	0.596	0.564	0.535	0.507	0.480
7	0.933	0.871	0.813	0.760	0.711	0.665	0.623	0.583	0.547	0.513	0.482	0.452	0.425
8	0.923	0.853	0.789	0.731	0.677	0.627	0.582	0.540	0.502	0.467	0.434	0.404	0.376
9	0.914	0.837	0.766	0.703	0.645	0.592	0.544	0.500	0.460	0.424	0.391	0.361	0.333
10	0.905	0.820	0.744	0.676	0.614	0.558	0.508	0.463	0.422	0.386	0.352	0.322	0.295
11	0.896	0.804	0.722	0.650	0.585	0.527	0.475	0.429	0.388	0.350	0.317	0.287	0.261
12	0.887	0.788	0.701	0.625	0.557	0.497	0.444	0.397	0.356	0.319	0.286	0.257	0.231
13	0.879	0.773	0.681	0.601	0.530	0.469	0.415	0.368	0.326	0.290	0.258	0.229	0.204
14	0.870	0.758	0.661	0.577	0.505	0.442	0.388	0.340	0.299	0.263	0.232	0.205	0.181
15	0.861	0.743	0.642	0.555	0.481	0.417	0.362	0.315	0.275	0.239	0.209	0.183	0.160
16	0.853	0.728	0.623	0.534	0.458	0.394	0.339	0.292	0.252	0.218	0.188	0.163	0.141
17	0.844	0.714	0.605	0.513	0.436	0.371	0.317	0.270	0.231	0.198	0.170	0.146	0.125
18	0.836	0.700	0.587	0.494	0.416	0.350	0.296	0.250	0.212	0.180	0.153	0.130	0.111
19	0.828	0.686	0.570	0.475	0.396	0.331	0.276	0.232	0.194	0.164	0.138	0.116	0.098
20	0.820	0.673	0.554	0.456	0.377	0.312	0.258	0.215	0.178	0.149	0.124	0.104	0.087
24	0.788	0.622	0.492	0.390	0.310	0.247	0.197	0.158	0.126	0.102	0.082	0.066	0.053
25	0.780	0.610	0.478	0.375	0.295	0.233	0.184	0.146	0.116	0.092	0.074	0.059	0.047
30	0.742	0.552	0.412	0.308	0.231	0.174	0.131	0.099	0.075	0.057	0.044	0.033	0.026
40	0.672	0.453	0.307	0.208	0.142	0.097	0.067	0.046	0.032	0.022	0.015	0.011	0.008
50	0.608	0.372	0.228	0.141	0.087	0.054	0.034	0.021	0.013	0.009	0.005	0.003	0.002
60	0.550	0.305	0.170	0.095	0.054	0.030	0.017	0.010	0.006	0.003	0.002	0.001	0.001

APPENDIX C (Continued)

$$PVIF = \frac{1}{(1 + i)^n}$$

$$PV = FV_n(PVIF_{i,n})$$

PERIOD n	14%	15%	16%	17%	18%	19%	20%	24%	28%	32%	36%	40%
0	1.000	1.000	1.000	1.000	1.000	1.000	1.000	1.000	1.000	1.000	1.000	1.000
1	0.877	0.870	0.862	0.855	0.847	0.840	0.833	0.806	0.781	0.758	0.735	0.714
2	0.769	0.756	0.743	0.731	0.718	0.706	0.694	0.650	0.610	0.574	0.541	0.510
3	0.675	0.658	0.641	0.624	0.609	0.593	0.579	0.524	0.477	0.435	0.398	0.364
4	0.592	0.572	0.552	0.534	0.516	0.499	0.482	0.423	0.373	0.329	0.292	0.260
5	0.519	0.497	0.476	0.456	0.437	0.419	0.402	0.341	0.291	0.250	0.215	0.186
6	0.456	0.432	0.410	0.390	0.370	0.352	0.335	0.275	0.227	0.189	0.158	0.133
7	0.400	0.376	0.354	0.333	0.314	0.296	0.279	0.222	0.178	0.143	0.116	0.095
8	0.351	0.327	0.305	0.285	0.266	0.249	0.233	0.179	0.139	0.108	0.085	0.068
9	0.308	0.284	0.263	0.243	0.225	0.209	0.194	0.144	0.108	0.082	0.063	0.048
10	0.270	0.247	0.227	0.208	0.191	0.176	0.162	0.116	0.085	0.062	0.046	0.035
11	0.237	0.215	0.195	0.178	0.162	0.148	0.135	0.094	0.066	0.047	0.034	0.025
12	0.208	0.187	0.168	0.152	0.137	0.124	0.112	0.076	0.052	0.036	0.025	0.018
13	0.182	0.163	0.145	0.130	0.116	0.104	0.093	0.061	0.040	0.027	0.018	0.013
14	0.160	0.141	0.125	0.111	0.099	0.088	0.078	0.049	0.032	0.021	0.014	0.009
15	0.140	0.123	0.108	0.095	0.084	0.074	0.065	0.040	0.025	0.016	0.010	0.006
16	0.123	0.107	0.093	0.081	0.071	0.062	0.054	0.032	0.019	0.012	0.007	0.005
17	0.108	0.093	0.080	0.069	0.060	0.052	0.045	0.026	0.015	0.009	0.005	0.003
18	0.095	0.081	0.069	0.059	0.051	0.044	0.038	0.021	0.012	0.007	0.004	0.002
19	0.083	0.070	0.060	0.051	0.043	0.037	0.031	0.017	0.009	0.005	0.003	0.002
20	0.073	0.061	0.051	0.043	0.037	0.031	0.026	0.014	0.007	0.004	0.002	0.001
24	0.043	0.035	0.028	0.023	0.019	0.015	0.013	0.006	0.003	0.001	0.001	0.000
25	0.038	0.030	0.024	0.020	0.016	0.013	0.010	0.005	0.002	0.001	0.000	0.000
30	0.020	0.015	0.012	0.009	0.007	0.005	0.004	0.002	0.001	0.000	0.000	0.000
40	0.005	0.004	0.003	0.002	0.001	0.001	0.001	0.000	0.000	0.000	0.000	0.000
50	0.001	0.001	0.001	0.000	0.000	0.000	0.000	0.000	0.000	0.000	0.000	0.000
60	0.000	0.000	0.000	0.000	0.000	0.000	0.000	0.000	0.000	0.000	0.000	0.000

APPENDIX D:

Present Value Interest Factor of an Annuity (PVIFA) ($1 per Periods at i% for n Periods)

$$PV_n = A(PVIFA_{i,n})$$

PERIOD n	1%	2%	3%	4%	5%	6%	7%	8%	9%	10%	11%	12%	13%
1	0.990	0.980	0.971	0.962	0.952	0.943	0.935	0.926	0.917	0.909	0.901	0.893	0.885
2	1.970	1.942	1.913	1.886	1.859	1.833	1.808	1.783	1.759	1.736	1.713	1.690	1.668
3	2.941	2.884	2.829	2.775	2.723	2.673	2.624	2.577	2.531	2.487	2.444	2.402	2.361
4	3.902	3.808	3.717	3.630	3.546	3.465	3.387	3.312	3.240	3.170	3.102	3.037	2.974
5	4.853	4.713	4.580	4.452	4.329	4.212	4.100	3.993	3.890	3.791	3.696	3.605	3.517
6	5.795	5.601	5.417	5.242	5.076	4.917	4.766	4.623	4.486	4.355	4.231	4.111	3.998
7	6.728	6.472	6.230	6.002	5.786	5.582	5.389	5.206	5.033	4.868	4.712	4.564	4.423
8	7.652	7.325	7.020	6.733	6.463	6.210	5.971	5.747	5.535	5.335	5.146	4.968	4.799
9	8.566	8.162	7.786	7.435	7.108	6.802	6.515	6.247	5.995	5.759	5.537	5.328	5.132
10	9.471	8.983	8.530	8.111	7.722	7.360	7.024	6.710	6.418	6.145	5.889	5.650	5.426
11	10.368	9.787	9.253	8.760	8.306	7.887	7.499	7.139	6.805	6.495	6.207	5.938	5.687
12	11.255	10.575	9.954	9.385	8.863	8.384	7.943	7.536	7.161	6.814	6.492	6.194	5.918
13	12.134	11.348	10.635	9.986	9.394	8.853	8.358	7.904	7.487	7.103	6.750	6.424	6.122
14	13.004	12.106	11.296	10.563	9.899	9.295	8.745	8.244	7.786	7.367	6.982	6.628	6.302
15	13.865	12.849	11.938	11.118	10.380	9.712	9.108	8.559	8.060	7.606	7.191	6.811	6.462
16	14.718	13.578	12.561	11.652	10.838	10.106	9.447	8.851	8.312	7.824	7.379	6.974	6.604
17	15.562	14.292	13.166	12.166	11.274	10.477	9.763	9.122	8.544	8.022	7.549	7.120	6.729
18	16.398	14.992	13.754	12.659	11.690	10.828	10.059	9.372	8.756	8.201	7.702	7.250	6.840
19	17.226	15.678	14.324	13.134	12.085	11.158	10.336	9.604	8.950	8.365	7.839	7.366	6.938
20	18.046	16.351	14.877	13.590	12.462	11.470	10.594	9.818	9.128	8.514	7.963	7.469	7.025
24	21.243	18.914	16.936	15.247	13.799	12.550	11.469	10.529	9.707	8.985	8.348	7.784	7.283
25	22.023	19.523	17.413	15.622	14.094	12.783	11.654	10.675	9.823	9.077	8.422	7.843	7.330
30	25.808	22.397	19.600	17.292	15.373	13.765	12.409	11.258	10.274	9.427	8.694	8.055	7.496
40	32.835	27.355	23.115	19.793	17.159	15.046	13.332	11.925	10.757	9.779	8.951	8.244	7.634
50	39.196	31.424	25.730	21.482	18.256	15.762	13.801	12.233	10.962	9.915	9.042	8.304	7.675
60	44.955	34.761	27.676	22.623	18.929	16.161	14.039	12.377	11.048	9.967	9.074	8.324	7.687

APPENDIX D (Continued)

$$PV_n = A(PVIFA_{i,n})$$

PERIOD n	14%	15%	16%	17%	18%	19%	20%	24%	28%	32%	36%	40%
1	0.877	0.870	0.862	0.855	0.847	0.840	0.833	0.806	0.781	0.758	0.735	0.714
2	1.647	1.626	1.605	1.585	1.566	1.547	1.528	1.457	1.392	1.332	1.276	1.224
3	2.322	2.283	2.246	2.210	2.174	2.140	2.106	1.981	1.868	1.766	1.674	1.589
4	2.914	2.855	2.798	2.743	2.690	2.639	2.589	2.404	2.241	2.096	1.966	1.849
5	3.433	3.352	3.274	3.199	3.127	3.058	2.991	2.745	2.532	2.345	2.181	2.035
6	3.889	3.784	3.685	3.589	3.498	3.410	3.326	3.020	2.759	2.534	2.399	2.168
7	4.288	4.160	4.039	3.922	3.812	3.706	3.605	3.242	2.937	2.678	2.455	2.263
8	4.639	4.487	4.344	4.207	4.078	3.954	3.837	3.421	3.076	2.786	2.540	2.331
9	4.946	4.772	4.607	4.451	4.303	4.163	4.031	3.566	3.184	2.868	2.603	2.379
10	5.216	5.019	4.883	4.659	4.494	4.339	4.193	3.682	3.269	2.930	2.650	2.414
11	5.453	5.234	5.029	4.836	4.656	4.486	4.327	3.776	3.335	2.978	2.683	2.438
12	5.660	5.421	5.197	4.988	4.793	4.611	4.439	3.851	3.387	3.013	2.708	2.456
13	5.842	5.583	5.342	5.118	4.910	4.715	4.533	3.912	3.427	3.040	2.727	2.469
14	6.002	5.724	5.468	5.229	5.008	4.802	4.611	3.962	3.459	3.061	2.740	2.478
15	6.142	5.847	5.575	5.324	5.092	4.876	4.675	4.001	3.483	3.076	2.750	2.484
16	6.265	5.954	5.669	5.405	5.162	4.938	4.730	4.033	3.503	3.088	2.758	2.489
17	5.373	6.047	5.749	5.475	5.222	4.990	4.775	4.059	3.518	3.097	2.763	2.492
18	6.467	6.128	5.818	5.534	5.273	5.033	4.812	4.080	3.529	3.104	2.767	2.494
19	6.550	6.198	5.877	5.584	5.316	5.070	4.844	4.097	3.539	3.109	2.770	2.496
20	6.623	6.259	5.929	5.628	5.353	5.101	4.870	4.110	3.546	3.113	2.772	2.497
24	6.835	6.434	6.073	5.746	5.451	5.182	4.937	4.143	3.562	3.121	2.776	2.499
25	6.873	6.464	6.097	5.766	5.467	5.195	4.948	4.147	3.564	3.122	2.776	2.499
30	7.003	6.566	6.177	5.829	5.517	5.235	4.979	4.160	3.569	3.124	2.778	2.500
40	7.105	6.642	6.233	5.871	5.548	5.258	4.997	4.166	3.571	3.125	2.778	2.500
50	7.133	6.661	6.246	5.880	5.554	5.262	4.999	4.167	3.571	3.125	2.778	2.500
60	7.140	6.665	6.249	5.882	5.555	5.263	5.000	4.167	3.571	3.125	2.778	2.500

APPENDIX E:
Standard Normal Probability Distribution

z	0.00	0.01	0.02	0.03	0.04	0.05	0.06	0.07	0.08	0.09
0.0	0.0000	0.0040	0.0080	0.0120	0.0160	0.0199	0.0239	0.0279	0.0319	0.0359
0.1	0.0398	0.0438	0.0478	0.0517	0.0557	0.0596	0.0636	0.0675	0.0714	0.0753
0.2	0.0793	0.0832	0.0871	0.0910	0.0948	0.0987	0.1026	0.0164	0.1103	0.1141
0.3	0.1179	0.1217	0.1255	0.1293	0.1331	0.1368	0.1406	0.1443	0.1480	0.1517
0.4	0.1554	0.1591	0.1628	0.1664	0.1700	0.1736	0.1772	0.1808	0.1844	0.1879
0.5	0.1915	0.1950	0.1985	0.2019	0.2054	0.2088	0.2123	0.2157	0.2190	0.2224
0.6	0.2257	0.2291	0.2324	0.2357	0.2389	0.2422	0.2454	0.2486	0.2517	0.2549
0.7	0.2580	0.2611	0.2642	0.2673	0.2703	0.2734	0.2764	0.2794	0.2823	0.2852
0.8	0.2881	0.2910	0.2939	0.2967	0.2995	0.3023	0.3051	0.3078	0.3106	0.3133
0.9	0.3159	0.3186	0.3212	0.3238	0.3264	0.3289	0.3315	0.3340	0.3365	0.3389
1.0	0.3413	0.3438	0.3461	0.3485	0.3508	0.3531	0.3554	0.3577	0.3599	0.3621
1.1	0.3643	0.3665	0.3686	0.3708	0.3729	0.3749	0.3770	0.3790	0.3810	0.3830
1.2	0.3849	0.3869	0.3888	0.3907	0.3925	0.3944	0.3962	0.3980	0.3997	0.4015
1.3	0.4032	0.4049	0.4066	0.4082	0.4099	0.4115	0.4131	0.4147	0.4162	0.4177
1.4	0.4192	0.4207	0.4222	0.4236	0.4251	0.4265	0.4279	0.4292	0.4306	0.4319
1.5	0.4332	0.4345	0.4357	0.4370	0.4382	0.4394	0.4406	0.4418	0.4429	0.4441
1.6	0.4452	0.4463	0.4474	0.4484	0.4495	0.4505	0.4515	0.4525	0.4535	0.4545
1.7	0.4554	0.4564	0.4573	0.4582	0.4591	0.4599	0.4608	0.4616	0.4625	0.4633
1.8	0.4641	0.4649	0.4656	0.4664	0.4671	0.4678	0.4686	0.4693	0.4699	0.4706
1.9	0.4713	0.4719	0.4726	0.4732	0.4738	0.4744	0.4750	0.4756	0.4761	0.4767
2.0	0.4772	0.4778	0.4783	0.4788	0.4793	0.4798	0.4803	0.4808	0.4812	0.4817
2.1	0.4821	0.4826	0.4830	0.4834	0.4838	0.4842	0.4846	0.4850	0.4854	0.4857
2.2	0.4861	0.4864	0.4868	0.4871	0.4875	0.4878	0.4881	0.4884	0.4887	0.4890
2.3	0.4893	0.4896	0.4898	0.4901	0.4904	0.4906	0.4909	0.4911	0.4913	0.4916
2.4	0.4918	0.4920	0.4922	0.4925	0.4927	0.4929	0.4931	0.4932	0.4934	0.4936
2.5	0.4938	0.4940	0.4941	0.4943	0.4945	0.4946	0.4948	0.4949	0.4951	0.4952
2.6	0.4953	0.4955	0.4956	0.4957	0.4959	0.4960	0.4961	0.4962	0.4963	0.4964
2.7	0.4965	0.4966	0.4967	0.4968	0.4969	0.4970	0.4971	0.4972	0.4973	0.4974
2.8	0.4974	0.4975	0.4976	0.4977	0.4977	0.4978	0.4979	0.4979	0.4980	0.4981
2.9	0.4981	0.4982	0.4982	0.4983	0.4984	0.4984	0.4985	0.4985	0.4986	0.4986
3.0	0.4987	0.4987	0.4987	0.4988	0.4988	0.4989	0.4989	0.4989	0.4990	0.4990

The total area under the normal curve applies to both positive and negative z values.

GLOSSARY

Accounting Equation   Assets equal liabilities plus owners' equity.

Accounting Rate of Return   A measure of a firm's profitability from a conventional accounting standpoint.

Accounts Receivable Turnover   Ratio that indicates how many times receivables are collected during a year.

Accrual Basis   Method of accounting that recognizes expenses as they are incurred and revenues as they are earned, even though they may have not been received or actually paid in cash.

Accruals   Current liabilities for services received but for which complete payments have not been made.

Acid-Test Ratio   See Quick Ratio.

Aging Schedule   A report of how long accounts receivable have been outstanding.

Amortization   The systematic allocation of the cost of an intangible asset at a given rate over a specified period of time.

Amortization Schedule   A report that breaks down payments into interest and principal.

Annual Cleanup Period   A continuous period of a specified length which the firm must be out of debt to the bank.

Annuity   A series of equal deposits or withdrawals made over equal time periods.

Annuity in Arrears   See Ordinary Annuity.

Articles of Incorporation   Document filed with the state, outlining all important data concerning a proposed business.

Asked Price   The lowest price at which a security will be sold.

Asset   Resource that a company has control over, that may provide future benefit, and that can be objectively valued.

Asset Management Ratios   Ratios that measure how effectively a firm manages its assets.

Auction Market   System by which securities are bought and sold through brokers on the securities exchanges.

Authorized Stock   Maximum number of shares of stock a corporation may issue without amending its charter.

Average Collection Period   The number of days it takes a firm to convert receivables into cash.

Average Daily Demand   The usage of inventory per day.

erage Tax Rate   See Effective Tax Rate.

Bad Debt Loss Ratio   The portion of the total receivables that is not paid.

Balance Sheet   Financial statement that shows a firm's financial condition at a specific point in time.

Banker's Acceptance   A trade acceptance in which the firm's bank, not the firm itself, guarantees payment.

Bankruptcy   Extreme form of financial distress involving a legal procedure to liquidate a business.

Basis Point   One-hundredth of one percent interest.

Best Efforts (Underwriting)   Arrangement under which an investment banker serves as a selling agent and not an underwriter.

Beta (Coefficient)   An index of the sensitivity of a given stock's return relative to the returns of the market portfolio.

Beta Estimation   An approach to risk estimation based on the CAPM.

Bid Price   The highest price at which prospective buyers are willing to pay for a given security.

Bird-in-the-hand Theory   Concept that asserts dividends are more reliable than capital gains.

Blanket Lien   An arrangement that gives the lender a lien against the borrower's entire inventory.

Blue Sky Law   State law governing public offerings of securities to protect investors against fraud.

Bond   A long-term debt security in which the issuer promises to pay a series of interest payments in addition to returning the principal at maturity.

Bond Rating   An evaluation of a bond issuer's possibility of defaulting.

Book Value   The accounting value of an asset liability, or equity.

Book Value Per Share   The value of each share of common stock based on the firm's accounting records.

Book Value Weight   A measure of the actual proportion of each type of permanent capital based on accounting values.

Breakeven Analysis   Evaluation of the relationships among sales, costs, and profits at various levels of output.

Broker   Person hired to buy and sell securities for investors.

Brokerage Commission   Fee for completing a stock transaction.

Budget   A financial expression of management's plans.

Budgeted Statement   See Pro Forma Statement.

Budgeting The process of formulating a written statement that details the firm's financial plans in numerical terms for a limited future period.

Business Finance See Financial Management.

Business Risk The variability or uncertainty of operating profits.

Business Strategy Plan by which the firm hopes to achieve its goals in a changing environment.

Call Premium The additional amount that are issuer must pay to call a bond before maturity.

Call Price Par value plus any call premium.

Call Provision The right to repurchase a bond prior to maturity under specified terms.

Capital Funds used to finance the firm's assets and operations.

Capital Asset A long-term asset that is not bought or sold in the ordinary course of business.

Capital Asset Pricing Model (CAPM) Model which provides the general framework for analyzing risk-return relationships for all types of assets.

Capital Budgeting Process of analyzing investment opportunities and making long-term investment decisions.

Capital Expenditure An outlay whose benefits are expected to extend beyond one year.

Capital Impairment Rule Legal restriction that prohibits corporations from paying dividends that would impair the initial capital contributions of the firm.

Capital Lease A long-term, noncancelable lease that meets the requirements of FASB-13.

Capital Markets Financial markets in which intermediate and long-term securities are bought and sold.

Capital Rationing Placement of an upper limit on capital expenditures.

Capital Structure All permanent sources of capital available to a firm.

Capitalized Value See Intrinsic Value.

Capitalizing A Lease Converting a lease obligation to an asset/liability form of expression on the balance sheet.

Carrying Cost Cost of holding items in inventory for a specific time period.

Cash The amount of currency a firm has on hand or deposited in a checking account.

Cash Breakeven Analysis Cost-profit-volume analysis based on cash receipts and payments.

Cash Breakeven Point The level of sales where cash revenues equal cash expenditures.

Cash Budget A projection of a firm's cash receipts and disbursements over some future time period.

Cash Cycle See Operating Cycle.

Cash Deductible Expenses Expenses that are tax-deductible and involve actual cash outlay.

Cash Discount A reduction in price given for early payment.

Cash Discount Period The length of time a customer has to pay for a purchase and still receive the cash discount.

Cash Flow A value equal to income after taxes plus noncash expenses.

Cash Management The process of managing a firm's liquid assets.

Cash Summary Report that shows whether a firm needs additional financing or has excess cash over a specific time horizon.

Certainty Equivalent Net Present Value Method Method of discounting cash flows by modifying a project's risky cash flows.

Certainty Equivalent Coefficient The ratio of a certain amount of cash flow to an alternate risky amount.

Characteristics Line A regression line used to estimate a security's beta.

Charter Certificate issued by the state establishing a corporation as a legal entity.

Chattel Mortgage A lien on personal property, which gives the lender the right to sieze and sell the equipment in the event of default.

Checkbook Float The difference between the cash balance on the bank's books and the firm's books.

Clientele Effect Implication that investors are attracted to firms whose dividend policies meet their particular needs.

Coefficient of Variation The ratio of the standard deviation to the expected value.

Collateral Assets promised to a lender by a borrower until a loan is repaid.

Collateral Trust Bond Bond secured by other securities owned by the issuer.

Collection Float See Negative Float.

Collection Float Time The length of time between a customer mailing a check and the firm receiving it and having the funds available.

Collection Policy A sets of procedures used to collect late accounts.

Combined Leverage The variability of earnings per share from a given change in sales.

Commercial Paper Short-term, unsecured debt issued by firms having a high credit standing.

Commitment Fee A fee charged by a bank on any funds not borrowed during the commitment period.

Common-size Balance Sheet Balance sheet with all amounts expressed as a percentage of total assets.

Common-size Income Statement Income statement with all balances expresses as a percentage of net sales.

Common-size Statements Financial statements with account balances expressed as a percentage of a base total.

Common Stock Stock held by the owners of the corporation.

Company Risk See Unsystematic Risk.

Compensating Balance A minimum average balance that the lending bank requires the borrower to maintain in either a checking account or a time deposit as a condition for making a loan.

Competitive Bid Underwriting An arrangement in which the issuer sells the securities to the underwriter with the highest bid (price).

Compound Interest Interest computed on two or more periods of time.

Compound Value See Future Value.

Compound Period The calendar period over which compounding occurs.

Conditional Sales Contract A financing agreement in which the seller of the equipment retains title to the equipment until all payments have been made.

Constant Growth Dividend Model A common stock valuation model that assumes dividends will grow at a constant rate each period.

Consumer (or Retail) Credit Credit which a firm extends to its final customers.

Controller Individual responsible for internal financial matters of a firm.

Contemporary Approach Theory which asserts that every firm has an optimal capital structure or at least an optimal range of structures.

Conventional Cash Flow Time series of net cash flows that contains only one change in sign (+ or −).

Conversion Feature Right to exchange a bond for a certain number of shares of preferred or common stock.

Conversion Premium The percentage or dollar difference between the market price and the conversion price of a security.

Conversion Price The effective price paid per share of common stock upon conversion.

Conversion Ratio The ratio in which a convertible security can be converted into common stock.

Conversion Value The value of a convertible security based on the market value of the underlying shares of common stock.

Convertible Security A bond or preferred stock that may be exchanged for common stock.

Corporate Finance See Financial Management.

Corporation A legal entity created by the state and owned by many persons.

Correlation Coefficient A relative statistical measure of correlation in the degree and direction of change between two variables.

Cost-balancing Model See Deterministic Model.

Cost of Capital See Required Rate of Return.

Cost of Debt Minimum rate of return required by suppliers of debt.

Coupon Rate The stated rate of interest on a bond.

Covariance An absolute statistical measure of the extent to which two variables move together.

Credit Period The period over which credit is granted.

Credit Policy A set of guidelines for extending credit to customers.

Credit Quality The probability of payment.

Credit Risk The risk that the issuing firm's financial position will worsen.

Credit Sales Noncash sales resulting from extending credit to customers.

Credit Standards Criteria and guidelines used by the firm to determine which customers get credit and how much each credit customer will get.

Credit Terms The repayment terms required of all customers.

Cross-sectional Analysis Evaluation of a firm's financial condition at a particular point in time.

Cumulative Voting Voting system that permits the stock holder to cast mutliple votes for a single director.

Current Asset An asset which will be converted into cash, sold, exchanged, or expensed, usually within one year.

Current Liability Liability that will fall due within one year.

Current Ratio A measure of a firm's ability to meet short-term obligations based only on current assets.

Current Yield The annual amount of interest on a bond divided by the current market price.

Date of Record The date a corporation examines its records to determine who will receive dividends or stock rights.

Dealer An individual or firm who purchases securities for its own accounts and then resells them.

Dealer-placed Issued An issue bought by investment banking group and resold at a higher price to investors.

Debenture An unsecured debt obligation that is backed only by the issuer's creditworthiness.

Debt-Equity Ratio Ratio that expresses the relationship between the amount of a firm's total assets financed by creditors and owners.

Debt Management Ratios Ratios that show the extent to which a firm uses debt to finance its investments and to meet interest charges and other fixed payments.

Debt Ratio The percentage of total assets financed by debt.

Debt Securities Obligations of the borrower to return the borrowed funds at a specified time and to pay interest to the lender.

Declaration Date Day on which the company's board of directors announces that a dividend will be paid.

Default Risk The risk that a debt's interest or principal will not be repaid.

Deferred Annuity See Ordinary Annuity.

Deferred Call Provision Call provision which can only take place after a certain date.

Degree of Combined Leverage The percentage change in EPS per percentage change in sales.

Degree of Financial Leverage The percentage change in EPS per percentage change in EBIT.

Degree of Operating Leverage The percentage change in EBIT per percentage change in sales.

Delivery Time See Lead Time.

Depository Institution Financial institution that accepts deposits and lends money.

Depository Transfer Check An unsigned, nonnegotiable check drawn against a bank deposit with the purpose of concentrating funds.

Depreciable Basis The cost of the asset plus all cost related to the asset's purchase.

Depreciation The systematic allocation of the cost of an asset over time.

Depreciation Rate The annual percentage rate at which an asset is depreciated or its cost recovered.

Deterministic Model Cash management model that assumes the firm has steady, predictable cash flows over some time period.

Direct Lease A lease that is initiated when a firm acquires the use of an asset that it did not previously own.

Direct Placement Placement in which the issuer sells directly to the public.

Disbursement Float See Positive Float.

Disbursement Float Time The length of time a firm can still use funds disbursed to, but not yet received by, other parties.

Discount Paper A money market instrument in which the buyer pays less than par or face value for the instrument.

Discount Rate The rate of interest used to find present values.

Discounted Loan A loan on which the bank deducts the interest in advance and distributes the remaining amount of the loan to the borrower.

Discounting The process of determining present values of future amounts.

Diversifiable Risk See Unsystematic Risk.

Diversification Investing in more than one type of asset to reduce risk.

Dividend Payout Ratio The percentage of earnings distributed to stockholders in the form of cash dividends.

Dividend Reinvestment Plan Arrangement whereby exisiting stockholders may reinvest all or part of their cash dividends in the firm's stock.

Dividend Yield The rate earned by shareholders from dividends relative to the current market price of the stock.

Dividends per Share Dollar amount of dividends paid on a share of common stock during the reporting period.

Draft An order for payment issued by one party to another.

DuPont Formula Formula that breaks down return on investment into net profit-margin and asset turnover ratio.

Earnings per Share The dollar amount earned on a share of common stock outstanding during a reporting period.

EBIT-EPS Analysis An analytical technique used to evaluate various capital structures in order to select the one that best maximizes the firm's EPS.

Economic Ordering Quantity The level at which the total cost of inventory is at its lowest.

Effective Interest Rate The actual interest rate; sometimes called the annual percentage rate.

Effective Tax Rate The percentage of total taxable income paid in tax.

Efficient Market Market in which the instrinsic value of an asset is equal to its market value.

Efficient Portfolio A portfolio that provides the highest return for a given level of risk or the least risk for a given level of return.

Equipment Financing Loan A loan used to finance the purchase of new equipment in which the equipment is used as collateral.

Equipment Trust Certificate A bond secured by and used to pay for specific equipment.

Equity Security Ownership share of the firm receiving the funds in the form of preferred or common stock.

Executory Costs The lessor's insurance, tax, and maintenance payments.

Expected Portfolio Return The weighted average of the expected returns from the individual assets in a portfolio.

Expected Rate of Return See Expected Value.

Expected Value The weighted average of all possible returns.

Expenses Costs incurred to produce revenues.

Ex-dividend Date Date on which the right to the most recently declared dividend no longer goes along with the sale of the stock.

Ex-rights Without the right to buy a firm's stock at a discount from the prevailing market price.

Face Value See Par Value.

Factoring The sale of accounts receivable to a financial institution, who manages and collects the accounts.

Factoring Commissions Payments for credit checking, collections, and risk-taking.

Fair Value See instrinsic value.

Federal Agency Security A debt issue of federally sponsored agencies that supply credit economic purposes such as aiding housing and agriculture.

Field Warehouse A warehouse operated by a warehousing company on the premises of the borrower.

Finance The body of facts, principles, and theories relating to the raising and using of money by individuals, businesses, and governments.

Financial Analysis The judgmental process of evaluating a firm's past financial performance and its future prospects.

Financial Asset A claim against the issuers future income and assets.

Financial Breakeven Point Level of EBIT where EPS equals zero.

Financial Distress Broad spectrum of problems, ranging from relatively minor liquidity shortages to bankruptcy.

Financial Forecasting The process of projecting or estimating some future financial event or condition of the firm.

Financial Intermediary A firm, such as a commercial bank, that facilitate the flow of funds from suppliers to demanders.

Financial Lease See Capital Lease.

Financial Leverage The extent to which a firm uses debt financing in its capital structure.

Financial Management The decision making process concerned with planning, and utilizing funds in a way that achieves the firm's desired goals.

Financial Manager The individual charged with financial management.

Financial Markets Mechanisms through which financial assets are bought, sold, or exchanged.

Financial Planning The development of a set of plans for the orderly acquisition and utilization of capital.

Financial Ratio The mathematical relationship among several numbers.

Financial Risk The variability or uncertainty of earnings per share.

Finished Goods Items that have been produced but not sold.

Fixed Annuity See Annuity.

Fixed Asset Turnover Ratio that indicates a firm's efficiency in managing fixed assets.

Fixed-Charge-Coverage Ratio Ratio that measures a firm's ability to meet total other fixed obligations plus interest payments.

Fixed Costs Expenditures that do not vary over a relevant range of activity.

Fixed Rate Note A note on which the rate of interest remains constant until maturity.

Float An amount of money represented by checks outstanding and in process of collection.

Float Time Time lag or delay between the moment of disbursement of funds by one party and receipt by another.

Floating Rate Note A note whose interest rate adjusts with the market.

Floor Broker Person that trades and bargains with various sellers on the floor of the exchange.

Flotation Costs Any costs associated with selling new securities.

Fluctuating Assets Current assets that vary over the year due to seasonal or cyclical needs.

Forecasted Statements See Pro Forma Statements.

Free Trade Credit Credit received during the discount period.

Fully-Diluted Earnings per Share The EPS with conversions, warrants, options, and other contracts included.

Funds Capital needed by a firm in order to operate.

Future Value The amount to which a present amount of money or a series of payments will grow when compounded at a given interest rate over a given period of time.

Generalized Risk Premium Approach Subjective method used to estimate the required rate of return.

Going-concern Value The value of a firm as an operating business.

Gordon Constant Growth Model Theory which assumes dividends perpetually grow at a constant annual rate.

Gross Profit Margin The percentage of each sales dollar remaining after deducting cost of goods sold.

Guaranteed Residual Value The lessee's purchase price at the end of the lease arrangement.

Holding Costs The opportunity costs associated with holding larger than average cash balances or inventories.

Hurdle Rate Minimum rate of return.

Implicit Rate of Interest   The lessor's internal rate of return.

Income Bonds   Bonds that pay interest only if the issuer earns an income.

Income Statement   Financial statement that shows the results of operations over a given period of time.

Incremental After-tax Cash Flows   All changes in net cash flow.

Incremental Borrowing Rate   The cost that the lessee would have incurred to borrow funds elsewhere.

Incremental Costs   See Marginal Costs.

Incremental Returns   See Marginal Returns.

Indifference Point   Level of EBIT where EPS is the same under alternate capital structures.

Informational Content Effect   Dividends payments may impart informational effects to investors about management's future expectations for the firm.

Initial Cash Inflows   The proceeds from the disposal of existing assets in a replacement transaction.

Initial Cash Outflows   The purchase price of an asset plus all cost necessary for placing the asset into service.

Insolvency   Situation in which either a firm's liabilities exceed its assets or it is unable to pay its creditors as required.

Installment Loan   A loan which requires the borrower to make equal payments at regular intervals over the life of the loan.

Instrinsic Value   The present value of all an asset's expected future returns when discounted at the investor's required rate of return.

Insurance Companies   Firms that provide benefits in the event of various casualties for a set fee.

Interest   Fee charged for borrowing or earned for lending money.

Interest-Bearing Securities   Debt instruments which pay interest based on the security's face value.

Interest on Advances   Interest charges made against money lent to the seller prior to collecting the accounts receivable.

Interest Rate   The percentage of the principal that is paid or earned in interest.

Interest Rate Risk   The risk that a loss will be incurred on the sale of a security sold before the maturity date due to an increase in interest rates.

Internal Rate of Return   The discount rate that equates the present value of the net cash inflows from a project to its net investment.

Interpolation   Mathematical technique for finding an unknown value that falls between two known values.

Intersection Rate   Rate used to discount a project's cash flows in finding its NPV and profitability index.

Intraperiod Compounding   Compounding that occurs more than once a year.

Inventory Cycle   The time between placement of successive orders of an item.

Inventory Management   The process of managing the investment in inventory.

Inventory Turnover   Ratio that measures the efficiency of a firm in managing and selling inventory.

Inverted Yield Curve   A downward sloping yield curve in which short-term rates are higher than long-term rates.

Investment Banker   A financial specialist who acts as an agent between buyers and sellers of new security issues.

Investment Opportunities Schedule (IOS)   List of investments in descending order according to IRR.

Issued Shares   The number of a firm's authorized shares that have been sold.

Lead Time   The time between order placement and receipt.

Lease   A contract by which the owner of an asset allows another party the use of the asset for a specified time in exchange for payment.

Lessee   The party that leases an assets and makes lease payments.

Lessor   The party that owns the asset that is leased.

Leverage   The percentage change in a dependent variable divided by the percentage change in the independent variable.

Leveraged Lease   An arrangement in which the lessor borrows a substantial portion of the asset's purchase price and then leases it to a lessee.

Liabilities   Claims by nonowners against the assets of a firm.

Lien   Legal instrument that gives the lender the right to possession of a specific asset in the event that the borrower defaults.

Line of Credit   An informal borrowing arrangement for a specific time period in which a bank places a ceiling on the total amount of credit available.

Liquid Asset   Cash or asset easily convertible into cash.

Liquidating Value   The amount that a firm would realize by selling its assets and paying off its liabilities.

Liquidity   The ability to be converted into cash.

Liquidity Ratios   Ratios which measure a firm's ability to meet short-term obligations.

Lockbox   Special post office box to which customers are instructed to send payments.

Loss Carryback   Loss applied against the taxable income of a previous year so as to produce a refund to the firm of taxes previously paid.

Loss Carryforward Loss applied against a subsequent year's taxable income.

Mail Float The time between when a customer mails a check and the firm receives it.

Majority Voting Voting system that entitles each shareholder to cast one vote for each share owned.

Managerial Finance See Financial Management.

Mandatory Projects Safety or environmental projects required by government, labor unions, or insurance companies.

Marginal Cost of Capital (MCC) Cost of obtaining another dollar of new capital.

Marginal Returns The benefits associated with each additional dollar invested in accounts receivable.

Marginal Costs The costs associated with each additional dollar invested in accounts receivable.

Marginal Tax Rate The tax rate on the next dollar of taxable income.

Market Ratios Ratios used primarily for investment decisions and long range planning.

Market Risk See Systematic Risk.

Market Risk Premium The additional return expected for holding a market portfolio of average riskiness.

Market Value The price for which an asset could be sold on the open market.

Market Value Weights Measure of the actual proportion of each type of permanent capital based on current market prices.

Marketability The ability to sell a security quickly and with the minimum possibility of loss.

Marketable Securities Short-term investment instruments that are easily sold.

Maturity The length of time remaining before a security or loan is due to be repaid.

Minimum Purchase Size The lowest size of a security which can be purchased.

Modified DuPont Formula Formula which shows how financial leverage affects return on equity.

Modigliani and Miller Approach Theory which asserts that, in the absence of taxes and other market imperfections, both the WACC and its value are completely unaffected by its capital structure.

Money Market Market for short-term debt instruments.

Money Market Instrument High-grade security characterized by a high degree of safety of principal and maturities of one year or less.

Money Market Mutual Funds Funds set up to invest in money market instruments.

Mortgage Bonds Bonds backed by real property.

Mutually Exclusive Project Project considered an alternate way of performing the same function as another project.

Mutual Funds A type of investment company that pools money from shareholders and invests in securities and other assets.

National Association of Securities Dealers A nonprofit organization formed to regulate in the over-the-counter markets.

National Association of Securities Dealers Automated Quotation System (NASDAQ) A computerized system that provides brokers and dealers with price quotations for securities traded in the over-the-counter markets.

Negative Float Money received by the firm from its customers.

Negotiable Certificates of Deposit Large time deposits instruments at a depository institution.

Negotiated Sources Sources of short-term financing that require special arrangements.

Negotiated Underwriting An arrangement in which the issuing firm and its investment banker negotiate the terms of the issue.

Net Cash Flow The difference between the cash receipts and the cash disbursements for the period.

Net Investment The net cash outflow that occurs when an investment project is accepted and funds invested.

Net Operating Cash Flows Incremental changes in a firm's operating cash flows.

Net Present Value The sum of a project's present values of the net cash flows minus the net investment.

Net Profit Margin The percentage of each sales dollar remaining after deducting all expenses.

Net Working Capital Current assets minus current liabilities.

Nominal Interest Rate Annual dollar amount of income received from fixed income divided by the par value of the security; stated as a percentage.

Noncash Deductible Expenses Expenses that are tax deductible but do not involve an actual cash outlay.

Nonconventional Cash Flow Time series of net cash flows that contains more than one change in sign (+ or −).

Nondiversifiable Risk See Systematic Risk.

Nonlinear Breakeven Analysis Breakeven analysis that involves nonlinear revenue and cost functions.

Nonnotification Situation in which the borrower's customers are not notified that their receivables have been pledged by the firm.

Nonrecourse   Situation where the factor absorbs bad debts and cannot turn to the seller for payment. The factor receives title to the accounts receivable.

Nonrevenue-producing Projects   See Mandatory Projects.

Normal Curve   A bell-shaped distribution curve.

Notes Payable   Formal type of trade credit in which the buyer signs a promissory note indicating liability to the seller.

Notification   Situation in which the borrower's customers are notified to make payments to the lender.

Open Account   An informal, prearranged extension of short-term credit by a supplier to a firm.

Operating Breakeven Point   The level of sales where the operating profit equals zero.

Operating Cycle   The length of time required to buy raw materials, produce and sell a finished product, collect the sales receipts, and repay credit.

Off Balance Sheet Financing   The exclusion of financial transactions from the balance sheet.

Operating Lease   Lease for less than the asset's life in which the lessor handles all maintenance.

Operating Leverage   The extent to which fixed operating costs are used in operations. The variability of operating profit, given a change in sales.

Operating Loss   The excess of deductible expenses over ordinary gross income.

Operating Profit Margin   The percentage of each sales dollar remaining after deducting both cost of goods sold and operating expenses.

Operating Restrictions   Limitations placed on a firm in conducting its business operations.

Operating Risk   See Business Risk.

Opportunity Cost   Rate of return that funds could earn if they were invested in the best available alternative.

Optimal Capital Budget   Level of capital investment that maximizes the value of the firm.

Optimal Capital Structure   Capital structure that balances risk and return to maximize the value of a firm.

Ordering Costs   The cost of placing and receiving an order.

Ordinary Annuity   Payments made at the end of a period.

Ordinary Taxable Income   Ordinary gross income less tax deductible expenses.

Organized Security Exchange   A centralized market in which listed securities are bought and sold.

Outstanding Shares   Number of shares held by the public which is the number of issued shares less treasury stock.

Overall Breakeven Analysis   Evaluation made to determine the level of sales at which profit, net of all cost including nonoperating costs, is equal to zero.

Overall Risk   The variability or uncertainty of EPS resulting from both business and financial risk.

Over-the-counter Market   The market for trading securities listed on an organized security exchange.

Par Value   The amount that appears on the face of a note.

Partnership   A legal arrangement between two or more people.

Partnership Agreement   Written agreement which outlines the formal arrangement of a partnership.

Payback Period   The length of time for a project's accumulated net cash inflows to equal its net investment.

Payment Date   The date the company distributes its dividends to stockholders.

Pension Fund   Fund that provide income to retired and disabled persons.

Percent of Sale Forecast   Estimate based on the relationship between sales and some other financial variable.

Perpetuity   An annuity with an infinite life span.

Permanent Assets   Fixed assets plus the portion of the firm's current assets that remain unchanged over the year.

Placement Fee   The dealer commission for arranging the sale of the issue.

Pledging   The use of accounts receivable as collateral for short-term loans extended by financial institutions.

Point   One percent interest.

Portfolio   A collection of two or more assets or securities.

Portfolio Beta   The weighted average of the betas of a portfolio's individual securities.

Portfolio Effect   The favorable interaction of assets resulting in reduced risk through diversification.

Portfolio Risk   The variability of returns of a portfolio as a whole.

Positive Float   Money paid by a firm to its customers.

Preemptive Right   Right of existing shareholders to purchase shares of a new issue before it is offered to others.

Preferred Stock   Stock that has a claim against income and assets after debt but over of common stock.

Preliminary Prospectus   A condensed version of the registration statement.

Premium   A positive remainder when the par

value of a security is deducted from its market value.

Present Value The current value of a future amount of money, or series of payments, evaluated at a given discount rate.

Price/Earnings Ratio The ratio of market price per share to earnings per share.

Price-pegging Method used by syndicate managers to stabilize a security's resale price.

Primary Markets Financial markets in which newly issued securities are bought and sold for the first time.

Prime Rate The minimum interest rate charged by banks on short-term loans to business borrowers with the highest possible credit rating.

Principal Face value of an obligation.

Private Placement The direct sale of an entire issue to a few investors rather than the public.

Private Security Issue Nonpublic sale of new securities to a few investors.

Privileged Subscription Right to buy a new issue of securities before sale to the general public.

Pro Forma Statements Statements that forecast future events as opposed to historical events.

Probability The percentage chance that an event will occur.

Probability Distribution A set of possible outcomes with their respective probabilities assigned.

Probabilistic Models Cash management models that incorporate the uncertainty of cash flows.

Processing Float The time between the receipt of a check and depositing it at a bank for collection.

Profit Maximization The goal of increasing a firm's total profits as much as possible in the shortest period of time.

Profitability Index The ratio of the sum of a project's present values of the net cash flows divided by its net investment.

Profitability Ratios Ratios that measure the earning power of a firm.

Promissory Note A formal document specifying the terms and conditions of the loan.

Protective Covenants Restrictions in a debt agreement designed to protect the lender's interest.

Proxy A temporary transfer of the voting rights of one party to another.

Public Security Issue Sale of new securities by a firm to the general public.

Public Warehouse A licensed storage facility operated by bonded managers.

Purchasing Power Risk The risk that inflation will reduce the purchasing power of the sum of money to be repaid.

Quick Assets Current assets minus inventories.

Quick Ratio Ratio that measures a firm's ability to meet short-term obligations based only on its quick assets.

Rate of Return The yield of a security.

Ratio Analysis Process of evaluating financial data by converting dollar amounts to ratios.

Raw Materials Items of input to the production process.

Record Date See date of record.

Recourse Situation in which the borrower is responsible for defaults on the accounts receivable pledged to the lender.

Recovery Period The length of time over which the cost of an asset is recovered.

Red Herring See Preliminary Prospectus.

Registration Statement Document that provides full disclosure of all material facts relating to a security issue.

Reorder Point Level of inventory at which an order is placed to replenish an item.

Repurchase Agreement Arrangement by which a bank or security dealer sells specific financial assets and agrees to repurchase them on a specified future date at a price set higher than the selling price.

Required Rate of Return The amount of return demanded on an investment.

Retained Earnings Net profits accumulated in a business after dividends are paid.

Return on Assets See Return on Investments.

Return on Equity Ratio that measures the rate of return realized by a firm's stockholders on their investment.

Return on Investment Ratio that measures the overall effectiveness of management in generating profits from its total investment in assets.

Revenues Inflows of assets resulting from the sale of goods or services.

Revolving Credit Agreement A contractual and binding obligation by a bank to provide a specific amount of funds for a certain time period.

Right An option to buy a specified number of shares of common stock at a certain price for a fixed period of time.

Right of Offset Right to use compensating balances as payment on a loan in default.

Rights Offering See Privileged Subscription.

Risk The measurable probability that actual future returns will be below expected future returns.

Risk Averter Investor who is unwilling to pay an amount equal to the expected value of an uncertain investment.

Risk Premium The rate of return required in excess of the risk-free rate due to systematic risk.

Risk-adjusted Net Present Value Method Method of discounting cash flows by adjusting the discount rate based on the amount of risk.

Risk-free Rate of Return The return required for a security having no systematic risk and is generally measured by the yield on short-term U.S. Treasury securities.

Risk-Return Tradeoff Higher returns in exchange for taking greater risk.

Safety Stock Additional inventory carried to meet unexpected demand and unanticipated delays in shipping or production.

Sale and Leaseback An arrangement in which a firm sells an asset it already owns to another party and then leases it back.

Sales Forecast An estimate of a firm's sales for a future period.

Schedule of Changes in Net Working Capital Statement which shows the increase or decrease in a firm's working capital over a period of time.

Seasonal Dating Special credit term that permit discounts on payments made during the purchaser's selling season, regardless of when the goods were shipped.

Seat Membership on an exchange.

Secondary Market Financial market in which previously issued securities are bought and sold.

Secured Debt A debt obligation having specific assets pledged as collateral.

Securities and Exchange Commission Federal agency that regulates both primary and secondary markets for publicly traded securities.

Security Agreement A standardized form which indicates the specific assets pledged for the purpose of securing a loan.

Security Market Line A capital asset pricing model expressed graphically.

Security Valuation The valuation of financial assets.

Selling Concession Compensation earned by investment banker for selling securities.

Semivariable Costs Costs that contain both fixed and semivariable elements.

Sensitivity Analysis Evaluation of the affect of changes in certain assumptions on forecasts.

Service Charge The fee charged by the lender to cover the administrative costs.

Service Lease See Operating Lease.

Shelf Registration Two-year registration of securities that allows immediate sales to the public.

Simple Interest Interest computed for a specified single period of time. Principal × interest rate × time.

Simple Interest Loan A loan on which interest is calculated on the face amount or unpaid balance of the loan and is only paid with the principal at maturity.

Simulation Analysis A statistically based approach for dealing with risk that provides information about the variability of a project's return.

Single Loan A loan for a specific amount and maturity for a specific purpose.

Sinking Fund An amount of money set aside, or to be set aside, to redeem debt securities or preferred stock issues.

Skewed Distribution A distribution which is not symmetrical.

Sole Proprietorship A business owned by one person.

Specialist Member of an organized security exchange who maintains a fair and orderly market in one or more securities.

Spontaneous Sources Sources of short-term financing that arise out of normal business operations.

Standard Deviation A statistical measure of the variability of a probability distribution around its expected value.

Standard Normal Distribution The distribution of a normal random variable with an expected value of zero and standard deviation equal to one.

Standby Underwriting Purchase of shares, not bought through a rights offering, by the investment banker at a specified price.

Statement of Changes in Financial Position (SCFP) Financial statement that shows a firm's financing and investing activities over a specific period of time.

Statement of Retained Earnings Financial statement that reports the amount of profits reinvested in the firm.

Stock Dividend A distribution of additional shares of stock to existing stockholders on a pro rata basis.

Stock Option Plan Benefit program that allows certain managers of a firm to purchase stock at a specified price for a stated period of time.

Stock Purchase Plan Benefit program which allows employees to purchase a firm's stock.

Stock Split Method of increasing the number of shares of common stock outstanding without any change in stockholder's equity or the aggregate market value at the time of the split.

Stockholders' Equity Claims by owners against the assets of a firm.

Stockouts Inventory shortages.

Stretching Accounts Payable Postponement of payment beyond the end of the credit period.

Subordinated Debentures Unsecured bonds

that rank behind other debts as claims on assets.

Subscription Price A price below market at which new shares may be purchased in a rights offering by current stockholders.

Sunk Costs Cash flows that have occurred and cannot be changed by an investment decision.

Supergrowth Dividend Model A common stock valuation model that assumes dividends will grow at an above-normal rate over some time period and then grow at a normal rate thereafter.

Symmetrical Distribution A distribution in which one half is the mirror image of the other.

Systematic Risk That part of a security's risk that is common to all securities of the same class and thus cannot be eliminated by diversification.

Target Capital Structure The desired range of values over which the firm's financial leverage varies.

Target Weight Measure of the proportion of each type of permanent capital based on desired optimal capital structure.

Tender Offer Formal offer to buy shares of a corporation, usually at a premium above the share's market price.

Term Loan A business loan with an original maturity of more than one year.

Terminal Warehouse See Public Warehouse.

Third-party Lease See leveraged lease.

Time Horizon The time period covered by a project, investment, or cash budget.

Time Value of Money The price put on the time an investor has to wait until a project matures.

Time-series Analysis Evaluation of a firm's performance over a period of time.

Times Interest Earned Ratio that measures a firm's ability to meet its interest payments from operating profit.

Total Asset Turnover Ratio that measures management's efficiency in managing total assets to generate sales.

Trade Acceptances Formal agreements in which the delivery of goods is not completed until the buyer accepts a draft drawn by the seller.

Trade Credit Short-term credit extended by suppliers and subject to certain terms and conditions.

Transactions Costs Costs associated with inadequate cash balances such as the cost of selling securities (brokerage fees) or borrowing to raise cash (interest expenses).

Treasurer Individual responsible for external financial matters of a firm.

Treasury Bills Short-term obligations of the United States government.

Treasury Stock Previously issued shares that have reacquired by the firm.

Trend Analysis See Time-Series Analysis.

Trend Forecast A projection of historical values of a single variable into the future.

Trend Line A line that best fits the overall data on a scatter diagram.

Trust Receipt A security agreement under which the borrower holds the inventory in trust for the lender.

Trustee A person responsible for certifying an issue, seeing that the issuer fulfills the terms of the indenture, and represents the bondholder in case of default.

Underpricing Sale of common stock at a price below the current market price.

Underwriting The process used by an investment bank of selling securities, guaranteeing the issuing firm a specified price within a specified time period.

Underwriting Profit Compensation earned by investment banker for risk-bearing.

Underwriting Spread The difference between the actual proceeds from security sales and the amount the issuing firm actually receives.

Underwriting Syndicate A group of investment bankers that is formed to share the risk of a security offering and to underwrite the security issue.

Unsecured Debt A debt obligation not having specific assets pledged as collateral.

Unsystematic Risk That part of a security's risk that is caused by factors unique to a particular firm and can be eliminated by diversification.

Usable Funds The net amount of the loan that the firm can use after taking into consideration the amount borrowed, any interest and fees paid in advance, required compensating balances, and the firm's normal bank balance.

Valuation The process of estimating what an asset is worth.

Valuation Model A model that attempts to isolate significant factors affecting security prices and rates of return.

Variance A measure of the dispersion of a distribution which is the standard deviation squared.

Variable Costs Costs that change as the level of activity changes.

Warehouse Receipt Loan Arrangement whereby the lender receives control of the pledged collateral.

Warrant An option to buy securities at a set price for a given period of time.

Weighted Average Cost of Capital (WACC) Cost of capital computed with each long-term source of capital weighted by its relative importance to total capital.

Weighted Marginal Cost of Capital (WMCC) Cost of obtaining another dollar of new capital from more than one source.

Wire Transfer Electronic transference of money between banks.

Work-in-process Inventory Items in the production process which have not yet been completed.

Working Capital A firm's investment in current assets.

Working Capital Management The management of a firm's current assets and liabilities.

Yield The actual return received by an investment in a security.

Yield Curve A graph showing the relationship between interest rates and debt maturities at a point in time.

Yield To Maturity The required rate of return an investor will receive if a long-term, interest-bearing investment is held to its maturity date.

Zero Balance System A payment system that uses a master disbursing account that service all other disbursing accounts.

Zero Coupon Bonds Bonds that accrue interest until the maturity date. Interest is not paid periodically but included in the principal.

Zero Growth Dividend Model A common stock valuation model that assumes dividends remain fixed.

INDEX